Data Structures and Algorithms in Java

Third Edition

Data Structures and Algorithms in Java

Third Edition

Michael T. Goodrich
Department of Computer Science
University of California, Irvine

Roberto Tamassia
Department of Computer Science
Brown University

John Wiley & Sons, Inc.

ACQUISITIONS EDITOR	Paul Crockett
ASSOCIATE MARKETING DIRECTOR	Ilse Wolfe
EDITORIAL ASSISTANT	Simon Durkin
SENIOR PRODUCTION EDITOR	Ken Santor
COVER DESIGNER	David Levy

About the cover: Anatjari Tjampitjinpa, "Snake Dreaming," 1988. Reproduced courtesy of Patrick Corbally Stourton of Corbally Stourton Contemporary Art Ltd.

This book was set in LaTeX by the authors and printed and bound by Von Hoffmann, Inc. The cover was printed by Von Hoffmann, Inc.

This book is printed on acid free paper. ∞

ISBN 0-471-46983-1

Printed in the United States of America

10 9 8 7 6 5 4 3 2 1

To Karen, Paul, Anna, and Jack
— *Michael T. Goodrich*

To Isabel
— *Roberto Tamassia*

Preface to the Third Edition

This third edition is designed to provide an introduction to data structures and algorithms, including their design, analysis, and implementation. With respect to computer science and computer engineering curricula, we have written this book to be primarily for Freshman-Sophomore level data structures courses. In terms of curricula based on the *IEEE/ACM 2001 Computing Curriculum*, this book is appropriate for use in the courses CS102 (I/O/B versions), CS103 (I/O/B versions), CS111 (A version), and CS112 (A/I/O/F/H versions). In terms of curricula based on the *1978 ACM Computer Science Curriculum*, this book is intended for the CS2 course. We discuss its use for such courses in more detail later in this preface.

The major changes, with respect to the second edition, are the following:

- Expanded coverage of recursion
- Streamlined mathematics to the seven most used functions
- Inclusion of HTML tag matching and favorites list applications
- Simplification of the Java interfaces associated with ADTs
- Better integration with the Java Collections Framework
- Simplified binary tree and priority queue ADTs
- Addition of the map ADT
- Addition of splay trees
- Addition of the union/find partition data structure
- Simplified graph ADT
- Expanded and revised exercises.

This book is related to the following books:

- M.T. Goodrich, R. Tamassia, and D.M. Mount, *Data Structures and Algorithms in C++*, John Wiley & Sons, Inc., 2004. This book has a similar overall structure to the present book, but uses C++ as the underlying language (with some modest, but necessary pedagogical differences required by this approach). Thus, it could make for a handy companion book in a curriculum that allows for either a Java or C++ track in the introductory courses.
- M.T. Goodrich and R. Tamassia, *Algorithm Design: Foundations, Analysis, and Internet Examples*, John Wiley & Sons, Inc., 2002. This is a textbook for a more advanced algorithms and data structures course, such as CS7 in the ACM 1978 curriculum or CS210 (T/W/C/S versions) in the IEEE/ACM 2001 curriculum.

vii

Use as a Textbook

The design and analysis of efficient data structures has long been recognized as a vital subject in computing, for the study of data structures is part of the core of every collegiate computer science and computer engineering major program we are familiar with. Typically, the introductory courses are presented as a two- or three-course sequence. Elementary data structures are often briefly introduced in the first programming or introduction to computer science course and this is followed by a more in-depth introduction to data structures in the following course(s). Furthermore, this course sequence is typically followed at a later point in the curriculum by a more in-depth study of data structures and algorithms. We feel that the central role of data structure design and analysis in the curriculum is fully justified, given the importance of efficient data structures in most software systems, including the Web, operating systems, databases, compilers, and scientific simulation systems.

With the emergence of the object-oriented paradigm as the framework of choice for building robust and reusable software, we have tried to take a consistent object-oriented viewpoint throughout this text. One of the main ideas of the object-oriented approach is that data should be presented as being encapsulated with the methods that access and modify them. That is, rather than simply viewing data as a collection of bytes and addresses, we think of data as instances of an ***abstract data type*** (***ADT***) that includes a repertory of methods for performing operations on the data. Likewise, object-oriented solutions are often organized utilizing common ***design patterns***, which facilitate software reuse and robustness. Thus, we present each data structure using ADTs and their respective implementations and we introduce important design patterns as means to organize those implementations into classes, methods, and objects.

For each ADT presented in this book, we provide an associated Java interface. Also, concrete data structures realizing the ADTs are provided as Java classes implementing the above interfaces. We also give Java implementations of fundamental algorithms (such as sorting and graph traversals) and of sample applications of data structures (such as HTML tag matching and a photo album). Due to space limitations, we sometimes show only code fragments in the book and make the full source code available on the companion Web site http://java.datastructures.net.

The Java code in this the book implementing fundamental data structures is organized in a single Java package, net.datastructures. This package forms a coherent library of data structures and algorithms in Java specifically designed for educational purposes in a way that is complementary with the Java Collections Framework.

Web Added-Value Education

This book is accompanied by an extensive Web site:

http://java.datastructures.net

Students are encouraged to use this site along with the book, to help with exercises and increase understanding of the subject. Instructors are likewise welcome to use the site to help plan, organize, and present their course materials.

For the Student

For all readers, and specifically for students, we include:

- All the Java source code presented in this book
- The student version of the net.datastructures package
- Slide handouts (four-per-page) in PDF format
- A database of hints to *all* exercises, indexed by problem number
- Java animations and interactive applets for data structures and algorithms
- Hyperlinks to other data structures and algorithms resources.

We feel that the Java animations and interactive applets should be of particular interest, since they allow readers to interactively "play" with different data structures, which leads to better understanding of the different ADTs. In addition, the hints should be of considerable use to anyone needing a little help getting started on certain exercises.

For the Instructor

For instructors using this book, we include the following additional teaching aids:

- Solutions to over two hundred of the book's exercises
- A keyword-searchable database of additional exercises
- The complete net.datastructures package
- Additional Java source code
- Slides in Powerpoint and PDF (one-per-page) format
- Self-contained special-topic supplements, including discussions on convex hulls, range trees, and orthogonal segment intersection.

The slides are fully editable, so as to allow an instructor using this book full freedom in customizing his or her presentations.

For the Instructor

This book contains many Java code and pseudo-code fragments, and over six hundred exercises, which are divided into roughly 40% reinforcement exercises, 40% creativity exercises, and 20% programming projects.

Relation to the IEEE/ACM 2001 Computing Curriculum

This book can be used for the CS2 course in the 1978 ACM Computer Science Curriculum or courses CS102 (I/O/B versions), CS103 (I/O/B versions), CS111 (A version), and/or CS112 (A/I/O/F/H versions) in the IEEE/ACM 2001 Computing Curriculum, with instructional units as outlined in Table 0.1.

Instructional Unit	Relevant Material
PL1. Overview of Programming Languages	Chapters 1 & 2
PL2. Virtual Machines	Sections 4.2.3, 4.3.4, & 12.4.4
PL3. Introduction to Language Translation	Section 1.9
PL4. Declarations and Types	Sections 1.1, 2.4, & 2.4.4
PL5. Abstraction Mechanisms	Sections 2.4, 4.2, 4.3, 4.5, 5.1.1, 5.2, 5.3, 5.5, 6.1, 6.3.1, 7.1, 8.1, 8.3, 10.6, & 12.1
PL6. Object-Oriented Programming	Chapters 1 & 2 and Sections 5.2.2, 5.5, 6.3.5, 7.1.2, & 12.3.1
PF1. Fundamental Programming Constructs	Chapters 1 & 2
PF2. Algorithms and Problem-Solving	Sections 1.9, 3.2, & 3.4
PF3. Fundamental Data Structures	Sections 1.5, 4.2–4.4, 4.5, , 5.1–5.3, 6.1, 6.3, 6.4, 7.1, 7.3, 8.1–8.4, 9.1–9.6, 12.1, & 12.2
PF4. Recursion	Sections 2.5.1 & 4.1
SE1. Software Design	Chapter 2 and Sections 5.2.2, 5.5, 6.3.5, 7.1.2, & 12.3.1
SE2. Using APIs	Sections 2.4, 2.4.4, 4.2, 4.3, 4.5, 5.1.1, 5.2, 5.3, 5.5, 6.1, 6.3.1, 7.1, 8.1, 8.3, 10.6, & 12.1
AL1. Basic Algorithmic Analysis	Chapter 3
AL2. Algorithmic Strategies	Sections 10.1.1, 10.7.1, 11.2.1, 11.4.2, & 11.5.2
AL3. Fundamental Computing Algorithms	Sections 7.1.4, 7.2.3, 7.3.5, 8.2, & 8.3.3, and Chapters 10, 11, & 12
DS1. Functions, Relations, and Sets	Sections 3.3, 7.1, & 10.6
DS3. Proof Techniques	Sections 3.5, 5.1.3, 6.3.3, 7.3, 9.2, 9.3, 9.4, 9.5, 10.2.1, 10.3, 10.6.2, 12.1, 12.3.1, 12.4, & 12.5
DS4. Basics of Counting	Sections 2.2.3 & 10.1.5
DS5. Graphs and Trees	Chapters 6, 7, 9, & 12
DS6. Discrete Probability	Appendix A and Sections 8.2.2, 8.4.2, 10.2.1, & 10.7

Table 0.1: Material for Units in the IEEE/ACM 2001 Computing Curriculum.

Teaching Options

This book is also structured to allow instructors a great deal of freedom in organizing and presenting the material. In Table 0.2, we illustrate some possible uses of this book for an intermediate-paced data structures course.

Chapter	Possible Options
1. Java Programming	skip if students know it already
2. Object-Oriented Design	omit the adapter pattern
3. Analysis Tools	omit justification methods
4. Stacks, Queues & Recursion	omit Java-thread queue application
5. Vectors, Lists, and Sequences	omit list iterators
6. Trees	omit template method pattern
7. Priority Queues	omit bottom-up heap construction
8. Maps and Dictionaries	omit extensions of dictionaries
9. Search Trees	omit (2,4) and red-black trees or splay trees
10. Sorting, Sets, and Selection	omit sorting lower bound
11. Text Processing	omit tries, compression, and/or LCS
12. Graphs	omit directed graphs or MSTs

Table 0.2: Options for a Freshman-Sophomore data structures course.

Prerequisites

We have written this book assuming that the reader comes to it with certain knowledge. That is, we assume that the reader is at least vaguely familiar with a high-level programming language, such as C, C++, or Java, and that he or she understands the main constructs from such a high-level language, including:

- Variables and expressions
- Methods (also known as functions or procedures)
- Decision structures (such as if-statements and switch-statements)
- Iteration structures (for-loops and while-loops).

For readers who are familiar with these concepts, but not with how they are expressed in Java, we provide a primer on the Java language in Chapter 1. Still, this book is primarily a data structures book, not a Java book; hence, it does not provide a comprehensive treatment of Java. Nevertheless, we do not assume that the reader is necessarily familiar with object-oriented design or with linked structures, such as linked lists, for these topics are covered in the core chapters of this book.

In terms of mathematical background, we assume the reader is somewhat familiar with topics from high-school mathematics. Even so, in Chapter 3, we discuss the seven most-important functions for algorithm analysis. In fact, sections that use something other than one of these seven functions are considered optional, and are indicated with a star ($\star$). We give a summary of other useful mathematical facts, including elementary probability, in Appendix A.

About the Authors

Professors Goodrich and Tamassia are well-recognized researchers in algorithms and data structures, having published many papers in this field, with applications to Internet computing, information visualization, computer security, and geometric computing. They have served as principal investigators in several joint projects sponsored by the National Science Foundation, the Army Research Office, and the Defense Advanced Research Projects Agency. They are also active in educational technology research, with special emphasis on algorithm visualization systems.

Michael Goodrich received his Ph.D. in Computer Science from Purdue University in 1987. He is currently a professor in the Department of Computer Science at University of California, Irvine. Previously, he was a professor at Johns Hopkins University. He is an editor for the *International Journal of Computational Geometry & Applications* and *Journal of Graph Algorithms and Applications*.

Roberto Tamassia received his Ph.D. in Electrical and Computer Engineering from the University of Illinois at Urbana-Champaign in 1988. He is currently a professor in the Department of Computer Science at Brown University. He is editor-in-chief for the *Journal of Graph Algorithms and Applications* and an editor for *Computational Geometry: Theory and Applications*. He previously served on the editorial board of *IEEE Transactions on Computers*.

In addition to their research accomplishments, the authors also have extensive experience in the classroom. For example, Dr. Goodrich has taught data structures and algorithms courses, including Data Structures as a freshman-sophomore level course and Introduction to Algorithms as an upper level course. He has earned several teaching awards in this capacity. His teaching style is to involve the students in lively interactive classroom sessions that bring out the intuition and insights behind data structuring and algorithmic techniques. Dr. Tamassia has taught Data Structures and Algorithms as an introductory freshman-level course since 1988. One thing that has set his teaching style apart is his effective use of interactive hypermedia presentations integrated with the Web.

The instructional Web sites, datastructures.net and algorithmdesign.net, supported by Drs. Goodrich and Tamassia are used as reference material by students, teachers, and professionals worldwide.

Acknowledgments

There are a number of individuals who have made contributions to this book.

We are grateful to all our research collaborators and teaching assistants, who provided feedback on early drafts of chapters and have helped us in developing exercises, programming assignments, and algorithm animation systems. In particular, we would like to thank Jeff Achter, James Baker, Ryan Baker, Benjamin Boer, Mike Boilen, Devin Borland, Lubomir Bourdev, Stina Bridgeman, Bryan Cantrill, Yi-Jen Chiang, Robert Cohen, David Emory, Jody Fanto, Ashim Garg, Natasha Gelfand, Mark Handy, Michael Horn, Benoît Hudson, Jovanna Ignatowicz, Seth Padowitz, James Piechota, Dan Polivy, Susannah Raub, Andy Schwerin, Michael Shapiro, Michael Shin, Christian Straub, Galina Shubina, Nikos Triandopoulos, and Luca Vismara. Lubomir Bourdev, Mike Demmer, Mark Handy, Michael Horn, and Scott Speigler developed a basic Java tutorial, which ultimately led to Chapter 1, Java Programming.

Special thanks go to Eric Zamore, who contributed to the development of the Java code examples in this book and to the design, implementation and testing of the net.datastructures library of data structures and algorithms in Java.

Many students and instructors have used the two previous editions of this book and their experiences and responses have helped shape this third edition.

There have been a number of friends and colleagues whose comments have lead to improvements in the text. We are particularly thankful to Karen Goodrich, Art Moorshead, David Mount, Scott Smith and Ioannis Tollis for their insightful comments. In addition, contributions by David Mount to Section 2.5.1 and to several figures are gratefully acknowledged.

We are also truly indebted to the outside reviewers and readers for their copious comments, emails, and constructive criticism, which were extremely useful in writing the third edition. We specifically thank the following reviewers for their comments and suggestions: Divy Agarwal, University of California, Santa Barbara; Terry Andres, University of Manitoba; Bobby Blumofe, University of Texas, Austin; Michael Clancy, University of California, Berkeley; Larry Davis, University of Maryland; Scott Drysdale, Dartmouth College; Arup Guha, University of Central Florida; Chris Ingram, University of Waterloo; Stan Kwasny, Washington University; Calvin Lin, University of Texas at Austin; John Mark Mercer, McGill University; Laurent Michel, University of Connecticut; Leonard Myers, California Polytechnic State University, San Luis Obispo; David Naumann, Stevens Institute of Technology; Robert Pastel, Michigan Technological University; Bina Ramamurthy, SUNY Buffalo; Ken Slonneger, University of Iowa; C.V. Ravishankar, University of Michigan; Val Tannen, University of Pennsylvania; Paul Van Arragon, Messiah College; and Christopher Wilson, University of Oregon.

We are grateful to our editor, Paul Crockett, for his enthusiastic support of this project. The team at Wiley has been great. Many thanks go to Lilian Brady, Ken Santor, Simon Durkin, Madelyn Lesure, Dawn Stanley, and Jeri Warner.

The computing systems and excellent technical support staff in the departments of computer science at Brown University and University of California, Irvine gave us reliable working environments. This manuscript was prepared primarily with the LaTeX typesetting package for the text and Adobe FrameMaker® and Microsoft Visio® for the figures.

Finally, we would like to warmly thank Isabel Cruz, Karen Goodrich, Giuseppe Di Battista, Franco Preparata, Ioannis Tollis, and our parents for providing advice, encouragement, and support at various stages of the preparation of this book. We also thank them for reminding us that there are things in life beyond writing books.

Michael T. Goodrich
Roberto Tamassia

Contents

Chapter

1

Java Programming

Contents

Building data structures and algorithms requires that we communicate detailed instructions to a computer, and an excellent way to perform such communication is using a high-level computer language, such as Java. In this chapter, we give a brief overview of the Java programming language, assuming the reader is somewhat familiar with an existing high-level language.

Java possesses a number of features that make it an excellent tool for exploring the implementation of data structures and algorithms. It was designed to allow for secure, platform-independent software execution, which is a big advantage in heterogeneous educational computing environments. Java allows us to use pointers for implementing sophisticated linked structures, but it restricts potentially dangerous programming styles, such as pointer arithmetic and arbitrary array indexing. In addition, it provides for several levels of data protection (such as public and private variables and methods), and it has an extensive collection of meaningfully named error conditions. It has a simple built-in mechanism for memory management and garbage collection, which can be used transparently by the novice programmer, but has several "behind-the-scenes" hooks for expert programmers. And, finally, it contains simple constructs for performing fairly sophisticated kinds of computing, such as multiprocessing, network computing, and graphical user interfaces.

The specific topics of the Java language we focus on in this chapter, and the next, are those that are directly related to the implementation of data structures and algorithms, including the following:

- Classes and objects (Section 1.1)
- Methods (Section 1.2)
- Variables and expressions (Section 1.3)
- Control flow (Section 1.4)
- Arrays (Section 1.5)
- Input and Output (Section 1.6)
- Packages (Section 1.8)
- Exceptions (Section 2.3)
- Interfaces (Section 2.4)
- Casting (Section 2.4.4).

This book does not provide a complete description of the Java language, however. There are major aspects of the language that are not directly relevant to data structure and algorithm design. These language features are therefore not included here, but are nevertheless fundamental parts of the language. These include graphical user interfaces, threads, JavaBeans, and sockets. For the reader interested in learning more about these topics, please see the notes at the end of this chapter.

1.1 Classes, Types, and Objects

The first digital computer, ENIAC, did not use any data structures to speak of. Its primary function was to quickly perform long sequences of mathematical calculations at speeds that were truly remarkable for its time. As important an achievement as this was, the major impact of ENIAC was not in the actual calculations it performed, but in the computational era it ushered in.

Computers are utilized today in myriad different ways. For consumers, computers provide real-time control of washing machines, automobiles, and ovens. For scientists and engineers, computers are used to design new airplanes, model complex molecules, and simulate galaxies. Computers are essential for modern-day commerce. They are used to perform most financial transactions and to facilitate a host of different modes of communication, including the Internet. Indeed, we have come a long way since 1945 when ENIAC was first built.

Modern computers routinely have memory capacities that are billions of times larger than ENIAC ever had,[1] and memory capacities continue to grow at astonishing rates. This growth in capacity has brought with it a new and exciting role for computers. Rather than simply being fast calculators, modern computers are *information processors*. They store, analyze, search, transfer, and update huge collections of complex data. Quickly performing these tasks requires that data be well organized and that the methods for accessing and maintaining data be fast and efficient. In short, modern computers need good data structures and algorithms.

In Java, data structures and algorithms are implemented using classes and objects. The main "actors" in a Java program are *objects*. Objects store data and provide methods for accessing and modifying this data. Every object is an instance of a *class*, which defines the *type* of data that the object stores, as well as the kinds of operations that can act on that data. In particular, the allowable *members* of a class in Java are the following:

- Data of Java objects are stored in *instance variables* (also called *fields*). Therefore, if an object from some class is to store data, then its class must specify the instance variables for such objects. Instance variables can either come from base types (such as integers, floating-point numbers, or Booleans) or they can refer to objects of other classes.
- The operations that can act on data, and which express the "messages" that objects respond to, are called *methods*. The methods of a class consist of constructors, procedures, and functions. They define the behavior of objects from that class.

---

[1]ENIAC's memory was upgraded around 1952 to be able to store a program of 1,800 two-digit instructions and a data set of 100 ten-digit numbers.

In short, an object is a specific combination of data and the methods that can process and communicate that data. Classes define the *types* for objects; hence, objects are sometimes referred to as instances of their defining class, for they take on the name of that class as their type.

How Classes Are Declared

The syntax for a Java class definition is as follows:

```
[⟨class_modifiers⟩] class ⟨class_name⟩
                   [extends ⟨superclass_name⟩]
                   [implements ⟨interface_1⟩, ⟨interface_2⟩, . . . ] {

    // class methods and instance variable definitions go here . . .

}
```

where we use a syntax shorthand where optional material is enclosed in square brackets ("[" and "]") and identifiers are indicated by words inside angle brackets ("⟨" and "⟩"). In Java, identifiers, such as ⟨class_name⟩, must begin with a letter and be a string of letters, numbers, and underscore characters (where "letter" and "number" can be from any written language defined in the Unicode character set). We list the exceptions to this general rule for Java identifiers in Table 1.1. We discuss the optional **extends** and **implements** clauses in Sections 2.2.1 and 2.4, respectively.

A simple example template for a class definition without these optional clauses is as follows:

```
class Gnome {

    // instance variable definitions would go here...

    // method definitions would go here...

}
```

In this example, we do not use any class modifiers (which we discuss next). Notice that the class definition is delimited by braces, that is, it begins with a "{" and ends with a "}." In Java, any set of statements between the braces "{" and "}" define a program *block*.

Reserved Words			
abstract	else	interface	switch
boolean	extends	long	synchronized
break	false	native	this
byte	final	new	throw
case	finally	null	throws
catch	float	package	transient
char	for	private	true
class	goto	protected	try
const	if	public	void
continue	implements	return	volatile
default	import	short	while
do	instanceof	static	
double	int	super	

Table 1.1: A listing of the reserved words in Java. These names cannot be used as method or variable names in Java.

Class Modifiers

Class modifiers are optional keywords that precede the **class** keyword. They modify a class's scope and status in a program in the following ways:

- The **abstract** class modifier describes a class that has abstract methods. Abstract methods are declared with the **abstract** keyword and are empty (that is, they have no block defining a body of code for this method). A class that has nothing but abstract methods and no instance variables is more properly called an interface (see Section 2.4), so an **abstract** class usually has a mixture of abstract methods and actual methods. (We discuss abstract classes and their uses in Section 2.4.)

- The **final** class modifier describes a class that can have no subclasses.

- The **public** class modifier describes a class that can be instantiated or extended by anything in the same package or by anything that *imports* the class. (This is explained in more detail in Section 1.8.) All public classes are declared in their own separate file called ⟨classname⟩.java. There can only be one public class per file.

- If the **public** class modifier is not used, the class is considered *friendly*. This means that it can be used and instantiated by all classes in the same *package*. This is the default class modifier.

1.1.1 Base Types

The types of objects are determined by the class they come from. For the sake of efficiency and simplicity, Java also has the following *base types* (also called *primitive types*), which are not objects:

boolean	Boolean value: true or false
char	16-bit Unicode character
byte	8-bit signed two's complement integer
short	16-bit signed two's complement integer
int	32-bit signed two's complement integer
long	64-bit signed two's complement integer
float	32-bit floating-point number (IEEE 754-1985)
double	64-bit floating-point number (IEEE 754-1985)

A variable declared to have one of these types simply stores a value of that type, rather than a reference to some object. Integer constants, like 14 or 195, are of type **int**, unless followed immediately by an 'L' or 'l', in which case they are of type **long**. Floating-point constants, like 3.1415 or 2.158*e*5, are of type **double**, unless followed immediately by an 'F' or 'f', in which case they are of type **float**.

Even though they themselves do not refer to objects, base-type variables are useful in the context of objects, for they often make up the instance variables (or fields) inside an object. They also provide an additional safety feature of Java, in that such instance variables are always given an initial value whenever an object containing them is created.

1.1.2 Objects

In Java, a new object is created from a defined class by using the **new** operator. The **new** operator creates a new object from a specified class and returns a *reference* to that object. Here is the syntax for using the **new** operator in an expression:

> **new** ⟨class_type⟩([param, param, . . .])

Typically, such an expression would appear in an assignment statement, having the following form:

> ⟨variable_name⟩ = **new** ⟨class_type⟩([param, param, . . .]);

We use ⟨variable_name⟩ here to denote an identifier that is the name of an object variable, which is a reference to the object just created. The ⟨class_type⟩ name refers to a special *constructor* method (with the same name as the class), which initializes the object being created. (We say more about constructor methods in Section 1.2.) The ⟨class_type⟩ is an identifier defining the name of the class, and the list of parameters is optional. Calling the **new** operator on a class type as shown above causes three events to occur:

- A new object is dynamically allocated in memory, and all instance variables are initialized to standard default values. The default values are **null** for object variables and 0 for all base types except **boolean** variables (which are **false** by default).
- The constructor for the new object is called with the parameters specified. The constructor fills in meaningful values for the instance variables and performs any additional computations that must be done to create this object.
- After the constructor returns, the **new** operator returns a reference (that is, a memory address) to the newly created object. If the expression is in the form of an assignment statement, then this address is stored in the object variable, so the object variable *refers* to this newly created object.

In the following statement, a new Point object is created with a constructor that takes the coordinates of the point as arguments, and variable myPoint becomes a reference to that object:

```
myPoint = new Point (3,6);
```

Number Objects

We sometimes want to store numbers as objects, but base type numbers are not themselves objects, as we have noted. To get around this obstacle, Java defines a wrapper class for each numeric base type. We call these classes *number classes*. In Table 1.2, we show the numeric base types and their corresponding number class, along with examples of how number objects are created and accessed.

Base Type	Class Name	Creation Example	Access Example
byte	Byte	n = **new** Byte((**byte**)34);	n.byteValue()
short	Short	n = **new** Short((**short**)100);	n.shortValue()
int	Integer	n = **new** Integer(1045);	n.intValue()
long	Long	n = **new** Long(10849L);	n.longValue()
float	Float	n = **new** Float(3.934F);	n.floatValue()
double	Double	n = **new** Double(3.934);	n.doubleValue()

Table 1.2: Java number classes. Each class is given with its corresponding base type and example expressions for creating and accessing such objects. For each row, we assume the variable n is declared with the corresponding class name.

String Objects

A string is a sequence of characters that come from some ***alphabet***, which is a set Σ of ***characters***. Each character c that makes up a string s can be referenced by its index in the string, which is equal to the number of characters that come before c in s (so the first character is at index 0). In Java, the alphabet Σ used to define strings is the Unicode international character set, a 16-bit character encoding that covers the most used written languages. Other programming languages tend to use the smaller ASCII character set (which is a proper subset of the Unicode alphabet based on a 7-bit encoding). In addition, Java defines a special built-in class of objects called String objects.

Let P be a string of m characters, which we write as $P[0]P[1]P[2]\ldots P[m-1]$. For example, P could be the string `"hogs and dogs"`, which has length 13 and could have come from someone's Web page. In this case, $P[2] = $ 'g' and $P[5] = $ 'a'. Alternately, P could be the string `"CGTAATAGTTAATCCG"`, which has length 16 and could have come from a scientific application for DNA sequencing, where $\Sigma = \{G, C, A, T\}$.

String processing involves dealing with both large strings and smaller ones. It also involves combining smaller strings into larger ones. The primary operation for combining strings is called ***concatenation***, which takes a string

$$P = P[0]P[1]\ldots P[m-1]$$

and a string

$$Q = Q[0]Q[1]\ldots Q[n-1]$$

and combines them into a new string, denoted $P + Q$, with the following sequence of characters:

$$P[0]P[1]\ldots P[m-1]Q[0]Q[1]\ldots Q[n-1].$$

In Java, the "+" operation works exactly like this when acting on two strings. Thus, it is legal (and even useful) in Java to write an assignment statement like

```
String s = "kilo" + "meters";
```

This statement defines a variable s that references objects of the String class, and assigns it the string `"kilometers"`. (We will discuss assignment statements and expressions such as that above in more detail later in this chapter.) Every object in Java is assumed to have a built-in method toString() that returns a string associated with the object. This description of the String class should be sufficient for most uses; we discuss the String class and its "relative" the StringBuffer class in more detail in Section 11.1.

Instance Variables

Java classes can define *instance variables*, also called *fields*. These variables represent the data associated with the objects of a class. Instance variables must have a *type*, which can either be a *base type* (such as **int, float, double**) or a *reference type*, that is, a class, such as String, an interface (see Section 2.4), or an array (see Section 1.5). The syntax for declaring an instance variable is as follows:

[⟨variable_modifier⟩] ⟨variable_type⟩ ⟨variable_name⟩ [=⟨initial_value⟩];

The syntax of the ⟨variable_name⟩ parameter is the same as any other Java identifier. The ⟨variable_type⟩ parameter is either a base type, indicating that this variable stores values of this type, or a class name, indicating that this variable is a *reference* to an object from this class. The optional ⟨initial_value⟩ must match the variable's type. Our running example, the Gnome class, with some definitions of instance variables, could look like the following:

```java
class Gnome {
    // Instance variables:
    protected String name;
    protected int age;
    protected Gnome gnome_buddy;
    private boolean magical;
    public double height = 2.6;           // an initialization
    public static final int MAX_HEIGHT = 3; // a constant

    // Method definitions would go here...

}
```

Note the use of comments in this and other examples. These comments are annotations provided for human readers and are not processed by a Java compiler. Java allows for two kinds of comments—block comments and inline comments—which define text ignored by the compiler. Java uses a /* to begin a block comment and a */ to close it. In addition, Java uses a // to begin inline comments and ignores everything else on the line. For example:

```java
/*
 *  This is a block comment.
 */

// This is an inline comment.
```

Also note the use of instance variables in the Gnome example. The variables age, magical, and height are base types, the variable name is a reference to an instance of the built in class String, and the variable gnome_buddy is a reference to an object of the class we are now defining. Our declaration of the instance variable MAX_HEIGHT is taking advantage of a number of variable modifiers to define a "variable" that has a fixed constant value. Next, we describe the precise meaning of these and other variable modifiers that can be used in Java.

Variable Modifiers

The scope (visibility) of instance variables can be controlled through the use of the following *variable modifiers*:

- **public**: Anyone can access public instance variables.
- **protected**: Only methods of the same package or of subclasses can access protected instance variables.
- **private**: Only methods of the same class (not methods of a subclass) can access private instance variables.
- If none of the above modifiers are used, the instance variable is considered friendly. Friendly instance variables can be accessed by any class in the same package. Packages are discussed in more detail in Section 1.8.

In addition to scope variable modifiers, there are also the following usage modifiers:

- **static**: The **static** keyword is used to declare a variable that is associated with the class, not with individual instances of that class. Static variables are used to store "global" information about a class (for example, a static variable could be used to maintain the total number of Gnome objects created). Static variables exist even if no instance of their class is created.
- **final**: A final instance variable is one that *must* be assigned an initial value, and then can never be assigned a new value after that. If it is a base type, then it is a constant (like the MAX_HEIGHT constant in the Gnome class above). If an object variable is **final**, then it will always refer to the same object (even if that object changes its internal state).

Constant values associated with a class should be declared to be both **static** and **final**. Before we go into more detail about instance variables and their uses, however (which we do in Section 1.3), let us discuss the methods that can act on instance variables in a class.

1.2   Methods

Methods in Java are conceptually similar to functions and procedures in other high-level languages. In general, they are "chunks" of code that can be called on a particular object (from some class). Methods can accept parameters as arguments, and their behavior depends on the object they belong to and the values of any parameters that are passed. Every method in Java is specified in the body of some class. A method definition has two parts: the ***signature***, which defines the name and parameters for a method, and the ***body***, which defines what the method does.

A method allows a programmer to send a message to an object. The method signature specifies how such a message should look and the method body specifies what the object will do when it receives such a message.

Declaring Methods

The syntax for defining a method is as follows:

```
[⟨method_modifiers⟩] ⟨return_type⟩ ⟨method_name⟩ ([⟨params⟩]) {
    // method body . . .
}
```

where ⟨params⟩ is an optional comma-separated list of parameter declarations that has the following syntax:

```
⟨param_type⟩ ⟨param_name⟩ [, ⟨param_type⟩ ⟨param_name⟩ [, . . .] ]
```

When a method of a class is invoked, it is invoked on a specific instance of that class and can change the state of that object (except for a **static** method, which is associated with the class itself). For example, invoking the following method on a particular gnome changes its name.

```
public void renameGnome (String s) {
    name = s;      // Reassign the name instance variable of this gnome.
}
```

The syntax rule for the return type of a method is the same as for instance variables, and this rule also applies to parameter names. In the example above, we use the keyword **void** to indicate that this method has no return value. Parameters that are passed to a method can be either base types or object references. These variables and the instance variables of the class can be referenced inside the body of the method. Likewise, other methods of this class can be called from inside the body of a method. We discuss each of the components of a method declaration in more detail below.

Method Modifiers

As with instance variables, method modifiers can restrict the scope of a method as follows:

- **public**: Anyone can call public methods.
- **protected**: Only methods of the same package or of subclasses can call a protected method.
- **private**: Only methods of the same class (not methods of a subclass) can call a private method.
- If none of the above modifiers are used, then the method is friendly. Friendly methods can only be called by objects of classes in the same package.

The above method modifiers may be preceded by the following additional modifiers, which further restrict a method:

- **abstract**: A method declared as **abstract** will have no code. The signature of an abstract method is followed by a semicolon with no method body. For example:

  public abstract void setHeight (**double** newHeight);

  Abstract methods may only appear within an abstract class. We discuss the usefulness of this construct in Section 2.4.
- **final**: This is a method that cannot be overridden by a subclass.
- **static**: This is a method that is associated with the class itself, and not with a particular instance of the class. Static methods can also be used to change the state of static variables associated with a class (provided these variables are not declared to be **final**).

Return Types

A method definition must specify the type of value the method will return. If the method does not return a value, then the keyword **void** must be used. If the return type is **void**, the method is called a *procedure*; otherwise, it is called a *function*. To return a value in Java, a method must use the **return** keyword (and the type returned must match the return type of the method). Here is an example of a method (from inside the Gnome class) that is a function:

```
public boolean isMagical () {
    return magical;
}
```

As soon as a **return** is performed in a Java function, the method invocation ends.

Java functions can return only one value. To return multiple values in Java, we should instead combine all the values we wish to return in a ***compound object***, whose instance variables include all the values we want to return, and then return a reference to that compound object. In addition, we can change the internal state of an object that is passed to a method as another way of "returning" multiple results.

Parameters

A method's parameters are defined in a comma-separated list enclosed in parentheses after the name of the method. A parameter consists of two parts, the parameter type and the parameter name. If a method has no parameters, then only an empty pair of parentheses is used.

All parameters in Java are passed ***by value***, that is, any time we pass a parameter to a method, a copy of that parameter is made for use within the method body. So if we pass an **int** variable to a method, then that variable's integer value is copied. The method can change the copy but not the original. If we pass an object reference as a parameter to a method, then the reference is copied as well. Remember that we can have many different variables that all refer to the same object. Changing the internal reference inside a method will not change the reference that was passed in. For example, if we pass a Gnome reference g to a method that calls this parameter h, then this method can change the reference h to point to a different object, but g will still refer to the same object it did before. Of course, the method can use the reference h to change the internal state of the object, and this will change g's object as well (since g and h are currently referring to the same object).

Constructor Methods

A ***constructor*** is a special kind of method that is used to initialize newly created objects. Java has a special way to declare the constructor and a special way to invoke the constructor. First, let's look at the syntax for declaring a constructor:

```
[constructor_modifiers] ⟨constructor_name⟩ ([⟨params⟩]) {
    // Constructor body . . .
}
```

Thus, its syntax is essentially the same as that of any other method. The name of the constructor must be the same as the name of the class it constructs, however. So, if the class is called Fish, the constructor must be called Fish as well. In addition, a constructor has no return value. So its return type is implicitly void. The constructor modifier follows the same rules as for normal methods. An **abstract**, **static**, or **final** constructor is not allowed, however.

Here is an example:

```
public Fish (int w, String n) {
  weight = w;
  name = n;
}
```

The body of a constructor is like a normal method's body (with one exception that we discuss in the next chapter). This body is intended to be used to initialize the data associated with objects of this class so that they may be in a stable initial state when first created.

Constructors are invoked in a unique way: they *must* be called using the **new** operator. So, upon invocation, a new instance of this class is automatically created and its constructor is then called, to initialize its instance variables and perform other setup tasks. For example, consider the following constructor invocation (which is also a declaration for the myFish variable):

```
Fish myFish = new Fish (7, "Wally");
```

A class can have many constructors, but each must have a different *signature*, that is, each must be distinguished by the type and number of the parameters it takes.

The main Method

Some Java classes are meant to be utilized by other classes, others are meant to define stand-alone programs. Classes that define stand-alone programs must contain one other special kind of method for a class—the main method. When we wish to execute a stand-alone Java program, we reference the name of the class that defines this program, say, by issuing the following command (in DOS, Linux, or UNIX):

```
java Aquarium
```

In this case, the Java run-time system looks for a compiled version of the Aquarium class, and then invokes the special main method in that class. This method must be declared as follows:

```
public static void main(String[] args) {
  // main method body . . .
}
```

The arguments passed as the parameter args to the main method are the command-line arguments given when the program is called. The args variable is an array of String objects; that is, a collection of indexed strings, with the first string being args[0], the second being args[1], and so on. (We say more about arrays in Section 1.5.) For example, we may have defined the Aquarium program to take an optional argument that specifies the number of fish in the aquarium. We could then invoke the program by typing

```
java Aquarium 45
```

to specify that we want an aquarium with 45 fish in it. In this case, args[0] refers to the string "45". One nice feature of the main method is that it allows each class to define a stand-alone program, and one of the uses for this method is to test all the other methods in a class. Thus, thorough use of the main method is an effective tool for debugging collections of Java classes.

Statement Blocks and Local Variables

The body of a method is a ***statement block***, which is a sequence of statements and declarations to be performed between the braces "{" and "}". Method bodies and other statement blocks can themselves have statement blocks nested inside of them. In addition to statements that perform some action, like calling the method of some object, statement blocks can contain declarations of ***local variables***. These variables are declared inside the statement body, usually at the beginning (but between the braces "{" and "}"). Local variables are similar to instance variables, but they only exist while the statement block is being executed. As soon as control flow exits out of that block, all local variables inside it can no longer be referenced. A local variable can be either a ***base type*** (such as **int**, **float**, **double**) or a ***reference*** to an instance of some class. Single statements and declarations in Java are always terminated by a semicolon, that is, a ";".

Here is the syntax for declaring local variables:

⟨variable_type⟩ ⟨variable_name⟩ [= ⟨initial_value⟩];

where the rules for the type, name, and initial value are the same as for instance variables. Here are some examples of local variable declarations:

```
{
    double r;
    Point p1 = new Point (3, 4);
    Point p2 = new Point (8, 2);
    int i = 512;
    double e = 2.71828;
}
```

Notice that we can assign an initial value to a variable when we declare it.

We show a complete example definition of the Gnome class in Code Fragment 1.1.

```java
public class Gnome {
  // Instance variables:
  protected String name;
  protected int age;
  protected Gnome gnome_buddy;
  private boolean magical = false;
  public double height = 2.6;              // in feet
  public static final int MAX_HEIGHT = 3; // maximum height

  // Constructors:
  Gnome(String nm, int ag, Gnome bud, double hgt) { // fully parameterized
    name = nm;
    age = ag;
    gnome_buddy = bud;
    height = hgt;
  }
  Gnome() { // Default constructor
    name = "Rumple";
    age = 204;
    gnome_buddy = null;
    height = 2.1;
  }

  // Methods:
  public static void makeKing (Gnome h) {
    h.name = "King " + h.getRealName();
    h.magical = true;   // Only the Gnome class can reference this field.
  }
  public void makeMeKing () {
    name = "King " + getRealName();
    magical = true;
  }
  public boolean isMagical() { return magical; }
  public void setHeight(int newHeight) { height = newHeight; }
  public String getName() { return "I won't tell!"; }
  public String getRealName() { return name; }
  public void renameGnome(String s) { name = s; }
}
```

Code Fragment 1.1: The Gnome class.

1.3 Expressions

Variables and constants are used in *expressions* to define new values and to modify variables. In this section, we discuss how expressions work in Java in more detail. Expressions involve the use of *literals*, *variables*, and *operators*. Since we have already discussed variables, let us briefly focus on literals and then discuss operators in some detail.

1.3.1 Literals

A *literal* is any "constant" value that can be used in an assignment or other expression. Java allows the following kinds of literals:

- The **null** object reference (this is the only object literal, and it is defined to be from the general Object class).
- Boolean: **true** and **false**.
- Integer: The default for an integer like 176 or -52 is that it is of type **int**, which is a 32-bit integer. A long integer literal must end with an "L" or "l," for example, 176L or -52l, and defines a 64-bit integer.
- Floating Point: The default for floating point numbers, such as 3.1415 and 10035.23, is that they are **double**. To specify that a literal is a **float**, it must end with an "F" or "f." Floating-point literals in exponential notation are also allowed, such as 3.14E2 or .19e10; the base is assumed to be 10.
- Character: In Java character constants are assumed to be taken from the Unicode alphabet. Typically, a character is defined as an individual symbol enclosed in single quotes, for example, 'a' and '?'. In addition, Java defines the following special character constants:

'\n'	(newline)	'\t'	(tab)
'\b'	(backspace)	'\r'	(return)
'\f'	(form feed)	'\\'	(backslash)
'\''	(single quote)	'\"'	(double quote).

- Strings literal: A string literal is a sequence of characters enclosed in double quotes, for example, "dogs all around" or "jump".

1.3.2 Operators

Java expressions involve composing literals and variables with operators. We survey the operators in Java in this section.

The Assignment Operator

The standard assignment operator in Java is " =". It is used to assign a value to an instance variable or local variable. Its syntax is as follows:

⟨variable⟩ = ⟨expression⟩

Where ⟨variable⟩ refers to a variable that can be referenced by the statement block containing this expression. The value of an assignment operation is the value of the expression that was assigned. Thus, if i and j are both declared as type **int**, it is correct to have an assignment statement like the following:

i = j = 25;   // works because '=' operators are evaluated right-to-left

The Dot Operator

As we have mentioned above, creating a new object in Java involves the use of the **new** operator to allocate space for the object, and then the use of a constructor of the object to initialize this space. The location (or *address*) of this space is then assigned to a *reference* variable. Therefore, a reference variable can be viewed as a link or "pointer" to some object. Every object reference variable must refer to some object, even if it is the **null** object. There can, in fact, be many references to the same object, and each reference to a specific object can be used to call methods on that object.

One of the primary uses of an object reference variable is to access the members of the class for this object, an instance of its class. That is, an object reference variable is useful for accessing the methods and instance variables associated with an object. This access is performed with the dot (".") operator. We call a method associated with an object by using the following syntax:

⟨object_reference⟩.⟨method_name⟩([⟨param⟩,⟨param⟩, ...]);

This calls the method with the specified name for the object referred to by this object reference. It can optionally be passed multiple parameters. If there are several methods with this same name defined for this object, then the Java runtime system uses the one that matches the number of parameters and most closely matches their respective types. As mentioned earlier, a method's name combined with the number and types of its parameters is called a method's *signature*, for it takes all of these parts to determine the actual method to perform for a certain method call. Consider the following examples:

```
oven.cookDinner();
oven.cookDinner(food);
oven.cookDinner(food,seasoning);
```

Each of these method calls is actually referring to a different method with the same name defined in the class that oven belongs to. Note, however, that the signature of a method in Java does not include the type that the method returns, so Java does not allow two methods with the same signature to return different types.

We refer to the instance variables associated with an object using the dot operator, with the following syntax:

$$\langle object\_reference\rangle.\langle variable\_name\rangle$$

Assuming, of course, that the scope specification for such a variable allows access, then this use can appear anywhere in an expression. Nevertheless, the name $\langle variable\_name\rangle$ must be a member of the object to which $\langle object\_reference\rangle$ refers.

If an object reference is not **final**, then it can appear on the left-hand side of an assignment as well. Consider the following examples:

```
gnome.name = "Professor Smythe";
gnome.age = 132;
```

The $\langle object\_reference\rangle$ can also be any expression that returns an object reference. So the following is also syntactically correct:

```
Gnome g = new Gnome();
String buddyName = (g.gnome_buddy).name;
```

Arithmetic Operators

The following are binary arithmetic operators in Java:

+	addition
−	subtraction
*	multiplication
/	division
%	the modulo operator

This last operator, modulo, is also known as the "remainder" operator, for it is the remainder left after an integer division. We often use "mod" to denote the modulo operator, and we define it formally as

$$n \bmod m = r, \text{ such that } n = mq + r, \text{ for an integer } q \text{ and } 0 \le r < n.$$

Java also provides a unary minus ($-$), which can be placed in front of an arithmetic expression to invert its sign. Parentheses can be used in any expression to define the order of evaluation. Java also uses a fairly intuitive operator precedence rule to determine the order of evaluation when parentheses are not used. Unlike C++, Java does not allow operator overloading.

Increment and Decrement Operators

Like C and C++, Java provides increment and decrement operators. Specifically, it provides the plus-one increment (++) and decrement (−−) operators. If such an operator is used in front of a variable reference, then 1 is added to (or subtracted from) the variable and its value is read into the expression. If it is used after a variable reference, then the value is first read and then the variable is incremented or decremented by 1. So, for example, the code fragment

```
int i = 8;
int j = i++;
int k = ++i;
int m = i−−;
int n = 9 + i++;
```

assigns 8 to j, 10 to k, 10 to m, 18 to n, and leaves i with value 10.

Logical Operators

Java allows for the standard comparison operators between numbers:

$<$	less than
$<=$	less than or equal to
$==$	equal to
$!=$	not equal to
$>=$	greater than or equal to
$>$	greater than

The operators $==$ and $!=$ can also be used for object references. The type of the result of a comparison is a **boolean**.

Operators that operate on **boolean** values are the following:

!	not (prefix)
&&	conditional and
||	conditional or

The Boolean operators && and || will not evaluate the second operand (to the right) in their expression if it is not needed to determine the value of the expression. This feature is useful, for example, for constructing Boolean expressions where we first test that a certain condition holds (such as a reference not being null) and then we test a condition that could have otherwise generated an error condition had the prior test not succeeded.

Bitwise Operators

Java also provides the following bitwise operators for integers and Booleans:

~	bitwise complement (prefix unary operator)
&	bitwise and
|	bitwise or
^	bitwise exclusive-or
<<	shift bits left, filling in with zeros
>>	shift bits right, filling in with sign bit
>>>	shift bits right, filling in with zeros

Operational Assignment Operators

Besides the standard assignment operator ($=$), Java also provides a number of other assignment operators that have operational side effects. These other kinds of operators are of the following form:

⟨variable⟩ ⟨op⟩= ⟨expression⟩;

This is equivalent to

⟨variable⟩ = ⟨variable⟩ ⟨op⟩ ⟨expression⟩;

except that if ⟨variable⟩ contains an expression (for example, an array index), the expression is evaluated only once. Thus, the code fragment

```
a[5] = 10;
i = 5;
a[i++] += 2;
```

leaves a[5] with value 12 and i with value 6.

String Concatenation

Strings can be composed using the ***concatenation*** operator ($+$), so that the code

```
String rug = "carpet";
String dog = "spot";
String mess = rug + dog;
String answer = mess + " will cost me " + 5 + " dollars!";
```

would have the effect of making answer refer to the string

```
"carpetspot will cost me 5 dollars!"
```

This example also shows how Java converts nonstring constants into strings, when they are involved in a string concatenation operation.

Operator Precedence

Operators in Java are given preferences, or precedence, that determine the order in which operations are performed when the absence of parentheses brings up evaluation ambiguities.

We show the precedence of the operators in Java (which, incidentally, is the same as in C) in Table 1.3.

	Operator Precedence	
	Type	**Symbols**
1	postfix ops prefix ops cast	$\langle exp \rangle$ ++ $\langle exp \rangle$ $--$ $++\langle exp \rangle$ $--\langle exp \rangle$ $+\langle exp \rangle$ $-\langle exp \rangle$ $\tilde{}\langle exp \rangle$ $!\langle exp \rangle$ $(\langle type \rangle)\langle exp \rangle$
2	mult./div.	* / %
3	add./subt.	+ −
4	shift	<< >> >>>
5	comparison	< <= > >= **instanceof**
6	equality	== !=
7	bitwise-and	&
8	bitwise-xor	^
9	bitwise-or	|
10	and	&&
11	or	||
12	conditional	$\langle bool\_exp \rangle$? $\langle true\_val \rangle$: $\langle false\_val \rangle$
13	assignment	= += −= *= /= %= >>= <<= >>>= &= ^= |=

Table 1.3: The Java precedence rules. Operators in Java are evaluated according to the above ordering, if parentheses are not used to determine the order of evaluation. Operators on the same line are evaluated in left-to-right order (except for assignment and prefix operations, which are evaluated right-to-left), subject to the conditional evaluation rule for Boolean **and** and **or** operations. The operations are listed from highest to lowest precedence (we use $\langle exp \rangle$ to denote an atomic or parenthesized expression). Without parenthesization, higher precedence operators are performed before lower precedence operators.

We have now discussed almost all of the operators listed in Table 1.3. A notable exception is the conditional operator, which involves evaluating a Boolean expression and then taking on the appropriate value depending on whether this Boolean expression is true or false. (We discuss the use of the **instanceof** operator in the next chapter.)

1.3.3   Casting in Expressions

Casting is an operation that allows us to change the type of a variable. In essence, we can take a variable of one type and *cast* it into an equivalent variable of another type. Casting can be useful for doing certain numerical and input/output operations.
The syntax for casting a variable to a desired type is as follows:

$$((\text{desired\_type}))(\text{variable});$$

There are two fundamental types of casting that can be done in Java. We can either cast with respect to the base numerical types or we can cast with respect to objects. We discuss here how to perform casting of numerical and string types, and we discuss object casting in Section 2.4.4. For instance, it might be helpful to cast an **int** to a **double** in order to perform operations like division.

Ordinary Casting

When casting from a **double** to an **int**, we may lose precision. This means that the resulting double value will be rounded down. But we can cast an **int** to a **double** without this worry. For example, consider the following:

```
double d1 = 3.2;
double d2 = 3.9999;
int i1 = (int)d1;        // i1 has value 3
int i2 = (int)d2;        // i2 has value 3
double d3 = (double)i2;    // d3 has value 3.0
```

Casting with Operators

Certain binary operators, like division, will have different results depending on the variable types they are used with. We must take care to make sure operations perform their computations on values of the intended type. When used with integers, division does not keep track of the fractional part, for example. When used with doubles, division keeps this part, as is illustrated in the following example:

```
int i1 = 3;
int i2 = 6;
dresult = (double)i1 / (double)i2;    // dresult has value 0.5
dresult = i1 / i2;                    // dresult has value 0.0
```

Notice that when i1 and i2 were cast to doubles, regular division for real numbers was performed. When i1 and i2 were not cast, the " /" operator performed an integer division and the result of i1 / i2 was the **int** 0. Java then did an *implicit cast* to assign an **int** value to the **double** result. We discuss implicit casting next.

Implicit Casting

If an ***explicit cast***, that is, a cast included in the code, is not specified, then there are cases where Java will perform an ***implicit cast***. This means that Java will go ahead and change the types of variables, even though the programmer did not explicitly include the cast. Java will perform a cast according to the type of the assignment variable, provided there is no loss of precision. For example:

```
int iresult, i = 3;
double dresult, d = 3.2;
dresult = i / d;          // dresult is 0.9375. i was cast to a double
iresult = i / d;          // loss of precision -> this is a compilation error
```

Java will not perform implicit casts where precision is lost. So, the last line above should be

```
iresult = (int) i / d;    // iresult is 0, since the fractional part is lost
```

This explicit cast shows the programmer accepts the loss of precision.

The general rule with casting then is to ***play it safe***. If unsure about whether the compiler will be implicitly casting our variables, it is better to spell it out. Explicitly casting variables guarantees the right results.

Implicit Casting with String Objects

There is one situation in Java when only implicit casting is allowed, and that is in string concatenation. Any time a string is concatenated with any object or base type, that object or base type is automatically converted to a string. Explicit casting of an object or base type to a string is not allowed, however. Thus, the following assignments are incorrect:

```
String s = (String) 4.5;              // this is wrong!
String t = "Value = " + (String) 13;  // this is wrong!
String u = 22;                        // this is wrong!
```

To perform a conversion to a string, we must instead use the appropriate toString method or perform an implicit cast via the concatenation operation.

Thus, the following statements are correct:

```
String s = "" + 4.5;                  // correct, but poor style
String t = "Value = " + 13;           // this is good
String u = Integer.toString(22);      // this is good
```

As noted above, every object in Java supports a toString() method (with no arguments), which converts that object to a string. In addition, the Integer, Long, Short, Byte, Float, and Double classes each have a built-in static toString(x) method for converting the analogous base type to a string.

1.4 Control Flow

Control flow in Java is similar to that of other high-level languages. We review the basic structure and syntax of control flow in Java in this section, including method returns, **if** statements, **switch** statements, loops, and restricted forms of "jumps" (the **break** and **continue** statements).

1.4.1 The If and Switch Statements

In Java, conditionals work the same as in other languages. They provide a way to make a decision and then execute one or more different statement blocks based on the outcome of that decision.

The If Statement

The syntax of an **if** statement is as follows:

```
if (⟨boolean_expr⟩)
    ⟨true_statement⟩
[else if (⟨boolean_expr⟩)
    ⟨else_if_statement⟩]
[else
    ⟨else_statement⟩]
```

where each statement can be a block of statements enclosed in braces ("{" and "}"). In addition, the **else if** and **else** parts are optional; either or both may be omitted from a valid if statement.

Unlike C and C++, the expression in an **if** statement in Java *must* be a Boolean expression.

This requirement helps us avoid a common programming error, for the following bug will be caught by the compiler:

```
i = 5;
// intermediate code ...
if (i = 5)              // (THIS IS WRONG!)
    // ...
```

In the above example, the "condition" is really an assignment, which is of type **int**. Thus, this is not a correct **if** statement. The following is correct, however:

```java
if (snowLevel < 2) {
    goToClass();
    comeHome();
}
else if (snowLevel < 5) {
    goSledding();
    haveSnowballFight();
}
else
    stayAtHome();
```

Switch Statements

Java provides for multiple-value control flow using the **switch** statement. The following is an indicative example:

```java
public Candy getCandy (int money) {
    Candy candy;
    int tax=1;
    switch (money+tax) {
      case 5:
          candy = new Gumball ();
          break;
      case 25:
          candy = new Peanuts ();
          break;
      case 50:
          candy = new Candybar ();
          break;
      default:
          candy = new EmptyWrapper();
          break;
    }
    return candy;
}
```

The **switch** statement evaluates an integer expression (such as " money+tax") and causes control flow to jump to the code location labeled with the value of this expression. If there is no matching label, then control flow jumps to the location labeled "**default**." This is the only explicit jump performed by the **switch** statement, however, so flow of control "falls through" to other cases if the code for each case is not ended with a **break** statement (which causes control flow to jump to the next line after the **switch** statement).

1.4.2 Loops

Another important control flow mechanism in a programming language is looping. Java provides for three types of loops.

While Loops

The simplest kind of loop in Java is a **while** loop. Such a loop tests that a certain condition is satisfied and will perform the body of the loop each time this condition is evaluated to be **true**. The syntax for such a conditional test before a loop body is executed is as follows:

$$\textbf{while } (\langle \text{boolean\_expression} \rangle)$$
$$\langle \text{loop\_body\_statement} \rangle$$

At the beginning of each iteration, the loop tests the Boolean expression and then executes the loop body only if this expression evaluates to true. The loop body statement can also be a block of statements.

Consider, for example, a gnome that is trying to water all of the carrots in his carrot patch, which he does so long as his watering can is not empty. Since his can might be empty to begin with, we would write the code to perform this task as follows:

```
public void waterCarrots () {
    Carrot current = garden.findNextCarrot ();

    while (!waterCan.isEmpty ()) {
        water (current, waterCan);
        current = garden.findNextCarrot ();
    }
}
```

Recall that "!" in Java is the "not" operator.

For Loops

Another kind of loop is the **for** loop. In their simplest form, **for** loops provide for repeated code based on an integer index. In Java, we can do that and much more. The functionality of a **for** loop is significantly more flexible. In particular, the usage of a **for** loop is split into four sections: the initialization, the condition, the increment, and the body.

Here is the syntax for a Java **for** loop:

```
for ([⟨initialization⟩];[⟨condition⟩];[⟨increment⟩])
    ⟨body_statement⟩
```

In the ⟨initialization⟩ section, we can declare an index variable that will only be in the scope of the **for** loop. For example, if we want a loop that indexes on a counter, and we have no need for the counter variable outside of the **for** loop, then declaring

```
for (int counter = 0; ⟨condition⟩; ⟨increment⟩)
```

will declare a variable counter whose scope is the loop body only.

In the ⟨condition⟩ section, we specify the repeat (while) condition of the loop. This must be a Boolean expression. The body of the **for** loop will be executed each time the ⟨condition⟩ is **true** when evaluated at the beginning of a potential iteration. As soon as ⟨condition⟩ evaluates to **false**, then the loop body is not executed, and, instead, the program executes the next statement after the **for** loop.

In the ⟨increment⟩ section, we declare the incrementing statement for the loop. The incrementing statement can be any legal statement, allowing for significant flexibility in coding. Thus, the syntax of a **for** loop is equivalent to the following:

```
[⟨initialization⟩]
while (⟨condition⟩) {
    ⟨body_statement⟩
    [⟨increment⟩]
}
```

except that a **while** loop in Java cannot have an empty condition, whereas a **for** loop in Java can. The following example shows a simple **for** loop in Java:

```
public void eatApples (Apples apples) {
    numApples = apples.getNumApples ();
    for (int x = 0; x < numApples; x++) {
        eatApple (apples.getApple (x));
        spitOutCore ();
    }
}
```

In the Java example above, the loop variable x was declared as **int** x = 0. Before each iteration, the loop tests the condition " x < numApples" and executes the loop body only if this is true. Finally, at the end of each iteration the loop uses the statement x++ to increment the loop variable x before again testing the condition.

Do-While Loops

Java has another kind of loop besides the **for** loop and the standard **while** loop—the **do-while** loop. The former loops tests a condition before performing an iteration of the loop body, the **do-while** loop tests a condition after the loop body. The syntax for a **do-while** loop is as shown below:

```
do
    ⟨loop_body_statement⟩
while (⟨boolean_expression⟩)
```

Again, the loop body statement will typically be a block of statements, and the conditional must be a Boolean expression. In a **do-while** loop, we repeat the loop body for as long as the condition is true each time it is evaluated.

Consider, for example, that we want to prompt the user for input and then do something useful with that input. (We discuss Java input and output in more detail in Section 1.6.) A possible condition, in this case, for exiting the loop is when the user enters an empty string. However, even in this case, we may want to handle that input and inform the user that she has quit. The following example illustrates this case:

```java
public void getUserInput() {
    String input;
    do {
        input = getInputString();
        handleInput(input);
    } while (input.length()>0);
}
```

Notice the exit condition for the above example. Specifically, it is written to be consistent with the rule in Java that **do-while** loops exit when the condition is ***not*** true (unlike the repeat-until construct used in other languages).

1.4.3 Explicit Control-Flow Statements

Java also provides statements that allow for explicit change in the flow of control of a program.

Returning from a Method

If a Java method is declared with return type of **void**, then flow of control returns when it reaches the last line of code in the method or when it encounters a **return** statement with no argument. If a method is declared with a return type, however, the method is a function and it must exit by returning the function's value as an argument to a **return** statement. The following (correct) example illustrates returning from a function:

```java
// Check for a specific birthday
public boolean checkBDay (int date) {
    if (date == Birthdays.MIKES_BDAY) {
        return true;
    }
    return false;
}
```

It follows that the **return** statement *must* be the last statement executed in a function, as the rest of the code will never be reached.

Note that there is a significant difference between a statement being the last line of code that is *executed* in a method and the last line of code in the method itself. In the example above, the line **return true;** is clearly not the last line of code that is written in the function, but it may be the last line that is executed (if the condition involving date is **true**). Such a statement explicitly interrupts the flow of control in the method. There are two other such explicit control-flow statements, which are used in conjunction with loops and switch statements.

The break Statement

The typical use of a **break** statement has the following simple syntax:

```java
break;
```

It is used to "break" out of the innermost **switch**, **for**, **while**, or **do-while** statement body. When it is executed, a break statement causes the flow of control to jump to the next line after the loop or **switch** statement body containing the **break**.

The **break** statement can also be used in a labeled form to jump out of an outer-nested loop or **switch** statement. In this case, it has the syntax

break ⟨label⟩;

where ⟨label⟩ is a Java identifier that is used to label a loop or **switch** statement. Such a label can only appear at the beginning of the declaration of a loop; there are no other kinds of "go to" statements in Java.

We illustrate the use of a label with a **break** statement in the following simple example:

```
public static boolean hasZeroEntry (int[][] a) {
    boolean foundFlag = false;

zeroSearch:
  for (int i=0; i<a.length; i++) {
      for (int j=0; j<a[i].length; j++) {
          if (a[i][j] == 0) {
              foundFlag = true;
              break zeroSearch;
          }
      }
  }
    return foundFlag;
}
```

The above example also uses arrays, which are covered in Section 1.5.

The continue Statement

The other statement to explicitly change the flow of control in a Java program is the **continue** statement, which has the following syntax:

continue [⟨label⟩];

where ⟨label⟩ is a Java identifier that is used to label a loop. As mentioned above, there are no explicit "go to" statements in Java. Likewise, the **continue** statement can only be used inside loops (**for**, **while**, and **do-while**). The **continue** statement causes the execution to skip over the remaining steps of the loop body in the current iteration (but then continue the loop if its condition is satisfied).

1.5 Arrays

An *array* is a numbered collection of variables all of the same type. Each variable, or *cell*, in an array has an *index*, and the cells in an array are numbered consecutively starting with 0 and going to $N-1$, where N is the *length* of the array, which is also known as its *capacity*. A value stored in a cell of an array is called an *element*. Any index not in the range from 0 to $N-1$ is said to be *out of bounds*.

We show an example use of an array and the **continue** statement in the following code fragment:

```java
// count the number of times an integer x appears in an array a
public static int countInteger (int[ ] a, int x) {
    int count = 0;
    for (int i=0; i<a.length; i++) {
        if (a[i] != x) continue;
        count++;
    }
    return count;
}
```

As a safety feature, array indices are always checked in Java to see if they are ever out of bounds. If an array index is out of bounds, the run-time Java environment signals an error condition. This check helps Java avoid a number of security problems (including buffer overflow attacks) that other languages must cope with. We never need to guess the length of an array, however, to avoid the out-of-bounds error. The size of an array is stored in an instance variable, length, which can be accessed as follows:

⟨array_name⟩.length

We can avoid out-of-bounds errors by carefully using the early termination feature of Boolean operations in Java. For example, a statement like the following will never generate an index out-of-bounds error:

```java
if ((i >= 0) && (i < a.length) && (a[i] > 0.5) )
    x = a[i];
```

for the comparison " a[i] > 0.5" will only be performed if the first two comparisons succeed.

Declaring Arrays

The syntax for declaring an array is as follows:

⟨element_type⟩[] ⟨array_name⟩ [=
{⟨init_val_0⟩,⟨init_val_1⟩,...,⟨init_val_N−1⟩}];

where the first set of brackets, " []", are part of the syntax, and the second denotes an optional array initialization. The ⟨element_type⟩ can be any Java base type or class name, and ⟨array_name⟩ can be any value Java identifier. We can create the collection of cells for an array using the following syntax:

new ⟨element_type⟩[⟨length⟩]

where ⟨length⟩ is a positive integer denoting the length of the array created, and the brackets "[" and "]" are a nonoptional part of the syntax. Typically this expression appears in an assignment statement with an array name on the left-hand side of the assignment operator. So, for example, the following statement defines an array variable named a, and assigns it an array of 10 cells, each of type **int**:

int[] a = **new int**[10];

The cells of the new array "a" are indexed using the integer set $\{0, 1, 2, \ldots, 9\}$ (note that arrays in Java always start indexing at 0).

Arrays in Java are similar to objects, which explains our use of the dot operator to find an array's length, and are defined to be one-dimensional. Nevertheless, we can compose arrays to define multi-dimensional arrays. That is, a two-dimensional array is actually an array of arrays, which can be created with a declaration statement like the following:

float[][] x = **new float**[8][10];

This statement creates a two-dimensional "array of arrays." The following are then valid uses of the above arrays a and x:

```
i = 5;
a[i] = 138;
x[i][i+1] = 2.189 + x[i][i];
i = a.length;
j = x[4].length;
```

1.6   Simple Input and Output

Java provides a rich set of classes and methods for performing input and output within a program.

Graphical User Interfaces

There are classes in Java for doing graphical user interface design, complete with pop-up windows and pull-down menus, as well as methods for the display and input of text and numbers. Java also provides methods for dealing with graphical objects, images, sounds, Web pages, and mouse events (such as clicks, mouse overs, and dragging). Moreover, many of these input and output methods can be used in either stand-alone programs or in applets.

Using the Java Console

Unfortunately, going into the details on how all of the methods work for constructing sophisticated graphical user interfaces is beyond the scope of this book. Still, for the sake of completeness, we describe how simple input and output can be done in Java in this section.

Simple input and output in Java occurs within the Java console window. Depending on the Java environment we are using, this window is either a special pop-up window that can be used for displaying and inputting text, or it is a window used to issue commands to the operating system (such windows are referred to as shell windows, DOS windows, or terminal windows).

Simple Output Methods

Java provides a built-in static object, called System.out, that performs output to the "standard output" device. Operating systems, such as UNIX/Linux, allow users to redirect standard output to files or even as input to other programs, but the default output is to the Java console window. The System.out object is an instance of the java.io.PrintStream class. This class defines methods for a buffered output stream, meaning that characters are put in a temporary location, called a *buffer*, which is then emptied when the console window is ready to print characters.

Specifically, the java.io.PrintStream class provides the following methods for performing simple output (we use ⟨base_type⟩ here to refer to any of the possible base types):

- print(Object *o*): print the object *o* using its toString method.
- print(String *s*): print the string *s*.
- print(⟨base_type⟩ *b*): print the base type value *b*.
- println(String *s*): print the string *s*, followed by the newline character.
- flush(): print and empty the contents of the print buffer.

Consider, for example, the following code fragment:

```
System.out.print("Java values: ");
System.out.print(3.1415);
System.out.print(',');
System.out.print(15);
System.out.println(" (double,char,int).");
```

When executed, this fragment produces the following output:

```
Java values: 3.1415,15 (double,char,int).
```

This output will appear, of course, in the Java console window.

Simple Input Methods

Just as there is a special object for performing output to the Java console window, there is also a special object, called System.in, for performing input from the Java console window. Technically, the input is actually coming from the "standard input" device, which by default is the computer keyboard echoing its characters in the Java console. The System.in object is an instance of the java.io.InputStream class, which is defined to proceed one character at time.

This form of input is typically too primitive to be convenient, but it can be used to define another input object that processes input in a streaming and buffered way, using the java.io.BufferedReader and java.io.InputStreamReader classes.

For example, we can use the following template:

```
java.io.BufferedReader stndin;  // Standard input (buffered)
stndin=new java.io.BufferedReader(new java.io.InputStreamReader(System.in));
```

The details of the above code fragment are not critical for us; the important thing is that the above code creates an input stream object that we can use to read characters from the standard input device.

Specifically, the class java.io.BufferedReader supports the following simple input methods:

> **int** read(): Read a single character. If the input stream is at its end, this method returns -1. This method raises an error condition, "java.io.IOException," if an input error occurs.

> String readLine(): Read a line of text, that is, a string of characters up to the next newline character. The newline character is read, but it is not included in the string. If the input stream is at its end, this method returns **null**. This method raises the error condition "java.io.IOException" if an input error occurs.

Consider, for example, the following code fragment that combines input and output:

```java
java.io.BufferedReader stndin;   // Standard input (buffered)
String line;                     // A line of input text
double sum, d = 0.0;
int i = 0;
stndin=new java.io.BufferedReader(new
java.io.InputStreamReader(System.in));
System.out.print("Input a double: ");
System.out.flush();
if ((line = stndin.readLine()) != null)
  d = Double.valueOf(line).doubleValue();
System.out.print("Input an int: ");
System.out.flush();
if ((line = stndin.readLine()) != null)
  i = Integer.valueOf(line).intValue();
sum = d + i;
System.out.println("Their sum is " + sum + ".");
```

When executed, this code fragment could produce the following combination of input and output:

```
Input a double: 6.1078
Input an int: 209
Their sum is 215.1078.
```

1.7 An Example Program

In this section, we describe a simple example Java program that illustrates many of the constructs defined above. Our example consists of two classes, one, CreditCard, that defines credit card objects, and another, Test, that tests the functionality of CreditCard class. The credit card objects defined by the CreditCard class are simplified versions of traditional credit cards. They have identifying numbers, identifying information about their owners and their issuing bank, and information about their current balance and credit limit. They do not charge interest or late payments, however, but they do restrict charges that would cause a card's balance to go over its spending limit.

The CreditCard Class

We show the CreditCard class in Code Fragment 1.2. Note that the CreditCard class defines five instance variables, all of which are private to the class, and it provides a simple constructor that initializes these instance variables.

It also defines five *accessor methods* that provide access to the current values of these instance variables. Of course, we could have alternatively defined the instance variables as being public, which would have made the accessor methods moot. The disadvantage with this direct approach, however, is that it allows users to modify an object's instance variables directly, whereas in many cases such as this, we prefer to restrict the modification of instance variables to special *update methods*. We include two such update methods, chargeIt and makePayment in Code Fragment 1.2.

In addition, it is often convenient to include *action methods*, which define specific actions for that object's behavior. To demonstrate, we have defined such an action method, the printCard method, as a static method, which is also included in Code Fragment 1.2.

The Test Class

We test the CreditCard class in a Test class. Note the use of an array of CreditCard objects here, and how we are using iteration to make charges and payments. We show the complete code for the Test class in Code Fragment 1.3. For simplicity's sake, the Test class does not do any fancy graphical output, but simply sends its output to the Java console. We show this output in Code Fragment 1.4. Note the difference between the way we utilize the nonstatic chargeIt and makePayment methods and the static printCard method.

```java
public class CreditCard {
  // Instance variables:
  private String number;
  private String name;
  private String bank;
  private double balance;
  private int limit;
  // Constructor:
  CreditCard(String no, String nm, String bk, double bal, int lim) {
    number = no;
    name = nm;
    bank = bk;
    balance = bal;
    limit = lim;
  }
  // Accessor methods:
  public String getNumber() { return number; }
  public String getName() { return name; }
  public String getBank() { return bank; }
  public double getBalance() { return balance; }
  public int getLimit() { return limit; }
  // Action methods:
  public boolean chargeIt(double price) { // Make a charge
    if (price + balance > (double) limit)
      return false; // There is not enough money left to charge it
    balance += price;
    return true; // The charge goes through in this case
  }
  public void makePayment(double payment) { // Make a payment
    balance -= payment;
  }
  public static void printCard(CreditCard c) { // Print a card's information
    System.out.println("Number = " + c.getNumber());
    System.out.println("Name = " + c.getName());
    System.out.println("Bank = " + c.getBank());
    System.out.println("Balance = " + c.getBalance()); // Implicit cast
    System.out.println("Limit = " + c.getLimit()); // Implicit cast
  }
}
```

Code Fragment 1.2: The CreditCard class.

```java
public class Test {
  public static void main(String[] args) {
    CreditCard wallet[] = new CreditCard[10];
    wallet[0] = new CreditCard("5391 0375 9387 5309",
                        "John Bowman", "California Savings", 0.0, 2500);
    wallet[1] = new CreditCard("3485 0399 3395 1954",
                        "John Bowman", "California Federal", 0.0, 3500);
    wallet[2] = new CreditCard("6011 4902 3294 2994",
                        "John Bowman", "California Finance", 0.0, 5000);
    for (int i=1; i<=16; i++) {
      wallet[0].chargeIt((double)i);
      wallet[1].chargeIt(2.0*i);         // implicit cast
      wallet[2].chargeIt((double)3*i);   // explicit cast
    }
    for (int i=0; i<3; i++) {
      CreditCard.printCard(wallet[i]);
      while (wallet[i].getBalance() > 100.0) {
        wallet[i].makePayment(100.0);
        System.out.println("New balance = " + wallet[i].getBalance());
      }
    }
  }
}
```

Code Fragment 1.3: The Test class.

```
Number = 5391 0375 9387 5309
Name = John Bowman
Bank = Calfornia Savings
Balance = 136.0
Limit = 2500
New balance = 36.0
Number = 3485 0399 3395 1954
Name = John Bowman
Bank = Calfornia Federal
Balance = 272.0
Limit = 3500
New balance = 172.0
New balance = 72.0
Number = 6011 4902 3294 2994
Name = John Bowman
Bank = Calfornia Finance
Balance = 408.0
Limit = 5000
New balance = 308.0
New balance = 208.0
New balance = 108.0
New balance = 8.0
```

Code Fragment 1.4: Output from the Test class.

1.8   Packages

The Java language takes a general and useful approach to the organization of classes
into programs. Every public class defined in Java must be given in a separate file.
The file name is the name of the class with a *.java* extension. So a class, **public
class** SmartBoard, is defined in a file, *SmartBoard.java*. A set of related classes,
all defined in a common subdirectory, can be a Java **package**. Every file in a
package starts with the line:

      package ⟨package_name⟩;

The subdirectory containing the package must be named the same as the package.
We can also define a package in a single file that contains several class definitions,
but when it is compiled, all the classes will be compiled into separate files in the
same subdirectory.

Using Other Packages

In Java, we can use classes that are defined in other packages by prefixing class
names with dots (that is, using the '.' character) that correspond to the other packages' directory structure.

```
public boolean Temperature(TA.Measures.Thermometer thermometer,
                              int temperature) {
    // . . .
}
```

Here, the function Temperature takes a class Thermometer as a parameter.
Thermometer is defined in the TA package in a subpackage called Measures. The
dots in TA.Measures.Thermometer correspond directly to the directory structure
in the TA package.

The Import Command

All the extra typing needed to refer to a class outside of the current package can get
tiring. In Java, we can use the **import** keyword to include external classes or entire
packages in the current file. To import an individual class from a specific package,
we type the following at the beginning of the file:

      import ⟨packageName⟩.⟨classNames⟩;

For example, we could type

> **package** Project;
>
> **import** TA.Measures.Thermometer;
> **import** TA.Measures.Scale;

at the beginning of a Project package to indicate that we are importing the classes named TA.Measures.Thermometer and TA.Measures.Scale. The Java run-time environment will now search these classes to match identifiers to classes, methods, and instance variables that we use in our program.

Importing a Whole Package

We can also import an entire package, by using the following syntax:

> **import** ⟨packageName⟩.*;

For example:

> **package** student;
>
> **import** TA.Measures.*;
>
> **public boolean** Temperature(Thermometer thermometer, **int** temperature) {
>   *// . . .*
>   }

In the case where two packages have classes of the same name, we ***must*** specifically reference the package that contains a class. For example, suppose both the package Gnomes and package Cooking have a class named Mushroom.

If we provide an **import** statement for both packages, then we must specify which class we mean as follows:

> Gnomes.Mushroom shroom = **new** Gnomes.Mushroom (`"purple"`);
> Cooking.Mushroom topping = **new** Cooking.Mushroom ();

If we do not specify the package (that is, in the previous example we just use a variable of type Mushroom), the compiler will give an "ambiguous class" error.

To sum up the structure of a Java program, we can have instance variables and methods inside a class, and classes inside a package.

1.9   Writing a Java Program

The process of writing a Java program involves three fundamental steps:

1. Design
2. Coding
3. Testing and Debugging.

We briefly discuss each of these steps in this section.

1.9.1   Design

The design step is perhaps the most important step in the process of writing a program. For it is in the design step that we decide how to divide the workings of our program into classes, we decide how these classes will interact, what data each will store, and what actions each will perform. Indeed, one of the main challenges that beginning Java programmers face is deciding what classes to define to do the work of their program. While general prescriptions are hard to come by, there are some general rules of thumb that we can apply when determining how to define our classes:

- *Responsibilities*: divide the work into different *actors*, each with a different responsibility. Try to describe responsibilities using action verbs. These actors will form the classes for the program.
- *Independence*: define the work for each class to be as independent from other classes as possible. Subdivide responsibilities between classes so that each class has autonomy over some aspect of the program. Give data (as instance variables) to the class that has jurisdiction over the actions that require access to this data.
- *Behaviors*: so that the consequences of each action performed by a class will be well understood by other classes that interact with it, define the behaviors for each class carefully and precisely. These behaviors will define the methods that this class performs. The set of behaviors for a class is sometimes referred to as a *protocol*, for we expect the behaviors for a class to hold together as a cohesive unit.

Defining the classes, together with their instance variables and methods, determines the design of a Java program. A good programmer will naturally develop greater skill in performing these tasks over time, as experience teaches him or her to notice patterns in the requirements of a program that match patterns that he or she has seen before.

In order to accelerate the development of this skill, we discuss, at various points throughout this text, various ***design patterns*** for designing object-oriented programs. These patterns provide templates for defining classes and the interactions between these classes.

Many programmers do their initial designs using ***CRC cards***. Component-responsibility-collaborator, or CRC, cards are simple index cards that subdivide the work required of a program. The use of such cards allows a programmer to iteratively refine his or her organizational structure so as to ultimately arrive at a coherent set of classes. The main idea behind this tool is to have each card represent a component, which will ultimately become a class in our program. We write the name of each component on the top of its index card. On the left-hand side of its card we begin writing the responsibilities for this component. On the right-hand side, we list the collaborators for this component, that is, the other components that this component will have to interact with to perform its duties. The design process iterates through an action/actor cycle, where we first identify an action (that is, a responsibility), and we then determine an actor (that is, a component) that is best suited to perform that action. The design is complete when we have assigned all actions to actors.

By the way, in using index cards to perform our design, we are of course assuming that each component will have a small set of responsibilities and collaborators. This assumption is no accident, for it helps keep our programs manageable, even when they must necessarily be large.

An alternative to CRC cards is the use of UML (Unified Modeling Language) diagrams to express the design of a program. UML diagrams are a standard visual notation to express object-oriented software designs. Several computer-aided tools are available to build UML diagrams.

1.9.2 Coding

Once we have decided on the classes for our program, together with their responsibilities, we are ready to begin coding. We create the actual code for the classes in our program by using either an independent text editor (such as emacs, notepad, or vi), or the editor embedded in an ***integrated development environment*** (IDE), such as Borland JBuilder, Eclipse, IBM WebSphere Studio, or Sun ONE Studio.

Once we have completed coding for a class (or package) we then compile this file into working code by invoking a compiler. If we are not using an IDE, then we compile our program by calling a program, such as `javac`, on our file. If we are using an IDE, then we compile our program by clicking the appropriate compilation button. If we are fortunate, and our program has no syntax errors, then this compilation process will create files with a "`.class`" extension.

If our program contains syntax errors, then these will be identified, and we will have to go back into our editor to fix the offending lines of code. Once we have eliminated all syntax errors, and created the appropriate compiled code, we then run our program by either invoking a command, such as "java" (outside an IDE) or clicking on the appropriate "run" button (within an IDE). When a Java program is run in this way, the run-time environment locates the directories containing the named class and any other classes that are referenced from this class according to a special operating system environment variable. This variable is named "CLASS-PATH," and the ordering of directories to search in is given as a list of directories, which are separated by colons in Unix/Linux or semicolons in DOS/Windows. An example CLASSPATH assignment in the DOS/Windows operating system could be the following:

```
SET CLASSPATH=.;C:\java;C:\Program Files\Java\
```

Whereas an example CLASSPATH assignment in the Unix/Linux operating system could be the following:

```
setenv  CLASSPATH ".:/usr/local/java/lib:/usr/netscape/classes"
```

where, in both cases, the dot (".") refers to the current directory in which the run-time environment is invoked.

Javadoc

In order to encourage good use of block comments and the automatic production of documentation, the Java programming environment comes with a documentation production program called *javadoc*. This program takes a collection of Java source files that have been commented using certain keywords, called *tags*, and it produces a series of HTML documents that describe the classes, methods, variables, and constants contained in these files. For space reasons, we have not used javadoc-style comments in all the example programs included in this book, but we include a javadoc example in Code Fragment 1.5 as well as other examples at the Web site that accompanies this book.

Each javadoc comment is a block comment that starts with "/**" and ends with "*/," and such that each line between these two can begin with a single asterisk, "*," which is ignored. The block comment is assumed to start with a descriptive sentence, followed by a blank line, which is followed by special lines that begin with javadoc tags. A block comment that comes just before a class definition, instance variable declaration, or method definition, is processed by javadoc into a comment about that class, variable, or method.

```java
/**
 * This class defines an immutable (x,y) point in the plane.
 *
 * @author Michael Goodrich
 */
public class XYPoint {
  private double x,y;  // private instance variables for the coordinates

  /**
   * Construct an (x,y) point at a specified location.
   *
   * @param xCoor The x-coordinate of the point
   * @param yCoor The y-coordinate of the point
   */
  public XYPoint(double xCoor, double yCoor) {
    x = xCoor;
    y = yCoor;
  }

  /**
   * Return x-coordinate value.
   *
   * @return x-coordinate
   */
  public double getX() { return x; }

  /**
   * Return y-coordinate value.
   *
   * @return y-coordinate
   */
  public double getY() { return y; }
}
```

Code Fragment 1.5: An example class definition using javadoc-style comments. Note that this class includes two instance variables, one constructor, and two accessor methods.

The primary javadoc tags are the following:

- @author *text*: identifies each author (one per line) for a class
- @exception *exception-name description*: identifies an error condition that is signaled by this method (see Section 2.3)
- @param *parameter-name description*: identifies a parameter accepted by this method
- @return *description*: describes the return type and its range of values for a method.

There are other tags as well; the interested reader is referred to on-line documentation for javadoc for further discussion.

Readability and Style

Programs should be made easy to read and understand. Good programmers should therefore be mindful of their coding style, and develop a style that communicates the important aspects of a program's design for both humans and computers.

Much has been written about good coding style, with some of the main principles being the following:

- Use meaningful names for identifiers. Try to choose names that can be read aloud, and choose names that reflect the action, responsibility, or data each identifier is naming. The tradition in most Java circles is to capitalize the first letter of each word in an identifier, except for the first word in an identifier for a variable or method. So, in this tradition, "Date," "Vector," "DeviceManager" would identify classes, and 'isFull()," "insertItem()," "studentName," and "studentHeight" would respectively identify methods and variables.
- Use named constants instead of literals. Readability, robustness, and modifiability are enhanced if we include a series of definitions of named constant values in a class definition. These can then be used within this class and others to refer to special values for this class. The tradition in Java is to fully capitalize such constants, as shown below:

```
public class Student {
    public static final int MIN_CREDITS = 12; // min. credits in a term
    public static final int MAX_CREDITS = 24; // max. credits in a term
    public static final int FRESHMAN = 1;     // code for freshman
    public static final int SOPHOMORE = 2;    // code for sophomore
    public static final int JUNIOR = 3;       // code for junior
    public static final int SENIOR = 4;       // code for senior

    // Instance variables, constructors, and method definitions go here. . .
}
```

- Indent statement blocks. Typically programmers indent each statement block by 4 spaces; in this book we typically use 2 spaces, however, to avoid having our code overrun the book's margins.
- Organize each class in the following order:
    1. constants
    2. instance variables
    3. constructors
    4. methods.

  We note that some Java programmers prefer to put instance variable definitions last; we put them earlier so that we can read each class sequentially and understand the data each method is working with.

- Use comments that add meaning to a program and explain ambiguous or confusing constructs. In-line comments are good for quick explanations and do not need to be sentences. Block comments are good for explaining the purpose of a method and complex code sections.

1.9.3   Testing and Debugging

Testing is the process of experimentally checking the correctness of a program, while debugging is the process of tracking the execution of a program and discovering the errors in it. Testing and debugging are often the most time-consuming activity in the development of a program.

Testing

A careful testing plan is an essential part of writing a program. While verifying the correctness of a program over all possible inputs is usually infeasible, we should aim at executing the program on a representative subset of inputs. At the very minimum, we should make sure that every method in the program is tested at least once (method coverage). Even better, each code statement in the program should be executed at least once (statement coverage).

Programs often tend to fail on *special cases* of the input. Such cases need to be carefully identified and tested. For example, when testing a method that sorts (that is, puts in order) an array of integers, we should consider the following inputs:

- the array has zero length (no elements)
- the array has one element
- all the elements of the array are the same
- the array is already sorted
- the array is reverse sorted.

In addition to special inputs to the program, we should also consider special conditions for the structures used by the program. For example, if we use an array to store data, we should make sure that boundary cases, such as inserting/removing at the beginning or end of the subarray holding data, are properly handled.

While it is essential to use hand-crafted test suites, it is also advantageous to run the program on a large collection of randomly generated inputs. The Random class in the java.util package provides several methods to generate random numbers.

There is a hierarchy among the classes and methods of a program induced by the caller-callee relationship. Namely, a method *A* is above a method *B* in the hierarchy if *A* calls *B*. There are two main testing strategies, ***top-down*** and ***bottom-up***, which differ in the order in which methods are tested.

Bottom-up testing proceeds from lower-level methods to higher-level methods. Namely, bottom-level methods, which do not invoke other methods, are tested first, followed by methods that call only bottom-level methods, and so on. This strategy ensures that errors found in a method are not likely to be caused by lower-level methods nested within it.

Top-down testing proceeds from the top to the bottom of the method hierarchy. It is typically used in conjunction with ***stubbing***, a boot-strapping technique that replaces a lower-level method with a ***stub***, a replacement for the method that simulates the output of the original method. For example, if method *A* calls method *B* to get the first line of a file, when testing *A* we can replace *B* with a stub that returns a fixed string.

Debugging

The simplest debugging technique consists of using ***print statements*** (using method System.out.println($\langle$string$\rangle$)) to track the values of variables during the execution of the program. A problem with this approach is that the print statements need to be eventually removed or commented out before the software is finally released.

A better approach is to run the program within a ***debugger***, which is a specialized environment for controlling and monitoring the execution of a program. The basic functionality provided by a debugger is the insertion of ***breakpoints*** within the code. When the program is executed within the debugger, it stops at each breakpoint. While the program is stopped, the current value of variables can be inspected. In addition to fixed breakpoints, advanced debuggers allow for specification of ***conditional breakpoints***, which are triggered only if a given expression is satisfied.

The standard Java tools include a basic debugger called jdb, which is command-line oriented. IDEs for Java programming provide advanced debugging environments with graphical user interfaces.

1.10 Utilities in the java.lang Package

The java.lang package provides classes that are fundamental to the Java language. It also includes a number of static methods and predefined special classes that provide several useful utilities. We have already mentioned several classes that are defined in this package, including the String class and the number classes (Integer, Float, etc.). This package also includes *exceptions*, which are classes associated with error conditions and other intentional interruptions in the flow of control in a Java program, which we discuss in more detail in Section 2.3.

In this section, we list a few static methods and constants that are a part of some of the classes in the java.lang package. A complete listing of all utility classes in the java.lang package and other useful packages in Java can be found in a full reference work on Java or at a Java documentation Web site.

The Math Class

The java.lang package includes a useful Math class that provides a number of fundamental mathematical functions and constants, including the following (we use ⟨number⟩ to refer to any of the possible numeric base types):

- **double** E: The **double** number closest to e, the base of the natural logarithm function, ln.
- **double** PI: The **double** number closest to π, the ratio of the circumference of a circle to its diameter.
- ⟨number⟩ abs(⟨number⟩ x): The absolute value of x, unless x is the smallest negative integer that can be represented.
- **double** acos(**double** x): The arc cosine of the value x in radians.
- **double** asin(**double** x): The arc sine of the value x in radians.
- **double** atan(**double** x): The arc tangent of the value x in radians.
- **double** cos(**double** a): The cosine of the angle a.
- **double** exp(**double** x) The exponential function e^x.
- **double** log(**double** x) The natural logarithm (base e) ln x.
- ⟨number⟩ max(⟨number⟩ x, ⟨number⟩ y): The greater of x and y.
- ⟨number⟩ min(⟨number⟩ x, ⟨number⟩ y): The smaller of x and y.
- **double** pow(**double** x, **double** y): The power function, x^y.
- **double** random(): A (pseudo-)random number in the range $[0.0, 1.0)$.
- **long** round(**double** x): The **long** integer closest to x.
- **double** sin(**double** a): The sine of the angle a.
- **double** sqrt(**double** x): The value $\sqrt{x}$.
- **double** tan(**double** a): The tangent of the angle a.

All of the above methods and constants are static; hence, we reference them directly from the Math class. For example, to compute the absolute value of an **int** *x*, we could use the following statement:

int a = Math.abs(x);

String Conversions

Every class in Java has a method toString, which converts instances of that class to a string. Indeed, each of the number classes even has a static version of toString, which takes a base type of the corresponding number class as an argument, and returns a string representing that value. For example, Integer.toString(i) returns a string representation of the **int** i. Additionally, to provide for the same functionality in a uniform way, the String class includes a valueOf method, which can take any base type value as an argument and convert it to a string. This method is static; hence, we can call String.valueOf(i) to convert an **int** i to a string representing i's value.

For input functions, on the other hand, we desire methods for converting a string in the appropriate syntax to each of the various base types. To provide for this functionality, Java includes a method valueOf in each of the number classes, which takes a string as its argument and returns an object of the corresponding number class that represents that string. So, for example, to convert the string "3.1415F" to its corresponding **float** value, we could use the following statement:

float pi = Float.valueOf("3.1415F").floatValue();

Big Numbers

There are some numbers that are too big to fit in the standard number types defined in Java. Since it is often necessary to process such numbers, Java provides two arbitrary precision number types, which are both kinds of number classes. These are the java.math.BigDecimal and java.math.BigInteger classes. In addition to the usual operations provided by a number class, these classes also provide methods for performing various mathematical operations on big numbers. We do not list all the methods here, however, and instead refer the interested reader to a Java reference.

1.11　Exercises

For source code and help with exercises, please visit **java.datastructures.net**.

Reinforcement

R-1.1 Rewrite each of the following statements to achieve the intended result without a syntax error:

```
String o = 54.5;
String p = "Pi = " + (String) 3.1415;
String q = 1024;
```

R-1.2 Consider the following (***incorrect***) example for changing the state of an object reference passed to a method called makeDoctor:

```
public static void makeDoctor (Gnome h) {
    Gnome k = new Gnome("Doctor "+h.name,h.age,null,h.height);
    h = k;
    k.magical = true;
}
```

Rewrite the above code fragment so that it correctly updates the Gnome reference by variable h so that its name has the title "Doctor" and its magical flag is set to **true**.

R-1.3 Modify the CreditCard class from Code Fragment 1.2 to check that the price argument passed to method chargeIt and the payment argument passed to method makePayment are positive.

R-1.4 Modify the CreditCard class from Code Fragment 1.2 to charge interest on each payment.

R-1.5 Modify the CreditCard class from Code Fragment 1.2 to charge a late fee for any payment that is past its due date.

R-1.6 Modify the CreditCard class from Code Fragment 1.2 to include ***modifier methods***, which allow a user to modify internal variables in a CreditCard class in a controlled manner.

R-1.7 Modify the declaration of the first **for** loop in the Test class in Code Fragment 1.3 so that its charges will eventually cause exactly one of the three credit cards to go over its credit limit. Which credit card is it?

R-1.8 Write a short Java function, inputAllBaseTypes, that inputs a different value of each base type from the standard input device and prints it back to the standard output device.

R-1.9 Write a Java class, Flower, that has three instance variables of type **String**, **int**, and **float**, which respectively represent the name of the flower, its number of pedals, and price. Your class must include a constructor method that initializes each variable to an appropriate value, and your class should include methods for setting the value of each type, and getting the value of each type.

R-1.10 Write a short Java function, isMultiple, that takes two **long** values, n and m, and returns true if and only if n is a multiple of m, that is, $n = mi$ for some integer i.

R-1.11 Write a short Java function, isOdd, that takes an **int** i and returns true if and only if i is odd. Your function cannot use the multiplication, modulus, or division operators, however.

R-1.12 Write a short Java function that takes an integer n and returns the sum of all the integers smaller than n.

R-1.13 Write a short Java function that takes an integer n and returns the sum of all the odd integers smaller than n.

R-1.14 Write a short Java function that takes a positive **double** value x and returns the number of times we can divide x by 2 before we get a number less than 2.

Creativity

C-1.1 Write a short Java function that takes an array of **int** values and determines if there is a pair of numbers in the array whose product is odd.

C-1.2 Write a Java method that takes an array of **int** values and determines if all the numbers are different from each other (that is, they are distinct).

C-1.3 Write a Java method that takes an array containing the set of all integers in the range 1 to 52 and shuffles it into random order. Your method should output each possible order with equal probability.

C-1.4 Write a short Java program that outputs all possible strings formed by using the characters 'c', 'a', 'r', 'b', 'o', and 'n' exactly once.

C-1.5 Write a short Java program that takes all the lines input to standard input and writes them to standard output in reverse order. That is, each line is output in the correct order, but the ordering of the lines is reversed.

C-1.6 Write a short Java program that takes two arrays a and b of length n storing **int** values, and returns the dot product of a and b. That is, it returns an array c of length n such that $c[i] = a[i] \cdot b[i]$, for $i = 0, \ldots, n-1$.

C-1.7 Write a fast Java function that can take any int value, i, and return 2^i, as a long value. Your method should **not** multiply 2 by itself i times; there are much faster ways of computing 2^i.

C-1.8 The **greatest common divisor**, or GCD, of two positive integers n and m is the largest number j, such that n and m are both multiples of j. Euclid proposed a simple algorithm for computing $\text{GCD}(n, m)$, where $n > m$, which is based on a concept known as the Chinese Remainder Theorem. The main idea of the algorithm is to repeatedly perform modulo computations of consecutive pairs of the sequence that starts $(n, m, \ldots)$, until reaching zero. The last nonzero number in this sequence is the GCD of n and m. For example, for $n = 80,844$ and $m = 25,320$, the sequence is as follows:

$$
\begin{aligned}
80,844 \bmod 25,320 &= 4,884 \\
25,320 \bmod 4,884 &= 900 \\
4,884 \bmod 900 &= 384 \\
900 \bmod 384 &= 132 \\
384 \bmod 132 &= 120 \\
132 \bmod 120 &= 12 \\
120 \bmod 12 &= 0
\end{aligned}
$$

So, GCD of $80,844$ and $25,320$ is 12. Write a short Java function to compute $\text{GCD}(n, m)$ for two integers n and m.

Projects

P-1.1 A common punishment for school children is to write out the same sentence multiple times. Write a Java stand-alone program that will write out the following sentence one hundred times: "I will never spam my friends again." Your program should number each of the sentences and it should "accidentally" make eight different random-looking typos at various points in the listing, so that it looks like a human typed it all by hand.

P-1.2 (For those who know Java graphical user interface methods) Define a GraphicalTest class that tests the functionality of the CreditCard class from Code Fragment 1.2 using text fields and buttons.

P-1.3 The *birthday paradox* says that the probability that two people in a room will have the same birthday is more than half as long as n, the number of people in the room, is more than 23. This property is not really a paradox, but many people find it surprising. Design a Java program that can test this paradox by a series of experiments on randomly generated birthdays, which test this paradox for $n = 5, 10, 15, 20, \ldots, 100$. You should run at least 10 experiments for each value of n and it should output, for each n, the number of experiments for that n, such that two people in that test have the same birthday.

Chapter Notes

For more detailed information about the Java programming language, we refer the reader to some of the fine books about Java, including the books by Arnold and Gosling [7], Campione and Walrath [18], Cornell and Horstmann [25], Flanagan [33], and Horstmann [49], as well as Sun's Java Web site (http://www.java.sun.com).

Chapter

2

Object-Oriented Design

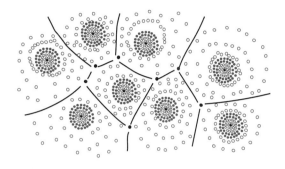

Contents

In the early days of the information age, computers were expensive and large, but had slow processors and small memories. It should come as no surprise then, that early computers had a limited number of applications, most of which dealt with numeric processing, not information management. Modern computers, on the other hand, are continually becoming cheaper and smaller, while also coming equipped with faster processors and larger memories. Consequently, modern computers are used for myriad different applications. Indeed, many modern toys, such as singing dolls and talking action figures, have embedded processors with more speed and memory than the first digital computer, ENIAC, which was the size of a large room. In addition, computing researchers of a couple decades ago used the term "supercomputers" to refer to computing devices that were slower and had smaller memories than today's personal computers. Thus, modern computers are significantly smaller, cheaper, faster, and higher-capacity than their predecessors. Yet these advances bring higher expectations for software.

Creating software has become a complex enterprise. Designing and implementing a new software application typically involves the interaction of pieces of software written by many different people in several different organizations. These people may not know each other and may not even be willing to share the source code for their respective software pieces. In addition, over time, there is a natural tendency to want to upgrade old software, adding new features for applications in new environments. The challenge for software engineers is to create software that is itself complex, but nevertheless appears conceptually simple, so as to easily integrate with other software and allow for future modifications.

Thus, a driving force in research in software engineering and programming languages has been the development of methodologies that can produce designs that are conceptually **simple** enough to be understandable while being **powerful** enough to solve hard problems efficiently. Achieving such a balance is not easy, but a methodology that is showing considerable promise is **object-oriented design**.

As the name implies, the main "actors" in the object-oriented design paradigm are called **objects**. An object comes from a **class**, which is a specification of the data **fields**, also called **instance variables**, that the object contains, as well as the **methods** (operations) that the object can execute. Each class presents to the outside world a concise and consistent view of the objects that are instances of this class, without going into too much unnecessary detail or giving others access to the inner workings of the objects. This view of computing is intended to fulfill several goals and incorporate several design principles, which we discuss in this chapter.

2.1 Goals and Principles

Dealing with the complexity of modern software naturally gives rise to several goals and principles directed at producing quality software.

2.1.1 Object-Oriented Design Goals

In particular, software implementations should achieve ***robustness***, ***adaptability***, and ***reusability***. (See Figure 2.1.)

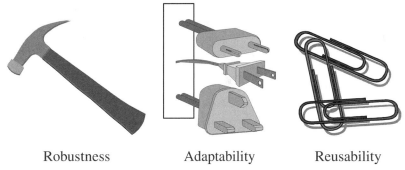

Robustness   Adaptability   Reusability

Figure 2.1: Goals of object-oriented design.

Robustness

Every good programmer wants to produce software that is correct, which means that a program produces the right output for all the anticipated inputs in the program's application. In addition, we want software to be ***robust***, that is, capable of handling unexpected inputs that are not explicitly defined for its application. For example, if a program is expecting a positive integer (for example, representing the price of an item) and instead is given a negative integer, then the program should be able to recover gracefully from this error. A program that does not gracefully handle such unexpected-input errors can be embarrassing for the programmer.

More importantly, in ***life-critical applications***, where a software error can lead to injury or loss of life, software that is not robust is deadly. This importance was driven home in the late 1980s in accidents involving Therac-25, a radiation-therapy machine, which severely overdosed six patients between 1985 and 1987, some of whom died from complications resulting from their radiation overdoses. All six accidents were traced to software errors, with one of the most troubling being a user-interface error involving unexpected inputs (a fast-typing radiologist could backspace over a radiation dosage on the screen without the previous characters actually being deleted from the input).

The goal of robustness goes beyond the need to handle unexpected inputs, however. Software should produce correct solutions, even given the well-known limitations of computers. For example, if a user wishes to store more elements in a data structure than originally expected, then the software should expand the capacity of this structure to handle more elements. This philosophy of robustness is present, for example, in the java.util.ArrayList class in Java, which defines an expandable array. In addition, if an application calls for numerical computations, those numbers should be represented fully and should not overflow or underflow. Indeed, software should achieve **correctness** for its full range of possible inputs, including boundary cases, such as when an integer value is 0 or 1 or the maximum or minimum possible values. Robustness and correctness do not come automatically, however, they must be designed in from the start.

Adaptability

Modern software projects, such as word processors, Web browsers, and Internet search engines, typically involve large programs that are expected to last for many years. Software, therefore, needs to be able to evolve over time in response to changing conditions in its environment. These changes can be expected, such as the need to adapt to an increase in CPU or network speed, or they can be unexpected, such as the need to add new functionality because of new market demands. Software should also be able to adapt to unexpected events that, in hindsight, really should have been expected, such as the coming of a new millennium and its effects on date calculations (the "year 2000" problem). Thus, another important goal of quality software is that it achieve **adaptability** (also called **evolvability**). Related to this concepts is **portability**, which is the ability of software to run with minimal change on different hardware and operating system platforms. An advantage of writing software in Java is the portability provided by the language itself.

Reusability

Going hand in hand with adaptability is the desire that software be reusable, that is, code should be usable as a component of different systems in various applications. Developing quality software can be an expensive enterprise, and its cost can be offset somewhat if the software is designed in a way that makes it easily reusable in future applications. Such reuse should be done with care, however, for one of the major sources of software errors in the Therac-25 came from inappropriate reuse of software from the Therac-20 (which was not object-oriented and not designed for the hardware platform used with the Therac-25). So, for software to be truly reusable, we must be clear about what it does and does not do. Given this clarity, however, software reuse can be a significant cost-saving technique.

2.1.2 Object-Oriented Design Principles

Chief among the principles of the object-oriented approach, which are intended to facilitate the goals outlined above, are the following (see Figure 2.2):

- Abstraction
- Encapsulation
- Modularity.

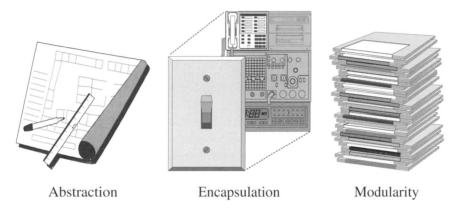

| Abstraction | Encapsulation | Modularity |

Figure 2.2: Principles of object-oriented design.

Abstraction

The notion of ***abstraction*** is to distill a complicated system down to its most fundamental parts and describe these parts in a simple, precise language. Typically, describing the parts of a system involves naming them and describing their functionality. For example, a typical text-editor graphical user interface (GUI) provides an abstraction of an "edit" menu that offers several text-editing operations, including cutting and pasting portions of text or other graphical objects. Without going into details about the ways a GUI represents and displays text and graphical objects, the concepts of cutting and pasting are simple and precise. A cut operation deletes the selected text and graphics and places them into an external storage buffer. A paste operation inserts the contents of the external storage buffer at a specific location in the text. Thus, the abstract functionality of an "edit" menu and its cutting and pasting operations is specified in a language precise enough to be clear, but simple enough to "abstract away" unnecessary details. This combination of clarity and simplicity benefits robustness, since it leads to understandable and correct implementations.

Applying this paradigm to the design of data structures gives rise to *abstract data types* (ADTs). An ADT is a mathematical model of a data structure that specifies the type of data stored, the operations supported on them, and the types of parameters of the operations. An ADT specifies *what* each operation does, but not *how* it does it. In Java, an ADT can be expressed by an *interface*, which is simply a list of method declarations. (We say more about Java interfaces in Section 2.4.)

An ADT is realized by a concrete data structure, which is modeled in Java by a *class*. A class defines the data being stored and the operations supported by the objects that are instances of the class. Also, unlike interfaces, classes specify *how* the operations are performed. A Java class is said to *implement an interface* if its methods give life to all of those of the interface.

Encapsulation

Another important principle of object-oriented design is the concept of *encapsulation*, or *information hiding*, which states that different components of a software system should not reveal the internal details of their respective implementations. Consider again our example of an edit menu with cutting and pasting functionality in a text-editor graphical user interface (GUI). One of the main reasons an edit menu is so useful is that we can completely understand how to use it without understanding exactly how it is implemented. For example, we do not need to know how the menu is drawn, how selected text to be cut or pasted is represented, how selected portions of text are stored in an external buffer, or how various graphical objects, such as graphs, images, or drawings, are identified, stored, and copied in and out of the external buffer. Indeed, the code associated with the edit menu should not depend on all of these details to work correctly. Instead, the edit menu should provide an interface that is sufficiently specified for other software components to use its methods effectively, while also requiring well-defined interfaces from other software components that it needs. In general terms, the principle of encapsulation states that all the different components of a large software system should operate on a strictly need-to-know basis.

One of the main advantages of encapsulation is that it gives the programmer freedom in implementing the details of a system. The only constraint on the programmer is to maintain the abstract interface that outsiders see. For example, the programmer of the edit menu code in a text-editor GUI might at first implement the cut and paste operations by copying actual screen images in and out of an external buffer. Later, he or she may be dissatisfied with this implementation, since it does not allow compact storage of the selection, and it does not distinguish text and graphic objects. If the programmer has designed the cut and paste interface with encapsulation in mind, switching the underlying implementation to one that stores text as text and graphic objects in an appropriate compact format should not cause any problems to methods that need to interface with this GUI. Thus, encapsulation yields adaptability, for it allows the implementation details of parts of a program to change without adversely affecting other parts.

Modularity

In addition to abstraction and encapsulation, a principle fundamental to object-oriented design is *modularity*. Modern software systems typically consist of several different components that must interact correctly in order for the entire system to work properly. Keeping these interactions straight requires that these different components be well organized. In the object-oriented approach, this structure centers around the concept of *modularity*. Modularity refers to an organizing structure in which different components of a software system are divided into separate functional units. For example, a house or apartment can be viewed as consisting of several interacting units: electrical, heating and cooling, plumbing, and structural. Rather than viewing these systems as one giant jumble of wires, vents, pipes, and boards, the organized architect designing a house or apartment will view them as separate modules that interact in well-defined ways. In so doing, he or she is using modularity to bring a clarity of thought that provides a natural way of organizing functions into distinct manageable units. In like manner, using modularity in a software system can also provide a powerful organizing framework that brings clarity to an implementation.

The structure imposed by modularity helps to enable software reusability. If software modules are written in an abstract way to solve general problems, then modules can be reused when instances of these same general problems may arise in other contexts. For example, the structural definition of a wall is the same from house to house, typically being defined in terms of 2- by 4-inch studs, spaced a certain distance apart, etc. Thus, an organized architect can reuse his or her wall definitions from one house to another. In reusing such a definition, some parts may require redefinition, for example, a wall in a commercial building may be similar to that of a house, but the electrical system and stud material might be different. Thus, our architect may wish to organize the various structural components, such as electrical and structural, in a *hierarchical* fashion, which groups similar abstract definitions together in a level-by-level manner that goes from specific to more general as one traverses up the hierarchy. A common use of such hierarchies is in an organizational chart, where each link going up can be read as "is a," as in "a ranch is a house is a building." Likewise, this kind of hierarchy is useful in software design, for it groups together common functionality at the most general level, and views specialized behavior as an extension of the general one.

2.2   Inheritance and Polymorphism

To take advantage of hierarchical relationships, which are common in software projects, the object-oriented design approach provides ways of reusing code in a software system. Reusing software saves programming time and reduces the probability of errors. Indeed, once a software component is completely debugged, it is better to reuse it than to copy it and slightly modify it at several different locations, for all this copying and modifying can introduce new errors into a program.

2.2.1   Inheritance

To avoid redundant code, the object-oriented paradigm provides a modular and hierarchical organizing structure for reusing code, through a technique called ***inheritance***. This technique allows the design of generic classes that can be specialized to more particular classes, with the specialized classes reusing the code from the generic class. For example, the Java Number class is specialized into the Float, Integer, and Long classes. The general class, which is also known as a ***base class*** or ***superclass***, can define "generic" instance variables and methods that apply in a multitude of situations. A class that ***specializes***, or ***extends***, or ***inherits from***, a superclass need not give new implementations for the general methods, for it inherits them. It should only define those methods that are specialized for this particular ***subclass*** (which is also known as a ***derived*** class). Such relationships often represent an "is a" hierarchy, as shown in Figure 2.3.

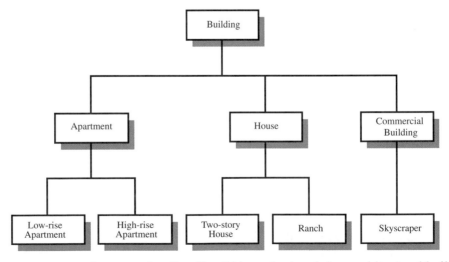

Figure 2.3: An example of an "is a" hierarchy involving architectural buildings.

Let us consider an example to illustrate these concepts.

Example 2.1: *Consider a class* S *that defines objects with a field,* x, *and three methods,* a(), b(), *and* c(). *(The particular type of* x *and the functionality of* a(), b(), *and* c() *are not important for this example.) Suppose we were to define a class* T *that extends* S *and includes an additional field,* y, *and two methods,* d() *and* e(). *This would imply that objects of the class* T *have two fields,* x *and* y, *and five methods,* a(), b(), c(), d(), *and* e(). *The class* T **inherits** *the instance variable* x *and the methods* a(), b(), *and* c() *from* S. *We illustrate the relationships between the class* S *and the class* T *in a* **class inheritance diagram** *in Figure 2.4. Each box in such a diagram denotes a class, with its name, fields (or instance variables), and methods included as subrectangles. An arrow from one box* T *to another box* S *indicates that class* T *extends (or inherits from) class* S.

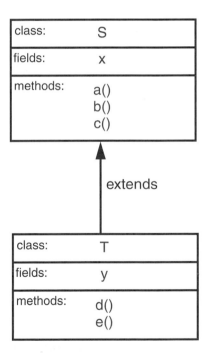

Figure 2.4: A class inheritance diagram. Each box denotes a class, with its name, fields, and methods. Some of these entries can be omitted if they are denoting unnecessary details. Likewise, as shown, we can optionally annotate the arrow between the two boxes to denote an inheritance relation.

Object Creation and Referencing

When an object o is created, memory is allocated for its data fields, and these same fields are initialized to specific beginning values. Typically, one associates the new object o with a variable, which serves as a "link" to object o, and is said to **reference** o. When we wish to access object o (for the purpose of getting at its fields or executing its methods), we can either request the execution of one of o's methods (defined by the class that o belongs to), or look up one of the fields of o. Indeed, the primary way that an object p interacts with another object o is for p to send a "message" to o that invokes one of o's methods, for example, for o to print a description of itself, for o to convert itself to a string, or for o to return the value of one of its data fields. The secondary way that p can interact with o is for p to access one of o's fields directly, but only if o has given other objects like p permission to do so. For example, an instance of the Java class Integer stores, as an instance variable, an integer, and it provides several operations for accessing this data, including methods for converting it into other number types, for converting it to a string of digits, and for converting strings of digits to a number. It does not allow for direct access of its instance variable, however, for such details are hidden.

Dynamic Dispatch

When a program wishes to invoke a certain method a() of some object o, it sends a message to o, which is usually denoted, using the dot-operator syntax (Section 1.3.2), as "o.a()." In the compiled version of this program, the code corresponding to this invocation directs the run-time environment to examine o's class T to determine if the class T supports an a() method, and, if so, to execute it. Specifically, the run-time environment examines the class T to see if it defines an a() method itself. If it does, then this method is executed. If T does not define an a() method, then the run-time environment examines the superclass S of T. If S defines a(), then this method is executed. If S does not define a(), on the other hand, then the run-time environment repeats the search at the superclass of S. This search continues up the hierarchy of classes until it either finds an a() method, which is then executed, or it reaches a topmost class (for example, the Object class in Java) without an a() method, which generates a run-time error. The algorithm that processes the message o.a() to find the specific method to invoke is called the **dynamic dispatch** (or **dynamic binding**) algorithm. This dynamic dispatch algorithm for finding a method a() to process the message "o.a()" provides an effective mechanism for locating reused software. It also allows for another powerful technique of object-oriented programming—**polymorphism**.

2.2.2 Polymorphism

Literally, "polymorphism" means "many forms." In the context of object-oriented design, it refers to the ability of an object variable to take different forms. Object-oriented languages, such as Java, address objects using reference variables. The reference variable o must define which class of objects it is allowed to refer to, in terms of some class S. But this implies that o can also refer to any object belonging to a class T that extends S. Now consider what happens if S defines an a() method and T also defines an a() method. The dynamic dispatch algorithm for method invocation always starts its search from the most restrictive class that applies. When o refers to an object from class T, then it will use T's a() method when asked for o.a(), not S's. In this case, T is said to *override* method a() from S. Alternatively, when o refers to an object from class S (that is not also a T object), it will execute S's a() method when asked for o.a(). Polymorphism such as this is useful because the caller of o.a() does not have to know whether the object o refers to an instance of T or S in order to get the a() method to execute correctly. Thus, the object variable o can be *polymorphic*, or take many forms, depending on the specific class of the objects it is referring to. This kind of functionality allows a specialized class T to extend a class S, inherit the "generic" methods from S, and redefine other methods from S to account for specific properties of objects of T.

Some object-oriented languages, such as Java, also provide a useful technique related to polymorphism, which is called method *overloading*. Overloading occurs when a single class T has multiple methods with the same name, provided each one has a different *signature*. The signature of a method is a combination of its name and the type and number of arguments that are passed to it. Thus, even though multiple methods in a class can have the same name, they can be distinguished by a compiler, provided they have different signatures, that is, are different in actuality. In languages that allow for method overloading, the run-time environment determines which actual method to invoke for a specific method call by searching up the class hierarchy to find the first method with a signature matching the method being invoked. For example, suppose a class T, which defines a method a(), extends a class U, which defines a method a(x, y). If an object o from class T receives the message "o.a(x, y)," then it is U's version of method a that is invoked (with the two parameters x and y). Thus, true polymorphism applies only to methods that have the same signature, but are defined in different classes.

Inheritance, polymorphism, and method overloading support the development of reusable software. We can define classes that inherit the generic instance variables and methods and can then define new more-specific instance variables and methods that deal with special aspects of objects of the new class.

2.2.3   Using Inheritance in Java

There are two primary ways of using the inheritance of classes in Java, *specialization* and *extension*. In using specialization we are specializing a general class to particular subclasses. Such subclasses typically possess an "is a" relationship to their superclass. Such subclasses then inherit all methods of the superclass. For each inherited method, if that method operates correctly independent of whether it is operating for a specialization, no additional work is needed. If, on the other hand, a general method of the superclass would not work correctly on the subclass, then we should override the method to have the correct functionality for the subclass. For example, we could have a general class, Dog, which has a method drink and a method sniff. Specializing this class to a Bloodhound class would probably not require that we override the drink method, as all dogs drink pretty much the same way. But it could require that we override the sniff method, as a Bloodhound has a much more sensitive sense of smell than a "generic" dog. In this way, the Bloodhound class specializes the methods of its superclass, Dog.

In using extension, on the other hand, we utilize inheritance to reuse the code written for methods of the superclass, but we then add new methods that are not present in the superclass, so as to extend its functionality. For example, returning to our Dog class, we might wish to create a subclass, BorderCollie, which inherits all the generic methods of the Dog class, but then adds a new method, herd, since Border Collies have a herding instinct that is not present in generic dogs. By adding the new method, we are extending the functionality of a generic dog.

Class Inheritance in Java

In Java, each class can extend exactly one other class. Even if a class definition makes no explicit use of the **extends** clause, it still inherits from exactly one other class, which in this case is java.lang.Object. Because of this property, Java is said to allow only for *single inheritance* among classes.

Types of Method Overriding

Inside the declaration of a new class, Java uses two kinds of method overriding, *refinement* and *replacement*. In the replacement type of overriding, a method completely replaces the method of the superclass that it is overriding (as in the sniff method of Bloodhound mentioned above). In Java, all regular methods of a class utilize this type of overriding behavior.

In the refinement type of overriding, however, a method does not replace the method of its superclass, but instead adds additional code to that of its superclass. In Java, all constructors utilize the refinement type of overriding, a scheme called

constructor chaining. Namely, a constructor begins its execution by calling a constructor of the superclass. This call can be made explicitly or implicitly. To call a constructor of the superclass explicitly, we use the keyword **super** to refer to the superclass. (For example, super() calls the constructor of the superclass with no arguments.) If no explicit call is made in the body of a constructor, however, the compiler automatically inserts, as the first line of the constructor, a call to the super() method. (There is an exception to this general rule, which is discussed in the next section.) Summarizing, in Java, constructors use the refinement type of method overriding whereas regular methods use replacement.

The Keyword **this**

Sometimes in a Java class it is convenient to reference the current instance of that class. Java provides such a reference, which is called **this**. Using such a construct is useful, for example, if we would like to pass the current object as a parameter to some method. The **this** keyword is also useful to reference a field inside the current object that has a name clash with a variable defined in the current block, as shown in the following program:

```java
public class ThisTester {
  // instance variable
  public int dog = 2;
  // constructor
  ThisTester() {  /* null constructor */
    }
  public void clobber() {
    double dog=5.0;
    this.dog = (int) dog;  // two different dogs!
    }
  public static void main(String args[ ]) {
    ThisTester t = new ThisTester();
    System.out.println("The dog field = " + t.dog);
    t.clobber();
    System.out.println("After clobbering, dog = " + t.dog);
  }
}
```

When this program is executed it prints the following:

```
The dog field = 2
After clobbering, dog = 5
```

An Illustration of Inheritance in Java

To make some of the above notions about inheritance and polymorphism more concrete, let us consider some simple examples in Java.

In particular, we consider some examples of several classes for stepping through and printing out numeric progressions. A numeric progression is a sequence of numbers, where the value of each number depends on one or more of the previous values. For example, an arithmetic progression determines a next number by addition and a geometric progression determines a next number by multiplication. In any case, a progression requires a way of defining its first value and it needs a way of identifying the current value as well.

We begin by defining a class, Progression, shown in Code Fragment 2.1, which defines the "generic" fields and methods of a numeric progression. Specifically, it defines the following two long-integer fields:

- first: first value of the progression;
- cur: current value of the progression;

and the following three methods:

firstValue(): Reset the progression to the first value, and return that value.
Input: None; *Output:* Long Integer.

nextValue(): Step the progression to the next value and return that value.
Input: None; *Output:* Long Integer.

printProgression(n): Reset the progression and print the first n values of the progression.
Input: Integer; *Output:* None.

We say that the method printProgression has no output in the sense that it does not return any value, whereas the methods firstValue and nextValue both return long-integer values. That is, firstValue and nextValue are functions, and printProgression is a procedure.

The Progression class also includes a method Progression(), which is a ***constructor***. Recall that constructors set up all the instance variables at the time an object of this class is created. The Progression class is meant to be a generic superclass from which specialized classes inherit, so this constructor is code that will be included in the constructors for each class that extends the Progression class.

```java
/**
 * A class for numeric progressions.
 */
public class Progression {

  /** First value of the progression. */
  protected long first;

  /** Current value of the progression. */
  protected long cur;

  /** Default constructor. */
  Progression() {
    cur = first = 0;
  }

  /** Resets the progression to the first value.
   *
   * @return first value
   */
  protected long firstValue() {
    cur = first;
    return cur;
  }

  /** Advances the progression to the next value.
   *
   * @return next value of the progression
   */
  protected long nextValue() {
    return ++cur; // default next value
  }

  /** Prints the first n values of the progression.
   *
   * @param n number of values to print
   */
  public void printProgression(int n) {
    System.out.print(firstValue());
    for (int i = 2; i <= n; i++)
      System.out.print(" " + nextValue());
    System.out.println(); // ends the line
  }
}
```

Code Fragment 2.1: Generic numeric progression class.

An Arithmetic Progression Class

Next, we consider the class ArithProgression, which we present in Code Fragment 2.2.

This class defines a progression where each value is determined by adding a fixed increment, inc, to the previous value. That is, ArithProgression defines an arithmetic progression.

Class ArithProgression inherits the fields first and cur and methods firstValue() and printProgression(*n*) from the Progression class. It adds a new field, inc, to store the increment, and two constructors for setting the increment. Finally, it overrides the nextValue() method to conform to the way we get a next value for an arithmetic progression.

Polymorphism is at work here. When a Progression reference is pointing to an ArithProgression object, then it is the ArithProgression methods firstValue() and nextValue() that will be used. This polymorphism is also true inside the inherited version of printProgression(*n*), for the calls to the firstValue() and nextValue() methods here are implicitly for the "current" object (called this in Java), which in this case will be of the ArithProgression class.

In the definition of the ArithProgression class, we have added two constructors, a default one, which takes no parameters, and a parametric one, which takes an integer parameter as the increment for the progression. The default constructor actually calls the parametric one, using the keyword **this** and passing 1 as the value of the increment parameter. These two constructors illustrate method overloading, where a method name can have multiple versions inside the same class, since a method is actually specified by its name, the class of the object that calls it, and the types of arguments that are passed to it—its signature. In this case, the overloading is for constructors (a default constructor and a parametric constructor).

The call **this**(1) to the parametric constructor as the first statement of the default constructor triggers an exception to the general constructor chaining rule discussed in Section 2.2.3. Namely, whenever the first statement of a constructor C' calls another constructor C'' of the same class using the **this** reference, the superclass constructor is not implicitly called for C'. Note that a superclass constructor will be eventually called along the chain, however, either explicitly or implicitly. In particular, for our ArithProgression class, the default constructor of the superclass (Progression) is implicitly called as the first statement of the parametric constructor of ArithProgression.

We discuss constructors in more detail in Section 1.2.

```java
/**
 * Arithmetic progression.
 */
class ArithProgression extends Progression {

  /** Increment. */
  protected long inc;

  // Inherits variables first and cur.

  /** Default constructor setting a unit increment. */
  ArithProgression() {
    this(1);
  }

  /** Parametric constructor providing the increment. */
  ArithProgression(long increment) {
    inc = increment;
  }

  /** Advances the progression by adding the increment to the current value.
   *
   * @return next value of the progression
   */
  protected long nextValue() {
    cur += inc;
    return cur;
  }

  // Inherits methods firstValue() and printProgression(int).
}
```

Code Fragment 2.2: Class for arithmetic progressions.

A Geometric Progression Class

Let us next define a class, GeomProgression, shown in Code Fragment 2.3, which steps through and prints out a geometric progression, determined by multiplying the previous value by a base b. A geometric progression is like a generic progression, except for the way we determine the next value. Hence, GeomProgression is declared as a subclass of the Progression class. As with the ArithProgression class, the GeomProgression class inherits the fields first and cur, and the methods firstValue and printProgression from the Progression class.

```java
/**
 * Geometric Progression
 */
class GeomProgression extends Progression {

  // Inherits variables first and cur.

  /** Default constructor setting base 2. */
  GeomProgression() {
    this(2);
  }

  /** Parametric constructor providing the base.
   *
   * @param base base of the progression.
   */
  GeomProgression(long base) {
    first = base;
    cur = first;
  }

  /** Advances the progression by multiplying the base with the current value.
   *
   * @return next value of the progression
   */
  protected long nextValue() {
    cur *= first;
    return cur;
  }

  // Inherits methods firstValue() and printProgression(int).
}
```

Code Fragment 2.3: Class for geometric progressions.

A Fibonacci Progression Class

As a further example, we define a FibonacciProgression class that represents another kind of progression, the *Fibonacci progression*, where the next value is defined as the sum of the current and previous values. We show class FibonacciProgression in Code Fragment 2.4. Note our use of a parameterized constructor in the FibonacciProgression class to provide a different way of starting the progression.

```
/**
 * Fibonacci progression.
 */
class FibonacciProgression extends Progression {
  /** Previous value. */
  long prev;
  // Inherits variables first and cur.

  /** Default constructor setting 0 and 1 as the first two values. */
  FibonacciProgression() {
    this(0, 1);
  }
  /** Parametric constructor providing the first and second values.
   *
   * @param value1 first value.
   * @param value2 second value.
   */
  FibonacciProgression(long value1, long value2) {
      first = value1;
      prev = value2 − value1; // fictitious value preceding the first
  }

  /** Advances the progression by adding the previous value to the current value.
   *
   * @return next value of the progression
   */
  protected long nextValue() {
    long temp = prev;
    prev = cur;
    cur += temp;
    return cur;
  }
  // Inherits methods firstValue() and printProgression(int).
}
```

Code Fragment 2.4: Class for the Fibonacci progression.

In order to visualize how the three different progression classes are derived from the generic Progression class, we give their inheritance diagram in Figure 2.5.

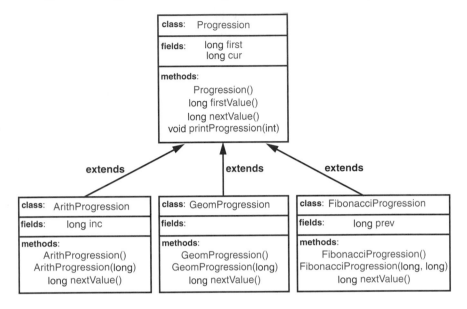

Figure 2.5: Inheritance diagram for class Progression and its subclasses.

To complete our example, we define a class Tester, shown in Code Fragment 2.5, which performs a simple test of each of the three classes. In this class, variable prog is polymorphic during the execution of the main method, since it references objects of class ArithProgression, GeomProgression, and FibonacciProgression in turn. When the main method of the Tester class is invoked by the Java run-time system, the output shown in Code Fragment 2.6 is produced.

The example presented in this section is admittedly small, but it provides a simple illustration of inheritance in Java. The Progression class, its subclasses, and the tester program have a number of shortcomings, however, which might not be immediately apparent. One problem is that the geometric and Fibonacci progressions grow quickly, and there is no provision for handling the inevitable overflow of the long integers involved. For example, since $3^{40} > 2^{63}$, a geometric progression with base $b = 3$ will overflow a long integer after 40 iterations. Likewise, the 94th Fibonacci number is greater than 2^{63}; hence, the Fibonacci progression will overflow a long integer after 94 iterations. Another problem is that we may not allow arbitrary starting values for a Fibonacci progression. For example, do we allow a Fibonacci progression starting with 0 and -1? Dealing with input errors or error conditions that occur during the running of a Java program requires that we have some mechanism for handling them. We discuss this topic next.

```
/** Test program for the progression classes */
class Tester {
  public static void main(String[] args) {
    Progression prog;
    // test ArithProgression
    System.out.println("Arithmetic progression with default increment:");
    prog = new ArithProgression();
    prog.printProgression(10);
    System.out.println("Arithmetic progression with increment 5:");
    prog = new ArithProgression(5);
    prog.printProgression(10);
    // test GeomProgression
    System.out.println("Geometric progression with default base:");
    prog = new GeomProgression();
    prog.printProgression(10);
    System.out.println("Geometric progression with base 3:");
    prog = new GeomProgression(3);
    prog.printProgression(10);
    // test FibonacciProgression
    System.out.println("Fibonacci progression with default start values:");
    prog = new FibonacciProgression();
    prog.printProgression(10);
    System.out.println("Fibonacci progression with start values 4 and 6:");
    prog = new FibonacciProgression(4,6);
    prog.printProgression(10);
  }
}
```

Code Fragment 2.5: Program for testing the progression classes.

```
Arithmetic progression with default increment:
0 1 2 3 4 5 6 7 8 9
Arithmetic progression with increment 5:
0 5 10 15 20 25 30 35 40 45
Geometric progression with default base:
2 4 8 16 32 64 128 256 512 1024
Geometric progression with base 3:
3 9 27 81 243 729 2187 6561 19683 59049
Fibonacci progression with default start values:
0 1 1 2 3 5 8 13 21 34
Fibonacci progression with start values 4 and 6:
4 6 10 16 26 42 68 110 178 288
```

Code Fragment 2.6: Output of the Tester program shown in Code Fragment 2.5.

2.3 Exceptions

Exceptions are unexpected events that occur during the execution of a program. An exception can be the result of an error condition or simply an unanticipated input. In any case, in an object-oriented language, such as Java, exceptions can be thought of as being objects themselves.

2.3.1 Throwing Exceptions

In Java, exceptions are objects that are "***thrown***" by code that encounters some sort of unexpected condition. They can also be thrown by the Java run-time environment should it encounter an unexpected condition, like running out of object memory. A thrown exception is ***caught*** by other code that "handles" the exception somehow, or the program is terminated unexpectedly. (We will say more about catching exceptions shortly.)

Exceptions originate when a piece of Java code finds some sort of problem during execution and ***throws*** an exception object, which is identified with a descriptive name. For instance, if we try to delete the tenth element from a sequence that has only five elements, the code may throw a BoundaryViolationException. This action could be done, for example, using the following code fragment:

```
if (insertIndex > size()) {
  throw new
    BoundaryViolationException("No element at index " + insertIndex);
}
```

It is often convenient to instantiate an exception object at the time the exception has to be thrown. Thus, a **throw** statement is typically written as follows:

```
throw new ⟨exception_constructor⟩([⟨param⟩,⟨param⟩,...]);
```

Exceptions are also thrown by the Java run-time environment itself. For example, the counterpart to the example above is ArrayIndexOutOfBoundsException. If we have a six-element array and ask for the 9th element, then this exception will be thrown by the Java run-time system.

The Throws Clause

When a method is declared, it is appropriate to specify the exceptions it might throw. This convention has both a functional and courteous purpose. For one, it lets users know what to expect. It also lets the Java compiler know which exceptions to prepare for. The following is an example of such a method definition:

```
public void goShopping() throws ShoppingListTooSmallException,
                                OutOfMoneyException {
    // method body . . .
}
```

By specifying all the exceptions that might be thrown by a method, we prepare others to be able to handle all of the exceptional cases that might arise from using this method. Another benefit of declaring exceptions is that we do not need to catch those exceptions in our method. Sometimes this is appropriate in the case where other code is responsible for causing the circumstances leading up to the exception. The following illustrates an exception that is "passed through":

```
public void getReadyForClass() throws ShoppingListTooSmallException,
                                      OutOfMoneyException {
    goShopping();   // I don't have to try or catch the exceptions
                    // which goShopping() might throw because
                    // getReadyForClass() will just pass these along.

    makeCookiesForTA();
}
```

A function can declare that it throws as many exceptions as it likes. Such a listing can be simplified somewhat if all exceptions that can be thrown are subclasses of the same exception. In this case, we only have to declare that a method throws the appropriate superclass.

Kinds of Throwables

Java defines classes Exception and Error as subclasses of Throwable, which denotes any object that can be thrown and caught. Also, it defines class RuntimeException as a subclass of Exception.

The Error class is used for abnormal conditions occurring in the run-time environment, such as running out of memory. Errors can be caught, but they probably should not be, because they usually signal problems that cannot be handled gracefully. An error message or a sudden program termination is about as much grace as we can expect.

The Exception class is the root of the exception hierarchy. Specialized exceptions (for example, BoundaryViolationException) should be defined by subclassing from either Exception or RuntimeException. Note that exceptions that are not subclasses of RuntimeException must be declared in the **throws** clause of any method that can throw them.

2.3.2   Catching Exceptions

When an exception is thrown, it must be *caught* or the program will terminate. In any particular method, an exception in that method can be passed through to the calling method or it can be caught in that method. When an exception is caught, it can be analyzed and dealt with. The general methodology for dealing with exceptions is to "*try*" to execute some fragment of code that might throw an exception. If it does throw an exception, then that exception is *caught* by having the flow of control jump to a predefined **catch** block. Within the catch block we can then deal with the exceptional circumstance.

The general syntax for a *try-catch block* in Java is as follows:

```
try
     ⟨block_of_statements_1⟩
catch (⟨exception_type⟩ ⟨identifier⟩)
     ⟨block_of_statements_2⟩
[catch (⟨exception_type⟩ ⟨identifier⟩)
     ⟨block_of_statements_3⟩]
     . . .
[finally
     ⟨block_of_statements_n⟩]
```

The Java environment begins by executing ⟨block_of_statements_1⟩. If this execution generates no exceptions, then the flow of control continues with the first statement after the last line of the entire **try-catch** block, unless the **try-catch** block includes an optional **finally** block. The **finally** block, if it exists, is executed regardless of whether any exceptions are thrown or caught. Thus, in this case, if no exception is thrown, execution progresses through the **try** block, jumps to the **finally** block, and then continues with the first statement after the last line of the **try** block.

If, on the other hand, ⟨block_of_statements_1⟩ generates an exception, then execution in the **try** block terminates at that point and execution jumps to the **catch** block most closely matching the exception thrown. The ⟨identifier⟩ for this catch statement identifies the exception object itself, which can be referenced in the block of the matching **catch** statement. Once execution of that **catch** block completes, control flow is passed to the optional **finally** block, if it exists, or immediately to the first statement after the last line of the entire **try-catch** block if there is no **finally** block. Otherwise, if there is no **catch** block matching the exception thrown, then control is passed to the optional **finally** block, if it exists, and then the exception is thrown back to the calling method.

Consider the following example code fragment:

```
int index = Integer.MAX_VALUE;    // 2.14 Billion
try                               // This code might have a problem...
{
    String toBuy = shoppingList[index];
}
catch (ArrayIndexOutOfBoundsException aioobx)
{
    System.out.println("The index "+index+" is outside the array.");
}
```

If this code does not catch a thrown exception, the flow of control will immediately exit the method and return to the code that called our method. There, the Java run-time environment will look again for a catch block. If there is no catch block in the code that called this method, the flow of control will jump to the code that called this, and so on. Eventually, if no code catches the exception, the Java run-time system (the origin of our program's flow of control) will catch the exception. At this point, an error message and a stack trace is printed to the screen and the program is terminated.

The following is an actual (hopefully unfamiliar) run-time error message:

```
java.lang.NullPointerException: Returned a null locator
    at java.awt.Component.handleEvent(Component.java:900)
    at java.awt.Component.postEvent(Component.java:838)
    at java.awt.Component.postEvent(Component.java:845)
    at sun.awt.motif.MButtonPeer.action(MButtonPeer.java:39)
    at java.lang.Thread.run(Thread.java)
```

Once an exception is caught, there are several things a programmer might want to do. One possibility is to print out an error message and terminate the program. There are also some interesting cases in which the best way to handle an exception is to ignore it (this can be done by having an empty **catch** block).

Ignoring an exception is usually done, for example, when the programmer does not care whether there was an exception or not. Another legitimate way of handling exceptions is to create and throw another exception, possibly one that specifies the exceptional condition more precisely. The following is an example of this approach:

```
catch (ArrayIndexOutOfBoundsException aioobx) {
    throw new ShoppingListTooSmallException(
            "Product index is not in the shopping list");
}
```

Perhaps the best way to handle an exception (although this is not always possible) is to find the problem, fix it, and continue execution.

2.4   Interfaces, Abstract Classes, and Casting

In order for two objects to interact, they must "know" about the various messages that each will accept, that is, the methods each object supports. To enforce this "knowledge," the object-oriented design paradigm asks that classes specify the ***application programming interface*** (API), or simply ***interface***, that their objects present to other objects. In the ***ADT-based*** approach (see Section 2.1.2) to data structures followed in this book, an interface defining an ADT is specified as a type definition and a collection of methods for this type, with the arguments for each method being of specified types. This specification is, in turn, enforced by the compiler or run-time system, which requires that the types of parameters that are actually passed to methods rigidly conform with the type specified in the interface. This requirement is known as ***strong typing***. Having to define interfaces and then having those definitions enforced by strong typing admittedly places a burden on the programmer, but this burden is offset by the rewards it provides, for it enforces the encapsulation principle and often catches programming errors that would otherwise go unnoticed.

2.4.1   Implementing Interfaces

The main structural element in Java that enforces an API is the ***interface***. An interface is a collection of method declarations with no data and no bodies. That is, the methods of an interface are always empty (that is, they are simply method signatures). When a class implements an interface, it must implement all of the methods declared in the interface. In this way, interfaces enforce requirements that an implementing class have methods with certain specified signatures.

Suppose, for example, that we want to create an inventory of antiques we own, categorized as objects of various types and with various properties. We might, for instance, wish to identify some of our objects as sellable, in which case they could implement the Sellable interface shown in Code Fragment 2.7.

We can then define a concrete class, Photograph, shown in Code Fragment 2.8, that implements the Sellable interface, indicating that we would be willing to sell any of our Photograph objects: This class defines an object that implements each of the methods of the Sellable interface, as required. In addition, it adds a method, isColor, which is specialized for Photograph objects.

Another kind of object in our collection might be something we could transport. For such objects, we define the interface shown in Code Fragment 2.9.

```
/** Interface for objects that can be sold. */
public interface Sellable {

  /** description of the object */
  public String description();

  /** list price in cents */
  public int listPrice();

  /** lowest price in cents we will accept */
  public int lowestPrice();
}
```

Code Fragment 2.7: Interface Sellable.

```
/** Class for photographs that can be sold */
public class Photograph implements Sellable {
  private String descript;      // description of this photo
  private int price;            // the price we are setting
  private boolean color;        // true if photo is in color

  public Photograph(String desc, int p, boolean c) { // constructor
    descript = desc;
    price = p;
    color = c;
  }

  public String description() { return descript; }
  public int listPrice() { return price; }
  public int lowestPrice() { return price/2;  }
  public boolean isColor() { return color; }
}
```

Code Fragment 2.8: Class Photograph implementing the Sellable interface.

```
/** Interface for objects that can be transported. */
public interface Transportable {
  /** weight in grams */
  public int weight();
  /** whether the object is hazardous */
  public boolean isHazardous();
}
```

Code Fragment 2.9: Interface Transportable.

We could then define the class BoxedItem, shown in Code Fragment 2.10, for miscellaneous antiques that we can sell, pack, and ship. Thus, the class BoxedItem implements the methods of the Sellable interface and the Transportable interface, while also adding specialized methods to set an insured value for a boxed shipment and to set the dimensions of a box for shipment.

```java
/** Class for objects that can be sold, packed, and shipped. */
public class BoxedItem implements Sellable, Transportable {
  private String descript;      // description of this item
  private int price;            // list price in cents
  private int weight;           // weight in grams
  private boolean haz;          // true if object is hazardous
  private int height=0;         // box height in centimeters
  private int width=0;          // box width in centimeters
  private int depth=0;          // box depth in centimeters
  /** Constructor */
  public BoxedItem(String desc, int p, int w, boolean h) {
    descript = desc;
    price = p;
    weight = w;
    haz = h;
  }
  public String description() { return descript; }
  public int listPrice() { return price; }
  public int lowestPrice() { return price/2;  }
  public int weight() { return weight; }
  public boolean isHazardous() { return haz; }
  public int insuredValue() { return price*2; }
  public void setBox(int h, int w, int d) {
    height = h;
    width = w;
    depth = d;
  }
}
```

Code Fragment 2.10: Class BoxedItem.

The class BoxedItem shows another feature of classes and interfaces in Java, as well—a class can implement multiple interfaces—which allows us a great deal of flexibility when defining classes that should conform to multiple APIs. For, while a class in Java can extend only one other class, it can nevertheless implement many interfaces.

2.4.2 Multiple Inheritance in Interfaces

The ability of extending from more than one class is known as *multiple inheritance*. In Java, multiple inheritance is allowed for interfaces but not for classes. The reason for this rule is that the methods of an interface never have bodies, while methods in a class always do. Thus, if Java were to allow for multiple inheritance for classes, there could be a confusion if a class tried to extend from two classes that contained methods with the same signatures. This confusion does not exist for interfaces, however, since their methods are empty. So, since no confusion is involved, and there are times when multiple inheritance of interfaces is useful, Java allows for interfaces to use multiple inheritance.

One use for multiple inheritance of interfaces is to approximate a multiple inheritance technique called the *mixin*. Unlike Java, some object-oriented languages, such as Smalltalk and C++, allow for multiple inheritance of concrete classes, not just interfaces. In such languages, it is common to define classes, called *mixin* classes, that are never intended to be created as stand-alone objects, but are instead meant to provide additional functionality to existing classes. Such inheritance is not allowed in Java, however, so programmers must approximate it with interfaces. In particular, we can use multiple inheritance of interfaces as a mechanism for "mixing" the methods from two or more unrelated interfaces to define an interface that combines their functionality, possibly adding more methods of its own. Returning to our example of the antique objects, we could define an interface for insurable items as follows:

```
public interface InsurableItem extends Transportable, Sellable {
    public int insuredValue();     // Return insured Value in cents
}
```

This interface mixes the methods of the Transportable interface with the methods of the Sellable interface, and adds an extra method, insuredValue. Such an interface could allow us to define the BoxedItem alternately as follows:

```
public class BoxedItem implements InsurableItem {
    // ... rest of code exactly as before
}
```

In this case, note that the method insuredValue is not optional, whereas it was optional in the declaration of BoxedItem given previously.

Java interfaces that approximate the mixin include java.lang.Cloneable, which adds a copy feature to a class, java.lang.Comparable, which adds a comparability feature to a class (imposing a natural order on its instances), and java.util.Observer, which adds an update feature to a class that wishes to be notified when certain "observable" objects change state.

2.4.3   Abstract Classes

An abstract class is a class that contains empty method declarations (that is, declarations of methods without bodies) as well as concrete definitions of methods and/or instance variables. Thus, an abstract class lies between an interface and a complete concrete class. Like an interface, an abstract class may not be instantiated, that is, no object can be created from an abstract class. A subclass of an abstract class must provide an implementation for the abstract methods of its superclass, unless it is itself abstract. But, like a concrete class, an abstract class A can extend another abstract class, and abstract and concrete classes can further extend A, as well. Ultimately, we must define another class that is not abstract and extends (subclasses) the abstract superclass, and this new class must fill in code for all abstract methods. Thus, an abstract class uses the specification style of inheritance, but also allows for the specialization and extension styles as well.

The java.lang.Number Class

It turns out that we have already seen an example of an abstract class. Namely, the Java number classes (shown in Table 1.2) specialize an abstract class called java.lang.Number. Each concrete number class, such as java.lang.Integer and java.lang.Double, extends the java.lang.Number class and fills in the details for the abstract methods of the superclass. In particular, the methods intValue, floatValue, doubleValue, and longValue are all abstract in java.lang.Number. Each concrete number class must specify the details of these methods.

2.4.4   Strong Typing

An object variable can be viewed as being of various types, but it can be declared as only one type (either a class or an interface). Moreover, the type in which a variable is declared determines how it is used, and even determines how certain methods will act on it. By enforcing that all variables be typed and that operations declare the types they expect, Java uses the technique of **strong typing** to help prevent bugs. But with such strong types, it is sometimes necessary to explicitly change, or **cast**, a variable from one type to another. We have already discussed, in Section 1.3.3, how casting works for base types. We discuss next how it works for object variables.

2.4.5 Casting in an Inheritance Hierarchy

In Java, we can cast an object reference o of type T into a type S, provided the object o is referring to is actually of type S. If, on the other hand, o is referring to a T object that is not also of type S, then attempting to cast o to type S will throw an exception called "ClassCastException." We illustrate this rule in the following example code fragment:

```
Number n;
Integer i;
n = new Integer(3);
i = (Integer) n;      // This is legal
n = new Double(3.1415);
i = (Integer) n;      // This is illegal!
```

To help avoid potentially embarrassing problems such as this, and to avoid peppering our code with **try-catch** blocks every time we wish to perform a cast, Java provides a simple way to make sure an object cast will be correct. Namely, it provides an operator, **instanceof**, which allows us to test whether an object variable is referring to an object of a certain class (or implementing a certain interface). The syntax for using this operator is as follows:

⟨object_reference⟩ **instanceof** ⟨reference_type⟩

where ⟨object_reference⟩ is an expression that evaluates to an object reference, and ⟨reference_type⟩ is the name of some existing class or interface. If ⟨object_reference⟩ is indeed an instance of ⟨class_type⟩, then the above expression returns **true**. Otherwise, it returns **false**. Thus, we can avoid a class-cast exception from being raised in the above code fragment by modifying it as follows:

```
Number n;
Integer i;
n = new Integer(3);
if (n instanceof Integer)
   i = (Integer) n;      // This is legal
n = new Double(3.1415);
if (n instanceof Integer)
   i = (Integer) n;      // This will not be attempted
```

In addition to being simpler than surrounding each cast by a **try-catch** block, using the **instanceof** in this way is also more efficient.

2.4.6   Casting with Interfaces

In Java, we can define generic data structures that organize elements of a common class or a common interface. We can use these data structures to hold elements of any class we like, as long as the class extends the common class or implements the common interface. Suppose, for example, we want to declare a Person interface for all classes that are associated with persons. We could specify this as shown in Code Fragment 2.11.

```
public interface Person {
    public boolean equalTo (Person other); // is this the same person?
    public String getName(); // get this person's name
    public int getAge(); // get this person's age
}
```
Code Fragment 2.11: Interface Person.

Thus, the Person interface declares three functions. The first of these functions takes one parameter of type Person. So, any class implementing the Person comparison function is passed another object from a class implementing the Person interface to compare to.

Suppose we want to build a directory for Student objects that implement the Person interface shown in Code Fragment 2.12. But a Student object only knows how to compare itself to other Student objects. To resolve this difficulty, we must cast a Person object into a Student. We can do this because we know that only Student objects are in our directory; hence, we know that a reference to a given Person object in this case is also a reference to a Student. This knowledge assures us that the run-time environment will let us perform the cast in method equalTo.

In order to compare two student names, we did an explicit cast of the Person parameter other into a Student. This cast is allowed in this case, but, in general, there are limited circumstances when we can perform a cast to a concrete class S of an object variable v that is declared as an interface type U. In particular, such a cast is allowed only if v is referring an object taken from a concrete class T such that T extends S (or $T = S$) and S implements U.

This type of generic casting also allows us to write general kinds of data structures, which only make minimal assumptions about the elements they store. In Code Fragment 2.13, we sketch how to build a person-pair directory storing pairs of objects implementing the Person interface. This directory contains pairs of elements implementing the interface Person. The remove method performs a search on the directory contents and removes the specified person pair, if it exists, and, like the findOther method, it uses the equalTo method to do this.

```
public class Student implements Person {
  String id;
  String name;
  int age;
  public Student (String i, String n, int a) { // simple constructor
    id = i;
    name = n;
    age = a;
  }
  protected int studyHours() { return age/2; } // just a guess
  public String getID () { return id; } // ID of the student
  public String getName() { return name; } // from Person interface
  public int getAge() { return age; } // from Person interface
  public boolean equalTo (Person other) { // from Person interface
    Student otherStudent = (Student) other;   // cast Person to Student
    return (id.equals (otherStudent.getID()));   // compare IDs
  }
}
```

Code Fragment 2.12: Class Student implementing interface Person.

```
public class PersonPairDirectory {
  // ... instance variables would go here ...
  public PersonPairDirectory() { /* default constructor goes here */ }
  public void insert (Person person, Person other) { /* insert code goes here */ }
  public Person findOther (Person person) { return null; } // stub for find
  public void remove (Person person, Person other) { /* remove code goes here */ }
}
```

Code Fragment 2.13: Class PersonPairDirectory.

Now, suppose we have filled a directory, myDirectory, full of pairs of Student objects that represent roommate pairs. In order to find the roommate of a given Student object, smart_one, we may try to do the following (which is ***wrong***):

Student cute_one = myDirectory.findOther(smart_one); // wrong!

The above statement causes an "explicit-cast-required" compilation error. The problem here is that we are trying to assign a value of declared type Person to a variable of type Student. To solve this problem, we write something like the following:

Student cute_one = (Student) (myDirectory.findOther(smart_one));

We cast the Person value of method findOther to Student. This works fine as long as we are sure that myDirectory.findOther is really giving us a Student object. In general, interfaces can be a valuable tool for the design of general data structures, which can then be specialized by other programmers through the use of casting.

2.5   Recursion and Other Design Patterns

One of the advantages of object-oriented design is that it facilitates reusable, robust, and adaptable software. Designing good code takes more than simply understanding object-oriented methodologies, however. It requires the effective use of object-oriented design techniques.

Computing researchers and practitioners have developed a variety of organizational concepts and methodologies for designing quality object-oriented software that is concise, correct, and reusable. Of special relevance to this book is the concept of a ***design pattern***, which describes a solution to a "typical" software design problem. A pattern provides a general template for a solution that can be applied in many different situations. It describes the main elements of a solution in an abstract way that can be specialized for a specific problem at hand. It consists of a name, which identifies the pattern, a context, which describes the scenarios for which this pattern can be applied, a template, which describes how the pattern is applied, and a result, which describes and analyzes what the pattern produces.

We present several design patterns in this book, and we show how they can be consistently applied to implementations of data structures and algorithms. These design patterns fall into two groups—patterns for solving algorithm design problems and patterns for solving software engineering problems. Some of the algorithm design patterns we discuss include the following:

- Recursion (Sections 2.5.1 and 4.1)
- Amortization (Section 5.1.3)
- Divide-and-conquer (Section 10.1.1)
- Prune-and-search, also known as decrease-and-conquer (Section 10.7.1)
- Brute force (Section 11.2.1)
- The greedy method (Section 11.4.2)
- Dynamic programming (Section 11.5.2).

Likewise, some of the software engineering design patterns we discuss include:

- Position (Section 5.2.2)
- Iterator (Section 5.5)
- Template method (Section 6.3.5)
- Composition (Section 7.1.2)
- Comparator (Section 7.1.2)
- Decorator (Section 12.3.1).

Rather than explain each of these concepts here, however, we introduce them throughout the text as noted above. Nevertheless, we include in this section a brief discussion of an algorithmic design pattern (recursion) and a software engineering design pattern (adapter). Neither of these discussions require prior experience with data structures or algorithms.

2.5.1 Recursion

We have seen that repetition can be achieved by writing loops, such as **for** loops and **while** loops. Another way to achieve repetition is through *recursion*, which occurs when a function calls itself. We have seen examples of methods calling other methods, so it should come as no surprise that most modern programming languages, including Java, allow a method to call itself. In this section, we will see why this capability provides an elegant and powerful alternative for performing repetitive tasks.

The Factorial Function

To illustrate recursion, let us begin with a simple example of computing the value of the *factorial function*. The factorial of a positive integer n, denoted $n!$, is defined as the product of the integers from 1 to n. If $n = 0$, then $n!$ is defined as 1 by convention. More formally, for any integer $n \geq 0$,

$$n! = \begin{cases} 1 & \text{if } n = 0 \\ n \cdot (n-1) \cdot (n-2) \cdots 3 \cdot 2 \cdot 1 & \text{if } n \geq 1. \end{cases}$$

For example, $5! = 5 \cdot 4 \cdot 3 \cdot 2 \cdot 1 = 120$. To make the connection with methods clearer, we use the notation $\text{factorial}(n)$ to denote $n!$.

The factorial function can be defined in a manner that suggests a recursive formulation. To see this, observe that

$$\text{factorial}(5) = 5 \cdot (4 \cdot 3 \cdot 2 \cdot 1) = 5 \cdot \text{factorial}(4).$$

Thus, we can define $\text{factorial}(5)$ in terms of $\text{factorial}(4)$. In general, for a positive integer n, we can define $\text{factorial}(n)$ to be $n \cdot \text{factorial}(n-1)$. This leads to the following *recursive definition*.

$$\text{factorial}(n) = \begin{cases} 1 & \text{if } n = 0 \\ n \cdot \text{factorial}(n-1) & \text{if } n \geq 1. \end{cases}$$

This definition is typical of many recursive definitions. First, it contains one or more *base cases*, which are defined nonrecursively in terms of fixed quantities. In this case, $n = 0$ is the base case. It also contains one or more *recursive cases*, which are defined by appealing to the definition of the function being defined. Observe that there is no circularity in this definition, because each time the function is invoked, its argument is smaller by one.

A Recursive Implementation of the Factorial Function

Let us consider a Java implementation of the factorial function shown in Code Fragment 2.14 under the name recursiveFactorial(). Notice that no looping was needed here. The repeated recursive invocations of the function takes the place of looping.

```java
public static int recursiveFactorial(int n) {    // recursive factorial function
    if (n == 0) return 1;                         // basis case
    else return n * recursiveFactorial(n−1);      // recursive case
}
```

Code Fragment 2.14: A recursive implementation of the factorial function.

We can illustrate the execution of a recursive function definition by means of a *recursion trace*. Each entry of the trace corresponds to a recursive call. Each new recursive function call is indicated by an arrow to the newly called function. When the function returns, an arrow showing this return is drawn and the return value may be indicated with this arrow. An example of a trace is shown in Figure 2.6.

What is the advantage of using recursion? Although the recursive implementation of the factorial function is somewhat simpler than the iterative version, in this case there is no compelling reason for preferring recursion over iteration. For some problems, however, a recursive implementation can be significantly simpler and easier to understand than an iterative implementation. Such an example follows.

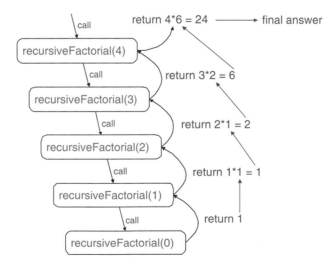

Figure 2.6: A recursion trace for the call recursiveFactorial(4).

Drawing an English Ruler

As a more complex example of the use of recursion, consider how to draw the markings of a typical English ruler. A ruler is broken up into 1-inch intervals, and each interval consists of a set of *ticks* placed at intervals of $1/2$ inch, $1/4$ inch, and so on. As the size of the interval decreases by half, the tick length decreases by one. (See Figure 2.7.)

```
      ---- 0             ----- 0           --- 0
      -                  -                  -
      --                 --                 --
      -                  -                  -
      --- 1              ---                --- 1
      -                  -                  -
      --                 --                 --
      -                  -                  -
      ---- 1             ----               --- 2
      -                  -                  -
      --                 --                 --
      -                  -                  -
      --- 1              ---                --- 3
      -                  -
      --                 --
      -                  -
      ---- 2             ----- 1

      (a)                (b)                (c)
```

Figure 2.7: Three sample outputs of the ruler-drawing function: (a) a 2-inch ruler with major tick length 4; (b) a 1-inch ruler with major tick length 5; (c) a 3-inch ruler with major tick length 3.

Each multiple of 1 inch also has a numeric label. The longest tick length is called the ***major tick length***. We will not worry about actual distances, however, and just print one tick per line.

A Recursive Approach to Ruler Drawing

Our approach to drawing such a ruler consists of three methods. The main method drawRuler draws the entire ruler. Its arguments are the total number of inches in the ruler, nInches, and the major tick length, majorLength. The utility method drawOneTick draws a single tick of the given length. It can also be given an optional integer label, which is printed if it is nonnegative.

The interesting work is done by the recursive method drawTicks, which draws the sequence of ticks within some interval. Its only argument is the tick length associated with the interval's central tick. Consider the 1-inch ruler with major tick length 5 shown in Figure 2.7(b). Ignoring the lines containing 0 and 1, let us consider how to draw the sequence of ticks lying between these lines. The central tick (at 1/2 inch) has length 4. Observe that the two patterns of ticks above and below this central tick are identical, and each has a central tick of length 3. In general, an interval with a central tick length $L \geq 1$ is composed of the following:

- an interval with a central tick length $L - 1$,
- a single tick of length L,
- an interval with a central tick length $L - 1$.

With each recursive call, the length decreases by one. When the length drops to zero, we simply return. As a result, this recursive process will always terminate. This suggests a recursive process, in which the first and last steps are performed by calling drawTicks$(L - 1)$ recursively. The middle step is performed by calling drawOneTick(L). This recursive formulation is shown in Code Fragment 2.15. As in the factorial example, the code has a base case (when $L = 0$). In this instance we make two recursive calls to the method.

```
                                                            // draw a tick with no label
public static void drawOneTick(int tickLength) { drawOneTick(tickLength, −1); }
                                                            // draw one tick
public static void drawOneTick(int tickLength, int tickLabel) {
  for (int i = 0; i < tickLength; i++)
    System.out.print("-");
  if (tickLabel >= 0) System.out.print(" " + tickLabel);
  System.out.print("\n");
}
public static void drawTicks(int tickLength) {   // draw ticks of given length
  if (tickLength > 0) {                          // stop when length drops to 0
    drawTicks(tickLength−1);                      // recursively draw left ticks
    drawOneTick(tickLength);                      // draw center tick
    drawTicks(tickLength−1);                      // recursively draw right ticks
  }
}
public static void drawRuler(int nInches, int majorLength) { // draw ruler
  drawOneTick(majorLength, 0);                    // draw tick 0 and its label
  for (int i = 1; i <= nInches; i++) {
    drawTicks(majorLength−1);                      // draw ticks for this inch
    drawOneTick(majorLength, i);                   // draw tick i and its label
  }
}
```

Code Fragment 2.15: A recursive implementation of a method that draws a ruler.

Illustrating Ruler Drawing using a Recursion Trace

The recursive execution of the recursive drawTicks method, defined above, can be visualized using a recursion trace.

The trace for drawTicks is more complicated than in the factorial example, however, because each instance makes two recursive calls. To illustrate this, we will show the recursion trace in a form that is reminiscent of an outline for a document. See Figure 2.8.

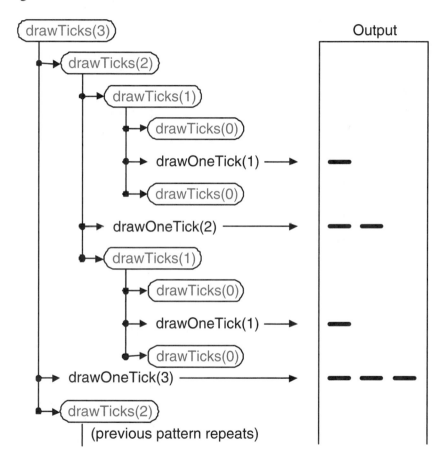

Figure 2.8: A partial recursion trace for the call drawTicks(3). The second pattern of calls for drawTicks(2) is not shown, but it is identical to the first.

Throughout this book we shall see many other examples of how recursion can be used in the design of data structures and algorithms. Section 4.1 contains more examples and a more detailed investigation of issues arising in recursion.

2.5.2   The Adapter Pattern

Classes are often written to provide similar functionality to other classes. For example, we may have a class that performs insertion and removal operations on a directory of Person objects, whereas we might wish to have a directory that operates exclusively on Student objects. We could, of course, rewrite a complete directory program for processing Student objects, but that would be a waste.

The *adapter pattern* applies to any context where we want to modify an existing class so that its methods match those of a related, but different, class or interface. One general way for applying the adapter pattern is to define the new class in such a way that it contains an instance of the old class as a hidden field, and implement each method of the new class using methods of this hidden instance variable.

In the example of a Person directory adapted so that it operates exclusively on Student objects, we can define an adapter class that uses the existing generic directory as a protected instance variable in such a way that it guarantees only objects of the correct type go in and out of our directory. In particular, to adapt a directory designed to handle Person objects, we can write a simple StudentPairDirectory class guaranteeing that only Student pairs go into our directory, as shown in Code Fragment 2.16. Such an adapter class *specializes*, or "adapts," the generic directory data structure to only work for pairs of Student objects.

The result of applying the adapter pattern is that a new class that performs almost the same functions as a previous class, but in a more convenient way, has been created. Analyzing this solution, we see that it adds to the length of an existing program, and performs two method calls in the place of one (one to the method with the desired signature and one to the method inside this method to do the actual computation). Thus, if our directory data structure is to be used infrequently in another program, then it is probably reasonable to do the casting explicitly with each use, and not use the above adapter class. If our directory data structure is to be used extensively, however, it saves typing time and eases readability to design an adapter class such as that above, which hides the casting inside its internal methods.

```
/** Class for a directory storing pairs of Student objects. */
public class StudentPairDirectory {
  protected PersonPairDirectory directory;
  public StudentPairDirectory() { directory = new PersonPairDirectory (); }
  public void insert(Student s, Student t) { directory.insert(s,t); }
  public Student findOther(Student s) { return (Student) directory.findOther(s); }
  public void remove(Student s, Student t) { directory.remove(s, t); }
}
```

Code Fragment 2.16: Class StudentPairDirectory adapting class PersonPairDirectory of Code Fragment 2.13.

2.6 Exercises

For source code and help with exercises, please visit **java.datastructures.net**.

Reinforcement

R-2.1 Give three examples of life-critical software applications.

R-2.2 Give an example of a software application where adaptability can mean the difference between a prolonged sales lifetime and bankruptcy.

R-2.3 Describe a component from a text-editor GUI (other than an "edit" menu) and the methods that it encapsulates.

R-2.4 Draw a class inheritance diagram for the following set of classes:

- Class Goat extends Object and adds an instance variable tail and methods milk() and jump().
- Class Pig extends Object and adds an instance variable nose and methods eat() and wallow().
- Class Horse extends Object and adds instance variables height and color, and methods run() and jump() (which overrides the Object clone() method).
- Class Racer extends Horse and adds a method race().
- Class Equestrian extends Horse and adds an instance variable weight and methods trot() and isTrained().

R-2.5 Give a short fragment of Java code that uses the progression classes from Section 2.2.3 to find the 8th value of a Fibonacci progression that starts with 2 and 2 as its first two values.

R-2.6 If we choose inc = 128, how many calls to the nextValue method from the ArithProgression class of Section 2.2.3 can we make before we cause a long-integer overflow?

R-2.7 Suppose we have an instance variable p that is declared of type Progression, using the classes of Section 2.2.3. Suppose further that p actually refers to an instance of the class GeomProgression that was created with the default constructor. If we cast p to type Progression and call p.firstValue(), what will be returned? Why?

R-2.8 Consider the inheritance of classes from Exercise R-2.4, and let *d* be an object variable of type Horse. If *d* refers to an actual object of type Equestrian, can it be cast to the class Racer? Why or why not?

R-2.9 Give an example of a Java code fragment that performs an array reference that is possibly out of bounds, and if it is out of bounds, the program catches that exception and prints the following error message:
"Don't try buffer overflow attacks in Java!"

R-2.10 Consider the following code fragment, taken from some package:

```java
public class Maryland extends State {
  Maryland() { /* null constructor */ }
  public void printMe() { System.out.println("Read it."); }
  public static void main(String[] args) {
    Region mid = new State();
    State md = new Maryland();
    Object obj = new Place();
    Place usa = new Region();
    md.printMe();
    mid.printMe();
    ((Place) obj).printMe();
    obj = md;
    ((Maryland) obj).printMe();
    obj = usa;
    ((Place) obj).printMe();
    usa = md;
    ((Place) usa).printMe();
  }
}
class State  extends Region {
  State() { /* null constructor */ }
  public void printMe() { System.out.println("Ship it."); }
}
class Region extends Place {
  Region() { /* null constructor */ }
  public void printMe() { System.out.println("Box it."); }
}
class Place extends Object {
  Place() { /* null constructor */ }
  public void printMe() { System.out.println("Buy it."); }
}
```

What is the output from calling the main() method of the Maryland class?

R-2.11 Write a short recursive Java method that counts the number of vowels in character string *s*.

R-2.12 Write a short recursive Java method that removes all the punctuation from a string *s* storing a sentence. For example, this operation would transform "Let's eat, Mike." to "Lets eat Mike".

R-2.13 Write a short recursive Java method for computing the product of the first *k* positive integers.

Creativity

C-2.1 Explain why the Java dynamic dispatch algorithm, which looks for the method to invoke for a message *o*.a(), will never get into an infinite loop.

C-2.2 Write a Java class that extends the Progression class to produce a progression where each value is the absolute value of the difference between the previous two values. You should include a default constructor that starts with 2 and 200 as the first two values and a parametric constructor that starts with a specified pair of numbers as the first two values.

C-2.3 Write a Java class that extends the Progression class to produce a progression where each value is the square root of the previous value. (Note that you can no longer represent each value with an integer.) You should include a default constructor that starts with $65,536$ as the first value and a parametric constructor that starts with a specified (**double**) number as the first value.

C-2.4 Rewrite all the classes in the Progression hierarchy so that all values are from the BigInteger class, in order to avoid overflows all together.

C-2.5 Write a short recursive Java method that finds the minimum and maximum values in an array of **int** values without using any loops.

C-2.6 Write a short recursive Java method that will check if an array of **int** values has any repeated entries.

C-2.7 Write a short recursive Java method that will rearrange an array of **int** values so that all the even values appear before all the odd values.

C-2.8 Write a short recursive Java method that takes a character string *s* and outputs its reverse. So for example, the reverse of "pots&pans" would be "snap&stop".

C-2.9 Write a short recursive Java method that determines if a string *s* is a palindrome, that is, it is equal to its reverse. For example, `"racecar"` and `"gohangasalamiimalasagnahog"` are palindromes.

C-2.10 Use recursion to write a Java method for determining if a string *s* has more vowels than consonants.

Projects

P-2.1 Fill in code for the PersonPairDirectory class of Code Fragment 2.13, assuming person pairs are stored in an array with capacity 1,000. The directory should keep track of how many person pairs are actually in it.

P-2.2 Write a Java program that can take a positive integer greater than 2 as input and write out the number of times one must repeatedly divide this number by 2 before getting a value less than 2.

P-2.3 Write a Java program that can "make change." Your program should take two numbers as input, one that is a monetary amount charged and the other that is a monetary amount given. It should then return the number of each kind of bill and coin to give back as change for the difference between the amount given and the amount charged. The values assigned to the bills and coins can be based on the monetary system of any current or former government. Try to design your program so that it returns the fewest number of bills and coins as possible.

Chapter Notes

The reader interested in learning more about the contribution to computing that was made by ENIAC and other historical computing devices is referred to the book by Williams [97] or the Web site (`http://ftp.arl.mil/~mike/comphist/`) for the Army Research Laboratory's "History of Computing Information." For a broad overview of recent developments in computer science and engineering, we refer the reader to *The Computer Science and Engineering Handbook* [90]. For more information about the Therac-25 incident, please see the paper by Leveson and Turner [62].

The reader interested in further studying object-oriented programming is referred to the books by Booch [14], Budd [17], and Liskov and Guttag [66]. Liskov and Guttag [66] also provide a nice discussion of abstract data types, as does the survey paper by Cardelli and Wegner [19] and the book chapter by Demurjian [27] in the *The Computer Science and Engineering Handbook* [90]. Design patterns are described in the book by Gamma, *et al.* [37]. The class inheritance diagram notation we use is derived from the book by Gamma, *et al.*

Chapter
3

Analysis Tools

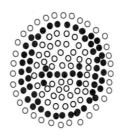

Contents

In a classic story, the famous mathematician Archimedes was asked to determine if a golden crown commissioned by the king was indeed pure gold, and not part silver, as an informant had claimed. Archimedes discovered a way to perform this analysis while stepping into a (Greek) bath. He noted that water spilled out of the bath in proportion to the amount of him that went in. Realizing the implications of this fact, he immediately got out of the bath and ran naked through the city shouting, "Eureka, eureka!," for he had discovered an analysis tool (displacement), which, when combined with a simple scale, could determine if the king's new crown was good or not. That is, Archimedes could dip the crown and an equal-weight amount of gold into a bowl of water to see if they both displaced the same amount. This discovery was unfortunate for the goldsmith, however, for when Archimedes did his analysis, the crown displaced more water than an equal-weight lump of pure gold, indicating that the crown was not, in fact, pure gold.

In this book, we are interested in the design of "good" data structures and algorithms. Simply put, a ***data structure*** is a systematic way of organizing and accessing data, and an ***algorithm*** is a step-by-step procedure for performing some task in a finite amount of time. These concepts are central to computing, but to be able to classify some data structures and algorithms as "good," we must have precise ways of analyzing them.

The primary analysis tool we will use in this book involves characterizing the running times of algorithms and data structure operations, with space usage also being of interest. Running time is a natural measure of "goodness," since time is a precious resource—computer solutions should run as fast as possible.

In general, the running time of an algorithm or data structure method increases with the input size, although it may also vary for different inputs of the same size. Also, the running time is affected by the hardware environment (as reflected in the processor, clock rate, memory, disk, etc.) and software environment (as reflected in the operating system, programming language, compiler, interpreter, etc.) in which the algorithm is implemented, compiled, and executed. All other factors being equal, the running time of the same algorithm on the same input data will be smaller if the computer has, say, a much faster processor or if the implementation is done in a program compiled into native machine code instead of an interpreted implementation run on a virtual machine. Nevertheless, in spite of the possible variations that come from different environmental factors, we would like to focus on the relationship between the running time of an algorithm and the size of its input.

But focusing on running time as a primary measure of goodness raises an interesting question.

3.1   What Is Running Time Anyway?

If we are interested in characterizing an algorithm's running time as a function of the input size, what is the proper way of measuring it?

3.1.1   Experimental Studies

If an algorithm has been implemented, we can study its running time by executing it on various test inputs and recording the actual time spent in each execution. Fortunately, such measurements can be taken in an accurate manner by using system calls that are built into the language or operating system (for example, by using the System.currentTimeMillis() method or calling the run-time environment with profiling enabled). Such tests assign a specific running time to a specific input size, but we are interested in determining the general dependence of running time on the size of the input. In order to determine this dependence, we should perform several experiments on many different test inputs of various sizes. Then we can visualize the results of such experiments by plotting the performance of each run of the algorithm as a point with x-coordinate equal to the input size, n, and y-coordinate equal to the running time, t. (See Figure 3.1.) From this visualization and the data that supports it, we can perform a statistical analysis that seeks to fit the best function of the input size to the experimental data. To be meaningful, this analysis requires that we choose good sample inputs and test enough of them to be able to make sound statistical claims about the algorithm's running time.

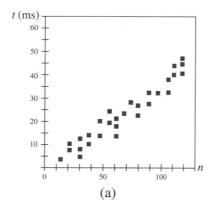

(a)

Figure 3.1: Results of an experimental study on the running time of an algorithm. A dot with coordinates (n,t) indicates that on an input of size n, the running time of the algorithm is t milliseconds (ms).

3.1.2   Requirements for a General Analysis Methodology

While experimental studies of running times are useful, they have three major limitations:

- Experiments can be done only on a limited set of test inputs; hence, they leave out the running times of inputs not included in the experiment (and these inputs may be important).
- We will have difficulty comparing the experimental running times of two algorithms unless the experiments were performed in the same hardware and software environments.
- We have to fully implement and execute an algorithm in order to study its running time experimentally.

This last requirement is obvious, but it is probably the most time consuming aspect of performing an experimental analysis of an algorithm. The other limitations impose serious hurdles too, of course. Thus, we would ideally like to have an analysis tool that allows us to avoid performing experiments.

In the rest of this chapter, we develop a general methodology for analyzing the running times of algorithms that:

- Takes into account all possible inputs
- Allows us to evaluate the relative efficiency of any two algorithms in a way that is independent from the hardware and software environment
- Can be performed by studying a high-level description of the algorithm without actually implementing it or running experiments on it.

This methodology aims at associating with each algorithm a function $f(n)$ that characterizes the running time of the algorithm as a function of the input size n. Typical functions that will be encountered include n and n^2. For example, we will write statements of the type "Algorithm A runs in time proportional to n," meaning that if we were to perform experiments, we would find that the actual running time of algorithm A on **any** input of size n never exceeds cn, where c is a constant that depends on the hardware and software environment used in the experiment. Given two algorithms A and B, where A runs in time proportional to n and B runs in time proportional to n^2, we will prefer A to B, since function n grows at a smaller rate than function n^2. We will say more in this chapter about these and other important functions, and our methodology will make such notions precise.

Before we "roll up our sleeves" and start developing our methodology for algorithm analysis, we present a high-level notation for describing algorithms (Section 3.2) and review the seven important functions that we will use most in this book (Section 3.3).

3.2 Pseudo-Code

Programmers are often asked to describe algorithms in a way that is intended for human eyes only. Such descriptions are not computer programs, but instead are "high-level" explanations, combining natural language and familiar structures from a programming language in a way that is both clear and informative. Such descriptions also facilitate the high-level analysis of a data structure or algorithm. We call these descriptions ***pseudo-code***.

Let us illustrate pseudo-code with an easy example of finding the maximum element in an array A storing n integers. We can use an algorithm called arrayMax, which scans through the elements of A as shown in Code Fragment 3.1. We give a complete Java implementation in Code Fragment 3.2.

Algorithm arrayMax(A, n):

    Input: An array A storing $n \geq 1$ integers.

    Output: The maximum element in A.

    currentMax $\leftarrow A[0]$

    for $i \leftarrow 1$ **to** $n-1$ **do**

      if *currentMax* $< A[i]$ **then**

        currentMax $\leftarrow A[i]$

    return *currentMax*

Code Fragment 3.1: Algorithm arrayMax.

```java
/** Program for finding the maximum element in an array A of n integers. */
public class ArrayMaxProgram {
  static int arrayMax(int[] A, int n) {
    int currentMax = A[0];       // executed once
    for (int i=1; i < n; i++)    // executed once; n times; n-1 times, resp.
      if (currentMax < A[i])     // executed n-1 times
        currentMax = A[i];       // executed at most n-1 times
    return currentMax;           // executed once
  }
  /** Testing method called when the program is executed. */
  public static void main(String args[]) {
    int[] num = { 10, 15, 3, 5, 56, 107, 22, 16, 85 };
    int n = num.length;
    System.out.println("The maximum element is " + arrayMax(num,n) + ".");
  }
}
```

Code Fragment 3.2: Algorithm arrayMax within a complete Java program.

3.2.1   What Is Pseudo-Code?

As shown in the example above, pseudo-code is generally more compact than Java code and is easier to read and understand. Nevertheless, by inspecting pseudo-code, we can argue about the correctness and running time of an algorithm. For example, in arrayMax, the variable *currentMax* starts out being equal to the first element of *A*. We claim that at the beginning of the *i*th iteration of the loop, *currentMax* is equal to the maximum of the first *i* elements in *A*. Since we compare *currentMax* to $A[i]$ in iteration *i*, if this claim is true before this iteration, it will be true after it for $i + 1$ (which is the next value of counter *i*). Thus, after $n - 1$ iterations, *currentMax* will equal the maximum element in *A*.

Pseudo-code is a mixture of natural language and high-level programming constructs to describe the main ideas behind a generic implementation of a data structure or algorithm. There really is no precise definition of the ***pseudo-code*** language, however, because of its reliance on natural language. At the same time, to help achieve clarity, pseudo-code mixes natural language with some formal programming language constructs. In this book, we use the following:

- Expressions: We use standard mathematical symbols to express numeric and Boolean expressions. We use the left arrow sign ($\leftarrow$) as the assignment operator in assignment statements (equivalent to the Java = operator) and we use the equal sign (=) as the equality relation in Boolean expressions (which is equivalent to the "==" relation in Java).
- Method declarations: **Algorithm** name(*param1, param2, . . .*) declares a new method name and its parameters.
- Decision structures: **if** condition **then** true-actions [**else** false-actions]. We use indentation to indicate what actions should be included in the true-actions and false-actions.
- While-loops: **while** condition **do** actions. We use indentation to indicate what actions should be included in the loop actions.
- Repeat-loops: **repeat** actions **until** condition. We use indentation to indicate what actions should be included in the loop actions.
- For-loops: **for** loop-control **do** actions. We use indentation to indicate what actions should be included among the loop actions.
- Array indexing: $A[i]$ represents the *i*th cell in the array *A*. The cells of an *n*-celled array *A* are indexed from $A[0]$ to $A[n - 1]$ (consistently with Java).
- Method calls: *object*.method(arguments) (*object* is optional if it is understood).
- Method returns: **return** expression. This operation returns the value of the given expression to the method that called this one.

3.3 The Seven Functions Used in This Book

In this section, we briefly discuss the seven most important functions used in the analysis of algorithms. We will use only these seven simple functions for almost all the analysis we do in this book. In fact, a section that uses a function other than one of these seven will be marked with a star ($\star$) to indicate that it is optional. In addition to these seven fundamental functions, Appendix A contains a list of other useful mathematical facts that apply in the context of data structure and algorithm analysis.

3.3.1 The Constant Function

The simplest function we can think of is the ***constant function***. This is the function,

$$f(n) = c,$$

for some fixed constant c, such as $c = 5$, $c = 27$, or $c = 2^{10}$. That is, for any argument n, the constant function $f(n)$ assigns the value c. In other words, it doesn't matter what the value of n is; $f(n)$ will always be equal to the constant value c.

Since we are most interested in integer functions, the most fundamental constant function is $g(n) = 1$, and this is the typical constant function we use in this book. Note that any other constant function, $f(n) = c$, can be written as a constant c times $g(n)$. That is, $f(n) = cg(n)$ in this case.

As simple as it is, the constant function is useful in algorithm analysis, because it characterizes the number of steps needed to do a basic operation on a computer, like adding two numbers, assigning a value to some variable, or comparing two numbers.

3.3.2 The Linear Function

Another simple yet important function is the ***linear function***,

$$f(n) = n.$$

That is, given an input value n, the linear function f assigns the value n itself.

This function arises in algorithm analysis any time we have to do a single basic operation for each of n elements. For example, comparing a number x to each element of an array of size n will require n comparisons. The linear function also represents the best running time we can hope to achieve for any algorithm that processes a collection of n objects that are not already in the computer's memory, since reading in the n objects itself requires n operations.

3.3.3   The Quadratic Function

Another function that appears quite often in algorithm analysis is the *quadratic function*,

$$f(n) = n^2.$$

That is, given an input value n, the function f assigns the product of n with itself (in other words, "n squared").

The main reason why the quadratic function appears in the analysis of algorithms is that there are many algorithms that have nested loops, where the inner loop performs a linear number of operations and the outer loop is performed a linear number of times. Thus, in such cases, the algorithm performs $n \cdot n = n^2$ operations.

Nested Loops and the Quadratic Function

The quadratic function can also arise in the context of nested loops where the first iteration of the inner loop uses one operation, the second uses two operations, the third uses three operations, and so on. In other words, the number of operations performed in such an algorithm is

$$1 + 2 + 3 + \cdots + (n-2) + (n-1) + n.$$

In other words, this is the total number of operations that will be performed by the nested loop if the number of operations performed inside the loop increases by one with each iteration of the outer loop. This quantity also has an interesting history.

In 1787, a German elementary schoolteacher decided to keep his 9- and 10-year-old pupils occupied with the task of adding up all the numbers from 1 to 100. But almost immediately after giving this assignment, one of the children claimed to have the answer! The teacher was suspicious, for the student had only the answer on his slate, with no calculations. But the answer was correct—5,050. That student was none other than Carl Gauss, who would grow up to be one of the greatest mathematicians of all times. It is widely suspected that young Gauss derived the answer to his teacher's assignment using the following identity.

Proposition 3.1: *For any integer $n \geq 1$, we have:*

$$1 + 2 + 3 + \cdots + (n-2) + (n-1) + n = \frac{n(n+1)}{2}.$$

We give two "visual" justifications of Proposition 3.1 in Figure 3.2.

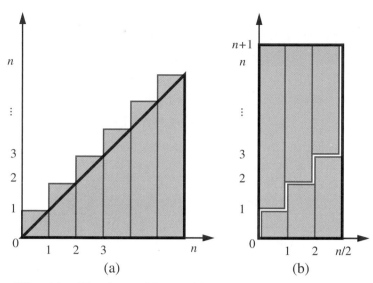

Figure 3.2: Visual justifications of Proposition 3.1. Both illustrations visualize the identity in terms of the total area covered by n unit-width rectangles with heights $1, 2, \ldots, n$. In (a) the rectangles are shown to cover a big triangle of area $n^2/2$ (base n and height n) plus n small triangles of area $1/2$ each (base 1 and height 1). In (b), which applies only when n is even, the rectangles are shown to cover a big rectangle of base $n/2$ and height $n + 1$.

The lesson to be learned from Proposition 3.1 is that if we perform an algorithm with nested loops such that the operations in the inner loop increase by one each time, then the total number of operations is quadratic in the number of times, n, we perform the outer loop. In particular, the number of operations is $n^2/2 + n/2$, in this case, which is a little more than a constant factor $(1/2)$ times the quadratic function n^2. In other words, such an algorithm is only slightly better than an algorithm that uses n operations each time the inner loop is performed. This observation might at first seem nonintuitive, but it is nevertheless true, as shown in Figure 3.2.

3.3.4 The Cubic Function and Other Polynomials

Continuing our discussion of functions that are powers of the input, we consider the **cubic function**,

$$f(n) = n^3,$$

which assigns to an input value n the product of n with itself three times. This function appears less frequently in the context of algorithm analysis than the constant, linear, and quadratic functions previously mentioned, but it does appear from time to time.

Polynomials

Interestingly, the functions we have listed so far can be viewed as all being part of a larger class of functions, the *polynomials*.

A *polynomial* function is a function of the form,

$$f(n) = a_0 + a_1 n + a_2 n^2 + a_3 n^3 + \cdots + a_d n^d,$$

where $a_0, a_1, \ldots, a_d$ are constants, called the *coefficients* of the polynomial, and $a_d \neq 0$. Integer d, which indicates the highest power in the polynomial, is called the *degree* of the polynomial.

For example, the following functions are all polynomials:

- $f(n) = 2 + 5n + n^2$
- $f(n) = 1 + n^3$
- $f(n) = 1$
- $f(n) = n$
- $f(n) = n^2$

Therefore, we could argue that this book presents just four important functions used in algorithm analysis, but we will stick to saying that there are seven, since the constant, linear, and quadratic functions are too important to be lumped in with other polynomials. Running times that are polynomials with degree, d, are generally better than polynomial running times with large degree.

Summations

A notation that appears again and again in the analysis of data structures and algorithms is the *summation*, which is defined as follows:

$$\sum_{i=a}^{b} f(i) = f(a) + f(a+1) + f(a+2) + \cdots + f(b),$$

where a and b are integers and $a \leq b$. Summations arise in data structure and algorithm analysis because the running times of loops naturally give rise to summations.

Using a summation, we can rewrite the formula of Proposition 3.1 as

$$\sum_{i=1}^{n} i = \frac{n(n+1)}{2}.$$

Likewise, we can write a polynomial $f(n)$ of degree d with coefficients $a_0, \ldots, a_d$ as

$$f(n) = \sum_{i=0}^{d} a_i n^i.$$

Thus, the summation notation gives us a shorthand way of expressing sums of increasing terms that have a regular structure.

3.3.5 The Exponential Function

Another function used in the analysis of algorithms is the *exponential function*,

$$f(n) = b^n,$$

where b is a positive constant, called the *base*, and the argument n is the *exponent*. That is, function $f(n)$ assigns to the input argument n the value obtained by multiplying the base b by itself n times. In algorithm analysis, the most common base for the exponential function is $b = 2$. For instance, if we have a loop that starts by performing one operation and then doubles the number of operations performed with each iteration, then the number of operations performed in the nth iteration is 2^n. In addition, an integer word containing n bits can represent all the nonnegative integers less than 2^n. Thus, the exponential function with base 2 is quite common. The exponential function will be also referred to as *exponent function*.

We sometimes have other exponents besides n, however; hence, it is useful for us to know a few handy rules for working with exponents. In particular, the following *exponent rules* are quite helpful.

Proposition 3.2 (Exponent Rules): *Given positive integers a, b, and c, we have*

1. $(b^a)^c = b^{ac}$
2. $b^a b^c = b^{a+c}$
3. $b^a / b^c = b^{a-c}$.

For example, we have the following:

- $256 = 16^2 = (2^4)^2 = 2^{4 \cdot 2} = 2^8 = 256$ (Exponent Rule 1)
- $243 = 3^5 = 3^{2+3} = 3^2 3^3 = 9 \cdot 27 = 243$ (Exponent Rule 2)
- $16 = 1024/64 = 2^{10}/2^6 = 2^{10-6} = 2^4 = 16$ (Exponent Rule 3).

We can extend the exponential function to exponents that are fractions or real numbers and to negative exponents, as follows. Given a positive integer k, we define $b^{1/k}$ to be kth root of b, that is, the number r such that $r^k = b$. For example, $25^{1/2} = 5$, since $5^2 = 25$. Likewise, $27^{1/3} = 3$ and $16^{1/4} = 2$. This approach allows us to define any power whose exponent can be expressed as a fraction, for $b^{a/c} = (b^a)^{1/c}$, by Exponent Rule 1. For example, $9^{3/2} = (9^3)^{1/2} = 729^{1/2} = 27$. Thus, a fractional exponent $b^{a/c}$ is really just the cth root of the integral exponent b^a. We need not restrict our exponents to powers that are expressed as fractions, however.

We can further extend the exponential function to define b^x for any real number x, by computing a series of numbers of the form $b^{a/c}$ for fractions a/c that get progressively closer and closer to x. Any real number x can be approximated arbitrarily close by a fraction a/c; hence, we can use the fraction a/c as the exponent of b to get arbitrarily close to b^x. So, for example, the number 2^π is well defined. Incidentally, this ability to approximate exponents is the reason why scientific calculators can have a button marked X^Y for computing the exponential function x^y.

Finally, given a negative exponent d, we define $b^d = 1/b^{-d}$, which corresponds to applying Exponent Rule 3 with $a = 0$ and $c = -d$.

Geometric Sums

Suppose we have a loop where each iteration takes a multiplicative factor longer than the previous one. This loop can be analyzed using the following proposition.

Proposition 3.3: *For any integer $n \geq 0$ and any real number a such that $a > 0$ and $a \neq 1$, consider the summation*

$$\sum_{i=0}^{n} a^i = 1 + a + a^2 + \cdots + a^n$$

(remembering that $a^0 = 1$ if $a > 0$). This summation is equal to

$$\frac{a^{n+1} - 1}{a - 1}.$$

Summations as shown in Proposition 3.3 are called **geometric** summations, because each term is geometrically larger than the previous one if $a > 1$. That is, the terms in such a geometric summation exhibit exponential growth. For example, everyone working in computing should know that

$$1 + 2 + 4 + 8 + \cdots + 2^{n-1} = 2^n - 1,$$

for this is the largest integer that can be represented in binary notation using n bits.

3.3.6 The Logarithm Function

One of the interesting and sometimes even surprising aspects of the analysis of data structures and algorithms is the ubiquitous presence of the **logarithm function**,

$$f(n) = \log_b n,$$

for some constant $b > 1$. This function is defined as follows:

$$x = \log_b n \quad \text{if and only if} \quad b^x = n.$$

By definition, $\log_b 1 = 0$. The value b is known as the **base** of the logarithm.

Calculating the Logarithm Function

Computing the logarithm function exactly for any integer n involves the use of calculus, but we can use an approximation that is good enough for our purposes without calculus. In particular, we can easily compute the smallest integer greater than or equal to $\log_a n$, for this number is equal to the number of times we can divide n by a until we get a number less than or equal to 1. For example, this evaluation of $\log_3 27$ is 3, since $27/3/3/3 = 1$. Likewise, this evaluation of $\log_4 64$ is 4, since $64/4/4/4/4 = 1$, and this approximation to $\log_2 12$ is 4, since $12/2/2/2/2 = 0.75 \leq 1$. This base-two approximation arises in algorithm analysis, actually, since a common operation in many algorithms is to repeatedly divide an input in half.

Indeed, since computers store integers in binary, the most common base for the logarithm function in computer science is 2. In fact, this base is so common that we will typically leave it off when it is 2. That is, for us,

$$\log n = \log_2 n.$$

We note that most handheld calculators have a button marked LOG, but this is typically for calculating the logarithm base-10, not base-two.

Rules for the Logarithm Function

There are some important rules for logarithms, similar to the exponent rules. We list them in the following proposition.

Proposition 3.4 (Logarithm Rules): *Given real numbers $a > 0$, $b > 1$, $c > 0$ and $d > 1$, we have:*

1. $\log_b ac = \log_b a + \log_b c$
2. $\log_b a/c = \log_b a - \log_b c$
3. $\log_b a^c = c \log_b a$
4. $\log_b a = (\log_d a)/\log_d b$
5. $b^{\log_d a} = a^{\log_d b}$

Also, as a notational shorthand, we use $\log^c n$ to denote the function $(\log n)^c$. Rather than show how we could derive each of the above identities, which all follow from the definition of logarithms and exponents, let us illustrate these identities with a few examples instead.

Example 3.5: *We demonstrate below some interesting applications of the logarithm rules from Proposition 3.4 (using the usual convention that the base of a logarithm is 2 if it is omitted).*

- $\log(2n) = \log 2 + \log n = 1 + \log n$, *by rule 1*
- $\log(n/2) = \log n - \log 2 = \log n - 1$, *by rule 2*
- $\log n^3 = 3\log n$, *by rule 3*
- $\log 2^n = n\log 2 = n \cdot 1 = n$, *by rule 3*
- $\log_4 n = (\log n)/\log 4 = (\log n)/2$, *by rule 4*
- $2^{\log n} = n^{\log 2} = n^1 = n$, *by rule 5*

As a practical matter, we note that rule 4 gives us a way to compute the base-two logarithm on a calculator that has a base-10 logarithm button, LOG, *for*

$$\log_2 n = \text{LOG}\, n\, / \,\text{LOG}\, 2.$$

One additional comment concerning logarithms is in order. The value of a logarithm is typically not an integer, yet the running time of an algorithm is usually expressed by means of an integer quantity, such as the number of operations performed. Thus, the analysis of an algorithm may sometimes involve the use of the *floor function* and *ceiling function*, which are defined respectively as follows:

- $\lfloor x \rfloor$ = the largest integer less than or equal to x.
- $\lceil x \rceil$ = the smallest integer greater than or equal to x.

These functions allow us to convert real-valued functions into integer-valued ones.[1]

3.3.7   The N-Log-N Function

The last function we discuss in this section is the *n-log-n function*,

$$f(n) = n\log n,$$

that is, the function that assigns to an input n the value of n times the logarithm base-two of n. This function grows a little faster than the linear function and a lot slower than the quadratic function. Thus, as we will show on several occasions, if we can improve the running time of solving some problem from quadratic to n-log-n, we will have an algorithm that runs much faster in general.

---

[1]Running times that are real valued are almost always used in conjunction with the asymptotic notation described in Section 3.4.1, for which the use of the ceiling function would usually be redundant anyway. (See Exercise R-3.24.)

3.3.8 Comparing Growth Rates

To sum up, Table 3.1 shows, in simplified terms, each of the seven common functions used in algorithm analysis, which we described above. The functions are shown in order by increasing growth rates.

constant	logarithm	linear	n-log-n	quadratic	cubic	exponent
1	$\log n$	n	$n \log n$	n^2	n^3	a^n

Table 3.1: Terminology for classes of functions. Here we assume that $a > 1$ is a constant.

Ideally, we would like data structure operations to run in times proportional to the constant or logarithm function, and we would like all of our algorithms to run in time proportional to the linear or n-log-n function. Algorithms with quadratic or cubic running times are less practical, but still feasible for reasonably small input sizes. But algorithms with exponential running times are generally considered infeasible for all but the smallest sized inputs.

Plots of the seven functions are shown in Figure 3.3.

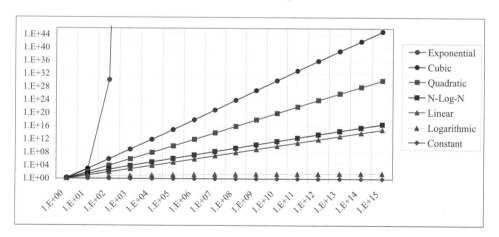

Figure 3.3: Growth rates for the seven fundamental functions used in algorithm analysis. We use base $a = 2$ for the exponential function. The functions are plotted in a log-log chart, to compare the growth rates primarily as slopes. Even so, the exponential function grows too fast to display all its values on the chart. Also, to we use the scientific notation for numbers, where, aE+b denotes $a10^b$.

3.4   Analysis of Algorithms

Having discussed a high-level way of describing algorithms and some necessary mathematics, let us now address ways of analyzing algorithms.

As we noted above, experimental analysis is valuable, but it has its limitations. If we wish to analyze a particular algorithm without performing experiments on its running time, we can take the following more analytical approach:

1. Code up the algorithm in some high-level computer language (like Java).
2. Compile the program into some low-level executable language (like the byte-code language of the Java Virtual Machine).
3. Determine, for each instruction i of the low-level language, the time t_i needed to execute the instruction.
4. Determine, for each instruction i of the low-level language, the number of times n_i that instruction i gets executed when the algorithm is run.
5. Sum up the products $n_i \cdot t_i$ over all the instructions, which yields the running time of the algorithm.

This approach can give us an accurate estimate of a running time, but it is very complicated. So, instead, we perform our analysis directly on the high-level pseudo-code. We define a set of ***primitive operations*** such as the following:

- Assigning a value to a variable
- Calling a method
- Performing an arithmetic operation (for example, adding two numbers)
- Comparing two numbers
- Indexing into an array
- Following an object reference
- Returning from a method.

Specifically, a primitive operation corresponds to a low-level instruction with an execution time that is constant. Instead of trying to determine the specific execution time of each primitive operation, we will simply ***count*** how many primitive operations are executed, and use this number t as a measure of the running-time of the algorithm. This operation count will correlate to an actual running time in a specific hardware and software environment, for each primitive operation corresponds to a constant-time instruction, and there are only a fixed number of primitive operations. The implicit assumption in this approach is that the running times of different primitive operations will be fairly similar. Thus, the number, t, of primitive operations an algorithm performs will be proportional to the actual running time of that algorithm.

Counting Primitive Operations

We now show how to count the number of primitive operations executed by an algorithm, using as an example algorithm arrayMax, whose pseudo-code and Java implementation are given in Code Fragments 3.1 and 3.2, respectively. The following analysis refers to the pseudo-code. A similar analysis can be conducted using the Java code.

- Initializing variable *currentMax* to $A[0]$ corresponds to two primitive operations (indexing into an array and assigning a value to a variable) and is executed only once at the beginning of the algorithm. Thus, it contributes two units to the count.
- At the beginning of the **for** loop, counter i is initialized to 1. This step corresponds to executing one primitive operation (assigning a value to a variable).
- Before entering the body of the **for** loop, condition $i \leq n - 1$ is verified. This action corresponds to executing two primitive instructions (one subtraction and comparing two numbers). Since counter i starts at 1 and is incremented by 1 at the end of each iteration of the loop, these two operations are performed n times. Thus, testing the loop condition contributes $2n$ units to the count.
- The body of the **for** loop is executed $n - 1$ times (for $i = 1, 2, \ldots, n - 1$ of the counter i). At each iteration, $A[i]$ is compared with *currentMax* (two primitive operations, indexing and comparing), $A[i]$ is possibly assigned to *currentMax* (two primitive operations, indexing and assigning), and the counter i is incremented (two primitive operations, summing and assigning). Hence, at each iteration of the loop, either four or six primitive operations are performed, depending on whether $A[i] \leq currentMax$ or $A[i] > currentMax$. Therefore, the body of the loop contributes between $4(n-1)$ and $6(n-1)$ units to the count.
- Returning the value of variable *currentMax* corresponds to one primitive operation, and is executed only once.

That is, the number of primitive operations $t(n)$ executed by arrayMax is at least

$$2 + 1 + 2n + 4(n - 1) + 1 = 6n$$

and at most

$$2 + 1 + 2n + 6(n - 1) + 1 = 8n - 2.$$

The best case ($t(n) = 6n$) occurs when $A[0]$ is the maximum element, so that variable *currentMax* is never reassigned. The worst case ($t(n) = 8n - 2$) occurs when the elements are sorted in increasing order, so that variable *currentMax* is reassigned at each iteration of the **for** loop.

Average-Case and Worst-Case Analysis

Like the arrayMax method, an algorithm may run faster on some inputs than it does on others of the same size. Thus, we may wish to express the running time of an algorithm as the function of the input size obtained by taking the average over all possible inputs of the same size. Unfortunately, such an ***average-case*** analysis is typically quite challenging. It requires us to define a probability distribution on the set of inputs, which is often a difficult task. Figure 3.4 schematically shows how, depending on the input distribution, the running time of an algorithm can be anywhere between the worst-case time and the best-case time. For example, what if inputs are really only of types "A" or "D"?

An average-case analysis also usually requires that we calculate expected running times based on a given input distribution. Such an analysis often requires heavy mathematics and probability theory. Therefore, for the remainder of this book, unless we specify otherwise, we will characterize running times in terms of the ***worst case***. We shall say that algorithm arrayMax executes $t(n) = 8n - 2$ primitive operations ***in the worst case***, meaning that the maximum number of primitive operations executed by the algorithm, taken over all inputs of size n, is $8n - 2$.

Worst-case analysis is much easier than average-case analysis, as it requires only the ability to identify the worst-case input, which is often simple. Also, this approach typically leads to better algorithms. Making the standard of success for an algorithm to perform well in the worst case necessarily requires that it will do well on ***every*** input. That is, designing for the worst case leads to stronger algorithmic "muscles," much like a track star who always practices by running up an incline.

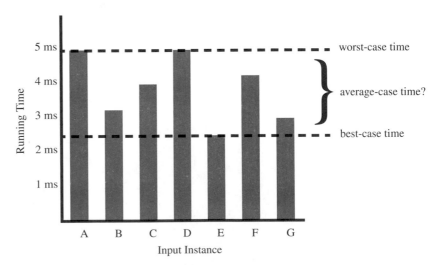

Figure 3.4: The difference between best-case and worst-case time. Each bar represents the running time of some algorithm on a different possible input.

3.4.1 Asymptotic Notation

We have clearly gone into laborious detail for evaluating the running time of such a simple algorithm as the arrayMax algorithm. There are a number of questions that this analysis raises:

- Is this level of detail really needed?
- How important is it to figure out the exact number of primitive operations performed by an algorithm?
- How carefully must we define the set of primitive operations? For example, how many primitive operations are used in the statement y = a*x + b? (We may argue that two arithmetic operations and one assignment are executed, but we may be disregarding the additional "hidden" assignment of the result of a*x to a temporary variable before performing the sum.)

In general, each basic step in a pseudo-code description or a high-level language implementation corresponds to a small number of primitive operations (except for method calls, of course). Thus, we can perform a simplified analysis that estimates the number of primitive operations executed up to a constant factor, by counting the constant-time steps of the pseudo-code or high-level language executed (but we must be careful, since a single line of pseudo-code may denote a nonconstant step). Going back to algorithm arrayMax, our simplified analysis indicates that between $6n$ and $8n - 2$ steps are executed on an input of size n.

Simplifying the Analysis Further

In algorithm analysis, we focus on the growth rate of the running time as a function of the input size n, taking a "big-picture" approach, rather than being bogged down with small details. It is often enough just to know that the running time of an algorithm such as arrayMax ***grows proportionally to*** n, with its true running time being n times a constant factor that depends on the hardware and software environment.

We analyze data structures and algorithms using a mathematical notation for functions that disregards constant factors. Namely, we characterize the running times of algorithms by using functions that map the size of the input, n, to values that correspond to the main factor that determines the growth rate in terms of n. We do not formally define what n means, however, and instead let n refer to a chosen measure of the input "size," which is allowed to be defined differently for each algorithm we are analyzing. This approach allows us to focus attention on the primary "big-picture" aspects in a running time function. In addition, the same approach lets us characterize space usage for data structures and algorithms, where we define ***space usage*** to be the total number of memory cells used.

The "Big-Oh" Notation

Let $f(n)$ and $g(n)$ be functions mapping nonnegative integers to real numbers. We say that $f(n)$ is $O(g(n))$ if there is a real constant $c > 0$ and an integer constant $n_0 \geq 1$ such that

$$f(n) \leq cg(n), \quad \text{for} \quad n \geq n_0.$$

This definition is often referred to as the "big-Oh" notation, for it is sometimes pronounced as "$f(n)$ is **big-Oh** of $g(n)$." Alternatively, we can also say "$f(n)$ is **order of** $g(n)$." (This definition is illustrated in Figure 3.5.)

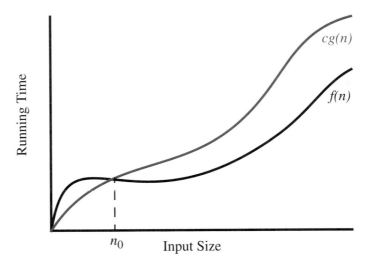

Figure 3.5: Illustrating the "big-Oh" notation. The function $f(n)$ is $O(g(n))$, since $f(n) \leq c \cdot g(n)$ when $n \geq n_0$.

Example 3.6: *The function $8n - 2$ is $O(n)$.*

Justification: By the big-Oh definition, we need to find a real constant $c > 0$ and an integer constant $n_0 \geq 1$ such that $8n - 2 \leq cn$ for every integer $n \geq n_0$. It is easy to see that a possible choice is $c = 8$ and $n_0 = 1$. Indeed, this is one of infinitely many choices available because any real number greater than or equal to 8 will work for c, and any integer greater than or equal to 1 will work for n_0.   ∎

The big-Oh notation allows us to say that a function $f(n)$ is "less than or equal to" another function $g(n)$ up to a constant factor and in the **asymptotic** sense as n grows toward infinity. This ability comes from the fact that the definition uses "$\leq$" to compare $f(n)$ to a $g(n)$ times a constant, c, for the asymptotic cases when $n \geq n_0$.

Characterizing Running Times using the Big-Oh Notation

The big-Oh notation is used widely to characterize running times and space bounds in terms of some parameter n, which varies from problem to problem, but is always defined as a chosen measure of the "size" of the problem. For example, if we are interested in finding the largest element in an array of integers, as in our running arrayMax example from Code Fragments 3.1 and 3.2, it would be most natural to let n denote the number of elements of the array.

The big-Oh notation allows us to ignore constant factors and lower order terms and focus on the main components of a function that affect its growth. Using the big-Oh notation, we can write the following mathematically precise statement on the running time of algorithm arrayMax for **any** hardware and software environment.

Proposition 3.7: *The running time of algorithm* arrayMax *for computing the maximum element in an array of n integers is $O(n)$.*

Justification: As shown in Section 3.4, the number of primitive operations executed by algorithm arrayMax is at most $8n - 2$. Hence, since each primitive operation runs in constant time, we can say that the running time of algorithm arrayMax on an input of size n is at most $d(8n - 2)$, for some positive constant d. We apply the big-Oh definition with $c = 8d$ and $n_0 = 1$ (see Example 3.6) and conclude that the running time of algorithm arrayMax is $O(n)$. ∎

In other words, the arrayMax algorithm runs in $O(n)$ time. Moreover, its running time is still $O(n)$, even if we slightly miscounted the number of worst-case primitive operations it performs and this value really should be $9n + 6$ or $4n - 5$.

Some Properties of the Big-Oh Notation

Let us consider an example that further illustrates the power of the big-Oh notation.

Example 3.8: $5n^4 + 3n^3 + 2n^2 + 4n + 1$ *is* $O(n^4)$.

Justification: *Note that*

$$5n^4 + 3n^3 + 2n^2 + 4n + 1 \le (5 + 3 + 2 + 4 + 1)n^4 = cn^4,$$

for $c = 15$, *when* $n \ge n_0 = 1$. ∎

In fact, we can easily characterize the main factor determining the growth rate of any polynomial function.

Proposition 3.9: *If $f(n)$ is a polynomial of degree d, that is,*

$$f(n) = a_0 + a_1 n + \cdots + a_d n^d,$$

and $a_d > 0$, then $f(n)$ is $O(n^d)$.

Justification: Note that, for $n \geq 1$, we have $1 \leq n \leq n^2 \leq \cdots \leq n^d$; hence,

$$a_0 + a_1 n + a_2 n^2 + \cdots + a_d n^d \leq (a_0 + a_1 + a_2 + \cdots + a_d) n^d.$$

Therefore, we can show $f(n)$ is $O(n^d)$ by defining $c = a_0 + a_1 + \cdots + a_d$ and $n_0 = 1$.
    ■

Thus, the highest-degree term in a polynomial is the term that determines the asymptotic growth rate of that polynomial. We consider some additional properties of the big-Oh notation in the exercises. Let us consider some further examples here, however, focusing on combinations of the seven fundamental functions used in algorithm design.

Example 3.10: $5n^2 + 3n \log n + 2n + 5$ *is $O(n^2)$.*
Justification: $5n^2 + 3n \log n + 2n + 5 \leq (5 + 3 + 2 + 5)n^2 = cn^2$, for $c = 15$, when $n \geq n_0 = 2$ (note that $n \log n$ is zero for $n = 1$).
    ■

Example 3.11: $20n^3 + 10n \log n + 5$ *is $O(n^3)$.*
Justification: $20n^3 + 10n \log n + 5 \leq 35n^3$, for $n \geq 1$.
    ■

Example 3.12: $3 \log n + 2$ *is $O(\log n)$.*
Justification: $3 \log n + 2 \leq 5 \log n$, for $n \geq 2$. Note that $\log n$ is zero for $n = 1$. That is why we use $n \geq n_0 = 2$ in this case.
    ■

Example 3.13: 2^{100} *is $O(1)$.*
Justification: $2^{100} \leq 2^{100} \cdot 1$, for $n \geq 1$. Note that variable n does not appear in the inequality, since we are dealing with constant-valued functions.
    ■

Example 3.14: 2^{n+2} *is $O(2^n)$.*
Justification: $2^{n+2} = 2^n 2^2 = 4 \cdot 2^n$; hence, we can take $c = 4$ and $n_0 = 1$ in this case.
    ■

Example 3.15: $2n + 100 \log n$ *is $O(n)$.*
Justification: $2n + 100 \log n \leq 102n$, for $n \geq n_0 = 2$; hence, we can take $c = 102$ in this case.
    ■

Characterizing Functions in Simplest Terms

In general, we should use the big-Oh notation to characterize a function as closely as possible. While it is true that the function $f(n) = 4n^3 + 3n^2$ is $O(n^5)$ or even $O(n^4)$, it is more accurate to say that $f(n)$ is $O(n^3)$. Consider, by way of analogy, a scenario where a hungry traveler driving along a long country road happens upon a local farmer walking home from a market. If the traveler asks the farmer how much longer he must drive before he can find some food, it may be truthful for the farmer to say, "certainly no longer than 12 hours," but it is much more accurate (and helpful) for him to say, "you can find a market just a few minutes drive up this road." Thus, even with the big-Oh notation, we should strive as much as possible to tell the whole truth.

It is also considered poor taste to include constant factors and lower order terms in the big-Oh notation. For example, it is not fashionable to say that the function $2n^2$ is $O(4n^2 + 6n\log n)$, although this is completely correct. We should strive instead to describe the function in the big-Oh in **simplest terms**.

The seven functions listed in Section 3.3 are the most common functions used in conjunction with the big-Oh notation to characterize the running times and space usage of algorithms. Indeed, we typically use the names of these functions to refer to the running times of the algorithms they characterize. So, for example, we would say that an algorithm that runs in worst-case time $4n^2 + n\log n$ as a **quadratic-time** algorithm, since it runs in $O(n^2)$ time. Likewise, an algorithm running in time at most $5n + 20\log n + 4$ would be called a **linear-time** algorithm.

Big-Omega

Just as the big-Oh notation provides an asymptotic way of saying that a function is "less than or equal to" another function, the following notations provide an asymptotic way of saying that a function grows at a rate that is "greater than or equal to" that of another.

Let $f(n)$ and $g(n)$ be functions mapping nonnegative integers to real numbers. We say that $f(n)$ is $\Omega(g(n))$ (pronounced "$f(n)$ is big-Omega of $g(n)$") if $g(n)$ is $O(f(n))$; that is, there is a real constant $c > 0$ and an integer constant $n_0 \geq 1$ such that

$$f(n) \geq cg(n), \quad \text{for} \quad n \geq n_0.$$

This definition allows us to say asymptotically that one function is greater than or equal to another, up to a constant factor.

Example 3.16: $3n\log n + 2n$ is $\Omega(n\log n)$.

Justification: $3n\log n + 2n \geq 3n\log n$, for $n \geq 2$. ∎

Big-Theta

In addition, there is a notation that allows us to say that two functions grow at the same rate, up to constant factors. We say that $f(n)$ is $\Theta(g(n))$ (pronounced "$f(n)$ is big-Theta of $g(n)$") if $f(n)$ is $O(g(n))$ and $f(n)$ is $\Omega(g(n))$; that is, there are real constants $c' > 0$ and $c'' > 0$, and an integer constant $n_0 \geq 1$ such that

$$c'g(n) \leq f(n) \leq c''g(n), \quad \text{for} \quad n \geq n_0.$$

Example 3.17: $3n\log n + 4n + 5\log n$ is $\Theta(n\log n)$.

Justification: $3n\log n \leq 3n\log n + 4n + 5\log n \leq (3+4+5)n\log n$ for $n \geq 2$. ∎

3.4.2 Asymptotic Analysis

Suppose two algorithms solving the same problem are available: an algorithm A, which has a running time of $O(n)$, and an algorithm B, which has a running time of $O(n^2)$. Which algorithm is better? We know that n is $O(n^2)$, which implies that algorithm A is *asymptotically better* than algorithm B, although for a small value of n, B may have a lower running time than A.

We can use the big-Oh notation to order classes of functions by asymptotic growth rate. Our seven functions are ordered by increasing growth rate in the sequence below, that is, if a function $f(n)$ precedes a function $g(n)$ in the sequence, then $f(n)$ is $O(g(n))$:

$$1 \quad \log n \quad n \quad n\log n \quad n^2 \quad n^3 \quad 2^n.$$

We have already illustrated the growth rates of these seven functions, in Figure 3.3. We give some sample values in Table 3.2.

n	$\log n$	n	$n\log n$	n^2	n^3	2^n
4	2	4	8	16	64	16
8	3	8	24	64	512	256
16	4	16	64	256	4,096	65,536
32	5	32	160	1,024	32,768	4,294,967,296
64	6	64	384	4,096	262,144	1.84×10^{19}
128	7	128	896	16,384	2,097,152	3.40×10^{38}
256	8	256	2,048	65,536	16,777,216	1.15×10^{77}
512	9	512	4,608	262,144	134,217,728	1.34×10^{154}
1,024	10	1,024	10,240	1,048,576	1,073,741,824	1.79×10^{308}

Table 3.2: Selected values of the seven fundamental functions in algorithm analysis.

Improving an Algorithm is Better than Improving Hardware

We further illustrate the importance of the asymptotic viewpoint in Table 3.3. This table explores the maximum size allowed for an input instance that is processed by an algorithm in 1 second, 1 minute, and 1 hour, for various running times of the algorithm, expressed microseconds (μs). It also shows the importance of good algorithm design, because an algorithm with an asymptotically slow running time (for example, one that is $O(n^2)$) is easily beaten in the long run by an algorithm with an asymptotically faster running time (for example, one that is $O(n \log n)$), even if the constant factor for the asymptotically faster algorithm is worse.

Running	Maximum Problem Size (n)		
Time (μs)	1 second	1 minute	1 hour
$400n$	2,500	150,000	9,000,000
$20n \lceil \log n \rceil$	4,096	166,666	7,826,087
$2n^2$	707	5,477	42,426
2^n	19	25	31

Table 3.3: Maximum size of a problem that can be solved in 1 second, 1 minute, and 1 hour, for various running times measured in microseconds.

The importance of good algorithm design goes beyond just what can be solved effectively on a given computer, however. As shown in Table 3.4, even if we achieve a dramatic speed-up in hardware, we still cannot overcome the handicap of an asymptotically slow algorithm. This table shows the new maximum problem size achievable for any fixed amount of time, assuming algorithms with the given running times are now run on a computer 256 times faster than the previous one.

Running Time	New Maximum Problem Size
$400n$	$256m$
$20n \lceil \log n \rceil$	approx. $256((\log m)/(7 + \log m))m$
$2n^2$	$16m$
2^n	$m + 8$

Table 3.4: Increase in the maximum size of a problem that can be solved in a certain fixed amount of time, by using a computer that is 256 times faster than the previous one, for various running times of the algorithm. Each entry is given as a function of m, the previous maximum problem size.

3.4.3   Using the Big-Oh Notation

Having made the case of using the big-Oh notation for analyzing algorithms, let us briefly discuss a few issues concerning its use. It is considered poor taste, in general, to say "$f(n) \leq O(g(n))$," since the big-Oh already denotes the "less-than-or-equal-to" concept. Likewise, although common, it is not fully correct to say "$f(n) = O(g(n))$" (with the usual understanding of the "$=$" relation), since there is no way to make sense of the statement "$O(g(n)) = f(n)$." In addition, it is completely wrong to say "$f(n) \geq O(g(n))$" or "$f(n) > O(g(n))$," since the $g(n)$ in the big-Oh expresses an upper bound on $f(n)$. It is best to say,

"$f(n)$ *is* $O(g(n))$."

For the more mathematically inclined, it is also correct to say,

"$f(n) \in O(g(n))$,"

for the big-Oh notation is, technically speaking, denoting a whole collection of functions. In this book, we will stick to saying big-Oh statements as "$f(n)$ *is* $O(g(n))$." Even with this interpretation, there is considerable freedom in how we can use arithmetic operations with the big-Oh notation, and with this freedom comes a certain amount of responsibility.

Some Words of Caution

A few words of caution about asymptotic notation are in order at this point. First, note that the use of the big-Oh and related notations can be somewhat misleading should the constant factors they "hide" be very large. For example, while it is true that the function $10^{100}n$ is $O(n)$, if this is the running time of an algorithm being compared to one whose running time is $10n \log n$, we should prefer the $O(n \log n)$ time algorithm, even though the linear-time algorithm is asymptotically faster. This preference is because the constant factor, 10^{100}, which is called "one googol," is believed by many astronomers to be an upper bound on the number of atoms in the observable universe. So we are unlikely to ever have a real-world problem that has this number as its input size. Thus, even when using the big-Oh notation, we should at least be somewhat mindful of the constant factors and lower order terms we are "hiding."

The above observation raises the issue of what constitutes a "fast" algorithm. Generally speaking, any algorithm running in $O(n \log n)$ time (with a reasonable constant factor) should be considered efficient. Even an $O(n^2)$ time method may be fast enough in some contexts, that is, when n is small. But an algorithm running in $O(2^n)$ time should almost never be considered efficient.

There is a famous story about the inventor of the game of chess. He asked only that his king pay him 1 grain of rice for the first square on the board, 2 grains for the second, 4 grains for the third, 8 for the fourth, and so on. It is an interesting test of programming skills to write a program to exactly compute the number of grains of rice the king would have to pay. In fact, any Java program written to compute this number in a single integer value will cause an integer overflow to occur (although the run-time machine will probably not complain). To represent this number exactly as an integer requires using a BigInteger class.

If we must draw a line between efficient and inefficient algorithms, therefore, it is natural to make this distinction be that between those algorithms running in polynomial time and those running in exponential time. That is, make the distinction between algorithms with a running time that is $O(n^c)$, for some constant $c > 1$, and those with a running time that is $O(b^n)$, for some constant $b > 1$. Like so many notions we have discussed in this section, this too should be taken with a "grain of salt," for an algorithm running in $O(n^{100})$ time should probably not be considered "efficient." Even so, the distinction between polynomial-time and exponential-time algorithms is considered a robust measure of tractability.

To summarize, the asymptotic notations of big-Oh, big-Omega, and big-Theta provide a convenient language for us to analyze data structures and algorithms. As mentioned earlier, these notations provide convenience because they let us concentrate on the "big picture" rather than low-level details.

Two Examples of Asymptotic Algorithm Analysis

We conclude this section by analyzing two algorithms that solve the same problem but have rather different running times. The problem we are interested in is the one of computing the so-called *prefix averages* of a sequence of numbers. Namely, given an array X storing n numbers, we want to compute an array A such that $A[i]$ is the average of elements $X[0], \ldots, X[i]$, for $i = 0, \ldots, n-1$, that is,

$$A[i] = \frac{\sum_{j=0}^{i} X[j]}{i+1}.$$

Computing prefix averages has many applications in economics and statistics. For example, given the year-by-year returns of a mutual fund, an investor will typically want to see the fund's average annual returns for the last year, the last three years, the last five years, and the last ten years. Likewise, given a stream of daily Web usage logs, a Web site manager may wish to track average usage trends over various time periods.

A Quadratic-Time Algorithm

Our first algorithm for the prefix averages problem, called prefixAverages1, is shown in Code Fragment 3.3. It computes every element of A separately, following the definition.

Algorithm prefixAverages1(X):
   Input: An n-element array X of numbers.
   Output: An n-element array A of numbers such that $A[i]$ is
      the average of elements $X[0], \ldots, X[i]$.
   Let A be an array of n numbers.
   for $i \leftarrow 0$ **to** $n-1$ **do**
      $a \leftarrow 0$
      for $j \leftarrow 0$ **to** i **do**
         $a \leftarrow a + X[j]$
      $A[i] \leftarrow a/(i+1)$
   return array A

Code Fragment 3.3: Algorithm prefixAverages1.

Let us analyze the prefixAverages1 algorithm.

- Initializing and returning array A at the beginning and end can be done with a constant number of primitive operations per element, and takes $O(n)$ time.
- There are two nested **for** loops, which are controlled by counters i and j, respectively. The body of the outer loop, controlled by counter i, is executed n times, for $i = 0, \ldots, n-1$. Thus, statements $a = 0$ and $A[i] = a/(i+1)$ are executed n times each. This implies that these two statements, plus the incrementing and testing of counter i, contribute a number of primitive operations proportional to n, that is, $O(n)$ time.
- The body of the inner loop, which is controlled by counter j, is executed $i+1$ times, depending on the current value of the outer loop counter i. Thus, statement $a = a + X[j]$ in the inner loop is executed $1 + 2 + 3 + \cdots + n$ times. By recalling Proposition 3.1, we know that $1 + 2 + 3 + \cdots + n = n(n+1)/2$, which implies that the statement in the inner loop contributes $O(n^2)$ time. A similar argument can be done for the primitive operations associated with incrementing and testing counter j, which also take $O(n^2)$ time.

The running time of algorithm prefixAverages1 is given by the sum of three terms. The first and the second term are $O(n)$, and the third term is $O(n^2)$. By a simple application of Proposition 3.9, the running time of prefixAverages1 is $O(n^2)$.

A Linear-Time Algorithm

In order to compute prefix averages more efficiently, we can observe that two consecutive averages $A[i-1]$ and $A[i]$ are similar:

$$
\begin{aligned}
A[i-1] &= (X[0]+X[1]+\cdots+X[i-1])/i \\
A[i] &= (X[0]+X[1]+\cdots+X[i-1]+X[i])/(i+1).
\end{aligned}
$$

If we denote with S_i the **prefix sum** $X[0]+X[1]+\cdots+X[i]$, we can compute the prefix averages as $A[i]=S_i/(i+1)$. It is easy to keep track of the current prefix sum while scanning array X with a loop. We are now ready to present Algorithm prefixAverages2 in Code Fragment 3.4.

Algorithm prefixAverages2(X):
   Input: An n-element array X of numbers.¡
   Output: An n-element array A of numbers such that $A[i]$ is
      the average of elements $X[0],\ldots,X[i]$.

Let A be an array of n numbers.
$s \leftarrow 0$
for $i \leftarrow 0$ **to** $n-1$ **do**
   $s \leftarrow s+X[i]$
   $A[i] \leftarrow s/(i+1)$
return array A

Code Fragment 3.4: Algorithm prefixAverages2.

The analysis of the running time of algorithm prefixAverages2 follows:

- Initializing and returning array A at the beginning and end can be done with a constant number of primitive operations per element, and takes $O(n)$ time.
- Initializing variable s at the beginning takes $O(1)$ time.
- There is a single **for** loop, which is controlled by counter i. The body of the loop is executed n times, for $i=0,\ldots,n-1$. Thus, statements $s=s+X[i]$ and $A[i]=s/(i+1)$ are executed n times each. This implies that these two statements plus the incrementing and testing of counter i contribute a number of primitive operations proportional to n, that is, $O(n)$ time.

The running time of algorithm prefixAverages2 is given by the sum of three terms. The first and the third term are $O(n)$, and the second term is $O(1)$. By a simple application of Proposition 3.9, the running time of prefixAverages2 is $O(n)$, which is much better than the quadratic-time algorithm prefixAverages1.

3.5   Simple Justification Techniques

We will sometimes wish to make strong claims about a certain data structure or algorithm. We may, for example, wish to show that our algorithm is correct or that it runs fast. In order to rigorously make such claims, we must use mathematical language, and in order to back up such claims, we must justify or **prove** our statements. Fortunately, there are several simple ways to do this.

3.5.1   By Example

Some claims are of the generic form, "There is an element x in a set S that has property P." To justify such a claim, we need only produce a particular $x \in S$ that has property P. Likewise, some hard-to-believe claims are of the generic form, "Every element x in a set S has property P." To justify that such a claim is false, we need to only produce a particular x from S that does not have property P. Such an instance is called a **counterexample**.

Example 3.18: *A certain Professor Amongus claims that every number of the form $2^i - 1$ is a prime, when i is an integer greater than* 1. *Professor Amongus is wrong.*

Justification: To prove Professor Amongus is wrong, we find a counter-example. Fortunately, we need not look too far, for $2^4 - 1 = 15 = 3 \cdot 5$. ∎

3.5.2   The "Contra" Attack

Another set of justification techniques involves the use of the negative. The two primary such methods are the use of the **contrapositive** and the **contradiction**. The use of the contrapositive method is like looking through a negative mirror. To justify the statement "if p is true, then q is true" we instead establish that "if q is not true, then p is not true." Logically, these two statements are the same, but the latter, which is called the **contrapositive** of the first, may be easier to think about.

Example 3.19: *Let a and b be integers. If ab is even, then a is even or b is even.*

Justification: To justify this claim, consider the contrapositive, "If a is odd and b is odd, then ab is odd." So, suppose $a = 2i + 1$ and $b = 2j + 1$, for some integers i and j. Then $ab = 4ij + 2i + 2j + 1 = 2(2ij + i + j) + 1$; hence, ab is odd. ∎

Besides showing a use of the contrapositive justification technique, the previous example also contains an application of *DeMorgan's Law*. This law helps us deal with negations, for it states that the negation of a statement of the form "*p* or *q*" is "not *p* and not *q*." Likewise, it states that the negation of a statement of the form "*p* and *q*" is "not *p* or not *q*."

Another negative justification technique is justification by **contradiction**, which also often involves using DeMorgan's Law. In applying the justification by contradiction technique, we establish that a statement *q* is true by first supposing that *q* is false and then showing that this assumption leads to a contradiction (such as $2 \neq 2$ or $1 > 3$). By reaching such a contradiction, we show that no consistent situation exists with *q* being false, so *q* must be true. Of course, in order to reach this conclusion, we must be sure our situation is consistent before we assume *q* is false.

Example 3.20: *Let a and b be integers. If ab is odd, then a is odd and b is odd.*

Justification: Let *ab* be odd. We wish to show that *a* is odd and *b* is odd. So, with the hope of leading to a contradiction, let us assume the opposite, namely, suppose *a* is even or *b* is even. In fact, without loss of generality, we can assume that *a* is even (since the case for *b* is symmetric). Then $a = 2i$ for some integer *i*. Hence, $ab = (2i)b = 2(ib)$, that is, *ab* is even. But this is a contradiction: *ab* cannot simultaneously be odd and even. Therefore *a* is odd and *b* is odd. ∎

3.5.3 Induction and Loop Invariants

Most of the claims we make about a running time or a space bound involve an integer parameter *n* (usually denoting an intuitive notion of the "size" of the problem). Moreover, most of these claims are equivalent to saying some statement $q(n)$ is true "for all $n \geq 1$." Since this is making a claim about an infinite set of numbers, we cannot justify this exhaustively in a direct fashion.

Induction

We can often justify claims such as those above as true, however, by using the technique of **induction**. This technique amounts to showing that, for any particular $n \geq 1$, there is a finite sequence of implications that starts with something known to be true and ultimately leads to showing that $q(n)$ is true. Specifically, we begin a justification by induction by showing that $q(n)$ is true for $n = 1$ (and possibly some other values $n = 2, 3, \ldots, k$, for some constant *k*). Then we justify that the inductive "step" is true for $n > k$, namely, we show "if $q(i)$ is true for $i < n$, then $q(n)$ is true." The combination of these two pieces completes the justification by induction.

Proposition 3.21: *Consider the Fibonacci function $F(n)$, where we define $F(1) = 1$, $F(2) = 2$, and $F(n) = F(n-1) + F(n-2)$ for $n > 2$. (See Section 2.2.3.) We claim that $F(n) < 2^n$.*

Justification: We will show our claim is right by induction.
Base cases: $(n \leq 2)$. $F(1) = 1 < 2 = 2^1$ and $F(2) = 2 < 4 = 2^2$.
Induction step: $(n > 2)$. Suppose our claim is true for $n' < n$. Consider $F(n)$. Since $n > 2$, $F(n) = F(n-1) + F(n-2)$. Moreover, since $n - 1 < n$ and $n - 2 < n$, we can apply the inductive assumption (sometimes called the "inductive hypothesis") to imply that $F(n) < 2^{n-1} + 2^{n-2}$, since

$$2^{n-1} + 2^{n-2} < 2^{n-1} + 2^{n-1} = 2 \cdot 2^{n-1} = 2^n.$$

■

Let us do another inductive argument, this time for a fact we have seen before.

Proposition 3.22: *(which is the same as Proposition 3.1)*

$$\sum_{i=1}^{n} i = \frac{n(n+1)}{2}.$$

Justification: We will justify this equality by induction.
Base case: $n = 1$. Trivial, for $1 = n(n+1)/2$, if $n = 1$.
Induction step: $n \geq 2$. Assume the claim is true for $n' < n$. Consider n.

$$\sum_{i=1}^{n} i = n + \sum_{i=1}^{n-1} i.$$

By the induction hypothesis, then

$$\sum_{i=1}^{n} i = n + \frac{(n-1)n}{2},$$

which we can simplify as

$$n + \frac{(n-1)n}{2} = \frac{2n + n^2 - n}{2} = \frac{n^2 + n}{2} = \frac{n(n+1)}{2}.$$

■

We may sometimes feel overwhelmed by the task of justifying something true for *all* $n \geq 1$. We should remember, however, the concreteness of the inductive technique. It shows that, for any particular n, there is a finite step-by-step sequence of implications that starts with something true and leads to the truth about n. In short, the inductive argument is a formula for building a sequence of direct justifications.

Loop Invariants

The final justification technique we discuss in this section is the ***loop invariant***. To prove some statement S about a loop is correct, define S in terms of a series of smaller statements $S_0, S_1, \ldots, S_k$, where:

1. The ***initial*** claim, S_0, is true before the loop begins.
2. If S_{i-1} is true before iteration i, then S_i will be true after iteration i.
3. The final statement, S_k, implies the statement S that we wish to be true.

We have, in fact, seen a loop-invariant argument in Section 3.2 (for the correctness of Algorithm arrayMax), but let us give one more example here. In particular, let us consider using a loop invariant to justify the correctness of arrayFind, shown in Code Fragment 3.5, for finding an element x in an array A.

Algorithm arrayFind(x, A):
    Input: An element x and an n-element array, A.
    Output: The index i such that $x = A[i]$ or -1 if no element of A is equal to x.
  $i \leftarrow 0$
  while $i < n$ **do**
    if $x = A[i]$ **then**
      return i
    else
      $i \leftarrow i + 1$
  return -1

Code Fragment 3.5: Algorithm arrayFind for finding a given element in an array.

To show that arrayFind is correct, we inductively define a series of statements, S_i, that lead to the correctness of our algorithm. Specifically, we claim the following is true at the beginning of iteration i of the **while** loop:

    S_i: x is not equal to any of the first i elements of A.

This claim is true at the beginning of the first iteration of the loop, since there are no elements among the first 0 in A (this kind of a trivially true claim is said to hold ***vacuously***). In iteration i, we compare element x to element $A[i]$ and return the index i if these two elements are equal, which is clearly correct and completes the algorithm in this case. If the two elements x and $A[i]$ are not equal, then we have found one more element not equal to x and we increment the index i. Thus, the claim S_i will be true for this new value of i; hence, it is true at the beginning of the next iteration. If the while-loop terminates without ever returning an index in A, then we have $i = n$. That is, S_n is true—there are no elements of A equal to x. Therefore, the algorithm correctly returns -1 to indicate that x is not in A.

3.6 Exercises

For source code and help with exercises, please visit **java.datastructures.net**.

Reinforcement

R-3.1 Graph the functions $8n$, $4n\log n$, $2n^2$, n^3, and 2^n using a logarithmic scale for the x- and y-axes; that is, if the function value $f(n)$ is y, plot this as a point with x-coordinate at $\log n$ and y-coordinate at $\log y$.

R-3.2 The number of operations executed by algorithms A and B is $8n\log n$ and $2n^2$, respectively. Determine n_0 such that A is better than B for $n \geq n_0$.

R-3.3 The number of operations executed by algorithms A and B is $40n^2$ and $2n^3$, respectively. Determine n_0 such that A is better than B for $n \geq n_0$.

R-3.4 Give an example of a function that is the plotted the same on a log-log scale as it is on a standard scale.

R-3.5 Explain why the plot of the function n^c is a straight line with slope c on a log-log scale.

R-3.6 What is the sum of all the even numbers from 0 to $2n$, for any positive integer n?

R-3.7 Show that the following two statements are equivalent:

(a) The running time of algorithm A is $O(f(n))$.

(b) In the worst case, the running time of algorithm A is $O(f(n))$.

R-3.8 Order the following functions by asymptotic growth rate.

$$4n\log n + 2n \qquad 2^{10} \qquad 2^{\log n}$$
$$3n + 100\log n \qquad 4n \qquad 2^n$$
$$n^2 + 10n \qquad n^3 \qquad n\log n$$

R-3.9 Bill has an algorithm, find2D, to find an element x in an $n \times n$ array A. The algorithm find2D iterates over the rows of A, and calls the algorithm arrayFind, of Code Fragment 3.5, on each row, until x is found or it has searched all rows of A. What is the worst-case running time of find2D in terms of n? What is the worst-case running time of find2D in terms of N, where N is the total size of A? Would it be correct to say that Find2D is a linear-time algorithm? Why or why not?

R-3.10 Show that if $d(n)$ is $O(f(n))$, then $ad(n)$ is $O(f(n))$, for any constant $a > 0$.

R-3.11 For each function $f(n)$ and time t in the following table, determine the largest size n of a problem P that can be solved in time t if the algorithm for solving P takes $f(n)$ microseconds. One entry has been completed to get you started.

	1 Second	1 Hour	1 Month	1 Century
$\log n$	$\approx 10^{300000}$			
n				
$n\log n$				
n^2				
n^3				
2^n				

R-3.12 Show that if $d(n)$ is $O(f(n))$ and $e(n)$ is $O(g(n))$, then $d(n) + e(n)$ is $O(f(n) + g(n))$.

R-3.13 Show that if $d(n)$ is $O(f(n))$ and $e(n)$ is $O(g(n))$, then $d(n) - e(n)$ is **not necessarily** $O(f(n) - g(n))$.

R-3.14 Show that if $d(n)$ is $O(f(n))$ and $e(n)$ is $O(g(n))$, then the product $d(n)e(n)$ is $O(f(n)g(n))$.

R-3.15 Show that if $d(n)$ is $O(f(n))$ and $f(n)$ is $O(g(n))$, then $d(n)$ is $O(g(n))$.

R-3.16 Show that $O(\max\{f(n), g(n)\}) = O(f(n) + g(n))$.

R-3.17 Show that $f(n)$ is $O(g(n))$ if and only if $g(n)$ is $\Omega(f(n))$.

R-3.18 Show that if $p(n)$ is a polynomial in n, then $\log p(n)$ is $O(\log n)$.

R-3.19 Show that $(n+1)^5$ is $O(n^5)$.

R-3.20 Show that 2^{n+1} is $O(2^n)$.

R-3.21 Show that n is $O(n\log n)$.

R-3.22 Show that n^2 is $\Omega(n\log n)$.

R-3.23 Show that $n\log n$ is $\Omega(n)$.

R-3.24 Show that $\lceil f(n) \rceil$ is $O(f(n))$, if $f(n)$ is a positive nondecreasing function that is always greater than 1.

R-3.25 Give a big-Oh characterization, in terms of n, of the running time of the Ex1 method shown in Code Fragment 3.6.

R-3.26 Give a big-Oh characterization, in terms of n, of the running time of the Ex2 method shown in Code Fragment 3.6.

R-3.27 Give a big-Oh characterization, in terms of n, of the running time of the Ex3 method shown in Code Fragment 3.6.

Algorithm Ex1(A):
   Input: An array A storing $n \geq 1$ integers.
   Output: The sum of the elements in A.
   $s \leftarrow A[0]$
   for $i \leftarrow 1$ **to** $n - 1$ **do**
     $s \leftarrow s + A[i]$
   return s

Algorithm Ex2(A):
   Input: An array A storing $n \geq 1$ integers.
   Output: The sum of the elements at even cells in A.
   $s \leftarrow A[0]$
   for $i \leftarrow 2$ **to** $n - 1$ **by** increments of 2 **do**
     $s \leftarrow s + A[i]$
   return s

Algorithm Ex3(A):
   Input: An array A storing $n \geq 1$ integers.
   Output: The sum of the prefix sums in A.
   $s \leftarrow 0$
   for $i \leftarrow 0$ **to** $n - 1$ **do**
     $s \leftarrow s + A[0]$
     for $j \leftarrow 1$ **to** i **do**
       $s \leftarrow s + A[j]$
   return s

Code Fragment 3.6: Some algorithms.

R-3.28 Give a big-Oh characterization, in terms of n, of the running time of the Ex4 method shown in Code Fragment 3.7.

R-3.29 Give a big-Oh characterization, in terms of n, of the running time of the Ex5 method shown in Code Fragment 3.7.

R-3.30 Algorithm A executes an $O(\log n)$-time computation for each entry of an n-element array. What is the worst-case running time of Algorithm A?

Algorithm Ex4(A):
  Input: An array A storing $n \geq 1$ integers.
  Output: The sum of the prefix sums in A.
  $s \leftarrow A[0]$
  $t \leftarrow s$
  for $i \leftarrow 1$ **to** $n-1$ **do**
    $s \leftarrow s + A[i]$
    $t \leftarrow t + s$
  return t

Algorithm Ex5(A, B):
  Input: Arrays A and B each storing $n \geq 1$ integers.
  Output: The number of elements in B equal to the sum of prefix sums in A.
  $c \leftarrow 0$
  for $i \leftarrow 0$ **to** $n-1$ **do**
    $s \leftarrow 0$
    for $j \leftarrow 0$ **to** $n-1$ **do**
      $s \leftarrow s + A[0]$
      for $k \leftarrow 1$ **to** j **do**
        $s \leftarrow s + A[k]$
    if $B[i] = s$ **then**
      $c \leftarrow c + 1$
  return c

Code Fragment 3.7: Some more algorithms.

R-3.31 Given an n-element array X, Algorithm B chooses $\log n$ elements in X at random and executes an $O(n)$-time calculation for each. What is the worst-case running time of Algorithm B?

R-3.32 Given an n-element array X of integers, Algorithm C executes an $O(n)$-time computation for each even number in X, and an $O(\log n)$-time computation for each odd number in X. What are the best-case and worst-case running times of Algorithm C?

R-3.33 Given an n-element array X, Algorithm D calls Algorithm E on each element $X[i]$. Algorithm E runs in $O(i)$ time when it is called on element $X[i]$. What is the worst-case running time of Algorithm D?

R-3.34 Al and Bill are arguing about the performance of their sorting algorithms. Al claims that his $O(n \log n)$-time algorithm is *always* faster than Bill's $O(n^2)$-time algorithm. To settle the issue, they implement and run the two algorithms on many randomly generated data sets. To Al's dismay, they find that if $n < 100$, the $O(n^2)$-time algorithm actually runs faster, and only when $n \geq 100$ is the $O(n \log n)$-time one better. Explain why this scenario is possible. You may give numerical examples.

Creativity

C-3.1 Show that $\sum_{i=1}^{n} i^2$ is $O(n^3)$.

C-3.2 Show that $\sum_{i=1}^{n} i/2^i < 2$.   (Hint: Try to bound this sum term by term with a geometric progression.)

C-3.3 Show that $\log_b f(n)$ is $\Theta(\log f(n))$ if $b > 1$ is a constant.

C-3.4 Describe a method for finding both the minimum and maximum of n numbers using fewer than $3n/2$ comparisons.   (Hint: First construct a group of candidate minimums and a group of candidate maximums.)

C-3.5 Bob built a Web site and gave the URL only to his n friends, which he numbered from 1 to n. He told friend number i that he/she can visit the Web site at most i times. Now Bob has a counter, C, keeping track of the total number of visits to the site (but not the identities of who visits). What is the minimum value for C such that Bob should know that one of his friends has visited his/her maximum allowed number of times?

C-3.6 Given a set $A = \{a_1, a_2, \ldots, a_n\}$ of n integers, describe in pseudo-code an efficient method for computing each of partial sums $s_k = \sum_{i=1}^{k} a_i$, for $k = 1, 2, \ldots, n$. What is the running time of this method?

C-3.7 Let $p(x)$ be a polynomial of degree n with coefficients $a_0, \ldots, a_n$, that is,

$$p(x) = \sum_{i=0}^{n} a_i x^i.$$

(a) Describe a simple $O(n^2)$ time method for computing $p(x)$.
(b) Consider now a rewriting of $p(x)$ as

$$p(x) = a_0 + x(a_1 + x(a_2 + x(a_3 + \cdots + x(a_{n-1} + x a_n) \cdots))),$$

which is known as **Horner's method**. Characterize, using the big-Oh notation, the number of arithmetic operations this method executes.

C-3.8 Al says he can prove that all sheep in a flock are the same color:

Base case: One sheep. It is clearly the same color as itself.

Induction step: A flock of n sheep. Take a sheep, a, out. The remaining $n - 1$ are all the same color by induction. Now put sheep a back in and take out a different sheep, b. By induction, the $n - 1$ sheep (now with a) are all the same color. Therefore, all the sheep in the flock are the same color.

What is wrong with Al's "justification"?

C-3.9 Consider the following "justification" that the Fibonacci function, $F(n)$ (see Proposition 3.21) is $O(n)$:
Base case ($n \leq 2$): $F(1) = 1$ and $F(2) = 2$.
Induction step ($n > 2$): Assume claim true for $n' < n$. Consider n. $F(n) = F(n-1) + F(n-2)$. By induction, $F(n-1)$ is $O(n-1)$ and $F(n-2)$ is $O(n-2)$. Then, $F(n)$ is $O((n-1) + (n-2))$, by the identity presented in Exercise R-3.12. Therefore, $F(n)$ is $O(n)$.
What is wrong with this "justification"?

C-3.10 Consider the Fibonacci function, $F(n)$ (see Proposition 3.21). Show by induction that $F(n)$ is $\Omega((3/2)^n)$.

C-3.11 Draw a visual justification of Proposition 3.1 analogous to that of Figure 3.2(b) for the case when n is odd.

C-3.12 An array A contains $n - 1$ unique integers in the range $[0, n-1]$; that is, there is one number from this range that is not in A. Design an $O(n)$-time algorithm for finding that number. You are allowed to use only $O(1)$ additional space besides the array A itself.

C-3.13 An evil king has a cellar containing n bottles of expensive wine, and his guards have just caught a spy trying to poison the king's wine. Fortunately, the guards caught the spy after he succeeded in poisoning only one bottle. Unfortunately, they don't know which one. To make matters worse, the poison the spy used was very deadly; just one drop diluted even a billion to one will still kill someone. Even so, the poison works slowly; it takes a full month for the person to die. Design a scheme for determining exactly which one of his wine bottles was poisoned in just one month's time while expending $O(\log n)$ taste testers.

C-3.14 Show that the summation $\sum_{i=1}^{n} \lceil \log_2 i \rceil$ is $O(n \log n)$.

C-3.15 Let S be a set of n lines in the plane such that no two are parallel and no three meet in the same point. Show by induction that the lines in S determine $\Theta(n^2)$ intersection points.

C-3.16 Suppose that each row of an $n \times n$ array A consists of 1's and 0's such that, in any row of A, all the 1's come before any 0's in that row. Assuming A is already in memory, describe a method running in $O(n)$ time (not $O(n^2)$ time) for finding the row of A that contains the most 1's.

C-3.17 Describe in pseudo-code a method for multiplying an $n \times m$ matrix A and an $m \times p$ matrix B. Recall that the product $C = AB$ is defined so that $C[i][j] = \sum_{k=1}^{m} A[i][k] \cdot B[k][j]$. What is the running time of your method?

C-3.18 Suppose each row of an $n \times n$ array A consists of 1's and 0's such that, in any row i of A, all the 1's come before any 0's. Also suppose that the number of 1's in row i is at least the number in row $i+1$, for $i = 0, 1, \ldots, n-2$. Assuming A is already in memory, describe a method running in $O(n)$ time (not $O(n^2)$) for counting the number of 1's in A.

Projects

P-3.1 Implement algorithms prefixAverages1 and prefixAverages2 from Section 3.4.3, and perform an experimental analysis of their running times. Visualize their running times as a function of the input size with a log-log chart. Choose representative values of the input size n, and run at least 5 tests for each size value n.

P-3.2 Perform a careful experimental analysis that compares the relative running times of the methods shown in Code Fragments 3.6 and 3.7.

Chapter Notes

The methodology for analyzing algorithms is traditionally within a model of computation called the ***RAM***, or ***random access machine*** (not to be confused with "random access memory"). Within this model, a computer consists of a ***central processing unit*** (or ***CPU***) and a ***memory***. The CPU performs elementary operations, such as loads, stores, additions, and comparisons, and the memory stores the program and data in ***cells*** that have integer addresses. The term "random access" refers to the ability of the CPU to access an arbitrary memory cell with one primitive operation. Each primitive operation executed by an algorithm corresponds to a constant number of elementary computations of the RAM. Our approach of counting primitive operations is equivalent to this approach theoretically, but does not require the conceptual burden of an abstract model like the RAM.

Our use of the big-Oh notation is consistent with most authors' usage, but we have taken a slightly more conservative approach than some. The big-Oh notation has prompted several discussions in the algorithms and computation theory community over its proper use [16, 46, 57]. Knuth [58, 57], for example, defines it using the notation $f(n) = O(g(n))$, but he refers to this "equality" as being only "one way," even though he mentions that the big-Oh is actually defining a set of functions. We have chosen to take a more standard view of equality and view the big-Oh notation truly as a set, following the suggestions of Brassard [16]. The reader interested in studying average-case analysis is referred to the book chapter by Vitter and Flajolet [94].

We include a number of useful mathematical facts in Appendix A. The reader interested in additional mathematical facts is referred to the books by Graham, Knuth, and Patashnik [44], and Sedgewick and Flajolet [83]. Our version of the story about Archimedes is taken from [74]. For some additional mathematical tools, refer to Appendix A.

Chapter

4

Stacks, Queues, and Recursion

Contents

Stacks and queues are among the simplest of all data structures, yet they are also among the most important. Stacks and queues are used in a host of different applications that include many more sophisticated data structures. In addition, stacks and queues are among the few kinds of data structures that are often implemented in the hardware microinstructions inside the CPU of a typical computer. Moreover, they are central to some important features of modern computing environments, like the Java run-time environment called the Java Virtual Machine (JVM).

As another indication of the importance of stacks and queues, we note that the Java Collections Framework provides a specific built-in class for a stack plus other classes that implement all the operations of stacks and queues. Nevertheless, our focus here is not just in learning how to use data structures that are included in Java itself, such as stacks and queues, but also in learning how to write our own data structures. For this reason, we use stacks and queues as examples of how to design simple data structures "from scratch." The principles that we learn here will be applicable to more complex data structures, which are not provided by the Java Collections Framework.

In this chapter, we define the stack and queue abstract data types in a general way, and we give two alternative implementations for them: arrays and linked lists. The array implementations use index-based access methods, while the linked list implementations are based on a "node" or "position" concept. In both cases, however, we show that the fundamental methods of stacks and queues can be implemented to run in constant time.

To illustrate the usefulness of stacks and queues, we present several examples of their application, including applications to the Java Virtual Machine model. We also present a generalization of stacks and queues, called the double-ended queue, and show how it can be implemented using a doubly linked list.

In addition, this chapter provides discussions of several programming concepts, including recursion, interfaces, casting, sentinels, and the adapter pattern. Indeed, we begin this chapter with a general discussion of how to use recursion and we explain in the subsequent section how recursion can be implemented with the stack data structure. We discuss linear recursion, binary recursion, and multiple recursion, as well as how to analyze recursive algorithms using recursion traces.

We also include several complete Java programs that illustrate how stacks and queues are implemented as well as how we can use stacks and queues to solve other problems. For example, we show how to use a stack to solve the well-known parenthesis matching problem and we show how essentially the same algorithm can be used to validate the syntax of documents written in the HTML format, which is the standard format used by documents on the World Wide Web.

4.1 Using Recursion

As we discussed in Section 2.5.1, *recursion* is the concept of defining a method that makes a call to itself. Whenever a method calls itself, we refer to this as a ***recursive*** call. We also consider a method M to be recursive if it calls another method that ultimately leads to a call back to M. In this section, we discuss how to use recursion to define efficient algorithms. The main benefit of this approach to algorithm design is that it allows us to take advantage of the repetitive structure present in many problems. By making our algorithm description exploit this repetitive structure in a recursive way, we can often avoid complex case analyses and nested loops. Therefore, this approach can lead to more readable algorithm descriptions, while still being quite efficient. In addition, recursion is a useful way for defining objects that have a repeated similar structural form, as shown in the following examples.

Example 4.1: *Modern operating systems define file-system directories (which are also sometimes called "folders") in a recursive way. Namely, a file system consists of a top-level directory, and the contents of this directory consists of files and other directories, which in turn can contain files and other directories, and so on. The base directories in the file system contain only files, but by using this recursive definition, the operating system allows for directories to be nested arbitrarily deep (as long as there is enough space in memory).*

Example 4.2: *Much of the syntax in modern programming languages is defined in a recursive way. For example, we can define an argument list in Java using the following notation:*

> *argument-list:*
> > *argument*
> > *argument-list , argument*

In other words, an argument list consists of either (i) an argument or (ii) an argument list followed by a comma and an argument. That is, an argument list consists of a comma-separated list of arguments. Similarly, arithmetic expressions can be defined recursively in terms of primitives (like variables and constants) and arithmetic expressions.

Example 4.3: *There are many examples of recursion in art and nature. One of the most classic examples of recursion used in art is in the Russian Matryoshka dolls. Each doll is made of solid wood or is hollow and contains another Matryoshka doll inside it.*

4.1.1   Linear Recursion

The simplest form of recursion is *linear recursion*, where a method is defined so that it makes at most one recursive call each time it is invoked. This type of recursion is useful when we view an algorithmic problem in terms of a first or last element plus a remaining set that has the same structure as the original set.

Summing the Elements of an Array Recursively

Suppose, for example, we are given an array, A, of n integers that we wish to sum together. We can solve this summation problem using linear recursion by observing that the sum of all n integers in A is equal to $A[0]$, if $n = 1$, or the sum of the first $n - 1$ integers in A plus the last element in A. In particular, we can solve this summation problem using the recursive algorithm described in Code Fragment 4.1.

Algorithm LinearSum(A, n):

   Input: A integer array A and an integer $n \geq 1$, such that A has at least n elements
   Output: The sum of the first n integers in A

   if $n = 1$ **then**
      return $A[0]$
   else
      return LinearSum($A, n - 1$) $+ A[n - 1]$

Code Fragment 4.1: Summing the elements in an array using linear recursion.

This example also illustrates an important property that a recursive method should always possess—the method terminates. We ensure this by writing a nonrecursive statement for the case $n = 1$. In addition, we always perform the recursive call on a smaller value of the parameter ($n - 1$) than that which we are given (n), so that, at some point (at the "bottom" of the recursion), we will perform the nonrecursive part of the computation (returning $A[0]$). In general, an algorithm that uses linear recursion typically has the following form:

- *Test for base cases.* We begin by testing for a set of base cases (there should be at least one). These base cases should be defined so that every possible chain of recursive calls will eventually reach a base case, and the handling of each base case should not use recursion.
- *Recur.* After testing for base cases, we then perform a single recursive call. This recursive step may involve a test that decides which of several possible recursive calls to make, but it should ultimately choose to make just one of these calls each time we perform this step. Moreover, we should define each possible recursive call so that it makes progress towards a base case.

Analyzing Recursive Algorithms using Recursion Traces

We can analyze the running of a recursive algorithm by using a visual tool known as a *recursion trace*. We used recursion traces, for example, to analyze and visualize the recursive Fibonacci function of Section 2.5.1, and we will similarly use recursion traces for the recursive sorting algorithms of Sections 10.1 and 10.2.

To draw a recursion trace, we create a box for each instance of the method and label it with the parameters of the method. Also, we visualize a recursive call by drawing an arrow from the box of the calling method to the box of the called method. For example, we illustrate the recursion trace of the LinearSum algorithm of Code Fragment 4.1 in Figure 4.1. We label each box in this trace with the parameters used to make this call. Each time we make a recursive call, we draw a line to the box representing the recursive call. We can also use this diagram to visualize our stepping through the algorithm, since it proceeds by going from the call for n to the call for $n-1$, to the call for $n-2$, and so on, all the way down to the call for 1. When the final call finishes, it returns its value back to the call for 2, which adds in its value, and returns this partial sum to the call for 3, and so on, until the call for $n-1$ returns its partial sum to the call for n.

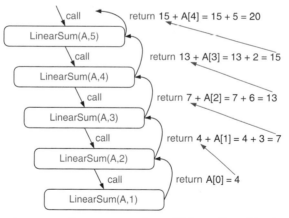

Figure 4.1: Recursion trace for an execution of $\text{LinearSum}(A, n)$ with input parameters $A = \{4, 3, 6, 2, 5\}$ and $n = 5$.

From Figure 4.1, it should be clear that for an input array of size n, Algorithm LinearSum runs in $O(n)$ time, since we spend a constant amount of time performing the nonrecursive part of each call. Moreover, we can also see that the memory space used by the algorithm (in addition to the array A) is also $O(n)$, since we need a constant amount of memory space for each of the n boxes in the trace at the time we make the final recursive call (for $n = 1$). Incidentally, another technique that can be used to analyze the running time of a recursive algorithm is to use a *recurrence equation*. This topic is discussed in Section 10.1.5.

Reversing an Array by Recursion

Let us consider next the problem of reversing the n elements of an array, A, so that the first element becomes the last, the second element becomes second to the last, and so on. We can solve this problem using linear recursion, by observing that the reversal of an array can be achieved by swapping the first and last elements and then recursively reversing the remaining elements in the array. We describe the details of this algorithm in Code Fragment 4.2, using the convention that the first time we call this algorithm we do so as ReverseArray$(A, 0, n - 1)$.

Algorithm ReverseArray(A, i, j):

    Input: An array A and nonnegative integer indices i and j
    Output: The reversal of the elements in A starting at index i and ending at j

    if $i < j$ **then**
        Swap $A[i]$ and $A[j]$
        ReverseArray$(A, i + 1, j - 1)$
    return

Code Fragment 4.2: Reversing the elements of an array using linear recursion.

Note that, in this algorithm, we actually have two base cases, namely, when $i = j$ and when $i > j$. Moreover, in either case, we simply terminate the algorithm, since a sequence with zero elements or one element is trivially equal to its reversal. Furthermore, note that in the recursive step we are guaranteed to make progress towards one of these two base cases. If n is odd, we will eventually reach the $i = j$ case, and if n is even, we will eventually reach the $i > j$ case. The above argument immediately implies that the recursive algorithm of Code Fragment 4.2 is guaranteed to terminate.

Defining Problems in Ways That Facilitate Recursion

To design a recursive algorithm for a given problem, it is useful to think of the different ways we can subdivide this problem so as to define problems that have the same general structure as the original problem. This process sometimes means we need to redefine the original problem so as to facilitate similar-looking subproblems. For example, with the ReverseArray algorithm, we added the parameters i and j so that a recursive call to reverse the inner part of the array A would have the same structure (and same syntax) as the call to reverse all of A. Then, rather than initially calling the algorithm as ReverseArray(A), we call it initially as ReverseArray$(A,0,n-1)$. In general, if one has difficulty finding the repetitive structure needed to design a recursive algorithm, it is sometimes useful to work out the problem on a few concrete examples to see how the subproblems should be defined.

Computing Powers via Linear Recursion

As a more interesting example of using linear recursion, let us consider the problem of raising a number x to an arbitrary nonnegative integer, n. That is, we wish to compute the **power function** $p(x,n)$, defined as $p(x,n) = x^n$. This function has an immediate recursive definition based on linear recursion:

$$p(x,n) = \begin{cases} 1 & \text{if } n = 0 \\ x \cdot p(x,n-1) & \text{otherwise.} \end{cases}$$

This definition leads immediately to a recursive algorithm that uses $O(n)$ method calls to compute $p(x,n)$. We can compute the power function much faster than this, however, by using the following alternative definition, also based on linear recursion, which employs a squaring technique:

$$p(x,n) = \begin{cases} 1 & \text{if } n = 0 \\ x \cdot p(x,(n-1)/2)^2 & \text{if } n > 0 \text{ is odd} \\ p(x,n/2)^2 & \text{if } n > 0 \text{ is even.} \end{cases}$$

To illustrate how this definition works, consider the following examples:

$$\begin{aligned}
2^4 &= 2^{(4/2)2} = (2^{4/2})^2 = (2^2)^2 = 4^2 = 16 \\
2^5 &= 2^{1+(4/2)2} = 2(2^{4/2})^2 = 2(2^2)^2 = 2(4^2) = 32 \\
2^6 &= 2^{(6/2)2} = (2^{6/2})^2 = (2^3)^2 = 8^2 = 64 \\
2^7 &= 2^{1+(6/2)2} = 2(2^{6/2})^2 = 2(2^3)^2 = 2(8^2) = 128.
\end{aligned}$$

This definition suggests the algorithm of Code Fragment 4.3.

Algorithm Power(x,n):

    Input: A number x and integer $n \geq 0$

    Output: The value x^n

    if $n = 0$ **then**

        return 1

    if n is odd **then**

        $y \leftarrow$ Power($x,(n-1)/2$)

        return $x \cdot y \cdot y$

    else

        $y \leftarrow$ Power($x,n/2$)

        return $y \cdot y$

Code Fragment 4.3: Computing the power function using linear recursion.

To analyze the running time of the algorithm, we observe that each recursive call of method Power(x,n) divides the exponent, n, by two. Thus, there are $O(\log n)$ recursive calls, not $O(n)$. That is, by using linear recursion and the squaring technique, we reduce the running time for the computation of the power function from $O(n)$ to $O(\log n)$, which is a big improvement.

Tail Recursion

Using recursion can often be a useful tool for designing algorithms that have elegant, short definitions. But this usefulness does come at a modest cost. When we use a recursive algorithm to solve a problem, we have to use some of the memory locations in our computer to keep track of the state of each active recursive call. When computer memory is at a premium, then, it is useful in some cases to be able to derive nonrecursive algorithms from recursive ones.

We can use the stack data structure, discussed in Section 4.2, to convert a recursive algorithm into a nonrecursive algorithm, but there are some instances when we can do this conversion more easily and efficiently. Specifically, we can easily convert algorithms that use **tail recursion**. An algorithm uses tail recursion if it uses linear recursion and the algorithm makes a recursive call as its very last operation. For example, the algorithm of Code Fragment 4.2 uses tail recursion to reverse the elements of an array.

It is not enough that the last statement in the method definition include a recursive call, however. In order for a method to use tail recursion, the recursive call must be the absolutely last thing the method does (unless we are in a base case, of course). For example, the algorithm of Code Fragment 4.1 does not use tail recursion, even though its last statement includes a recursive call. This recursive call is not actually the last thing the method does. After it receives the value returned from the recursive call, it adds this value to $A[n-1]$ and returns this sum. That is, the last thing this algorithm does is an add, not a recursive call.

When an algorithm uses tail recursion, we can convert the recursive algorithm into a nonrecursive one, by iterating through the recursive calls rather than calling them explicitly. We illustrate this type of conversion by revisiting the problem of reversing the elements of an array. In Code Fragment 4.4, we give a nonrecursive algorithm that performs this task by iterating through the recursive calls of the algorithm of Code Fragment 4.2. We initially call this algorithm as IterativeReverseArray($A, 0, n-1$).

Algorithm IterativeReverseArray(A, i, j):
　　Input: An array A and nonnegative integer indices i and j
　　Output: The reversal of the elements in A starting at index i and ending at j

　　while $i < j$ **do**
　　．　Swap $A[i]$ and $A[j]$
　　　　$i \leftarrow i + 1$
　　　　$j \leftarrow j - 1$
　　return

　　Code Fragment 4.4: Reversing the elements of an array using iteration.

4.1.2 Binary Recursion

When an algorithm makes two recursive calls, we say that it uses ***binary recursion***. These calls can, for example, be used to solve two similar halves of some problem, as we did in Section 2.5.1 for drawing an English ruler. As another application of binary recursion, let us revisit the problem of summing the n elements of an integer array A. In this case, we can sum the elements in A by: (*i*) recursively summing the elements in the first half of A; (*ii*) recursively summing the elements in the second half of A; and (*iii*) adding these two values together. We give the details in the algorithm of Code Fragment 4.5, which we initially call as BinarySum($A, 0, n$).

Algorithm BinarySum(A, i, n):
    Input: An array A and integers i and n
    Output: The sum of the n integers in A starting at index i
    if $n = 1$ **then**
        return $A[i]$
    return BinarySum($A, i, \lceil n/2 \rceil$) + BinarySum($A, i + \lceil n/2 \rceil, \lfloor n/2 \rfloor$)

Code Fragment 4.5: Summing the elements in an array using binary recursion.

To analyze Algorithm BinarySum, we consider, for simplicity, the case where n is a power of two. The general case of arbitrary n is considered in Exercise R-4.5. Figure 4.2 shows the recursion trace of an execution of method BinarySum$(0, 8)$. We label each box with the values of parameters i and n, which represent the starting index and length of the sequence of elements to be reversed, respectively. Notice that the arrows in the trace go from a box labeled (i, n) to another box labeled $(i, n/2)$ or $(i + n/2, n/2)$. That is, the value of parameter n is halved at each recursive call. Thus, the depth of the recursion, that is, the maximum number of method instances that are active at the same time, is $1 + \log_2 n$. Thus, Algorithm Binary-Sum uses $O(\log n)$ additional space. This is a big improvement over the $O(n)$ space needed by the LinearSum method of Code Fragment 4.1. The running time of Algorithm BinarySum is still $O(n)$, however, since visit each box in constant time when stepping through our algorithm and there are $O(n)$ boxes ($2n - 1$ to be exact).

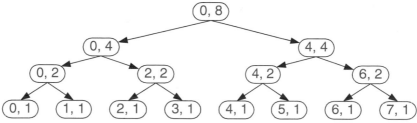

Figure 4.2: Recursion trace for the execution of BinarySum$(0, 8)$.

Computing Fibonacci Numbers via Binary Recursion

Let us consider the problem of computing the kth Fibonacci number. Recall from Section 2.2.3, that the Fibonacci numbers are recursively defined as follows:

$$
\begin{aligned}
F_0 &= 0 \\
F_1 &= 1 \\
F_i &= F_{i-1} + F_{i-2} \quad \text{for } i > 1.
\end{aligned}
$$

By applying directly this definition, Algorithm BinaryFib, shown in Code Fragment 4.6, computes the sequence of Fibonacci numbers using binary recursion.

Algorithm BinaryFib(k):

  Input: Nonnegative integer k
  Output: The kth Fibonacci number F_k

  if $k \leq 1$ **then**
    return k
  else
    return BinaryFib($k-1$) + BinaryFib($k-2$)

Code Fragment 4.6: Computing the kth Fibonacci number using binary recursion.

Unfortunately, in spite of the Fibonacci definition looking like a binary recursion, using this technique is inefficient in this case. In fact, it takes an exponential number of calls to compute the kth Fibonacci number in this way. Specifically, let n_k denote the number of calls performed in the execution of BinaryFib(k). Then, we have the following values for the n_k's:

$$
\begin{aligned}
n_0 &= 1 \\
n_1 &= 1 \\
n_2 &= n_1 + n_0 + 1 = 1 + 1 + 1 = 3 \\
n_3 &= n_2 + n_1 + 1 = 3 + 1 + 1 = 5 \\
n_4 &= n_3 + n_2 + 1 = 5 + 3 + 1 = 9 \\
n_5 &= n_4 + n_3 + 1 = 9 + 5 + 1 = 15 \\
n_6 &= n_5 + n_4 + 1 = 15 + 9 + 1 = 25 \\
n_7 &= n_6 + n_5 + 1 = 25 + 15 + 1 = 41 \\
n_8 &= n_7 + n_6 + 1 = 41 + 25 + 1 = 67.
\end{aligned}
$$

If we follow the pattern forward, we see that the number of calls more than doubles for each two consecutive indices. That is, n_4 is more than twice n_2, n_5 is more than twice n_3, n_6 is more than twice n_4, and so on. Thus, $n_k > 2^{k/2}$, which means that BinaryFib(k) makes a number of calls that are exponential in k. In other words, using binary recursion to compute Fibonacci numbers is very inefficient.

Computing Fibonacci Numbers via Linear Recursion

The main problem with the above approach, based on binary recursion, is that the computation of Fibonacci numbers is really a linearly recursive problem. It is not a good candidate for using binary recursion. We simply got tempted into using binary recursion because of the way the kth Fibonacci number, F_k, depends on the two previous values, F_{k-1} and F_{k-2}. But we can compute F_k much more efficiently using linear recursion.

In order to use linear recursion, however, we need to slightly redefine the problem. One way to accomplish this conversion is to define a recursive function that computes a pair of consecutive Fibonacci numbers (F_k, F_{k-1}), using the convention $F_{-1} = 0$. Then we can use the linearly recursive algorithm shown in Code Fragment 4.7.

Algorithm LinearFibonacci(k):

    Input: A nonnegative integer k

    Output: Pair of Fibonacci numbers (F_k, F_{k-1})

    if $k \leq 1$ **then**

        return $(k, 0)$

    else

        $(i, j) \leftarrow$ LinearFibonacci($k - 1$)

        return $(i + j, i)$

Code Fragment 4.7: Computing the kth Fibonacci number using linear recursion.

The algorithm given in Code Fragment 4.7 shows that using linear recursion to compute Fibonacci numbers is much more efficient than using binary recursion. Since each recursive call to LinearFibonacci decreases the argument k by 1, the original call LinearFibonacci(k) results in a series of $k - 1$ additional calls. That is, computing the kth Fibonacci number via linear recursion requires $O(k)$ method calls. This performance is significantly faster than the exponential time needed by the algorithm based on binary recursion, which was given in Code Fragment 4.6. Therefore, when using binary recursion, we should first try to fully partition the problem in two (as we did for summing the elements of an array) or, we should be sure that overlapping recursive calls are really necessary.

Usually, we can eliminate overlapping recursive calls by using more memory to keep track of previous values. In fact, this approach is a central part of a technique called ***dynamic programming***, which is related to recursion and is discussed in Section 11.5.2.

4.1.3 Multiple Recursion

Generalizing from binary recursion, we use ***multiple recursion*** when a method may make multiple recursive calls, with that number potentially being more than two. One of the most common applications of this type of recursion is used when we wish to enumerate various configurations in order to solve a combinatorial puzzle. For example, the following are all instances of ***summation puzzles***:

$$
\begin{aligned}
pot + pan &= bib \\
dog + cat &= pig \\
boy + girl &= baby
\end{aligned}
$$

To solve such a puzzle, we need to assign a unique digit (that is, $0, 1, \ldots, 9$) to each letter in the equation, in order to make the equation true. Typically, we solve such a puzzle by using our human observations of the particular puzzle we are trying to solve to eliminate configurations (that is, possible partial assignments of digits to letters) until we can work though the feasible configurations left, testing for the correctness of each one.

If the number of possible configurations is not too large, however, we can use a computer to simply enumerate all the possibilities and test each one, without employing any human observations. In addition, such an algorithm can use multiple recursion to work through the configurations in a systematic way. We show pseudo-code for such an algorithm in Code Fragment 4.8. To keep the description general enough to be used with other puzzles, the algorithm enumerates and tests all k-length sequences without repetitions of the elements of a given set U. We build the sequences of k elements by the following steps:

1. Recursively generating the sequences of $k-1$ elements
2. Appending to each such sequence an element not already contained in it.

Throughout the execution of the algorithm, we use the set U to keep track of the elements not contained in the current sequence, so that an element e has not been used yet if and only if e is in U.

Another way to look at the algorithm of Code Fragment 4.8 is that it enumerates every possible size-k ordered subset of U, and tests each subset for being a possible solution to our puzzle.

For summation puzzles, $U = \{0, 1, 2, 3, 4, 5, 6, 7, 8, 9\}$ and each position in the sequence corresponds to a given letter. For example, the first position could stand for b, the second for o, the third for y, and so on.

Algorithm PuzzleSolve(k, S, U):

    Input: An integer k, sequence S, and set U

    Output: An enumeration of all k-length extensions to S using elements in U without repetitions

    for all $e \in U$ **do**

        Remove e from U $\{e$ is now being used$\}$

        Add e to the end of S

        if $k = 1$ **then**

            Test whether S is a configuration that solves the puzzle

            if S solves the puzzle **then**

                return "Solution found: " S

        else

            PuzzleSolve($k - 1, S, U$)

        Add e back to U $\{e$ is now unused$\}$

        Remove e from the end of S

Code Fragment 4.8: Solving a combinatorial puzzle by enumerating and testing all possible configurations.

In Figure 4.3, we show a recursion trace of the execution of PuzzleSolve($3, S, U$), where S is empty and $U = \{a, b, c\}$. During the execution, all the permutations of the three characters are generated and tested. Note that the initial call makes three recursive calls, which each in turn makes two more. If we had executed PuzzleSolve($3, S, U$) on a set U consisting of four elements, the initial call would have made four recursive calls, each of which would have a trace looking like the one in Figure 4.3.

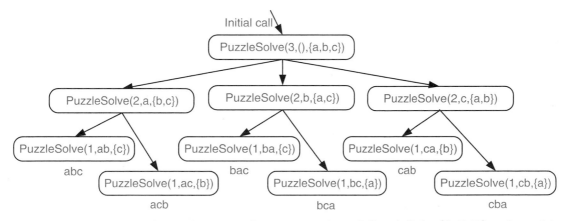

Figure 4.3: Recursion trace for an execution of PuzzleSolve($3, S, U$), where S is empty and $U = \{a, b, c\}$. This execution generates and tests all permutations of a, b, and c. We show the permutations generated directly below their respective boxes.

4.2   Stacks

A *stack* is a container of objects that are inserted and removed according to the *last-in first-out* (*LIFO*) principle. Objects can be inserted into a stack at any time, but only the most-recently inserted (that is, "last") object can be removed at any time. The name "stack" is derived from the metaphor of a stack of plates in a spring-loaded, cafeteria plate dispenser. In this case, the fundamental operations involve the "pushing" and "popping" of plates on the stack. When we need a new plate from the dispenser, we "pop" the top plate off the stack, and when we add a plate, we "push" it down on the stack to become the new top plate. Perhaps an even more amusing metaphor would be a PEZ® candy dispenser, which stores mint candies in a spring-loaded container that "pops" out the top-most candy in the stack when the top of the dispenser is lifted. (See Figure 4.4.) Stacks are a fundamental data structure. They are used in many applications, including the following.

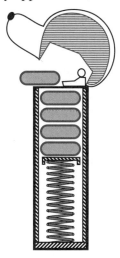

Figure 4.4: A schematic drawing of a PEZ® dispenser; a physical implementation of the stack ADT. (PEZ® is a registered trademark of PEZ Candy, Inc.)

Example 4.4: *Internet Web browsers store the addresses of recently visited sites on a stack. Each time a user visits a new site, that site's address is "pushed" onto the stack of addresses. The browser then allows the user to "pop" back to previously visited sites using the "back" button.*

Example 4.5: *Text editors usually provide an "undo" mechanism that cancels recent editing operations and reverts to former states of a document. This undo operation can be accomplished by keeping text changes in a stack.*

4.2.1 The Stack Abstract Data Type

A stack is an abstract data type (ADT) that supports the following two methods:

push(o): Insert object o at the top of the stack.
Input: Object; *Output:* None.

pop(): Remove from the stack and return the top object on the stack; an error occurs if the stack is empty.
Input: None; *Output:* Object.

Additionally, let us also define the following methods:

size(): Return the number of objects in the stack.
Input: None; *Output:* Integer.

isEmpty(): Return a Boolean indicating if the stack is empty.
Input: None; *Output:* Boolean.

top(): Return the top object on the stack, without removing it; an error occurs if the stack is empty.
Input: None; *Output:* Object.

Example 4.6: *The following table shows a series of stack operations and their effects on an initially empty stack S of integers.*

Operation	Output	Stack Contents
push(5)	–	(5)
push(3)	–	(5,3)
pop()	3	(5)
push(7)	–	(5,7)
pop()	7	(5)
top()	5	(5)
pop()	5	()
pop()	"error"	()
isEmpty()	true	()
push(9)	–	(9)
push(7)	–	(9,7)
push(3)	–	(9,7,3)
push(5)	–	(9,7,3,5)
size()	4	(9,7,3,5)
pop()	5	(9,7,3)
push(8)	–	(9,7,3,8)
pop()	8	(9,7,3)
pop()	3	(9,7)

A Stack Interface in Java

Because of its importance, the stack data structure is included as a "built-in" class in the java.util package of Java. Class java.util.Stack is a data structure that stores generic Java objects and includes, among others, the methods push(obj), pop(), peek() (equivalent to top()), size(), and empty() (equivalent to isEmpty()). Methods pop() and peek() throw exception EmptyStackException if they are called on an empty stack. While it is convenient to just use the built-in class java.util.Stack, it is instructive to learn how to design and implement a stack "from scratch."

Implementing an abstract data type in Java involves two steps. The first step is the definition of a Java *Application Programming Interface* (API), or simply *interface*, which describes the names of the methods that the ADT supports and how they are to be declared and used.

In addition, we must define exceptions for any error conditions that can arise. For instance, the error condition that occurs when calling method pop() or top() on an empty stack is signaled by throwing an exception of type EmptyStackException, which is defined in Code Fragment 4.9.

```
/**
 * Runtime exception thrown when one tries to perform operation top or
 * pop on an empty stack.
 */

public class EmptyStackException extends RuntimeException {
  public EmplyStackException(String err) {
    super(err);
  }
}
```

Code Fragment 4.9: Exception thrown by methods pop() and top() of the Stack interface when called on an empty stack.

A complete Java interface for the stack ADT is given in Code Fragment 4.10. Note that this interface is very general since it specifies that objects of arbitrary, and possibly heterogeneous, classes can be inserted into the stack.

For a given ADT to be of any use, we need to provide a concrete class that implements the methods of the interface associated with that ADT. We give a simple implementation of the Stack interface in the following subsection.

```
/**
 * Interface for a stack: a collection of objects that are inserted
 * and removed according to the last-in first-out principle.
 *
 * @author Roberto Tamassia
 * @author Michael Goodrich
 * @see EmptyStackException
 */

public interface Stack {
 /**
  * Return the number of elements in the stack.
  * @return number of elements in the stack.
  */
  public int size();
 /**
  * Return whether the stack is empty.
  * @return true if the stack is empty, false otherwise.
  */
  public boolean isEmpty();
 /**
  * Inspect the element at the top of the stack.
  * @return top element in the stack.
  * @exception EmptyStackException if the stack is empty.
  */
  public Object top()
    throws EmptyStackException;
 /**
  * Insert an element at the top of the stack.
  * @param element element to be inserted.
  */
  public void push (Object element);
 /**
  * Remove the top element from the stack.
  * @return element removed.
  * @exception EmptyStackException if the stack is empty.
  */
  public Object pop()
    throws EmptyStackException;
}
```

Code Fragment 4.10: Interface Stack documented with comments in Javadoc style. (See Section 1.9.2.)

4.2.2   A Simple Array-Based Implementation

We can implement a stack by storing its elements in an array. Specifically, the stack in this implementation consists of an N-element array S plus an integer variable t that gives the the index of the top element in array S. (See Figure 4.5.)

S 0   1   2 t $N{-}1$

Figure 4.5: Realization of a stack by means of an array S. The top element in the stack is stored in the cell $S[t]$.

Recalling that arrays start at index 0 in Java, we initialize t to -1, and we use this value for t to identify an empty stack. Likewise, we can use t to determine the number of elements $(t+1)$. We also introduce a new exception, called FullStack-Exception, to signal the error that arises if we try to insert a new element into a full array. Exception FullStackException is specific to this implementation and is not defined in the stack ADT, however. We give the details of the array-based stack implementation in Code Fragment 4.11.

Algorithm size():
    return $t+1$
Algorithm isEmpty():
    return $(t<0)$
Algorithm top():
    if isEmpty() **then**
        throw a EmptyStackException
    return $S[t]$
Algorithm push(o):
    if size() $= N$ **then**
        throw a FullStackException
    $t \leftarrow t+1$
    $S[t] \leftarrow o$
Algorithm pop():
    if isEmpty() **then**
        throw a EmptyStackException
    $e \leftarrow S[t]$.
    $S[t] \leftarrow$ **null**
    $t \leftarrow t-1$
    return e

Code Fragment 4.11: Implementing a stack using an array of a given size, N.

Analyzing the Array-Based Stack Implementation

The correctness of the methods in the array-based implementation follows immediately from the definition of the methods themselves. There is, nevertheless, a mildly interesting point here involving the implementation of the pop method.

Note that we could have avoided resetting the old $S[t]$ to **null** and we would still have a correct method. There is a trade-off in being able to avoid this assignment should we be thinking about implementing these algorithms in Java, however. The trade-off involves the Java *garbage collection* mechanism that searches memory for objects that are no longer referenced by active objects, and reclaims their space for future use. (For more details, see Section 12.4.4.) Let $e = S[t]$ be the top element before the pop method is called. By making $S[t]$ a null reference, we indicate that the stack no longer needs to hold a reference to object e. Indeed, if there are no other active references to e, then the memory space taken by e will be reclaimed by the garbage collector.

Table 4.1 shows the running times for methods in a realization of a stack by an array. Each of the stack methods in the array realization executes a constant number of statements involving arithmetic operations, comparisons, and assignments. In addition, pop also calls isEmpty, which itself runs in constant time. Thus, in this implementation of the Stack ADT, each method runs in constant time, that is, they each run in $O(1)$ time.

Method	Time
size	$O(1)$
isEmpty	$O(1)$
top	$O(1)$
push	$O(1)$
pop	$O(1)$

Table 4.1: Performance of a stack realized by an array. The space usage is $O(N)$, where N is the size of the array, determined at the time the stack is instantiated. Note that the space usage is independent from the number $n \leq N$ of elements that are actually in the stack.

A concrete Java implementation of the pseudo-code of Code Fragment 4.11, by means of Java class ArrayStack implementing the Stack interface, is given in Code Fragments 4.12 and 4.13. Note that we use a symbolic name, CAPACITY, to specify the capacity of the array. This allows us to specify the capacity of the array in one place in our code and have that value reflected throughout.

```java
/**
 * Implementation of the Stack interface using a fixed-length array.
 * An exception is thrown if a push operation is attempted when the
 * size of the stack is equal to the length of the array.
 *
 * @author Natasha Gelfand
 * @author Roberto Tamassia
 * @see FullStackException
 */
public class ArrayStack implements Stack {
  /**
   * Default length of the array used to implement the stack.
   */
  public static final int CAPACITY = 1000;
  /**
   * Length of the array used to implement the stack.
   */
  protected int capacity;
  /**
   * Array used to implement the stack.
   */
  protected Object S[];
  /**
   * Index of the top element of the stack in the array.
   */
  protected int top = -1;
  /**
   * Initialize the stack to use an array of default length CAPACITY.
   */
  public ArrayStack() {
    this(CAPACITY);
  }
  /**
   * Initialize the stack to use an array of given length.
   *
   * @param cap length of the array.
   */
  public ArrayStack(int cap) {
    capacity = cap;
    S = new Object[capacity];
  }
```

Code Fragment 4.12: Array-based Java implementation of the Stack interface. (Continues in Code Fragment 4.13.)

```java
/**
 * O(1) time.
 */
public int size() {
    return (top + 1);
}
/**
 * O(1) time.
 */
public boolean isEmpty() {
    return (top < 0);
}
/**
 * O(1) time.
 * @exception FullStackException if the array is full.
 */
public void push(Object obj) throws FullStackException {
    if (size() == capacity)
        throw new FullStackException("Stack overflow.");
    S[++top] = obj;
}
/**
 * O(1) time.
 */
public Object top() throws EmptyStackException {
    if (isEmpty())
        throw new EmptyStackException("Stack is empty.");
    return S[top];
}
/**
 * O(1) time.
 */
public Object pop() throws EmptyStackException {
    Object elem;
    if (isEmpty())
        throw new EmptyStackException("Stack is Empty.");
    elem = S[top];
    S[top--] = null; // dereference S[top] for garbage collection.
    return elem;
}
}
```

Code Fragment 4.13: Array-based Java implementation of the Stack interface. (Continued from Code Fragment 4.12.) Note that the Javadoc comments on methods of the Stack interface provide only class-specific information (the running time of the method) that is not already contained in Code Fragment 4.10.

A Drawback with the Array-Based Stack Implementation

The array implementation of a stack is both simple and efficient, and is widely used in a variety of computing applications. Nevertheless, this implementation has one negative aspect; it must assume a fixed upper bound N on the ultimate size of the stack. In Code Fragment 4.12, we chose the capacity value $N = 1,000$ more or less arbitrarily. An application may actually need much less space than this, in which case we would be wasting memory. Alternatively, an application may need more space than this, in which case our stack implementation may "crash" the application with an error as soon as it tries to push its $(N + 1)$st object on the stack. Thus, even with its simplicity and efficiency, the array-based stack implementation is not necessarily ideal.

Fortunately, there are other implementations, discussed later in this chapter, that do not have a size limitation and use space proportional to the actual number of elements stored in the stack. Still, in cases where we have a good estimate on the number of items needing to go in the stack, the array-based implementation is hard to beat. Stacks serve a vital role in a number of computing applications, so it is helpful to have a fast stack ADT implementation such as the simple array-based implementation.

Casting with a Generic Stack

One of the strong points of our realization of the stack ADT by means of a Java class that implements the Stack interface is that we can store generic objects in the stack, each belonging to an arbitrary class. (See Code Fragments 4.10 and 4.12–4.13.) Namely, an ArrayStack can store Integer objects, Student objects, or even Planet objects.

We must take care, however, that we are consistent in how we use our generic stack, because any elements that are stored in it are viewed as instances of the Java Object class. This causes no problem when we are adding elements to the stack, because every class in Java inherits from the Object class. However, when we retrieve an object from the stack (with either the top or pop method), we always get a reference of type Object back, no matter what the specific class of the object is. Thus, in order to use the retrieved element as an instance of the specific class it really belongs to, we must perform a *cast*, which forces the object to be viewed as a member of a specific class rather than the most general superclass Object. The issues and rules for casting in Java are discussed in more detail in Section 2.4.4.

Reversing an Array Using a Stack

We can use a stack to reverse the elements in an array, thereby producing yet another nonrecursive algorithm for the problem introduced in Section 4.1.1. The basic idea is simply to push all the elements of the array in order into a stack and then fill the array back up again by popping the elements off of the stack. In Code Fragment 4.14, we give a Java implementation of this algorithm. Incidentally, this method also illustrates the need for casting in a simple application that uses a generic stack. In particular, when the elements are popped off the stack, they are returned as elements of the Object type. So they must be casted back to the Integer type before we put them back into the input array.

```java
public static Integer[] reverse(Integer[] a) {
    ArrayStack S = new ArrayStack(a.length);
    Integer[] b = new Integer[a.length];
    for (int i=0; i < a.length; i++)
        S.push(a[i]);
    for (int i=0; i < a.length; i++)
        b[i] = (Integer) (S.pop());
    return b;
}
```

Code Fragment 4.14: A method that reverses the ordering of the elements in an array of Integer objects using an auxiliary stack of class ArrayStack. Casting is performed to force the object returned by pop to be viewed as an Integer object. Note that a Java array has a field length that stores the size of the array.

The reverse method, shown in Code Fragment 4.14, illustrates a small application of the stack data structure, but this data structure has many more important applications than this. In fact, the stack data structure plays an important role in the implementation of the Java language itself.

4.2.3   Stacks in the Java Virtual Machine

A Java program is typically compiled into a sequence of byte codes that are defined as "machine" instructions for a well-defined model—the *Java Virtual Machine* (*JVM*). The definition of the JVM is at the heart of the definition of the Java language itself. By compiling Java code into the JVM byte codes, rather than the machine language of a specific CPU, a Java program can be run on any computer, such as a personal computer or a server, that has a program that can emulate the JVM. Interestingly, the stack data structure plays a central role in the definition of the JVM.

The Java Method Stack

Stacks are an important application to the run-time environment of Java programs. A running Java program (more precisely, a running Java thread) has a private stack, called the *Java method stack* or just *Java stack* for short, which is used to keep track of local variables and other important information on methods as they are invoked during execution. (See Figure 4.6.)

More specifically, during the execution of a Java program, the Java Virtual Machine (JVM) maintains a stack whose elements are descriptors of the currently active (that is, nonterminated) invocations of methods. These descriptors are called *frames*. A frame for some invocation of method "fool" stores the current values of the local variables and parameters of method fool, as well as information on method "cool" that called fool and on what needs to be returned to method "cool".

The JVM keeps a special variable, called the *program counter*, to maintain the address of the statement the JVM is currently executing in the program. When a method "cool" invokes another method "fool", the current value of the program counter is recorded in the frame of the current invocation of cool (so the JVM will know where to return to when method fool is done). At the top of the Java stack is the frame of the *running method*, that is, the method that currently has control of the execution. The remaining elements of the stack are frames of the *suspended methods*, that is, methods that have invoked another method and are currently waiting for it to return control to them upon its termination. The order of the elements in the stack corresponds to the chain of invocations of the currently active methods. When a new method is invoked, a frame for this method is pushed onto the stack. When it terminates, its frame is popped from the stack and the JVM resumes the processing of the previously suspended method.

The JVM uses the Java stack to perform parameter passing to methods. Specifically, Java uses the *call-by-value* parameter passing protocol. This means that the current *value* of a variable (or expression) is what is passed as an argument to a called method.

In the case of a variable x of a primitive type, such as an int or float, the current value of x is simply the number that is associated with x. When such a value is passed to the called method, it is assigned to a local variable in the called method's frame. (This simple assignment is also illustrated in Figure 4.6.) Note that if the called method changes the value of this local variable, it will *not* change the value of the variable in the calling method.

In the case of a variable x that refers to an object, however, the current value of x is the memory address of object x. (We will say more about where this address actually is in Section 4.3.4.) Thus, when object x is passed as a parameter to some method, the address of x is actually passed. When this address is assigned to some local variable y in the called method, y will refer to the same object that x refers to.

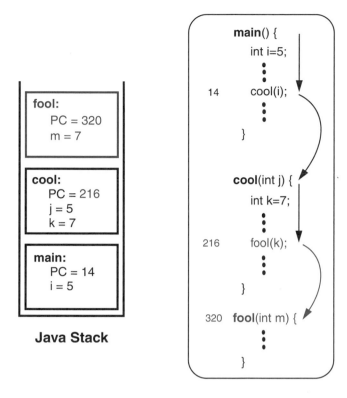

Java Stack

Java Program

Figure 4.6: An example of a Java method stack: Method fool has just been called by method cool, which itself was previously called by method main. Note the values of the program counter, parameters, and local variables stored in the stack frames. When the invocation of method fool terminates, the invocation of method cool will resume its execution at instruction 217, which is obtained by incrementing the value of the program counter stored in the stack frame.

Therefore, if the called method changes the internal state of the object that y refers to, it will simultaneously be changing the internal state of the object that x refers to (which is the same object). Nevertheless, if the called program changes y to refer to some other object, x will remain unchanged—it will still refer to the same object it was referencing before.

Thus, the Java method stack is used by the JVM to implement method calls and parameter passing. Incidentally, method stacks are not a specific feature of Java. They are used in the run-time environment of most modern programming languages, including C and C++.

Implementing Recursion

One of the benefits of using a stack to implement method invocation is that it allows programs to use *recursion*. That is, it allows a method to call itself, as discussed in Sections 2.5.1 and 4.1. Interestingly, early programming languages, such as Cobol and Fortran, did not originally use run-time stacks to implement method and procedure calls. But because of the elegance and efficiency that recursion allows, all modern programming languages, including the modern versions of classic languages like Cobol and Fortran, utilize a run-time stack for method and procedure calls.

In the execution of a recursive method, each box of the recursion trace corresponds to a frame of the Java method stack. Also, the content of the Java method stack corresponds to the chain of boxes from the initial method invocation to the current one.

To better illustrate how a run-time stack allows for recursive methods, let us consider a Java implementation of the classic recursive definition of the factorial function, $n! = n(n-1)(n-2)\cdots 1$, as shown in Code Fragment 4.15.

```java
public static long factorial(long n) {
  if (n <= 1)
    return 1;
  else
    return n*factorial(n−1);
}
```

Code Fragment 4.15: Recursive method factorial.

The first time we call method factorial, its stack frame includes a local variable storing the value n. Method factorial() recursively calls itself to compute $(n-1)!$, which pushes a new frame on the Java run-time stack. In turn, this recursive invocation calls itself to compute $(n-2)!$, etc. The chain of recursive invocations, and thus the run-time stack, only grows up to size n, because calling factorial(1) returns 1 immediately without invoking itself recursively. The run-time stack allows for method factorial() to exist simultaneously in several active frames (as many as n at some point). Each frame stores the value of its parameter n as well as the value to be returned. Eventually, when the first recursive call terminates, it returns $(n-1)!$, which is then multiplied by n to compute $n!$ for the original call of the factorial method.

The Operand Stack

Interestingly, there is actually another place where the JVM uses a stack. Arithmetic expressions, such as $((a+b)*(c+d))/e$, are evaluated by the JVM using an *operand stack*. A simple binary operation, such as $a+b$, is computed by pushing a on the stack, pushing b on the stack, and then calling an instruction that pops the top two items from the stack, performs the binary operation on them, and pushes the result back onto the stack. Likewise, instructions for writing and reading elements to and from memory involve the use of pop and push methods for the operand stack.

In Chapter 6 we discuss the evaluation of arithmetic expressions in a more general framework. For now, however, let us simply note that the operand stack plays a crucial role in this computation. Thus, the operand stack and the Java (method) stack are fundamental components of the Java Virtual Machine.

4.2.4 Matching Parentheses and HTML Tags

In this subsection, we explore two related applications of stacks, the first of which is for matching parentheses and grouping symbols in arithmetic expressions.

Arithmetic expressions can contain various pairs of grouping symbols, such as

- parentheses: "(" and ")"
- braces: "{" and "}"
- brackets: "[" and "]"
- floor function symbols: "⌊" and "⌋"
- ceiling function symbols: "⌈" and "⌉,"

and each opening symbol must match with its corresponding closing symbol. For example, a left bracket, "[," must match with a corresponding right bracket, "]," as in the following expression:

$$[(5+x)-(y+z)].$$

The following examples further illustrate this concept:

- correct: ( )(( )){([( )])}
- correct: ((( )(( )){([( )])}
- incorrect:)(( )){([( )])}
- incorrect: ({[])}
- incorrect: (

We leave the precise definition of matching of grouping symbols to Exercise R-4.10.

An important problem in processing arithmetic expressions, therefore, is to make sure their grouping symbols match up correctly.

An Algorithm for Parentheses Matching

We now present an algorithm that uses a stack S to perform the matching of grouping symbols in an arithmetic expression with a single left-to-right scan. The algorithm tests that left and right symbols match up and also that the left and right symbols are both of the same type. For example, they could respectively be left and right brackets, "[" and "]."

Suppose we are given a sequence $X = x_0 x_1 x_2 \ldots x_{n-1}$, where each x_i is a ***token*** that can be a grouping symbol, a variable name, an arithmetic operator, or a number. The basic idea behind checking that the grouping symbols in S match correctly, is to process the tokens in X in order. Each time we encounter an opening symbol, we push that symbol onto S, and each time we encounter a closing symbol, we pop the top symbol from the stack S (assuming S is not empty) and we check that these two symbols are of the same type. If the stack is empty after we have processed the whole sequence, then the symbols in X match. Assuming that the push and pop operations are implemented to run in constant time, this algorithm runs in $O(n)$, that is linear, time.

We give a pseudo-code description of this algorithm in Code Fragment 4.16.

Algorithm ParenMatch(X, n):

    Input: An array X of n tokens, each of which is either a grouping symbol, a variable, an arithmetic operator, or a number

    Output: **true** if and only if all the grouping symbols in X match

    Let S be an empty stack
    for $i \leftarrow 0$ to $n - 1$ **do**
        if $X[i]$ is an opening grouping symbol **then**
            S.push($X[i]$)
        else if $X[i]$ is a closing grouping symbol **then**
            if S.isEmpty() **then**
                return false　　　{nothing to match with}
            if S.pop() does not match the type of $X[i]$ **then**
                return false　　　{wrong type}
    if S.isEmpty() **then**
        return true　　　{every symbol matched}
    else
        return false　　　{some symbols were never matched}

Code Fragment 4.16: Algorithm for matching grouping symbols in an arithmetic expression.

Matching Tags in an HTML Document

Another application in which matching is important is in the validation of HTML documents. HTML is the standard format for hyperlinked documents on the Internet. In an HTML document, portions of text are delimited by ***HTML tags***. A simple opening HTML tag has the form "<name>" and the corresponding closing tag has the form "</name>." Commonly used HTML tags include

- body: document body
- h1: section header
- center: center justify
- p: paragraph
- ol: numbered (ordered) list
- li: list item.

Ideally, an HTML document should have matching tags, although most browsers tolerate a certain number of mismatching tags. We show a sample HTML document and its rendering by a browser in Figure 4.7.

```
<body>
<center>
<h1> The Little Boat </h1>
</center>
<p> The storm tossed the little
boat like a cheap sneaker in an
old washing machine.  The three
drunken fishermen were used to
such treatment, of course, but
not the tree salesman, who even as
a stowaway now felt that he
had overpaid for the voyage. </p>
<ol>
<li> Will the salesman die? </li>
<li> What color is the boat? </li>
<li> And what about Naomi? </li>
</ol>
</body>
```

The Little Boat

The storm tossed the little boat like a cheap sneaker in an old washing machine. The three drunken fishermen were used to such treatment, of course, but not the tree salesman, who even as a stowaway now felt that he had overpaid for the voyage.

1. Will the salesman die?
2. What color is the boat?
3. And what about Naomi?

(a)   (b)

Figure 4.7: Illustrating HTML tags. (a) A sample HTML document and (b) its rendering by a browser.

Fortunately, more or less the same algorithm as given in Code Fragment 4.16 can be used to match the tags in an HTML document. In Code Fragments 4.17 and 4.18, we give a complete Java program for matching tags in an HTML document read from standard input.

```java
import java.util.StringTokenizer;
import datastructures.Stack;
import datastructures.NodeStack;
import java.io.*;
/** Simplified test of matching tags in an HTML document. */
public class HTML {
  /** Nested class to store simple HTML tags */
  public static class Tag {
    String name;          // The name of this tag
    boolean opening;      // Is true iff this is an opening tag
    public Tag() {        // Default constructor
      name = "";
      opening = false;
    }
    public Tag(String nm, boolean op) {       // Preferred constructor
      name = nm;
      opening = op;
    }
    /** Is this an opening tag? */
    public boolean isOpening() { return opening; }
    /** Return the name of this tag */
    public String getName() {return name; }
  }
  /** Test if every opening tag has a matching closing tag. */
  public boolean isHTMLMatched(Tag[ ] tag) {
    Stack S = new NodeStack(); // Stack for matching tags
    for (int i=0; (i<tag.length) && (tag[i] != null); i++) {
      if (tag[i].isOpening())
        S.push(tag[i].getName()); // opening tag; push its name on the stack
      else {
        if (S.isEmpty()) // nothing to match
          return false;
        if (!((String) S.pop()).equals(tag[i].getName())) // wrong match
          return false;
      }
    }
    if (S.isEmpty())
      return true; // we matched everything
    return false; // we have some tags that never were matched
  }
```

Code Fragment 4.17: A complete Java program for testing if an HTML document has fully matching tags. (Continues in 4.18.) For simplicity, we assume that all tags are the simple opening or closing tags defined above and that no tags are formed incorrectly. We use Java's *nested class* mechanism to define class Tag inside the main class HTML. Method isHTMLMatched uses a stack to store the names of the opening tags seen so far, similar to how the stack was used in Code Fragment 4.16.

```java
    public final static int CAPACITY = 1000; // Tag array size upper bound
    /* Parse an HTML document into an array of html tags */
    public Tag[ ] parseHTML(BufferedReader r)
        throws IOException {
      String line;                            // a line of text
      boolean inTag = false;                  // true iff we are in a tag
      Tag[ ] tag = new Tag[CAPACITY]; // our tag array (initially all null)
      int count = 0;                          // tag counter
      while ((line = r.readLine()) != null) {
        // Create a string tokenizer for HTML tags (use < and > as delimiters)
        StringTokenizer st = new StringTokenizer(line,"<> \t",true);
        while (st.hasMoreTokens()) {
          String token = (String) st.nextToken();
          if (token.equals("<")) // opening a new HTML tag
            inTag = true;
          else if (token.equals(">"))  // ending an HTML tag
            inTag = false;
          else if (inTag) { // we have a opening or closing HTML tag
            if ( (token.length() == 0) || (token.charAt(0) != '/') )
              tag[count++] = new Tag(token, true); // opening tag
            else  // ending tag
              tag[count++] = new Tag(token.substring(1), false); // skip the '/'
          } // Note: we ignore anything not in an HTML tag
        }
      }
      return tag; // our array of tags
    }
    /** Tester method */
    public static void main(String[ ] args) throws IOException {
      BufferedReader stdr;        // Standard Input Reader
      stdr = new BufferedReader(new InputStreamReader(System.in));
      HTML tagChecker = new HTML();
      if (tagChecker.isHTMLMatched(tagChecker.parseHTML(stdr)))
        System.out.println("The input file is a matched HTML document.");
      else
        System.out.println("The input file is not a matched HTML document.");
    }
}
```

Code Fragment 4.18: A complete Java program for testing if an HTML document has fully matching tags. (Continued from 4.17.) Method parseHTML uses a string tokenizer to extract the tags from the HTML document. Method parseHTML performs a preliminary computation that builds an array of HTML tags by using a StringTokenizer (a built-in Java class) to break the input text into tokens, which it takes to be strings delimited by white space or the "<" or ">" characters (and the delimiters themselves). This method also uses a variable, inTag, to keep track of whether it is inside or outside an HTML tag.

4.3   Queues

Another fundamental data structure is the *queue*. It is a close "cousin" of the stack, as a queue is a container of objects that are inserted and removed according to the *first-in first-out* (*FIFO*) principle. That is, elements can be inserted at any time, but only the element that has been in the queue the longest can be removed at any time. We usually say that elements enter the queue at the *rear* and are removed from the *front*. The metaphor for this terminology is a line of people waiting to get on an amusement park ride. People enter at the rear of the line and get on the ride from the front of the line.

4.3.1   The Queue Abstract Data Type

Formally, the queue abstract data type defines a container that keeps objects in a sequence, where element access and deletion are restricted to the first element in the sequence, which is called the *front* of the queue, and element insertion is restricted to the end of the sequence, which is called the *rear* of the queue. This restriction enforces the rule that items are inserted and deleted in a queue according to the first-in first-out (FIFO) principle.

The *queue* abstract data type (ADT) supports the following two fundamental methods:

> enqueue(o): Insert object o at the rear of the queue.
> *Input:* Object; *Output:* None.

> dequeue(): Remove and return from the queue the object at the front; an error occurs if the queue is empty.
> *Input:* None; *Output:* Object.

Additionally, similar to the case with the Stack ADT, the queue ADT includes the following supporting methods:

> size(): Return the number of objects in the queue.
> *Input:* None; *Output:* Integer.

> isEmpty(): Return a Boolean value that indicates whether the queue is empty.
> *Input:* None; *Output:* Boolean.

> front(): Return, but do not remove, the front object in the queue; an error occurs if the queue is empty.
> *Input:* None; *Output:* Object.

Example 4.7: *The following table shows a series of queue operations and their effects on an initially empty queue Q of integer objects. For simplicity, we use integers instead of integer objects as arguments of the operations.*

Operation	Output	front ← Q ← rear
enqueue(5)	–	(5)
enqueue(3)	–	(5,3)
dequeue()	5	(3)
enqueue(7)	–	(3,7)
dequeue()	3	(7)
front()	7	(7)
dequeue()	7	()
dequeue()	"error"	()
isEmpty()	true	()
enqueue(9)	–	(9)
enqueue(7)	–	(9,7)
size()	2	(9,7)
enqueue(3)	–	(9,7,3)
enqueue(5)	–	(9,7,3,5)
dequeue()	9	(7,3,5)

Example Applications

There are several possible applications for queues. Stores, theaters, reservation centers, and other similar services typically process customer requests according to the FIFO principle. A queue would therefore be a logical choice for a data structure to handle transaction processing for such applications. For example, it would be a natural choice for handling calls to the reservation center of an airline or to the box office of a theater.

A Queue Interface in Java

A Java interface for the queue ADT is given in Code Fragment 4.19. This generic interface specifies that objects of arbitrary classes can be inserted into the queue. Thus, we may need to use casting when removing elements.

Note that the size and isEmpty methods have the same meaning as their counterparts in the Stack ADT. These two methods, as well as the front method, are known as ***accessor*** methods, for they return a value and do not change the contents of the data structure.

```java
public interface Queue {
  /**
   * Returns the number of elements in the queue.
   * @return number of elements in the queue.
   */
  public int size();
  /**
   * Returns whether the queue is empty.
   * @return true if the queue is empty, false otherwise.
   */
  public boolean isEmpty();
  /**
   * Inspects the element at the front of the queue.
   * @return element at the front of the queue.
   * @exception EmptyQueueException if the queue is empty.
   */
  public Object front() throws EmptyQueueException;
  /**
   * Inserts an element at the rear of the queue.
   * @param element new element to be inserted.
   */
  public void enqueue (Object element);
  /**
   * Removes the element at the front of the queue.
   * @return element removed.
   * @exception EmptyQueueException if the queue is empty.
   */
  public Object dequeue() throws EmptyQueueException;
}
```

Code Fragment 4.19: Interface Queue documented with comments in Javadoc style.

4.3.2   A Simple Array-Based Implementation

We present a simple realization of a queue by means of an array, Q, of fixed capacity, storing its elements. Since the main rule with the queue ADT is that we insert and delete objects according to the FIFO principle, we must decide how we are going to keep track of the front and rear of the queue.

One possibility is to adapt the approach we used for the stack implementation, letting $Q[0]$ be the front of the queue and then letting the queue grow from there. This is not an efficient solution, however, for it requires that we move all the elements forward one array cell each time we perform a dequeue operation. Such an implementation would therefore take $O(n)$ time to perform the dequeue method, where n is the current number of objects in the queue.

Using an Array in a Circular Way

To avoid moving objects once they are placed in Q, we define two variables f and r, which have the following meanings:

- f is an index to the cell of Q storing the first element of the queue (which is the next candidate to be removed by a dequeue operation), unless the queue is empty (in which case $f = r$).

- r is an index to the next available array cell in Q.

Initially, we assign $f = r = 0$, which indicates that the queue is empty. Now, when we remove an element from the front of the queue, we increment f to index the next cell. Likewise, when we add an element, we store it in cell $Q[r]$ and increment r to index the next available cell in Q. This scheme allows us to implement methods front, enqueue, and dequeue in constant time, that is, $O(1)$ time. However, there is still a problem with this approach.

Consider, for example, what happens if we repeatedly enqueue and dequeue a single element N different times. We would have $f = r = N$. If we were then to try to insert the element just one more time, we would get an array-out-of-bounds error (since the N valid locations in Q are from $Q[0]$ to $Q[N-1]$), even though there is plenty of room in the queue in this case. To avoid this problem and be able to utilize all of the array Q, we let the f and r indices "wrap around" the end of Q. That is, we now view Q as a "circular array" that goes from $Q[0]$ to $Q[N-1]$ and then immediately back to $Q[0]$ again. (See Figure 4.8.)

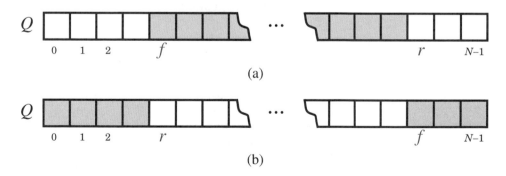

Figure 4.8: Using array Q in a circular fashion: (a) the "normal" configuration with $f \leq r$; (b) the "wrapped around" configuration with $r < f$. The cells storing queue elements are highlighted.

Using the Modulo Operator to Implement a Circular Array

Implementing this circular view of Q is actually pretty easy. Each time we increment f or r, we compute this increment as "$(f+1)$ mod N" or "$(r+1)$ mod N," respectively.

Recall that operator "mod" is the **modulo** operator, which is computed by taking the remainder after an integral division. For example, 14 divided by 4 is 3 with remainder 2, so 14 mod 4 = 2. Specifically, given integers x and y such that $x \geq 0$ and $y > 0$, we have x mod $y = x - \lfloor x/y \rfloor y$. That is, if $r = x$ mod y, then there is a nonnegative integer q, such that $x = qy + r$. Java uses "%" to denote the modulo operator. By using the modulo operator, we can view Q as a circular array and implement each queue method in a constant amount of time (that is, $O(1)$ time). We describe how to use this approach to implement a queue in Code Fragment 4.20.

Algorithm size():
    return $(N - f + r)$ mod N

Algorithm isEmpty():
    return $(f = r)$

Algorithm front():
    if isEmpty() **then**
        throw a QueueEmptyException
    return $Q[f]$

Algorithm dequeue():
    if isEmpty() **then**
        throw a QueueEmptyException
    $temp \leftarrow Q[f]$
    $Q[f] \leftarrow$ **null**
    $f \leftarrow (f+1)$ mod N
    return $temp$

Algorithm enqueue(o):
    if size() $= N - 1$ **then**
        throw a FullQueueException
    $Q[r] \leftarrow o$
    $r \leftarrow (r+1)$ mod N

Code Fragment 4.20: Implementation of a queue using a circular array. The implementation uses the modulo operator to "wrap" indices around the end of the array and it also includes two instance variables, f and r, which index the front of the queue and first empty cell after the rear of the queue respectively.

The implementation above contains an important detail, which might be missed at first. Consider the situation that occurs if we enqueue N objects into Q without dequeuing any of them. We would have $f = r$, which is the same condition that occurs when the queue is empty. Hence, we would not be able to tell the difference between a full queue and an empty one in this case. Fortunately, this is not a big problem, and a number of ways for dealing with it exist.

The solution we describe here is to insist that Q can never hold more than $N - 1$ objects. This simple rule for handling a full queue takes care of the final problem with our implementation, and leads to the pseudo-coded descriptions of the queue methods given in Code Fragment 4.20. Note our introduction of an implementation-specific exception, called FullQueueException, to signal that no more elements can be inserted in the queue. Also note the way we compute the size of the queue by means of the expression $(N - f + r) \bmod N$, which gives the correct result both in the "normal" configuration (when $f \leq r$) and in the "wrapped around" configuration (when $r < f$). The Java implementation of a queue by means of an array is similar to that of a stack, and is left as an exercise (P-4.4).

Table 4.2 shows the running times of methods in a realization of a queue by an array. As with our array-based stack implementation, each of the queue methods in the array realization executes a constant number of statements involving arithmetic operations, comparisons, and assignments. Thus, each method in this implementation runs in $O(1)$ time.

Method	Time
size	$O(1)$
isEmpty	$O(1)$
front	$O(1)$
enqueue	$O(1)$
dequeue	$O(1)$

Table 4.2: Performance of a queue realized by an array. The space usage is $O(N)$, where N is the size of the array, determined at the time the queue is created. Note that the space usage is independent from the number $n < N$ of elements that are actually in the queue.

As with the array-based stack implementation, the only real disadvantage of the array-based queue implementation is that we artificially set the capacity of the queue to be some fixed value. In a real application, we may actually need more or less queue capacity than this, but if we have a good capacity estimate, then the array-based implementation is quite efficient. One such possible application of a queue is for round robin schedulers, which we discuss next.

4.3.3   Round Robin Schedulers

A popular use of the queue data structure is to implement a ***round robin*** scheduler, where we iterate through a collection of elements in a circular fashion and "service" each element by performing a given action on it. Such a schedule is used, for example, to fairly allocate a resource that must be shared by a collection of clients. For instance, we can use a round robin scheduler to allocate a slice of CPU time to various applications running concurrently on a computer.

We can implement a round robin scheduler using a queue, Q, by repeatedly performing the following steps (see Figure 4.9):

1. $e \leftarrow Q.\text{dequeue}()$
2. Service element e
3. $Q.\text{enqueue}(e)$

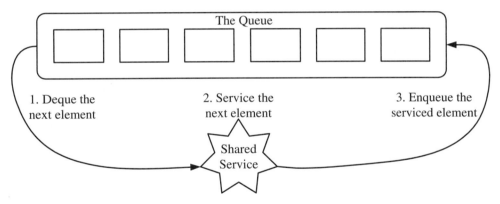

Figure 4.9: The three iterative steps for using a queue to implement a round robin scheduler.

The Josephus Problem

In the children's game "hot potato," a group of n children sit in a circle passing an object, called the "potato," around the circle. The potato begins with a starting child in the circle, and the children continue passing the potato until a leader rings a bell, at which point the child holding the potato must leave the game after handing the potato to the next child in the circle. After the selected child leaves, the other children close up the circle. This process is then continued until there is only one child remaining, who is declared the winner. If the leader always uses the strategy of ringing the bell after the potato has been passed k times, for some fixed value k, then determining the winner for a given list of children is known as the ***Josephus problem***.

We can solve the Josephus problem for a collection of *n* elements using a queue, by associating the potato with the element at the front of the queue and storing elements in the queue according to their order around the circle. Thus, passing the potato is equivalent to dequeuing an element and immediately enqueuing it again. After this process has been performed *k* times, we remove the front element by dequeuing it from the queue and discarding it. We show a complete Java program for solving the Josephus problem using this approach in Code Fragment 4.21, which describes a solution that runs in $O(nk)$ time. (We can solve this problem faster using techniques beyond the scope of this book.)

```java
import datastructures.Queue;
import datastructures.NodeQueue;
public class Josephus {
  /** Solution of the Josephus problem using a queue. */
  public static Object Josephus(Queue Q, int k) {
    if (Q.isEmpty()) return null;
    while (Q.size() > 1) {
      System.out.println(" Queue: " + Q + "  k = " + k);
      for (int i=0; i < k; i++)
        Q.enqueue(Q.dequeue());  // move the front element to the end
      Object e = Q.dequeue(); // remove the front element from the collection
      System.out.println("    " + e + " is out");
    }
    return Q.dequeue();  // the winner
  }
  /** Build a queue from an array of objects */
  public static Queue buildQueue(Object a[]) {
    Queue Q = new NodeQueue();
    for (int i=0; i<a.length; i++)
      Q.enqueue(a[i]);
    return Q;
  }
  /** Tester method */
  public static void main(String[] args) {
    String[] a1 = {"Alice", "Bob", "Cindy", "Doug", "Ed", "Fred"};
    String[] a2 = {"Gene", "Hope", "Irene", "Jack", "Kim", "Lance"};
    String[] a3 = {"Mike", "Roberto"};
    System.out.println("First winner is " + Josephus(buildQueue(a1), 3));
    System.out.println("Second winner is " + Josephus(buildQueue(a2), 10));
    System.out.println("Third winner is " + Josephus(buildQueue(a3), 7));
  }
}
```

Code Fragment 4.21: A complete Java program for solving the Josephus problem using a queue. Class NodeQueue is shown in Code Fragment 4.24.

4.3.4 Memory Allocation in Java

We have already discussed (in Section 4.2.3) how the Java Virtual Machine allocates a method's local variables in that method's frame on the Java run-time stack. The Java stack is not the only kind of memory available for program data in Java, however. Memory for an object can also be allocated dynamically during a method's execution, by having that method utilize the special **new** operator built into Java. For example, the following Java statement creates an array of integers whose size is given by the value of variable k:

$$\text{int[] items} = \textbf{new}\text{int[k];}$$

The size of the above array is known only at runtime. Moreover, the array may continue to exist even after the method that created it terminates. Thus, the memory for this array cannot be allocated on the Java stack.

The Memory Heap

Instead of using the Java stack for this object's memory, Java uses memory from another area of storage—the *memory heap* (which should not be confused with the "heap" data structure we will discuss in Chapter 7). We illustrate this memory area, together with the other memory areas, in a Java Virtual Machine in Figure 4.10. The storage available in the memory heap is divided into *blocks*, which are contiguous array-like "chunks" of memory that may be of variable or fixed sizes.

To simplify the discussion, let us assume that blocks in the memory heap are of a fixed size, say, 1,024 bytes, and that one block is big enough for any object we might want to create. (Efficiently handling the more general case is actually an interesting research problem.)

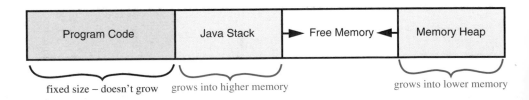

Figure 4.10: A schematic view of the layout of memory addresses in the Java Virtual Machine.

Using a Queue to Allocate Memory

The Java Virtual Machine definition requires that the memory heap be able to quickly allocate memory blocks for new objects, but it does not specify the data structure that we should use to do this. So each implementor of a JVM is free to choose the implementation thought to be best. For example, we can use a queue to manage the set of free (unused) blocks in the memory heap. When a method uses the **new** operator to request a block of memory for some new object, we perform a dequeue operation to retrieve a free block of memory. Likewise, when the Java Virtual Machine determines (by means of its "garbage collector") that a block of memory previously allocated is no longer being used, then the Java Virtual Machine performs an enqueue operation to return this block to the set of available blocks.

As long as there are enough data blocks available in the Java Virtual Machine's memory heap, this scheme is guaranteed to efficiently allocate memory for newly created objects. Thus, the queue data structure can be applied in the implementation of Java itself.

4.3.5   Java Threads ⋆

Multiprogramming is a way of achieving a limited form of parallelism, even on a computer that has only one CPU. This mechanism allows us to have multiple tasks or computational *threads* running at the same time, with each thread being responsible for some specific computation. Multiprogramming is useful in graphical applications. For example, one thread can be responsible for catching mouse clicks while another thread handles the motion of objects on the screen. Even if the computer has only one CPU, these different computational threads can all seem to be running at the same time because:

1. The CPU is so fast relative to our perception of time.

2. The operating system is providing each thread with a different "slice" of the CPU's time.

The time slices given to each different thread occur with such rapid succession that the different threads appear to be running simultaneously, in parallel.

⋆We use a star (⋆) to indicate sections containing material more advanced than the material in the rest of the chapter; this material can be considered optional in a first reading.

A Java Stack for Each Thread

Java has a built-in mechanism for achieving multiprogramming—Java threads. Java threads are computational objects that can cooperate and communicate with one another to share other objects in memory, the computer's screen, or other kinds of resources and devices. Switching between different threads in a Java program occurs rapidly because each thread has its own Java stack stored in the memory of the Java Virtual Machine. The Java stack for each thread contains the local variables and the frames for the methods that that thread is currently running. Thus, to switch from a thread T to another thread U, all the CPU needs to do is to "remember" where it left off in the thread T before it switches to the thread U. We have already discussed a way for this to be done, namely, by storing the current value of T's program counter, which is a reference to the next instruction T is to perform, at the top of T's Java stack. By saving the program counter for each active thread in the top of its Java stack, the CPU can pick up where it left off in some other thread U, by restoring the value of the program counter to the value that was stored at the top of U's Java stack (and using U's stack as the "current" Java stack).

Thread States

A Java thread will always be in one of four different states:

- New
- Runnable
- Blocked
- Dead.

When a thread is first created, it is in a ***new*** state, and it remains in this state until it receives a start message. Once it starts, a Java thread becomes ***runnable***, which means that it is a candidate to perform computations when given a slice of the CPU's time. When a thread is in the runnable state and it becomes the active thread, then it executes its instructions. These instructions can be regular primitive operations, or they can be special operations that put the thread into a ***blocked*** state so that it is no longer runnable (until some event or thread puts it back in the runnable state). These blocking operations include calls to sleep, suspend, and wait methods or any instruction that causes the thread to have to wait for some input-output (I/O) action. A thread can be brought back into the runnable state by having its sleep event terminate (that is, it "wakes up"), having some other thread send it a resume or notify message, or having an I/O it was waiting for complete. Finally, when a thread is done performing its computations, it enters a ***dead*** state.

Multiprogramming and the Round-Robin Protocol

When designing a program that uses multiple threads, we must be careful not to allow an individual thread to monopolize the CPU. Such CPU monopolization can lead to an application or applet *hanging*, where it is technically running, but not actually doing anything.

In some operating systems, CPU monopolizing by threads is not an issue. These operating systems utilize a queue to allocate CPU time to the runnable threads in the *round robin* protocol (see Section 4.3.3). The application of the round-robin protocol in this case involves having the operating system store all runnable threads in a queue.

Using a Queue for Multiprogramming

The mechanism for using a queue to implement multiprogramming is actually quite simple. When the CPU is ready to provide a time slice to a thread, the operating system performs a dequeue operation on the queue to get the next available runnable thread; let's call it T. Before the CPU actually begins executing instructions for T, however, the operating system starts a timer running in hardware that is set to expire a fixed amount of time later. The operating system then gives control of the CPU to T until either one of the following occurs:

- Thread T blocks itself (by one of the blocking methods mentioned above)
- The timer for T expires.

In the latter case, the operating system makes the CPU stop the execution of T and it performs an enqueue operation to place T at the end of the line of currently runnable threads. Likewise, whenever a thread returns to the runnable state, because an event that it is waiting on has occurred, it too is put back in the queue using an enqueue operation. In any case, when T loses control of the CPU, the operating system saves the current value of T's program counter at the top of T's Java stack and processes the next available runnable thread by extracting it from the queue with a dequeue operation. In this way, the operating system ensures that each runnable thread is given its fair share of the CPU's time. Thus, by using a simple queue data structure and a hardware timer, the operating system can avoid CPU monopolization.

While this queue-based solution solves the multiprogramming problem, we should mention that this solution is actually an oversimplification of the protocol used by most operating systems that do round-robin time slicing, as most systems give threads priorities. Thus, they use a *priority queue* to implement time slicing. We discuss priority queues in Chapter 7.

4.4   Linked Lists

In the previous sections, we presented the stack and queue ADTs and discussed some important applications of them. We also showed how to implement these abstract data types with concrete data structures based on arrays. While these implementations are quite simple, they have the drawback of not being very adaptable, since the size N of the array must be fixed in advance. There are other ways to implement these data structures, however, that do not have this drawback. In this section, we explore an important alternate implementation, which is known as the singly linked list.

4.4.1   Singly Linked Lists

A *linked list* in its simplest form is a collection of *nodes* that together form a linear ordering. The ordering is determined as in the children's game "Follow the Leader," in that each node is a compound object that stores a reference to an element and a reference, called next, to another node. (See Figure 4.11.)

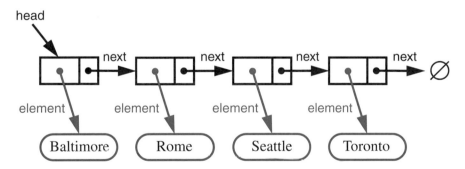

Figure 4.11: A singly linked list. References to elements are shown with blue arrows; next references are shown with black arrows. The **null** object is denoted as ∅. The head reference is a single instance variable.

It might seem like circular reasoning to have a node reference another node, but such a scheme easily works. The next reference inside a node can be viewed as a *link* or *pointer* to another node. Likewise, moving from one node to another by following a next reference is known as *link hopping* or *pointer hopping*. The first and last node of a linked list usually are called the *head* and *tail* of the list, respectively. We can identify the tail as the node having a null next reference, which indicates the termination of the list. A linked list defined in this way is known as a *singly linked list*.

Like an array, a singly linked list keeps the elements in a certain linear order, which is determined by the chain of next links between the nodes. Unlike an array, a singly linked list does not have a predetermined fixed size, and uses space proportional to the number of its elements.

More precisely, the space usage of a singly linked list with n elements is $O(n)$, since it has n nodes and each node uses $O(1)$ space to store references to an element and to the next node. To implement a singly linked list in Java, we define a Node class, as shown in Code Fragment 4.22, which specifies the format of the objects associated with the nodes of the list, and a class (not shown) that keeps a reference to the head node and a variable counting the total number of nodes. Note that to save space, Javadoc comments are not included in Code Fragment 4.22 and in most Java code fragments shown in the rest of this book.

```java
public class Node {
  // Instance variables:
  private Object element;
  private Node next;
  /** Creates a node with null references to its element and next node. */
  public Node() {
    this(null, null);
  }
  /** Creates a node with the given element and next node. */
  public Node(Object e, Node n) {
    element = e;
    next = n;
  }
  // Accessor methods:
  public Object getElement() {
    return element;
  }
  public Node getNext() {
    return next;
  }
  // Modifier methods:
  public void setElement(Object newElem) {
    element = newElem;
  }
  public void setNext(Node newNext) {
    next = newNext;
  }
}
```

Code Fragment 4.22: Implementation of a node of a singly linked list. To save space, Javadoc comments have been omitted.

With a singly linked list, we can easily insert or delete an element at the head of the list in $O(1)$ time, as shown in Figure 4.12. We create a new node, set its next link to refer to the same object as the head, and then set the head to point to the new node. Note that this simple procedure works even when the linked list is empty and the head refers to the **null** object.

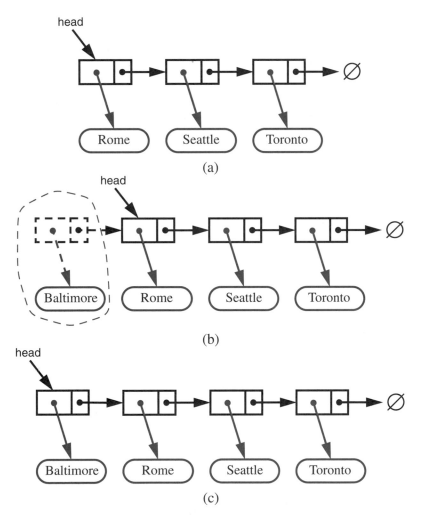

Figure 4.12: Insertion of an element at the head of a singly linked list: (a) before the insertion; (b) creation of a new node; (c) after the insertion. Deleting an element from the head of the list is a symmetric operation, which can be visualized by looking first at (c), then (b), and finally (a).

We can also insert an element at the tail of the list in $O(1)$ time, provided we keep a reference to the tail node, as shown in Figure 4.13. In this case, we create a new node, assign its next reference to point to the **null** object, set the next reference of the tail to point to this new object, and then assign the tail reference itself to this new node.

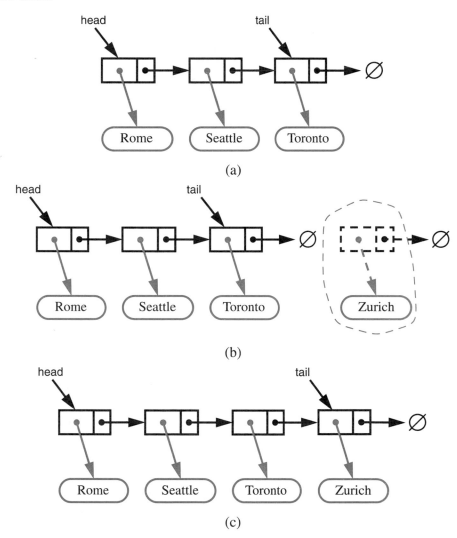

Figure 4.13: Insertion of an element at the tail of a singly linked list: (a) before the insertion; (b) creation of a new node; (c) after the insertion. Note that it is crucial that we set the next link for the tail in (b) before we assign the tail variable to point to the new node in (c).

We cannot delete the tail node of a singly linked list in $O(1)$ time, however. Even if we have a tail reference directly to the last node of the list, we must be able to access the node *before* the last node, in order to remove the last node. This is one time when it is appropriate to say, "you can't get there from here," for we cannot reach the node before a node v by following next links from v. The only way to access the node before v is to start from the head of the list and search all the way through the list until reaching a node whose next reference points to v. But if v is the last node, such link hopping takes an amount of time proportional to the number of elements in the list, that is, $O(n)$ time.

We next consider how one can use a singly linked list to implement the stack and queue ADTs .

4.4.2 Implementing a Stack with a Singly Linked List

Let us explore using a singly linked list to implement the stack ADT. In principle, the top of the stack could be either at the head or at the tail of the list. However, since we can insert and delete elements in $O(1)$ time only at the head, it is more efficient to have the top of the stack at the head. Also, in order to perform operation size in $O(1)$ time, we keep track of the current number of elements in an instance variable. A Java implementation of a stack, by means of a singly linked list, is given in Code Fragment 4.23. All the methods of the Stack interface are therefore executed in $O(1)$ time.

In addition to being time efficient, this linked list implementation has a space requirement that is $O(n)$, where n is the current number of elements in the stack. That is, its space usage depends on the number of elements in the stack and not on any artificial capacity constraint. Likewise, this implementation does not require that a new exception be created to handle any size overflow problems. It instead implicitly has the run-time environment deal with the general issue of whether our implementation will run out of memory, which involves the OutOfMemoryError error (see Section 2.3 for the difference between exceptions and errors). Thus, this implementation of a stack, by means of a singly linked list, has an important advantage over the array-based one: it does not require that we place an explicit upper bound on the size of the stack.

We use an instance variable top to refer to the head of the list (which points to the **null** object if the list is empty). When we push a new element e on the stack, we simply create a new node v for e, reference e from v, and insert v at the head of the list. Likewise, when we pop an element from the stack, we simply remove the node at the head of the list and return its element. Thus, we perform all insertions and removals of elements at the head of the list.

```
public class NodeStack implements Stack {
  protected Node top;           // reference to the head node
  protected int size;           // number of elements in the stack
  public NodeStack() { // constructs an empty stack
    top = null;
    size = 0;
  }
  public int size() {
    return size;
  }
  public boolean isEmpty() {
    if (top == null)
      return true;
    return false;
  }
  public void push(Object elem) {
    Node v = new Node(elem, top);   // create and link-in a new node
    top = v;
    size++;
  }
  public Object top() throws EmptyStackException {
    if (isEmpty())
      throw new EmptyStackException("Stack is empty.");
    return top.getElement();
  }
  public Object pop() throws EmptyStackException {
    if (isEmpty())
      throw new EmptyStackException("Stack is empty.");
    Object temp = top.getElement();
    top = top.getNext();        // link-out the former top node
    size--;
    return temp;
  }
}
```

Code Fragment 4.23: Class NodeStack, which implements the Stack interface using a singly linked list. The nodes of the list are objects of class Node shown in Code Fragment 4.22.

4.4.3   Implementing a Queue with a Singly Linked List

We can efficiently implement the queue ADT using a singly linked list, as well. For efficiency reasons, we choose the front of the queue to be at the head of the list, and the rear of the queue to be at the tail of the list. In this way, we remove from the head and insert at the tail. (Why would it be bad to insert at the head and remove at the tail?) Note that we need to maintain references to both the head and tail nodes of the list. Rather than go into every detail of this implementation, we simply give a Java implementation for the fundamental queue methods in Code Fragment 4.24.

```java
public void enqueue(Object obj) {
    Node node = new Node();
    node.setElement(obj);
    node.setNext(null); // node will be new tail node
    if (size == 0)
        head = node; // special case of a previously empty queue
    else
        tail.setNext(node); // add node at the tail of the list
    tail = node; // update the reference to the tail node
    size++;
}
...
public Object dequeue() throws EmptyQueueException {
    if (size == 0)
        throw new EmptyQueueException("Queue is empty.");
    Object obj = head.getElement();
    head = head.getNext();
    size--;
    if (size == 0)
        tail = null; // the queue is now empty
    return obj;
}
```

Code Fragment 4.24: Methods enqueue and dequeue in the implementation of the queue ADT by means of a singly linked list.

Each of the methods of the singly linked list implementation of the queue ADT runs in $O(1)$ time. We also avoid the need to specify a maximum size for the queue, as was done in the array-based queue implementation, but this benefit comes at the expense of increasing the amount of space used per element. Still, the methods in the singly linked list queue implementation are more complicated than we might like, for we must take extra care in how we deal with special cases where the queue is empty before an enqueue or where the queue becomes empty after a dequeue.

4.5 Double-Ended Queues

Consider now a queue-like data structure that supports insertion and deletion at both the front and the rear of the queue. Such an extension of a queue is called a ***double-ended queue***, or ***deque***, which is usually pronounced "deck" to avoid confusion with the dequeue method of the regular queue ADT, which is pronounced like the abbreviation "D.Q."

4.5.1 The Deque Abstract Data Type

The deque abstract data type is richer than both the stack and the queue ADTs. The fundamental methods of the deque ADT are as follows:

insertFirst(e): Insert a new element e at the beginning of the deque.
Input: Object; *Output:* None.

insertLast(e): Insert a new element e at the end of the deque.
Input: Object; *Output:* None.

removeFirst(): Remove and return the first element of the deque; an error occurs if the deque is empty.
Input: None; *Output:* Object.

removeLast(): Remove and return the last element of the deque; an error occurs if the deque is empty.
Input: None; *Output:* Object.

Additionally, the deque ADT may also include the following support methods:

first(): Return the first element of the deque; an error occurs if the deque is empty.
Input: None; *Output:* Object.

last(): Return the last element of the deque; an error occurs if the deque is empty.
Input: None; *Output:* Object.

size(): Return the number of elements of the deque.
Input: None; *Output:* Integer.

isEmpty(): Determine if the deque is empty.
Input: None; *Output:* Boolean.

Example 4.8: *The following table shows a series of operations and their effects on an initially empty deque D of integer objects. For simplicity, we use integers instead of integer objects as arguments of the operations.*

Operation	Output	D
insertFirst(3)	–	(3)
insertFirst(5)	–	(5,3)
removeFirst()	5	(3)
insertLast(7)	–	(3,7)
removeFirst()	3	(7)
removeLast()	7	()
removeFirst()	"error"	()
isEmpty()	true	()

4.5.2   Implementing a Deque with a Doubly Linked List

Since the deque requires insertion and removal at both ends of a list, using a singly linked list would be inefficient. (See Section 4.4.1.) There is a type of linked list, however, that allows for a great variety of operations, including insertion and removal at both ends, to run in $O(1)$ time—the **doubly linked** list. A node in a doubly linked list stores two references—a next link, which points to the next node in the list, and a prev link, which points to the previous node in the list. A Java implementation of a node of a doubly linked list is shown in Code Fragment 4.25.

```
public class DLNode {
  private Object element;
  private DLNode next, prev;
  DLNode() { this(null, null, null); }
  DLNode(Object e, DLNode p, DLNode n) {
    element = e;
    next = n;
    prev = p;
  }
  public void setElement(Object newElem) { element = newElem; }
  public void setNext(DLNode newNext) { next = newNext; }
  public void setPrev(DLNode newPrev) { prev = newPrev; }
  public Object getElement() { return element; }
  public DLNode getNext() { return next; }
  public DLNode getPrev() { return prev; }
}
```

Code Fragment 4.25: Implementation of a node of a doubly linked list.

To simplify programming, it is convenient to add special nodes at both ends of the list; a *header* node just before the head of the list, and a *trailer* node just after the tail of the list. These "dummy" or *sentinel* nodes do not store any element. The header has a valid next reference but a null prev reference, while the trailer has a valid prev reference but a null next reference. A doubly linked list with these sentinels is shown in Figure 4.14. Note that a linked list object would simply need to store references to these two sentinels and a size counter that keeps track of the number of elements (not counting sentinels) in the list.

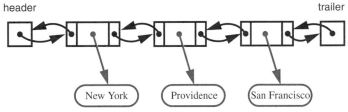

Figure 4.14: A doubly linked list with sentinels, header and trailer, marking the ends of the list. An empty list would have these sentinels pointing to each other. The null prev link for the header and the null next link for the trailer are not shown.

Inserting or removing elements at either end of a doubly linked list is straightforward to do in $O(1)$ time. (See Figure 4.15.) Indeed, the prev links eliminate the need to traverse the list to get to the node just before the tail.

For any insertion of a new element e, we can have access to the node p before the place e should go and the node q after the place e should go. To insert a new element between the two nodes p and q (either or both of which could be sentinels), we create a new node t, have t's prev and next links respectively refer to p and q, and then have p's next link refer to t, and have q's prev link refer to t.

Likewise, to remove an element stored at a node t, we can access the nodes p and q on either side of t (and these nodes must exist, since we are using sentinels). To remove node t between nodes p and q, we simply have p and q point to each other instead of t. We need not change any of the fields in t, for now t can be reclaimed by the garbage collector, since no one is pointing to t.

Table 4.3 shows the running times of methods for a deque implemented with a doubly linked list. Note that every method runs in $O(1)$ time.

Method	Time
size, isEmpty	$O(1)$
first, last	$O(1)$
insertFirst, insertLast	$O(1)$
removeFirst, removeLast	$O(1)$

Table 4.3: Performance of a deque realized by a doubly linked list.

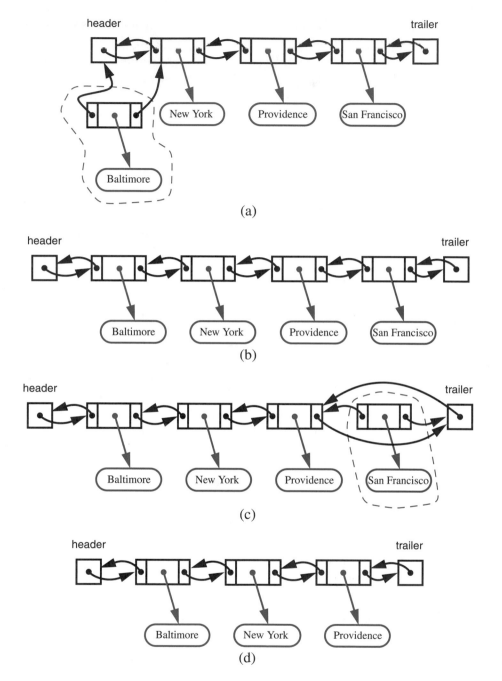

Figure 4.15: Update operations for a doubly linked list with header and trailer sentinels: (a) inserting at the head; (b) after the insertion and before deleting at the tail; (c) deleting at the tail; (d) after the deletion.

Thus, a doubly linked list can be used to implement all the methods of the deque ADT in $O(1)$ time. We show in Code Fragment 4.26 portions of the Java class MyDeque, which implements a deque by means of a doubly linked list. Note the use of sentinels and the way we initialize them in the constructor.

```java
public class NodeDeque implements Deque {
  protected DLNode header, trailer; // sentinels
  protected int size;     // number of elements
  public NodeDeque() {  // initialize an empty deque
    header = new DLNode();
    trailer = new DLNode();
    header.setNext(trailer); // make header point to trailer
    trailer.setPrev(header); // make trailer point to header
    size = 0;
  }
  public Object first() throws EmptyDequeException {
    if (isEmpty())
      throw new EmptyDequeException("Deque is empty.");
    return header.getNext().getElement();
  }
  public void insertFirst(Object o) {
    DLNode second = header.getNext();
    DLNode first = new DLNode(o, header, second);
    second.setPrev(first);
    header.setNext(first);
    size++;
  }
  public Object removeLast() throws EmptyDequeException {
    if (isEmpty())
      throw new EmptyDequeException("Deque is empty.");
    DLNode last = trailer.getPrev();
    Object o = last.getElement();
    DLNode secondtolast = last.getPrev();
    trailer.setPrev(secondtolast);
    secondtolast.setNext(trailer);
    size--;
    return o;
  }
```

Code Fragment 4.26: Portions of the implementation of the deque ADT by means of a doubly linked list. Note that thanks to the use of sentinels, we do not need to check for "special cases" of an empty, or about to become empty, list. Methods insertFirst and removeLast are illustrated in Figure 4.15.

4.6   Exercises

For source code and help with exercises, please visit **java.datastructures.net**.

Reinforcement

R-4.1   Draw the recursion trace for the execution of method ReverseArray$(A, 0, 4)$ (Code Fragment 4.2) on array $A = \{4, 3, 6, 2, 5\}$.

R-4.2   Give a pseudo-code description of the $O(n)$-time algorithm for computing the power function $p(x, n)$. Also, draw the recursion trace of this algorithm for the computation of $p(2, 5)$.

R-4.3   Give a Java description of Algorithm Power for computing the power function $p(x, n)$ (Code Fragment 4.3).

R-4.4   Draw the recursion trace of the Power algorithm (Code Fragment 4.3, which computes the power function $p(x, n)$) for computing $p(2, 9)$.

R-4.5   Analyze the running time of Algorithm BinarySum (Code Fragment 4.5) for arbitrary values of the input parameter n.

R-4.6   Describe a way to use recursion to add all the elements in a $n \times n$ (2-dimensional) array of integers.

R-4.7   Draw the recursion trace for the execution of method PuzzleSolve$(3, S, U)$ (Code Fragment 4.8), where S is empty and $U = \{a, b, c, d\}$.

R-4.8   Describe the output of the following series of stack operations: push(5), push(3), pop(), push(2), push(8), pop(), pop(), push(9), push(1), pop(), push(7), push(6), pop(), pop(), push(4), pop(), pop().

R-4.9   Give a recursive method for removing all the elements in a stack.

R-4.10   Give a precise and complete definition of the concept of matching for grouping symbols in an arithmetic expression.

R-4.11   Describe the output for the following sequence of queue operations: enqueue(5), enqueue(3), dequeue(), enqueue(2), enqueue(8), dequeue(), dequeue(), enqueue(9), enqueue(1), dequeue(), enqueue(7), enqueue(6), dequeue(), dequeue(), enqueue(4), dequeue(), dequeue().

R-4.12   Give a recursive definition of a singly linked list.

R-4.13 Describe the output for the following sequence of deque operations: insertFirst(3), insertLast(8), insertLast(9), insertFirst(5), removeFirst(), removeLast(), first(), insertLast(7), removeFirst(), last(), removeLast().

R-4.14 Describe a method for inserting an element at the beginning of a singly linked list. Assume that the list does **not** have a sentinel header node, and instead uses a variable head to reference the first node in the list.

R-4.15 Give an algorithm for finding the penultimate node in a singly linked list where the last element is indicated by a null next reference.

R-4.16 Describe a nonrecursive method for finding, by link hopping, the middle node of a doubly linked list with header and trailer sentinels. (Note: This method must only use link hopping; it cannot use a counter.) What is the running time of this method?

R-4.17 Describe a recursive algorithm for finding the maximum element in an array A of n elements. What is your running time and space usage?

Creativity

C-4.1 Give a recursive algorithm to compute the product of two positive integers, m and n, using only addition and subtraction.

C-4.2 Describe a recursive algorithm to compute the integer part of the base-two logarithm of n using only addition and integer division.

C-4.3 Describe how to implement the queue ADT using two stacks. What is the running time of the enqueue() and dequeue() methods in this case?

C-4.4 Suppose we are given an n-element array A whose elements are integers taken from the set $\{1, 2, \ldots, n-1\}$. Describe a recursive algorithm for finding a repeated element in A. What is the running time of your algorithm?

C-4.5 Suppose you are given an n-element array A containing distinct integers that are listed in increasing order. Given a number k, describe a recursive algorithm to find two integers in A that sum to k, if such a pair exists. What is the running time of your algorithm?

C-4.6 Given an n-element unsorted array A of n integers and an integer k, describe a recursive algorithm for rearranging the elements in A so that all elements less than or equal to k come before any elements larger than k. What is the running time of your algorithm?

C-4.7 In the **Towers of Hanoi** puzzle, we are given a platform with three pegs, a, b, and c, sticking out of it. On peg a is a stack of n disks, each larger than the next, so that the smallest is on the top and the largest is on the bottom. The puzzle is to move all the disks from peg a to peg c, moving one disk at a time, so that we never place a larger disk on top of a smaller one. See Figure 4.16 for an example of the case $n = 4$. Describe a recursive algorithm for solving the Towers of Hanoi puzzle for arbitrary n. (Hint: Consider first the subproblem of moving all but the nth disk from peg a to another peg using the third as "temporary storage.")

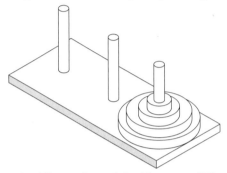

Figure 4.16: An illustration of the Towers of Hanoi puzzle.

C-4.8 Describe a recursive method for converting a string of digits into the integer it represents. For example, "13531" represents the integer $13,531$.

C-4.9 Describe a recursive method for computing the nth **Harmonic number**, $H_n = \sum_{i=1}^{n} 1/i$.

C-4.10 Describe a recursive algorithm that counts the number of nodes in a singly linked list.

C-4.11 Describe a linear-time algorithm for reversing a singly linked list L, so that the ordering of the nodes becomes opposite of what it was before.

C-4.12 Give an algorithm for concatenating two singly linked lists L and M, with header sentinels, into a single list L' that contains all the nodes of L (in their original order) followed by all the nodes of M (also in their original order). What is the running time of this method, if we let n denote the number of nodes in L and we let m denote the number of nodes in M?

C-4.13 Give an algorithm for concatenating two doubly linked lists L and M, with header and trailer sentinel nodes, into a single list L', as in the previous exercise. What is the running time of this method?

C-4.14 Describe a linear-time algorithm for reversing a queue Q. To access the queue, you are only allowed to use the methods of queue ADT.

C-4.15 Describe in pseudo-code how to swap two nodes x and y in a singly linked list L given references only to x and y. Repeat this exercise for the case when L is a doubly linked list. What are the running times of each of these methods in terms of n, the number of nodes in L?

C-4.16 Describe in pseudo-code an algorithm for reversing a singly linked list L using only a constant amount of additional space and not using any recursion. What is the running time of this method?

C-4.17 Give a pseudo-code description for an array-based implementation of the double-ended queue ADT. What is the running time for each operation?

C-4.18 Describe how to implement the stack ADT using two queues. What is the running time of the push() and pop() methods in this case?

Projects

P-4.1 Write a program for solving summation puzzles by enumerating and testing all possible configurations. Using your program, solve the three puzzles given in Section 4.1.3.

P-4.2 Implement the stack ADT with a doubly linked list.

P-4.3 Implement the stack ADT using the Java ArrayList class. (without using the built-in Java Stack class).

P-4.4 Implement the queue ADT using an array.

P-4.5 Implement the entire queue ADT using a singly linked list.

P-4.6 Design an ADT for a two-color, double-stack ADT that consists of two stacks—one "red" and one "blue"—and has as its operations color-coded versions of the regular stack ADT operations. For example, this ADT should allow for both a red push operation and a blue push operation. Give an efficient implementation of this ADT using a single array whose capacity is set at some value N that is assumed to always be larger than the sizes of the red and blue stacks combined.

P-4.7 Complete the implementation of class NodeDeque.

P-4.8 Implement the deque ADT with an array used in a circular fashion.

P-4.9 Implement the Stack and Queue interfaces with a unique class that extends class NodeDeque (Code Fragment 4.26).

P-4.10 When a share of common stock of some company is sold, the ***capital gain*** (or, sometimes, loss) is the difference between the share's selling price and the price originally paid to buy it. This rule is easy to understand for a single share, but if we sell multiple shares of stock bought over a long period of time, then we must identify the shares actually being sold. A standard accounting principle for identifying which shares of a stock were sold in such a case is to use a FIFO protocol—the shares sold are the ones that have been held the longest (indeed, this is the default method built into several personal finance software packages). For example, suppose we buy 100 shares at $20 each on day 1, 20 shares at $24 on day 2, 200 shares at $36 on day 3, and then sell 150 shares on day 4 at $30 each. Then applying the FIFO protocol means that of the 150 shares sold, 100 were bought on day 1, 20 were bought on day 2, and 30 were bought on day 3. The capital gain in this case would therefore be $100 \cdot 10 + 20 \cdot 6 + 30 \cdot (-6)$, or $940. Write a program that takes as input a sequence of transactions of the form "buy x share(s) at $\$y$ each" or "sell x share(s) at $\$y$ each," assuming that the transactions occur on consecutive days and the values x and y are integers. Given this input sequence, the output should be the total capital gain (or loss) for the entire sequence, using the FIFO protocol to identify shares.

Chapter Notes

The fundamental data structures of stacks, queues, and linked lists discussed in this chapter belong to the folklore of computer science. They were first chronicled by Knuth in his seminal book on *Fundamental Algorithms*, now in its third edition [58]. In this chapter, we have taken the approach of defining the fundamental data structures of stacks, queues, and deques, first in terms of their ADTs and then in terms of concrete implementations. This approach to data structure specification and implementation is an outgrowth of software engineering advances brought on by the object-oriented design approach, and is now considered a standard approach for teaching data structures. We were introduced to this approach to data structure design by the classic books by Aho, Hopcroft, and Ullman on data structures and algorithms [4, 5]. For further study of abstract data types, please see the book by Liskov and Guttag [66], the survey paper by Cardelli and Wegner [19], or the book chapter by Demurjian [27]. In this chapter, we motivated the study of stacks and queues from implementation issues in Java. The reader interested in learning more about the Java run-time environment known as the Java Virtual Machine (JVM) is referred to the book by Lindholm and Yellin [65] that defines the JVM.

Chapter

5

Vectors, Lists, and Sequences

Contents

The concept of a sequence, where each object comes before or after another, is fundamental. We see it in a line-by-line listing of the code of a computer program, where the order of instructions determines the computation that the program represents. Sequences are interesting, then, for they represent the important relationships of "next" and "previous" between related objects. In addition, sequences are widely used to realize and implement other data structures; hence, they are foundational building blocks for data structure design.

In this chapter, we present the *vector*, *list*, and *sequence* ADTs, each of which represents a collection of linearly arranged elements and provides methods for accessing, inserting, and removing arbitrary elements. The different types of sequences are distinguished from one another by the specific ways in which these operations are defined. Stacks, queues, and deques, studied in Chapter 4, can be viewed as restricted types of sequences that access only the first and/or last elements. An important property of a sequence is that, just as with stacks, queues, and deques, the order of the elements in a sequence is determined by the operations in the abstract data type specification, and not by the values of the elements.

A vector, which is also known as an *array list*, is an abstraction and extension of the concrete array data structure. It provides accessor methods that can index into the middle of a sequence and it also provides update methods for adding and removing elements by their indices. To avoid confusion with the way items are accessed in the concrete array data structure, we typically use the term *rank* to refer to the index of an element in a vector.

The list ADT, on the other hand, is an abstraction of the concrete linked list data structure. It provides accessor and update methods based on an object-oriented encapsulation of a list's node objects, which we call *positions*, for they provide an object-oriented way of referring to "places" where elements are stored.

Finally, we present the full sequence ADT, which is a unification of the vector and list ADTs. We show, however, that such a unification comes at a cost, for we give two basic ways of implementing a sequence, with an array and with a doubly linked list, and we point out performance trade-offs between these two implementations. We also discuss the *iterator* design pattern and mention its realization by means of a vector or list.

In this chapter, we illustrate the use of the list ADT in an extended Java example of a favorites list, which keeps a count of how many times an entry in a list has been accessed. Such a list is useful for maintaining logs of frequently visited Web pages, which is the example we illustrate, as well as most viewed photographs or commonly used menu items in a graphical user interface. We show two possible implementations of this idea, one based on maintaining entries ordered by access counts and the other based on the so called *move-to-front heuristic*, and we analyze the performance trade-offs of these two approaches.

5.1　Vectors and Array Lists

Suppose we have a collection S of n elements stored in a certain linear order, so that we can refer to the elements in S as first, second, third, and so on. Such a collection is generically referred to as a *sequence*. We can uniquely refer to each element e in S using an integer in the range $[0, n-1]$ that is equal to the number of elements of S that precede e in S. We define the *rank* of an element e in S to be the number of elements that are before e in S. Hence, the first element in S has rank 0 and the last element has rank $n-1$. Also, if an element of S has rank r, its previous element (if it exists) has rank $r-1$, and its next element (if it exists) has rank $r+1$. This definition is consistent with the way arrays are indexed in Java and other programming languages (such as C++).

A sequence that supports access to its elements by their ranks is called a *vector* or *array list*. Rank is a simple yet powerful notion, since it can be used to specify where to insert a new element into a vector or where to remove an old element.

5.1.1　The Vector Abstract Data Type

As an ADT, a *vector* S has the following methods (besides size() and isEmpty()):

elemAtRank(r): Return the element of S with rank r; an error condition occurs if $r < 0$ or $r >$ size() $- 1$.
Input: Integer; *Output:* Object.

replaceAtRank(r, e): Replace with e and return the element at rank r; an error condition occurs if $r < 0$ or $r >$ size() $- 1$.
Input: Integer and object; *Output:* Object.

insertAtRank(r, e): Insert a new element e into S to have rank r; an error condition occurs if $r < 0$ or $r >$ size().
Input: Integer and object; *Output:* None.

removeAtRank(r): Remove from S the element at rank r; an error condition occurs if $r < 0$ or $r >$ size() $- 1$.
Input: Integer; *Output:* Object.

We do *not* insist that an array should be used to implement a vector, so that the element at rank 0 is stored at index 0 in the array, although that is one possibility. The rank definition offers us a way to refer to the "index" of an element in a sequence without having to worry about the exact implementation of that sequence. The rank of an element may change whenever the sequence is updated, however, as we illustrate in the following example.

Example 5.1: *We show below some operations on an initially empty vector S.*

Operation	Output	S
insertAtRank(0, 7)	–	(7)
insertAtRank(0, 4)	–	(4, 7)
elemAtRank(1)	7	(4, 7)
insertAtRank(2, 2)	–	(4, 7, 2)
elemAtRank(3)	"error"	(4, 7, 2)
removeAtRank(1)	7	(4, 2)
insertAtRank(1, 5)	–	(4, 5, 2)
insertAtRank(1, 3)	–	(4, 3, 5, 2)

Our vector ADT is shown as a Java interface in Code Fragment 5.1. We use a BoundaryViolationException to signal an invalid rank argument.

```java
public interface Vector {
    /** Returns the number of elements in the vector. */
    public int size();
    /** Returns whether the vector is empty. */
    public boolean isEmpty();
    /** Returns the element stored at the given rank. */
    public Object elemAtRank(int r) throws BoundaryViolationException;
    /** Replaces the element stored at the given rank. */
    public Object replaceAtRank(int r, Object e) throws BoundaryViolationException;
    /** Inserts an element at the given rank. */
    public void insertAtRank(int r, Object e) throws BoundaryViolationException;
    /** Removes the element stored at the given rank. */
    public Object removeAtRank(int r) throws BoundaryViolationException;
}
```

Code Fragment 5.1: The Vector interface.

The set of vector methods is small, but it is sufficient to define an adapter class (Section 2.5.2) for the deque ADT, as shown in Table 5.1. (See Exercise C-5.9.)

Deque Method	Realization with Vector Methods
size(), isEmpty()	size(), isEmpty()
first()	elemAtRank(0)
last()	elemAtRank(size() − 1)
insertFirst(e)	insertAtRank(0, e)
insertLast(e)	insertAtRank(size(), e)
removeFirst()	removeAtRank(0)
removeLast()	removeAtRank(size() − 1)

Table 5.1: Realization of a deque by means of a vector.

5.1.2   A Simple Array-Based Implementation

An obvious choice for implementing the vector ADT is to use an array A (motivating the alternative term, "array list"), where $A[i]$ stores (a reference to) the element with rank i. We choose the size N of array A sufficiently large, and we maintain the number of elements in an instance variable, $n < N$.

The details of this implementation of the vector ADT are simple. To implement the elemAtRank(r) operation, for example, we just return $A[r]$. Implementations of methods insertAtRank(r, e) and removeAtRank(r) are given in Code Fragment 5.2. An important (and time-consuming) part of this implementation involves the shifting of elements up or down to keep the occupied cells in the array contiguous. These shifting operations are required to maintain our rule of always storing an element of rank i at index i in A. (See Figure 5.1 and also Exercise R-5.12.)

Algorithm insertAtRank(r, e):
    for $i = n - 1, n - 2, \ldots, r$ **do**
        $A[i+1] \leftarrow A[i]$ {make room for the new element}
    $A[r] \leftarrow e$
    $n \leftarrow n + 1$

Algorithm removeAtRank(r):
    $e \leftarrow A[r]$ {e is a temporary variable}
    for $i = r, r + 1, \ldots, n - 2$ **do**
        $A[i] \leftarrow A[i+1]$ {fill in for the removed element}
    $n \leftarrow n - 1$
    return e

Code Fragment 5.2: Methods insertAtRank(r, e) and removeAtRank(r) in the array implementation of the vector ADT. We denote with n the instance variable storing the number of elements in the vector.

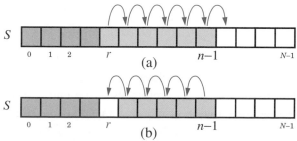

Figure 5.1: Array-based implementation of a vector S storing n elements: (a) shifting up for an insertion at rank r; (b) shifting down for a removal at rank r.

Table 5.2 shows the worst-case running times of the methods of a vector with n elements realized by means of an array. Methods isEmpty, size, elemAtRank and replaceAtRank clearly run in $O(1)$ time, but the insertion and removal methods can take much longer than this. In particular, insertAtRank(r, e) runs in time $O(n)$. Indeed, the worst case for this operation occurs when $r = 0$, since all the existing n elements have to be shifted forward. A similar argument applies to method removeAtRank(r), which runs in $O(n)$ time, because we have to shift backward $n - 1$ elements in the worst case $(r = 0)$. In fact, assuming that each possible rank is equally likely to be passed as an argument to these operations, their average running time is $O(n)$, for we will have to shift $n/2$ elements on average.

Method	Time
size()	$O(1)$
isEmpty()	$O(1)$
elemAtRank(r)	$O(1)$
replaceAtRank(r, e)	$O(1)$
insertAtRank(r, e)	$O(n)$
removeAtRank(r)	$O(n)$

Table 5.2: Performance of a vector with n elements realized by an array. The space usage is $O(N)$, where N is the size of the array.

Looking more closely at insertAtRank(r, e) and removeAtRank(r), we note that they each run in time $O(n - r + 1)$, for only those elements at rank r and higher have to be shifted up or down. Thus, inserting or removing an item at the end of a vector, using the methods insertAtRank(n, e) and removeAtRank$(n - 1)$, respectively take $O(1)$ time each. Moreover, this observation has an interesting consequence for the adaptation of the vector ADT to the deque ADT given in Section 5.1.1. If the vector ADT in this case is implemented by means of an array as described above, then methods insertLast and removeLast of the deque each run in $O(1)$ time. However, methods insertFirst and removeFirst of the deque each run in $O(n)$ time.

Actually, with a little effort, we can produce an array-based implementation of the vector ADT that achieves $O(1)$ time for insertions and removals at rank 0, as well as insertions and removals at the end of the vector. Achieving this requires that we give up on our rule that an element at rank i is stored in the array at index i, however, as we would have to use a circular array approach like the one we used in Section 4.3 to implement a queue. We leave the details of this implementation for an exercise (C-5.10).

5.1.3 An Extendable Array Implementation

A major weakness of the simple array implementation for the vector ADT given in Section 5.1.2 is that it requires advance specification of a fixed capacity, N, for the total number of elements that may be stored in the vector. If the actual number of elements, n, of the vector is much smaller than N, then this implementation will waste space. Worse, if n increases past N, then this implementation will crash. Fortunately, there is a simple way to fix this major drawback.

Let us provide a means to grow the array A that stores the elements of a vector S. Of course, in Java (and other programming languages) we cannot actually grow the array A; its capacity is fixed at some number N, as we have already observed. Instead, when an **overflow** occurs, that is, when $n = N$ and method insertAtRank is called, we perform the following steps:

1. Allocate a new array B of capacity $2N$
2. Let $B[i] \leftarrow A[i]$, for $i = 0, \ldots, N-1$
3. Let $A \leftarrow B$, that is, we use B as the array supporting S
4. Insert the new element in A.

This array replacement strategy is known as an **extendable array**, for it can be viewed as extending the end of the underlying array to make room for more elements. (See Figure 5.2.) Intuitively, this strategy is much like that of the hermit crab, which moves into a larger shell when it outgrows its previous one.

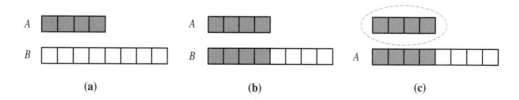

(a)   (b)   (c)

Figure 5.2: An illustration of the three steps for "growing" an extendable array: (a) create new array B; (b) copy elements from A to B; (c) reassign reference A to the new array. Not shown is the future garbage collection of the old array.

We give portions of a Java implementation of the vector ADT using an extendable array in Code Fragment 5.3. This class only provides means for the array to grow; there is no corresponding means to shrink the array. Exercise C-5.2 explores the realization of the vector ADT by means of an array that can grow and shrink so that its length is always no more than four times the number of elements in the vector.

```java
/** Realization of a vector by means of an array.  The array has
 * initial length 16 and is doubled when the size of the vector
 * exceeds the capacity of the array.  No shrinking of the array is
 * performed.
 */
public class ArrayVector implements Vector {
  private Object[] A;         // array storing the elements of the vector
  private int capacity = 16;  // initial length of array A
  private int size = 0;       // number of elements stored in the vector
  /** Creates the vector with initial capacity 16. */
  public ArrayVector() {
    A = new Object[capacity];
  }
  /** Inserts an element at the given rank. */
  public void insertAtRank(int r, Object e)
    throws BoundaryViolationException {
    checkRank(r, size() + 1);
    if (size == capacity) {               // an overflow
      capacity *= 2;
      Object[ ] B = new Object[capacity];
      for (int i=0; i<size; i++)
        B[i] = A[i];
      A = B;
    }
    for (int i=size−1; i>=r; i−−)        // shift elements up
      A[i+1] = A[i];
    A[r] = e;
    size++;
  }
  /** Removes the element stored at the given rank. */
  public Object removeAtRank(int r)
    throws BoundaryViolationException {
    checkRank(r, size());
    Object temp = A[r];
    for (int i=r; i<size−1; i++)         // shift elements down
      A[i] = A[i+1];
    size−−;
    return temp;
  }
```

Code Fragment 5.3: Portions of class ArrayVector realizing the vector ADT by means of an extendable array. Method checkRank(r, n) (not shown) checks whether r is in the range $[0, n − 1]$.

This array replacement strategy might at first seem slow, for performing a single array replacement required by some element insertion can take $O(n)$ time. Still, notice that after we perform an array replacement, our new array allows us to add n new elements to the vector before the array must be replaced again. This simple fact allows us to show that performing a series of operations on an initially empty vector is actually quite efficient. As a shorthand notation, let us refer to the insertion of an element to be the last element in a vector as a ***push*** operation.

We can show, using a design pattern called ***amortization***, that performing a sequence of such push operations on a vector implemented with an extendable array is actually quite efficient. To perform an ***amortized analysis***, we use an accounting technique where view the computer as a coin-operated appliance that requires the payment of one ***cyber-dollar*** for a constant amount of computing time. When an operation is executed, we should have enough cyber-dollars available in our current "bank account" to pay for that operation's running time. Thus, the total amount of cyber-dollars spent for any computation will be proportional to the total time spent on that computation. The beauty of using this analysis method is that we can overcharge some operations in order to save up cyber-dollars to pay for others.

Proposition 5.2: *Let S be a vector implemented by means of an extendable array with initial length one. The total time to perform a series of n push operations in S, starting from S being empty is $O(n)$.*

Justification: Let us assume that one cyber-dollar is enough to pay for the execution of each push operation in S, excluding the time spent for growing the array. Also, let us assume that growing the array from size k to size $2k$ requires k cyber-dollars for the time spent copying the elements. We shall charge each push operation three cyber-dollars. Thus, we overcharge each push operation that does not cause an overflow by two cyber-dollars. Think of the two cyber-dollars profited in an insertion that does not grow the array as being "stored" at the element inserted. An overflow occurs when the vector S has 2^i elements, for some integer $i \geq 0$, and the size of the array used by the vector representing S is 2^i. Thus, doubling the size of the array will require 2^i cyber-dollars. Fortunately, these cyber-dollars can be found at the elements stored in cells 2^{i-1} through $2^i - 1$. (See Figure 5.3.) Note that the previous overflow occurred when the number of elements became larger than 2^{i-1} for the first time, and thus the cyber-dollars stored in cells 2^{i-1} through $2^i - 1$ were not previously spent. Therefore, we have a valid amortization scheme in which each operation is charged three cyber-dollars and all the computing time is paid for. That is, we can pay for the execution of n push operations using $3n$ cyber-dollars. In other words, the amortized running time of each push operation is $O(1)$; hence, the total running time of n push operations is $O(n)$. ∎

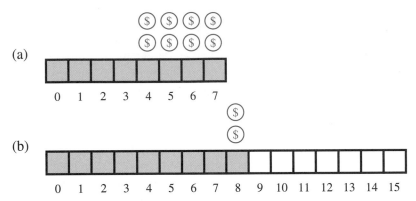

Figure 5.3: Illustration of a series of push operations on a vector: (a) an 8-cell array is full, with two cyber-dollars "stored" at cells 4 through 7; (b) a push operation causes an overflow and a doubling of capacity. Copying the eight old elements to the new array is paid for by the cyber-dollars already stored in the table; inserting the new element is paid for by one of the cyber-dollars charged to the push operation; and the two cyber-dollars profited are stored at cell 8.

5.1.4 The java.util.ArrayList and java.util.Vector Classes

Java has provides classes, java.util.ArrayList and java.util.Vector, that have similar functionality to our vector ADT. Moreover, the standard implementations of these two classes use extendable arrays as described in the previous subsection. The correspondence between these classes and our vector ADT is given in Table 5.3. Note that methods of the java.util classes have short names. This feature speeds up coding, at the slight expense of readability, since the exact meaning of how the vector is being accessed or updated must be inferred, in this case, from a method's complete signature, not just its name.

Vector ADT Methods	java.util.ArrayList Methods
size(), isEmpty()	size(), isEmpty()
elemAtRank(r)	get(r)
replaceAtRank(r, e)	set(r, e)
insertAtRank(r, e)	add(r, e)
removeAtRank(r)	remove(r)

Table 5.3: Correspondence between similar methods in the vector ADT and the java.util.ArrayList class. The corresponding methods in the java.util.Vector class are the same as in the java.util.ArrayList class.

The Java classes java.util.ArrayList and java.util.Vector have features in addition to those of our simplified vector ADT. For example, the class java.util.Vector provides an integer capacityIncrement parameter, which determines how the underlying extendable array grows. If the capacityIncrement parameter is set to 0, then the array doubles when it grows (like in our class ArrayVector). If this parameter is set to a positive value, k, however, then the array adds k new cells when it grows. We must utilize this parameter with caution, however. For most applications, leaving the capacityIncrement parameter set to 0 is the right choice, as the following proposition shows. In fact, the java.util.ArrayList does not provide this flexibility, possibly because of the negative consequences shown in the following.

Proposition 5.3: *If we create an initially empty* java.util.Vector *object with a fixed positive* capacityIncrement *value, then performing a series of n push operations on this vector takes $\Omega(n^2)$ time.*

Justification: Let $c > 0$ be the capacityIncrement value, and let $c_0 > 0$ be the initial size of the array. An overflow is caused by an add operation when the number of elements in the Vector is $c_0 + ic$, for $i = 0, \ldots, m-1$, where $m = \lfloor (n - c_0)/c \rfloor$. Thus, by Proposition 3.1, the time for handling the overflows is proportional to

$$\sum_{i=0}^{m-1} (c_0 + ci) = c_0 m + c \sum_{i=0}^{m-1} i = c_0 m + c \frac{m(m-1)}{2},$$

which is $\Omega(n^2)$. Therefore, performing the n push operations takes $\Omega(n^2)$ time. ∎

Figure 5.4 compares the running times of a series of push operations on an initially empty java.util.Vector, for two initial values of capacityIncrement.

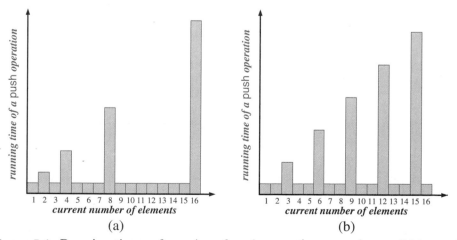

Figure 5.4: Running times of a series of push operations on a java.util.Vector instantiated with capacityIncrement equal to 0 in (a) and 3 in (b).

5.2   Lists

Using rank is not the only means of referring to the place where an element appears in a sequence. If we have a sequence S implemented with a (singly or doubly) linked list, then it could possibly be more natural and efficient to use a node instead of a rank as a means of identifying where to access and update S. In this section, we define the list ADT, which abstracts the concrete linked list data structure using a related position ADT that abstracts the notion of "place" in a list.

5.2.1   Node-Based Operations

Let S be a (singly or doubly) linked list. We would like to define methods for S that take nodes as parameters and provide nodes as return types. Such methods could provide significant speedups over rank-based methods, for finding the rank of an element in a linked list requires searching through the list incrementally from its beginning or end, counting elements as we go.

For instance, we could define a hypothetical method removeAtNode(v) that removes the element of S stored at node v of the list. Using a node as a parameter allows us to remove an element in $O(1)$ time by simply going directly to the place where that node is stored and then "linking out" this node through an update of the *next* and *prev* links of its neighbors. Similarly, we could insert, in $O(1)$ time, a new element e into S with an operation such as insertAfterNode(v,e), which specifies the node v after which the node of the new element should be inserted. In this case, we simply "link in" the new node.

Defining methods of a list ADT by adding such node-based operations raises the issue of how much information we should be exposing about the implementation of our list. Certainly, it is desirable for us to be able to use either a singly or doubly linked list without revealing this detail to a user. Likewise, we do not wish to allow a user to modify the internal structure of a list without our knowledge. Such modification would be possible, however, if we provided to a user a reference to a node in our list in a form that allowed the user to access internal data in that node (such as a *next* or *prev* field).

To abstract and unify the different ways of storing elements in the various implementations of a list, we introduce the concept of **position** in a list, which formalizes the intuitive notion of "place" of an element relative to others in the list.

5.2.2 Positions

So as to safely expand the set of operations for lists, we abstract a notion of "position" that allows us to enjoy the efficiency of doubly or singly linked list implementations without violating object-oriented design principles. In this framework, we view a list as a container of elements that stores each element at a position and that keeps these positions arranged in a linear order. A position is itself an abstract data type that supports the following simple method:

element(): Return the element stored at this position.
Input: None; *Output:* Object.

A position is always defined ***relatively***, that is, in terms of its neighbors. In a list, a position p will always be "after" some position q and "before" some position s (unless p is the first or last position). A position p, which is associated with some element e in a list S, does not change, even if the rank of e changes in S, unless we explicitly remove e (and, hence, destroy position p). Moreover, the position p does not change even if we replace or swap the element e stored at p with another element. These facts about positions allow us to define a set of position-based list methods that take position objects as parameters and also provide position objects as return values.

5.2.3 The List Abstract Data Type

Using the concept of position to encapsulate the idea of "node" in a list, we can define another type of sequence ADT, called simply the ***list*** ADT. This ADT supports the following methods for a list S:

first(): Return the position of the first element of S; an error occurs if S is empty.
Input: None; *Output:* Position.

last(): Return the position of the last element of S; an error occurs if S is empty.
Input: None; *Output:* Position.

prev(p): Return the position of the element of S preceding the one at position p; an error occurs if p is the first position.
Input: Position; *Output:* Position.

next(p): Return the position of the element of S following the one at position p; an error occurs if p is the last position.
Input: Position; *Output:* Position.

The above methods allow us to refer to relative positions in a list, starting at the beginning or end, and to move incrementally up or down the list. These positions can intuitively be thought of as nodes in the list, but note that there are no specific references to node objects. Moreover, if we provide a position as an argument to a list method, then that position must represent a valid position in that list.

List Update Methods

In addition to the above methods and the generic methods size and isEmpty, we also include the following update methods for the list ADT, which take position objects as parameters and/or provide position objects as return values.

replace(p,e): Replace the element at position p with e, returning the element formerly at position p.
Input: Position and object; **Output:** Object.

insertFirst(e): Insert a new element e into S as the first element and return the position of e.
Input: Object; **Output:** Position.

insertLast(e): Insert a new element e into S as the last element and return the position of e.
Input: Object; **Output:** Position.

insertBefore(p,e): Insert a new element e into S before position p and return the position of e.
Input: Position and object; **Output:** Position.

insertAfter(p,e): Insert a new element e into S after position p and return the position of e.
Input: Position and object; **Output:** Position.

remove(p): Remove from S the element at position p.
Input: Position; **Output:** Object.

The list ADT allows us to view an ordered collection of objects in terms of their places, without worrying about the exact way those places are represented. (See Figure 5.5.)

Also, note that there is some redundancy in the above repertory of operations for the list ADT. For example, we can perform operation insertFirst(e) with insertBefore(first(), e), and operation insertLast(e) with insertAfter(last(), e). The redundant methods can be viewed as shortcuts for common operations that help code readability.

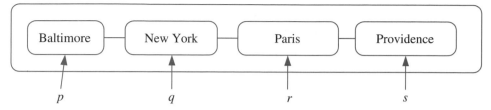

Figure 5.5: A list. The positions in the current order are p, q, r, and s.

Note that an error condition occurs if a position passed as argument to one of the list operations is invalid. Reasons for a position p to be invalid include:

- $p =$ **null**
- p was previously deleted from the list
- p is a position of a different list
- p is the first position of the list and we call prev(p)
- p is the last position of the list and we call next(p).

We illustrate the operations of the list ADT in the following example.

Example 5.4: *We show below a series of operations for an initially empty list S. We use variables p_1, p_2, and so on, to denote different positions, and we show the object currently stored at such a position in parentheses.*

Operation	Output	S
insertFirst(8)	$p_1(8)$	(8)
insertAfter(p_1,5)	$p_2(5)$	(8,5)
insertBefore(p_2,3)	$p_3(3)$	(8,3,5)
insertFirst(9)	$p_4(9)$	(9,8,3,5)
prev(p_3)	$p_1(8)$	(9,8,3,5)
last()	$p_2(5)$	(9,8,3,5)
remove(p_4)	9	(8,3,5)
replace(p_3,7)	3	(8,7,5)
insertAfter(first(),2)	$p_5(2)$	(8,2,7,5)

The list ADT, with its built-in notion of position, is useful in a number of settings. For example, a program that simulates a game of cards could model each person's hand as a list. Since most people keep cards of the same suit together, inserting and removing cards from a person's hand could be implemented using the methods of the list ADT, with the positions being determined by a natural ordering of the suits. Likewise, a simple text editor embeds the notion of positional insertion and removal, since such editors typically perform all updates relative to a *cursor*, which represents the current position in the list of characters of text being edited.

A Java interface representing the position ADT is given in Code Fragment 5.4 and an interface for the list ADT is given in Code Fragment 5.5. The List interface uses the following exceptions to indicate error conditions.

BoundaryViolationException: thrown if an attempt is made at accessing an element whose position is outside the range of positions of the list (for example, calling method next on the last position of the sequence).

InvalidPositionException: thrown if a position provided as argument is not valid (for example, it is a null reference or it has no associated list).

```java
public interface Position {
  /** Returns the element stored at this position. */
  Object element();
}
```

Code Fragment 5.4: Java interface for the position ADT.

```java
public interface List {
  /** Returns the number of elements in this list. */
  public int size();
  /** Returns whether the list is empty. */
  public boolean isEmpty();
  /** Returns the first node in the list. */
  public Position first();
  /** Returns the last node in the list. */
  public Position last();
  /** Returns the node after a given node in the list. */
  public Position next(Position p)
    throws InvalidPositionException, BoundaryViolationException;
  /** Returns the node before a given node in the list. */
  public Position prev(Position p)
    throws InvalidPositionException, BoundaryViolationException;
  /** Inserts an element at the front of the list. */
  public Position insertFirst(Object e);
  /** Inserts and element at the back of the list. */
  public Position insertLast(Object e);
  /** Inserts an element after the given node in the list. */
  public Position insertAfter(Position p, Object e)
    throws InvalidPositionException;
  /** Inserts an element before the given node in the list. */
  public Position insertBefore(Position p, Object e)
    throws InvalidPositionException;
  /** Removes a node from the list. */
  public Object remove(Position p) throws InvalidPositionException;
  /** Replaces the element stored at the given node. */
  public Object replace(Position p, Object e) throws InvalidPositionException;
}
```

Code Fragment 5.5: Java interface for the list ADT.

5.2.4 Doubly Linked List Implementation

Suppose we wish to implement the list ADT using a doubly linked list. We can simply make the nodes of the linked list implement the position ADT. That is, we have each node implement the Position interface and therefore define a method element(), which returns the element stored at the node. Thus, the nodes themselves act as positions. They are viewed internally by the linked list as nodes, but from the outside, they are viewed only as generic positions. In the internal view, we can give each node v instance variables prev and next that respectively refer to the predecessor and successor nodes of v (which could in fact be header or trailer sentinel nodes marking the beginning and end of the list). Instead of using variables prev and next directly, we define methods getPrev, setPrev, getNext, and setNext of a node to access and modify these variables. In Code Fragment 5.6, we show a Java class DNode for the nodes of a doubly linked list implementing the position ADT. Note that the prev and next instance variables in DNode are private references to other DNode objects.

```
public class DNode implements Position {
    private DNode prev, next;      // References to the nodes before and after
    private Object element;        // Element stored in this position
    // Constructor
    public DNode(DNode newPrev, DNode newNext, Object elem) {
        prev = newPrev;
        next = newNext;
        element = elem;
    }
    // Method from interface Position
    public Object element() throws InvalidPositionException {
        if ((prev == null) && (next == null))
            throw new InvalidPositionException("Position is not in a list!");
        return element;
    }
    // Accessor methods
    public DNode getNext() { return next; }
    public DNode getPrev() { return prev; }
    // Update methods
    public void setNext(DNode newNext) { next = newNext; }
    public void setPrev(DNode newPrev) { prev = newPrev; }
    public void setElement(Object newElement) { element = newElement; }
}
```

Code Fragment 5.6: Class DNode realizing a node of a doubly linked list and implementing the Position interface (ADT).

Given a position p in S, we can "unwrap" p to reveal the underlying node v. This is accomplished by *casting* the position to a node. Once we have node v, we can, for example, implement method prev(p) with v.getPrev (unless the node returned by v.getPrev is the header, in which case we signal an error). Therefore, positions in a doubly linked list implementation can be supported in an object-oriented way without any additional time or space overhead.

Consider how we might implement the insertAfter(p, e) method, for inserting an element e after position p. We create a new node v to hold the element e, link v into its place in the list, and then update the next and prev references of v's two new neighbors. This method is given in pseudo-code in Code Fragment 5.7, and is illustrated in Figure 5.6. Recalling the use of header and trailer sentinels (Section 4.5.2), note that this algorithm works even if p is the last real position.

Algorithm insertAfter(p, e):
    Create a new node v
    v.setElement(e)
    v.setPrev(p)   {link v to its predecessor}
    v.setNext(p.getNext())   {link v to its successor}
    (p.getNext()).setPrev(v)   {link p's old successor to v}
    p.setNext(v)   {link p to its new successor, v}
    return v {the position for the element e}

Code Fragment 5.7: Inserting an element e after a position p in a linked list.

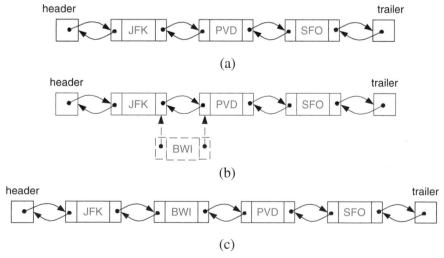

Figure 5.6: Adding a new node after the position for "JFK": (a) before the insertion; (b) creating node v with element "BWI" and linking it in; (c) after the insertion.

The algorithms for methods insertBefore, insertFirst, and insertLast are similar to that for method insertAfter; we leave their details as an exercise (R-5.4). Next, consider the remove(p) method, which removes the element e stored at position p. To perform this operation we link the two neighbors of p to refer to one another as new neighbors—linking out p. Note that after p is linked out, no nodes will be pointing to p; hence, the garbage collector can reclaim the space for p. This algorithm is given in Code Fragment 5.8 and is illustrated in Figure 5.7. Recalling our use of sentinels, note that this algorithm works even if p is the first, last, or only real position in the list.

Algorithm remove(p):

    $t \leftarrow p$.element   {a temporary variable to hold the return value}

    (p.getPrev()).setNext(p.getNext())   {linking out p}

    (p.getNext()).setPrev(p.getPrev())

    p.setPrev(**null**)   {invalidating the position p}

    p.setNext(**null**)

    return t

Code Fragment 5.8: Removing an element e stored at a position p in a linked list.

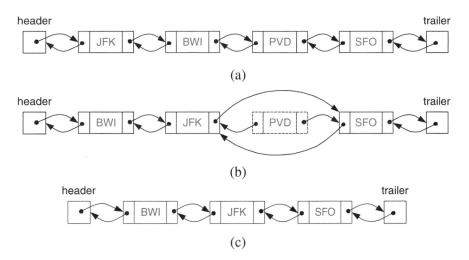

Figure 5.7: Removing the object stored at the position for "PVD": (a) before the removal; (b) linking out the old node; (c) after the removal (and garbage collection).

In conclusion, using a doubly linked list, we can perform all the methods of the list ADT in $O(1)$ time. Thus, a doubly linked list is an efficient implementation of the list ADT.

A List Implementation in Java

Portions of the Java class NodeList, which implements the list ADT using a doubly linked list, are shown in Code Fragments 5.9–5.11. Code Fragment 5.9 shows NodeList's instance variables, its constructor, and a "convenience" method, check-Position, which performs some safety checks and "unwraps" a position, casting it back to a DNode object. Code Fragment 5.10 shows additional accessor and update methods. Code Fragment 5.11 shows additional update methods.

```java
public class NodeList implements List {
  protected int numElts;                  // Number of elements in the list
  protected DNode header, trailer;        // Special sentinels
  /** Constructor that creates an empty list; O(1) time */
  public NodeList() {
    numElts = 0;
    header = new DNode(null, null, null);    // create header
    trailer = new DNode(header, null, null);  // create trailer
    header.setNext(trailer);        // make header and trailer point to each other
  }
  /** Checks if position is valid for this list and converts it to
   *  DNode if it is valid; O(1) time */
  protected DNode checkPosition(Position p) throws InvalidPositionException {
    if (p == null)
      throw new InvalidPositionException
        ("Null position passed to NodeList");
    if (p == header)
        throw new InvalidPositionException
          ("The header node is not a valid position");
    if (p == trailer)
        throw new InvalidPositionException
          ("The trailer node is not a valid position");
    try {
      DNode temp = (DNode)p;
      if ((temp.getPrev() == null) || (temp.getNext() == null))
        throw new InvalidPositionException
          ("Position does not belong to a valid NodeList");
      return temp;
    } catch (ClassCastException e) {
      throw new InvalidPositionException
        ("Position is of wrong type for this list");
    }
  }
}
```

Code Fragment 5.9: Portions of the NodeList class implementing the list ADT with a doubly linked list. (Continues in Code Fragments 5.10 and 5.11.)

```
/** Returns the number of elements in the list;   O(1) time */
public int size() { return numElts; }
/** Returns whether the list is empty;   O(1) time  */
public boolean isEmpty() { return (numElts == 0); }
/** Returns the first position in the list; O(1) time */
public Position first()
    throws EmptyListException {
  if (isEmpty())
    throw new EmptyListException("List is empty");
  return header.getNext();
}
/** Returns the position before the given one; O(1) time */
public Position prev(Position p)
    throws InvalidPositionException, BoundaryViolationException {
  DNode v = checkPosition(p);
  DNode prev = v.getPrev();
  if (prev == header)
    throw new BoundaryViolationException
      ("Cannot advance past the beginning of the list");
  return prev;
}
/** Insert the given element before the given position, returning
  * the new position; O(1) time  */
public Position insertBefore(Position p, Object element)
    throws InvalidPositionException {                    //
  DNode v = checkPosition(p);
  numElts++;
  DNode newNode = new DNode(v.getPrev(), v, element);
  v.getPrev().setNext(newNode);
  v.setPrev(newNode);
  return newNode;
}
```

Code Fragment 5.10: Portions of the NodeList class implementing the list ADT with a doubly linked list. (Continued from Code Fragment 5.9. Continues in Code Fragment 5.11.)

```
/** Insert the given element at the beginning of the list, returning
 * the new position; O(1) time  */
public Position insertFirst(Object element) {
  numElts++;
  DNode newNode = new DNode(header, header.getNext(), element);
  header.getNext().setPrev(newNode);
  header.setNext(newNode);
  return newNode;
}
/**Remove the given position from the list; O(1) time */
public Object remove(Position p)
    throws InvalidPositionException {
  DNode v = checkPosition(p);
  numElts--;
  DNode vPrev = v.getPrev();
  DNode vNext = v.getNext();
  vPrev.setNext(vNext);
  vNext.setPrev(vPrev);
  Object vElem = v.element();
  // unlink the position from the list and make it invalid
  v.setNext(null);
  v.setPrev(null);
  return vElem;
}
/** Replace the element at the given position with the new element
 * and return the old element; O(1) time  */
public Object replace(Position p, Object element)
    throws InvalidPositionException {
  DNode v = checkPosition(p);
  Object oldElt = v.element();
  v.setElement(element);
  return oldElt;
}
```

Code Fragment 5.11: Portions of the NodeList class implementing the list ADT with a doubly linked list. (Continued from Code Fragments 5.10 and 5.11.) Note that the mechanism used to invalidate a position in the remove method is consistent with one of the checks performed in the checkPosition convenience function.

5.3 Sequences

In this section, we define a generalized sequence ADT that includes all the methods of the vector and list ADTs. This ADT therefore provides access to its elements using both ranks and positions, and is a versatile data structure for a wide variety of applications.

5.3.1 The Sequence Abstract Data Type

A *sequence* is an ADT that supports all the methods of both the vector ADT (discussed in Section 5.1) and the list ADT (discussed in Section 5.2), plus the following two "bridging" methods that provide connections between ranks and positions:

atRank(r): Return the position of the element with rank r; an error condition occurs if $r < 0$ or $r > \text{size}() - 1$.
Input: Integer; *Output:* Position.

rankOf(p): Return the rank of the element at position p.
Input: Position; *Output:* Integer.

Multiple Inheritance in the Sequence ADT

The definition of the sequence ADT is an example of *multiple inheritance* (Section 2.4.2), since the sequence inherits methods from two other "super" ADTs. Therefore, its methods include the union of the methods of its super ADTs. See Code Fragment 5.12 for a Java specification.

```
/**
 * An interface for a sequence, a data structure supporting all
 * operations of a vector and a list.
 */
public interface Sequence extends List, Vector {
    /** Returns the position containing the element at the given rank. */
    public Position atRank(int r) throws BoundaryViolationException;
    /** Returns the rank of the element stored at the given position. */
    public int rankOf(Position p) throws InvalidPositionException;
}
```

Code Fragment 5.12: The Sequence interface defined via multiple inheritance.

5.3.2 Implementing a Sequence with a Doubly Linked List

One possible implementation of a sequence, of course, is with a doubly linked list. Then, all of the methods of the list ADT can be easily implemented to run in $O(1)$ time each. But the methods from the vector ADT can also be implemented with a doubly linked list, though in a less efficient manner. In particular, if we want the methods from the list ADT to run efficiently (using position objects to indicate where accesses and updates should occur), then we can no longer explicitly store the ranks of elements in the sequence. Hence, to perform the operation elemAtRank(r), we must perform link "hopping" from one of the ends of the list until we locate the node storing the element with rank r. As a slight optimization, we can start hopping from the closest end of the sequence, achieving a running time that is

$$O(\min(r+1, n-r)),$$

where n is the number of elements. The worst case occurs when

$$r = \lfloor n/2 \rfloor.$$

Thus, the running time is still $O(n)$.

Operations insertAtRank(r, e) and removeAtRank(r) also perform link hopping to locate the node storing the element with rank r, and then insert or delete a node, as shown in Figures 5.6. and 5.7. The running time of this implementation of insertAtRank(r, e) and removeAtRank(r) is

$$O(\min(r+1, n-r+1)),$$

which is $O(n)$. One advantage of this approach is that, if $r = 0$ or $r = n - 1$, as is the case in the adaptation of the vector ADT to the deque ADT given in Section 5.1.1, then insertAtRank and removeAtRank run in $O(1)$ time.

In Code Fragment 5.13, we show portions of a Java implementation of the Sequence interface by means of a doubly linked list. Note that this implementation is a class, NodeSequence, that extends (through class inheritance) the implementation of a list given in Section 5.3.2. Like its parent class, NodeList, the class NodeSequence uses class DNode for the implementation of the nodes of a doubly linked list. It also uses an internal convenience method, checkRank(r) that throws a BoundaryViolationException when its argument r is an invalid rank, that is, if $r < 0$ or $r > n - 1$.

```
/** Implementation of a sequence by means of a doubly linked list. */
public class NodeSequence extends NodeList implements Sequence {
  /** Checks whether the given rank is in the range [0, n - 1] */
  protected void checkRank(int r, int n)
    throws BoundaryViolationException {
    if (r < 0 || r >= n)
      throw new BoundaryViolationException("Illegal rank: " + r);
  }
  /** Returns the position containing the element at the given rank;
   * O(n) time. */
  public Position atRank (int rank) {
    DNode node;
    checkRank(rank, size());
    if (rank <= size()/2) { // scan forward from the head
      node = header.getNext();
      for (int i=0; i < rank; i++)
        node = node.getNext();
    }
    else { // scan backward from the tail
      node = trailer.getPrev();
      for (int i=1; i < size()−rank; i++)
        node = node.getPrev();
    }
    return node;
  }
  /** Inserts an element at the given rank; O(n) time. */
  public void insertAtRank (int rank, Object element)
    throws BoundaryViolationException {
    checkRank(rank, size() + 1);
    if (rank == size())
      insertLast(element);
    else {
      insertBefore(atRank(rank), element);
    }
  }
  /** Removes the element stored at the given rank; O(n) time. */
  public Object removeAtRank (int rank)
    throws BoundaryViolationException {
    checkRank(rank, size());
    return remove(atRank(rank));
  }
```

Code Fragment 5.13: Portions of an implementation of a sequence by means of a doubly linked-list. Class NodeSequence extends class NodeList shown in Code Fragments 5.9–5.11.

5.3.3   Implementing a Sequence with an Array

Suppose we want to implement a sequence S by storing each element e of S in a cell $A[i]$ of an array A. We can define a position object p to hold an index i and a reference to array A, as instance variables. We can then implement method element(p) by simply returning $A[i]$. A major drawback with this approach, however, is that the cells in A have no way to reference their corresponding positions. Thus, after performing an insertFirst operation, we have no way of informing the existing positions in S that their ranks each went up by 1 (remember that positions in a sequence are always defined relative to their neighboring positions, not their ranks). Hence, if we are going to implement a general sequence with an array, we need a different approach.

Consider an alternate solution in which, instead of storing the elements of S in array A, we store a new kind of position object in each cell of A, and we store elements in positions. The new position object p holds the index i and the element e associated with p.

With this data structure, illustrated in Figure 5.8, we can easily scan through the array to update the index variable i for each position whose rank changes because of an insertion or deletion.

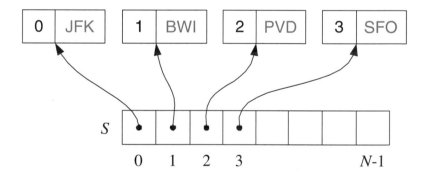

Figure 5.8: An array-based implementation of the sequence ADT.

Efficiency Trade-Offs with an Array-Based Sequence

In this array implementation of a sequence, the methods insertFirst, insertBefore, insertAfter, and remove take $O(n)$ time because we have to shift position objects to make room for the new position or to fill in the hole created by the removal of the old position (just as in the insert and remove methods based on rank). All the other position-based methods take $O(1)$ time.

5.4 Favorite Lists and the Move-to-Front Heuristic

Suppose we would like to maintain a collection of elements while keeping track of the number of times each element is accessed. Keeping such access counts allows us to know which elements are among the "top ten" most popular, for instance. Example of such scenarios include a Web browser that keeps track of the most popular Web addresses (or URLs) a user visits or a photo album program that maintains a list of the most popular images a user views. In addition, a favorites list could be used in a graphical user interface (GUI) to keep track of the most popular buttons used in a pull-down menu, and then present the user with condensed pull-downs containing the most popular options. Therefore, in this section, we consider how we can implement a *favorite list* ADT, which supports the size() and isEmpty() methods as well as the following:

> access(e): Access the element e, incrementing its access count, and adding it to the favorites list if it is not already present.
> ***Input:*** Object; ***Output:*** None.

> remove(e): Remove element e from the favorites list and return e.
> ***Input:*** Object; ***Output:*** Object.

> top(k): Return a list of the k most accessed elements.
> ***Input:*** None; ***Output:*** List.

5.4.1 Using a Sorted List and a Nested Class

The first implementation we consider (in Code Fragments 5.14–5.15) is to build a class, FavoriteList, storing references to accessed objects in a linked list ordered by nonincreasing access counts. This class also uses a feature of Java that allows us to define a related class nested inside an (enclosing) class definition. Such a *nested class* must be declared **static**, to indicate that this definition is related to the enclosing class, not any specific instance of that class. Using nested classes allows us to define "helper" or "support" classes that can be protected from outside use.

In this case, the nested class, Entry, stores, for each element e in our list, a pair (c, v), where c is the access count for e and v is a ***value*** reference to the element e itself. Each time an element is accessed, we find it in the linked list (adding it if is not already there) and increment its access count. Removing an element amounts to finding it and taking it out of our linked list. Returning the k most accessed elements simply involves our copying the entry values into an output list according to their order in the internal linked list.

```
public class FavoriteList {
  protected List fList;                    // List of entries
  /** Constructor; O(1) time */
  public FavoriteList() { fList = new NodeList(); }
  /** Return the number of elements in the list; O(1) time */
  public int size() { return fList.size(); }
  /** Return true iff the list is empty; O(1) time */
  public boolean isEmpty() { return fList.isEmpty(); }
  /** Find the position of an element; O(n) time */
  protected Position find(Object obj) {
    if (fList.isEmpty()) return null;
    Position p;
    for (p = fList.first(); p != fList.last(); p = fList.next(p))
      if (value(p).equals(obj)) return p; // found it
    if (value(p).equals(obj)) return p; // found it at end
    return null;            // we have not found it
    }
  /** Find and remove a given object if it's in the list; O(n) time */
  public Object remove(Object obj) {
    Position pos = find(obj);        // Search for obj in the favorites list
    if (pos == null) return null;    // obj is not in the list in this case
    Entry ent = entry(pos);
    fList.remove(pos);    // remove this entry from the favorites list
    return ent.value();   // return the removed object
    }
  /** Incr. access count for obj or insert it if it's not present; O(rank(obj)) time */
  public void access(Object obj) {
    Position pos = find(obj);          // search for obj in the favorites list
    if (pos != null)                   // obj is in the favorites list
      entry(pos).incrementCount();     // increment obj's access count
    else                               // obj is not in list, so add it at end
      pos = fList.insertLast(new Entry(obj));
    moveUp(pos);                       // We may want to move obj up in fList
    }
  /** Move up an entry in the favorites list if needed;  O(n) time */
  protected void moveUp(Position pos) {
    Entry ent = entry(pos);            // the entry for obj
    for (Position prev=null; pos != fList.first();) { // Move ent to correct position
      prev = fList.prev(pos);          // the position before obj's
      if (ent.count() <= entry(prev).count()) break; // obj now at correct position
      Object temp = prev.element();    // move obj up in the favorites list
      fList.replace(prev,pos.element());
      fList.replace(pos,temp);
      pos = fList.prev(pos);           // go to prev position (new pos. for ent)
      }
    }
  }
```

Code Fragment 5.14: A FavoritesList class. (Continues in Code Fragment 5.15.)

```
/** Return the k most accessed elements, for a given k;  O(k) time */
public List top(int k) {
  if (k < 0 || k > size())
    throw new IllegalArgumentException("Invalid argument");
  List T = new NodeList(); // top-k list
  if (!isEmpty()) {
    Position p = fList.first();
    for (int i = 1; i < k; i++) {
      T.insertLast(value(p));
      p = fList.next(p);
    }
    T.insertLast(value(p));
  }
  return T;
}
/** An overridden toString method, for visualization purposes */
public String toString() { return fList.toString(); }
/** Helper method */
protected Object value(Position p) { return ((Entry) p.element()).value(); }
/** Helper method */
protected Entry entry(Position p) { return (Entry) p.element(); }
/**
 * Our Entry class - an inner class to keep track of entries and
 * their access counts.
 */
protected static class Entry {
  private int count;
  private Object value;
  /** Default constructor */
  Entry() { }
  /** The expected constructor */
  Entry(Object v) { count = 1; value = v; }
  /** Increment the Entry's count */
  public int incrementCount() { return ++count; }
  /** Return the count */
  public int count() { return count; }
  /** Return the value */
  public Object value() { return value; }
  /** For visualization purposes */
  public String toString() { return "[" + count + "," + value + "]"; }
}
} // End of FavoriteList class
```

Code Fragment 5.15: A FavoriteList class, including a nested class, Entry, for representing elements and their access count. (Continued from Code Fragment 5.14.)

5.4.2   Using a List with the Move-to-Front Heuristic

The previous implementation of a favorite list performs the access(e) method in time proportional to the rank of e in the favorite list. That is, if e is the kth most popular element in the favorite list, then accessing it takes $O(k)$ time. In many real-life access sequences, including those formed by the visits that users make to Web pages, it is common that once an element is accessed, it is likely to be accessed again in the near future. Such scenarios are said to possess *locality of reference*.

A *heuristic*, or rule of thumb, that attempts to take advantage of the locality of reference that is present in an access sequence is the *move-to-front heuristic*. To apply this heuristic, each time we access an element we move it all the way to the front of the list. Our hope, of course, is that this element will then be accessed again in the near future. Consider, for example, a scenario in which we have n elements and the following series of n^2 accesses:

- element 1 is accessed n times
- element 2 is accessed n times
- $\cdots$
- element n is accessed n times.

If we store the elements sorted by their access counts, inserting each element the first time it is accessed, then

- each access to element 1 runs in $O(1)$ time
- each access to element 2 runs in $O(2)$ time
- $\cdots$
- each access to element n runs in $O(n)$ time.

Thus, the total time for performing the series of accesses is proportional to

$$n + 2n + 3n + \cdots + n \cdot n = n(1 + 2 + 3 + \cdots + n) = n \cdot \frac{n(n+1)}{2},$$

which is $O(n^3)$.

On the other hand, if we use the move-to-front heuristic, inserting each element the first time it is accessed, then

- each access to element 1 takes $O(1)$ time
- each access to element 2 takes $O(1)$ time
- $\cdots$
- each access to element n runs in $O(1)$ time.

So the running time for performing all the accesses in this case is $O(n^2)$. Thus, the move-to-front implementation has faster access times for this scenario. This benefit comes at a cost, however.

Implementing the Move-to-Front Heuristic in Java

In Code Fragment 5.16, we give an implementation of a favorite list using the move-to-front heuristic. We implement the move-to-front approach in this case by defining a new class, FavoriteListMTF, which extends the FavoriteList class and then overwrites the definitions of the moveUp and top methods. The moveUp method in this case simply removes the accessed element from its present position in the linked list and then inserts this element back in this list at the front. The top method, on the other hand, is more complicated.

The Trade-Offs with the Move-to-Front Heuristic

Now that we are no longer maintaining the favorite list as a list of entries ordered by their value's access counts, when we are asked to find the k most accessed elements, we need to search for them. In particular, we can implement method top(k) as follows:

1. We copy the entries of our favorite list into another list, C, and we create an empty list, T.
2. We scan list C k times. In each scan, we find an entry of C with the largest access count, remove this entry from C, and insert its value at the end of T.
3. We return list T.

This implementation of method top takes $O(kn)$ time. Thus, when k is a constant, method top runs in $O(n)$ time. This occurs, for example, when we want to get the "top ten" list. However, if k is proportional to n, then top runs in $O(n^2)$ time. This occurs, for example, when we want a "top 25%" list.

Still, the move-to-front approach is just a heuristic, or rule of thumb, for there are access sequences where using the move-to-front approach is slower than simply keeping the favorite list ordered by access counts. In addition, it trades off the potential speed of performing accesses that possess locality of reference, for a slower reporting of the top elements.

5.4.3 Possible Uses of a Favorites List

In Code Fragment 5.17, we use an example application of our favorite list implementations to solve the problem of maintaining the most popular URLs in a simulated sequence of Web page accesses. This program accesses a set of URLs in decreasing order and then pops up a window showing the most popular Web page accessed in the simulation.

```
public class FavoriteListMTF extends FavoriteList {
  /** Default constructor */
  public FavoriteListMTF() { }
  /** Helper method */
  protected int count(Position p) {
    return ((Entry) p.element()).count();
  }
  /** Move up an entry to the first position;  O(1) time  */
  protected void moveUp(Position pos) { fList.insertFirst(fList.remove(pos)); }
  /** Return the k most accessed elements, for a given k; O(kn) time */
  public List top(int k) {
    if (k < 0 || k > size())
      throw new IllegalArgumentException("Invalid argument");
    List T = new NodeList(); // top-k list
    if (!isEmpty()) {
      int n = fList.size();
      // copy entries into a temporary list
      List C = new NodeList(); // copy of the list of entries
      Position p = fList.first();
      for (int i = 1; i < n; i++) {
        C.insertLast(p.element());
        p = fList.next(p);
      }
      C.insertLast(p.element());
      // find the top k elements, one at a time
      for (int j = 1; j <= k; j++) {
        Position maxPos = null;
        int maxCount = 0;
        Position q = C.first();
        while (true) {
          if (count(q) > maxCount) {
            maxCount = count(q);
            maxPos = q;
          }
          if (q == C.last()) break;
          q = C.next(q);
        }
        T.insertLast(value(maxPos));
        C.remove(maxPos);
      }
    }
    return T;
  }
}
```

Code Fragment 5.16: Class FavoriteListMTF class, which implements the move-to-front heuristic.

```java
import java.io.*;
import javax.swing.*;
import java.awt.*;
import java.net.*;
import java.util.Random;
// Example program for the FavoriteList and FavoriteListMTF classes
public class FavoriteTester {
  public static void main(String[] args) {
    String[] urlArray = { "http://wiley.com",
      "http://datastructures.net", "http://algorithmdesign.net",
      "http://www.brown.edu", "http://uci.edu" };
    FavoriteList L1 = new FavoriteList();
    FavoriteListMTF L2 = new FavoriteListMTF();
    int n = 20;
    // Simulation scenario: access n times a random URL
    Random rand = new Random();
    for (int k=0;  k<n; k++) {
      int i = rand.nextInt(urlArray.length);
      String url = urlArray[i];
      System.out.println(url);
      L1.access(url);
      System.out.println("L1 = " + L1);
      L2.access(url);
      System.out.println("L2 = " + L2);
    }
    int t = L1.size()/2;
    System.out.println("Top " + t + " in L1 = " + L1.top(t));
    System.out.println("Top " + t + " in L2 = " + L2.top(t));
    // Pop up a window of the most popular Web site in L1
    try {
      String popular = (String) L1.top(1).first().element();
      JEditorPane jep = new JEditorPane(popular);
      jep.setEditable(false);
      JFrame frame = new JFrame(popular);
      frame.getContentPane().add(new JScrollPane(jep), BorderLayout.CENTER);
      frame.setSize(640, 480);
      frame.setVisible(true);
    } catch (IOException e) { // ignore I/O exceptions
    }
  }
}
```

Code Fragment 5.17: Illustrating the use of the FavoritesList and FavoritesListMTF classes for counting Web page access counts. This simulation randomly accesses several web pages and then displays the most popular page.

5.5 Iterators

A typical computation on a vector, list, or sequence is to march through its elements in order, one at a time, for example, to look for a specific element.

5.5.1 A Simple Iterator ADT

An *iterator* is a software design pattern that abstracts the process of scanning through a collection of elements one element at a time. An iterator consists of a sequence S, a current element in S, and a way of stepping to the next element in S and making it the current element. Thus, an iterator extends the concept of the position ADT we introduced in Section 5.2. In fact, a position can be thought of as an iterator that doesn't go anywhere. An iterator encapsulates the concepts of "place" and "next" in a collection of objects.

We define the *iterator* ADT as supporting the following two methods:

hasNext: Test whether there are elements left in the iterator.
Input: None; *Output:* Boolean.

next: Return the next element in the iterator.
Input: None; *Output:* Object.

Note that the iterator ADT has the notion of the "current" element in a traversal of a sequence. The first element in an iterator is returned by the first call to the method next, assuming of course that the iterator contains at least one element.

An iterator provides a unified scheme to access all the elements of a collection of objects in a way that is independent from the specific organization of the collection. An iterator for a vector, list, or sequence should return the elements according to their linear ordering.

Simple Iterators in Java

Java provides an iterator through its java.util.Iterator interface. This interface supports an additional method to remove the previously returned element from the collection. This functionality (removing elements through an iterator) is somewhat controversial from an object-oriented viewpoint, however, and it is not surprising that its implementation by classes is optional. Incidentally, Java also provides the java.util.Enumeration interface, which is historically older than the iterator interface and uses names hasMoreElements and nextElement.

Using Iterators in Lists and Other ADTs

In order to provide a unified generic mechanism for scanning through a data structure, ADTs storing collections of objects should support the following method:

> elements(): Return an iterator of the elements in the collection.
> ***Input:*** None; ***Output:*** Iterator.

This method is supported by the java.util.Vector class, for example (except that it returns an Enumeration). In Code Fragment 5.18, we show an example of using a java.util.Iterator for printing the elements of a java.util.Vector, using the iterator() method (which is similar to the elements() method, but returns a java.util.Iterator).

```
public static void printVector(java.util.Vector vec) {
  java.util.Iterator iter = vec.iterator();
  while (iter.hasNext()) {
    System.out.println(iter.next());
  }
}
```

Code Fragment 5.18: Example of a Java iterator used to print the elements of a vector.

For ADTs that support the notion of position, such as the list and sequence ADTs, we can also provide the following method:

> positions(): Return an iterator of the positions in the collection.
> ***Input:*** None; ***Output:*** Iterator.

This method can make it simple for us to specify computations that need to loop through the positions of a container.

To guarantee that a list supports the above methods, for example, we could add these methods to the List interface, as shown in Code Fragment 5.19.

```
public interface List {
  // ... the other List methods ...
  /** Returns an iterator of all the nodes in the list. */
  public Iterator positions();
  /** Returns an iterator of all the elements in the list. */
  public Iterator elements();
}
```

Code Fragment 5.19: Adding iterator methods to the List interface.

Therefore, let us assume that our vectors, lists, and sequences support the methods positions() and elements().

5.5.2 Implementing Iterators

A first approach to the implementation of an iterator for a collection of elements consists of taking a "snapshot" of the collection and storing it in a data structure that supports sequential access to its elements. For example, we can insert all the elements of the collection into a stack. In this case, method hasNext() corresponds to !isEmpty(), while method next() corresponds to pop(). If there is a given order in which the elements should be returned by the iterator, we should insert the elements into the stack in reverse order. Similarly, we can realize an iterator with a queue, which allows us to insert the elements in order. With this approach, methods positions() and elements() take $O(n)$ time when called on a collection of size n.

An alternative approach, shown in Code Fragment 5.20, consists of keeping track of the current element of the iterator. With this approach, methods positions() and elements() take $O(1)$ time. We show in Code Fragment 5.21 how this approach is used to implement methods elements() and positions() in class NodeList.

```
public class PositionIterator implements Iterator {
  protected List list; // the underlying list
  protected Position cur; // the current (next) position
  public PositionIterator() { } // default constructor
  public PositionIterator(List L) { // preferred constructor
    list = L;
    if (list.isEmpty()) cur = null; // list is empty
    else cur = list.first(); // start with the first position
  }
  public boolean hasNext() { return (cur != null); }
  public Object next() throws NoSuchElementException {
    if (!hasNext()) throw new NoSuchElementException("No next position");
    Position toReturn = cur;
    if (cur == list.last()) cur = null; // no positions left
    else cur = list.next(cur); // move cursor to the next position
    return toReturn;
  }
}
```

Code Fragment 5.20: A position iterator class.

```
/** Returns an iterator of all the nodes in the list. */
public Iterator positions() { return new PositionIterator(this); }
/** Returns an iterator of all the elements in the list. */
public Iterator elements() { return new ElementIterator(this); }
```

Code Fragment 5.21: The elements() and positions() methods of class NodeList.

5.5.3 Lists and Iterators in Java

It is generally considered dangerous practice to use an iterator while modifying the contents of its container. If insertions, deletions, or replacements are required at a certain "place" in a container, it is safer to use a position to specify this location. Indeed, most of the implementations of the java.util.Iterator have a "fail-fast" feature that immediately invalidates the iterator if its underlying container is modified unexpectedly. Of course, this danger is not shared by position objects, which are used in the list ADT to specify update locations, since position objects do not move.

The LinkedList class in the java.util package does not expose a position concept to users in its API. Instead, the preferred way to access and update a LinkedList object in Java, without using ranks, is to use a ListIterator that is generated by the linked list, using a listIterator() method. Such an iterator provides forward and backward traversal methods as well as local update methods. It views its current position as being before the first element, between two elements, or after the last element. That is, it uses a list *cursor*, much like a screen cursor is viewed as being located between two characters on a screen. Specifically, the java.util.ListIterator interface includes the following methods:

add(e):	Add the element e at the current position of the iterator.
hasNext():	True if and only if there is an element after the current position of the iterator.
hasPrevious():	True if and only if there is an element before the current position of the iterator.
previous():	Returns the element e before the current position and sets the current position to be before e.
next():	Returns the element e after the current position and sets the current position to be after e.
nextIndex():	Return the index (rank) of the next element.
previousIndex():	Return the index (rank) of the previous element.
set(e):	Replaces the element returned by the previous next or previous operation with e.
remove():	Removes the element returned by the previous next or previous operation.

Java allows many list iterators to be traversing a linked list at the same time. But if one of them modifies the linked list (using an add or remove method), then all the other iterators become invalid.

The java.util.List Interface and Its Implementations

Java provides functionality similar to our sequence ADT in the java.util.List interface, which is implemented with an array in the java.util classes ArrayList and Vector and with a linked list in the LinkedList class. There are naturally some trade-offs between these two implementations. Moreover, Java uses iterators to achieve a similar functionality that our sequence ADT derives from positions. Table 5.4 shows corresponding methods between our sequence ADT and the java.util interfaces List and ListIterator interfaces, with notes about these correspondences and their implementations in the java.util classes ArrayList and LinkedList.

Sequence ADT Method	java.util List Method	java.util ListIterator Method	Notes
size()	size()		$O(1)$ time
isEmpty()	isEmpty()		$O(1)$ time
atRank(i)	listIterator(i)		cursor is before index i
rankOf(p)		nextIndex()	index after the cursor
elemAtRank(i)	get(i)		A is $O(1)$, L is $O(\min\{i, n-i\})$
first()	listIterator()		first element is next
last()	listIterator(size())		last element is previous
prev(p)		previous()	$O(1)$ time
next(p)		next()	$O(1)$ time
replace(p, e)		set(e)	$O(1)$ time
replaceAtRank(i, e)	set(i, e)		A is $O(1)$, L is $O(\min\{i, n-i\})$
insertAtRank(i, e)	add(i, e)		$O(n)$ time
removeAtRank(i, e)	remove(i)		A is $O(1)$, L is $O(\min\{i, n-i\})$
insertFirst(e)	add($0, e$)		A is $O(n)$, L is $O(1)$
insertLast(e)	add(e)		$O(1)$ time
insertAfter(p, e)		add(e)	insertion is at cursor; A is $O(n)$, L is $O(1)$
insertBefore(p, e)		add(e)	insertion is at cursor; A is $O(n)$, L is $O(1)$
remove(p)		remove()	deletion is at cursor; A is $O(n)$, L is $O(1)$

Table 5.4: Correspondences between methods in the sequence ADT and the java.util interfaces List and ListIterator. We use A to denote the running time of a method in java.util.ArrayList and L for the corresponding time in java.util.LinkedList.

5.6 Exercises

For source code and help with exercises, please visit **java.datastructures.net**.

Reinforcement

R-5.1 Give a justification of the running times shown in Table 5.2 for the methods of a vector implemented with an array that does not expand in size.

R-5.2 Give an adapter class to support the Stack interface using the methods of the vector ADT.

R-5.3 Redo the justification of Proposition 5.2 assuming that the the cost of growing the array from size k to size $2k$ is $3k$ cyber-dollars. How much should each push operation be charged to make the amortization work?

R-5.4 Give pseudo-code descriptions of algorithms for performing the methods insertBefore(p, e), insertFirst(e), and insertLast(e) of the list ADT, assuming the list is implemented using a doubly linked list.

R-5.5 Draw pictures illustrating each of the major steps in the algorithms given in the previous exercise.

R-5.6 Draw a picture illustrating the final state of a doubly linked list after performing the algorithm for insertAfter(p, e), but with the order of the last two assignment statements in Code Fragment 5.7 reversed, so that the pseudo-code (which is now incorrect) would become:

> Create a new node v
> v.setElement(e)
> v.setPrev(p)
> v.setNext(p.getNext())
> p.setNext(v)
> (p.getNext()).setPrev(v)
> **return** v

R-5.7 Provide the details of an array implementation of the list ADT. In particular, describe how the index fields of the position objects are updated after an insertion or deletion of an element.

R-5.8 Provide Java code fragments for the methods of the List interface of Code Fragment 5.5 that are not included in Code Fragments 5.9–5.11.

R-5.9 Describe a method for reversing the contents of a list represented with a doubly linked list using a single pass through the list.

R-5.10 Given the set of element $\{a,b,c,d,e,f\}$ stored in a list, show the final state of the list, assuming we use the move-to-front heuristic and access the elements according to the following sequence: $(a,b,c,d,e,f,a,c,f,b,d,e)$.

R-5.11 Suppose we are keeping track of access counts in a list L of n elements. Suppose further that we have made kn total accesses to the elements in L, for some integer $k \geq 1$. What are the minimum and maximum number of elements that have been accessed fewer than k times?

R-5.12 Give pseudo-code describing how to implement all the operations in the vector ADT using an array in a circular fashion. What is the running time for each of these methods?

R-5.13 Using the Sequence interface methods, describe a recursive method for determining if a sequence S of n integers contains a given integer k. Your method should not contain any loops. How much space does your method use in addition to the space used for S?

R-5.14 Briefly describe how to perform a new sequence method makeFirst(p) that moves the element of a sequence S at position p to be the first element in S while keeping the relative ordering of the remaining elements in S unchanged. That is, makeFirst(p) performs a move-to-front. Your method should run in $O(1)$ time if S is implemented with a doubly linked list.

R-5.15 Describe how to use a vector and an **int** field to implement an iterator. Include pseudo-code fragments describing hasNext() and next().

R-5.16 Describe how to use the PositionIterator class to create an iterator for a snapshot of a list. That is, the iterator should be for the version of the list that existed when the iterator was created.

R-5.17 Suppose we are maintaining a collection C of elements such that each time we add a new element to the collection, we copy the contents of C into a new vector of just the right size. What is the running time of adding n elements to an initially empty collection C in this case?

R-5.18 Describe an implementation of the methods insertLast and insertBefore realized by using only methods in the set {isEmpty, checkPosition, first, last, prev, next, insertAfter, insertFirst}.

R-5.19 Let L be maintained to be a list of n items ordered by decreasing access count. Describe a series of $O(n^2)$ accesses that will reverse L.

R-5.20 Let L be a list of n items maintained according to the move-to-front heuristic. Describe a series of $O(n)$ accesses that will reverse L.

Creativity

C-5.1 Give pseudo-code for the methods of a new class, ShrinkingArrayVector, that extends the class ArrayVector shown in Code Fragment 5.3 and adds a method, shrinkToFit(), which replaces the underlying array with an array whose capacity is exactly equal to the number of elements currently in the vector.

C-5.2 Describe what changes need to be made to the extendable array implementation given in Code Fragment 5.3 in order to shrink by half the size N of the array any time the number of elements in the vector goes below $N/4$.

C-5.3 Show that, using an extendable array that grows and shrinks as described in the previous exercise, the following series of $2n$ operations takes $O(n)$ time: (i) n push operations on a vector with initial capacity $N = 1$; (ii) n pop (removal of the last element) operations.

C-5.4 Show how to improve the implementation of method insertAtRank in Code Fragment 5.3 so that, in case of an overflow, the elements are copied into their final place in the new array; that is, no shifting should be done in this case.

C-5.5 Consider an implementation of the vector ADT using an extendable array, but instead of copying the elements of the vector into an array of double the size (that is, from N to $2N$) when its capacity is reached, we copy the elements into an array with $\lceil N/4 \rceil$ additional cells, going from capacity N to $N + \lceil N/4 \rceil$. Show that performing a sequence of n push operations (that is, insertions at the end) still runs in $O(n)$ time in this case.

C-5.6 The NodeList implementation given in Code Fragments 5.9–5.11 does not do any error checks to test if a given position p is actually a member of this particular list. For example, if p is a position in list S and we call T.insertAfter(p, e) on a different list T, then we actually will add the element to S just after p. Describe how to change the NodeList implementation in an efficient manner to disallow such misuses.

C-5.7 Suppose we want to extend the Sequence abstract data type with methods rankOfElement(e) and positionOfElement(e), which respectively return the rank and the position of the (first occurrence of) element e in the sequence. Show how to implement these methods by expressing them in terms of other methods of the Sequence interface.

C-5.8 Design algorithms for reversing a sequence that access the sequence only through a restricted set of methods, as indicated below. Each algorithm should rearrange the elements of the sequence. Returning a new sequence is not allowed. However, using other sequences is allowed.

   a. {size, first, last, remove, insertFirst}.

   b. {size, first, remove, insertFirst}.

C-5.9 Give an adaptation of the vector ADT to the deque ADT that is different from that given in Table 5.1.

C-5.10 Describe the structure and pseudo-code for an array-based implementation of the vector ADT that achieves $O(1)$ time for insertions and removals at rank 0, as well as insertions and removals at the end of the vector. Your implementation should also provide for a constant-time elemAtRank method. (Hint: Think about how to extend the circular array implementation of the queue ADT given in the previous chapter.)

C-5.11 Give a Java code fragment for the method rankOf(p), which is missing from the implementation given in Code Fragment 5.13.

C-5.12 Describe an efficient way of putting a vector representing a deck of n cards into random order. You may use a function, randomInteger(n), which returns a random number between 0 and $n-1$, inclusive. Your method should guarantee that every possible ordering is equally likely. What is the running time of your method?

C-5.13 Describe a method for maintaining a favorites list L such that every element in L has been accessed at least once in the last n accesses, where n is the size of L. Your scheme should add only $O(1)$ additional amortized time to each operation.

C-5.14 Suppose we have an n-element list L maintained according to the move-to-front heuristic. Describe a sequence of n^2 accesses that is guaranteed to take $\Omega(n^3)$ time to perform on L.

C-5.15 A (singly linked) *circular list* is a collection C of n positions such that each has a next variable and following next links starting from any position in C can visit all the positions in C. Describe how to perform insertAfter(p,e) and insertBefore($p.e$), for a position p and element e, in such a scheme. What are the running times for these operations?

C-5.16 Describe a scheme for creating list iterators that *fail fast*, that is, they all become invalid as soon as the underlying list changes.

C-5.17 An array is *sparse* if most of its entries are **null**. A list L can be used to implement such an array, A, efficiently. In particular, for each nonnull cell $A[i]$, we can store an entry (i,e) in L, where e is the element stored at $A[i]$. This approach allows us to represent A using $O(m)$ storage, where m is the number of nonnull entries in A. Describe and analyze efficient ways of performing the methods of the vector ADT on such a representation. Is it better to store the entries in L by increasing indices or not?

C-5.18 There is a simple, but inefficient, algorithm, called ***bubble-sort***, for sorting a sequence S of n comparable elements. This algorithm scans the sequence $n-1$ times, where, in each scan, the algorithm compares the current element with the next one and swaps them if they are out of order. Give a pseudo-code description of bubble-sort that is as efficient as possible assuming S is implemented with a doubly linked list. What is the running time of this algorithm?

C-5.19 Answer Exercise C-5.18 assuming S is implemented with an array.

C-5.20 A useful operation in databases is the ***natural join***. If we view a database A as a list of pairs of objects (x,y) and a database B as a list of pairs (y,z), then the natural join of A and B is the list of all triples (x,y,z) such that (x,y) is in A and (y,z) is in B. Describe and analyze an efficient algorithm for computing the natural join of a list A of n pairs and a list B of m pairs.

C-5.21 When Bob wants to send Alice a message M on the Internet, he breaks M into n ***data packets***, numbers the packets consecutively, and injects them into the network. When the packets arrive at Alice's computer, they may be out of order, so Alice must assemble the sequence of n packets in order before she can be sure she has the entire message. Describe an efficient scheme for Alice to do this. What is the running time of this algorithm?

C-5.22 Given a list L of n positive integers, each represented with $k = \lceil \log n \rceil + 1$ bits, describe an $O(n)$-time method for finding a k-bit integer not in L.

C-5.23 Argue why any solution to the previous problem must run in $\Omega(n)$ time.

C-5.24 Given a list L of n arbitrary integers, design an $O(n)$-time method for finding an integer that cannot be formed as the sum of two integers in L.

C-5.25 Isabel has an interesting way of summing up the values in an array A of n integers, where n is a power of two. She creates an array B of half the size of A and sets $B[i] = A[2i] + A[2i+1]$, for $i = 0, 1, \ldots, (n/2) - 1$. If B has size 1, then she outputs $B[0]$. Otherwise, she replaces A with B, and repeats the process. What is the running time of her algorithm?

Projects

P-5.1 Implement the vector ADT by means of an extendable array used in a circular fashion, so that insertions and deletions at the beginning and end of the vector run in constant time.

P-5.2 Implement the vector ADT using a doubly linked list. Show experimentally that this implementation is worse than the array-based approach.

P-5.3 Write a simple text editor, which stores and displays a string of characters using the list ADT, together with a cursor object that highlights a position in this string. Your editor should support the following operations:

- left: move cursor left one character (or do nothing if at text end).
- right: move cursor right one character (or do nothing if at text end).
- delete: delete the character to the right of the cursor (or do nothing if at text end).
- insert c: insert the character c just after the cursor.

P-5.4 Implement a ***phased favorites list***. A phase consists of N accesses in the list, for a given parameter N. During a phase the list should maintain itself so that elements are ordered by decreasing access counts during that phase. At the end of a phase, it should clear all the access counts and start the next phase. Determine experimentally what are the best values of N for various list sizes.

P-5.5 Write a complete adapter class that implements the sequence ADT using a java.util.ArrayList object.

P-5.6 Implement the favorites list application using a vector instead of a list. Compare it experimentally to the list-based implementation.

Chapter Notes

The concept of viewing data structures as containers (and other principles of object-oriented design) can be found in object-oriented design books by Booch [14] and Budd [17]. The concept also exists under the name "collection class" in books by Golberg and Robson [39] and Liskov and Guttag [66]. Sequences and iterators are pervasive concepts in the Java Collection Framework. The sequence ADT is a generalization and extension of the Java java.util.Vector API (for example, see the book by Arnold and Gosling [7]) and the list ADTs proposed by several authors, including Aho, Hopcroft, and Ullman [5], who introduce the "position" abstraction, and Wood [98], who defines a list ADT similar to ours. Implementations of sequences via arrays and linked lists are discussed by Knuth [58].

Chapter

6

Trees

Contents

Productivity experts say that breakthroughs come by thinking "nonlinearly." In this chapter, we discuss one of the most important nonlinear data structures in computing—*trees*. Tree structures are indeed a breakthrough in data organization, for they allow us to implement a host of algorithms much faster than when using linear data structures, such as list, vectors, and sequences. Trees also provide a natural organization for data, and consequently have become ubiquitous structures in file systems, graphical user interfaces, databases, Web sites, and other computer systems.

It is not always clear what productivity experts mean by "nonlinear" thinking, but when we say that trees are "nonlinear," we are referring to an organizational relationship that is richer than the simple "before" and "after" relationships between objects in sequences. The relationships in a tree are *hierarchical*, with some objects being "above" and some "below" others. Actually, the main terminology for tree data structures comes from family trees, with the terms "parent," "child," "ancestor," and "descendent" being the most common words used to describe relationships. We show an example of a family tree in Figure 6.1.

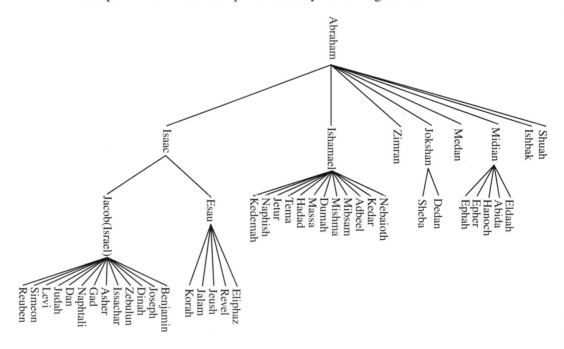

Figure 6.1: A family tree showing some descendents of Abraham, as recorded in Genesis, chapters 25–36.

6.1   The Tree Abstract Data Type

A *tree* is an abstract data type that stores elements hierarchically. With the exception of the top element, each element in a tree has a *parent* element and zero or more *children* elements. A tree is usually visualized by placing elements inside ovals or rectangles, and by drawing the connections between parents and children with straight lines. (See Figure 6.2.) We typically call the top element the *root* of the tree, but it is drawn as the highest element, with the other elements being connected below (just the opposite of a botanical tree).

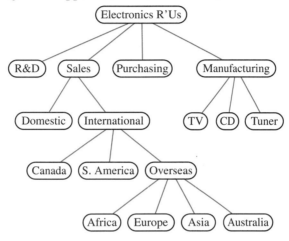

Figure 6.2: A tree with 17 nodes representing the organization of a fictitious corporation. The root stores *Electronics R'Us*. The children of the root store *R&D*, *Sales*, *Purchasing*, and *Manufacturing*. The internal nodes store *Sales*, *International*, *Overseas*, *Electronics R'Us*, and *Manufacturing*.

6.1.1   Terminology and Basic Properties

Formally, we define a *tree T* as a set of *nodes* storing elements such that the nodes have a *parent-child* relationship, that satisfies the following properties:

- If T is nonempty, it has a special node, called the *root* of T, that has no parent.
- Each node v of T different from the root has a unique *parent* node w; every node with parent w is a *child* of w.

For simplicity, we sometimes refer to a node in terms of the element stored at that node. For example, for Figure 6.2, we may say that "*TV* is a child of *Manufacturing*." instead of 'The node storing *TV* is a child of the node storing *Manufacturing*."

Two nodes that are children of the same parent are *siblings*. A node *v* is *external* if *v* has no children. A node *v* is *internal* if it has one or more children. External nodes are also known as *leaves*.

Example 6.1: *In most operating systems, files are organized hierarchically into nested directories (also called folders), which are presented to the user in the form of a tree. (See Figure 6.3.) More specifically, the internal nodes of the tree are associated with directories and the external nodes are associated with regular files. In the UNIX and Linux operating systems, the root of the tree is appropriately called the "root directory," and is represented by the symbol "/."*

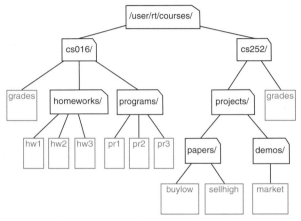

Figure 6.3: Tree representing a portion of a file system.

A node *u* is an *ancestor* of a node *v* if *u* = *v* or *u* is an ancestor of the parent of *v*. (Note the recursive definition.) Conversely, we say that a node *v* is a *descendent* of a node *u* if *u* is an ancestor of *v*. For example, in Figure 6.3, cs252/ is an ancestor of papers/, and pr3 is a descendent of cs016/. The *subtree* of *T* *rooted* at a node *v* is the tree consisting of all the descendents of *v* in *T* (including *v* itself). For example, in the tree of Figure 6.3, the subtree rooted at cs016/ consists of the nodes cs016/, grades, homeworks/, programs/, hw1, hw2, hw3, pr1, pr2, and pr3.

Example 6.2: *The inheritance relation between classes in a Java program forms a tree. The root, java.lang.Object, is an ancestor of all other classes. Each class, C, is a descendent of this root and is the root of a subtree of the classes that extend C.*

Note that according to our definition, a tree can be empty, meaning that it doesn't have any nodes. This convention allows us to alternatively define a tree recursively, such that a tree *T* is either empty or consists of a node *r*, called the root of *T*, and a set of trees, called the subtrees of *T*, such that the roots of the nonempty subtrees are the children of *r*.

A tree is ***ordered*** if there is a linear ordering defined for the children of each node; that is, we can identify children of a node as being the first, second, third, and so on. Such an ordering is usually indicated in a drawing of a tree by arranging siblings left to right, according to their ordering. Ordered trees typically indicate the linear order existing between siblings by listing them in a sequence or iterator in the correct order.

Example 6.3: *The parts of a structured document, such as a book, are hierarchically organized as a tree whose internal nodes are chapters, sections, and subsections, and whose external nodes are paragraphs, tables, figures, and so on. (See Figure 6.4.) The root of the tree corresponds to the book itself. Such a tree is an example of an ordered tree, because there is a well-defined ordering among the children of each node.*

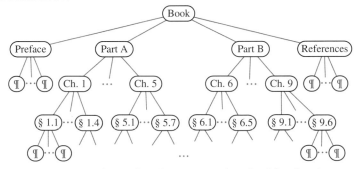

Figure 6.4: An ordered tree associated with a book.

A ***binary tree*** is an ordered tree with the following properties:

1. Every node has at most two children.
2. Each child node is labeled as being either a ***left child*** or a ***right child***.
3. The left child precedes the right child in the ordering of the children of a node.

The subtree rooted at a left or right child of an internal node *v* is called a ***left subtree*** or ***right subtree***, respectively, of *v*. A binary tree is ***proper*** if each node has either zero or two children. Some people also refer to such trees as being ***full*** binary trees. Thus, in a proper binary tree, every internal node has exactly two children. A binary tree that is not proper is ***improper***.

Alternatively, we can define a binary tree in a recursive way such that a binary tree is either empty or consists of:

- A node *r*, called the root of *T* and storing an element
- A binary tree, called the left subtree of *T*
- A binary tree, called the right subtree of *T*.

An *edge* of tree T is a pair of nodes (u, v) such that u is the parent of v. A *path* of T is a sequence of nodes such that any two consecutive nodes in the sequence form an edge.

Example 6.4: *An important class of binary trees arises in contexts where we wish to represent a number of different outcomes that can result from answering a series of yes-or-no questions. Each internal node is associated with a question. Starting at the root, we go to the left or right child of the current node, depending on whether the answer to the question is "Yes" or "No." With each decision, we follow an edge from a parent to a child, eventually tracing a path in the tree from the root to an external node. Such binary trees are known as **decision trees**, because each external node v in such a tree represents a decision of what to do if the questions associated with v's ancestors are answered in a way that leads to v. A decision tree is a proper binary tree. Figure 6.5 illustrates a decision tree that provides recommendations to a prospective investor.*

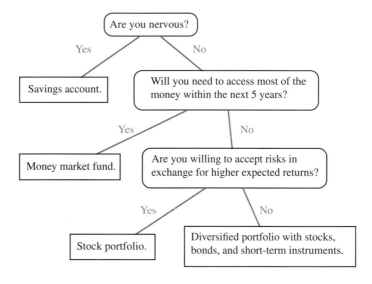

Figure 6.5: A decision tree providing investment advice.

Example 6.5: *An arithmetic expression can be represented by a binary tree whose external nodes are associated with variables or constants, and whose internal nodes are associated with one of the operators $+$, $-$, $\times$, and $/$. (See Figure 6.6.) Each node in such a tree has a value associated with it.*

- *If a node is external, then its value is that of its variable or constant.*
- *If a node is internal, then its value is defined by applying its operation to the values of its children.*

An arithmetic expression tree is a proper binary tree, since each of the operators $+$, $-$, $\times$, and $/$ take exactly two operands. Of course, if we were to allow for unary operators, like negation $(-)$, as in "$-x$," then we could have an improper binary tree.

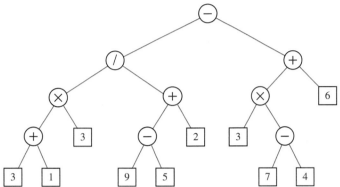

Figure 6.6: A binary tree representing an arithmetic expression. This tree represents the expression $((((3+1)\times 3)/((9-5)+2))-((3\times(7-4))+6))$. The value associated with the internal node labeled "$/$" is 2.

6.1.2 Tree Methods

The tree ADT stores elements at positions, which, as with positions in a list, are defined relative to neighboring positions. The *positions* in a tree are its *nodes*, and neighboring positions satisfy the parent-child relationships that define a valid tree. Therefore we use the terms "position" and "node" interchangeably for trees. As with a list position, a position object for a tree supports the method:

> element(): Return the object stored at this position.
> *Input:* None; *Output:* Object.

The real power of node positions in a tree, however, comes from the *accessor methods* of the tree ADT that return and accept positions, such as the following:

> root(): Return the tree's root; an error occurs if the tree is empty.
> *Input:* None; *Output:* Position.

> parent(v): Return the parent of v; an error occurs if v is the root.
> *Input:* Position; *Output:* Position.

> children(v): Return an iterator of the children of node v.
> *Input:* Position; *Output:* Iterator of positions.

If a tree T is ordered, then the iterator children(v) provides access to the children of v in order. If v is an external node, then children(v) is an empty iterator.

In addition to the above fundamental accessor methods, we also include the following *query methods*:

isInternal(v): Test whether node v is internal.
Input: Position; *Output:* Boolean.

isExternal(v): Test whether node v is external.
Input: Position; *Output:* Boolean.

isRoot(v): Test whether node v is the root.
Input: Position; *Output:* Boolean.

These methods make programming with trees easier and more readable, since we can use them in the conditionals of **if** statements and **while** loops, rather than using a nonintuitive conditional.

There are also a number of *generic methods* a tree should probably support that are not necessarily related to its tree structure, including the following:

size(): Return the number of nodes in the tree.
Input: None; *Output:* Integer.

isEmpty(): Test whether the tree has any nodes or not.
Input: None; *Output:* Boolean.

elements(): Return an iterator of all the elements stored at nodes of the tree.
Input: None; *Output:* Iterator.

positions(): Return an iterator of all the nodes of the tree.
Input: None; *Output:* Iterator.

replace(v, e): Replace with e and return the element stored at node v.
Input: Position and object (new element); *Output:* Object (old element).

Any method that takes a position as an argument should generate an error condition if that position is invalid. For example, if v is not a tree position object, then a call to T.isRoot(v) or T.parent(v) should generate an error.

We do not define any specialized update methods for trees here. Instead, we prefer to describe different tree update methods in conjunction with specific applications of trees in subsequent chapters. In fact, we can imagine several kinds of tree update operations beyond those given in this book. Even though we are not including any update operations here, we nevertheless will consider how we might organize this collection of tree ADT methods into a Java interface.

6.1.3 A Tree Interface in Java

The Java interface shown in Code Fragment 6.1 represents the tree ADT. Error conditions are handled as follows: Each method that can take a position as an argument, may throw an InvalidPositionException, to indicate that the position is invalid. Method parent throws a BoundaryViolationException if it is called on the root. Method root throws an EmptyTreeException if it called on an empty tree.

```java
/**
 * An interface for a tree where nodes can have an arbitrary number of children.
 */
public interface Tree {
  /** Returns the number of nodes in the tree. */
  public int size();
  /** Returns whether the tree is empty. */
  public boolean isEmpty();
  /** Return an iterator of the elements stored in the tree. */
  public Iterator elements();
  /** Returns an iterator of the nodes stored in the tree. */
  public Iterator positions();
  /** Replaces the element stored at a given node. */
  public Object replace(Position v, Object e)
    throws InvalidPositionException;
  /** Returns the root of the tree. */
  public Position root() throws EmptyTreeException;
  /** Returns the parent of a given node. */
  public Position parent(Position v)
    throws InvalidPositionException, BoundaryViolationException;
  /** Returns an iterator of the children of a given node. */
  public Iterator children(Position v)
    throws InvalidPositionException;
  /** Returns whether a given node is internal. */
  public boolean isInternal(Position v)
    throws InvalidPositionException;
  /** Returns whether a given node is external. */
  public boolean isExternal(Position v)
    throws InvalidPositionException;
  /** Returns whether a given node is the root of the tree. */
  public boolean isRoot(Position v)
    throws InvalidPositionException;
}
```

Code Fragment 6.1: Java interface Tree representing the tree ADT. Additional update methods may be added, depending on the application. We do not include such methods in the interface, however.

6.2   Basic Algorithms on Trees

In this section, we present algorithms for performing computations on a tree by accessing it through the tree ADT methods, which correspond to the methods of the Tree interface. We describe methods for computing the height and depth of nodes in a tree, as well as various methods for efficiently traversing the nodes of a tree.

6.2.1   Performance Assumptions

In order to analyze the running time of the algorithms presented throughout this section, we make the following assumptions on the running times of the methods of the tree ADT.

- The accessor methods root() and parent(v) take $O(1)$ time.

- The query methods isInternal(v), isExternal(v), and isRoot(v) take $O(1)$ time, as well.

- The accessor method children(v) takes $O(c_v)$ time, where c_v is the number of children of v.

- The generic methods size() and isEmpty() take $O(1)$ time.

- The generic method replace(v, e) runs in $O(1)$ time.

- The generic methods elements() and positions(), which each return an iterator, take $O(n)$ time, where n is the number of nodes in the tree.

- For the iterators returned by methods elements(), positions() and children(v), the methods hasNext() and next() each take $O(1)$ time.

In Section 6.4, we will present data structures for trees that satisfy the above assumptions.

Before we describe how to implement the tree ADT using a concrete data structure, however, let us describe how we can use the methods of the tree ADT to solve some interesting problems for trees.

6.2.2 Depth and Height

Let v be a node of a tree T. The ***depth*** of v is the number of ancestors of v, excluding v itself. For example, in the tree of Figure 6.2, the node storing *International* has depth 2. Note that this definition implies that the depth of the root of T is 0.

The depth of a node v can also be recursively defined as follows:

- If v is the root, then the depth of v is 0.
- Otherwise, the depth of v is one plus the depth of the parent of v.

Based on the above definition, the recursive algorithm depth, shown in Code Fragment 6.2, computes the depth of a node v of T by calling itself recursively on the parent of v, and adding 1 to the value returned. Thus, each ancestor of v is visited by a recursive call, and contributes a value of 1 to the depth, as it should.

Algorithm depth(T, v):
  if T.isRoot(v) **then**
    return 0
  else
    return $1 +$ depth$(T, T$.parent$(v))$

Code Fragment 6.2: Algorithm depth for computing the depth of a node v in a tree T.

A simple Java implementation of algorithm depth is shown in Code Fragment 6.3.

```
public static int depth (Tree T, Position v) {
  if (T.isRoot(v))
    return 0;
  else
    return 1 + depth(T, T.parent(v));
}
```

Code Fragment 6.3: Method depth written in Java.

The running time of algorithm depth(T, v) is $O(d_v)$, where d_v denotes the depth of the node v in the tree T, because the algorithm performs a constant-time recursive step for each ancestor of v. Thus, algorithm depth(T, v) runs in $O(n)$ time, where n is the total number of nodes of T, since a node of T may have depth $n - 1$ in the worst case. Although such a running time is a function of the input size, it is more accurate to characterize the running time in terms of the parameter d_v, since this parameter can be much smaller than n.

The *height* of a node v in a tree T is also defined recursively:

- If v is an external node, then the height of v is 0.
- Otherwise, the height of v is one plus the maximum height of a child of v.

The *height* of a nonempty tree T is the height of the root of T. For example, the tree of Figure 6.2 has height 4. In addition, height can also be viewed as follows.

Proposition 6.6: *The height of a nonempty tree T is equal to the maximum depth of an external node of T.*

We leave the justification of this fact to an exercise (R-6.6). We present here an algorithm, height1, shown in Code Fragment 6.4 and implemented in Java in Code Fragment 6.5, for computing the height of a nonempty tree T based on the above proposition. This algorithm utilizes an iterator of all the nodes in the tree to aid the computation of the depth of each external node by using algorithm depth (Code Fragment 6.2), keeping track of the maximum depth seen so far.

Algorithm height1(T):
  $h = 0$
  for each $v \in T$.positions() **do**
    if T.isExternal(v) **then**
      $h = \max(h, \text{depth}(T, v))$
  return h

Code Fragment 6.4: Algorithm height1 for computing the height of a nonempty tree T. Note that this algorithm calls algorithm depth (Code Fragment 6.2).

```
public static int height1 (Tree T) {
    int h = 0;
    Iterator positer = T.positions();
    while (positer.hasNext()) {
        Position v = (Position) positer.next();
        if (T.isExternal(v))
            h = Math.max(h, depth(T, v));
    }
    return h;
}
```

Code Fragment 6.5: Method height1 written in Java. Note the use of the max method of class java.lang.Math.

Unfortunately, algorithm height1 is not very efficient. Since height1 calls algorithm depth(v) on each external node v of T, the running time of height1 is given by $O(n + \sum_{v \in E}(1 + d_v))$, where n is the number of nodes of T, d_v is the depth of node v, and E is the set of external nodes of T. In the worst case, we have that $\sum_{v \in E}(1 + d_v)$ is proportional to n^2. (See Exercise C-6.5.) Thus, algorithm height1 runs in $O(n^2)$ time.

Algorithm height2, shown in Code Fragment 6.6 and implemented in Java in Code Fragment 6.7, computes the height of tree T in a more efficient manner by using the recursive definition of height. The algorithm is expressed by a recursive method height2(T, v) that computes the height of the subtree of T rooted at a node v. If the node v is external, then the algorithm returns 0. Otherwise, it gets an iterator of the children of v, recursively computes the height of each child, and returns 1 plus the maximum height returned from a recursive call. The height of tree T is obtained by calling height2(T, T.root()).

Algorithm height2(T, v):
    if T.isExternal(v) **then**
        return 0
    else
        $h = 0$
        for each $w \in T$.children(v) **do**
            $h = \max(h, \text{height2}(T, w))$
        return $1 + h$

Code Fragment 6.6: Algorithm height2 for computing the height of the subtree of tree T rooted at a node v.

```java
public static int height2 (Tree T, Position v) {
  if (T.isExternal(v))
    return 0;
  else {
    int h = 0;
    Iterator children = T.children(v);
    while (children.hasNext())
      h = Math.max(h, height2(T, (Position) children.next()));
    return 1 + h;
  }
}
```

Code Fragment 6.7: Method height2 written in Java.

Algorithm height2 is much more efficient than Algorithm height1 (from Code Fragment 6.4). The algorithm is recursive, and if it is initially called on the root of T, it will eventually be called once on each node of T. Thus, we can determine the running time of this method by first determining the amount of time spent at each node (on the nonrecursive part), and then summing this time bound over all the nodes. The computation of an iterator children(v) takes $O(c_v)$ time, where c_v denotes the number of children of node v. Also, the **while** loop has c_v iterations, and each iteration of the loop takes $O(1)$ time plus the time for the recursive call on a child of v. Thus, algorithm height2 spends $O(1 + c_v)$ time at each node v, and its running time is $O(\sum_{v \in T}(1 + c_v))$. In order to complete the analysis, we make use of the following property.

Proposition 6.7: *Let T be a tree with n nodes, and let c_v denote the number of children of a node v of T. Then*

$$\sum_{v \in T} c_v = n - 1.$$

Justification: Each node of T, with the exception of the root, is a child of another node, and thus contributes one unit to the above sum. ∎

By Proposition 6.7, the running time of algorithm height2, when called on the root of T, is $O(n)$, where n is the number of nodes of T.

6.2.3 Preorder Traversal

A *traversal* of a tree T is a systematic way of accessing, or "visiting," all the nodes of T. In this section, we present a basic traversal scheme for trees, called preorder traversal. In the next section, we will study another basic traversal scheme, called postorder traversal.

In a *preorder traversal* of a tree T, the root of T is visited first and then the subtrees rooted at its children are traversed recursively. If the tree is ordered, then the subtrees are traversed according to the order of the children. The specific action associated with the "visit" of a node v depends on the application of this traversal, and could involve anything from incrementing a counter to performing some complex computation for v. The pseudo-code for the preorder traversal of the subtree rooted at a node v is shown in Code Fragment 6.8. We initially call this algorithm with preorder(T, T.root()).

The preorder traversal algorithm is useful for producing a linear ordering of the nodes of a tree where parents must always come before their children in the ordering. Such orderings have several different applications; we explore a simple instance of such an application in the next example.

Algorithm preorder(T, v):

    perform the "visit" action for node v

    for each $w \in T$.children(v) **do**

        preorder(T, w)　　　{recursively traverse the subtree rooted at w}

Code Fragment 6.8: Algorithm preorder for performing the preorder traversal of the subtree of a tree T rooted at a node v.

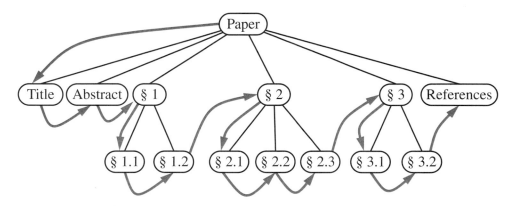

Figure 6.7: Preorder traversal of an ordered tree, where the children of each node are ordered from left to right.

Example 6.8: *The preorder traversal of the tree associated with a document, as in Example 6.3, examines an entire document sequentially, from beginning to end. If the external nodes are removed before the traversal, then the traversal examines the table of contents of the document. (See Figure 6.7.)*

The preorder traversal is also an efficient way to access all the nodes of a tree. To justify this, let us consider the running time of the preorder traversal of a tree T with n nodes under the assumption that visiting a node takes $O(1)$ time. The analysis of the preorder traversal algorithm is actually similar to that of algorithm height2 (Code Fragment 6.7), given in Section 6.2.2. At each node v, the nonrecursive part of the preorder traversal algorithm requires time $O(1 + c_v)$, where c_v is the number of children of v. Thus, by Proposition 6.7, the overall running time of the preorder traversal of T is $O(n)$.

Algorithm preorderPrint(T, v), implemented in Java in Code Fragment 6.9, performs a preorder printing of the subtree of a node v of T, that is, it performs the preorder traversal of the subtree rooted at v and prints the element stored at a node when the node is visited. Recall that, for an ordered tree T, method T.children(v) returns an iterator that accesses the children of v in order.

```java
public static String preorderPrint(Tree T, Position v) {
    String s = v.element().toString(); // elements must implement toString
    Iterator children = T.children(v);
    while (children.hasNext())
        s += " " + preorderPrint(T, (Position) children.next());
    return s;
}
```

Code Fragment 6.9: Method preorderPrint(T,v) that performs a preorder print-ing of the elements in the subtree of node v of T. The method implicitly calls the standard Java method toString to return a string associated with an element, that is, its "name" or "label." Method toString has a default implementation in java.lang.Object, which is typically overridden by subclasses to print useful infor-mation about instances of each such subclass.

There is an interesting variation of the preorderPrint method that produces a string representation of an entire tree. Let us assume again that for each element e stored in tree T, calling e.toString() returns a string associated with e. The *paren-thetic string representation* $P(T)$ of tree T is recursively defined as follows. If T consists of a single node v, then

$$P(T) = v.\text{element}().\text{toString}().$$

Otherwise,

$$P(T) = v.\text{element}().\text{toString}() + "\,(\," + P(T_1) + "\,,\," + \cdots + "\,,\," + P(T_k) + "\,)\,",$$

where v is the root of T and $T_1, T_2, \ldots, T_k$ are the subtrees rooted at the children of v, which are given in order if T is an ordered tree. Note that the definition of $P(T)$ is recursive. Also, we are using "+" here to denote string concatenation. (See Section 1.3.2 for details.) The parenthetic representation of the tree of Figure 6.2 is shown in Figure 6.8.

> *Electronics R'Us (R&D*
> *Sales (Domestic*
> *International (Canada S. America*
> *Overseas (Africa Europe Asia Australia)))*
> *Purchasing*
> *Manufacturing (TV CD Tuner))*

Figure 6.8: Parenthetic representation of the tree of Figure 6.2. Indentation, line breaks and spaces have been added for clarity.

Note that, technically speaking, there are some computations that occur between and after the recursive calls at a node's children in the above algorithm. We still consider this algorithm to be a preorder traversal, however, since the primary action of printing a node's contents occurs prior to the recursive calls.

The Java method parentheticRepresentation, shown in Code Fragment 6.10, is a variation of method preorderPrint (Code Fragment 6.9). It implements the definition given above to output a parenthetic string representation of a tree T. As with the method preorderPrint, the method parentheticRepresentation makes use of the toString method that is defined for every Java object. In fact, we can view this method as a kind of toString() method for tree objects.

```java
public static String parentheticRepresentation(Tree T, Position v) {
    String s = v.element().toString(); // elements must implement toString
    if (T.isInternal(v)) {
        Iterator children = T.children(v);
        // open parenthesis and recursively process the first subtree
        s += " ( " + parentheticRepresentation(T, (Position) children.next());
        while (children.hasNext())
            // recursively process the remaining subtrees
            s += ", " + parentheticRepresentation(T, (Position) children.next());
        s += " )"; // close parenthesis
    }
    return s;
}
```

Code Fragment 6.10: Algorithm parentheticRepresentation. Note the use of the $+$ operator to concatenate two strings.

We explore a modification to Code Fragment 6.10 in Exercise R-6.9, to display a tree in a fashion more closely matching that given in Figure 6.8.

The preorder traversal is useful for solving a tree problem where we must perform a computation for a node before performing any computations for its descendents.

6.2.4 Postorder Traversal

Another important tree traversal algorithm is the *postorder traversal*. This algorithm can be viewed as the opposite of the preorder traversal, because it recursively traverses the subtrees rooted at the children of the root first, and then visits the root. Still, as with the preorder traversal, if the tree is ordered, we make recursive calls for the children of a node v according to their specified order. Pseudo-code for the postorder traversal is given in Code Fragment 6.11.

Algorithm postorder(T, v):

   for each $w \in T$.children(v) **do**

      postorder(T, w)   {recursively traverse the subtree rooted at w}

   perform the "visit" action for node v

Code Fragment 6.11: Algorithm postorder for performing the postorder traversal of the subtree of a tree T rooted at a node v.

The name of the postorder traversal comes from the fact that this traversal method will visit a node v after it has visited all the other nodes in the subtree rooted at v. (See Figure 6.9.)

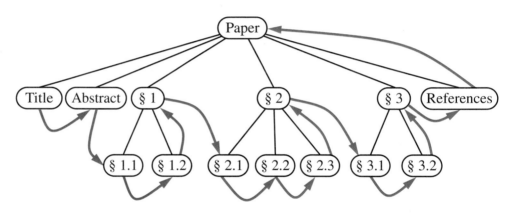

Figure 6.9: Postorder traversal of the ordered tree of Figure 6.7.

The analysis of the running time of a postorder traversal is analogous to that of a preorder traversal. (See Section 6.2.3.) The total time spent in the nonrecursive portions of the algorithm is proportional to the time spent visiting the children of each node in the tree. Thus, a postorder traversal of a tree T with n nodes takes $O(n)$ time, assuming that visiting each node takes $O(1)$ time. That is, the postorder traversal runs in linear time.

As an example instance of a postorder traversal, we show a Java method postorderPrint in Code Fragment 6.12, which performs a postorder traversal of a tree T. This method prints the element stored at a node when it is visited.

The postorder traversal method is useful for solving problems where we wish to compute some property for each node v in a tree, but computing that property for v requires that we have already computed that same property for v's children. Such an application is illustrated in the following example.

```
public static String postorderPrint(Tree T, Position v) {
  String s = "";
  Iterator children = T.children(v);
  while (children.hasNext())
    s += postorderPrint(T, (Position) children.next()) + " ";
  s += v.element();         // elements must implement toString
  return s;
}
```

Code Fragment 6.12: Method postorderPrint(T, v) that performs a postorder print-ing of the elements in the subtree of node v of T. The method implicitly calls toString on elements, when they are involved in a string concatenation operation.

Example 6.9: *Consider a file system tree T, where external nodes represent files and internal nodes represent directories (Example 6.1). Suppose we want to com-pute the disk space used by a directory, which is recursively given by the sum of:*
- *The size of the directory itself*
- *The sizes of the files in the directory*
- *The space used by the children directories.*

(See Figure 6.10.) *This computation can be done with a postorder traversal of tree T. After the subtrees of an internal node v have been traversed, we compute the space used by v by adding the sizes of the directory v itself and of the files contained in v to the space used by each internal child of v, which was computed by the recursive postorder traversals of the children of v.*

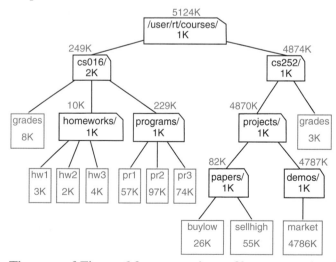

Figure 6.10: The tree of Figure 6.3 representing a file system, showing the name and size of the associated file/directory inside each node, and the disk space used by the associated directory above each internal node.

A Recursive Java Method for Computing Disk Space

Motivated by Example 6.9, Java method diskSpace, shown in Code Fragment 6.13, performs a postorder traversal of a file-system tree T, printing the name and disk space used by the directory associated with each internal node of T. When called on the root of tree T, diskSpace runs in time $O(n)$, where n is the number of nodes of T, provided the auxiliary methods name and size take $O(1)$ time.

```java
public static int diskSpace (Tree T, Position v) {
    int s = size(v);              // start with the size of the node itself
    Iterator children = T.children(v);
    while (children.hasNext()) {
        // add the recursively computed space used by the children of v
        s += diskSpace(T, (Position) children.next());
    }
    if (T.isInternal(v)) {
        // print name and disk space used
        System.out.print(name(v) + ": " + s);
    }
    return s;
}
```

Code Fragment 6.13: Method diskSpace prints the name and disk space used by the directory associated with each internal node of a file-system tree. This method calls the auxiliary methods name and size, which should be defined to return the name and size of the file/directory associated with a node.

Other Kinds of Traversals

Although the preorder and postorder traversals are common ways of visiting the nodes of a tree, we can also imagine other traversals. For example, we could traverse a tree so that we visit all the nodes at depth d before we visit the nodes at depth $d + 1$. Consecutively numbering the nodes of a tree T as we visit them in this kind of traversal is called the **level numbering** of the nodes of T (see Section 6.4.1). Such a traversal could be implemented, for example, using a queue, whereas the preorder and postorder traversals use a stack (this stack is implicit in our use of recursion to describe these methods, but we could make this use explicit, as well, to avoid recursion).

In addition, binary trees, which we discuss next, support an additional traversal method, known as the inorder traversal.

6.3 Binary Trees

One kind of tree that is of particular interest is the binary tree. As we mentioned in Section 6.1.1, a ***binary tree*** is an ordered tree in which each node has most two children and each child node is labeled as being either a ***left child*** or a ***right child***. Also, we recall that a binary tree is ***proper*** if each internal node has exactly two children and ***improper*** otherwise. When we draw a proper binary tree, we shall use different symbols for the internal and external nodes, such as ovals for internal nodes and rectangles for external nodes. Note that we can easily convert any binary tree into an equivalent proper one, as we explore in Exercise R-6.3. Even without such a conversion, we can consider an improper binary tree as proper, simply by viewing missing external nodes as "null nodes" or place holders that still count as nodes.

Binary trees arise naturally in many different applications. For example, an arithmetic expression tree (Example 6.5) is a binary tree. Also, a decision tree (see Example 6.4) is a binary tree, since the outcome of a decision is always "yes" or "no."

We discuss some of the specialized topics for binary trees below.

6.3.1 The Binary Tree ADT

As an abstract data type, a binary tree is a specialization of a tree that supports three additional accessor methods:

> left(v): Return the left child of v; an error condition occurs if v has no left child.
> ***Input:*** Position; ***Output:*** Position.

> right(v): Return the right child of v; an error condition occurs if v has no right child.
> ***Input:*** Position; ***Output:*** Position.

> hasLeft(v): Test whether v has a left child.
> ***Input:*** Position; ***Output:*** Boolean.

> hasRight(v): Test whether v has a right child.
> ***Input:*** Position; ***Output:*** Boolean.

Just as in Section 6.1.2 for the tree ADT, we do not define specialized update methods for binary trees here. Instead, we will consider some possible update methods when we describe specific implementations and applications of binary trees.

6.3.2 A Binary Tree Interface in Java

We model a binary tree as an abstract data type that extends the tree ADT and adds the three specialized methods for a binary tree. In Code Fragment 6.14, we show the simple Java interface we can define using this approach. By the way, since binary trees are ordered trees, the iterator returned by method children(v) (inherited from the Tree interface) accesses the left child of v before the right child of v.

```
/**
 * An interface for a binary tree, where each node can have zero, one,
 * or two children.
 */
public interface BinaryTree extends Tree {
  /** Returns the left child of a node. */
  public Position left(Position v)
    throws InvalidPositionException, BoundaryViolationException;
  /** Returns the right child of a node. */
  public Position right(Position v)
    throws InvalidPositionException, BoundaryViolationException;
  /** Returns whether a node has a left child. */
  public boolean hasLeft(Position v) throws InvalidPositionException;
  /** Returns whether a node has a right child. */
  public boolean hasRight(Position v) throws InvalidPositionException;
}
```

Code Fragment 6.14: A BinaryTree interface in Java, which extends the Tree interface (Code Fragment 6.1).

We make the following assumptions on the running time of the methods of any class that implements the BinaryTree interface.

- All the assumptions on the running time of the tree ADT methods made in Section 6.2 hold. In particular, for a binary tree, method children(v) takes $O(1)$ time, because each node has at most two children.
- Methods left(v), right(v), hasLeft(v) and hasRight(v) each take $O(1)$ time.

6.3.3 Properties of Binary Trees

Binary trees have several interesting properties dealing with relationships between their heights and number of nodes. We denote the set of all nodes of a tree T at the same depth d as the *level* d of T. In a binary tree, level 0 has one node (the root), level 1 has at most two nodes (the children of the root), level 2 has at most four nodes, and so on. (See Figure 6.11.) In general, level d has at most 2^d nodes.

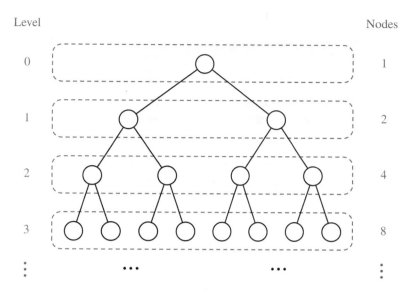

Figure 6.11: Maximum number of nodes in the levels of a binary tree.

We can see that the maximum number of nodes on the levels of a binary tree grows exponentially as we go down the tree. From this simple observation, we can derive the following properties relating the height of a binary T with its number of nodes. A detailed justification of these properties is left as an exercise (R-6.15).

Proposition 6.10: *Let T be a binary tree, and let n, n_E, n_I and h denote the number of nodes, number of external nodes, number of internal nodes and height of T, respectively. Then T has the following properties:*

1. $h + 1 \le n \le 2^{h+1} - 1$
2. $1 \le n_E \le 2^h$
3. $h \le n_I \le 2^h - 1$
4. $\log(n+1) - 1 \le h \le n - 1$

Also, if T is proper, then T has the following properties:

1. $2h + 1 \le n \le 2^{h+1} - 1$
2. $h + 1 \le n_E \le 2^h$
3. $h \le n_I \le 2^h - 1$
4. $\log(n+1) - 1 \le h \le (n-1)/2$

In addition, we also have the following relationship between the number of internal nodes and external nodes in a proper binary tree.

Proposition 6.11: *In a proper binary tree* T, *with* n_E *external nodes and* n_I *internal nodes, we have* $n_E = n_I + 1$.

Justification: We justify this proposition by removing nodes from T and dividing them up into two "piles", an internal-node pile and an external-node pile, until T becomes empty. The piles are initially empty. At the end, the external-node pile will have one more node than the internal-node pile. We consider two cases:

Case 1: If T has only one node v, we remove v and place it on the external-node pile. Thus, the external-node pile has one node and the internal-node pile is empty.

Case 2: Otherwise (T has more than one node), we remove from T an (arbitrary) external node w and its parent v, which is an internal node. We place w on the external-node pile and v on the internal-node pile. If v has a parent u, then we reconnect u with the former sibling z of w, as shown in Figure 6.12. This operation, removes one internal node and one external node, and leaves the tree being a proper binary tree.

Repeating this operation, we eventually are left with a final tree consisting of a single node. Note that the same number of external and internal nodes have been removed and placed on their respective piles by the sequence of operations leading to this final tree. Now, we remove the node of the final tree and we place it on the external-node pile. Thus, the the external-node pile has one more node than the internal-node pile. ∎

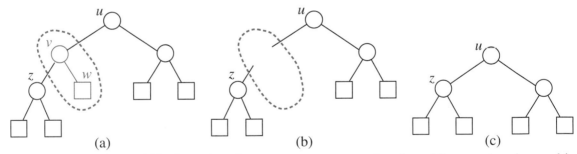

Figure 6.12: Operation that removes an external node and its parent node, used in the justification of Proposition 6.11.

Note that the above relationship does not hold, in general, for improper binary tree and nonbinary trees, although there are other interesting relationships that can hold, as we explore in an exercise (C-6.6).

In subsequent chapters, we explore some important applications of the above facts. Before we can discuss such applications, however, we should first understand more about how binary trees are traversed and represented.

6.3.4 Traversals of a Binary Tree

As with general trees, computations performed on binary trees often involve traversals. In this section, we present algorithms that perform traversals of binary trees, using the binary tree ADT methods.

Preorder Traversal of a Binary Tree

Since any binary tree can also be viewed as a general tree, the preorder traversal for general trees (Code Fragment 6.8) can be applied to any binary tree. We can simplify the algorithm in the case of a binary tree traversal, however, as we show in Code Fragment 6.15.

Algorithm binaryPreorder(T, v):
    perform the "visit" action for node v
    if T.hasLeft(v) **then**
        binaryPreorder(T, T.left(v))   {recursively traverse left subtree}
    if T.hasRight(v) **then**
        binaryPreorder(T, T.right(v))   {recursively traverse right subtree}

Code Fragment 6.15: Algorithm binaryPreorder for performing the preorder traversal of the subtree of a binary tree T rooted at a node v.

As is the case for general trees, there are many applications of the preorder traversal for binary trees.

Postorder Traversal of a Binary Tree

Analogously, the postorder traversal for general trees (Code Fragment 6.11) can be specialized for binary trees, as shown in Code Fragment 6.16.

Algorithm binaryPostorder(T, v):
    if T.hasLeft(v) **then**
        binaryPostorder(T, T.left(v))   {recursively traverse left subtree}
    if T.hasRight(v) **then**
        binaryPostorder(T, T.right(v))   {recursively traverse right subtree}
    perform the "visit" action for node v

Code Fragment 6.16: Algorithm binaryPostorder for performing the postorder traversal of the subtree of a binary tree T rooted at node v.

Expression Tree Evaluation

The postorder traversal of a binary tree can be used to solve the expression tree evaluation problem. In this problem, we are given an arithmetic expression tree, that is, a binary tree where each external node has a value associated with it and each internal node has an arithmetic operation associated with it (see Example 6.5), and we want to compute the value of the arithmetic expression represented by the tree.

Algorithm evaluateExpression, given in Code Fragment 6.17, evaluates the expression associated with the subtree rooted at a node v of an arithmetic expression tree T by performing a postorder traversal of T starting at v. In this case, the "visit" action consists of performing a single arithmetic operation. Note that we use the fact that an arithmetic expression tree is a proper binary tree.

Algorithm evaluateExpression(T, v):
   if T.isInternal(v) **then**
      let $\circ$ be the operator stored at v
      $x \leftarrow$ evaluateExpression(T, T.left(v))
      $y \leftarrow$ evaluateExpression(T, T.right(v))
      return $x \circ y$
   else
      return the value stored at v

Code Fragment 6.17: Algorithm evaluateExpression for evaluating the expression represented by the subtree of an arithmetic expression tree T rooted at node v.

The expression-tree evaluation application of the postorder traversal provides an $O(n)$-time algorithm for evaluating an arithmetic expression represented by a binary tree with n nodes. Indeed, like the general postorder traversal, the postorder traversal for binary trees can be applied to other "bottom-up" evaluation problems (such as the size computation given in Example 6.9) as well. The specialization of the postorder traversal for binary trees simplifies that for general trees, however, because we use the left and right methods to avoid a loop that iterates through the children of an internal node.

Interestingly, the specialization of the general preorder and postorder traversal methods to binary trees suggests a third traversal of a binary tree that is different from both the preorder and postorder traversals.

Inorder Traversal of a Binary Tree

An additional traversal method for a binary tree is the ***inorder*** traversal. In this traversal, we visit a node between the recursive traversals of its left and right subtrees. The inorder traversal of the subtree rooted at a node v in a binary tree T is given in Code Fragment 6.18.

Algorithm inorder(T, v):
    if T.hasLeft(v) **then**
        inorder(T, T.left(v))   {recursively traverse left subtree}
    perform the "visit" action for node v
    if T.hasRight(v) **then**
        inorder(T, T.right(v))   {recursively traverse right subtree}

Code Fragment 6.18: Algorithm inorder for performing the inorder traversal of the subtree of a binary tree T rooted at a node v.

The inorder traversal of a binary tree T can be informally viewed as visiting the nodes of T "from left to right." Indeed, for every node v, the inorder traversal visits v after all the nodes in the left subtree of v and before all the nodes in the right subtree of v. (See Figure 6.13.)

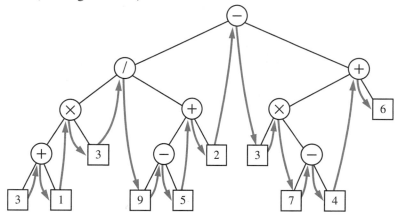

Figure 6.13: Inorder traversal of a binary tree.

The inorder traversal algorithm also has several applications. One of the most important ones arises when we store an ordered sequence of elements in a binary tree, defining a structure we call a binary search tree.

Binary Search Trees

Let S be a set whose elements have an order relation. For examples, S could be a set of integers. A ***binary search*** tree for S is a proper binary tree T such that

- Each internal node v of T stores an element of S, denoted with $x(v)$.
- For each internal node v of T, the elements stored in the left subtree of v are less than or equal to $x(v)$ and the elements stored in the right subtree of v are greater than or equal to $x(v)$.
- The external nodes of T do not store any element.

An inorder traversal of the internal nodes of a binary search tree T visits the elements in nondecreasing order. (See Figure 6.14.)

We can use a binary search tree T for set S to find whether a given search value y is in S, by traversing a path down the tree T, starting at the root. (See Figure 6.14.) At each internal node v encountered, we compare our search value y with the element $x(v)$ stored at v. If $y \leq x(v)$, then the search continues in the left subtree of v. If $y = x(v)$, then the search terminates successfully. If $y \geq x(v)$, then the search continues in the right subtree of v. Finally, if we reach an external node, the search terminates unsuccessfully. In other words, a binary search tree can be viewed as a binary decision tree (recall Example 6.4), where the question asked at each internal node is whether the element at that node is less than, equal to, or larger than the element being searched for. Indeed, it is exactly this correspondence to a binary decision tree that motivates restricting binary search trees to be proper binary trees (with "place-holder" external nodes).

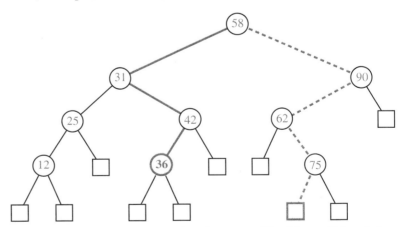

Figure 6.14: A binary search tree storing integers. The blue solid path is traversed when searching (successfully) for 36. The blue dashed path is traversed when searching (unsuccessfully) for 70.

Note that the running time of searching in a binary search tree T is proportional to the height of T. Recall from Proposition 6.10 that the height of a proper binary tree with n nodes can be as small as $\log(n+1) - 1$ or as large as $(n-1)/2$. Thus, binary search trees are most efficient when they have small height. We illustrate an example search operation in a binary search tree in Figure 6.14, and we study binary search trees in more detail in Section 9.1.

Using Inorder Traversal for Tree Drawing

The inorder traversal can also be applied to the problem of computing a drawing of a binary tree. We can draw a binary tree T with an algorithm that assigns x- and y-coordinates to a node v of T using the following two rules (see Figure 6.15):

- $x(v)$ is the number of nodes visited before v in the inorder traversal of T.
- $y(v)$ is the depth of v in T.

In this application, we take the convention common in computer graphics that x-coordinates increase left to right and y-coordinates increase top to bottom. So the origin is in the upper left corner of the computer screen.

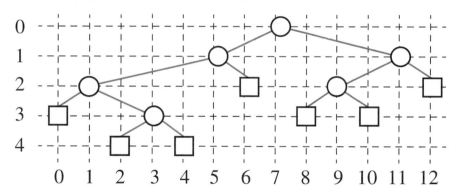

Figure 6.15: An inorder drawing of a binary tree.

A Unified Tree Traversal Framework

The tree-traversal algorithms we have discussed so far are all forms of iterators. Each traversal visits the nodes of a tree in a certain order, and is guaranteed to visit each node exactly once. We can unify the tree-traversal algorithms given above into a single framework, however, by relaxing the requirement that each node be visited exactly once. The resulting traversal method is called the ***Euler tour traversal***, which we study next. The advantage of this traversal is that it allows for more general kinds of algorithms to be expressed easily.

The Euler Tour Traversal of a Binary Tree

The Euler tour traversal of a binary tree T can be informally defined as a "walk" around T, where we start by going from the root toward its left child, viewing the edges of T as being "walls" that we always keep to our left. (See Figure 6.16.) Each node v of T is encountered three times by the Euler tour:

- "On the left" (before the Euler tour of v's left subtree)
- "From below" (between the Euler tours of v's two subtrees)
- "On the right" (after the Euler tour of v's right subtree).

If v is external, then these three "visits" actually all happen at the same time.

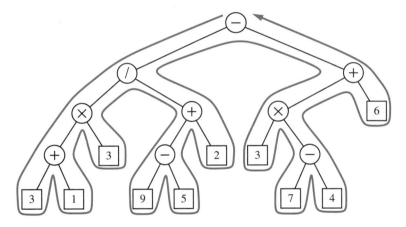

Figure 6.16: Euler tour traversal of a binary tree.

We give pseudo-code for the Euler tour of the subtree rooted at a node v in Code Fragment 6.19.

The preorder traversal of a binary tree is equivalent to an Euler tour traversal such that each node has an associated "visit" action occur only when it is encountered on the left. Likewise, the inorder and postorder traversals of a binary tree are equivalent to an Euler tour such that each node has an associated "visit" action occur only when it is encountered from below or on the right, respectively.

The Euler tour traversal extends the preorder, inorder, and postorder traversals, but it can also perform other kinds of traversals. For example, suppose we wish to compute the number of descendents of each node v in an n-node binary tree. We start an Euler tour by initializing a counter to 0, and then increment the counter each time we visit a node on the left. To determine the number of descendents of a node v, we compute the difference between the values of the counter when v is

Algorithm eulerTour(T, v):

    perform the action for visiting node v on the left

    if T.hasLeft(v) **then**

        eulerTour(T, T.left(v))   { recursively tour the left subtree of v }

    perform the action for visiting node v from below

    if T.hasRight(v) **then**

        eulerTour(T, T.right(v))   { recursively tour the right subtree of v }

    perform the action for visiting node v on the right

Code Fragment 6.19: Algorithm eulerTour for computing the Euler tour traversal of the subtree of a binary tree T rooted at a node v.

visited on the left and when it is visited on the right, and add 1. This simple rule gives us the number of descendents of v, because each node in the subtree rooted at v is counted between v's visit on the left and v's visit on the right. Therefore, we have an $O(n)$-time method for computing the number of descendents of each node.

The running time of the Euler tour traversal is easy to analyze, assuming each visit action takes $O(1)$ time. Namely, in each traversal, we spend a constant amount of time at each node of the tree during the traversal, so the overall running time is $O(n)$ for an n-node tree.

Another application of the Euler tour traversal is to print a fully parenthesized arithmetic expression from its expression tree (Example 6.5). Algorithm printExpression, shown in Code Fragment 6.20, accomplishes this task by performing the following actions in an Euler tour:

- "On the left" action: if the node is internal, print "("
- "From below" action: print the value or operator stored at the node
- "On the right" action: if the node is internal, print ")".

Algorithm printExpression(T, v):

    if T.isExternal(v) **then**

        print the value stored at v

    else

        print "("

        printExpression(T, T.left(v))

        print the operator stored at v

        printExpression(T, T.right(v))

        print ")"

Code Fragment 6.20: An algorithm for printing the arithmetic expression associated with the subtree of an arithmetic expression tree T rooted at v.

6.3.5 The Template Method Pattern

The tree traversal methods described above are actually examples of an interesting object-oriented software design pattern, the ***template method pattern***. The template method pattern describes a generic computation mechanism that can be specialized for a particular application by redefining certain steps.

Euler Tour with the Template Method Pattern

Following the template method pattern, we design an algorithm that implements a generic Euler tour traversal of a binary tree. This algorithm, called templateEuler-Tour, is shown in Code Fragment 6.21.

When called on a node v, method templateEulerTour calls several other auxiliary methods at different phases of the traversal. Namely, it

- Creates a local variable r of type TraversalResult, which is used to store intermediate results of the computation and has fields left, right and out
- Calls auxiliary method visitLeft(T, v, r), which performs the computations associated with encountering the node on the left
- If v has a left child, recursively calls itself on the left child of v and stores the returned value in r.left
- Calls auxiliary method visitBelow(T, v, r), which performs the computations associated with encountering the node from below
- If v has a right child, recursively calls itself on the right child and stores the returned value in r.right
- Calls auxiliary method visitRight(T, v, r), which performs the computations associated with encountering the node on the right
- Returns r.out.

Method templateEulerTour can be viewed as a ***template*** or "skeleton" of an Euler tour. (See Code Fragment 6.21.)

In an object-oriented context, we can then write a class EulerTour that:

- Contains a recursive method templateEulerTour(T, v)
- Contains all the auxiliary methods called by templateEulerTour as empty place holders (that is, with no instructions or returning null).

Class EulerTour itself does not perform any useful computation. However, we can extend it with the inheritance mechanism and override the empty methods to do useful tasks.

Algorithm templateEulerTour(T, v):

> $r \leftarrow$ new object of type TraversalResult
> visitLeft(T, v, r)
> **if** T.hasLeft(v) **then**
> > r.left $\leftarrow$ templateEulerTour(T, T.left(v))
> visitBelow(T, v, r)
> **if** T.hasRight(v) **then**
> > r.right $\leftarrow$ templateEulerTour(T, T.right(v))
> visitRight(T, v, r)
> **return** r.out

Code Fragment 6.21: Method templateEulerTour for computing a generic Euler tour traversal of the subtree of a binary tree T rooted at a node v, following the template method pattern. This method calls the auxiliary methods visitLeft, visitBelow, and visitRight.

Template Method Examples

As a first example, we can evaluate the expression associated with an arithmetic expression tree (see Example 6.5) by writing a new class EvaluateExpression that extends class EulerTour and overrides auxiliary method visitRight(T, v, r) with the following computation:

- If v is an external node, set r.out equal to the value of the variable stored at v
- Else (v is an internal node), combine r.left and r.right with the operator stored at v, and set r.out equal to the result of the operation.

This approach should be compared with the direct implementation of the algorithm shown in Code Fragment 6.17.

As a second example, we can print the expression associated with an arithmetic expression tree (see Example 6.5) using a new class PrintExpression that extends class EulerTour and overrides methods visitLeft, visitBelow, and visitRight as follows:

- visitLeft prints "(" if the current node is internal
- visitBelow prints the variable or the operator stored at the current node
- visitRight prints ")" if the current node is internal.

This approach should be compared with the direct implementation of the algorithm shown in Code Fragment 6.20.

Java Implementation of Euler Tour Traversal

Java class EulerTour, which implements a generic Euler tour traversal, and its specializations EvaluateExpressionTour and PrintExpressionTour are shown in Code Fragments 6.22–6.24. Class EulerTour is an abstract class and thus cannot be instantiated. It contains an abstract method, called execute, which needs to be specified in concrete subclass of EulerTour. Class TraversalResult, with fields left, right, and out, is not shown.

```
/**
 * Template for algorithms traversing a binary tree using an Euler
 * tour. The subclasses of this class will redefine some of the
 * methods of this class to create a specific traversal.
 */
public abstract class EulerTour {
  protected BinaryTree tree;
  /** Execution of the traversal. This abstract method must be
   * specified in a concrete subclass. */
  public abstract Object execute(BinaryTree T);
  /** Initialization of the traversal */
  protected void init(BinaryTree T) { tree = T; }
  /** Template method */
  protected Object eulerTour(Position v) {
    TraversalResult r = new TraversalResult();
    visitLeft(v, r);
    if (tree.hasLeft(v))
      r.left = eulerTour(tree.left(v)); // recursive traversal
    visitBelow(v, r);
    if (tree.hasRight(v))
      r.right = eulerTour(tree.right(v)); // recursive traversal
    visitRight(v, r);
    return r.out;
  }
  // Auxiliary methods that can be redefined by subclasses:
  /** Method called for the visit on the left */
  protected void visitLeft(Position v, TraversalResult r) {}
  /** Method called for the visit on from below */
  protected void visitBelow(Position v, TraversalResult r) {}
  /** Method called for the visit on the right */
  protected void visitRight(Position v, TraversalResult r) {}
}
```

Code Fragment 6.22: Java class EulerTour defining a generic Euler tour of a binary tree. This class realizes the template method pattern and must be specialized in order to get an interesting computation.

```
/** This traversal specializes EulerTour to compute the value of the
  * expression represented by an arithmetic expression tree. It
  * assumes that the elements stored at the external nodes are of type
  * Integer and the elements stored at the internal nodes are of type
  * OperatorInfo, with method operation(Integer x, Integer y), which
  * returns the result of applying an arithmetic operation.  */
public class EvaluateExpressionTour extends EulerTour {
  public Object execute(BinaryTree T) {
    init(T); // calls method of superclass
    System.out.print("Value of the expression: ");
    System.out.println(eulerTour(tree.root()));
    return null;   // nothing interesting to return
  }
  protected void visitRight(Position v, TraversalResult r) {
    if (tree.isExternal(v)) r.out = v.element();
    else {
      OperatorInfo op = (OperatorInfo) v.element();
      r.out = op.operation((Integer) r.left, (Integer) r.right);
    }
  }
}
```

Code Fragment 6.23: Class EvaluateExpressionTour that specializes EulerTour to evaluate the expression associated with an arithmetic expression tree.

```
/** This traversal specializes EulerTour to print out the expression
  * stored in an arithmetic expression tree. It assumes that method
  * toString, when called on a node v, prints the value stored at v if
  * v is external and the operator stored at v, if v is internal.  */
public class PrintExpressionTour extends EulerTour {
  public Object execute(BinaryTree T) {
    init(T);
    System.out.print("Expression: ");
    eulerTour(T.root());
    System.out.println();
    return null;    // nothing interesting to return
  }
  protected void visitLeft(Position v, TraversalResult r) {
    if (tree.isInternal(v)) System.out.print("("); }
  protected void visitBelow(Position v, TraversalResult r) {
    System.out.print(v.element()); }
  protected void visitRight(Position v, TraversalResult r) {
    if (tree.isInternal(v)) System.out.print(")"); }
}
```

Code Fragment 6.24: Class PrintExpressionTour that specializes EulerTour to print the expression associated with an arithmetic expression tree.

6.4 Data Structures for Representing Trees

In this section, we describe concrete data structures for representing trees.

6.4.1 A Vector-Based Structure for Binary Trees

A simple structure for representing a binary tree T is based on a way of numbering the nodes of T. For every node v of T, let $p(v)$ be the integer defined as follows.

- If v is the root of T, then $p(v) = 1$.
- If v is the left child of node u, then $p(v) = 2p(u)$.
- If v is the right child of node u, then $p(v) = 2p(u) + 1$.

The numbering function p is known as a ***level numbering*** of the nodes in a binary tree T, for it numbers the nodes on each level of T in increasing order from left to right, although it may skip some numbers. (See Figure 6.17.)

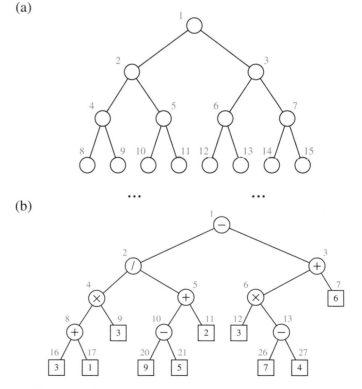

Figure 6.17: Binary tree level numbering: (a) general scheme; (b) an example.

The level numbering function p suggests a representation of a binary tree T by means of a vector S such that node v of T is the element of S at rank $p(v)$. (See Figure 6.18.) Typically, we realize the vector S by means of an extendable array. (See Section 5.1.3.) Such an implementation is simple and efficient, for we can use it to easily perform the methods root, parent, left, right, hasLeft, hasRight, isInternal, isExternal, and isRoot by using simple arithmetic operations on the numbers $p(v)$ associated with each node v involved in the operation. That is, each position object v is simply a "wrapper" for the index $p(v)$ into the vector S. We leave the details of this implementation as an exercise (R-6.26).

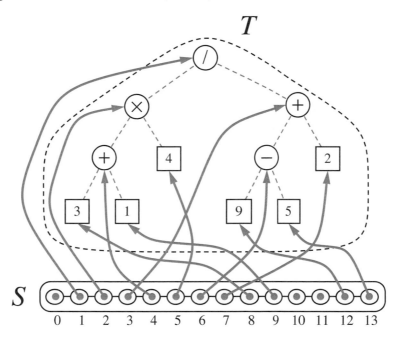

Figure 6.18: Representation of a binary tree T by means of a vector S.

Let n be the number of nodes of T, and let p_M be the maximum value of $p(v)$ over all the nodes of T. Vector S has size $N = p_M + 1$ since the element of S at rank 0 is not associated with any node of T. Also, vector S will have, in general, a number of empty elements that do not refer to existing nodes of T. In fact, in the worst case, $N = 2^n$, the justification of which is left as an exercise (R-6.23). In Section 7.3, we will see a class of binary trees, called "heaps" for which $N = n + 1$. Thus, in spite of the worst-case space usage, there are applications for which the vector representation of a binary tree is space efficient. Still, for general binary trees, the exponential worst-case space requirement of this representation is prohibitive.

Table 6.1 summarizes the running times of the methods of a binary tree implemented with a vector. We do not include any tree update methods in this table.

Operation	Time
size, isEmpty	$O(1)$
elements, positions	$O(n)$
replace	$O(1)$
root, parent, children, left, right	$O(1)$
hasLeft, hasRight, isInternal, isExternal, isRoot	$O(1)$

Table 6.1: Running times for a binary tree T implemented with a vector S. We denote with n the number of nodes of T, and N denotes the size of S. Methods hasNext() and next() of the iterators elements(), positions() and children(v) take $O(1)$ time. The space usage is $O(N)$, which is $O(2^n)$ in the worst case.

6.4.2   A Linked Structure for Binary Trees

A natural way to realize a binary tree T is to use a ***linked structure***, where we represent each node v of T by an object (see Figure 6.19a) with fields storing references to the element stored at v and to the position objects associated with the children and parent of v. If v is the root of T, then the parent field of v is null. If v has no left child, then the left field of v is null. If v has no right child, then the right field of v is null. Also, we store the number of nodes of T in a variable, called size. We show the linked structure representation of a binary tree in Figure 6.19b.

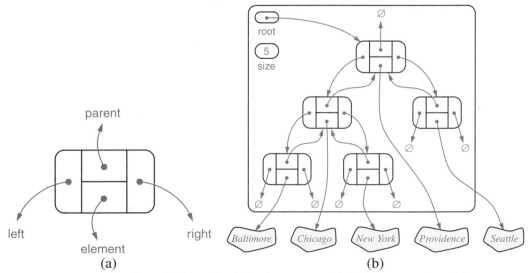

(a)   (b)

Figure 6.19: A node (a) and a linked structure (b) for representing a binary tree.

A Java Implementation of a Linked Binary Tree Structure

We use a Java interface BTPosition (not shown) to represent a node of a binary tree. This interfaces extends Position, thus inheriting method element, and has additional methods for setting the element stored at the node (setElement) and for setting and returning the left child (setLeft and getLeft), right child (setRight and getRight) and parent (setParent and getParent) of the node. Class BTNode (Code Fragment 6.25) implements interface BTPosition by an object with fields element, left, right, and parent, which, for a node v, reference the element at v, the left child of v, the right child of v, and the parent of v, respectively.

```
/**
 * Class implementing a node of a binary tree by storing references to
 * an element, a parent node, a left node, and a right node.
 */
public class BTNode implements BTPosition {
  private Object element;   // element stored at this node
  private BTPosition left, right, parent;  // adjacent nodes
  /** Main constructor */
  public BTNode(Object element, BTPosition parent,
          BTPosition left, BTPosition right) {
    setElement(element);
    setParent(parent);
    setLeft(left);
    setRight(right);
  }
  public Object element() { return element; }
  public void setElement(Object o) {
    element=o;
  }
  public BTPosition getLeft() { return left; }
  public void setLeft(BTPosition v) {
    left=v;
  }
  public BTPosition getRight() { return right; }
  public void setRight(BTPosition v) {
    right=v;
  }
  public BTPosition getParent() { return parent; }
  public void setParent(BTPosition v) {
    parent=v;
  }
}
```

Code Fragment 6.25: Auxiliary class BTNode for implementing binary tree nodes.

In Code Fragments 6.26–6.28, we show class LinkedBinaryTree that implements the BinaryTree interface (Code Fragment 6.14) using a linked data structure. This class stores the size of the tree and a reference to the BTNode object associated with the root of the tree in internal variables. In addition to the BinaryTree interface methods, LinkedBinaryTree has various other methods, including accessor method sibling(v), which returns the sibling of a node v, and the following update methods:

addRoot(e): Create and return a new node r storing element e and make r the root; an error occurs if the tree is not empty.
Input: Element; *Output:* Position.

insertLeft(v, e): Create and return a new node w storing element e, add w as the the left child of v and return w; an error occurs if v already has a left child.
Input: Position and element; *Output:* Position.

insertRight(v, e): Create and return a new node z storing element e, add z as the the right child of v and return z; an error occurs if v already has a right child.
Input: Position and element; *Output:* Position.

remove(v): Remove node v, replace it with its child, if any, and return the element stored at v; an error occurs if v has two children.
Input: Position; *Output:* Object.

attach(v, T_1, T_2): Attach T_1 and T_2, respectively, as the left and right subtrees of the external node v; an error condition occurs if v is not external.
Input: Position and two binary trees; *Output:* None.

Class LinkedBinaryTree has a constructor with no arguments that returns an empty binary tree. Starting from this empty tree, we can build any binary tree by creating the first node with method addRoot and repeatedly applying the insertLeft and insertRight methods and/or the attach method. Likewise, we can dismantle any binary tree T using the remove operation, ultimately reducing such a tree T to an empty binary tree.

When a position v is passed as an argument to one of the methods of class LinkedBinaryTree, its validity is checked by calling an auxiliary helper method, checkPosition(v). A list of the nodes visited in an inorder traversal of the tree is constructed by recursive method inorderPositions. Error conditions are indicated by throwing exceptions InvalidPositionException, BoundaryViolationException, EmptyTreeException and NonEmptyTreeException.

```java
/**
 * An implementation of the BinaryTree interface by means of a linked structure.
 */
public class LinkedBinaryTree implements BinaryTree {
  protected Position root;        // reference to the root
  protected int size;             // number of nodes
  /**  Creates an empty binary tree. */
  public LinkedBinaryTree() {
    root = null;  // start with an empty tree
    size = 0;
  }
  // BinaryTree interface methods
  /** Returns the number of nodes in the tree. */
  public int size() {
    return size;
  }
  /** Returns whether the tree is empty. */
  public boolean isEmpty() {
    return (size==0);
  }
  /** Returns whether a node is internal. */
  public boolean isInternal(Position v) throws InvalidPositionException {
    checkPosition(v);    // auxiliary method
    return (hasLeft(v) || hasRight(v));
  }
  /** Returns whether a node is external. */
  public boolean isExternal(Position v) throws InvalidPositionException {
    return !isInternal(v);
  }
  /** Returns whether a node is the root. */
  public boolean isRoot(Position v) throws InvalidPositionException {
    checkPosition(v);
    return (v == root());
  }
  /** Returns whether a node has a left child. */
  public boolean hasLeft(Position v) throws InvalidPositionException {
    BTPosition vv = checkPosition(v);
    return (vv.getLeft() != null);
  }
  /** Returns whether a node has a right child. */
  public boolean hasRight(Position v) throws InvalidPositionException {
    BTPosition vv = checkPosition(v);
    return (vv.getRight() != null);
  }
```

Code Fragment 6.26: Class LinkedBinaryTree, implementing the BinaryTree interface. (Continues in Code Fragment 6.27.)

```java
/** Returns the root of the tree. */
public Position root() throws EmptyTreeException {
  if (root == null)
    throw new EmptyTreeException("The tree has no root");
  return root;
}
/** Returns the left child of a node. */
public Position left(Position v)
  throws InvalidPositionException, BoundaryViolationException {
  if (!hasLeft(v))
    throw new BoundaryViolationException("No left child");
  return ((BTPosition)v).getLeft();
}
/** Returns the right child of a node. */
public Position right(Position v)
  throws InvalidPositionException, BoundaryViolationException {
  if (!hasRight(v))
    throw new BoundaryViolationException("No right child");
  return ((BTPosition)v).getRight();
}
/** Returns the parent of a node. */
public Position parent(Position v)
  throws InvalidPositionException, BoundaryViolationException {
  if (isRoot(v))
    throw new BoundaryViolationException("Root has no parent");
  return ((BTPosition)v).getParent();
}
/** Returns an iterator of the children of a node. */
public Iterator children(Position v)
  throws InvalidPositionException {
  List children = new NodeList();
  if (hasLeft(v))
    children.insertLast(left(v));
  if (hasRight(v))
    children.insertLast(right(v));
  return children.elements();
}
/** Returns an iterator of the tree nodes. */
public Iterator positions() {
  List positions = new NodeList();
  if(size != 0)
    inorderPositions(root(), positions);  // assign positions in inorder
  return positions.elements();
}
```

Code Fragment 6.27: Class LinkedBinaryTree, implementing the BinaryTree interface. (Continued from Code Fragment 6.26; continues in Code Fragment 6.28.)

```
/** Returns an iterator of the elements stored at the nodes */
public Iterator elements() {
  Iterator positer = positions();
  List elements = new NodeList();
  for (int i = 0; i < size; i++)
    elements.insertLast(((Position) positer.next()).element());
  return elements.elements();  // An iterator of elements
}
/** Replaces the element at a node. */
public Object replace(Position v, Object o)
  throws InvalidPositionException {
  BTPosition vv = checkPosition(v);
  Object temp = v.element();
  vv.setElement(o);
  return temp;
}
// Additional accessor method
/** Return the sibling of a node */
public Position sibling(Position v)
  throws InvalidPositionException, BoundaryViolationException {
  try {
    Position p = parent(v);
    Position lc = left(p);
    if (v == lc)
      return right(p);
    else
      return lc;
  }
  catch(BoundaryViolationException e) {
    throw new BoundaryViolationException("Node has no sibling");
  }
}
// Additional update methods
/** Inserts a left child at a given node. */
public Position  insertLeft(Position v, Object e)
  throws InvalidPositionException {
  if (hasLeft(v))
    throw new InvalidPositionException("Node already has a left child");
  BTPosition vv = (BTPosition)v;
  BTPosition ww = createNode(e, vv, null, null);
  vv.setLeft(ww);
  size++;
  return ww;
}
```

Code Fragment 6.28: Class LinkedBinaryTree, implementing the BinaryTree interface. (Continued from Code Fragment 6.27; continues in Code Fragment 6.29.)

```
/** Inserts a right child at a given node. */
public Position  insertRight(Position v, Object e)
  throws InvalidPositionException {
  if (hasRight(v))
    throw new InvalidPositionException("Node already has a right child");
  BTPosition vv = (BTPosition)v;
  BTPosition w = createNode(e, vv, null, null);
  vv.setRight(w);
  size++;
  return w;
}
/** Removes a node with zero or one child. */
public Object remove(Position v)
  throws InvalidPositionException {
  if (hasLeft(v) && hasRight(v))
    throw new InvalidPositionException("Cannot remove node w/ 2 children");
  BTPosition vv = (BTPosition)v;
  BTPosition ww; // the only child of v, if any
  if (hasLeft(v))
    ww = (BTPosition) left(v);
  else if (hasRight(v))
    ww = (BTPosition) right(v);
  else
    ww = null;
  if (v == root()) {
    if (ww != null)
      ww.setParent(null);
    root = ww;
  }
  else {
    BTPosition uu = (BTPosition) parent(v);
    if (hasLeft(uu) && v == left(uu))
      uu.setLeft(ww);
    else
      uu.setRight(ww);
    if(ww != null)
      ww.setParent(uu);
  }
  size--;
  return v.element();
}
```

Code Fragment 6.29: Class LinkedBinaryTree, implementing the BinaryTree interface. (Continued from Code Fragment 6.28; continues in Code Fragment 6.30.)

```
/** Adds a root node to an empty tree */
public Position addRoot(Object e) throws NonEmptyTreeException {
  if(!isEmpty())
    throw new NonEmptyTreeException("Tree already has a root");
  size = 1;
  root = createNode(e,null,null,null);
  return root;
}
/** Attaches two trees to be subtrees of an external node. */
public void attach(Position v, BinaryTree T1, BinaryTree T2)
  throws InvalidPositionException {
  if (isInternal(v))
    throw new InvalidPositionException("Cannot attach from internal node");
  BTPosition vv = (BTPosition)v;
  if (!T1.isEmpty()) {
    vv.setLeft((BTPosition) T1.root());
    ((BTPosition)T1.root()).setParent(vv);  // T1 should be invalidated
  }
  if (!T2.isEmpty()) {
    vv.setRight((BTPosition) T2.root());
    ((BTPosition)T2.root()).setParent(vv);  // T2 should be invalidated
  }
}
/** If v is a good binary tree node, cast to BTPosition, else throw exception */
protected BTPosition checkPosition(Position v)
  throws InvalidPositionException {
  if (v == null || !(v instanceof BTPosition))
    throw new InvalidPositionException("The position is invalid");
  return (BTPosition) v;
}
/** Creates a new binary tree node */
protected BTPosition createNode(Object element, BTPosition parent,
                                BTPosition left, BTPosition right) {
  return new BTNode(element,parent,left,right); }
/** Creates a list storing the the nodes in the subtree of a node,
  * ordered according to the inorder traversal of the subtree. */
protected void inorderPositions(Position v, List pos)
  throws InvalidPositionException {
  if (hasLeft(v))
    inorderPositions(left(v), pos);  // recurse on left child
  pos.insertLast(v);
  if (hasRight(v))
    inorderPositions(right(v), pos); // recurse on right child
}
```

Code Fragment 6.30: Class LinkedBinaryTree, implementing the BinaryTree interface. (Continued from Code Fragment 6.29.)

Performance of the LinkedBinaryTree Implementation

Let us now analyze the running times of the methods of class LinkedBinaryTree, which uses a linked structure representation:

- Methods size() and isEmpty() use an instance variable storing the number of nodes of T, and each take $O(1)$ time.
- The accessor methods root, left, right, sibling and parent take $O(1)$ time.
- Method replace(v, e) takes $O(1)$ time.
- Methods elements() and positions() are implemented by performing an inorder traversal of the tree. While any one of the three traversals discussed in Section 6.3.4 (preorder, inorder, and postorder) would serve the purpose, we chose the inorder traversal, as it is possibly the most natural for binary trees. The nodes visited by the traversal are stored in a list implemented by class NodeList (Section 5.2.4) and the output iterator is generated with method elements() of class NodeList. Methods elements() and positions() takes $O(n)$ time and methods hasNext() and next() of the returned iterators run in $O(1)$ time.
- Method children uses a similar approach to construct the returned iterator, but it runs in $O(1)$ time, since there are at most two children for any node in a binary tree.
- The update methods insertLeft, insertRight, attach, and remove all run in $O(1)$ time, as they involve constant-time manipulation of a constant number of nodes.

Considering the space required by this data structure, note that there is an object of class BTNode (Code Fragment 6.25) for every node of tree T. Thus, the overall space requirement is $O(n)$. Table 6.2 summarizes the performance of the linked structure implementation of a binary tree.

Operation	Time
size, isEmpty	$O(1)$
elements, positions	$O(n)$
replace	$O(1)$
root, parent, children, left, right, sibling	$O(1)$
hasLeft, hasRight, isInternal, isExternal, isRoot	$O(1)$
insertLeft, insertRight, attach, remove	$O(1)$

Table 6.2: Running times for the methods of an n-node binary tree implemented with a linked structure. Methods hasNext() and next() of the iterators returned by elements(), positions() and children(v) run in $O(1)$ time. The space usage is $O(n)$.

Building an Expression Tree

As an example use of the attach(v, T_1, T_2) method, consider the problem of constructing an expression tree from a fully parenthesized arithmetic expression of size n. (Recall Example 6.5 and Code Fragment 6.17.) In Code Fragment 6.31, we give algorithm buildExpression for building such an expression tree, assuming all arithmetic operations are binary and variables are not parenthesized. Thus, every parenthesized subexpression contains an operator in the middle. The algorithm uses a stack S while scanning the input expression E looking for variables, operators, and right parentheses.

- When we see a variable or operator x, we create a single-node binary tree T, whose root stores x and we push T on the stack.
- When we see a right parenthesis, ")", we pop the top three trees from the stack S, which represent a subexpression $(E_1 \circ E_2)$. We then attach the trees for E_1 and E_2 to the one for $\circ$, and push the resulting tree back on S.

We repeat this until the expression E has been processed, at which time the top element on the stack is the expression tree for E. The total running time is $O(n)$.

Algorithm buildExpression(E):

    Input: A fully-parenthesized arithmetic expression $E = e_0, e_1, \ldots, e_{n-1}$, with each e_i being a variable, operator, or parenthetic symbol

    Output: A binary tree T representing arithmetic expression E

  $S \leftarrow$ a new initially-empty stack
  for $i \leftarrow 0$ to $n - 1$ **do**
    if e_i is a variable or an operator **then**
      $T \leftarrow$ a new empty binary tree
      T.addRoot(e_i)
      S.push(T)
    else if $e_i =$ '(' **then**
      Continue looping
    else $\{e_i =$ ')'$\}$
      $T_2 \leftarrow S$.pop()   {the tree representing E_2}
      $T \leftarrow S$.pop()   {the tree representing $\circ$}
      $T_1 \leftarrow S$.pop()   {the tree representing E_1}
      T.attach$(T$.root$(), T_1, T_2)$
      S.push(T)
  return S.pop()

Code Fragment 6.31: Algorithm buildExpression.

Cloning a Tree

The methods insertLeft and insertRight can be used to make an exact copy, or "clone," T' of a binary tree T. In Code Fragment 6.32 we show how to do this recursively using a preorder traversal. (In Java, every object implementing the java.lang.Cloneable interface must be able to duplicate itself using the clone method.)

Algorithm clone(T, T', v, v'):

    Input: Binary trees T and T', a node v in T, and an external node v' in T'

    Output: An augmentation of T' that replaces v' with an exact copy of the subtree of T rooted at v

T'.replace$(v', v$.element$())$
if T.hasLeft(v) **then**
    clone$(T, T', T$.left$(v), T'$.insertLeft$(v', \text{null}))$
if T.hasRight(v) **then**
    clone$(T, T', T$.right$(v), T'$.insertRight$(v', \text{null}))$

        Code Fragment 6.32: Algorithm clone for cloning a binary tree.

6.4.3   A Linked Structure for General Trees

We can extend the linked structure for binary trees to represent general trees. Since there is no limit on the number of children that a node v in a general tree can have, we use a container (for example, a list or vector) to store the children of v, instead of using instance variables. This structure is schematically illustrated in Figure 6.20.

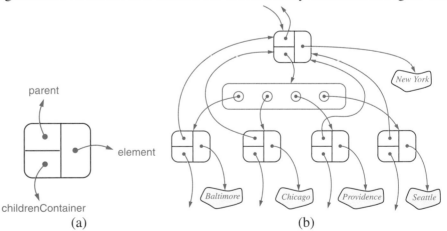

(a)   (b)

Figure 6.20: The linked structure for a general tree: (a) the object associated with a node; (b) the portion of the data structure associated with a node and its children.

Table 6.3 summarizes the performance of the implementation of a general tree using a linked structure. The analysis is left as an exercise (C-6.23), but we note that, by using a container to store the children of each node v, we can implement children(v) simply by calling the elements() method of the children container of v.

Operation	Time
size, isEmpty	$O(1)$
elements, positions	$O(n)$
replace	$O(1)$
root, parent	$O(1)$
children(v)	$O(c_v)$
isInternal, isExternal, isRoot	$O(1)$

Table 6.3: Running times of the methods of an n-node general tree implemented with a linked structure. We let c_v denote the number of children of a node v. Methods hasNext() and next() of the iterators returned by elements(), positions() and children(v) take $O(1)$ time. The space usage is $O(n)$.

6.4.4 Representing General Trees with Binary Trees

An alternative representation of a general tree T is obtained by transforming T into a binary tree T'. (See Figure 6.21.)

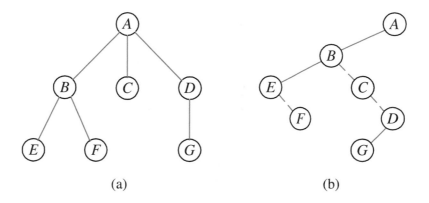

(a)   (b)

Figure 6.21: Representation of a tree by means of a binary tree: (a) tree T; (b) binary tree T' representing T. The dashed edges connect nodes of T' associated with sibling nodes of T.

In order to facilitate this representation, we assume that either T is ordered or that it has been arbitrarily ordered. The transformation is as follows:

- For each node u of T, there is a node u' of T' associated with u.

- If u is an internal node of T and v is the first child of u in T, then v' is the left child of u' in T'.

- If v has a sibling w immediately following v, then w' is the right child of v' in T'.

It is easy to maintain the correspondence between T and T', and to express operations in T in terms of corresponding operations in T'. Intuitively, we can think of the correspondence in terms of a conversion of T into T' that takes each set of siblings $\{v_1, v_2, \ldots, v_k\}$ in T with parent u and replaces it with a chain of right children rooted at v_1, which then becomes the left child of u.

Table 6.4 summarizes the performance of the implementation of a tree by means of a binary tree. The analysis is left as an exercise (C-6.24).

Operation	Time
size, isEmpty	$O(1)$
elements, positions	$O(n)$
replace	$O(1)$
root	$O(1)$
parent(v)	$O(s_v)$
children(v)	$O(c_v)$
isInternal, isExternal, isRoot	$O(1)$

Table 6.4: Running times of the methods of a tree represented by means of a binary tree, which is in turn implemented with a linked structure. We denote with n the number of nodes of the tree, with c_v the number of children of a node v, and with s_v the number of siblings of v. The methods hasNext() and next() of the iterators returned by methods elements(), positions() and children(v) take $O(1)$ time. The space usage is $O(n)$.

6.5 Exercises

For source code and help with exercises, please visit **java.datastructures.net**.

Reinforcement

R-6.1 The following questions refer to the tree of Figure 6.3.

    a. Which node is the root?
    b. What are the internal nodes?
    c. How many descendents does node cs016/ have?
    d. How many ancestors does node cs016/ have?
    e. What are the siblings of node homeworks/?
    f. Which nodes are in the subtree rooted at node projects/?
    g. What is the depth of node papers/?
    h. What is the height of the tree?

R-6.2 Find the value of the arithmetic expression associated with each subtree of the binary tree of Figure 6.6.

R-6.3 Let T be an n-node binary tree that may be improper. Describe how to represent T by means of a **proper** binary tree T' with $O(n)$ nodes.

R-6.4 What are the minimum and maximum number of internal and external nodes in an improper binary tree with n nodes?

R-6.5 Show a tree achieving the worst-case running time for algorithm depth.

R-6.6 Give a justification of Proposition 6.6.

R-6.7 What is the running time of algorithm height2(T, v) (Code Fragment 6.6) when called on a node v distinct from the root of T?

R-6.8 Let T be the tree of Figure 6.3.

    a. Give the output of preorderPrint(T, T.root()) (Code Fragment 6.9).
    b. Give the output of parentheticRepresentation(T, T.root()) (which is shown in Code Fragment 6.10).

R-6.9 Describe a modification to parentheticRepresentation, from Code Fragment 6.10, so that it uses the length() method for String objects to output the parenthetic representation of a tree with line breaks and spaces added to display the tree in a text window that is 80 characters wide.

R-6.10 Draw an arithmetic expression tree that has four external nodes, storing the numbers 1, 5, 6, and 7 (with each number stored in a distinct external node, but not necessarily in this order), and has three internal nodes, each storing an operator from the set $\{+, -, \times, /\}$, so that the value of the root is 21. The operators may return and act on fractions, and an operator may be used more than once.

R-6.11 Let T be an ordered tree with more than one node. Is it possible that the preorder traversal of T visits the nodes in the same order as the postorder traversal of T? If so, give an example; otherwise, argue why this cannot occur. Likewise, is it possible that the preorder traversal of T visits the nodes in the reverse order of the postorder traversal of T? If so, give an example; otherwise, argue why this cannot occur.

R-6.12 Answer the previous question for the case when T is a proper binary tree with more than one node.

R-6.13 What is the running time of parentheticRepresentation(T, T.root()) (Code Fragment 6.10) for a tree T with n nodes?

R-6.14 Draw a (single) binary tree T such that

- Each internal node of T stores a single character
- A *preorder* traversal of T yields EXAMFUN
- An *inorder* traversal of T yields MAFXUEN.

R-6.15 Answer the following questions so as to justify Proposition 6.10.

a. What is the minimum number of external nodes for a proper binary tree with height h? Justify your answer.
b. What is the maximum number of external nodes for a proper binary tree with height h? Justify your answer.
c. Let T be a proper binary tree with height h and n nodes. Show that

$$\log(n+1) - 1 \leq h \leq (n-1)/2.$$

d. For which values of n and h can the above lower and upper bounds on h be attained with equality?

R-6.16 Describe a generalization of the Euler tour traversal to trees such that each internal node has three children. Describe how you could use this traversal to compute the height of each node in such a tree.

R-6.17 Compute the output of algorithm postorderPrint(T, T.root()), from Code Fragment 6.12, on the tree T of Figure 6.3.

R-6.18 Illustrate the execution of algorithm diskSpace(T, T.root()) (Code Fragment 6.13) on the tree T of Figure 6.10.

R-6.19 Let T be the binary tree of Figure 6.6.

a. Give the output of preorderPrint(T, T.root()) (Code Fragment 6.9).

b. Give the output of parentheticRepresentation(T, T.root()) (Code Fragment 6.10).

R-6.20 Let T be the binary tree of Figure 6.6.

a. Give the output of postorderPrint(T, T.root()) (Code Fragment 6.12).

b. Give the output of printExpression(T, T.root()) (Code Fragment 6.20).

R-6.21 Describe, in pseudo-code, an algorithm for computing the number of descendents of each node of a binary tree. The algorithm should be based on the Euler tour traversal.

R-6.22 Let T be a (possibly improper) binary tree with n nodes, and let D be the sum of the depths of all the external nodes of T. Show that if T has the minimum number of external nodes possible, then D is $O(n)$ and if T has the maximum number of external nodes possible, then D is $O(n \log n)$.

R-6.23 Let T be a binary tree with n nodes, and let p be the level numbering of the nodes of T, as given in Section 6.4.1.

a. Show that, for every node v of T, $p(v) \leq 2^n - 1$.

b. Show an example of a binary tree with seven nodes that attains the above upper bound on $p(v)$ for some node v.

R-6.24 Show how to use the Euler tour traversal to compute the level number, defined in Section 6.4.1, of each node in a binary tree T.

R-6.25 Draw the binary tree representation of the tree shown in Figure 6.2 using the binary-tree representation scheme described in Section 6.4.4.

R-6.26 Let T be a binary tree with n nodes that is realized with a vector, S, and let p be the level numbering of the nodes in T, as given in Section 6.4.1. Give pseudo-code descriptions of each of the methods root, parent, leftChild, rightChild, hasLeft, hasRight, isInternal, isExternal, and isRoot.

Creativity

C-6.1 For each node v in a tree T, let $\text{pre}(v)$ be the rank of v in a preorder traversal of T, let $\text{post}(v)$ be the rank of v in a postorder traversal of T, let $\text{depth}(v)$ be the depth of v, and let $\text{desc}(v)$ be the number of descendents of v, not counting v itself. Derive a formula defining $\text{post}(v)$ in terms of $\text{desc}(v)$, $\text{depth}(v)$, and $\text{pre}(v)$, for each node v in T.

C-6.2 Let T be a tree whose nodes store strings. Give an efficient algorithm that computes and prints, for every node v of T, the string stored at v and the height of the subtree rooted at v.

C-6.3 Design algorithms for the following operations for a binary tree T:

- preorderNext(v): return the node visited after node v in a preorder traversal of T
- inorderNext(v): return the node visited after node v in an inorder traversal of T
- postorderNext(v): return the node visited after node v in a postorder traversal of T.

What are the worst-case running times of your algorithms?

C-6.4 Give an $O(n)$-time algorithm for computing the depth of all the nodes of a tree T, where n is the number of nodes of T.

C-6.5 Let T be a (possibly improper) binary tree with n nodes, and let D be the sum of the depths of all the external nodes of T. Describe a configuration for T such that D is $\Omega(n^2)$. Such a tree would be the worst case for the asymptotic running time of Algorithm height1 (Code Fragment 6.5).

C-6.6 For a tree T, let n_I denote the number of its internal nodes, and let n_E denote the number of its external nodes. Show that if every internal node in T has exactly 3 children, then $n_E = 2n_I + 1$.

C-6.7 Describe how to clone a proper binary tree using the attach method instead of methods insertLeft and insertRight.

C-6.8 The *balance factor* of an internal node v of a proper binary tree is the difference between the heights of the right and left subtrees of v. Show how to specialize the Euler tour traversal of Section 6.3.5 to print the balance factors of all the internal nodes of a proper binary tree.

C-6.9 Two ordered trees T' and T'' are said to be *isomorphic* if one of the following holds:

- Both T' and T'' are empty
- Both T' and T'' consist of a single node
- Both T' and T'' have the same number $k \geq 1$ of subtrees, and the ith subtree of T' is isomorphic to the ith subtree of T'', for $i = 1, \ldots, k$.

Design an algorithm that tests whether two given ordered trees are isomorphic. What is the running time of your algorithm?

C-6.10 Extend the concept of an Euler tour to an ordered tree that is not necessarily a binary tree.

C-6.11 Given a proper binary tree T, define the *reflection* of T to be the binary tree T' such that each node v in T is also in T', but the left child of v in T is v's right child in T' and the right child of v in T is v's left child in T'. Show that a preorder traversal of a proper binary tree T is the same as the postorder traversal of T's reflection, but in reverse order.

C-6.12 Algorithm preorderDraw draws a binary tree T by assigning x- and y-coordinates to each node v such that $x(v)$ is the number of nodes preceding v in the preorder traversal of T and $y(v)$ is the depth of v in T. Algorithm postorderDraw is similar to preorderDraw but assigns x-coordinates using a postorder traversal.

  a. Show that the drawing of T produced by preorderDraw has no pairs of crossing edges.
  b. Redraw the binary tree of Figure 6.15 using algorithm preorder-Draw.
  c. Show that the drawing of T produced by postorderDraw has no pairs of crossing edges.
  d. Redraw the binary tree of Figure 6.15 using algorithm postorder-Draw.

C-6.13 Design an algorithm for drawing general trees that generalizes the inorder traversal approach for drawing binary trees.

C-6.14 Let a visit action in the Euler tour traversal be denoted by a pair (v, a), where v is the visited node and a is one of *left*, *below*, or *right*. Design and analyze an algorithm for performing operation tourNext(v, a), which returns the visit action (w, b) following (v, a).

C-6.15 Consider a variation of the linked data structure for binary trees where each node object has references to the node objects of the children but not to the node object of the parent. Describe an implementation of the methods of a binary tree with this data structure and analyze the time complexity for these methods.

C-6.16 The *indented parenthetic representation* of a tree T is a variation of the parenthetic representation of T (see Figure 6.8) that uses indentation and line breaks as illustrated in Figure 6.22. Give an algorithm that prints this representation of a tree.

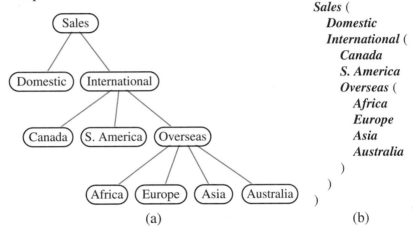

(a)   (b)

Figure 6.22: (a) Tree T; (b) indented parenthetic representation of T.

C-6.17 Design an alternative implementation of the linked data structure for proper binary trees using a class for nodes that specializes into subclasses for an internal node, an external node, and the root node.

C-6.18 Within the linked data structure for binary trees, explore an alternative design for implementing the iterators returned by methods elements(), positions(), and children(v) such that each of these methods takes $O(1)$ time. Can you still achieve constant time implementations for the methods hasNext() and next() of the iterators returned?

C-6.19 Let T be a tree with n nodes. Define the *lowest common ancestor* (LCA) between two nodes v and w as the lowest node in T that has both v and w as descendents (where we allow a node to be a descendent of itself). Given two nodes v and w, describe an efficient algorithm for finding the LCA of v and w. What is the running time of your algorithm?

C-6.20 Let T be a binary tree with n nodes, and, for any node v in T, let d_v denote the depth of v in T. The ***distance*** between two nodes v and w in T is $d_v + d_w - 2d_u$, where u is the lowest common ancestor (LCA) u of v and w. The ***diameter*** of T is the maximum distance between two nodes in T. Describe an efficient algorithm for finding the diameter of T. What is the running time of your algorithm?

C-6.21 Suppose each node v of a binary tree T is labeled with its value $p(v)$ in a level numbering of T. Design a fast method for determining $p(u)$ for the lowest common ancestor (LCA), u, of two nodes v and w in T, given $p(v)$ and $p(w)$. You do not need to find node u, just compute its level-numbering label.

C-6.22 Justify the bounds in Table 6.1 by providing a detailed analysis of the running times of the methods of a binary tree T implemented with a vector S, where S is realized by means of an array.

C-6.23 Justify Table 6.3, summarizing the running time of the methods of a tree represented with a linked structure, by providing, for each method, a description of its implementation, and an analysis of its running time.

C-6.24 Justify the bounds in Table 6.4 for the running times of the methods of a tree represented by means of a binary tree, which is in turn implemented with a linked structure, by providing, for each method, a description of its implementation and an analysis of its running time.

C-6.25 Let T be a binary tree with n nodes. Define a ***Roman node*** to be a node v in T, such that the number of descendents in v's left subtree differ from the number of descendents in v's right subtree by at most 5. Describe a linear-time method for finding each node v of T, such that v is not a Roman node, but all of v's descendents are Roman nodes.

C-6.26 Let T' be the binary tree representing a tree T (see Section 6.4.4).

    a. Is a preorder traversal of T' equivalent to a preorder traversal of T?
    b. Is a postorder traversal of T' equivalent to a postorder traversal of T?
    c. Is an inorder traversal of T' equivalent to one of the standard traversals of T? If so, which one?

C-6.27 Describe a nonrecursive method for performing an Euler tour traversal of a binary tree that runs in linear time and does not use a stack.

C-6.28 Describe in pseudo-code a nonrecursive method for performing an inorder traversal of a binary tree in linear time.

C-6.29 Let T be a binary tree with n nodes (T may be realized with a vector or a linked structure). Give a linear-time algorithm that uses the methods of the BinaryTree interface to traverse the nodes of T by increasing values of the level numbering function p given in Section 6.4.1. This traversal is known as the *level order traversal*.

C-6.30 The *path length* of a tree T is the sum of the depths of all the nodes in T. Describe a linear-time method for computing the path length of a tree T (which is not necessarily binary).

C-6.31 Define the *internal path length*, $I(T)$, of a tree T to be the sum of the depths of all the internal nodes in T. Likewise, define the *external path length*, $E(T)$, of a tree T to be the sum of the depths of all the external nodes in T. Show that if T is a proper binary tree with n nodes, then $E(T) = I(T) + n - 1$.

Projects

P-6.1 Implement the binary tree ADT using a vector.

P-6.2 Implement the tree ADT using a linked structure.

P-6.3 Write a program that draws a binary tree.

P-6.4 Write a program that draws a general tree.

P-6.5 Write a program that can input and display a person's family tree.

P-6.6 Implement the binary tree representation of the tree ADT. You may reuse the LinkedBinaryTree implementation of a binary tree.

P-6.7 A *slicing floorplan* divides a rectangle with horizontal and vertical sides using horizontal and vertical *cuts*. (See Figure 6.23a.) A slicing floorplan can be represented by a proper binary tree, called a *slicing tree*, whose internal nodes represent the cuts, and whose external nodes represent the *basic rectangles* into which the floorplan is decomposed by the cuts. (See Figure 6.23b.) The *compaction problem* for a slicing floorplan is defined as follows. Assume that each basic rectangle of a slicing floorplan is assigned a minimum width w and a minimum height h. The compaction problem is to find the smallest possible height and width for each rectangle of the slicing floorplan that is compatible with the minimum dimensions of the basic rectangles. Namely, this problem requires the assignment of values $h(v)$ and $w(v)$ to each node v of the slicing tree such that:

$$w(v) = \begin{cases} w & \text{if } v \text{ is an external node whose basic rectangle has minimum width } w \\ \max(w(w), w(z)) & \text{if } v \text{ is an internal node associated with a horizontal cut with left child } w \text{ and right child } z \\ w(w) + w(z) & \text{if } v \text{ is an internal node associated with a vertical cut with left child } w \text{ and right child } z \end{cases}$$

$$h(v) = \begin{cases} h & \text{if } v \text{ is an external node whose basic rectangle has minimum height } h \\ h(w) + h(z) & \text{if } v \text{ is an internal node associated with a horizontal cut with left child } w \text{ and right child } z \\ \max(h(w), h(z)) & \text{if } v \text{ is an internal node associated with a vertical cut with left child } w \text{ and right child } z \end{cases}$$

Design a data structure for slicing floorplans that supports the operations:
- Create a floorplan consisting of a single basic rectangle.
- Decompose a basic rectangle by means of a horizontal cut.
- Decompose a basic rectangle by means of a vertical cut.
- Assign minimum height and width to a basic rectangle.
- Draw the slicing tree associated with the floorplan.
- Compact and draw the floorplan.

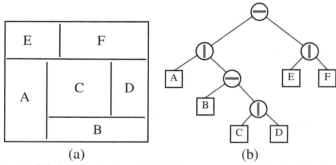

(a)   (b)

Figure 6.23: (a) Slicing floorplan; (b) slicing tree associated with the floorplan.

P-6.8 Write a program that takes as input a fully parenthesized, arithmetic expression and converts it to a binary expression tree. Your program should display the tree in some way and also print the value associated with the root. For an additional challenge, allow for the leaves to store variables of the form x_1, x_2, x_3, and so on, which are initially 0 and which can be updated interactively by your program, with the corresponding update in the printed value of the root of the expression tree.

P-6.9 Write a program that visualizes an Euler tour traversal of a proper binary tree, including the movements from node to node and the actions associated with visits on the left, from below, and on the right. Illustrate your program by having it compute and display preorder labels, inorder labels, postorder labels, ancestor counts, and descendent counts for each node in the tree (not necessarily all at the same time).

Chapter Notes

Discussions of the classic preorder, inorder, and postorder tree traversal methods can be found in Knuth's *Fundamental Algorithms* book [58]. The Euler tour traversal technique comes from the parallel algorithms community, as it is introduced by Tarjan and Vishkin [87] and is discussed by JáJá [51] and by Karp and Ramachandran [55]. The algorithm for drawing a tree is generally considered to be a part of the "folklore" of graph drawing algorithms. The reader interested in graph drawing is referred to works by Tamassia [86] and Di Battista *et al.* [29]. The puzzler in Exercise R-6.10 was communicated by Micha Sharir.

Chapter 7

Priority Queues

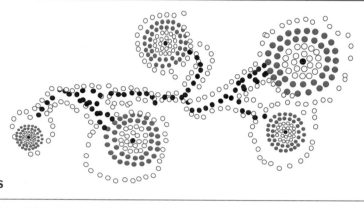

Contents

Having the right priorities is important to succeeding in life. On a quiet Saturday afternoon, presented with the opportunity of taking a nap, watching TV, playing soccer, or studying this chapter, the zealous student will certainly give first priority to the latter task. Outside of comfortable campus boundaries, priorities are an even more serious matter. Consider, for example, an air-traffic control center that has to decide which flight to clear for landing from among many approaching the airport. The priority of a flight may depend not only on the plane's distance from the runway, but also on the amount of fuel it has left. Another example is a standby passenger who is told she is "first" in line for a fully-booked flight. Thus, she thinks she has top priority if seats become available. Little does she know that the airline will give first priority to a standby passenger who has arrived later, if such a passenger is given a better priority by the agent (priority here is measured in terms of the fare paid, frequent-flyer status, and check-in time).

In this chapter, we study data structures that store "prioritized elements," that is, elements that have priorities assigned to them. Such a priority is typically a numerical value, and we take the view that the smallest numerical value should have first priority. However, as we show in this chapter, we can support the opposite viewpoint just as easily. More generally, priorities can be viewed as arbitrary objects, so long as there is a consistent way of comparing pairs of such objects to see if one is less than or equal to the other. This general viewpoint allows us to define a fairly generic ADT for storing prioritized elements.

A *priority queue* is an abstract data type for storing a collection of prioritized elements that supports arbitrary element insertion but supports removal of elements in order of priority; that is, the element with first priority can be removed at any time. This ADT is fundamentally different from the position-based data structures we discussed in previous chapters, such as stacks, queues, deques, sequences, and even trees. These other data structures store elements at specific positions, which are often positions in a linear arrangement of the elements determined by the insertion and deletion operations performed. The priority queue ADT stores elements according to their priorities, and exposes no notion of "position" to the user.

We present the priority queue ADT in Section 7.1. In Section 7.2, we present two implementations of a priority queue using lists. These implementations are simple, but unfortunately not very efficient. Even so, they allow us to easily describe two well-known sorting algorithms, insertion-sort and selection-sort. In Section 7.3, we give a more efficient implementation of a priority queue, based on a concrete data structure known as a *heap*. A heap uses the hierarchical power of binary trees to support the priority queue operations in logarithmic time, which leads to a fast sorting algorithm known as heap-sort. We conclude this chapter with a discussion of an adaptable version of the priority queue, which allows users to change the keys associated with values in the queue.

7.1 The Priority Queue Abstract Data Type

In this section, we provide the framework for studying priority queues, based on the concepts of key and comparator, and we define the methods of a priority queue as an abstract data type (ADT).

7.1.1 Keys, Priorities, and Total Order Relations

Applications commonly require that we compare and rank objects according to parameters or properties, called "keys," that are assigned for each object in a collection. Formally, we define a *key* to be an object that is assigned to an element as a specific attribute for that element, which can be used to identify, rank, or weigh that element. Note that the key is assigned to an element, typically by a user or application; hence, a key might represent a property that an element did not originally possess.

The key an application assigns to an element is not necessarily unique, however, and an application may even change an element's key if it needs to. For example, we can compare companies by earnings or by number of employees; hence, either of these parameters can be used as a key for a company, depending on the information we wish to extract. Likewise, we can compare restaurants by a critic's food quality rating or by average entrée price. To achieve the most generality, then, we allow a key to be of any type that is appropriate for a particular application.

As in the above motivating examples from an airport, the key used for comparisons is often more than a single numerical value, such as price, length, weight, or speed. That is, a key can sometimes be a more complex property that cannot be quantified with a single number. For example, the priority of standby passengers is usually determined by taking into account a host of different factors, including frequent-flyer status, the fare paid, and check-in time. In some applications, the key for an object is part of the object itself (for example, it might be an instance variable storing the list price of a book, or the weight of a car). In other applications, the key is not part of the object but the object gets assigned its key by the application (for example, the quality rating given to a stock by a financial analyst, or the priority assigned to a standby passenger by a gate agent).

The concept of a key as an arbitrary object type is therefore quite general. But, in order to deal consistently with such a general definition for keys and still be able to discuss when one key has priority over another, we need a way of robustly defining a rule for comparing keys.

Comparing Keys with Total Orders

A priority queue needs a comparison rule that will never contradict itself. In order for a comparison rule, which we denote by $\leq$, to be robust in this way, it must define a *total order* relation, which is to say that the comparison rule is defined for every pair of keys and it must satisfy the following properties:

- **Reflexive property**: $k \leq k$.
- **Antisymmetric property**: if $k_1 \leq k_2$ and $k_2 \leq k_1$, then $k_1 = k_2$.
- **Transitive property**: if $k_1 \leq k_2$ and $k_2 \leq k_3$, then $k_1 \leq k_3$.

Any comparison rule, $\leq$, that satisfies these three properties will never lead to a comparison contradiction. In fact, such a rule defines a linear ordering relationship among a set of keys; hence, if a (finite) collection of elements has a total order defined for it, then the notion of a *smallest* key, k_{min}, is well defined, as a key in which $k_{min} \leq k$, for any other key k in our collection.

A *priority queue* is a container of elements, called *values*, each having an associated key that is provided at the time the element is inserted. A key-value pair inserted into a priority queue is called an *entry* of the priority queue. The name "priority queue" comes from the fact that keys determine the "priority" used to pick entries to be removed. The two fundamental methods of a priority queue P are as follows:

- insert(k,x): insert a value x with key k into P.
- removeMin(): return and remove from P an entry with the smallest key, that is, an entry whose key is less than or equal to that of every other entry in P.

By the way, some people refer to the removeMin method as the "extractMin" method, so as to stress that this method simultaneously removes and returns an entry P. There are many applications where the insert and removeMin operations play an important role. We consider such an application in the example that follows.

Example 7.1: *Suppose a certain flight is fully booked an hour prior to departure. Because of the possibility of cancellations the airline maintains a priority queue of standby passengers hoping to get a seat. The priority of each standby passenger is determined by the airline taking into account the fare paid, the frequent-flyer status, and the time that the passenger is inserted into the priority queue. A standby passenger reference is inserted into the priority queue with an insert operation as soon as he or she requests to fly standby. Shortly before the flight departure, if seats become available (for example, due to no-shows or last-minute cancellations), the airline removes a standby passenger with first priority from the priority queue, using a removeMin operation and lets this person board. This process is then repeated until all available seats have been filled or the priority queue becomes empty.*

7.1.2 Entries and Comparators

There are still two important issues that we have left undetermined to this point:

- How do we keep track of the associations between keys and values?
- How do we compare keys so as to determine a smallest key?

Answering these questions involves the use of two interesting design patterns.

The definition of a priority queue implicitly makes use of two special kinds of objects that answer the above questions, the *entry* and *comparator*, which we discuss in this subsection.

Entries

An entry is an association between a key k and a value x, that is, an *entry* is simply a key-value pair. We use entries in a priority queue Q to keep track of the way Q is associating keys and their corresponding values.

An entry is actually an example of a more general object-oriented design pattern, the *composition pattern*, which defines a single object that is composed of other objects. We use this pattern in a priority queue when we define the entries being stored in the priority queue to be pairs consisting of a key k and a value x. A pair is the simplest composition, for it combines two objects into a single pair object. To implement this concept, we define a class that stores two objects in its first and second instance variables, respectively, and provides methods to access and update these variables.

In Code Fragment 7.1, we show a Java implementation of the composition pattern for entries storing key-value pairs in a priority queue. Other kinds of compositions include triples, which store three objects, quadruples, which store four objects, and general compositions, which can store an arbitrary number of objects (using, say, a list).

```
/** Interface for a key-value pair entry **/
public interface Entry {
  public Object key();
  public Object value();
}
```

Code Fragment 7.1: Java interface for an entry storing key-value pairs in a priority queue.

Comparators

Another important issue in the priority queue ADT that we need to define is how to specify the total order relation for comparing keys. We have a number of design choices concerning how to compare keys that we can make at this point.

One possibility, and the one that is the most concrete, is to implement a different priority queue for each key type we want to use and each possible way of comparing keys of such types. The problem with this approach is that it is not very general and it requires that we create a lot of similar code.

An alternative strategy is to require that keys be able to compare themselves to one another. This solution allows us to write a general priority queue class that can store instances of a key class that implements some kind of Comparable interface and encapsulates all the usual comparison methods. This solution is an improvement over the specialized approach, for it allows us to write a single priority queue class that can handle lots of different types of keys. But there are contexts in which this solution is asking too much of the keys, as keys often do not "know" how they ought to be compared. Two examples follow.

Example 7.2: *Given keys 4 and 11 we have that $4 \leq 11$ if the keys are integer objects (to be compared in the usual manner), but $11 \leq 4$ if the keys are string objects (to be compared lexicographically).*

Example 7.3: *A geometric algorithm may compare points p and q in the plane, by their x-coordinate (that is, $p \leq q$ if $x(p) \leq x(q)$), to sort them from left to right, while another algorithm may compare them by their y-coordinate (that is, $p \leq q$ if $y(p) \leq y(q)$), to sort them from bottom to top. In principle, there is nothing pertaining to the concept of a point that says whether points should be compared by x- or y-coordinate. Also, many other ways of comparing points can be defined (for example, we can compare the distances of p and q from the origin).*

Thus, for the most general and reusable form of a priority queue, we should not rely on the keys to provide their comparison rules. Instead, we use special ***comparator*** objects that are external to the keys to supply the comparison rules. A comparator is an object that compares two keys. We assume that a priority queue P is given a comparator when P is constructed, and we might also imagine the ability of a priority queue to be given a new comparator if its old one ever becomes "out of date." When P needs to compare two keys, it uses the comparator it was given to perform the comparison. Thus, a programmer can write a general priority queue implementation that works correctly in a wide variety of contexts.

The Comparator ADT

Formally, the comparator ADT provides a streamlined comparison mechanism, based on a single method that takes two keys and compares them (or reports an error if the keys are incomparable):

> compare(a, b): Returns an integer i such that $i < 0$ if $a < b$, $i = 0$ if $a = b$, and $i > 0$ if $a > b$; an error occurs if a and b cannot be compared.
> **Input:** Pair of objects; **Output:** Integer.

The standard Java interface java.util.Comparator corresponds to the above comparator ADT, which offers a general, dynamic, reusable way to compare objects. In Code Fragment 7.2, we provide an example of a comparator for two-dimensional points (Code Fragment 7.3), which is also an example of the composition pattern.

```java
/** Comparator for 2D points under the standard lexicographic order. */
public class Lexicographic implements Comparator {
  int xa, ya, xb, yb;
  public int compare(Object a, Object b) throws ClassCastException {
    xa = ((Point2D) a).getX();
    ya = ((Point2D) a).getY();
    xb = ((Point2D) b).getX();
    yb = ((Point2D) b).getY();
    if (xa != xb)
      return (xb − xa);
    else
      return (yb − ya);
  }
}
```

Code Fragment 7.2: A comparator for two-dimensional points based on the lexicographic order.

```java
/** Class represeting a point in the plane with integer coordinates */
public class Point2D {
  protected int xc, yc;         // coordinates
  public Point2D(int x, int y) {
    xc = x;
    yc = y;
  }
  public int getX() { return xc; }
  public int getY() { return yc; }
}
```

Code Fragment 7.3: Class representing points in the plane with integer coordinates.

7.1.3   The Priority Queue ADT

Having described the composition and comparator patterns, we now define the priority queue ADT in more detail. As an ADT, a priority queue P supports the following methods:

size(): Return the number of entries in P.
Input: None; *Output:* Integer.

isEmpty(): Test whether P is empty.
Input: None; *Output:* Boolean.

min(): Return (but do not remove) an entry of P with smallest key; an error condition occurs if P is empty.
Input: None; *Output:* Entry.

insert(k,x): Insert into P key k with value x and return the entry storing them; an error condition occurs if k is invalid (that is, k cannot be compared with other keys.
Input: Objects k (key) and x (value); *Output:* Entry.

removeMin(): Remove from P and return an entry with smallest key; an error condition occurs if P is empty.
Input: None; *Output:* Entry.

As mentioned above, the primary methods of the priority queue ADT are the insert and removeMin operations. The other methods are query operation min and the generic container operations size and isEmpty. Note that we allow a priority queue to have multiple entries with the same key.

A Java Priority Queue Interface

A Java interface, called PriorityQueue, for the priority queue ADT is shown in Code Fragment 7.4. The following exceptions are used to represent error conditions:

- EmptyPriorityQueueException: thrown when method min or removeMin is called on an empty priority queue.
- InvalidKeyException: thrown when method insert(k,x) is called with an invalid key k that cannot be compared by the comparator of the priority queue. This may occur, for example, if k is **null** or k is of a class that is incompatible with the class of the other keys in the priority queue.

```
/** Interface for the priority queue ADT */
public interface PriorityQueue {
  /** Returns the number of items in the priority queue. */
  public int size();
  /** Returns whether the priority queue is empty. */
  public boolean isEmpty();
  /** Returns but does not remove an entry with minimum key. */
  public Entry min() throws EmptyPriorityQueueException;
  /** Inserts a key-value pair and return the entry created. */
  public Entry insert(Object key, Object value) throws InvalidKeyException;
  /** Removes and returns an entry with minimum key. */
  public Entry removeMin() throws EmptyPriorityQueueException;
}
```

Code Fragment 7.4: Java interface for the priority queue ADT.

The Simplicity of the Priority Queue ADT

It should now be obvious that the priority queue ADT is much simpler than the sequence ADT. This simplicity is due to the fact that elements in a priority queue are inserted and removed based entirely on their keys, whereas elements are inserted and removed in a sequence based on their positions and ranks. Thus, only one insertion method and one deletion method are needed in the priority queue ADT, whereas the sequence ADT has many such methods.

Example 7.4: *The following table shows a series of operations and their effects on an initially empty priority queue P. We denote with e_i an entry object returned by method* insert. *The "Priority Queue" column is somewhat deceiving since it shows the entries sorted by key. This is more than is required of a priority queue. The way the entries are stored is implementation dependent. A priority queue need only have an algorithm to retrieve an entry with minimum key.*

Operation	*Output*	*Priority Queue*
insert($5,A$)	$e_1[=(5,A)]$	$\{(5,A)\}$
insert($9,C$)	$e_2[=(9,C)]$	$\{(5,A),(9,C)\}$
insert($3,B$)	$e_3[=(3,B)]$	$\{(3,B),(5,A),(9,C)\}$
insert($7,D$)	$e_4[=(7,D)]$	$\{(3,B),(5,A),(7,D),(9,C)\}$
min()	e_3	$\{(3,B),(5,A),(7,D),(9,C)\}$
removeMin()	e_3	$\{(5,A),(7,D),(9,C)\}$
size()	3	$\{(5,A),(7,D),(9,C)\}$
removeMin()	e_1	$\{(7,D),(9,C)\}$
removeMin()	e_4	$\{(9,C)\}$
removeMin()	e_2	$\{\}$
removeMin()	"error"	$\{\}$
isEmpty()	true	$\{\}$

7.1.4 Sorting with a Priority Queue

Another important application of a priority queue is sorting, where we are given a collection S of n elements that can be compared according to a total order relation, and we want to rearrange them in increasing order (or at least in nondecreasing order if there are ties). The algorithm for sorting S with a priority queue Q, called PriorityQueueSort, is quite simple and consists of the following two phases:

1. In the first phase, we put the elements of S into an initially empty priority queue P by means of a series of n insert operations, one for each element.

2. In the second phase, we extract the elements from P in nondecreasing order by means of a series of n removeMin operations, putting them back into S in order.

We give pseudo-code for this algorithm in Code Fragment 7.5, assuming that S is a sequence (pseudo-code for a different type of collection, such as a list or vector, would be similar). The algorithm works correctly for any priority queue P, no matter how P is implemented. However, the running time of the algorithm is determined by the running times of operations insert and removeMin, which do depend on how P is implemented. Indeed, PriorityQueueSort should be considered more a sorting "scheme" than a sorting "algorithm," because it does not specify how the priority queue P is implemented. The PriorityQueueSort scheme is the paradigm of several popular sorting algorithms, including selection-sort, insertion-sort, and heap-sort, which we discuss in this chapter.

Algorithm PriorityQueueSort(S, P):

    Input: A sequence S storing n elements, on which a total order relation is defined, and a priority queue, P, that compares keys using the same total order relation

    Output: The sequence S sorted by the total order relation

    while !S.isEmpty() **do**

        $e \leftarrow S$.removeFirst()

        P.insert($e, \emptyset$)   {a null value is used}

    while !S.isEmpty() **do**

        $e \leftarrow P$.removeMin().key()

        S.insertLast(e)   {the smallest key in P is added to the end of S}

Code Fragment 7.5: Algorithm PriorityQueueSort. Note that the elements of the input sequence S serve as keys of the priority queue P.

7.2 Implementing a Priority Queue with a List

In this section, we show how to implement a priority queue by storing its entries in a list S. (See Chapter 5.2.) We provide two realizations, depending on whether or not we keep the entries in S sorted by key. When analyzing the running time of the methods of a priority queue implemented with a list, we will assume that a comparison of two keys takes $O(1)$ time.

7.2.1 Implementation with an Unsorted List

As our first implementation of a priority queue P, let us consider storing the entries of P in a list S, where S is implemented with a doubly linked list. Thus, the elements of S are entries (k,x), where k is the key and x is the value.

Fast Insertions and Slow Removals

A simple way of performing operation insert(k,x) on P is to create a new entry object $e = (k,x)$ and add it at the end of list S, by executing method insertLast(e) on S. This implementation of method insert takes $O(1)$ time.

The above insertion algorithm implies that S will be unsorted, for always inserting entries at the end of S does not take into account the ordering of the keys. As a consequence, to perform operation min or removeMin on P, we must inspect all the elements of list S to find an entry (k,x) of S with minimum k. Thus, methods min and removeMin each take $O(n)$ time, where n is the number of entries in P at the time the method is executed. Moreover, these methods run in time proportional to n even in the best case, since they each require searching the entire list to find a minimum-key entry. That is, using the notation of Section 3.4.1, we can say that these methods run in $\Theta(n)$ time. Finally, we implement methods size and isEmpty by simply returning the output of the corresponding methods executed on list S.

Thus, by using an unsorted list to implement a priority queue, we achieve constant-time insertion, but linear-time search and removal.

7.2.2 Implementation with a Sorted List

An alternative implementation of a priority queue P also uses a list S, except that this time let us store the entries sorted by key. Specifically, we represent the priority queue P by using a list S of entries sorted by nondecreasing keys, which means that the first element of S is an entry with smallest key.

Fast Removals and Slow Insertions

We can implement method min in this case simply by accessing the first element of the list with the first method of S. Likewise, we can implement the removeMin method of P as S.remove(S.first()). Assuming that S is implemented with a doubly linked list, operations min and removeMin in P takes $O(1)$ time. Thus, using a sorted list allows for simple and fast implementations of priority queue access and removal methods.

This benefit comes at a cost, however, for now method insert of P requires that we scan through the list S to find the appropriate position to insert the new entry. Thus, implementing the insert method of P now takes $O(n)$ time, where n is the number of entries in P at the time the method is executed. In summary, when using a sorted list to implement a priority queue, insertion runs in linear time whereas finding and removing the minimum can be done in constant time.

Comparing the Two List-Based Implementations

Table 7.1 compares the running times of the methods of a priority queue realized by means of a sorted and unsorted list, respectively. We see an interesting trade-off when we use a list to implement the priority queue ADT. An unsorted list allows for fast insertions but slow queries and deletions, while a sorted list allows for fast queries and deletions, but slow insertions.

Method	Unsorted List	Sorted List
size, isEmpty	$O(1)$	$O(1)$
insert	$O(1)$	$O(n)$
min, removeMin	$O(n)$	$O(1)$

Table 7.1: Worst-case running times of the methods of a priority queue of size n, realized by means of an unsorted or sorted list, respectively. We assume that the list is implemented by a doubly linked list. The space requirement is $O(n)$.

Java Implementation

In Code Fragments 7.6 and 7.7, we show a Java implementation of a priority queue based on a sorted list. This implementation uses a nested class, called MyEntry, to implement the Entry interface (see Section 5.4.1). We do not show auxiliary method checkKey(k), which throws an InvalidKeyException if key k cannot be inserted into the priority queue.

```
/** Implementation of a priority queue by means of a sorted list */
public class SortedListPriorityQueue implements PriorityQueue {
  protected List L;
  protected Comparator c;
  protected Position actionPos; // variable used by subclasses
  /** Inner class for entries */
  protected static class MyEntry implements Entry {
    protected Object k; // key
    protected Object v; // value
    public MyEntry(Object key, Object value) {
      k = key;
      v = value;
    }
    // methods of the Entry interface
    public Object key() { return k; }
    public Object value() { return v; }
  }
  /** Inner class for a default comparator using the natural ordering */
  protected static class DefaultComparator implements Comparator {
    public DefaultComparator() { /* default constructor */ }
    public int compare(Object a, Object b) throws ClassCastException {
      return ((Comparable) a).compareTo(b);
    }
  }
  /** Creates the priority queue with the default comparator. */
  public SortedListPriorityQueue () {
    L = new NodeList();
    c = new DefaultComparator();
  }
  /** Creates the priority queue with the given comparator. */
  public SortedListPriorityQueue (Comparator comp) {
    L = new NodeList();
    c = comp;
  }
```

Code Fragment 7.6: Portions of the Java class SortedListPriorityQueue, which implements the PriorityQueue interface. The nested class MyEntry implements the Entry interface. (Continues in Code Fragment 7.7.)

```java
/** Returns but does not remove an entry with minimum key. */
public Entry min () throws EmptyPriorityQueueException {
  if (L.isEmpty())
    throw new EmptyPriorityQueueException("priority queue is empty");
  else
    return (Entry) L.first().element();
}
/** Inserts a key-value pair and return the entry created. */
public Entry insert (Object k, Object v) throws InvalidKeyException {
  checkKey(k); // auxiliary key-checking method (could throw exception)
  Entry entry = new MyEntry(k, v);
  insertEntry(entry); // auxiliary insertion method
  return entry;
}
/** Auxiliary method used for insertion. */
protected void insertEntry(Entry e) {
  Object k = e.key();
  if (L.isEmpty()) {
    actionPos = L.insertFirst(e);        // insert into empty list
  }
  else if (c.compare(k, key(L.last())) > 0) {
    actionPos = L.insertLast(e);         // insert at the end of the list
  }
  else {
    Position curr = L.first();
    while (c.compare(k, key(curr))> 0) {
      curr = L.next(curr);               // advance toward insertion position
    }
    actionPos = L.insertBefore(curr, e); // useful for subclasses
  }
}
/** Removes and returns an entry with minimum key. */
public Entry removeMin() throws EmptyPriorityQueueException {
  if (L.isEmpty())
    throw new EmptyPriorityQueueException("priority queue is empty");
  else
    return (Entry) (L.remove(L.first()));
}
protected Object key(Position pos) { return ((Entry) pos.element()).key(); }
```

Code Fragment 7.7: Portions of the Java class SortedListPriorityQueue, which implements the PriorityQueue interface. (Continued from Code Fragment 7.6.)

7.2.3 Selection-Sort and Insertion-Sort

Recall the PriorityQueueSort scheme introduced in Section 7.1.4. We are given an unsorted sequence S containing n elements, which we sort using a priority queue P in two phases. In Phase 1 we insert all the elements, one by one, and in Phase 2 we repeatedly remove elements using the removeMin operation. In this section, we consider two variations of the PriorityQueueSort algorithm. Again, we make the assumption that comparing two keys takes $O(1)$ time.

Selection-Sort

If we implement the priority queue P with an unsorted list, then Phase 1 of PriorityQueueSort takes $O(n)$ time, for we can insert each element in $O(1)$ time. In Phase 2, the running time of each removeMin operation is proportional to the number of elements currently in P. Thus, the bottleneck computation in this implementation is the repeated "selection" of the minimum element from an unsorted sequence in Phase 2. For this reason, this algorithm is better known as **selection-sort**. (See Figure 7.1.)

		Sequence S	*Priority Queue P*
Input		$(7,4,8,2,5,3,9)$	$()$
Phase 1	(a)	$(4,8,2,5,3,9)$	(7)
	(b)	$(8,2,5,3,9)$	$(7,4)$
	⋮	⋮	⋮
	(g)	$()$	$(7,4,8,2,5,3,9)$
Phase 2	(a)	(2)	$(7,4,8,5,3,9)$
	(b)	$(2,3)$	$(7,4,8,5,9)$
	(c)	$(2,3,4)$	$(7,8,5,9)$
	(d)	$(2,3,4,5)$	$(7,8,9)$
	(e)	$(2,3,4,5,7)$	$(8,9)$
	(f)	$(2,3,4,5,7,8)$	(9)
	(g)	$(2,3,4,5,7,8,9)$	$()$

Figure 7.1: Execution of selection-sort on sequence $S = (7,4,8,2,5,3,9)$. In Phase 1, we repeatedly remove the first element from S and insert it into priority queue P (as the last element of the list implementing P). Note that at the end of the first phase, P is a copy of what was initially S. In Phase 2, we repeatedly perform removeMin operations on P (each of which requires that we scan the entire list implementing P) and we add the elements returned at the end of S.

Let us analyze the selection-sort algorithm. As noted above, the bottleneck is in Phase 2 where we repeatedly remove an entry with smallest key from the priority queue P. The size of P starts at n and incrementally decreases with each removeMin until it becomes 0. Thus, the first removeMin operation takes time $O(n)$, the second one takes time $O(n-1)$, and so on, until the last (nth) operation takes time $O(1)$. Therefore, the total time needed for the second phase is

$$O(n + (n-1) + \cdots + 2 + 1) = O\left(\sum_{i=1}^{n} i\right).$$

By Proposition 3.1, we have

$$\sum_{i=1}^{n} i = \frac{n(n+1)}{2}.$$

Thus, Phase 2 takes time $O(n^2)$, as does the entire selection-sort algorithm.

Insertion-Sort

If we implement the priority queue P using a sorted list, then we improve the running time of Phase 2 to $O(n)$, for each operation removeMin on P now takes $O(1)$ time. Unfortunately, Phase 1 now becomes the bottleneck for the running time. Indeed, in the worst case, each insert operation takes time proportional to the number of entries that are currently in the priority queue, which starts out having size zero and increases in size until it has size n. The first insert operation takes time $O(1)$, the second one takes time $O(2)$, and so on, until the last (nth) operation takes time $O(n)$, in the worst case. Thus, if we use a sorted list to implement P, then the first phase is the computational bottleneck. This sorting algorithm is therefore better known as ***insertion-sort*** (see Figure 7.2), for the bottleneck in this sorting algorithm involves the repeated "insertion" of a new element at the appropriate position in a sorted list.

Analyzing the running time of Phase 1 of insertion-sort, we note that it is

$$O(1 + 2 + \ldots + (n-1) + n) = O\left(\sum_{i=1}^{n} i\right).$$

Again, by recalling Proposition 3.1, Phase 1 runs in $O(n^2)$ time, and hence, so does the entire insertion-sort algorithm.

In other words, the running time of the PriorityQueueSort scheme implemented with a sorted list is $O(n^2)$. Therefore, both selection-sort and insertion-sort have running time $O(n^2)$.

		Sequence S	*Priority queue P*
Input		$(7,4,8,2,5,3,9)$	$()$
Phase 1	(a)	$(4,8,2,5,3,9)$	(7)
	(b)	$(8,2,5,3,9)$	$(4,7)$
	(c)	$(2,5,3,9)$	$(4,7,8)$
	(d)	$(5,3,9)$	$(2,4,7,8)$
	(e)	$(3,9)$	$(2,4,5,7,8)$
	(f)	(9)	$(2,3,4,5,7,8)$
	(g)	$()$	$(2,3,4,5,7,8,9)$
Phase 2	(a)	(2)	$(3,4,5,7,8,9)$
	(b)	$(2,3)$	$(4,5,7,8,9)$
	$\vdots$	$\vdots$	$\vdots$
	(g)	$(2,3,4,5,7,8,9)$	$()$

Figure 7.2: Execution of insertion-sort on sequence $S = (7,4,8,2,5,3,9)$. In Phase 1, we repeatedly remove the first element of S and insert it into P, by scanning the list implementing P, until we find the correct position for the element. In Phase 2, we repeatedly perform removeMin operations on P, each of which returns the first element of the list implementing P, and we add the element at the end of S.

Although selection-sort and insertion-sort are similar, they actually have some interesting differences. For instance, note that selection-sort always takes time proportional to n^2. Indeed, selecting the minimum in each step of Phase 2 requires scanning the entire priority-queue list. The running time of insertion-sort, on the other hand, varies depending on the input sequence. For example, if the input sequence S is in reverse order, then insertion-sort runs in $O(n)$ time, for we are always inserting the next element at the beginning of the priority-queue list in Phase 1.

Alternatively, we could change our definition of insertion-sort so that we insert elements starting from the end of the priority-queue list in Phase 1, in which case performing insertion-sort on a sequence that is already sorted would run in $O(n)$ time. Indeed, the running time of insertion-sort in this case is $O(n+I)$, where I is the number of ***inversions*** in the sequence, that is, the number of pairs of elements that start out in the input sequence in the wrong relative order. The number of inversions in a small sequence is relatively small; hence, insertion-sort is fairly efficient for small sequences. Its $O(n^2)$ worst-case performance makes insertion-sort inefficient for sorting large sequences, however.

7.3   Heaps

The two implementations of the PriorityQueueSort scheme presented in the previous section suggest a possible way of improving the running time for priority-queue sorting. For one algorithm (selection-sort) achieves a fast running time for Phase 1, but has a slow Phase 2, whereas the other algorithm (insertion-sort) has a slow Phase 1, but achieves a fast running time for Phase 2. If we can somehow balance the running times of the two phases, we might be able to significantly speed up the overall running time for sorting. This is, in fact, exactly what we can achieve using the priority-queue implementation discussed in this section.

An efficient realization of a priority queue uses a data structure called a ***heap***. This data structure allows us to perform both insertions and removals in logarithmic time, which is a significant improvement over the list-based implementations discussed in Section 7.2. The fundamental way the heap achieves this improvement is to abandon the idea of storing entries in a list and take the approach of storing entries in a binary tree instead.

7.3.1   The Heap Data Structure

A heap (see Figure 7.3) is a binary tree T that stores a collection of entries at its nodes and that satisfies two additional properties: a relational property defined in terms of the way keys are stored in T and a structural property defined in terms of the nodes of T itself. We assume that a total order relation on the keys is given, for example, by a comparator.

The relational property of T, defined in terms of the way keys are stored, is the following:

Heap-Order Property: In a heap T, for every node v other than the root, the key stored at v is greater than or equal to the key stored at v's parent.

As a consequence of the heap-order property, the keys encountered on a path from the root to an external node of T are in nondecreasing order. Also, a minimum key is always stored at the root of T. This is the most important key and is informally said to be "at the top of the heap"; hence, the name "heap" for the data structure. By the way, the heap data structure defined here has nothing to do with the memory heap (Section 4.3.4) used in the run-time environment supporting a programming language like Java.

If we define our comparator to indicate the opposite of the standard total order relation between keys (so that, for example, compare(3, 2) < 0), then the root of the heap stores the largest key. This versatility comes essentially "for free" from

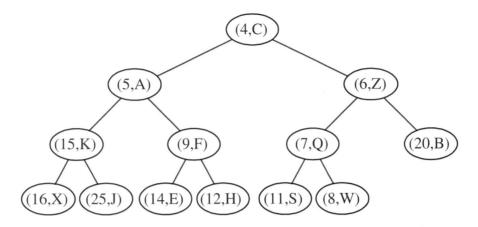

Figure 7.3: Example of a heap storing 13 entries with integer keys. The last node is the one storing entry $(8, W)$.

our use of the comparator pattern. By defining the minimum key in terms of the comparator, the "minimum" key with a "reverse" comparator is in fact the largest. Thus, without loss of generality, we assume that we are always interested in the minimum key, which will always be at the root of the heap.

For the sake of efficiency, as will become clear later, we want the heap T to have as small a height as possible. We enforce this requirement by insisting that the heap T satisfy an additional structural property: it must be **complete**. Before we define this structural property, we need some definitions. We recall from Section 6.3.3 that level i of a binary tree T is the set of nodes of T that have depth i. Given nodes v and w on the same level of T, we say that v is **to the left of** w if v is encountered before w in an inorder traversal of T. That is, there is a node u of T such that v is in the left subtree of u and w is in the right subtree of u. For example, in the binary tree of Figure 7.3, the node storing entry $(15, K)$ is to the left of the node storing entry $(7, Q)$. In a standard drawing of a binary tree, the "to the left of" relation is visualized by the relative horizontal placement of the nodes.

Complete Binary Tree Property: A heap T with height h is a **complete** binary tree if levels $0, 1, 2, \ldots, h-1$ of T have the maximum number of nodes possible (namely, level i has 2^i nodes, for $0 \le i \le h-1$) and in level $h-1$, all the internal nodes are to the left of the external nodes and there is at most one node with one child, which must be a left child.

By insisting that a heap T be complete, we identify another important node in a heap T, other than the root, namely, the **last node** of T, which we define to be the right-most, deepest external node of T (see Figure 7.3).

The Height of a Heap

Let h denote the height of T. Another way of defining the last node of T is that it is the node on level h such that all the other nodes of level h are the left of it. Insisting that T be complete also has an important consequence, as shown in Proposition 7.5.

Proposition 7.5: *A heap T storing n entries has height*

$$h = \lfloor \log n \rfloor.$$

Justification: From the fact that T is complete, we know that the number of nodes of T is at least

$$\begin{aligned} 1+2+4+\cdots+2^{h-1}+1 &= 2^h-1+1 \\ &= 2^h. \end{aligned}$$

This lower bound is achieved when there is only one node on level h. In addition, also following from T being complete, we have that the number of nodes of T is at most

$$1+2+4+\cdots+2^h = 2^{h+1}-1.$$

This upper bound is achieved when level h has 2^h. nodes. Since the number of nodes is equal to the number n of entries, we obtain

$$2^h \leq n$$

and

$$n \leq 2^{h+1}-1.$$

Thus, by taking logarithms of both sides of these two inequalities, we see that

$$h \leq \log n$$

and

$$\log(n+1) - 1 \leq h.$$

Since h is an integer, the two inequalities above imply that

$$h = \lfloor \log n \rfloor.$$

∎

Proposition 7.5 has an important consequence, for it implies that if we can perform update operations on a heap in time proportional to its height, then those operations will run in logarithmic time. Let us therefore turn to the problem of how to efficiently perform various priority queue methods using a heap.

7.3.2 Complete Binary Trees and Their Representation

Let us discuss more about complete binary trees and how they are represented.

The Complete Binary Tree ADT

As an abstract data type, a complete binary T supports all the methods of binary tree ADT (Section 6.3.1), plus the following two methods:

add(o): Add to T and return a new external node v storing element o such that the resulting tree is a complete binary tree with last node v.
Input: Object; ***Output:*** Position (inserted node).

remove(): Remove the last node of T and return its element.
Input: None; ***Output:*** Object.

Using only these update operations guarantees that we will always have a complete binary tree. As shown in Figure 7.4, there are two cases for the effect of an add of remove. Specifically, for an add, we have the following (remove is similar).

- If the bottom level of T is not full, then add inserts a new node on the bottom level of T, immediately after the rightmost node of this level (that is, the last node); hence, T's height remains the same.
- If the bottom level is full, then add inserts a new node as the left child of the leftmost node of the bottom level of T; hence, T's height increases by one.

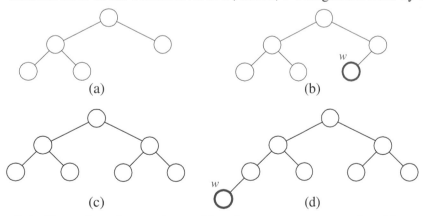

Figure 7.4: Examples of operations add and remove on a complete binary tree, where w denotes the node inserted by add or deleted by remove. The trees shown in (b) and (d) are the results of performing add operations on the trees in (a) and (c), respectively. Likewise, the trees shown in (a) and (c) are the results of performing remove operations on the trees in (b) and (d), respectively.

The Vector Representation of a Complete Binary Tree

The vector-based implementation (Section 6.4.1) is especially suitable for a complete binary tree T. We recall that in this implementation, the nodes of T are stored in a vector V such that node v is the element of V with rank equal to the level number $p(v)$ of v, defined as follows:

- If v is the root of T, then $p(v) = 1$.
- If v is the left child of node u, then $p(v) = 2p(u)$.
- If v is the right child of node u, then $p(v) = 2p(u) + 1$.

With this implementation, the nodes of T have contiguous ranks in the range $[1, n]$ and the last node of T has always rank n, where n is the number of nodes of T. Figure 7.5 shows two examples illustrating this property of the last node.

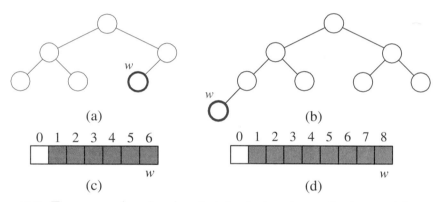

Figure 7.5: Two examples showing that the last node w of a heap with n nodes has level number n: (a) heap T_1 with more than one node on the bottom level; (b) heap T_2 with one node on the bottom level; (c) vector-based representation of T_1; (d) vector-based representation of T_2.

The simplifications that come from representing a complete binary tree T with a vector aid in the implementation of methods add and remove. Assuming that no vector expansion is necessary, methods add and remove can be performed in $O(1)$ time, for they simply involve adding or removing the last element of the vector. Moreover, the vector associated with T has $n + 1$ elements (the element at rank 0 is a place-holder). If we use an extendable array that grows and shrink for the implementation of the vector (Section 5.1.3 and Exercise C-5.2), the space used by the vector-based data structure for a complete binary tree with n nodes is $O(n)$ and operations add and remove take $O(1)$ amortized time.

Java Implementation of a Complete Binary Tree

We represent the complete binary tree ADT in interface CompleteBinaryTree shown in Code Fragment 7.8. We provide a Java class VectorCompleteBinaryTree that implements the CompleteBinaryTree interface with a vector and supports methods add and remove in $O(1)$ time in Code Fragments 7.9–7.11.

```java
public interface CompleteBinaryTree extends BinaryTree {
  public Position add(Object elem);
  public Object remove();
}
```

Code Fragment 7.8: Interface CompleteBinaryTree for a complete binary tree.

```java
public class VectorCompleteBinaryTree implements CompleteBinaryTree  {
  protected Vector T;  // vector of elements stored in the tree
  /** Nested class for a vector-based complete binary tree node. */
  protected static class VectorNode implements Position {
    Object element; // element stored at this position
    int index;       // index of this position in the vector
    public VectorNode(Object elt, int i) {
      element = elt;
      index = i;
    }
    public Object element() { return element; }
    public int index() { return index; }
    public Object setElement(Object elt) {
      Object temp = element;
      element = elt;
      return temp;
    }
  }
  /** default constructor */
  public VectorCompleteBinaryTree() {
    T = new ArrayVector();
    T.insertAtRank(0,null); // the location at rank 0 is deliberately empty
  }
  /** Returns the number of (internal and external) nodes. */
  public int size() { return T.size()-1; }
  /** Returns whether the tree is empty. */
  public boolean isEmpty() { return (size()==0); }
```

Code Fragment 7.9: Class VectorCompleteBinaryTree implementing interface CompleteBinaryTree using a java.util.Vector. (Continues in Code Fragment 7.10.)

```java
/** Returns whether v is an internal node. */
public boolean isInternal(Position v) throws InvalidPositionException {
  return hasLeft(v);   // if v has a right child it will have a left child
}
/** Returns whether v is an external node. */
public boolean isExternal(Position v) throws InvalidPositionException {
  return !isInternal(v);
}
/** Returns whether v is the root node. */
public boolean isRoot(Position v) throws InvalidPositionException {
  VectorNode vv = checkPosition(v);
  return vv.index() == 1;
}
/** Returns whether v has a left child. */
public boolean hasLeft(Position v) throws InvalidPositionException {
  VectorNode vv = checkPosition(v);
  return 2*vv.index() <= size();
}
/** Returns whether v has a right child. */
public boolean hasRight(Position v) throws InvalidPositionException {
  VectorNode vv = checkPosition(v);
  return 2*vv.index() + 1 <= size();
}
/** Returns the root of the tree. */
public Position root() throws EmptyTreeException {
  if (isEmpty()) throw new EmptyTreeException("Tree is empty");
  return (Position)T.elemAtRank(1);
}
/** Returns the left child of v. */
public Position left(Position v)
    throws InvalidPositionException, BoundaryViolationException {
  if (!hasLeft(v)) throw new BoundaryViolationException("No left child");
  return (Position)T.elemAtRank(2*((VectorNode) v).index());
}
/** Returns the right child of v. */
public Position right(Position v)
    throws InvalidPositionException {
  if (!hasRight(v)) throw new BoundaryViolationException("No right child");
  return (Position)T.elemAtRank(2*((VectorNode) v).index() + 1);
}
```

Code Fragment 7.10: Class VectorCompleteBinaryTree implementing the complete binary tree ADT. (Continues in Code Fragment 7.11.)

```
/** Returns the parent of v. */
public Position parent(Position v)
  throws InvalidPositionException, BoundaryViolationException {
  if (isRoot(v)) throw new BoundaryViolationException("No parent");
  return (Position)T.elemAtRank(((VectorNode) v).index() / 2);
}
/** Replaces the element at v. */
public Object replace(Position v, Object o) throws InvalidPositionException {
  VectorNode vv = checkPosition(v);
  return vv.setElement(o);
}
/** Add an element just after the last node (in a level numbering). */
public Position add(Object e) {
  int rankToInsert = size()+1;
  Position p = new VectorNode(e,rankToInsert);
  T.insertAtRank(rankToInsert,p);
  return p;
}
/** Removes and returns the element at the last node. */
public Object remove() throws EmptyTreeException {
  if(isEmpty()) throw new EmptyTreeException("Tree is empty");
  return ((Position)T.removeAtRank(size())).element();
}
/** Determine whether v is a valid node. */
protected VectorNode checkPosition(Position v)
  throws InvalidPositionException
{
  if (v == null || !(v instanceof VectorNode))
    throw new InvalidPositionException("Position is invalid");
  return (VectorNode)v;
}
/** Returns an iterator of the elements stored at all nodes in the tree. */
public Iterator elements() {
  List list = new NodeList();
  for(int i = 0; i < size(); i++)
    list.insertLast(((Position)T.elemAtRank(i+1)).element());
  return list.elements();
}
} // methods children and positions are omitted here (same as LinkedBinaryTree)
```

Code Fragment 7.11: Class VectorCompleteBinaryTree implementing the complete binary tree ADT. (Continued from Code Fragment 7.10.)

7.3.3 Implementing a Priority Queue with a Heap

We now discuss how to implement a priority queue using a heap. Our heap-based representation for a priority queue P consists of the following (see Figure 7.6):

- **heap**, a complete binary tree T whose internal nodes store entries so that the heap-order property is satisfied. We assume T is implemented using a vector, as described in Section 7.3.2. For each internal node v of T, we denote the key of the entry stored at v as $k(v)$.
- **comp**, a comparator that defines the total order relation among the keys.

With this data structure, methods size and isEmpty take $O(1)$ time, as usual. In addition, method min can also be easily performed in $O(1)$ time by accessing the entry stored at the root of the heap (which is at rank 1 in the vector).

Insertion

Let us consider how to perform insert on a priority queue implemented with a heap T. To store a new entry (k, x) into T we add a new node z to T with operation add so that this new node becomes the last node of T and stores entry (k, x).

After this action, the tree T is complete, but it may violate the heap-order property. Hence, unless node z is the root of T (that is, the priority queue was empty before the insertion), we compare key $k(z)$ with the key $k(u)$ stored at the parent u of z. If $k(z) \geq k(u)$, the heap-order property is satisfied and the algorithm terminates. If instead $k(z) < k(u)$, then we need to restore the heap-order property, which can be locally achieved by swapping the entries stored at z and u. (See Figure 7.7c and d.) This swap causes the new entry (k, e) to move up one level. Again, the heap-order property may be violated, and we continue swapping, going up in T until no violation of the heap-order property occurs. (See Figure 7.7e and h.)

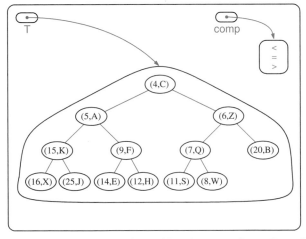

Figure 7.6: Illustration of the heap-based implementation of a priority queue.

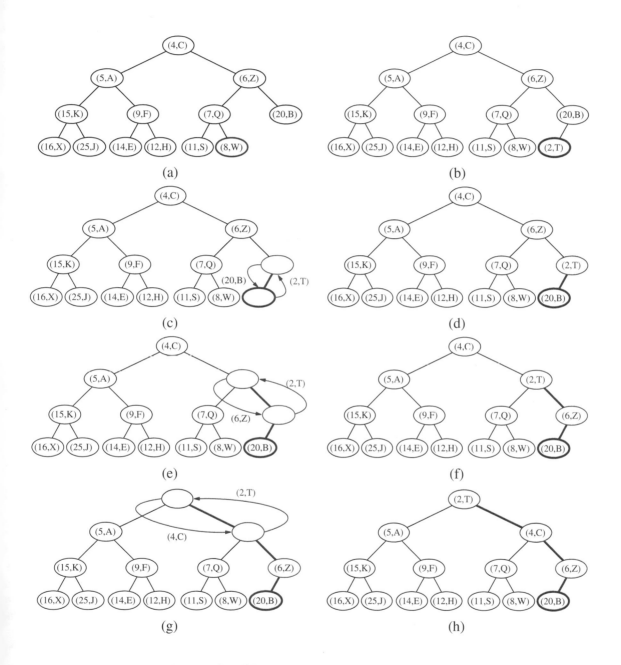

Figure 7.7: Insertion of a new entry with key 2 into the heap of Figure 7.6: (a) initial heap; (b) after performing operation add; (c and d) swap to locally restore the partial order property; (e and f) another swap; (g and h) final swap.

The upward movement of the newly inserted entry by means of swaps is conventionally called ***up-heap bubbling***. A swap either resolves the violation of the heap-order property or propagates it one level up in the heap. In the worst case, up-heap bubbling causes the new entry to move all the way up to the root of heap T. (See Figure 7.7.) Thus, in the worst case, the number of swaps performed in the execution of method insert is equal to the height of T, that is, it is $\lfloor \log n \rfloor$ by Proposition 7.5.

Removal

Let us now turn to method removeMin of the priority queue ADT. The algorithm for performing method removeMin using heap T is illustrated in Figure 7.8.

We know that an entry with the smallest key is stored at the root r of T (even if there is more than one entry with smallest key). However, unless r is the only internal node of T, we cannot simply delete node r, because this action would disrupt the binary tree structure. Instead, we access the last node w of T, copy its entry to the root r, and then delete the last node by performing operation remove of the complete binary tree ADT. (See Figure 7.8a and b.)

Down-Heap Bubbling after a Removal

We are not necessarily done, however, for, even though T is now complete, T may now violate the heap-order property. If T has only one node (the root), then the heap-order property is trivially satisfied and the algorithm terminates. Otherwise, we distinguish two cases, where r denotes the root of T:

- If r has no right child, let s be the left child of r.
- Otherwise (r has both children), let s be a child of r with the smallest key.

If $k(r) \leq k(s)$, the heap-order property is satisfied and the algorithm terminates. If instead $k(r) > k(s)$, then we need to restore the heap-order property, which can be locally achieved by swapping the entries stored at r and s. (See Figure 7.8c and d.) (Note that we shouldn't swap r with s's sibling.) The swap we perform restores the heap-order property for node r and its children, but it may violate this property at s; hence, we may have to continue swapping down T until no violation of the heap-order property occurs. (See Figure 7.8e and h.)

This downward swapping process is called ***down-heap bubbling***. A swap either resolves the violation of the heap-order property or propagates it one level down in the heap. In the worst case, an entry moves all the way down to the bottom level. (See Figure 7.8.) Thus, the number of swaps performed in the execution of method removeMin is, in the worst case, equal to the height of heap T, that is, it is $\lfloor \log n \rfloor$ by Proposition 7.5.

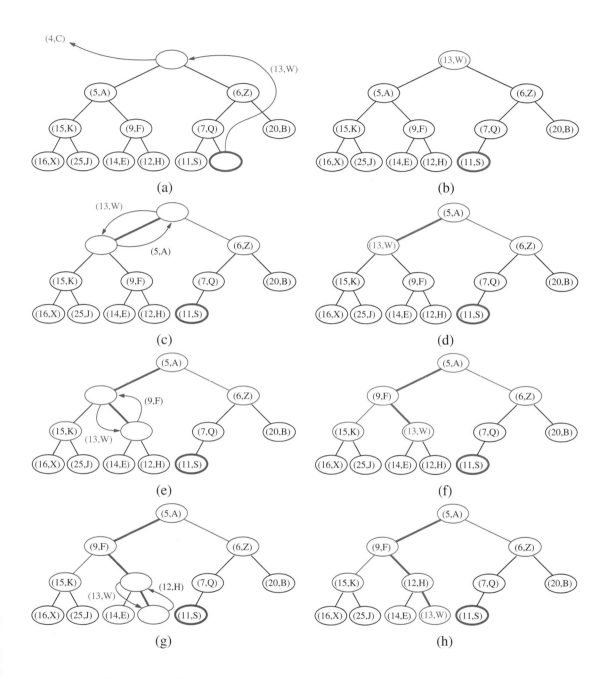

Figure 7.8: Removal of the entry with the smallest key from a heap: (a and b) deletion of the last node, whose entry gets stored into the root; (c and d) swap to locally restore the heap-order property; (e and f) another swap; (g and h) final swap.

Analysis

Table 7.2 shows the running time of the priority queue ADT methods for the heap implementation of a priority queue, assuming that two keys can be compared in $O(1)$ time and that the heap T is is implemented with either the vector-based or linked structure.

Operation	Time
size, isEmpty	$O(1)$
min,	$O(1)$
insert	$O(\log n)$
removeMin	$O(\log n)$

Table 7.2: Performance of a priority queue realized by means of a heap, which is in turn implemented with a vector-based or linked structure. We denote with n the number of entries in the priority queue at the time a method is executed. The space requirement is $O(n)$. The running time of operations insert and removeMin is worst-case for the vector-based implementation of the heap and amortized for the linked representation.

In short, each of the priority queue ADT methods can be performed in $O(1)$ or in $O(\log n)$ time, where n is the number of entries at the time the method is executed. The analysis of the running time of the methods is based on the following:

- The heap T has n nodes, each storing a reference to an entry.
- Operations add and remove on T take either $O(1)$ amortized time (vector-based representation) or $O(\log n)$ worst-case time.
- In the worst case, up-heap and down-heap bubbling perform a number of swaps equal to the height of T.
- The height of heap T is $O(\log n)$, since T is complete (Proposition 7.5).

We conclude that the heap data structure is a very efficient realization of the priority queue ADT, independent of whether the heap is implemented with a linked structure or a vector. The heap-based implementation achieves fast running times for both insertion and removal, unlike the list-based priority queue implementations. Indeed, an important consequence of the efficiency of the heap-based implementation is that it can speed up priority-queue sorting to be much faster than the list-based insertion-sort and selection-sort algorithms.

7.3.4 A Java Heap Implementation

A Java implementation of a heap-based priority queue is shown in Code Fragments 7.12–7.14. To aid in modularity, we delegate the maintenance of the structure of the heap itself to a complete binary tree.

```
/** Realization of a priority queue by means of a heap.  The heap is
  * built upon a vector-based complete binary tree.
  */
public class HeapPriorityQueue implements PriorityQueue {
  protected CompleteBinaryTree T;
  protected Comparator comp;
  /** Inner class for heap entries. */
  protected static class  MyEntry implements Entry {
    protected Object key, value;
    public MyEntry(Object k, Object v) { key = k; value = v; }
    public Object key() { return key; }
    public Object value() { return value; }
  }
  /** Inner class for a comparator that uses the natural ordering of keys. */
  protected static class DefaultComparator implements Comparator {
    public DefaultComparator() { /* default constructor */ }
    public int compare(Object a, Object b) throws ClassCastException {
      return ((Comparable) a).compareTo(b); // use the natural order for a
    }
  }
  /** Creates an empty heap with the default comparator. */
  public HeapPriorityQueue() {
    T = new VectorCompleteBinaryTree(); // use a vector-based tree
    comp = new DefaultComparator();      // use the default comparator
  }
  /** Creates an empty heap with the given comparator. */
  public HeapPriorityQueue(Comparator c) {
    T = new VectorCompleteBinaryTree();
    comp = c;
  }
  /** Returns the size of the heap. */
  public int size() { return T.size(); }
  /** Returns whether the heap is empty. */
  public boolean isEmpty() { return T.size() == 0; }
```

Code Fragment 7.12: Class HeapPriorityQueue, which implements a priority queue with a heap. A nested class MyEntry is used for the entries of the priority queue, which form the elements in the heap tree. (Continues in Code Fragment 7.14.)

```java
/** Returns but does not remove an entry with minimum key. */
public Entry min() throws EmptyPriorityQueueException {
  if (isEmpty())
    throw new EmptyPriorityQueueException("Priority queue is empty");
  return entry(T.root());
}
/** Inserts a key-value pair and return the entry created. */
public Entry insert(Object k, Object x) throws InvalidKeyException {
  checkKey(k);  // may throw an InvalidKeyException
  Entry entry = new MyEntry(k,x);
  upHeap(T.add(entry));
  return entry;
}
/** Removes and returns an entry with minimum key. */
public Entry removeMin() throws EmptyPriorityQueueException {
  if (isEmpty())
    throw new EmptyPriorityQueueException("Priority queue is empty");
  Entry min = entry(T.root());
  if (size() == 1)
    T.remove();
  else {
    T.replace(T.root(), T.remove());
    downHeap(T.root());
  }
  return min;
}
/** Returns the entry stored at a heap node. */
protected Entry entry (Position p) {
  return (Entry) p.element();
}
/** Returns the key stored at a heap node. */
protected Object key (Position p) {
  return ((Entry) p.element()).key();
}
/** Determines whether a given key is valid. */
protected void checkKey(Object key) throws InvalidKeyException {
  try {
    comp.compare(key,key);
  }
  catch(Exception e) {
    throw new InvalidKeyException("Invalid key");
  }
}
```

Code Fragment 7.13: Methods min, insert and removeMin and some auxiliary methods of class HeapPriorityQueue. (Continued from Code Fragment 7.12.)

```
/** Performs up-heap bubbling. */
protected void upHeap(Position v) {
  Position u;
  while (!T.isRoot(v)) {
    u = T.parent(v);
    if (comp.compare(key(u), key(v)) <= 0) break;
    swapElements(u, v);
    v = u;
  }
}
/** Performs down-heap bubbling. */
protected void downHeap(Position r) {
  while (T.isInternal(r)) {
    Position s;                    // the position of the smaller child
    if (!T.hasRight(r))
      s = T.left(r);
    else if (comp.compare(key(T.left(r)), key(T.right(r))) <=0)
      s = T.left(r);
    else
      s = T.right(r);
    if (comp.compare(key(s), key(r)) < 0) {
      swapElements(r, s);
      r = s;
    }
    else
      break;
  }
}
/** Swaps the elements of the two positions. */
protected void swapElements(Position x, Position y) {
  Object temp = x.element();
  T.replace(x, y.element());
  T.replace(y, temp);
}
/** Text visualization for debugging purposes */
public String toString() {
  return T.toString();
}
```

Code Fragment 7.14: Remaining auxiliary methods of class HeapPriorityQueue. (Continued from Code Fragment 7.13.)

7.3.5 Heap-Sort

As we have previously observed, realizing a priority queue with a heap has the advantage that all the methods in the priority queue ADT run in logarithmic time or better. Hence, this realization is suitable for applications where fast running times are sought for all the priority queue methods. Therefore, let us again consider the PriorityQueueSort sorting scheme from Section 7.1.4, which uses a priority queue P to sort a sequence S with n elements.

During Phase 1, the i-th insert operation $(1 \le i \le n)$ takes $O(1 + \log i)$ time, since the heap has i entries after the operation is performed. Likewise, during Phase 2, the j-th removeMin operation $(1 \le j \le n)$ runs in time $O(1 + \log(n - j + 1))$, since the heap has $n - j + 1$ entries at the time the operation is performed. Thus, each phase takes $O(n \log n)$ time, so the entire priority-queue sorting algorithm runs in $O(n \log n)$ time when we use a heap to implement the priority queue. This sorting algorithm is better known as **_heap-sort_**, and its performance is summarized in the following proposition.

Proposition 7.6: *The heap-sort algorithm sorts a sequence S of n elements in $O(n \log n)$ time, assuming two elements of S can be compared in $O(1)$ time.*

Let us stress that the $O(n \log n)$ running time of heap-sort is considerably better than the $O(n^2)$ running time of selection-sort and insertion-sort (Section 7.2.3).

Implementing Heap-Sort In-Place

If the sequence S to be sorted is implemented by means of an array, we can speed up heap-sort and reduce its space requirement by a constant factor using a portion of the sequence S itself to store the heap, thus avoiding the use of an external heap data structure. This is accomplished by modifying the algorithm as follows:

1. We use a reverse comparator, which corresponds to a heap where an entry with the largest key is at the top. At any time during the execution of the algorithm, we use the left portion of S, up to a certain rank $i - 1$, to store the entries of the heap, and the right portion of S, from rank i to $n - 1$, to store the elements of the sequence. Thus, the first i elements of S (at ranks $0, \ldots, i - 1$) provide the vector representation of the heap (with modified level numbers starting at 0 instead of 1), that is, the element at rank k is greater than or equal to its "children" at ranks $2k + 1$ and $2k + 2$.
2. In the first phase of the algorithm, we start with an empty heap and move the boundary between the heap and the sequence from left to right, one step at a time. In step i $(i = 1, \ldots, n)$, we expand the heap by adding the element at rank $i - 1$.

3. In the second phase of the algorithm, we start with an empty sequence and move the boundary between the heap and the sequence from right to left, one step at a time. At step i ($i = 1, \ldots, n$), we remove a maximum element from the heap and store it at rank $n - i$.

The above variation of heap-sort is said to be **in-place** because we use only a small amount of space in addition to the sequence itself. Instead of transferring elements out of the sequence and then back in, we simply rearrange them. We illustrate in-place heap-sort in Figure 7.9. In general, we say that a sorting algorithm is in-place if it uses only a small amount of memory in addition to the sequence storing the objects to be sorted.

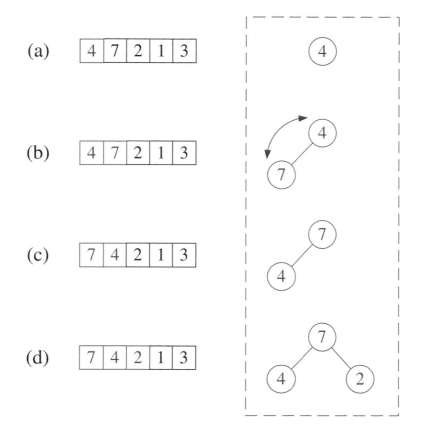

Figure 7.9: First three steps of Phase 1 of in-place heap-sort. The heap portion of the sequence is highlighted in blue. We draw next to the sequence a binary tree view of the heap, even though this tree is not actually constructed by the in-place algorithm.

7.3.6 Bottom-Up Heap Construction ⋆

The analysis of the heap-sort algorithm shows that we can construct a heap storing n entries in $O(n \log n)$ time, by means of n successive insert operations, and then use that heap to extract the entries in order by nondecreasing key. However, if all the n key-value pairs to be stored in the heap are given in advance, there is an alternative **bottom-up** construction method that runs in $O(n)$ time. We describe this method in this section, observing that it could be included as one of the constructors of a class implementing a heap-based priority queue. For simplicity of exposition, we describe this bottom-up heap construction assuming the number n of keys is an integer of the type $n = 2^{h+1} - 1$. That is, the heap is a complete binary tree with every level being full, so the heap has height $h = \log(n+1) - 1$. Viewed nonrecursively, bottom-up heap construction consists of the following $h + 1 = \log(n+1)$ steps:

1. In the first step (see Figure 7.10a), we construct $(n+1)/2$ elementary heaps storing one entry each.

2. In the second step (see Figure 7.10b–c), we form $(n+1)/4$ heaps, each storing three entries, by joining pairs of elementary heaps and adding a new entry. The new entry is placed at the root and may have to be swapped with the entry stored at a child to preserve the heap-order property.

3. In the third step (see Figure 7.10d–e), we form $(n+1)/8$ heaps, each storing 7 entries, by joining pairs of 3-entry heaps (constructed in the previous step) and adding a new entry. The new entry is placed initially at the root, but may have to move down with a down-heap bubbling to preserve the heap-order property.

$$\vdots$$

i. In the generic ith step, $2 \le i \le h$, we form $(n+1)/2^i$ heaps, each storing $2^i - 1$ entries, by joining pairs of heaps storing $(2^{i-1} - 1)$ entries (constructed in the previous step) and adding a new entry. The new entry is placed initially at the root, but may have to move down with a down-heap bubbling to preserve the heap-order property.

$$\vdots$$

$h+1$. In the last step (see Figure 7.10f–g), we form the final heap, storing all the n entries, by joining two heaps storing $(n-1)/2$ entries (constructed in the previous step) and adding a new entry. The new entry is placed initially at the root, but may have to move down with a down-heap bubbling to preserve the heap-order property.

We illustrate bottom-up heap construction in Figure 7.10 for $h = 3$.

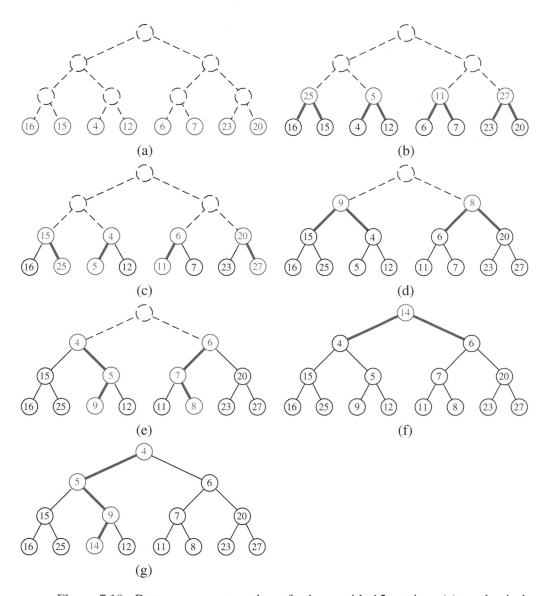

Figure 7.10: Bottom-up construction of a heap with 15 entries: (a) we begin by constructing 1-entry heaps on the bottom level; (b and c) we combine these heaps into 3-entry heaps and then (d and e) 7-entry heaps, until (f and g) we create the final heap. The paths of the down-heap bubblings are highlighted in blue. For simplicity, we only show the key within each node instead of the entire entry.

Recursive Bottom-Up Heap Construction

We can also describe bottom-up heap construction as a recursive algorithm, as shown in Code Fragment 7.15, which we call by passing a list storing the key-value pairs for which we wish to build a heap.

Algorithm BottomUpHeap(S):

> *Input:* A list L storing $n = 2^{h+1} - 1$ entries
>
> *Output:* A heap T storing the entries in L.
>
> **if** S.isEmpty() **then**
>> **return** an empty heap
>
> $e \leftarrow L$.remove(L.first())
>
> Split L into two lists, L_1 and L_2, each of size $(n-1)/2$
>
> $T_1 \leftarrow$ BottomUpHeap(L_1)
>
> $T_2 \leftarrow$ BottomUpHeap(L_2)
>
> Create binary tree T with root r storing e, left subtree T_1, and right subtree T_2
>
> Perform a down-heap bubbling from the root r of T, if necessary
>
> **return** T

Code Fragment 7.15: Recursive bottom-up heap construction.

Bottom-up heap construction is asymptotically faster than incrementally inserting n keys into an initially empty heap, as the following proposition shows.

Proposition 7.7: *Bottom-up construction of a heap with n entries takes $O(n)$ time, assuming two keys can be compared in $O(1)$ time.*

Justification: We analyze bottom-up heap construction using a "visual" approach, which is illustrated in Figure 7.11.

Let T be the final heap, let v be a node of T, and let $T(v)$ denote the subtree of T rooted at v. In the worst case, the time for forming $T(v)$ from the two recursively formed subtrees rooted at v's children is proportional to the height of $T(v)$. The worst case occurs when down-heap bubbling from v traverses a path from v all the way to a bottom-most node of $T(v)$.

Now consider the path $p(v)$ of T from node v to its inorder successor external node, that is, the path that starts at v, goes to the right child of v, and then goes down leftward until it reaches an external node. We say that path $p(v)$ is *associated with* node v. Note that $p(v)$ is not necessarily the path followed by down-heap bubbling when forming $T(v)$. Clearly, the size (number of nodes) of $p(v)$ is equal to the height of $T(v)$ plus one. Hence, forming $T(v)$ takes time proportional to the size of of $p(v)$, in the worst case. Thus, the total running time of bottom-up heap construction is proportional to the sum of the sizes of the paths associated with the nodes of T.

Observe that each node v of T distinct from the root belongs to exactly two such paths: the path $p(v)$ associated with v itself and the path $p(u)$ associated with the parent u of v. (See Figure 7.11.) Also, the root r of T belongs only to path $p(r)$ associated with r itself. Therefore, the sum of the sizes of the paths associated with the internal nodes of T is $2n - 1$. We conclude that the bottom-up construction of heap T takes $O(n)$ time. ∎

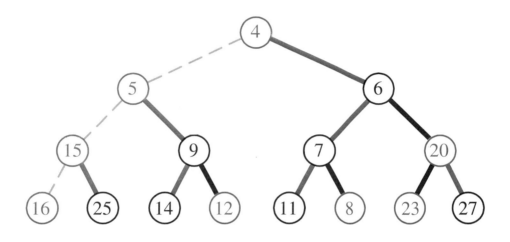

Figure 7.11: Visual justification of the linear running time of bottom-up heap construction, where the paths associated with the internal nodes have been highlighted with alternating colors. For example, the path associated with the root consists of the nodes storing keys 4, 6, 7, and 11. Also, the path associated with the right child of the root consists of the internal nodes storing keys 6, 20, and 23.

To summarize, Proposition 7.7 states that the running time for the first phase of heap-sort can be reduced to be $O(n)$. Unfortunately, the running time of the second phase of heap-sort cannot be made asymptotically better than $O(n \log n)$ (that is, it will always be $\Omega(n \log n)$ in the worst case). We will not justify this lower bound until Chapter 10, however. Instead, we conclude this chapter by discussing a design pattern that allows us to extend the priority queue ADT to have additional functionality.

7.4 Adaptable Priority Queues

The methods of the priority queue ADT given in Section 7.1.3 are sufficient for most basic applications of priority queues, such as sorting. However, there are situations where additional methods would be useful, as shown in the scenarios below, which refer to the standby airline passenger application.

- A standby passenger with a pessimistic attitude may become tired of waiting and decide to leave ahead of the boarding time, requesting to be removed from the waiting list. Thus, we would like to remove from the priority queue the entry associated with this passenger. Operation removeMin is not suitable for this purpose since the passenger leaving is unlikely to have first priority. Instead, we would like to have a new operation remove(e) that removes an arbitrary entry e.

- Another standby passenger finds her gold frequent-flyer card and shows it to the agent. Thus, her priority has to be modified accordingly. To achieve this change of priority, we would like to have a new operation replaceKey(e, k) that replaces with k the key of entry e in the priority queue.

- Finally, a third standby passenger notices her name is misspelled on the ticket and asks it to be corrected. To perform the change, we need to update the passenger's record. Hence, we would like to have a new operation replaceValue(e, x) that replaces with x the value of entry e in the priority queue.

7.4.1 Methods of the Adaptable Priority Queue ADT

The above scenarios motivate the definition of a new ADT that extends the priority queue ADT with methods remove, replaceKey, and replaceValue. Namely, an *adaptable priority queue* P supports the following methods in addition to those of the priority queue ADT:

remove(e): Remove from P and return entry e.
Input: Entry; ***Output:*** Entry.

replaceKey(e, k): Replace with k and return the key of entry e of P; an error condition occurs if k is invalid (that is, k cannot be compared with other keys).
Input: Entry, object; ***Output:*** Object.

replaceValue(e, x): Replace with x and return the value of entry e of P.
Input: Entry, object; ***Output:*** Object.

Example 7.8: *The following table shows a series of operations and their effects on an initially empty adaptable priority queue P.*

Operation	Output	P
insert$(5,A)$	e_1	$\{(5,A)\}$
insert$(3,B)$	e_2	$\{(3,B),(5,A)\}$
insert$(7,C)$	e_3	$\{(3,B),(5,A),(7,C)\}$
min$()$	e_2	$\{(3,B),(5,A),(7,C)\}$
key(e_2)	3	$\{(3,B),(5,A),(7,C)\}$
remove(e_1)	e_1	$\{(3,B),(7,C)\}$
replaceKey$(e_2,9)$	3	$\{(7,C),(9,B)\}$
replaceValue(e_3,D)	C	$\{(7,D),(9,B)\}$
remove(e_2)	e_2	$\{(7,D)\}$

7.4.2 Location-Aware Entries

In order to implement methods remove, replaceKey, and replaceValue of an adaptable priority queue P, we need a mechanism for finding the position of an entry of P. Namely, given the entry e of P passed as an argument to one of the above methods, we need to find the position storing e in the the data structure implementing P (for example, a doubly linked list or a heap). This position is called the *location* of the entry.

Instead of searching for the location of a given entry e, we augment the entry object with an instance variable of type Position storing the location. This implementation of an entry that keeps track of its position is called a *location-aware entry*. A summary description of the the use of location-aware entries for the sorted list and heap implementations of an adaptable priority queue is provided below. We denote with n the number of entries in the priority queue at the time an operation is performed.

- *Sorted list implementation*. In this implementation, after an entry is inserted, we set the location of the entry to refer to the position of the list containing the entry. Also, we update the location of the entry whenever it changes position in the list. Operations remove(e) and replaceValue(e,x) take $O(1)$ time, since we can obtain the position p of entry e in $O(1)$ time following the location reference stored with the entry. Instead, operation replaceKey(e,k) runs in $O(n)$ time, because the modification of the key of entry e may require moving the entry to a different position in the list to preserve the ordering of the keys. The use of location-aware entries increases the running time of the standard priority queue operations by a constant factor.

- *Heap implementation*. In this implementation, after an entry is inserted, we set the location of the entry to refer to the node of the heap containing the entry. Also, we update the location of the entry whenever it changes node in the heap (for example, because of the swaps in a down-heap or up-heap bubbling). Operation replaceValue(e,x) takes $O(1)$ time since we can obtain the position p of entry e in $O(1)$ time following the location reference stored with the entry. Operations remove(e) and replaceKey(e,k) run instead in $O(\log n)$ (details are explored in Exercise C-7.22). The use of location-aware entries increases the running time of operations insert and removeMin by a constant factor overhead.

The use of location-aware entries for the unsorted list implementation is explored in Exercise C-7.21.

Performance of Adaptable Priority Queue Implementations

The performance of an adaptable priority queue implemented by means of various data structures with location-aware entries is summarized in Table 7.3.

Method	Unsorted List	Sorted List	Heap
size, isEmpty	$O(1)$	$O(1)$	$O(1)$
insert	$O(1)$	$O(n)$	$O(\log n)$
min	$O(n)$	$O(1)$	$O(1)$
removeMin	$O(n)$	$O(1)$	$O(\log n)$
remove	$O(1)$	$O(1)$	$O(\log n)$
replaceKey	$O(1)$	$O(n)$	$O(\log n)$
replaceValue	$O(1)$	$O(1)$	$O(1)$

Table 7.3: Running times of the methods of an adaptable priority queue of size n, realized by means of an unsorted list, sorted list, and heap, respectively. The space requirement is $O(n)$.

7.4.3 Implementing an Adaptable Priority Queue

In Code Fragment 7.16 and 7.17, we show the Java implementation of an adaptable priority queue based on a sorted list. This implementation is obtained by extending class SortedListPriorityQueue shown in Code Fragment 7.6. In particular, Code Fragment 7.17 shows how to realize a location-aware entry in Java by extending a regular entry.

```java
/** Implementation of a priority queue by means of a sorted list */
public class SortedListAdaptablePriorityQueue
  extends SortedListPriorityQueue implements AdaptablePriorityQueue {
  /** Creates the priority queue with the default comparator. */
  public SortedListAdaptablePriorityQueue() {
    super();
  }
  /** Creates the priority queue with the given comparator. */
  public SortedListAdaptablePriorityQueue(Comparator comp) {
    super(comp);
  }
  /** Inserts a key-value pair and returns the entry created. */
  public Entry insert (Object k, Object v) throws InvalidKeyException {
    checkKey(k);
    LocationAwareEntry entry = new LocationAwareEntry(k,v);
    insertEntry(entry);
    entry.setLocation(actionPos);
    return entry;
  }
  /** Removes and returns the given entry. */
  public Entry remove(Entry entry) {
    checkEntry(entry);
    LocationAwareEntry e = (LocationAwareEntry) entry;
    Position p = e.location();
    L.remove(p);
    e.setLocation(null);
    return e;
  }
  /** Replaces the key of the given entry. */
  public Object replaceKey(Entry entry, Object k) {
    checkKey(k);
    checkEntry(entry);
    LocationAwareEntry e = (LocationAwareEntry) remove(entry);
    Object oldKey = e.setKey(k);
    insertEntry(e);
    e.setLocation(actionPos);
    return oldKey;
  }
}
```

Code Fragment 7.16: Java implementation of an adaptable priority queue by means of a sorted list storing location-aware entries. Class SortedListAdaptablePriorityQueue extends class SortedListPriorityQueue (Code Fragment 7.6) and implements interface AdaptablePriorityQueue. (Continues in Code Fragment 7.17.)

```
/** Replaces the value of the given entry. */
public Object replaceValue(Entry e, Object value) {
  checkEntry(e);
  Object oldValue = ((LocationAwareEntry) e).setValue(value);
  return oldValue;
}
/** Determines whether a given entry is valid. */
protected void checkEntry(Entry ent) throws InvalidEntryException {
  if(ent == null || !(ent instanceof LocationAwareEntry))
    throw new InvalidEntryException("invalid entry");
}
/** Inner class for a location-aware entry. */
protected static class LocationAwareEntry
  extends MyEntry implements Entry {
  /** Position where the entry is stored. */
  private Position loc;
  public LocationAwareEntry(Object key, Object value) {
    super(key, value);
  }
  public LocationAwareEntry(Object key, Object value, Position pos) {
    super(key, value);
    loc = pos;
  }
  protected Position location() {
    return loc;
  }
  protected Position setLocation(Position pos) {
    Position oldPosition = location();
    loc = pos;
    return oldPosition;
  }
  protected Object setKey(Object key) {
    Object oldKey = key();
    k = key;
    return oldKey;
  }
  protected Object setValue(Object value) {
    Object oldValue = value();
    v = value;
    return oldValue;
  }
 }
}
```

Code Fragment 7.17: An adaptable priority queue implemented with a sorted list storing location-aware entries. (Continued from Code Fragment 7.16.) The nested class LocationAwareEntry realizes a location-aware entry and extends nested class MyEntry of SortedListPriorityQueue shown in Code Fragment 7.6.

7.5 Exercises

For source code and help with exercises, please visit **java.datastructures.net**.

Reinforcement

R-7.1 An airport is developing a computer simulation of air-traffic control that handles events such as landings and takeoffs. Each event has a *time-stamp* that denotes the time when the event occurs. The simulation program needs to efficiently perform the following two fundamental operations:

- Insert an event with a given time-stamp (that is, add a future event).
- Extract the event with smallest time-stamp (that is, determine the next event to process).

Which data structure should be used for the above operations? Why?

R-7.2 Although it is correct to use a "reverse" comparator with the priority queue ADT so that we retrieve and remove an entry with the maximum key each time, it is confusing to have an entry with maximum key returned by a method named "removeMin." Write a short adapter class that can take any priority queue P and an associated comparator C and implement a priority queue that concentrates on the element with maximum key, using methods with names like removeMax.

R-7.3 Illustrate the execution of the selection-sort algorithm on the following input sequence: $(22, 15, 36, 44, 10, 3, 9, 13, 29, 25)$.

R-7.4 Illustrate the execution of the insertion-sort algorithm on the input sequence of the previous problem.

R-7.5 Give an example of a worst-case sequence with n elements for insertion-sort, and show that insertion-sort runs in $\Omega(n^2)$ time on such a sequence.

R-7.6 At which nodes of a heap can an entry with largest key be stored?

R-7.7 In defining the relation "to the left of" for two nodes of a binary tree (Section 7.3.1), can we use a preorder traversal instead of an inorder traversal? How about a postorder traversal?

R-7.8 Illustrate the execution of the heap-sort algorithm on the following input sequence: $(2, 5, 16, 4, 10, 23, 39, 18, 26, 15)$.

R-7.9 Let T be a complete binary tree such that node v stores the entry $(p(v), 0)$, where $p(v)$ is the level number of v. Is tree T a heap? Why or why not?

R-7.10 Explain why the case where node r has a right child but not a left child was not considered in the description of down-heap bubbling.

R-7.11 Is there a heap T storing seven entries with distinct keys such that a pre-order traversal of T yields the entries of T in increasing or decreasing order by key? How about an inorder traversal? How about a postorder traversal? If so, give an example; if not, say why.

R-7.12 Show that the sum

$$\sum_{i=1}^{n} \log i,$$

which appears in the analysis of heap-sort, is $\Omega(n \log n)$.

R-7.13 Bill claims that a preorder traversal of a heap will list its keys in nondecreasing order. Draw an example of a heap that proves him wrong.

R-7.14 Hillary claims that a postorder traversal of a heap will list its keys in nonincreasing order. Draw an example of a heap that proves her wrong.

R-7.15 Show all the steps of the algorithm for removing key 16 from the heap of Figure 7.3.

R-7.16 Show all the steps of the algorithm for replacing key 5 with 18 in the heap of Figure 7.3.

R-7.17 Draw an example of a heap whose keys are all the odd numbers from 1 to 59 (with no repeats), such that the insertion of an entry with key 32 would cause up-heap bubbling to proceed all the way up to a child of the root (replacing that child's key with 32).

R-7.18 Complete Figure 7.9 by showing all the steps of the in-place heap-sort algorithm. Show both the array and the associated heap at the end of each step.

R-7.19 Give a pseudo-code description of a nonrecursive in-place heap-sort algorithm.

R-7.20 A group of children want to play a game, called *Unmonopoly*, where in each turn the player with the most money must give half of his/her money to the player with the least amount of money. What data structure(s) should be used to play this game efficiently? Why?

Creativity

C-7.1 An online stock trading system needs to process orders of the form "buy 100 shares at x each" or "sell 100 shares at y each." A buy order for x can only be processed if there is an existing sell order with price y such that $y \leq x$. Likewise, a sell order for y can only be processed if there is an existing buy order with price x such that $y \leq x$. If a buy or sell order is entered but cannot be processed, it must wait for a future order that allows it to be processed. Describe a scheme that allows for buy and sell orders to be entered in $O(\log n)$ time, independent of whether or not they can be immediately processed.

C-7.2 Extend a solution to the previous problem so that users are allowed to update the prices for their buy or sell orders that have yet to be processed.

C-7.3 Write a comparator for nonnegative integers that determines order based on the number of 1's in each integer's binary expansion, so that $i < j$ if the number of 1's in the binary representation of i is less than the number of 1's in the binary representation of j.

C-7.4 Show how to implement the stack ADT using only a priority queue and one additional integer instance variable.

C-7.5 Show how to implement the (standard) queue ADT using only a priority queue and one additional integer instance variable.

C-7.6 Describe in detail an implementation of a priority queue based on a sorted array. Show that this implementation achieves $O(1)$ time for operations min and removeMin and $O(n)$ time for operation insert.

C-7.7 Describe an in-place version of the selection-sort algorithm that uses only $O(1)$ space for instance variables in addition to an input array itself.

C-7.8 Assuming the input to the sorting problem is given in an array A, describe how to implement the insertion-sort algorithm using only the array A and, at most, six additional (base-type) variables.

C-7.9 Describe how to implement the heap-sort algorithm using at most six integer variables in addition to an input array itself.

C-7.10 Describe a sequence of n insertions in a heap that requires $\Omega(n \log n)$ time to process.

C-7.11 An alternative method for finding the last node during an insertion in a heap T is to store in the last node and each external node of T a reference to the external node immediately to its right (wrapping to the first node in the next lower level for the right-most external node). Show how to maintain such references in $O(1)$ time per operation of the priority queue ADT assuming T is implemented as a linked structure.

C-7.12 Describe an implementation of complete binary tree T by means of a linked structure and a reference to the last node. In particular, show how to update the reference to the last node after operations add and remove in $O(\log n)$ time, where n is the current number of nodes of T. Be sure and handle all possible cases, as illustrated in Figure 7.12.

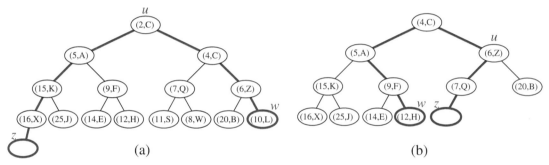

Figure 7.12: Updating the last node in a complete binary tree after operation add or remove. Node w is the last node before operation add or after operation remove. Node z is the last node after operation add or before operation remove.

C-7.13 We can represent a path from the root to a given node of a binary tree by means of a binary string, where 0 means "go to the left child" and 1 means "go to the right child." For example, the path from the root to the node storing 8 in the heap of Figure 7.3 is represented by "101." Design an $O(\log n)$-time algorithm for finding the last node of a complete binary tree with n nodes, based on the above representation. Show how this algorithm can be used in the implementation of a complete binary tree by means of a linked structure that does not keep a reference to the last node.

C-7.14 Given a heap T and a key k, give an algorithm to compute all the entries in T with key less than or equal to k. For example, given the heap of Figure 7.3 and query $k = 7$, the algorithm should report the entries with keys 4, 5, 6, and 7. Your algorithm should run in time proportional to the number of entries returned.

C-7.15 Provide a justification of the time bounds in Table 7.3.

C-7.16 Tamarindo Airlines wants to give a first-class upgrade coupon to their top $\log n$ frequent flyers, based on the number of miles accumulated, where n is the total number of the airlines' frequent flyers. The algorithm they currently use, which runs in $O(n \log n)$ time, sorts the flyers by the number of miles flown and then scans the sorted list to pick the top $\log n$ flyers. Describe an algorithm that identifies the top $\log n$ flyers in $O(n)$ time.

C-7.17 Develop an algorithm that computes the kth smallest element of a set of n distinct integers in $O(n + k \log n)$ time.

C-7.18 Suppose two binary trees, T_1 and T_2, hold entries satisfying the heap-order property. Describe a method for combining T_1 and T_2 into a tree T whose internal nodes hold the union of the entries in T_1 and T_2 and also satisfy the heap-order property. Your algorithm should run in time $O(h_1 + h_2)$ where h_1 and h_2 are the respective heights of T_1 and T_2.

C-7.19 Give an alternative analysis of bottom-up heap construction by showing the following summation is $O(1)$, for any positive integer h:

$$\sum_{i=1}^{h} (i/2^i).$$

C-7.20 Give an alternate description of the in-place heap-sort algorithm that uses a standard comparator instead of a reverse one.

C-7.21 Describe efficient algorithms for performing operations remove(e) and replaceKey(e,k) on an adaptable priority queue realized by means of an unsorted list with location-aware entries.

C-7.22 Describe efficient algorithms for performing operations remove(e) and replaceKey(e,k) on an adaptable priority queue realized by means of a heap with location-aware entries.

C-7.23 Let S be a set of n points in the plane with distinct integer x- and y-coordinates. Let T be a complete binary tree storing the points from S at its external nodes, such that the points are ordered left-to-right by increasing x-coordinates. For each node v in T, let $S(v)$ denote the subset of S consisting of points stored in the subtree rooted at v. For the root r of T, define $top(r)$ to be the point in $S = S(r)$ with maximum y-coordinate. For every other node v, define $top(r)$ to be the point in S with highest y-coordinate in $S(v)$ that is not also the highest y-coordinate in $S(u)$, where u is the parent of v in T (if such a point exists). Such a labeling of turns T into a ***priority search tree***. Describe a linear-time algorithm for turning T into a priority search tree.

Projects

P-7.1 Give a Java implementation of a priority queue based on an unsorted list.

P-7.2 Write an applet or stand-alone graphical program that animates both the insertion-sort and selection-sort algorithms. Your animation should visualize the movement of elements to their correct locations.

P-7.3 Write an applet or stand-alone graphical program that animates a heap. Your program should support all the priority queue operations and should visualize the swaps in the up-heap and down-heap bubblings. (Extra: visualize bottom-up heap construction as well.)

P-7.4 Implement the heap-sort algorithm using bottom-up heap construction.

P-7.5 Implement the in-place heap-sort algorithm. Experimentally compare its running time with that of the standard heap-sort that is not in-place.

P-7.6 Implement a heap-based priority queue that supports the following additional operation in linear time:

replaceComparator(c): Replace the current comparator with c.
Input: Comparator; *Output:* None.

(Hint: Utilize the bottom-up heap construction algorithm.)

P-7.7 Develop a Java implementation of an adaptable priority queue that is based on an unsorted list and supports location-aware entries.

P-7.8 Develop a Java implementation of an adaptable priority queue that is based on a heap and supports location-aware entries.

Chapter Notes

Knuth's book on sorting and searching [59] describes the motivation and history for the selection-sort, insertion-sort, and heap-sort algorithms. The heap-sort algorithm is due to Williams [96], and the linear-time heap construction algorithm is due to Floyd [35]. Additional algorithms and analyses for heaps and heap-sort variations can be found in papers by Bentley [13], Carlsson [20], Gonnet and Munro [41], McDiarmid and Reed [68], and Schaffer and Sedgewick [82]. The design pattern of using location-aware entries (also described in [42]) appears to be new.

Chapter

8

Maps and Dictionaries

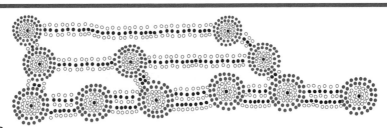

Contents

The familiar phrase, "Go look it up," might be heard when a lazy student asks for the definition of a word from an equally lazy teacher. This phrase is also the principle behind the *map* and *dictionary* abstract data types, which we discuss in this chapter. The primary use of a map or dictionary is to store elements so they can be located quickly using keys. The motivation for such searches is that each element typically stores additional useful information besides its search key, but the only way to get at that information is to use the search key. For example, we may wish to store a collection of bank account records. Each account is an object that is identified by an account number and stores a wealth of additional information, including the current balance, the name and address of the account holder, and the history of deposits and withdrawals performed. A software application wishing to operate on an account would have to provide the account number as a search key to get the rest of the account's information.

As another example, we may wish to store a set of windows that are open in a user's graphical interface. The window objects would be stored in our map according to some identifier (like a process number), to determine a unique *key*, but additional information is stored with each window object, including its dimensions, descriptions of its fonts, and colors. This additional information could be encapsulated in a *value* object associated with a window's key.

Like priority queues, maps and dictionaries store key-value pairs, called *entries*. Maps require that each key be unique, while dictionaries allow multiple entries to have the same key, just like priority queues. Nevertheless, while a total order relation is always required for keys in priority queues, it is optional for dictionaries. When a total order relation on the keys is defined, then we can talk about an *ordered dictionary*, and we can specify additional ADT methods.

A computer dictionary is similar to a paper dictionary of words in the sense that both are used to look things up. The paper dictionary metaphor is not fully appropriate, however, for we typically desire a computer dictionary to be dynamic, so as to support element insertion and removal. Thus, the dictionary abstract data type has methods for the insertion, removal, and searching of elements with keys.

In this chapter, we describe several different techniques for realizing maps and dictionaries. We show, for example, how to realize a map using a simple data structure known as a hash table, which often has very fast performance in practice. We also show how to implement a dictionary using an unordered list. This implementation is simple, and gives rise to a structure that is also known as an audit trail, but it is not very efficient in most applications. So we introduce skip lists, showing how these data structures can be used to realize ordered dictionaries with fast query and update times.

Incidentally, in Chapter 9, we discuss other data structures that achieve fast dictionary-operation performance by using various kinds of balanced search trees.

8.1 The Map Abstract Data Type

A ***map*** stores key-value pairs (k, v), which we call ***entries***, where k is the key and v is its corresponding value. In addition, the map ADT requires that each key be unique.

In order to achieve the highest level of generality, we allow both the keys and the values stored in a map to be of any object type. (See Figure 8.1.) In a map storing student records (such as the student's name, address, and course grades), the key might be the student's ID number. In some applications, the key and the value may be the same. For example, if we had a map storing prime numbers, we could use each number itself as both a key and its value.

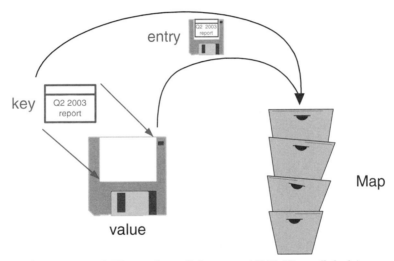

Figure 8.1: A conceptual illustration of the map ADT. Keys (labels) are assigned to values (diskettes) by a user. The resulting entries (labeled diskettes) are inserted into the map (file cabinet). The keys can be used later to retrieve or remove values.

In either case, we use a ***key*** as a unique identifier that is assigned by an application or user to an associated value object. Thus, a map is most appropriate in situations where each key is to be viewed as a kind of unique ***index*** address for its value, that is, an object that serves as a kind of location for that value. For example, if we wish to store student records, we would probably want to use student ID objects as keys (and disallow two students having the same student ID). In other words, the key associated with an object can be viewed as an "address" in memory for that object. Indeed, maps are sometimes referred to as ***associative stores***, for the key associated with an object determines its "location" in the data structure.

The Map ADT

Since a map stores a collection of objects, it should be viewed as a container of key-value pairs. As an ADT, a *map M* supports the following methods:

size(): Return the number of entries in M.
Input: None; *Output:* Integer.

isEmpty(): Test whether M is empty.
Input: None; *Output:* Boolean.

get(k): If M contains an entry e with key equal to k, then return the value of e, else return **null**.
Input: Object (key); *Output:* Object (its associated value).

put(k, v): If M does not have an entry with key equal to k, then add entry (k, v) to M and return **null**; else, replace with v the existing value of the entry with key equal to k and return the old value.
Input: Objects k (key) and v (value); *Output:* Object (value).

remove(k): Remove from M the entry with key equal to k, and return its value; if M has no such entry, then return **null**.
Input: Object (key); *Output:* Object (value).

keys(): Return an iterator of the keys stored in M.
Input: None; *Output:* Iterator of objects (keys in M).

values(): Return an iterator of the values associated with keys stored in M.
Input: None; *Output:* Iterator of objects (values in M).

When operations get(k), put(k, v) and remove(k) are performed on a map M that has no entry with key equal to k, we use the convention of returning **null**. A special value such as this is known as a *sentinel*. The disadvantage with using **null** as such a sentinel is that this choice can create ambiguity should we every want to have in the map an entry $(k, $**null**$)$ with value **null**. Another choice, of course, would be to throw an exception when someone requests a key that is not in our map. This would probably not be an appropriate use of an exception, however, since it is normal to ask for something that might not be in our map. Moreover, throwing and catching an exception is typically slower than a test against a sentinel; hence, using a sentinel is more efficient (and, in this case, conceptually more appropriate).

Example 8.1: *In the following, we show the effect of a series of operations on an initially empty map storing entries with integer keys and single-character values.*

Operation	*Output*	*Map*
isEmpty()	**true**	$\emptyset$
put(5,A)	**null**	$\{(5,A)\}$
put(7,B)	**null**	$\{(5,A),(7,B)\}$
put(2,C)	**null**	$\{(5,A),(7,B),(2,C)\}$
put(8,D)	**null**	$\{(5,A),(7,B),(2,C),(8,D)\}$
put(2,E)	C	$\{(5,A),(7,B),(2,E),(8,D)\}$
get(7)	B	$\{(5,A),(7,B),(2,E),(8,D)\}$
get(4)	**null**	$\{(5,A),(7,B),(2,E),(8,D)\}$
get(2)	E	$\{(5,A),(7,B),(2,E),(8,D)\}$
size()	4	$\{(5,A),(7,B),(2,E),(8,D)\}$
remove(5)	A	$\{(7,B),(2,E),(8,D)\}$
remove(2)	E	$\{(7,B),(8,D)\}$
get(2)	**null**	$\{(7,B),(8,D)\}$
isEmpty()	**false**	$\{(7,B),(8,D)\}$

Equality Testers

Each of the standard map ADT methods given above requires that we have a mechanism for deciding whether two keys are equal. If the keys come from a total order that is determined by some comparator C (Section 7.1.2), then we can use that comparator to decide equality by testing whether C.compare(k_1,k_2) returns 0. Otherwise, for a generic map, we can use an *equality tester* object that supports operation isEqualTo(k_1,k_2) on keys. Alternatively, we could use the built-in equals method that all Java Objects must implement to decide equality. This latter approach is not as general as would be possible using an equality tester, but it would make use of a natural equality-testing method. How ever we do it, implementing the map ADT requires that we have a way for testing the equality of keys. When a map M is first created, we can satisfy this requirement by associating an equality tester with M, such that this tester is based on a comparator, a special equality tester, or a default equality tester based on the equals method.

For the sake of simplicity, the pseudo-code examples in this chapter use the standard operator "=" in tests for equality of two keys, thus hiding the existence of an equality tester. In the Java implementation examples, we explicitly use equality tester objects, characterized by interface EqualityTester.

8.1.1 Maps in the java.util Package

The Java package java.util includes an interface for the map ADT, which is called java.util.Map and is defined so that an implementing class enforces unique keys. Interface java.util.Map does not have any methods to directly return iterators of a map's keys or values, but it does have methods to return a set of keys or values, which can, in turn, provide an iterator.

One additional minor point is that the java.util.Map interface does not use an external equality tester—it only uses method equals, which is supported by any Java object. Thus, if we store in a java.util.Map objects for which the default equals method is not appropriate, we must override this method by "hard-coding" it within the key class. This approach is not completely flexible, of course, since there are contexts in which keys do not "know" when they are equal. For example, a geometric algorithm may consider points as "equal" if they have the same x-coordinate, while another algorithm may consider them equal if they have the same y-coordinate. (See the related discussion in Section 7.1.2.)

Instead, we advocate the use of an equality tester (or a comparator) to test whether two keys in a map are equal, with the use of the equals method being possibly embedded in a default equality tester. This approach yields a general, reusable, and adaptable way of testing for object equality, while still providing for users who do not wish to define their own equality tester. Indeed, the equality tester can always use the equals method of the key class, if this use is appropriate.

Corresponding Methods

Other than these subtle points, the correspondences between the map ADT and the java.util.Map interface are as shown in Table 8.1.

Map ADT Methods	java.util.Map Methods
size()	size()
isEmpty()	isEmpty()
get(k)	get(k)
put(k,v)	put(k,v)
remove(k)	remove(k)
keys()	keySet().iterator()
values()	values().iterator()

Table 8.1: Correspondences between methods of the map ADT and the methods of the java.util.Map interface, which supports other methods as well.

8.1.2   A Simple List-Based Map Implementation

A simple way of implementing a map is to store its n entries in a list S, implemented as a doubly linked list. Performing the fundamental methods, get(k), put(k,v), and remove(k), involves simple scans down S looking for an entry with key k. We give pseudo-code for performing these methods in Code Fragment 8.1.

This list-based map implementation is simple, but it is only efficient for very small maps. Every one of the fundamental methods takes $O(n)$ time on a map with n entries, because each method involves searching through the entire list in the worst case. Thus, we would like something faster.

Algorithm get(k):
> $B \leftarrow S$.positions() $\{B$ is an iterator of the positions in the list $S\}$
> **while** B.hasNext() **do**
>> $p \leftarrow B$.next() $\{$the next position in $B\}$
>> **if** p.element().key() $= k$ **then**
>>> **return** p.element().value()
>
> **return null** $\{$there is no entry with key equal to $k\}$

Algorithm put(k,v):
> $B \leftarrow S$.positions()
> **while** B.hasNext() **do**
>> $p \leftarrow B$.next()
>> **if** p.element().key() $= k$ **then**
>>> $t \leftarrow p$.element().value()
>>> B.replace$(p,(k,v))$
>>> **return** t $\{$return the old value$\}$
>
> S.insertLast$((k,v))$
> $n \leftarrow n+1$ $\{$increment variable storing number of entries$\}$
> **return null** $\{$there was no previous entry with key equal to $k\}$

Algorithm remove(k):
> $B \leftarrow S$.positions()
> **while** B.hasNext() **do**
>> $p \leftarrow B$.next()
>> **if** p.element().key() $= k$ **then**
>>> $t \leftarrow p$.element().value()
>>> S.remove(p)
>>> $n \leftarrow n-1$ $\{$decrement variable storing number of entries$\}$
>>> **return** t $\{$return the removed value$\}$
>
> **return null** $\{$there is no entry with key equal to $k\}$

Code Fragment 8.1: Algorithms for the fundamental map methods with a list S.

8.2   Hash Tables

The keys associated with values in a map are typically thought of as "addresses" for those values. Examples of such applications include a compiler's symbol table and a registry of environment variables. Both of these structures consist of a collection of symbolic names where each name serves as the "address" for properties about a variable's type and value. One of the most efficient ways to implement a map in such circumstances is to use a ***hash table***. Although, as we will see, the worst-case running time of map operations in an *n*-entry hash table is $O(n)$, a hash table can usually perform these operations in $O(1)$ expected time. In general, a hash table consists of two major components, a ***bucket array*** and a ***hash function***.

8.2.1   Bucket Arrays

A ***bucket array*** for a hash table is an array *A* of size *N*, where each cell of *A* is thought of as a "bucket" (that is, a container of key-value pairs) and the integer *N* defines the ***capacity*** of the array. If the keys are integers well distributed in the range $[0, N-1]$, this bucket array is all that is needed. An entry *e* with key *k* is simply inserted into the bucket $A[k]$. (See Figure 8.2.) To save space, an empty bucket may be replaced by a **null** object.

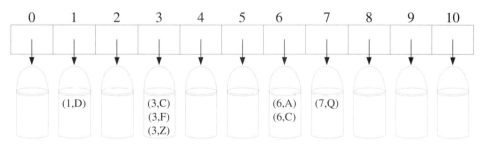

Figure 8.2: A bucket array of size 11 for the entries (1,D), (3,C), (3,F), (3,Z), (6,A), (6,C) and (7Q),

If our keys are unique integers in the range $[0, N-1]$, then each bucket holds at most one entry. Thus, searches, insertions, and removals in the bucket array take $O(1)$ time. This sounds like a great achievement, but it has two drawbacks. First, the space used is proportional to *N*. Thus, if *N* is much larger than the number of entries *n* actually present in the map, we have a waste of space. The second drawback is that keys are required to be integers in the range $[0, N-1]$, which is often not the case. Because of these two drawbacks, we use the bucket array in conjunction with a "good" mapping from the keys to the integers in the range $[0, N-1]$.

8.2.2 Hash Functions

The second part of a hash table structure is a function, h, called a ***hash function***, that maps each key k in our map to an integer in the range $[0, N-1]$, where N is the capacity of the bucket array for this table. Equipped with such a hash function, h, we can apply the bucket array method to arbitrary keys. The main idea of this approach is to use the hash function value, $h(k)$, as an index into our bucket array, A, instead of the key k (which is most likely inappropriate for use as a bucket array index). That is, we store the entry (k, v) in the bucket $A[h(k)]$.

Of course, if there are two or more keys with the same hash value, then two different entries will be mapped to the same bucket in A. In this case, we say that a ***collision*** has occurred. Clearly, if each bucket of A can store only a single entry, then we cannot associate more than one entry with a single bucket, which is a problem in the case of collisions. To be sure, there are ways of dealing with collisions, which we will discuss later, but the best strategy is to try to avoid them in the first place. We say that a hash function is "good" if it maps the keys in our map so as to minimize collisions as much as possible. For practical reasons, we also would like a hash function to be fast and easy to compute.

Following the convention in Java, we view the evaluation of a hash function, $h(k)$, as consisting of two actions—mapping the key k to an integer, called the ***hash code***, and mapping the hash code to an integer within the range of indices ($[0, N-1]$) of a bucket array, called the ***compression function***. (See Figure 8.3.)

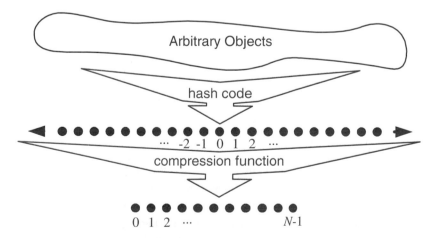

Figure 8.3: The two parts of a hash function: a hash code and a compression function.

8.2.3   Hash Codes

The first action that a hash function performs is to take an arbitrary key k in our map and assign it an integer value. The integer assigned to a key k is called the **hash code** for k. This integer value need not be in the range $[0, N-1]$, and may even be negative, but we desire that the set of hash codes assigned to our keys should avoid collisions as much as possible. For if the hash codes of our keys cause collisions, then there is no hope for our compression function to avoid them. In addition, to be consistent with all of our keys, the hash code we use for a key k should be the same as the hash code for any key that is equal to k (as determined by the equality tester for our map).

Hash Codes in Java

The generic Object class defined in a Java comes with a default hashCode() method for mapping each object instance to an integer that is a "representation" of that object. Specifically, the hashCode() method returns a 32-bit integer of type **int**. Unless specifically overridden, this method is inherited by every object used in a Java program. We should be careful in using the default Object version of hashCode(), however, as this could just be an integer interpretation of the object's location in memory (as is the case in many Java implementations). This type of hash code works poorly with character strings, for example, because two different string objects in memory might actually be equal, in which case we would like them to have the same hash code. Indeed, the Java String class overrides the hashCode method of the Object class to be something more appropriate for character strings. Likewise, if we intend to use certain objects as keys in a map, then we should override the built-in hashCode() method for these objects, replacing it with a mapping that assigns well-spread, consistent integers to these types of objects.

Let us consider, then, several common data types and some example methods for assigning hash codes to objects of these types.

Casting to an Integer

To begin, we note that, for any data type X that is represented using at most as many bits as our integer hash codes, we can simply take as a hash code for X an integer interpretation of its bits. Thus, for Java base types **byte**, **short**, **int**, and **char**, we can achieve a good hash code simply by casting this type to **int**. Likewise, for a variable x of base type **float**, we can convert x to an integer using a call to Float.floatToIntBits(x), and then use this integer as x's hash code.

Summing Components

For base types, such as **long** and **double**, whose bit representation is double that of a hash code, the above scheme is not immediately applicable. Still, one possible hash code, and indeed one that is used by many Java implementations, is to simply cast a (long) integer representation of the type down to an integer the size of a hash code. This hash code, of course, ignores half of the information present in the original value, and if many of the keys in our map only differ in these bits, then they will collide using this simple hash code. An alternative hash code, then, which takes all the original bits into consideration, is to sum an integer representation of the high-order bits with an integer representation of the low-order bits. Such a hash code can be written in Java as follows:

```
static int hashCode(long i) {return (int)((i >> 32) + (int) i);}
```

Indeed, the approach of summing components can be extended to any object x whose binary representation can be viewed as a k-tuple $(x_0, x_1, \ldots, x_{k-1})$ of integers, for we can then form a hash code for x as $\sum_{i=0}^{k-1} x_i$. For example, given any floating-point number, we can sum its mantissa and exponent as long integers, and then apply a hash code for long integers to the result.

Polynomial Hash Codes

The summation hash code, described above, is not a good choice for character strings or other variable-length objects that can be viewed as tuples of the form $(x_0, x_1, \ldots, x_{k-1})$, where the order of the x_i's is significant. For example, consider a hash code for a character string s that sums the ASCII (or Unicode) values of the characters in s. This hash code unfortunately produces lots of unwanted collisions for common groups of strings. In particular, `"temp01"` and `"temp10"` collide using this function, as do `"stop"`, `"tops"`, `"pots"`, and `"spot"`. A better hash code should somehow take into consideration the positions of the x_i's. An alternative hash code, which does exactly this, is to choose a nonzero constant, $a \neq 1$, and use as a hash code the value

$$x_0 a^{k-1} + x_1 a^{k-2} + \cdots + x_{k-2} a + x_{k-1}.$$

Mathematically speaking, this is simply a polynomial in a that takes the components $(x_0, x_1, \ldots, x_{k-1})$ of an object x as its coefficients. This hash code is therefore called a ***polynomial hash code***. By Horner's rule (see Exercise C-3.7), this polynomial can be written as

$$x_{k-1} + a(x_{k-2} + a(x_{k-3} + \cdots + a(x_2 + a(x_1 + ax_0)) \cdots)).$$

Intuitively, a polynomial hash code uses multiplication by the constant a as a way of "making room" for each component in a tuple of values while also preserving a characterization of the previous components. Of course, on a typical computer, evaluating a polynomial will be done using the finite bit representation for a hash code; hence, the value will periodically overflow the bits used for an integer. Since we are more interested in a good spread of the object x with respect to other keys, we simply ignore such overflows. Still, we should be mindful that such overflows are occurring and choose the constant a so that it has some nonzero, low-order bits, which will serve to preserve some of the information content even as we are in an overflow situation.

We have done some experimental studies that suggest that 33, 37, 39, and 41 are particularly good choices for a when working with character strings that are English words. In fact, in a list of over 50,000 English words formed as the union of the word lists provided in two variants of Unix, we found that taking a to be 33, 37, 39, or 41 produced less than 7 collisions in each case! It should come as no surprise, then, to learn that many Java implementations choose the polynomial hash function, using one of these constants for a, as a default hash code for strings. For the sake of speed, however, some Java implementations only apply the polynomial hash function to a fraction of the characters in long strings.

Cyclic Shift Hash Codes

A variant of the polynomial hash code replaces multiplication by a with a cyclic shift of a partial sum by a certain number of bits. Such a function, applied to character strings in Java could, for example, look like the following:

```java
static int hashCode(String s) {
  int h=0;
  for (int i=0; i<s.length(); i++) {
    h = (h << 5) | (h >>> 27);  // 5-bit cyclic shift of the running sum
    h += (int) s.charAt(i);   // add in next character
  }
  return h;
}
```

As with the traditional polynomial hash code, using the cyclic-shift hash code requires some fine-tuning. In this case, we must wisely choose the amount to shift by for each new character. We show in Table 8.2 the results of some experiments run on a list of just over 25,000 English words, which compare the number of collisions for various shift amounts. These and our previous experiments show that if we choose our constant a or our shift value wisely, then either the polynomial hash code or its cyclic-shift variant are suitable for any object that can be written as a tuple $(x_0, x_1, \ldots, x_{k-1})$, where the order in tuples matters.

Shift	Collisions	
	Total	**Max**
0	23739	86
1	10517	21
2	2254	6
3	448	3
4	89	2
5	4	2
6	6	2
7	14	2
8	105	2
9	18	2
10	277	3
11	453	4
12	43	2
13	13	2
14	135	3
15	1082	6
16	8760	9

Table 8.2: Comparison of collision behavior for the cyclic shift variant of the polynomial hash code as applied to a list of just over 25,000 English words. The "Total" column records the total number of collisions and the "Max" column records the maximum number of collisions for any one hash code. Note that with a cyclic shift of 0, this hash code reverts to the one that simply sums all the characters.

8.2.4 Compression Functions

The hash code for a key k will typically not be suitable for immediate use with a bucket array, because the range of possible hash codes for our keys will typically exceed the range of legal indices of our bucket array A. That is, incorrectly using a hash code as an index into our bucket array may result in an array out-of-bounds exception being thrown, either because the index is negative or it exceeds the capacity of A. Thus, once we have determined an integer hash code for a key object k, there is still the issue of mapping that integer into the range $[0, N-1]$. This mapping is the second action that a hash function performs, and a good compression function is one that minimizes the possible number of collisions in a given set of hash codes.

The Division Method

One simple *compression function* is the *division method*, which maps an integer i to

$$|i| \bmod N,$$

where N, the size of the bucket array, is a fixed positive integer. Additionally, if we take N to be a prime number, then this compression function helps "spread out" the distribution of hashed values. Indeed, if N is not prime, then there is a higher likelihood that patterns in the distribution of hash codes will be repeated in the distribution of hash values, thereby causing collisions. For example, if we insert keys with hash codes $\{200, 205, 210, 215, 220, \ldots, 600\}$ into a bucket array of size 100, then each hash code will collide with three others. But if we use a bucket array of size 101, then there will be no collisions. If a hash function is chosen well, it should ensure that the probability of two different keys getting hashed to the same bucket is $1/N$. Choosing N to be a prime number is not always enough, however, for if there is a repeated pattern of hash codes of the form $pN + q$ for several different p's, then there will still be collisions.

The MAD Method

A more sophisticated compression function, which helps eliminate repeated patterns in a set of integer keys is the *multiply add and divide* (or "MAD") method. This method maps an integer i to

$$|ai + b| \bmod N,$$

where N is a prime number, and $a > 0$ and $b \geq 0$ are integer constants randomly chosen at the time the compression function is determined so that $a \bmod N \neq 0$. This compression function is chosen in order to eliminate repeated patterns in the set of hash codes and get us closer to having a "good" hash function, that is, one such that the probability any two different keys collide is $1/N$. This good behavior would be the same as we would have if these keys were "thrown" into A uniformly at random.

With a compression function such as this, which spreads integers fairly evenly in the range $[0, N-1]$, and a hash code that transforms the keys in our map into integers, we have an effective hash function. Together, such a hash function and a bucket array define the main ingredients of the hash table implementation of the map ADT.

But before we can give the details of how to perform such operations as put, get, and remove, we must first resolve the issue of how we will be handling collisions.

8.2.5   Collision-Handling Schemes

The main idea of a hash table is to take a bucket array, A, and a hash function, h, and use them to implement a map by storing each entry (k,v) in the "bucket" $A[h(k)]$. This simple idea is challenged, however, when we have two distinct keys, k_1 and k_2, such that $h(k_1) = h(k_2)$. The existence of such **collisions** prevents us from simply inserting a new entry (k,v) directly in the bucket $A[h(k)]$. They also complicate our procedure for performing the $get(k)$, $put(k,v)$, and $remove(k)$ operations.

Separate Chaining

A simple and efficient way for dealing with collisions is to have each bucket $A[i]$ store a small map, M_i, implemented using a list, as described in Section 8.1.2, holding entries (k,v) such that $h(k) = i$. That is, each separate M_i chains together the entries that hash to index i in a linked list. This **collision resolution** rule is known as **separate chaining**. Assuming that we initialize each bucket $A[i]$ to be an empty list-based map, we can easily use the separate chaining rule to perform the fundamental map operations, as shown in Code Fragment 8.2.

Algorithm $get(k)$:

> *Output:* The value associated with the key k in the map, or **null** if there is no entry with key equal to k in the map

> **return** $A[h(k)].get(k)$ {delegate the get to the list-based map at $A[h(k)]$}

Algorithm $put(k,v)$:

> *Output:* If there is an existing entry in our map with key equal to k, then we return its value (replacing it with v); otherwise, we return **null**

> $t \leftarrow A[h(k)].put(k,v)$ {delegate the put to the list-based map at $A[h(k)]$}
> **if** $t = $ **null then** {k is a new key}
> > $n \leftarrow n + 1$

> **return** t

Algorithm $remove(k)$:

> *Output:* The (removed) value associated with key k in the map, or **null** if there is no entry with key equal to k in the map

> $t \leftarrow A[h(k)].remove(k)$ {delegate the remove to the list-based map at $A[h(k)]$}
> **if** $t \neq $ **null then** {k was found}
> > $n \leftarrow n - 1$

> **return** t

Code Fragment 8.2: The fundamental methods of the map ADT, implemented with a hash table that uses separate chaining to resolve collisions among its n entries.

For each fundamental map operation, involving a key k, the separate-chaining approach delegates the handling of this operation to the miniature list-based map stored at $A[h(k)]$. So, put(k,v) will scan this list looking for an entry with key equal to k; if it finds one, it replaces its value with v, otherwise, it puts (k,v) at the end of this list. Likewise, a get(k) will search through this list until it reaches the end or finds an entry with key equal to k. And a remove(k) will perform a similar search but additionally remove an entry after it is found. We can "get away" with this simple list-based approach, because the spreading properties of the hash function help keep each bucket's list small. Indeed, a good hash function will try to minimize collisions as much as possible, which will imply that most of our buckets are either empty or store just a single entry. This observation allows us to make a slight change to our implementation so that, if a bucket $A[i]$ is empty, it stores **null**, and if $A[i]$ stores just a single entry (k,v), we can simply have $A[i]$ point directly to the entry (k,v) rather than to a list-based map holding only the one entry. We leave the details of this final space optimization to an exercise (C-8.5). In Figure 8.4, we give an illustration of a hash table with separate chaining.

Assuming we use a good hash function to index the n entries of our map in a bucket array of capacity N, we expect each bucket to be of size n/N. This value, called the ***load factor*** of the hash table (and denoted with λ), should be bounded by a small constant, preferably below 1. For, given a good hash function, the expected running time of operations get, put, and remove in a map implemented with a hash table that uses this function is $O(\lceil n/N \rceil)$. Thus, we can implement these operations to run in $O(1)$ expected time, provided n is $O(N)$.

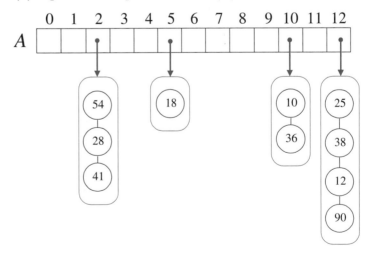

Figure 8.4: A hash table of size 13, storing 10 entries with integer keys, with collisions resolved by separate chaining. The compression function is $h(k) = k \bmod 13$. For simplicity, we do not show the values associated with the keys.

Open Addressing

The separate chaining rule has many nice properties, such as allowing for simple implementations of map operations, but it nevertheless has one slight disadvantage: it requires the use of an auxiliary data structure—a list—to hold entries with colliding keys. We can handle collisions in other ways besides using the separate chaining rule, however. In particular, if space is at a premium (for example, if we are writing a program for a small handheld device), then we can use the alternative approach of always storing each entry directly in a bucket, at most one entry per bucket. This approach saves space because no auxiliary structures are employed, but it requires a bit more complexity to deal with collisions. There are several variants of this approach, collectively referred to as *open addressing* schemes, which we discuss next. Open addressing requires that the load factor be always at most 1 and that entries be stored directly in the cells of the bucket array itself.

Linear Probing

A simple open addressing method for collision handling is *linear probing*. In this method, if we try to insert an entry (k, v) into a bucket $A[i]$ that is already occupied, where $i = h(k)$, then we try next at $A[(i + 1) \bmod N]$. If $A[(i + 1) \bmod N]$ is also occupied, then we try $A[(i + 2) \bmod N]$, and so on, until we find an empty bucket that can accept the new entry. Once this bucket is located, we simply insert the entry there. Of course, this collision resolution strategy requires that we change the implementation of the get(k, v) operation. In particular, to perform such a search, followed by either a replacement or insertion, we must examine consecutive buckets, starting from $A[h(k)]$, until we either find an entry with key equal to k or we find an empty bucket. (See Figure 8.5.) The name "linear probing" comes from the fact that accessing a cell of the bucket array can be viewed as a "probe".

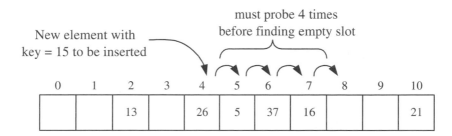

Figure 8.5: Insertion into a hash table with integer keys using linear probing. The hash function is $h(k) = k \bmod 11$. Values associated with keys are not shown.

To implement remove(k), we might, at first, think we need to do a consider-able amount of shifting of entries to make it look as though the entry with key k was never inserted, which would be very complicated. A typical way to get around this difficulty is to replace a deleted entry with a special "available" marker object. With this special marker possibly occupying buckets in our hash table, we modify our search algorithm for remove(k) or get(k) so that the search for a key k will skip over cells containing the available marker and continue probing until reaching the desired entry or an empty bucket (or returning back to where we started from). Additionally, our algorithm for put(k,v) should remember an available cell encountered during the search for k, since this is a valid place to put a new entry (k,v). Thus, linear probing saves space, but it complicates removals.

Even with the use of the available marker object, linear probing suffers from an additional disadvantage. It tends to cluster the entries of the map into contiguous runs, which may even overlap (particularly if more than half of the cells in the hash table are occupied). Such contiguous runs of occupied hash cells causes searches to slow down considerably.

Quadratic Probing

Another open addressing strategy, known as *quadratic probing*, involves iteratively trying the buckets $A[(i + f(j)) \bmod N]$, for $j = 0, 1, 2, \ldots$, where $f(j) = j^2$, until finding an empty bucket. As with linear probing, the quadratic probing strategy complicates the removal operation, but it does avoid the kinds of clustering patterns that occur with linear probing. Nevertheless, it creates its own kind of clustering, called *secondary clustering*, where the set of filled array cells "bounces" around the array in a fixed pattern. If N is not chosen as a prime, then the quadratic probing strategy may not find an empty bucket in A even if one exists. In fact, even if N is prime, this strategy may not find an empty slot, if the bucket array is at least half full; we explore the cause of this type of clustering in an exercise (C-8.8).

Double Hashing

Another open addressing strategy that does not cause clustering of the kind pro-duced by linear probing or the kind produced by quadratic probing is the *double hashing* strategy. In this approach, we choose a secondary hash function, h', and if h maps some key k to a bucket $A[i]$, with $i = h(k)$, that is already occupied, then we iteratively try the buckets $A[(i + f(j)) \bmod N]$ next, for $j = 1, 2, 3, \ldots$, where $f(j) = j \cdot h'(k)$. In this scheme, the secondary hash function is not allowed to eval-uate to zero; a common choice is $h'(k) = q - (k \bmod q)$, for some prime number $q < N$. Also, N should be a prime. Moreover, we should choose a secondary hash function that will attempt to minimize clustering as much as possible.

These ***open addressing*** schemes save some space over the separate chaining method, but they are not necessarily faster. In experimental and theoretical analyses, the chaining method is either competitive or faster than the other methods, depending on the load factor of the bucket array. So, if memory space is not a major issue, the collision-handling method of choice seems to be separate chaining. Still, if memory space is in short supply, then one of these open addressing methods might be worth implementing, provided our probing strategy minimizes the clustering that can occur from open addressing.

8.2.6 A Java Hash Table Implementation

In Code Fragments 8.3–8.5, we show class HashTable, which implements the map ADT using a hash table with linear probing to resolve collisions. These code fragments include the entire implementation of the map ADT, except for the values() method, which we leave as an Exercise (R-8.9).

The main design elements of the Java class HashTable are as follows:

- We maintain in instance variables the size, n, of the map, the bucket array, A, the capacity, N, of A and the ***equality tester***, T.
- A nested class, DefaultEqualityTester, provides a default equality tester based on the built-in equals method of the key class.
- We use method hashValue to compute the hash function of a key by means of the built-in hashCode method and the multiply-add-and-divide (MAD) compression function.
- We define a sentinel, AVAILABLE, as a marker for deactivated entries.
- We provide an optional constructor that allows us to specify the equality tester and the initial capacity of the bucket array.
- If the current bucket array is full and one tries to insert a new entry, we rehash the entire contents into a new array that is twice the size as the old version.
- The following (protected) auxiliary methods are used:
    - checkKey(k), which checks if the key k is valid or not. This method currently just checks that k is not **null**, but a class that extends HashTable can override this method with a more elaborate test.
    - rehash(), which computes a new MAD hash function with random parameters and rehashes the entries into a new array with double capacity.
    - findEntry(k), which looks for an entry with key equal to k, starting at the index $A[h(k)]$ and going through the array in a circular fashion. If the method finds a cell with such an entry, then it returns the index i of this cell. Otherwise, it returns $-i-1$, where i is the index of the last empty or available cell encountered.

```java
/** A hash table with linear probing and the MAD hash function */
public class HashTable implements Map {
  protected static class HashEntry implements Entry {
    Object key, value;
    HashEntry () { /* default constructor */ }
    HashEntry(Object k, Object v) { key = k; value = v; }
    public Object key() { return key; }
    public Object value() { return value; }
    protected Object setValue(Object v) {  // set a new value, returning old
      Object temp = value;
      value = v;
      return temp;  // return old value
    }
  }
  /** Nested class for a default equality tester */
  protected static class DefaultEqualityTester implements EqualityTester {
    DefaultEqualityTester() { /* default constructor */ }
    /** Returns whether the two objects are equal.  */
    public boolean isEqualTo(Object a, Object b) { return a.equals(b); }
  }
  protected static Entry AVAILABLE = new HashEntry(null, null); // empty marker
  protected int n = 0;          // number of entries in the dictionary
  protected int N;              // capacity of the bucket array
  protected Entry[ ] A;         // bucket array
  protected EqualityTester T; // the equality tester
  protected int scale, shift;   // the shift and scaling factors
  /** Creates a hash table with initial capacity 1023. */
  public HashTable() {
    N = 1023; // default capacity
    A = new Entry[N];
    T = new DefaultEqualityTester(); // use the default equality tester
    java.util.Random rand = new java.util.Random();
    scale = rand.nextInt(N-1) + 1;
    shift = rand.nextInt(N);
  }
  /** Creates a hash table with the given capacity and equality tester. */
  public HashTable(int bN, EqualityTester tester) {
    N = bN;
    A = new Entry[N];
    T = tester;
    java.util.Random rand = new java.util.Random();
    scale = rand.nextInt(N-1) + 1;
    shift = rand.nextInt(N);
  }
```

Code Fragment 8.3: Class HashTable implementing the map ADT using a hash table with linear probing. (Continues in Code Fragment 8.4.)

```
/** Determines whether a key is valid. */
protected void checkKey(Object k) {
  if (k == null) throw new InvalidKeyException("Invalid key: null.");
}
/** Hash function applying MAD method to default hash code. */
public int hashValue(Object key) {
  return Math.abs(key.hashCode()*scale + shift) % N;
}
/** Returns the number of entries in the hash table. */
public int size() { return n; }
/** Returns whether or not the table is empty. */
public boolean isEmpty() { return (n == 0); }
/** Helper search method - returns index of found key or -index-1,
 * where index is the index of an empty or available slot. */
protected int findEntry(Object key) throws InvalidKeyException {
  int avail = 0;
  checkKey(key);
  int i = hashValue(key);
  int j = i;
  do {
    if (A[i] == null)   return −i − 1;  // entry is not found
    if (A[i] == AVAILABLE) { // bucket is deactivated
      avail = i;                  // remember that this slot is available
      i = (i + 1) % N;        // keep looking
    }
    else if (T.isEqualTo(key,A[i].key()))  // we have found our entry
      return i;
    else // this slot is occupied–we must keep looking
      i = (i + 1) % N;
  } while (i != j);
  return −avail − 1;  // entry is not found
}
/** Returns the value associated with a key. */
public Object get (Object key) throws InvalidKeyException {
  int i = findEntry(key);  // helper method for finding a key
  if (i < 0) return null;  // there is no value for this key
  return A[i].value();     // return the found value in this case
}
```

Code Fragment 8.4: Class HashTable implementing the map ADT using a hash table with linear probing. (Continues in Code Fragment 8.5.)

```
/** Put a key-value pair in the map, replacing previous one if it exists. */
public Object put (Object key, Object value) throws InvalidKeyException {
  if (n >= N/2) rehash(); // rehash to keep the load factor <= 0.5
  int i = findEntry(key); //find the appropriate spot for this entry
  if (i < 0) {           // this key does not already have a value
    A[−i−1] = new HashEntry(key, value); // convert to the proper index
    n++;
    return null;      // there was no previous value
  }
  else                  // this key has a previous value
    return ((HashEntry) A[i]).setValue(value); // set new value & return old
}
/** Doubles the size of the hash table and rehashes all the entries. */
protected void rehash() {
  N = 2*N;
  Entry[ ] B = A;
  A = new Entry[N]; // allocate a new version of A twice as big as before
  java.util.Random rand = new java.util.Random();
  scale = rand.nextInt(N−1) + 1;    // new hash scaling factor
  shift = rand.nextInt(N);          // new hash shifting factor
  for (int i=0; i<B.length; i++)
    if ((B[i] != null) && (B[i] != AVAILABLE)) { // if we have a valid entry
      int j = findEntry(B[i].key());  // find the appropriate spot
      A[−j−1] = B[i];                 // copy into the new array
    }
}
/** Removes the key-value pair with a specified key. */
public Object remove (Object key) throws InvalidKeyException {
  int i = findEntry(key);      // find this key first
  if (i < 0) return null;      // nothing to remove
  Object toReturn = A[i].value();
  A[i] = AVAILABLE;            // mark this slot as deactivated
  n−−;
  return toReturn;
}
/** Returns an iterator of keys. */
public java.util.Iterator keys() {
  List keys = new NodeList();
  for (int i=0; i<N; i++)
    if ((A[i] != null) && (A[i] != AVAILABLE))
      keys.insertLast(A[i].key());
  return keys.elements();
}
} // ... values() is similar to keys() and is omitted here ...
```

Code Fragment 8.5: Class HashTable implementing the map ADT using a hash table with linear probing. (Continued from Code Fragment 8.4.)

8.2.7 Load Factors and Rehashing

In the hash table schemes described above, we should desire that the load factor, $\lambda = n/N$, be kept below 1. Experiments and average-case analyses suggest that we should maintain $\lambda < 0.5$ for the open addressing schemes and we should maintain $\lambda < 0.9$ for separate chaining. The built-in class java.util.HashMap, which implements the map ADT, uses the threshold 0.75 as a default maximum load factor and rehashes any time the load factor exceeds this (or an optional user-set load factor). The choice of 0.75 is fine for separate chaining (which is the likely implementation in java.util.HashMap), but, as we explore in Exercise C-8.8, some open addressing schemes can start to fail when $\lambda \geq 0.5$. Although the details of the average-case analysis of hashing are beyond the scope of this book, its probabilistic basis is quite intuitive. If our hash function is good, then we expect the entries to be uniformly distributed in the N cells of the bucket array. Thus, to store n entries, the expected number of keys in a bucket would be $\lceil n/N \rceil$, which is $O(1)$ if n is $O(N)$.

With separate chaining, as λ gets very close to 1, the probability of a collision also approaches 1, which adds overhead to our operations, since we must revert to linear-time list-based methods in buckets that have collisions. Of course, in the worst case, a poor hash function could map every entry to the same bucket, which would result in linear-time performance for all map operations, but this is unlikely.

With open addressing, on the other hand, as the load factor λ grows beyond 0.5 and starts approaching 1, clusters of entries in the bucket array start to grow as well. These clusters cause the probing strategies to "bounce around" the bucket array for a considerable amount of time before they can finish.

Thus, keeping the load factor below a certain threshold is vital for open addressing schemes and is also of concern with the separate chaining method. If the load factor of a hash table goes significantly above the specified threshold, then it is common to require that the table be resized (to regain the specified load factor) and all the objects inserted into this new table. When *rehashing* to a new table, it is a good requirement for the new array's size to be at least double the previous size. Once we have allocated this new bucket array, we must define a new hash function to go with it, possibly computing new parameters. We then reinsert every entry from the old array into the new array using this new hash function. In our implementation of a hash table with linear probing given in Code Fragments 8.3–8.5, rehashing is used to keep the load factor less than or equal to 0.5.

Even with periodic rehashing, a hash table is an efficient means of implementing a map. Indeed, if we always double the size of the table with each rehashing operation, then we can amortize the cost of rehashing all the entries in the table against the time used to insert them in the first place. (See Section 5.1.3.) Each rehashing will generally scatter the entries throughout the new bucket array.

8.3   The Dictionary Abstract Data Type

Like a map, a dictionary stores key-value pairs (k, v), which we call *entries*, where k is the key and v is the value. Similarly, a dictionary allows for keys and values to be of any object type. But, whereas a map insists that entries have unique keys, a dictionary allows for multiple entries to have the same key, much like an English dictionary, which allows for multiple definitions for the same word.

We distinguish two types of dictionaries, the ***unordered dictionary*** and the ***ordered dictionary***. In the ordered dictionary, we assume that a total order relation is defined by some comparator for the keys, and we provide additional methods that refer to this ordering (see Section 8.5.2). In an unordered dictionary, however, no order relation is assumed on the keys; hence, only equality testing between keys is used. Likewise, the methods included in the abstract data type of the unordered dictionary form a proper subset of those included in the ordered dictionary ADT.

The Dictionary ADT

As an ADT, an (unordered) ***dictionary*** D supports the following methods:

size(): Return the number of entries in D.
Input: None; *Output:* Integer.

isEmpty(): Test whether D is empty.
Input: None; *Output:* Boolean.

find(k): If D contains an entry with key equal to k, then return such an entry, else return **null**.
Input: Object (key); *Output:* Entry (key-value pair).

findAll(k): Return an iterator of all entries with key equal to k.
Input: Object (key); *Output:* Iterator (of entries).

insert(k, v): Insert an entry with key k and value v into D, returning the entry created.
Input: Objects k (key) and v (value); *Output:* Entry.

remove(e): Remove from D an entry e, returning the removed entry or **null** if e was not in D.
Input: Entry; *Output:* Entry.

entries(): Return the key-value entries stored in D.
Input: None; *Output:* Iterator of entries.

Notice that our dictionary operations make explicit use of entries, which are the key-value pairs stored in the dictionary. We assume each entry comes equipped with key() and value() methods to respectively access its key and value components.

When the method find(k) is unsuccessful (that is, there is no entry with key equal to k), we use the convention of returning a sentinel **null**. We could have also used the alternative convention of returning a special marker object. Another choice, of course, would be to throw an exception when someone requests a key that is not in our dictionary. This would probably not be an appropriate use of an exception, however, since it is normal to ask for something that might not be in our dictionary. Moreover, throwing and catching an exception is typically slower than a test against a sentinel; hence, using a sentinel is more efficient (and, in this case, conceptually more appropriate).

Note that, as we have defined it, a dictionary D can contain different entries with equal keys. In this case, operation find(k) returns an *arbitrary* entry (k,v), whose key is equal to k. We mention in passing that our dictionary ADT should not be confused with the abstract class java.util.Dictionary, which actually corresponds to the map ADT given above and is now considered obsolete. Indeed, as was the case with the priority queue ADT, there is no data structure similar to our dictionary ADT built into Java. Instead, Java provides a map ADT, which requires keys to be unique. Even so, Java includes the entry concept, in the class java.util.Map.Entry, and it allows a user to get an iterator of entries in a java.util.Map, M, by calling M.entrySet().iterator().

Example 8.2: *In the following, we show the effect of a series of operations on an initially empty dictionary storing entries with integer keys and single-character values.*

Operation	*Output*	*Dictionary*
insert$(5,A)$	$(5,A)$	$\{(5,A)\}$
insert$(7,B)$	$(7,B)$	$\{(5,A),(7,B)\}$
insert$(2,C)$	$(2,C)$	$\{(5,A),(7,B),(2,C)\}$
insert$(8,D)$	$(8,D)$	$\{(5,A),(7,B),(2,C),(8,D)\}$
insert$(2,E)$	$(2,E)$	$\{(5,A),(7,B),(2,C),(8,D),(2,E)\}$
find(7)	$(7,B)$	$\{(5,A),(7,B),(2,C),(8,D),(2,E)\}$
find(4)	**null**	$\{(5,A),(7,B),(2,C),(8,D),(2,E)\}$
find(2)	$(2,C)$	$\{(5,A),(7,B),(2,C),(8,D),(2,E)\}$
findAll(2)	$\{(2,C),(2,E)\}$	$\{(5,A),(7,B),(2,C),(8,D),(2,E)\}$
size$()$	5	$\{(5,A),(7,B),(2,C),(8,D),(2,E)\}$
remove$($find$(5))$	$(5,A)$	$\{(7,B),(2,C),(8,D),(2,E)\}$
find(5)	**null**	$\{(7,B),(2,C),(8,D),(2,E)\}$

8.3.1   List-Based Dictionaries and Audit Trails

A simple way of realizing a dictionary uses an unordered list to store the key-value entries. Such an implementation is often called a ***log file*** or ***audit trail***. The primary applications of audit trails are situations where we wish to archive structured data. For example, many financial database systems store a dictionary of all their transactions in this way. Likewise, many operating system programs, such as Web servers and remote login programs, store log files of all requests they process over the Internet (using an array to implement the list).

The typical scenario in such applications is that there are many insertions into the dictionary but few searches. For example, searching such an operating system log file typically occurs only after something goes wrong, such as a system crash. Thus, a list-based dictionary supports simple and fast insertions, possibly at the expense of search time, by storing entries of a dictionary in arbitrary order. (See Figure 8.6.)

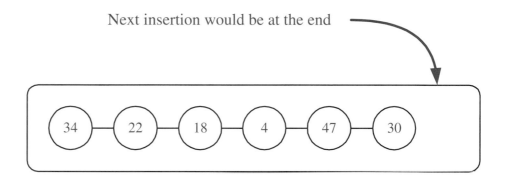

Figure 8.6: Realization of a dictionary D by means of a log file. We show only the keys in this dictionary, so as to highlight its unordered list implementation.

Implementing a Dictionary with an Unordered List

We assume that the list S used for a list-based dictionary is implemented with a doubly linked list (see Section 5.2.4). We give pseudo-code descriptions of the main dictionary methods for a list-based implementation in Code Fragment 8.6. In this simple implementation, we don't assume that an entry stores a reference to its location in S.

Algorithm findAll(k):

    Input: A key k

    Output: An iterator of entries with key equal to k

    Create an initially-empty list L

    $B \leftarrow D$.entries()

    while B.hasNext() **do**

      $e \leftarrow B$.next()

      if e.key() $= k$ **then**

        L.insertLast(e)

    return L.elements()   {the elements in L are the selected entries}

Algorithm insert(k, v):

    Input: A key k and value v

    Output: The entry (k, v) added to D

    Create a new entry $e = (k, v)$

    Call S.insertLast(e)   {S is unordered}

    return e

Algorithm remove(e):

    Input: An entry e

    Output: The removed entry e or **null** if e was not in D

    {We don't assume here that e stores its location in S}

    $B \leftarrow S$.positions()

    while B.hasNext() **do**

      $p \leftarrow B$.next()

      if p.element() $= e$ **then**

        Call S.remove(p)

        return e

    return null   {there is no entry e in D}

Algorithm entries():

    Input: None

    Output: An iterator of the entries in the dictionary D

    return S.elements()   {The elements of S are the entries in D}

Code Fragment 8.6: Some of the main methods for a dictionary D, implemented with an unordered list S. This implementation makes minimal assumptions about entries, and implements insert in $O(1)$ time, findAll in $O(n)$ time, remove in $O(n)$ time, and entries in $O(n)$ time, where n is the number of entries in D.

Analysis of a List-Based Dictionary

The space required for a list-based dictionary with n entries is $O(n)$, since the linked list data structures has memory usage proportional to its size. In addition, with this implementation of the dictionary ADT, we can realize operation insert(k, v) easily and efficiently, just by a single call to the insertLast method on S, which simply adds the new entry to the end of the list. Thus, we achieve $O(1)$ time for the insert(k, v) operation on D.

Unfortunately, this implementation does not allow for an efficient execution of the find method. A find(k) operation requires, in the worst case, scanning through the entire list S, examining each of its n entries. For example, we could use an iterator on the positions in S, stopping as soon as we encounter an entry with key equal to k (or reach the end of the list). The worst case for the running time of this method clearly occurs when the search is unsuccessful, and we reach the end of the list having examined all of its n entries. Thus, the find method runs in $O(n)$ time.

Similarly, time proportional to n is needed in the worst case to perform a remove(e) operation on D, if we assume that entries do not keep track of their positions in S. Thus the running time for performing operation remove(e) is $O(n)$. Alternatively, if we use location-aware entries that store their position in S, then we can perform operation remove(e) in $O(1)$ time. (See Section 8.5.1.)

The operation findAll always requires scanning through the entire list S, and hence its running time is $O(n)$. More precisely, using the big-Theta notation (Section 3.4.1), we say that operation findAll runs in $\Theta(n)$ time since it takes time proportional to n in both the best and worst case.

In conclusion, implementing a dictionary with an unordered list provides for fast insertions, but at the expense of slow searches and removals. Thus, we should only use this implementation where we either expect the dictionary to always be small or we expect the number of insertions to be large relative to the number of searches and removals. Of course, archiving database and operating system transactions are precisely situations such as this.

Nevertheless, there are many other scenarios where the number of insertions in a dictionary will be roughly proportional to the number of searches and removals, and in these cases the list implementation is clearly inappropriate. The unordered dictionary implementation we discuss next can often be used, however, to achieve fast insertions, removals, and searches in many such cases.

8.3.2 Hash Table Dictionary Implementation

We can use a hash table to implement the dictionary ADT, much in the same way as we did for the map ADT. The main difference, of course, is that a dictionary allows for entries with duplicate keys. Assuming that the load factor of our hash table is kept below 1, our hash function spreads entries fairly uniformly, and we use separate chaining to resolve collisions, then we can achieve $O(1)$-time performance for the find, remove, and insert methods and $O(1+m)$-time performance for the findAll method, where m is the number of entries returned.

In addition, we can simplify the algorithms for implementing this dictionary, if we assume we have a list-based dictionary storing the entries at each cell in the bucket array A. Such an assumption would be in keeping with our use of separate chaining, since each cell would be a list. This approach allows us to implement the main dictionary methods as shown in Code Fragment 8.7.

Algorithm insert(k,v):
    Input: A key k and value v
    Output: The entry (k,v) added to D
    if $(n+1)/N > \lambda$ **then**
        Double the size of A and rehash all the existing entries
    $e \leftarrow A[h(k)]$.insert(k,v)
    $n \leftarrow n+1$
    return e

Algorithm findAll(k):
    Input: A key k
    Output: An iterator of entries with key equal to k
    return $A[h(k)]$.findAll(k)

Algorithm remove(e):
    Input: An entry e
    Output: The removed entry e or **null** if e was not in D
    $t \leftarrow A[h(k)]$.remove(e)
    if $t \neq$ **null then**
        $n \leftarrow n-1$
    return t

Code Fragment 8.7: Some of the main methods for a dictionary D, implemented with a hash table that uses a bucket array, A, and an unordered list for each cell in A. We use n to denote the number of entries in D, N to denote the capacity of A, and λ to denote the maximum load factor for the hash table.

8.3.3 Ordered Search Tables and Binary Search

If the keys in a dictionary D come from a total order, we can store D's entries in a vector S by nondecreasing order of the keys. (See Figure 8.7.) We specify that S is a vector, rather than a list, for the ordering of the keys in the vector S allows for faster searching than would be possible had S been, say, implemented with a linked list. Admittedly, a hash table has good expected running time for searching. But its worst-case time for searching is no better than a linked list, and in some applications, such as in real-time processing, we need to guarantee a worst-case searching bound. The fast algorithm for searching in an ordered vector, which we discuss in this subsection, has a good worst-case guarantee on its running time. So it might be preferred over a hash table in certain applications. We refer to this ordered vector implementation of a dictionary D as an ***ordered search table***.

0	1	2	3	4	5	6	7	8	9	10
4	6	9	12	15	16	18	28	34		

Figure 8.7: Realization of a dictionary D by means of an ordered search table. We show only the keys for this dictionary, so as to highlight their ordering.

The space requirement of an ordered search table is $O(n)$, which is similar to the list-based dictionary implementation (Section 8.3.1), assuming we grow and shrink the array supporting the vector S to keep the size of this array proportional to the number of entries in S. Unlike an unordered list, however, performing updates in a search table takes a considerable amount of time. In particular, performing the insert(k, v) operation in a search table requires $O(n)$ time, since we need to shift up all the entries in the vector with key greater than k to make room for the new entry (k, v). Similar observations apply to operations remove(k) and removeAll(k), since it takes $O(n)$ time to shift all the entries in the vector with key greater than k to close the "hole" left by the removed entry (or entries). The search table implementation is therefore inferior to the log file in terms of the worst-case running times of the dictionary update operations. Nevertheless, we can perform the find method much faster in a search table.

Binary Search

A significant advantage of using an ordered array-based vector S to implement a dictionary D with n entries is that accessing an element of S by its ***rank*** takes $O(1)$ time. We recall from Section 5.1 that the rank of an element in a vector is the number of elements preceding it. Thus, the first element in S has rank 0, and the last element has rank $n - 1$.

The elements stored in S are the entries of dictionary D, and since S is ordered, the entry at rank i has a key no smaller than the keys of the entries at ranks $0, \ldots, i - 1$, and no larger than the keys of the entries at ranks $i+1, \ldots, n-1$. This observation allows us to quickly "home in" on a search key k using a variant of the children's game "high-low." We call an entry of D a **candidate** if, at the current stage of the search, we cannot rule out that this entry has key equal to k. The algorithm maintains two parameters, low and high, such that all the candidate entries have rank at least low and at most high in S. Initially, low $= 0$ and high $= n - 1$. We then compare k to the key of the median candidate e, that is, the entry e with rank

$$\text{mid} = \lfloor (\text{low} + \text{high})/2 \rfloor.$$

We consider three cases:

- If $k = e.\text{key}()$, then we have found the entry we were looking for, and the search terminates successfully returning e.
- If $k < e.\text{key}()$, then we recur on the first half of the vector, that is, on the range of ranks from low to mid $- 1$.
- If $k > e.\text{key}()$, we recur on the range of ranks from mid $+ 1$ to high.

This search method is called **binary search**, and is given in pseudo-code in Code Fragment 8.8. Operation find(k) on an n-entry dictionary implemented with an ordered vector S consists of calling BinarySearch$(S, k, 0, n-1)$.

Algorithm BinarySearch$(S, k, \text{low}, \text{high})$:
    Input: An ordered vector S storing n entries and integers low and high
    Output: An entry of S with key equal to k and rank between low and high, if
        such an entry exists, and otherwise **null**

    if low $>$ high **then**
        return null
    else
        mid $\leftarrow \lfloor (\text{low} + \text{high})/2 \rfloor$
        $e \leftarrow S.\text{elemAtRank}(\text{mid})$
        if $k = e.\text{key}()$ **then**
            return e
        else if $k < e.\text{key}()$ **then**
            return BinarySearch$(S, k, \text{low}, \text{mid} - 1)$
        else
            return BinarySearch$(S, k, \text{mid} + 1, \text{high})$

Code Fragment 8.8: Binary search in an ordered vector.

We illustrate the binary search algorithm in Figure 8.8.

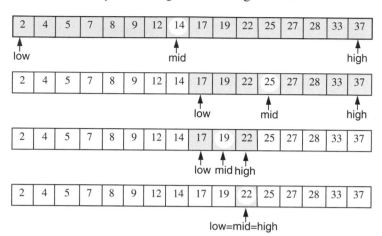

Figure 8.8: Example of a binary search to perform operation find(22), in a dictionary with integer keys, implemented with an array-based ordered vector. For simplicity, we show the keys stored in the dictionary but not the whole entries.

Considering the running time of binary search, we observe that a constant number of primitive operations are executed at each recursive call of method Binary-Search. Hence, the running time is proportional to the number of recursive calls performed. A crucial fact is that with each recursive call the number of candidate entries still to be searched in the vector S is given by the value

$$\text{high} - \text{low} + 1.$$

Moreover, the number of remaining candidates is reduced by at least one half with each recursive call. Specifically, from the definition of mid, the number of remaining candidates is either

$$(\text{mid} - 1) - \text{low} + 1 = \left\lfloor \frac{\text{low} + \text{high}}{2} \right\rfloor - \text{low} \leq \frac{\text{high} - \text{low} + 1}{2}$$

or

$$\text{high} - (\text{mid} + 1) + 1 = \text{high} - \left\lfloor \frac{\text{low} + \text{high}}{2} \right\rfloor \leq \frac{\text{high} - \text{low} + 1}{2}.$$

Initially, the number of candidate entries is n; after the first call to BinarySearch, it is at most $n/2$; after the second call, it is at most $n/4$; and so on. In general, after the ith call to BinarySearch, the number of candidate entries remaining is at most $n/2^i$. In the worst case (unsuccessful search), the recursive calls stop when there are no more candidate entries. Hence, the maximum number of recursive calls performed, is the smallest integer m such that

$$n/2^m < 1.$$

In other words (recalling that we omit a logarithm's base when it is 2), $m > \log n$. Thus, we have

$$m = \lfloor \log n \rfloor + 1,$$

which implies that binary search runs in $O(\log n)$ time.

There is a simple variation of binary search that performs findAll(k) in time $O(\log n + s)$, where s is the number of entries in the iterator returned. The details are left as an exercise (C-8.4).

Thus, we can use an ordered search table to perform fast dictionary searches, but using such a table for lots of dictionary updates would take a considerable amount of time. For this reason, the primary applications for search tables are in situations where we expect few updates to the dictionary but many searches. Such a situation could arise, for example, in an ordered list of English words we use to order entries in an encyclopedia or help file.

Comparing Dictionary Implementations

Table 8.3 compares the running times of the methods of a dictionary realized by either an unordered list, a hash table, or an ordered search table. Note that an unordered list allows for fast insertions but slow searches and removals, whereas a search table allows for fast searches but slow insertions and removals. Incidentally, although we don't explicitly discuss it, we note that a sorted list implemented with a doubly linked list would be slow in performing almost all the dictionary operations. (See Exercise R-8.2.)

Method	List	Hash Table	Search Table
size, isEmpty	$O(1)$	$O(1)$	$O(1)$
entries	$O(n)$	$O(n)$	$O(n)$
find	$O(n)$	$O(1)$ exp., $O(n)$ worst-case	$O(\log n)$
findAll	$O(n)$	$O(1+s)$ exp., $O(n)$ worst-case	$O(\log n + s)$
insert	$O(1)$	$O(1)$	$O(n)$
remove	$O(n)$	$O(1)$ exp., $O(n)$ worst-case	$O(n)$

Table 8.3: Comparison of the running times of the methods of a dictionary realized by means of an unordered list, a hash table, or an ordered search table. We let n denote the number of entries in the dictionary, N denote the capacity of the bucket array in the hash table implementations, and s denote the size of iterator returned by operation findAll. The space requirement of all the implementations is $O(n)$, assuming that the arrays supporting the hash table and search table implementations are maintained such that their capacity is proportional to the number of entries in the dictionary.

8.4   Skip Lists

An interesting data structure for efficiently realizing the dictionary ADT is the *skip list*. This data structure makes random choices in arranging the entries in such a way that search and update times are $O(\log n)$ *on average*, where n is the number of entries in the dictionary. Interestingly, the notion of average time complexity used here does not depend on the probability distribution of the keys in the input. Instead, it depends on the use of a random-number generator in the implementation of the insertions to help decide where to place the new entry. The running time is averaged over all possible outcomes of the random numbers used when inserting entries.

Because they are used extensively in computer games, cryptography, and computer simulations, methods that generate numbers that can be viewed as random numbers are built into most modern computers. Some methods, called *pseudorandom number generators*, generate random-like numbers deterministically, starting with an initial number called a *seed*. Other methods use hardware devices to extract "true" random numbers from nature. In any case, we will assume that our computer has access to numbers that are sufficiently random for our analysis.

The main advantage of using *randomization* in data structure and algorithm design is that the structures and methods that result are usually simple and efficient. We can devise a simple randomized data structure, called the skip list, which has the same logarithmic time bounds for searching as is achieved by the binary searching algorithm. Nevertheless, the bounds are *expected* for the skip list, while they are *worst-case* bounds for binary searching in a look-up table. On the other hand, skip lists are much faster than look-up tables for dictionary updates.

A *skip list* S for dictionary D consists of a series of lists $\{S_0, S_1, \ldots, S_h\}$. Each list S_i stores a subset of the entries of D sorted by a nondecreasing key plus entries with two special keys, denoted $-\infty$ and $+\infty$, where $-\infty$ is smaller than every possible key that can be inserted in D and $+\infty$ is larger than every possible key that can be inserted in D. In addition, the lists in S satisfy the following:

- List S_0 contains every entry of dictionary D (plus the special entries with keys $-\infty$ and $+\infty$).
- For $i = 1, \ldots, h-1$, list S_i contains (in addition to $-\infty$ and $+\infty$) a randomly generated subset of the entries in list S_{i-1}.
- List S_h contains only $-\infty$ and $+\infty$.

An example of a skip list is shown in Figure 8.9. It is customary to visualize a skip list S with list S_0 at the bottom and lists $S_1, \ldots, S_h$ above it. Also, we refer to h as the *height* of skip list S.

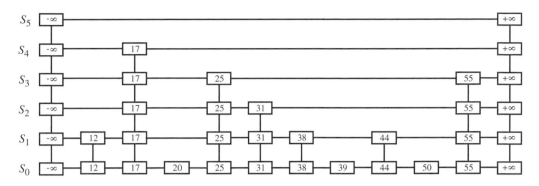

Figure 8.9: Example of a skip list storing 10 entries. For simplicity, we show only the keys of the entries.

Intuitively, the lists are set up so that S_{i+1} contains more or less every other entry in S_i. As we shall see in the details of the insertion method, the entries in S_{i+1} are chosen at random from the entries in S_i by picking each entry from S_i to also be in S_{i+1} with probability $1/2$. That is, in essence, we "flip a coin" for each entry in S_i and place that entry in S_{i+1} if the coin comes up "heads." Thus, we expect S_1 to have about $n/2$ entries, S_2 to have about $n/4$ entries, and, in general, S_i to have about $n/2^i$ entries. In other words, we expect the height h of S to be about $\log n$. The halving of the number of entries from one list to the next is not enforced as an explicit property of skip lists, however. Instead, randomization is used.

Using the position abstraction used for lists and trees, we view a skip list as a two-dimensional collection of positions arranged horizontally into *levels* and vertically into *towers*. Each level is a list S_i and each tower contains positions storing the same entry across consecutive lists. The positions in a skip list can be traversed using the following operations:

next(p): Return the position following p on the same level.

prev(p): Return the position preceding p on the same level.

below(p): Return the position below p in the same tower.

above(p): Return the position above p in the same tower.

We conventionally assume that the above operations return a **null** position if the position requested does not exist. Without going into the details, we note that we can easily implement a skip list by means of a linked structure such that the above traversal methods each take $O(1)$ time, given a skip-list position p. Such a linked structure is essentially a collection of h doubly linked lists aligned at towers, which are also doubly linked lists.

8.4.1   Search and Update Operations in a Skip List

The skip list structure allows for simple dictionary search and update algorithms. In fact, all of the skip list search and update algorithms are based on an elegant SkipSearch method that takes a key k and finds the position p of the entry e in list S_0 such that e has the largest key (which is possibly $-\infty$) less than or equal to k .

Searching in a Skip List

Suppose we are given a search key k. We begin the SkipSearch method by setting a position variable p to the top-most, left position in the skip list S, called the *start position* of S. That is, the start position is the position of S_h storing the special entry with key $-\infty$. We then perform the following steps (see Figure 8.10), where key(p) denotes the key of the entry at position p:

1. If $S.$below(p) is null, then the search terminates—we are *at the bottom* and have located the largest entry in S with key less than or equal to the search key k. Otherwise, we *drop down* to the next lower level in the present tower by setting $p \leftarrow S.$below(p).

2. Starting at position p, we move p forward until it is at the right-most position on the present level such that key$(p) \leq k$. We call this the *scan forward* step. Note that such a position always exists, since each level contains the keys $+\infty$ and $-\infty$. In fact, after we perform the scan forward for this level, p may remain where it started. In any case, we then repeat the previous step.

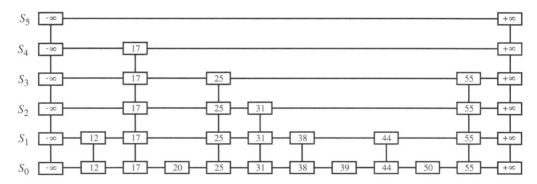

Figure 8.10: Example of a search in a skip list. The positions visited when searching for key 50 are highlighted in blue.

We give a pseudo-code description of the skip-list search algorithm, SkipSearch, in Code Fragment 8.9. Given this method, it is now easy to implement the operation find(k)—we simply perform $p \leftarrow$ SkipSearch(k) and test whether or not key$(p) = k$. If these two keys are equal, we return p; otherwise, we return **null**.

Algorithm SkipSearch(k):

   Input: A search key k

   Output: Position p in the bottom list S_0 such that the entry at p has the largest
     key less than or equal to k

   $p \leftarrow s$
   while below(p) $\neq$ **null do**
     $p \leftarrow$ below(p)   {drop down}
     while $k \geq$ key(next(p)) **do**
       $p \leftarrow$ next(p)   {scan forward}
   return p.

Code Fragment 8.9: Search in a skip list S. Variable s holds the start position of S.

As it turns out, the expected running time of algorithm SkipSearch on a skip
list with n entries is $O(\log n)$. We postpone the justification of this fact, however,
until after we discuss the implementation of the update methods for skip lists.

Insertion in a Skip List

The insertion algorithm for skip lists uses randomization to decide the height of the
tower for the new entry. We begin the insertion of a new entry (k, v) by performing
a SkipSearch(k) operation. This gives us the position p of the bottom-level entry
with the largest key less than or equal to k (note that p may hold the special entry
with key $-\infty$). We then insert (k, v) immediately after position p. After inserting
the new entry at the bottom level, we "flip" a coin. If the flip comes up tails, then
we stop here. Else (the flip comes up heads), we backtrack to the previous (next
higher) level and insert (k, v) in this level at the appropriate position. We again
flip a coin; if it comes up heads, we go to the next higher level and repeat. Thus,
we continue to insert the new entry (k, v) in lists until we finally get a flip that
comes up tails. We link together all the references to the new entry (k, v) created
in this process to create the tower for the new entry. A coin flip can be simulated
with Java's built-in pseudo-random number generator java.util.Random by calling
nextInt(2), which returns 0 of 1, each with probability $1/2$.

We give the insertion algorithm for a skip list S in Code Fragment 8.10 and we
illustrate it in Figure 8.11. The algorithm uses method insertAfterAbove($p, q, (k, v)$)
that inserts a position storing the entry (k, v) after position p (on the same level as
p) and above position q, returning the position r of the new entry (and setting internal references so that next, prev, above, and below methods will work correctly
for p, q, and r). The expected running time of the insertion algorithm on a skip list
with n entries is $O(\log n)$, which we show in Section 8.4.2.

Algorithm SkipInsert(k, v):

    Input: Key k and value v

    Output: Entry inserted in the skip list

    $p \leftarrow$ SkipSearch(k)

    $q \leftarrow$ insertAfterAbove(p, **null**, (k, v))   {we are at the bottom level}

    $e \leftarrow q$.element()

    $i \leftarrow 0$

    while coinFlip() $=$ heads **do**

        $i \leftarrow i + 1$

        if $i \geq h$ **then**

            $h \leftarrow h + 1$ {add a new level to the skip list}

            $t \leftarrow$ next(s)

            $s \leftarrow$ insertAfterAbove(**null**, s, $(-\infty, $**null**$)$)

            insertAfterAbove(s, t, $(+\infty, $**null**$)$)

        while above(p) $=$ **null do**

            $p \leftarrow$ prev(p)   {scan backward}

        $p \leftarrow$ above(p)   {jump up to higher level}

        $q \leftarrow$ insertAfterAbove(p, q, e) {add a position to the tower of the new entry}

    $n \leftarrow n + 1$

    return e

Code Fragment 8.10: Insertion in a skip list. Method coinFlip() returns "heads" or "tails", each with probability $1/2$. Variables n, h and s hold the number of entries, the height and the start node of the skip list.

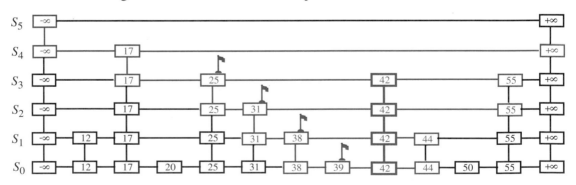

Figure 8.11: Insertion of an entry with key 42 into the skip list of Figure 8.9. We assume that the random "coin flips" for the new entry came up heads three times in a row, followed by tails. The positions visited are highlighted in blue. The positions inserted to hold the new entry are drawn with thick lines, and the positions preceding them are flagged.

Removal in a Skip List

Like the search and insertion algorithms, the removal algorithm for a skip list is quite simple. In fact, it is even easier than the insertion algorithm. That is, to perform a remove(k) operation, we begin by executing method SkipSearch(k). If the position p returned stores an entry with key different from k, we return **null**. Otherwise, we remove p and all the positions above p, which are easily accessed by using above operations to climb up the tower of this entry in S starting at position p. The removal algorithm is illustrated in Figure 8.12 and a detailed description of it is left as an exercise (R-8.15). As we show in the next subsection, operation remove in a skip list with n entries has $O(\log n)$ expected running time.

Before we give this analysis, however, there are some minor improvements to the skip list data structure we would like to discuss. First, we don't actually need to store references to entries at the levels of the skip list above the bottom level, because all that is needed at these levels are references to keys. Second, we don't actually need the above method. In fact, we don't need the prev method either. We can perform entry insertion and removal in strictly a top-down, scan-forward fashion, thus saving space for "up" and "prev" references. We explore the details of this optimization in Exercise C-8.9. Neither of these optimizations improve the asymptotic performance of skip lists by more than a constant factor, but these improvements can, nevertheless, be meaningful in practice. In fact, experimental evidence suggests that optimized skip lists are faster in practice than AVL trees and other balanced search trees, which are discussed in Chapter 9.

The expected running time of the removal algorithm is $O(\log n)$, which we show in Section 8.4.2.

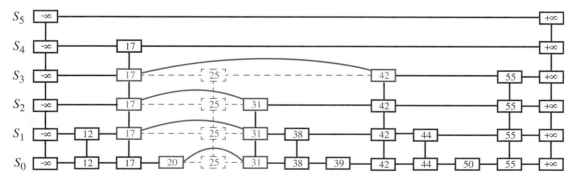

Figure 8.12: Removal of the entry with key 25 from the skip list of Figure 8.11. The positions visited after the search for the position of S_0 holding the entry are highlighted in blue. The positions removed are drawn with dashed lines.

Maintaining the Top-most Level

A skip-list S must maintain a reference to the start position (the top-most, left position in S) as an instance variable, and must have a policy for any insertion that wishes to continue inserting a new entry past the top level of S. There are two possible courses of action we can take, both of which have their merits.

One possibility is to restrict the top level, h, to be kept at some fixed value that is a function of n, the number of entries currently in the dictionary (from the analysis we will see that $h = \max\{10, 2\lceil \log n \rceil\}$ is a reasonable choice, and picking $h = 3\lceil \log n \rceil$ is even safer). Implementing this choice means that we must modify the insertion algorithm to stop inserting a new position once we reach the top-most level (unless $\lceil \log n \rceil < \lceil \log(n+1) \rceil$, in which case we can now go at least one more level, since the bound on the height is increasing).

The other possibility is to let an insertion continue inserting a new position as long it keeps getting heads returned from the random number generator. This is the approach taken in Algorithm SkipInsert of Code Fragment 8.10. As we show in the analysis of skip lists, the probability that an insertion will go to a level that is more than $O(\log n)$ is very low, so this design choice should also work.

Either choice will still result in expected $O(\log n)$ time to perform search, insertion, and removal, however, which we show in the next section.

8.4.2   A Probabilistic Analysis of Skip Lists ⋆

As we have shown above, skip lists provide a simple implementation of an ordered dictionary. In terms of worst-case performance, however, skip lists are not a superior data structure. In fact, if we don't officially prevent an insertion from continuing significantly past the current highest level, then the insertion algorithm can go into what is almost an infinite loop (it is not actually an infinite loop, however, since the probability of having a fair coin repeatedly come up heads forever is 0). Moreover, we cannot infinitely add positions to a list without eventually running out of memory. In any case, if we terminate position insertion at the highest level h, then the ***worst-case*** running time for performing the find, insert, and remove operations in a skip list S with n entries and height h is $O(n+h)$. This worst-case performance occurs when the tower of every entry reaches level $h-1$, where h is the height of S. However, this event has very low probability. Judging from this worst case, we might conclude that the skip list structure is strictly inferior to the other dictionary implementations discussed earlier in this chapter. But this would not be a fair analysis, for this worst-case behavior is a gross overestimate.

⋆We use a star (⋆) to indicate sections containing material more advanced than the material in the rest of the chapter; this material can be considered optional in a first reading.

Bounding the Height of a Skip List

Because the insertion step involves randomization, a more accurate analysis of skip lists involves a bit of probability. At first, this might seem like a major undertaking, for a complete and thorough probabilistic analysis could require deep mathematics (and, indeed, there are several such deep analyses that have appeared in data structures research literature). Fortunately, such an analysis is not necessary to understand the expected asymptotic behavior of skip lists. The informal and intuitive probabilistic analysis we give below uses only basic concepts of probability theory.

Let us begin by determining the expected value of the height h of a skip list S with n entries (assuming that we do not terminate insertions early). The probability that a given entry has a tower of height $i \geq 1$ is equal to the probability of getting i consecutive heads when flipping a coin, that is, this probability is $1/2^i$. Hence, the probability P_i that level i has at least one position is at most

$$P_i \leq \frac{n}{2^i},$$

for the probability that any one of n different events occurs is at most the sum of the probabilities that each occurs.

The probability that the height h of S is larger than i is equal to the probability that level i has at least one position, that is, it is no more than P_i. This means that h is larger than, say, $3 \log n$ with probability at most

$$
\begin{aligned}
P_{3\log n} \quad &\leq \quad \frac{n}{2^{3\log n}} \\
&= \quad \frac{n}{n^3} = \frac{1}{n^2}.
\end{aligned}
$$

For example, if $n = 1000$, this probability is a one-in-a-million long shot. More generally, given a constant $c > 1$, h is larger than $c \log n$ with probability at most $1/n^{c-1}$. That is, the probability that h is smaller than $c \log n$ is at least $1 - 1/n^{c-1}$. Thus, with high probability, the height h of S is $O(\log n)$.

Analyzing Search Time in a Skip List

Next, consider the running time of a search in skip list S, and recall that such a search involves two nested **while** loops. The inner loop performs a scan forward on a level of S as long as the next key is no greater than the search key k, and the outer loop drops down to the next level and repeats the scan forward iteration. Since the height h of S is $O(\log n)$ with high probability, the number of drop-down steps is $O(\log n)$ with high probability.

So we have yet to bound the number of scan-forward steps we make. Let n_i be the number of keys examined while scanning forward at level i. Observe that, after the key at the starting position, each additional key examined in a scan-forward at level i cannot also belong to level $i+1$. If any of these keys were on the previous level, we would have encountered them in the previous scan-forward step. Thus, the probability that any key is counted in n_i is $1/2$. Therefore, the expected value of n_i is exactly equal to the expected number of times we must flip a fair coin before it comes up heads. This expected value is 2. Hence, the expected amount of time spent scanning forward at any level i is $O(1)$. Since S has $O(\log n)$ levels with high probability, a search in S takes expected time $O(\log n)$. By a similar analysis, we can show that the expected running time of an insertion or a removal is $O(\log n)$.

Space Usage in a Skip List

Finally, let us turn to the space requirement of a skip list S with n entries. As we observed above, the expected number of positions at level i is $n/2^i$, which means that the expected total number of positions in S is

$$\sum_{i=0}^{h} \frac{n}{2^i} = n \sum_{i=0}^{h} \frac{1}{2^i}.$$

Using Proposition 3.3 on geometric summations, we have

$$\sum_{i=0}^{h} \frac{1}{2^i} = \frac{\left(\frac{1}{2}\right)^{h+1} - 1}{\frac{1}{2} - 1} = 2 \cdot \left(1 - \frac{1}{2^{h+1}}\right) < 2 \quad \text{for all } h \geq 0.$$

Hence, the expected space requirement of S is $O(n)$.

Table 8.4 summarizes the performance of a dictionary realized by a skip list.

Operation	Time
size, isEmpty	$O(1)$
entries	$O(n)$
find, insert, remove	$O(\log n)$ (expected)
findAll	$O(\log n + s)$ (expected)

Table 8.4: Performance of a dictionary implemented with a skip list. We denote the number of entries in the dictionary at the time the operation is performed with n, and the size of the iterator returned by operation findAll with s. The expected space requirement is $O(n)$.

8.5 Extensions and Applications of Dictionaries

In this section, we explore several extensions and applications of dictionaries.

8.5.1 Supporting Location-Aware Dictionary Entries

As we did for priority queues (Section 7.4.2), we can also use location-aware entries to speed up the running time for some operations in a dictionary. In particular, a location-aware entry can greatly speed up entry removal in a dictionary. For in removing a location-aware entry e, we can simply go directly to the place in our data structure where we are storing e and remove it. We could implement a location-aware entry, for example, by augmenting our entry class with a private location variable and protected methods, location() and setLocation(p), which respectively return and set this variable. We then require that the location variable for an entry e to always refer to e's position or rank in the data structure is implementing our dictionary. We would, of course, have to update this variable any time we moved an entry, so it would probably make the most sense for this entry class to be closely related to the class implementing the dictionary (the location-aware entry class could even be nested inside the dictionary class). Below, we show how to set up location-aware entries for several data structures presented in this chapter.

- *Unordered list*. In an unordered list, L, implementing a dictionary, we can maintain the location variable of each entry e to point to e's position in the underlying linked list for L. This choice allows us to perform remove(e) as L.remove(e.location()), which would run in $O(1)$ time.
- *Hash table with separate chaining*. Consider a hash table, with bucket array A and hash function h, that uses separate chaining for handling collisions. We use the location variable of each entry e to point to e's position in the list L implementing the mini-map $A[h(k)]$. This choice allows us to perform the main work of a remove(e) as L.remove(e.location()), which would run in constant expected time.
- *Ordered search table*. In an ordered search table, T, implementing a dictionary, we should maintain the location variable of each entry e to be e's rank (index) in T. This choice would allow us to perform remove(e) as T.removeAtRank(e.location()). (Recall that location() now returns an integer.) This approach would run fast if entry e was stored near the end of T.
- *Skip list*. In a skip list, S, implementing a dictionary, we should maintain the location variable of each entry e to point to e's position in the bottom level of S. This choice would allow us to skip the search step in our algorithm for performing remove(e) in a skip list.

We summarize the performance of entry removal in a dictionary with location-aware entries in Table 8.5.

List	Hash Table	Search Table	Skip List
$O(1)$	$O(1)$ (expected)	$O(n)$	$O(\log n)$ (expected)

Table 8.5: Performance of the remove method in dictionaries implemented with location-aware entries. We use n to denote the number of entries in the dictionary.

8.5.2 The Ordered Dictionary ADT

In an ordered dictionary, we wish to perform the usual dictionary operations, but also maintain an order relation for the keys in our dictionary. We can use a comparator to provide the order relation among keys, as we did for the ordered search table and skip list dictionary implementations described above. Indeed, all of the dictionary implementations discussed in Chapter 9 use a comparator to store the dictionary in nondecreasing key order.

When the entries of a dictionary are stored in order, we can provide efficient implementations for additional methods in the dictionary ADT. For example, we could consider adding the following methods to the dictionary ADT so as to define the ***ordered dictionary*** ADT.

first(): Return an entry with smallest key.
  Input: None; ***Output:*** Entry.

last(): Return an entry with largest key.
  Input: None; ***Output:*** Entry.

successors(k): Return an iterator of the entries with keys greater than or equal to k, in nondecreasing order.
  Input: Object (key); ***Output:*** Iterator (of entries).

predecessors(k): Return an iterator of the entries with keys less than or equal to k, in nonincreasing order.
  Input: Object (key); ***Output:*** Iterator (of entries).

Implementing an Ordered Dictionary

The ordered nature of the above operations makes the use of an unordered list or a hash table inappropriate for implementing the dictionary, for neither of these data structures maintains any ordering information for the keys in the dictionary. Indeed, hash tables achieve their best search speeds when their keys are distributed almost at random. Thus, we should consider an ordered search table or skip list (or a data structure from Chapter 9) when dealing with ordered dictionaries.

For example, using a skip list to implement an ordered dictionary, we can implement methods first() and last() in $O(1)$ time by accessing the second and second to last positions of the bottom list. Also methods successors(k) and predecessors(k) can be implemented to run in $O(\log n)$ expected time. Moreover, the iterators returned by the successors(k) and predecessors(k) methods could be implemented using a reference to a current position in the bottom level of the skip list. Thus, the hasNext and next methods of these iterators would each run in constant time using this approach.

The java.util.SortedMap Interface

Java provides an ordered version of the java.util.Map interface in its interface called java.util.SortedMap. This interface extends the java.util.Map interface with methods that take order into account. Like the parent interface, a SortedMap does not allow for duplicate keys.

Ignoring the fact that dictionaries allow for multiple entries with the same key, possible correspondences between methods of our ordered dictionary ADT and methods of interface java.util.SortedMap are shown in Table 8.6.

Ordered Dictionary Methods	java.util.SortedMap **Methods**
first().key()	firstKey()
first().value()	get(firstKey())
last().key()	lastKey()
last().value()	get(lastKey())
successors(k)	tailMap(k).entrySet().iterator()
predecessors(k)	headMap(k).entrySet().iterator()

Table 8.6: Loose correspondences between methods of the ordered dictionary ADT and methods of the java.util.SortedMap interface, which supports other methods as well. The java.util.SortedMap expression for predecessors(k) is not an exact correspondence, however, as the iterator returned would be by increasing keys and would not include the entry with key equal to k. There appears to be no efficient way of getting a true correspondence to predecessors(k) using java.util.SortedMap methods.

8.5.3   Flight Databases and Maxima Sets

As we have mentioned in the preceding sections, unordered and ordered dictionaries have many applications.

In this section, we explore some specific applications of ordered dictionaries.

Flight Databases

There are several web sites on the Internet that allow users to perform queries on flight databases to find flights between various cities, typically with the intent to buy a ticket. To make a query, a user specifies origin and destination cities, a departure date, and a departure time. To support such queries, we can model the flight database as a dictionary, where keys are Flight objects that contain fields corresponding to these four parameters. That is, a key is a *tuple*

$$k = (\text{origin}, \text{destination}, \text{date}, \text{time}).$$

Additional information about a flight, such as the flight number, the number of seats still available in first (F) and coach (Y) class, the flight duration, and the fare, can be stored in the value object.

Finding a requested flight is not simply a matter of finding a key in the dictionary matching the requested query, however. The main difficulty is that, although a user typically wants to exactly match the origin and destination cities, as well as the departure date, he or she will probably be content with any departure time that is close to his or her requested departure time. We can handle such a query, of course, by ordering our keys lexicographically. Thus, given a user query key k, we can call successors(k) to return an iteration of all the flights between the desired cities on the desired date, with departure times in strictly increasing order from the requested departure time. A similar use of predecessors(k) would give us flights with times before the requested time. Therefore, an efficient implementation for an ordered dictionary, say, one that uses a skip list, would be a good way to satisfy such queries. For example, calling successors(k) on a query key $k = (\text{ORD, PVD, 05May, 09:30})$, we could get an iterator with the following entries:

```
( (ORD, PVD, 05May, 09:53),   (AA 1840, F5, Y15, 02:05, $251) )
( (ORD, PVD, 05May, 13:29),   (AA 600, F2, Y0, 02:16, $713) )
( (ORD, PVD, 05May, 17:39),   (AA 416, F3, Y9, 02:09, $365) )
( (ORD, PVD, 05May, 19:50),   (AA 1828, F9, Y25, 02:13, $186) )
```

Maxima Sets

Life is full of trade-offs. We often have to trade off a desired performance measure against a corresponding cost. Suppose, for the sake of an example, we are interested in maintaining a database rating automobiles by their maximum speeds and their cost. We would like to allow someone with a certain amount to spend to query our database to find the fastest car they can possibly afford.

We can model such a trade-off problem as this by using a key-value pair to model the two parameters that we are trading off, which in this case would be the pair (cost, speed) for each car. Notice that some cars are strictly better than other cars using this measure. For example, a car with cost-speed pair $(20,000, 100)$ is strictly better than a car with cost-speed pair $(30,000, 90)$. At the same time, there are some cars that are not strictly dominated by another car. For example, a car with cost-speed pair $(20000, 100)$ may be better or worse than a car with cost-speed pair $(30000, 120)$, depending on how much money we have to spend. (See Figure 8.13.)

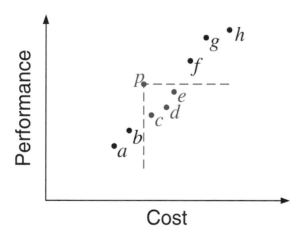

Figure 8.13: Illustrating the cost-performance trade-off with key-value pairs represented by points in the plane. Notice that point p is strictly better than points c, d, and e, but may be better or worse than points a, b, f, g, and h, depending on the price we are willing to pay. Thus, if we were to add p to our set, we could remove the points c, d, and e, but not the others.

Formally, we say a price-performance pair (a, b) **dominates** a pair (c, d) if $a < c$ and $b > d$. A pair (a, b) is called a **maximum** pair if it is not dominated by any other pairs. We are interested in maintaining the set of maxima of a collection C of price-performance pairs. That is, we would like to add new pairs to this collection (for example, when a new car is introduced), and we would like to query this collection for a given dollar amount d to find the fastest car that costs no more than d dollars.

We can store the set of maxima pairs in an ordered dictionary, D, ordered by cost, so that the cost is the key field and performance (speed) is the value field. We can then implement operations add(c,p), which adds a new cost-performance pair (c,p), and best(c), which returns the best pair with cost at most c, as shown in Code Fragment 8.11.

Algorithm best(c):

    Input: A cost c

    Output: The cost-performance pair in D with largest cost less than or equal to
        c or or **null** if there is no such pair

    $B \leftarrow D$.predecessors(c)

    if B.hasNext() **then**

        return B.next()   {the first entry in the predecessors iterator}

    else

        return null

Algorithm add(c,p):

    Input: A cost-performance pair (c,p)

    Output: None

    $B \leftarrow D$.predecessors(c) {iterator of pairs with cost at most c}

    if B.hasNext() **then**

        $e \leftarrow B$.next()   {predecessor of c}

        if e.value() $> p$ **then**

            return   {(c,p) is dominated, so don't insert it in D}

    $C \leftarrow D$.successors(c) {iterator of pairs with cost at least c}

    while C.hasNext() **do**

        $e \leftarrow C$.next()   {successor of c}

        if e.value() $< p$ **then**

            D.remove(e) {this pair is dominated by (c,p)}

        else

            break from this **while** loop   {no more pairs dominated by (c,p)}

    D.insert(c,p) {Add the pair (c,p), which is not dominated}

Code Fragment 8.11: The methods for maintaining a set of maxima, as implemented with an ordered dictionary D.

If we implement D using a skip list, then we can perform best(c) queries in $O(\log n)$ expected time and add(c,p) updates in $O((1+r)\log n)$ expected time, where r is the number of points removed. Thus, we are able to achieve good running times for the methods that maintain our set of maxima.

8.6 Exercises

For source code and help with exercises, please visit **java.datastructures.net**.

Reinforcement

R-8.1 Describe how to use a map to implement the dictionary ADT, assuming that the user does not attempt to insert entries with the same key.

R-8.2 Describe how an ordered list implemented as a doubly linked list could be used to implement the map ADT.

R-8.3 What would be a good hash code for a vehicle identification that is a string of numbers and letters of the form "9X9XX99X9XX999999," where a "9" represents a digit and an "X" represents a letter?

R-8.4 Draw the 11-entry hash table that results from using the hash function, $h(i) = (2i + 5) \bmod 11$, to hash the keys 12, 44, 13, 88, 23, 94, 11, 39, 20, 16, and 5, assuming collisions are handled by chaining.

R-8.5 What is the result of the previous exercise, assuming collisions are handled by linear probing?

R-8.6 Show the result of Exercise R-8.4, assuming collisions are handled by quadratic probing, up to the point where the method fails.

R-8.7 What is the result of Exercise R-8.4 when collisions are handled by double hashing using the secondary hash function $h'(k) = 7 - (k \bmod 7)$?

R-8.8 Give a pseudo-code description of an insertion into a hash table that uses quadratic probing to resolve collisions, assuming we also use the trick of replacing deleted entries with a special "deactivated entry" object.

R-8.9 Give a Java description of the values() method that could be included in the hash table implementation of Code Fragments 8.3–8.5.

R-8.10 Explain how to modify class HashTable given in Code Fragments 8.3–8.5, so that it implements the dictionary ADT instead of the map ADT.

R-8.11 Show the result of rehashing the hash table shown in Figure 8.4 into a table of size 19 using the new hash function $h(k) = 2k \bmod 19$.

R-8.12 Argue why a hash table is not suited to implement an ordered dictionary.

R-8.13 What is the worst-case running time for inserting n entries into an initially empty hash table, where collisions are resolved by chaining? What if each bucket's list is stored in sorted order?

R-8.14 Draw an example skip list that results from performing the following series of operations on the skip list shown in Figure 8.12: remove(38), insert(48,x), insert(24,y), remove(55). Assume the coin flips for the first insertion yield two heads followed by tails, and those for the second insertion yield three heads followed by tails.

R-8.15 Give a pseudo-code description of the remove operation in a skip list.

R-8.16 What is the expected running time of the methods for maintaining a maxima set if we insert n pairs such that each pair has lower cost and performance than one before it? What is contained in the ordered dictionary at the end of this series of operations? What if each pair had a lower cost and higher performance than the one before it?

R-8.17 Argue why location-aware entries are not really needed for a dictionary implemented with a good hash table.

Creativity

C-8.1 Describe how to use a map to implement the dictionary ADT, assuming that the user may attempt to insert entries with the same key.

C-8.2 Suppose we are given two ordered search tables S and T, each with n entries (with S and T being implemented with array-based vectors). Describe an $O(\log^2 n)$-time algorithm for finding the kth smallest key in the union of the keys from S and T (assuming no duplicates).

C-8.3 Give an $O(\log n)$-time solution for the previous problem.

C-8.4 Design a variation of binary search for performing operation findAll(k) in a dictionary implemented with an ordered search table, and show that it runs in time $O(\log n + s)$, where n is the number of elements in the dictionary and s is the size of the iterator returned.

C-8.5 Describe the changes that must be made in the pseudo-code descriptions of the fundamental dictionary methods when we implement a dictionary with a hash table such that collisions are handled via separate chaining, but we add the space optimization that if a bucket stores just a single entry, then we simply have the bucket reference that entry directly.

C-8.6 The hash table dictionary implementation requires that we find a prime number between a number M and a number $2M$. Implement a method for finding such a prime by using the *sieve algorithm*. In this algorithm, we allocate a $2M$ cell Boolean array A, such that cell i is associated with the integer i. We then initialize the array cells to all be "true" and we "mark off" all the cells that are multiples of 2, 3, 5, 7, and so on. This process can stop after it reaches a number larger than $\sqrt{2M}$.   (Hint: Consider a bootstrapping method for finding the primes up to $\sqrt{2M}$.)

C-8.7 Give the pseudo-code description for performing a removal from a hash table that uses linear probing to resolve collisions where we do not use a special marker to represent deleted elements. That is, we must rearrange the contents of the hash table so that it appears that the removed entry was never inserted in the first place.

C-8.8 The quadratic probing strategy has a clustering problem that relates to the way it looks for open slots after a collision. Namely, when a collision occurs at bucket $h(k)$, we check buckets $A[(h(k) + j^2) \bmod N]$, for $j = 1, 2, \ldots, N-1$.

  a. Show that $j^2 \bmod N$ will assume at most $(N+1)/2$ distinct values, for N prime, as j ranges from 1 to $N-1$. As a part of this justification, note that $j^2 \bmod N = (N-j)^2 \bmod N$ for all j.
  b. A better strategy is to choose a prime N such that $N \bmod 4 = 3$ and then to check the buckets $A[(h(k) \pm j^2) \bmod N]$ as j ranges from 1 to $(N-1)/2$, alternating between addition and subtraction. Show that this alternate type of quadratic probing is guaranteed to check every bucket in A.

C-8.9 Show that the methods above(p) and prev(p) are not actually needed to efficiently implement a dictionary using a skip list. That is, we can implement entry insertion and removal in a skip list using a strictly top-down, scan-forward approach, without ever using the above or prev methods. (Hint: In the insertion algorithm, first repeatedly flip the coin to determine the level where you should start inserting the new entry.)

C-8.10 Suppose we are given a collection C of n cost-performance pairs (c, p). Describe an algorithm for finding the maxima pairs of C in $O(n \log n)$ time.

C-8.11 Describe how to implement method successors(k) in an ordered dictionary realized using an ordered search table. What is the running time of this method?

C-8.12 Repeat the previous exercise using a skip list. What is the expected running time in this case?

C-8.13 Suppose that each row of an $n \times n$ array A consists of 1's and 0's such that, in any row of A, all the 1's come before any 0's in that row. Assuming A is already in memory, describe a method running in $O(n \log n)$ time (not $O(n^2)$ time!) for counting the number of 1's in A.

C-8.14 Describe an efficient dictionary structure for storing n entries that have an associated set of $r < n$ keys that come from a total order. That is, the set of keys is smaller than the number of entries. Your structure should perform operation findAll in $O(\log r + s)$ expected time, where s is the number of entries returned, operation entries() in $O(n)$ time, and the remaining operations of the dictionary ADT in $O(\log r)$ expected time.

C-8.15 Describe an efficient dictionary structure for storing n entries whose $r < n$ keys have distinct hash codes. Your structure should perform operation findAll in $O(1 + s)$ expected time, where s is the number of entries returned, operation entries() in $O(n)$ time, and the remaining operations of the dictionary ADT in $O(1)$ expected time.

C-8.16 Describe an efficient data structure for implementing the *bag* ADT, which supports a method add(e), for adding an element e to the bag, and a method remove(), which removes an arbitrary element in the bag. Show that both of these methods can be done in $O(1)$ time.

C-8.17 Describe how to modify the skip list data structure to support the method atRank(i), which returns the position of the element in the "bottom" list S_0 at rank i, for $i \in [0, n-1]$. Show that your implementation of this method runs in $O(\log n)$ expected time.

Projects

P-8.1 Implement a class that implements the dictionary ADT by adapting the java.util.HashMap class.

P-8.2 Implement a class that realizes the Comparator ADT so as to be able to compare objects that are numeric strings (see Section 11.1). In this case, the character strings should be interpreted as numbers in some base, such as base 2 (binary strings) or base 10 (decimal numbers). In addition to the comparator operations, the StringNumberComparator should support a method setBase(b) that takes a positive integer less than or equal to 10 as the base for the numeric strings to be compared.

P-8.3   Implement the map ADT with a hash table with separate chaining collision handling (do not adapt any java.util classes).

P-8.4   Implement the ordered dictionary ADT using an ordered list.

P-8.5   Implement the methods of the ordered dictionary ADT using a skip list.

P-8.6   Extend the previous project by providing a graphical animation of the skip list operations. Visualize how entries move up the skip list during insertions and are linked out of the skip list during removals. Also, in a search operation, visualize the scan-forward and drop-down actions.

P-8.7   Implement a dictionary that supports location-aware entries by means of an ordered list.

P-8.8   Perform a comparative analysis that studies the collision rates for various hash codes for character strings, such as various polynomial hash codes for different values of the parameter a. Use a hash table to determine collisions, but only count collisions where different strings map to the same hash code (not if they map to the same location in this hash table). Test these hash codes on text files found on the Internet.

P-8.9   Perform a comparative analysis as in the previous exercise but for 10-digit telephone numbers instead of character strings.

P-8.10   Design a Java class that implements the skip list data structure. Use this class to create implementations of both the map and dictionary ADTs, including location-aware methods for the dictionary.

Chapter Notes

Hashing is a well-studied technique in data structures, and the reader interested in further study on this topic is encouraged to explore the classic book by Knuth on sorting and searching, now in its second edition [59] (which discusses hashing in more detail and traces the history of hashing back to the 1950's), as well as the book by Vitter and Chen [93].

Interestingly, binary search was first published in 1946, but was not published in a fully correct form until 1962. For further discussions on lessons learned, please see the discussions in Knuth's book [59] and the papers by Bentley [12] and Levisse [63].

Skip lists were introduced by Pugh [80]. Our analysis of skip lists is a simplification of a presentation given in the book by Motwani and Raghavan [76]. For a more in-depth analysis of skip lists, the reader is referred to papers on skip lists that have appeared in the data structures literature [56, 77, 78]. Exercise C-8.8 was contributed by James Lee.

Chapter

9

Search Trees

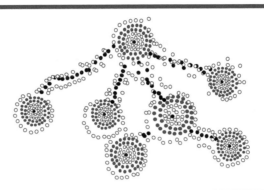

Contents

People like choices. We like to have different ways of solving the same problem, so that we can explore different trade-offs and efficiencies. This chapter is devoted to the exploration of different ways of solving a problem we discussed previously—the implementation of a dictionary (Chapter 8). Namely, we study several alternative data structures based on search trees for realizing the ordered dictionary ADT.

We begin this chapter by discussing binary search trees, in Section 9.1, and how they support a simple tree-based implementation of an ordered dictionary, but do not guarantee efficient worst-case performance. Nevertheless, they form the basis of many tree-based dictionary implementations, and we discuss several in this chapter. One of the classic implementations is the AVL tree, presented in Section 9.2, which is a binary search tree that achieves guaranteed logarithmic-time search and update operations.

In Section 9.3, we present splay trees, which are attractive due to the simplicity of their search and update methods. Splay trees are binary search trees that after each search, insertion, or deletion, move up the accessed node to the root by means of a carefully choreographed series of restructurings. This simple "move-to-the-top" heuristic helps this data structure to *adapt* itself to the kinds of operations being performed. One of the results of this approach is that splay trees guarantee that the amortized running time of each dictionary operation is logarithmic.

Section 9.4 is devoted to the discussion of $(2,4)$ trees, which are also known as 2-4 trees or 2-3-4 trees. These are multi-way search trees, such that all the external nodes have the same depth and each node stores 1, 2, or 3 keys and has 2, 3, or 4 children, respectively. That is, they are a type of multi-way search tree, which is an ordered tree where each internal node can store several entries and have several children. A multi-way search tree is a generalization of a binary search tree, and like the binary search tree, it can be specialized into an efficient data structure for dictionaries by imposing additional constraints. One of the advantages of using these multi-way trees is that they often require fewer internal nodes than binary search trees to store entries. But, just as with binary search trees, multi-way trees require additional methods to make them efficient for all dictionary methods. The advantage of these trees is that they have algorithms for inserting and removing keys that are simple and intuitive. In the case of $(2,4)$ trees, the update operations rearrange a given tree by means of operations that split and merge "nearby" nodes or transfer entries between them. A $(2,4)$ tree storing n entries uses $O(n)$ space and supports searches, insertions, and removals in $O(\log n)$ worst-case time.

We present red-black trees in Section 9.5. These are binary search trees whose nodes are colored "red" and "black" in such a way that the coloring scheme guarantees logarithmic height. There is a simple, yet illuminating, correspondence between red-black and $(2,4)$ trees. In fact, we use this correspondence to motivate and provide intuition for the somewhat more complex algorithms for insertion and removal in red-black trees, which are based on rotations and recolorings. Like an AVL tree, a red-black tree storing n entries uses $O(n)$ space and supports searches, insertions, and removals in $O(\log n)$ worst-case time. The advantage that a red-black tree achieves over an AVL tree is that it can be restructured after an insertion or removal with only $O(1)$ rotations, although at the expense of more complex operations.

Finally, in Section 9.6, we discuss external searching, that is, searching in external memory (which will usually be a disk). We introduce a type of multi-way tree called the B-tree and we show how it can be used to store and search entries so as to minimize the number of input-output (I/O) operations.

There are admittedly quite a few kinds of search trees discussed in this chapter, and we recognize that a reader or instructor with limited time might be interested in studying only selected topics. For this reason, in Figure 9.1, we show the conceptual dependencies between the sections in this chapter. Of the efficient implementations, AVL trees are conceptually the simplest, splay trees are the easiest to implement, (2,4) trees and red-black trees have good worst-case guarantees on update times, and B-trees are the most efficient for large-scale dictionaries.

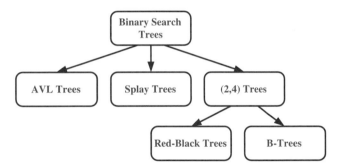

Figure 9.1: Dependencies between the sections in this chapter.

Since all of the data structures discussed in this chapter implement the dictionary ADT, let us briefly review its fundamental methods before we begin:

- find(k): Return an entry with key k, if it exists.
- findAll(k): Return an iterator of all entries with keys equal to k.
- insert(k,x): Insert an entry with key k and value x.
- remove(e): Remove an entry e, and return it.

Method find returns **null** if k is not found. The ordered dictionary ADT includes some additional methods for searching through predecessors and successors of a key or entry, but their performance is similar to that for find. So we will be focusing on find as the primary search operation in this chapter.

9.1 Binary Search Trees

Binary trees are an excellent data structure for storing the entries of a dictionary, assuming we have an order relation defined on the keys. As mentioned previously (Section 6.3.4), a ***binary search tree*** is a binary tree T such that each internal node v of T stores an entry (k,x) such that:

- Keys stored at nodes in the left subtree of v are less than or equal to k.
- Keys stored at nodes in the right subtree of v are greater than or equal to k.

As we show below, the keys stored at the nodes of T provide a way of performing a search by making a comparison at each internal node v, which can stop at v or continue at v's left or right child. Thus, we take the view here that binary search trees are nonempty proper binary trees. That is, we store entries only at the internal nodes of a binary search tree, and the external nodes serve only as "placeholders." This approach simplifies several of our search and update algorithms. Incidentally, we could have allowed for improper binary search trees, which have better space usage, but at the expense of more complicated search and update methods.

Independent of whether we view binary search trees as proper or not, the important property of a binary search tree is the realization of an ordered dictionary (or map). That is, a binary search tree should hierarchically represent an ordering of its keys, using relationships between parent and children. Specifically, an inorder traversal (Section 6.3.4) of the nodes of a binary search tree T should visit the keys in nondecreasing order. (See Figure 9.2a.)

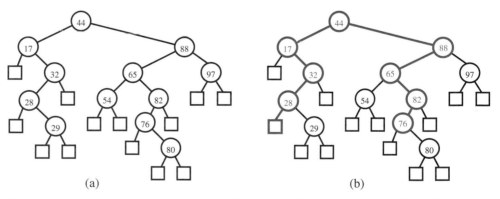

Figure 9.2: (a) A binary search tree T representing a dictionary D with integer keys; (b) nodes of T visited when executing operations find(76) (successful) and find(25) (unsuccessful) on D. For simplicity, we show the keys but not the values of the entries of D.

9.1.1 Searching

To perform operation find(k) in a dictionary D that is represented with a binary search tree T, we view the tree T as a decision tree (recall Figure 6.5). In this case, the question asked at each internal node v of T is whether the search key k is less than, equal to, or greater than the key stored at node v, denoted with key(v). If the answer is "smaller," then the search continues in the left subtree. If the answer is "equal," then the search terminates successfully. If the answer is "greater," then the search continues in the right subtree. Finally, if we reach an external node, then the search terminates unsuccessfully. (See Figure 9.2b.)

In Code Fragment 9.1, we give a recursive method TreeSearch, based on the above strategy for searching in a binary search tree T. Given a search key k and a node v of T, method TreeSearch returns a node (position) w of the subtree $T(v)$ of T rooted at v, such that one of the following two cases occurs:

- w is an internal node and w's entry has key equal to k.
- w is an external node and all the internal nodes of $T(v)$ that precede w in an inorder traversal have keys smaller than k and all the internal nodes of $T(v)$ that follow w in an inorder traversal have keys greater than k.

Thus, method find(k) can be performed on a dictionary D by calling the method TreeSearch(k, T.root()). Let w be the node of T returned by this call. If w is an internal node (hence, is storing an entry (k,x)), then we return w's entry; otherwise, we return **null**.

Algorithm TreeSearch(k, v):

    Input: A search key k, and a node v of a binary search tree T

    Output: A node w of the subtree $T(v)$ of T rooted at v, such that either w's entry has a key equal to k or w is an external node at the place where an entry with key k would belong if it existed

    if T.isExternal(v) **then**

        return v

    if $k < $ key(v) **then**

        return TreeSearch(k, T.left(v))

    else if $k > $ key(v) **then**

        return TreeSearch(k, T.right(v))

    else {we know $k = $ key(v)}

        return v

        Code Fragment 9.1: Recursive search in a binary search tree.

Analysis of Binary Tree Searching

The analysis of the worst-case running time of searching in a binary search tree T is simple. Algorithm TreeSearch is recursive and executes a constant number of primitive operations for each recursive call. Each recursive call of TreeSearch is made on a child of the previous node. That is, TreeSearch is called on the nodes of a path of T that starts at the root and goes down one level at a time. Thus, the number of such nodes is bounded by $h + 1$, where h is the height of T. In other words, since we spend $O(1)$ time per node encountered in the search, method find on dictionary D runs in $O(h)$ time, where h is the height of the binary search tree T used to implement D. (See Figure 9.3.)

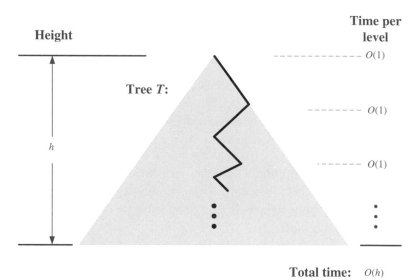

Figure 9.3: Illustrating the running time of searching in a binary search tree. The figure uses standard visualization shortcuts of viewing a binary search tree as a big triangle and a path from the root as a zig-zag line.

We can also show that a variation of the above algorithm performs operation findAll(k) in time $O(h + s)$, where s is the number of entries in the iterator returned. However, this method is slightly more complicated, and the details are left as an exercise (C-9.1).

Admittedly, the height h of T can be as large as n, but we expect that it is usually much smaller. Indeed, we will show how to maintain an upper bound of $O(\log n)$ on the height of a search tree T in Section 9.2. Before we describe such a scheme, however, let us describe implementations for dictionary update methods.

9.1.2 Update Operations

Binary search trees allow implementations of the insert and remove operations using algorithms that are fairly straightforward, but not trivial.

Insertion

Let us assume a proper binary tree T supports the following update operation:

insertAtExternal(v, e): Insert the element e at the external node v, and expand v to be internal, having new (empty) external node children; an error occurs if v is an internal node.

Given this method, we perform insert(k, x) for a dictionary implemented with a binary search tree T by calling TreeInsert$(k, x, T.\text{root}())$, which is given below:

Algorithm TreeInsert(k, x, v):

    Input: A search key k, an associated value, x, and a node v of T
    Output: A new node w in the subtree $T(v)$ that stores the entry (k, x)

    $w \leftarrow$ TreeSearch(k, v)
    if $k = \text{key}(w)$ **then** {the key at w is equal to k, so recurse at a child}
        return TreeInsert$(k, x, T.\text{left}(v))$ {going to the right would be correct too}
    $T.\text{insertAtExternal}(w, (k, x))$ {this is an appropriate place to put (k, x)}
    return w

This algorithm traces a path from T's root to an external node, which is expanded into a new internal node accommodating the new entry. An example of insertion into a binary search tree is shown in Figure 9.4.

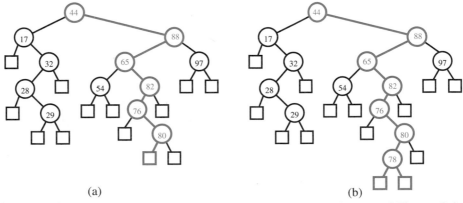

(a)   (b)

Figure 9.4: Insertion of an entry with key 78 into the search tree of Figure 9.2. Finding the position to insert is shown in (a), and the resulting tree is shown in (b).

Removal

The implementation of the remove(k) operation on a dictionary D implemented with a binary search tree T is a bit more complex, since we do not wish to create any "holes" in the tree T. We assume, in this case, that a proper binary tree supports the following additional update operation:

removeExternal(v): Remove an external node v and its parent, replacing v's parent with v's sibling; an error occurs if v is not external.

Given this operation, we begin our implementation of operation remove(k) of the dictionary ADT by calling TreeSearch(k, T.root()) on T to find a node of T storing an entry with key equal to k. If TreeSearch returns an external node, then there is no entry with key k in dictionary D, and we return **null** (and we are done). If TreeSearch returns an internal node w instead, then w stores an entry we wish to remove, and we distinguish two cases (of increasing difficulty):

- If one of the children of node w is an external node, say node z, we simply remove w and z from T by means of operation removeExternal(z) on T. This operation restructures T by replacing w with the sibling of z, removing both w and z from T. (See Figure 9.5.)
- If both children of node w are internal nodes, we cannot simply remove the node w from T, since this would create a "hole" in T. Instead, we proceed as follows (see Figure 9.6):
  - We find the first internal node y that follows w in an inorder traversal of T. Node y is the left-most internal node in the right subtree of w, and is found by going first to the right child of w and then down T from there, following left children. Also, the left child x of y is the external node that immediately follows node w in the inorder traversal of T.
  - We save the entry stored at w in a temporary variable t, and move the entry of y into w. This action has the effect of removing the former entry stored at w.
  - We remove nodes x and y from T by calling removeExternal(x) on T. This action replaces y with x's sibling, and removes both x and y from T.
  - We return the entry previously stored at w, which we had saved in the temporary variable t.

As with searching and insertion, this removal algorithm traverses a path from the root to an external node, possibly moving an entry between two nodes of this path, and then performs a removeExternal operation at that external node.

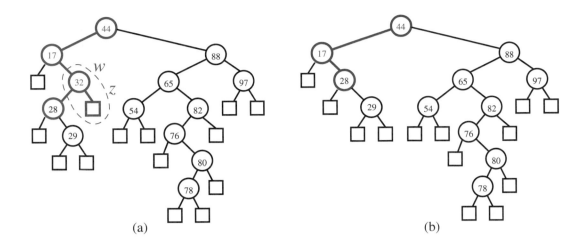

Figure 9.5: Removal from the binary search tree of Figure 9.4b, where the entry to remove (with key 32) is stored at a node (*w*) with an external child: (a) before the removal; (b) after the removal.

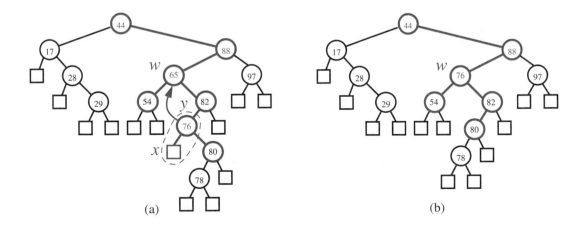

Figure 9.6: Removal from the binary search tree of Figure 9.4b, where the entry to remove (with key 65) is stored at a node (*w*) whose children are both internal: (a) before the removal; (b) after the removal.

Performance of a Binary Search Tree

The analysis of the search, insertion, and removal algorithms are similar. We spend $O(1)$ time at each node visited, and, in the worst case, the number of nodes visited is proportional to the height h of T. Thus, in a dictionary D implemented with a binary search tree T, the find, insert, and remove methods run in $O(h)$ time, where h is the height of T. Thus, a binary search tree T is an efficient implementation of a dictionary with n entries only if the height of T is small. In the best case, T has height $h = \lceil \log(n+1) \rceil$, which yields logarithmic-time performance for all the dictionary operations. In the worst case, however, T has height n, in which case it would look and feel like an ordered list implementation of a dictionary. Such a worst-case configuration arises, for example, if we insert a series of entries with keys in increasing or decreasing order. (See Figure 9.7.)

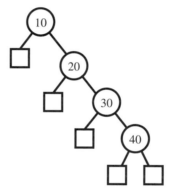

Figure 9.7: Example of a binary search tree with linear height, obtained by inserting entries with keys in increasing order.

The performance of a dictionary implemented with a binary search tree is summarized in Table 9.1.

Method	Time
size, isEmpty	$O(1)$
find, insert, remove	$O(h)$
findAll	$O(h+s)$

Table 9.1: Running times of the main methods of a dictionary realized by a binary search tree. We denote the current height of the tree with h and the size of the iterator returned by findAll with s. The space usage is $O(n)$, where n is the number of entries stored in the dictionary.

Note that the running time of search and update operations in a binary search tree varies dramatically depending on the tree's height. We can nevertheless take comfort that, on average, a binary search tree with n keys generated from a random series of insertions and removals of keys has expected height $O(\log n)$. Such a statement requires careful mathematical language to precisely define what we mean by a random series of insertions and removals, and sophisticated probability theory to prove; hence, its justification is beyond the scope of this book. Nevertheless, keep in mind the poor worst-case performance and take care in using standard binary search trees in applications where updates are not random. There are, after all, applications where it is essential to have a dictionary with fast worst-case search and update times. The data structures presented in the next sections address this need.

9.1.3 Java Implementation

In Code Fragments 9.2 through 9.4, we describe a binary search tree class, BinarySearchTree, which stores objects of class BSTEntry (implementing the Entry interface) at its nodes. Class BinarySearchTree extends class LinkedBinaryTree from Code Fragments 6.26 through 6.28, thus taking advantage of code reuse.

This class makes use of several auxiliary methods to do much of the heavy lifting. The auxiliary method treeSearch, based on the TreeSearch algorithm (Code Fragment 9.1), is invoked by the find, findAll, and insert methods. We use a recursive addAll method as the main engine for the findAll(k) method, in that it performs an inorder traversal of all the entries with keys equal to k (although not using the fast algorithm, since it performs a failed search for every entry it finds). We use two additional update methods, insertAtExternal, which inserts a new entry at an external node, and removeExternal, which removes an external node and its parent.

Class BinarySearchTree uses location-aware entries (see Section 7.4.2). Thus, its update methods inform any moved BSTEntry objects of their new positions. We also use several simple auxiliary methods for accessing and testing data, such as checkKey, which checks if a key is valid (albeit using a fairly simple rule in this case). We also use an instance variable, actionPos, which stores the position where the most recent search, insertion, or removal ended. This instance variable is not necessary to the implementation of a binary search tree, but is useful to classes that will extend BinarySearchTree (see Code Fragments 9.6 and 9.7 and 9.9 and 9.10) to identify the position where the previous search, insertion, or removal has taken place. Position actionPos has the intended meaning provided it is used right after executing the method find, insert, or remove.

```
// Realization of a dictionary by means of a binary search tree
public class BinarySearchTree extends LinkedBinaryTree implements Dictionary {
  // Instance variables:
  protected Comparator C;      // comparator
  protected Position actionPos; // insertion node or parent of removed node
  protected int numEntries = 0; // number of entries
  /** Creates a BinarySearchTree with a default comparator. */
  public BinarySearchTree()  {
    C = new DefaultComparator();
    addRoot(null);
  }
  public BinarySearchTree(Comparator c)  {
    C = c;
    addRoot(null);
  }
  /** Nested class for location-aware binary search tree entries */
  protected static class BSTEntry implements Entry {
    protected Object key;
    protected Object value;
    protected Position pos;
    BSTEntry() { /* default constructor */ }
    BSTEntry(Object k, Object v, Position p) { key = k; value = v; pos = p;}
    public Object key() { return key; }
    public Object value() { return value; }
    public Position position() { return pos; }
  }
  // Auxiliary methods:
  /** Extract the key of the entry at a given node of the tree. */
  protected Object key(Position position)  {
    return ((Entry) position.element()).key();
  }
  /** Extract the value of the entry at a given node of the tree. */
  protected Object value(Position position)  {
    return ((Entry) position.element()).value();
  }
  /** Extract the entry at a given node of the tree. */
  protected Entry entry(Position position)  {
    return (Entry) position.element();
  }
  /** Replace an entry with a new entry (and reset the entry's location) */
  protected void replaceEntry(Position pos, Entry ent) {
    ((BSTEntry) ent).pos = pos;
    replace(pos, ent);
  }
```

Code Fragment 9.2: Class BinarySearchTree. (Continues in Code Fragment 9.3.)

```
/** Check whether a given key is valid. */
protected void checkKey(Object key) throws InvalidKeyException {
  if(key == null)  // just a simple test for now
    throw new InvalidKeyException("null key");
}
/** Check whether a given entry is valid. */
protected void checkEntry(Entry ent) throws InvalidEntryException {
  if(ent == null || !(ent instanceof BSTEntry))
    throw new InvalidEntryException("invalid entry");
}
/** Auxiliary method for inserting an entry at an external node */
protected Entry insertAtExternal(Position v, Entry e) {
  expandExternal(v,null,null);
  replace(v, e);
  numEntries++;
  return e;
}
/** Auxiliary method for removing an external node and its parent */
protected void removeExternal(Position v) {
  removeAboveExternal(v);
  numEntries--;
}
/** Auxiliary method used by find, insert, and remove. */
protected Position treeSearch(Object key, Position pos) {
  if (isExternal(pos)) return pos; // key not found; return external node
  else {
    Object curKey = key(pos);
    int comp = C.compare(key, curKey);
    if (comp < 0)
      return treeSearch(key, left(pos));      // search left subtree
    else if (comp > 0)
      return treeSearch(key, right(pos));     // search right subtree
    return pos;                 // return internal node where key is found
  }
}
// Adds to L all entries in the subtree rooted at v having keys equal to k
protected void addAll(List L, Position v, Object k) {
  if (isExternal(v)) return;
  Position pos = treeSearch(k, v);
  if (!isExternal(pos)) {  // we found an entry with key equal to k
    addAll(L, left(pos), k);
    L.insertLast(pos.element());       // add entries in inorder
    addAll(L, right(pos), k);
  } // this recursive algorithm is simple, but it's not the fastest
}
```

Code Fragment 9.3: Class BinarySearchTree. (Continues in Code Fragment 9.4.)

```java
// methods of the dictionary ADT
public int size() { return numEntries; }
public boolean isEmpty() { return size() == 0; }
public Entry find(Object key) throws InvalidKeyException {
  checkKey(key);                // may throw an InvalidKeyException
  Position curPos = treeSearch(key, root());
  actionPos = curPos;           // node where the search ended
  if (isInternal(curPos)) return entry(curPos);
  return null;
}
public Iterator findAll(Object key) throws InvalidKeyException {
  checkKey(key);                // may throw an InvalidKeyException
  List L = new NodeList();
  addAll(L, root(), key);
  return L.elements();
}
public Entry insert(Object k, Object x) throws InvalidKeyException {
  checkKey(k);            // may throw an InvalidKeyException
  Position insPos = treeSearch(k, root());
  while (!isExternal(insPos))  // iterative search for insertion position
    insPos = treeSearch(k, left(insPos));
  actionPos = insPos; // node where the new entry is being inserted
  return insertAtExternal(insPos, new BSTEntry(k, x, insPos));
}
public Entry remove(Entry ent) throws InvalidEntryException {
  checkEntry(ent);                 // may throw an InvalidEntryException
  Position remPos = ((BSTEntry) ent).position();
  Entry toReturn = entry(remPos);   // entry to be returned
  if (isExternal(left(remPos))) remPos = left(remPos);  // left easy case
  else if (isExternal(right(remPos))) remPos = right(remPos); // right easy case
  else {                      // entry is at a node with internal children
    Position swapPos = remPos;      // find node for moving entry
    remPos = right(swapPos);
    do
      remPos = left(remPos);
    while (isInternal(remPos));
    replaceEntry(swapPos, (Entry) parent(remPos).element());
  }
  actionPos = sibling(remPos);      // sibling of the leaf to be removed
  removeExternal(remPos);
  return toReturn;
}
}      // entries() method is omitted here
```

Code Fragment 9.4: Class BinarySearchTree. (Continued from Code Fragment 9.3.)

9.2 AVL Trees

In the previous section, we discussed what should be an efficient dictionary data structure, but the worst-case performance it achieves for the various operations is linear time, which is no better than the performance of list- and vector-based dictionary implementations (such as unordered lists and search tables discussed in Chapter 8). In this section, we describe a simple way of correcting this problem so as to achieve logarithmic time for all the fundamental dictionary operations.

Definition of an AVL Tree

The simple correction is to add a rule to the binary search tree definition that will maintain a logarithmic height for the tree. The rule we consider in this section is the following *height-balance property*, which characterizes the structure of a binary search tree T in terms of the heights of its internal nodes (recall from Section 6.2.2 that the height of a node v in a tree is the length of a longest path from v to an external node):

Height-Balance Property: For every internal node v of T, the heights of the children of v differ by at most 1.

Any binary search tree T that satisfies the height-balance property is said to be an *AVL tree*, named after the initials of its inventors: Adel'son-Vel'skii and Landis. An example of an AVL tree is shown in Figure 9.8.

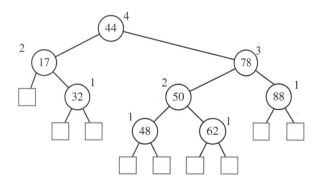

Figure 9.8: An example of an AVL tree. The keys of the entries are shown inside the nodes, and the heights of the nodes are shown next to the nodes.

An immediate consequence of the height-balance property is that a subtree of an AVL tree is itself an AVL tree. The height-balance property has also the important consequence of keeping the height small, as shown in the following proposition.

Proposition 9.1: *The height of an AVL tree storing n entries is $O(\log n)$.*

Justification: Instead of trying to find an upper bound on the height of an AVL tree directly, it turns out to be easier to work on the "inverse problem" of finding a lower bound on the minimum number of internal nodes $n(h)$ of an AVL tree with height h. We will show that $n(h)$ grows at least exponentially. From this, it will be an easy step to derive that the height of an AVL tree storing n entries is $O(\log n)$.

To start with, notice that $n(1) = 1$ and $n(2) = 2$, because an AVL tree of height 1 must have at least one internal node and an AVL tree of height 2 must have at least two internal nodes. Now, for $h \geq 3$, an AVL tree with height h and the minimum number of nodes is such that both its subtrees are AVL trees with the minimum number of nodes: one with height $h-1$ and the other with height $h-2$. Taking the root into account, we obtain the following formula that relates $n(h)$ to $n(h-1)$ and $n(h-2)$, for $h \geq 3$:

$$n(h) = 1 + n(h-1) + n(h-2). \tag{9.1}$$

At this point, the reader familiar with the properties of Fibonacci progressions (Section 2.2.3 and Exercise C-3.10) will already see that $n(h)$ is a function exponential in h. For the rest of the readers, we will proceed with our reasoning.

Formula 9.1 implies that $n(h)$ is a strictly increasing function of h. Thus, we know that $n(h-1) > n(h-2)$. Replacing $n(h-1)$ with $n(h-2)$ in Formula 9.1 and dropping the 1, we get, for $h \geq 3$,

$$n(h) > 2 \cdot n(h-2). \tag{9.2}$$

Formula 9.2 indicates that $n(h)$ at least doubles each time h increases by 2, which intuitively means that $n(h)$ grows exponentially. To show this fact in a formal way, we apply Formula 9.2 repeatedly, yielding the following series of inequalities:

$$
\begin{aligned}
n(h) \;&>\; 2 \cdot n(h-2) \\
&>\; 4 \cdot n(h-4) \\
&>\; 8 \cdot n(h-6) \\
&\;\;\vdots \\
&>\; 2^i \cdot n(h-2i). \tag{9.3}
\end{aligned}
$$

That is, $n(h) > 2^i \cdot n(h-2i)$, for any integer i, such that $h-2i \geq 1$. Since we already know the values of $n(1)$ and $n(2)$, we pick i so that $h-2i$ is equal to either 1 or 2. That is, we pick

$$i = \left\lceil \frac{h}{2} \right\rceil - 1.$$

By substituting the above value of i in formula 9.3, we obtain, for $h \geq 3$,

$$
\begin{aligned}
n(h) \quad &> \quad 2^{\lceil \frac{h}{2} \rceil - 1} \cdot n \left(h - 2 \left\lceil \frac{h}{2} \right\rceil + 2 \right) \\
&\geq \quad 2^{\lceil \frac{h}{2} \rceil - 1} n(1) \\
&\geq \quad 2^{\frac{h}{2} - 1}.
\end{aligned}
\tag{9.4}
$$

By taking logarithms of both sides of formula 9.4, we obtain

$$
\log n(h) \; > \; \frac{h}{2} - 1,
$$

from which we get

$$
h \; < \; 2 \log n(h) + 2,
\tag{9.5}
$$

which implies that an AVL tree storing n entries has height at most $2 \log n + 2$. ∎

By Proposition 9.1 and the analysis of binary search trees given in Section 9.1, the operations find and findAll, in a dictionary implemented with an AVL tree, run in time $O(\log n)$ and $O(\log n + s)$, respectively, where n is the number of entries in the dictionary and s is the size of the iterator returned. Of course, we still have to show how to maintain the height-balance property after an insertion or removal.

9.2.1 Update Operations

The insertion and removal operations for AVL trees are similar to those for binary search trees, but with AVL trees we must perform additional computations.

Insertion

An insertion in an AVL tree T begins as in an insert operation described in Section 9.1.2 for a (simple) binary search tree. Recall that this operation always inserts the new entry at a node w in T that was previously an external node, and it makes w become an internal node with operation insertAtExternal. That is, it adds two external node children to w. This action may violate the height-balance property, however, for some nodes increase their heights by one. In particular, node w, and possibly some of its ancestors, increase their heights by one. Therefore, let us describe how to restructure T to restore its height balance.

Given a binary search tree T, we say that an internal node v of T is **balanced** if the absolute value of the difference between the heights of the children of v is at most 1, and we say that it is **unbalanced** otherwise. Thus, the height-balance property characterizing AVL trees is equivalent to saying that every internal node is balanced.

Suppose that T satisfies the height-balance property, and hence is an AVL tree, prior to our inserting the new entry. As we have mentioned, after performing the operation insertAtExternal on T, the heights of some nodes of T, including w, increase. All such nodes are on the path of T from w to the root of T, and these are the only nodes of T that may have just become unbalanced. (See Figure 9.9a.) Of course, if this happens, then T is no longer an AVL tree; hence, we need a mechanism to fix the "unbalance" that we have just caused.

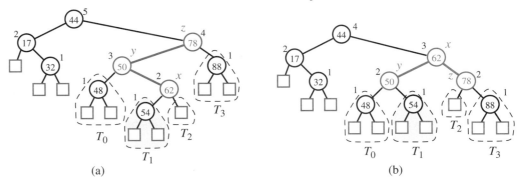

Figure 9.9: An example insertion of an entry with key 54 in the AVL tree of Figure 9.8: (a) after adding a new node for key 54, the nodes storing keys 78 and 44 become unbalanced; (b) a trinode restructuring restores the height-balance property. We show the heights of nodes next to them, and we identify the nodes x, y, and z participating in the trinode restructuring.

We restore the balance of the nodes in the binary search tree T by a simple "search-and-repair" strategy. In particular, let z be the first node we encounter in going up from w toward the root of T such that z is unbalanced. (See Figure 9.9a.) Also, let y denote the child of z with higher height (and note that node y must be an ancestor of w). Finally, let x be the child of y with higher height (there cannot be a tie and node x must be an ancestor of w). We have that node x is a grandchild of z and could be equal to w. Since z became unbalanced because of an insertion in the subtree rooted at its child y, the height of y is 2 greater than its sibling.

We now rebalance the subtree rooted at z by calling the ***trinode restructuring*** method, restructure(x), given in Code Fragment 9.5 and illustrated in Figures 9.9 and 9.10. A trinode restructuring temporarily renames the nodes x, y, and z as a, b, and c, so that a precedes b and b precedes c in an inorder traversal of T. There are four possible ways of mapping x, y, and z to a, b, and c, as shown in Figure 9.10, which are unified into one case by our relabeling. The trinode restructuring then replaces z with the node called b, makes the children of this node be a and c, and makes the children of a and c be the four previous children of x, y, and z (other than x and y) while maintaining the inorder relationships of all the nodes in T.

Algorithm restructure(x):

    Input: A node x of a binary search tree T that has both a parent y and a grand-parent z

    Output: Tree T after a trinode restructuring (which corresponds to a single or double rotation) involving nodes x, y, and z

1: Let (a, b, c) be a left-to-right (inorder) listing of the nodes x, y, and z, and let (T_0, T_1, T_2, T_3) be a left-to-right (inorder) listing of the four subtrees of x, y, and z not rooted at x, y, or z.

2: Replace the subtree rooted at z with a new subtree rooted at b.

3: Let a be the left child of b and let T_0 and T_1 be the left and right subtrees of a, respectively.

4: Let c be the right child of b and let T_2 and T_3 be the left and right subtrees of c, respectively.

Code Fragment 9.5: The trinode restructuring operation in a binary search tree.

The modification of a tree T caused by a trinode restructuring operation is often called a ***rotation***, because of the geometric way we can visualize the way it changes T. If $b = y$, the trinode restructuring method is called a ***single rotation***, for it can be visualized as "rotating" y over z. (See Figure 9.10a and b.) Otherwise, if $b = x$, the trinode restructuring operation is called a ***double rotation***, for it can be visualized as first "rotating" x over y and then over z. (See Figure 9.10c and d, and Figure 9.9.) Some computer researchers treat these two kinds of rotations as separate methods, each with two symmetric types; we have chosen, however, to unify these four types of rotations into a single trinode restructuring operation. No matter how we view it, however, note that the trinode restructuring method modifies parent-child relationships of $O(1)$ nodes in T, while preserving the inorder traversal ordering of all the nodes in T.

In addition to its order-preserving property, a trinode restructuring changes the heights of several nodes in T, so as to restore balance. Recall that we execute the method restructure(x) because z, the grandparent of x, is unbalanced. Moreover, this unbalance is due to one of the children of x now having too large a height relative to the height of z's other child. As a result of a rotation, we move up the "tall" child of x while pushing down the "short" child of z. Thus, after performing restructure(x), all the nodes in the subtree now rooted at the node we called b are balanced. (See Figure 9.10.) Thus, we restore the height-balance property ***locally*** at the nodes x, y, and z. In addition, since after performing the new entry insertion the subtree rooted at b replaces the one formerly rooted at z, which was taller by one unit, all the ancestors of z that were formerly unbalanced become balanced. (See Figure 9.9.) (The justification of this fact is left as Exercise C-9.11.) Therefore, this one restructuring also restores the height-balance property ***globally***.

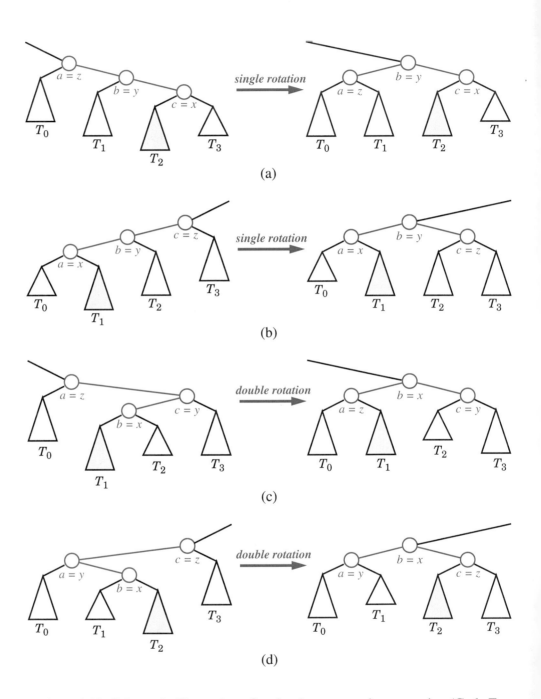

Figure 9.10: Schematic illustration of a trinode restructuring operation (Code Fragment 9.5): (a) and (b) a single rotation; (c) and (d) a double rotation.

Removal

As was the case for the insert dictionary operation, we begin the implementation of the remove dictionary operation on an AVL tree T by using the algorithm for performing this operation on a regular binary search tree. The added difficulty in using this approach with an AVL tree is that it may violate the height-balance property. In particular, after removing an internal node with operation removeExternal and elevating one of its children into its place, there may be an unbalanced node in T on the path from the parent w of the previously removed node to the root of T. (See Figure 9.11a.) In fact, there can be one such unbalanced node at most. (The justification of this fact is left as Exercise C-9.10.)

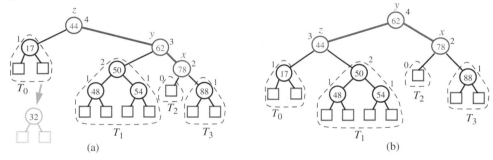

Figure 9.11: Removal of the entry with key 32 from the AVL tree of Figure 9.8: (a) after removing the node storing key 32, the root becomes unbalanced; (b) a (single) rotation restores the height-balance property.

As with insertion, we use trinode restructuring to restore balance in the tree T. In particular, let z be the first unbalanced node encountered going up from w toward the root of T. Also, let y be the child of z with larger height (note that node y is the child of z that is not an ancestor of w), and let x be the child of y defined as follows: if one of the children of y is taller than the other, let x be the taller child of y; else (both children of y have the same height), let x be the child of y on the same side as y (that is, if y is a left child, let x be the left child of y, else let x be the right child of y). In any case, we then perform a restructure(x) operation, which restores the height-balance property **locally**, at the subtree that was formerly rooted at z and is now rooted at the node we temporarily called b. (See Figure 9.11b.)

Unfortunately, this trinode restructuring may reduce the height of the subtree rooted at b by 1, which may cause an ancestor of b to become unbalanced. So, after rebalancing z, we continue walking up T looking for unbalanced nodes. If we find another, we perform a restructure operation to restore its balance, and continue marching up T looking for more, all the way to the root. Still, since the height of T is $O(\log n)$, where n is the number of entries, by Proposition 9.1, $O(\log n)$ trinode restructurings are sufficient to restore the height-balance property.

Performance of AVL Trees

We summarize the analysis of the performance of an AVL tree T as follows. Operations find, insert, and remove visit the nodes along a root-to-leaf path of T, plus, possibly, their siblings, and spend $O(1)$ time per node. Thus, since the height of T is $O(\log n)$ by Proposition 9.1, each of the above operations takes $O(\log n)$ time. We leave the implementation and analysis of an efficient version of the operation findAll as an interesting exercise. In Table 9.2, we summarize the performance of a dictionary implemented with an AVL tree. We illustrate this performance in Figure 9.12.

Operation	Time
size, isEmpty	$O(1)$
find, insert, remove	$O(\log n)$
findAll	$O(\log n + s)$

Table 9.2: Performance of an n-entry dictionary realized by an AVL tree, where s denotes the size of the iterator returned by findAll. The space usage is $O(n)$.

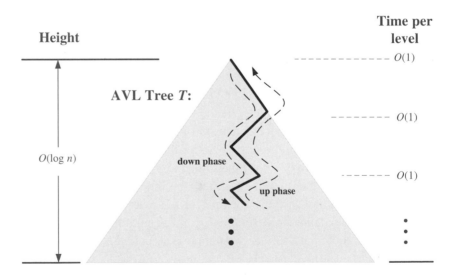

Figure 9.12: Illustrating the running time of searches and updates in an AVL tree. The time performance is $O(1)$ per level, broken into a down phase, which typically involves searching, and an up phase, which typically involves updating height values and performing local trinode restructurings (rotations).

9.2.2 Java Implementation

Let us now turn to the implementation details and analysis of using an AVL tree T with n internal nodes to implement an ordered dictionary of n entries. The insertion and removal algorithms for T require that we are able to perform trinode restructurings and determine the difference between the heights of two sibling nodes. Regarding restructurings, we now need to make sure our underlying implementation of a binary search tree includes the method restructure(x), which performs a tri-node restructuring operation (Code Fragment 9.5). It is easy to see that a restructure operation can be performed in $O(1)$ time if T is implemented with a linked structure (Section 6.4.2). In our case, we assume that the BinarySearchTree class includes this method.

Regarding height information, we can explicitly store the height of each internal node, v, in the node itself. Alternatively, we can store the **balance factor** of v at v, which is defined as the height of the left child of v minus the height of the right child of v. Thus, the balance factor of v is always equal to -1, 0, or 1, except during an insertion or removal, when it may become **temporarily** equal to -2 or $+2$. During the execution of an insertion or removal, the heights and balance factors of $O(\log n)$ nodes are affected and can be maintained in $O(\log n)$ time.

In Code Fragments 9.6 and 9.7, we show a complete Java class, AVLTree, implementing a dictionary using an AVL tree (assuming the parent class includes an implementation of the restructure method). This class extends BinarySearchTree (Code Fragments 9.2–9.4) and includes a nested class, AVLNode, which extends the BTNode class used to represent the nodes of a binary tree. The AVLNode class defines an additional instance variable height, representing the height of the node. We get our binary tree to use this node class instead of the BTNode class simply by overriding the createNode method, which is used exclusively to create new binary tree nodes. Class AVLTree inherits methods size, isEmpty, find, and findAll from its superclass, BinarySearchTree, but overrides methods insert and remove to keep the search tree balanced.

Method insert (Code Fragment 9.7) begins by calling the superclass's insert method, which inserts the new entry and assigns the insertion position (for example, the node storing key 54 in Figure 9.9) to the instance variable actionPos. The auxiliary method rebalance is then used to traverse the path from the insertion position to the root. This traversal updates the heights of all the nodes visited, and performs a trinode restructuring if necessary. Similarly, method remove (Code Fragment 9.7) begins by calling the superclass's remove method, which performs the removal of the entry and assigns the position replacing the deleted one to instance variable actionPos. The auxiliary method rebalance is then used to traverse the path from the removed position to the root, performing any needed restructurings.

```
/** Implementation of an AVL tree. */
public class AVLTree extends BinarySearchTree implements Dictionary {
  public AVLTree(Comparator c)  { super(c); }
  public AVLTree() { super(); }
  /** Nested class for the nodes of an AVL tree. */
  protected static class AVLNode extends BTNode {
    protected int height;  // we add a height field to a BTNode
    AVLNode() {/* default constructor */}
    /** Preferred constructor */
    AVLNode(Object element, BTPosition parent,
            BTPosition left, BTPosition right) {
      super(element, parent, left, right);
      height = 0;
      if (left != null)
        height = Math.max(height, 1 + ((AVLNode) left).getHeight());
      if (right != null)
        height = Math.max(height, 1 + ((AVLNode) right).getHeight());
    } // we assume that the parent will revise its height if needed
    public void setHeight(int h) { height = h; }
    public int getHeight() { return height; }
  }
  /** Creates a new binary search tree node (overrides super's version). */
  protected BTPosition createNode(Object element, BTPosition parent,
            BTPosition left, BTPosition right) {
    return new AVLNode(element,parent,left,right);  // now use AVL nodes
  }
  /** Returns the height of a node (call back to an AVLNode). */
  protected int height(Position p)  {
    return ((AVLNode) p).getHeight();
  }
  /** Sets the height of an internal node (call back to an AVLNode). */
  protected void setHeight(Position p)  { // called only if p is internal
    ((AVLNode) p).setHeight(1+Math.max(height(left(p)), height(right(p))));
  }
  /** Returns whether a node has balance factor between -1 and 1. */
  protected boolean isBalanced(Position p)  {
    int bf = height(left(p)) − height(right(p));
    return ((−1 <= bf) &&  (bf <= 1));
  }
```

Code Fragment 9.6: Constructor and auxiliary methods of class AVLTree.

```
/** Returns a child of p with height no smaller than that of the other child */
protected Position tallerChild(Position p)  {
  if (height(left(p)) > height(right(p))) return left(p);
  else if (height(left(p)) < height(right(p))) return right(p);
  // equal height children - break tie using parent's type
  if (isRoot(p)) return left(p);
  if (p == left(parent(p))) return left(p);
  else return right(p);
}
/**
  * Rebalance method called by insert and remove.  Traverses the path from
  * zPos to the root. For each node encountered, we recompute its height
  * and perform a trinode restructuring if it's unbalanced.
  */
protected void rebalance(Position zPos) {
  if(isInternal(zPos))
     setHeight(zPos);
  while (!isRoot(zPos)) {  // traverse up the tree towards the root
    zPos = parent(zPos);
    setHeight(zPos);
    if (!isBalanced(zPos)) {
      // perform a trinode restructuring at zPos's tallest grandchild
      Position xPos =  tallerChild(tallerChild(zPos));
      zPos = restructure(xPos); // tri-node restructure (from parent class)
      setHeight(left(zPos));  // recompute heights
      setHeight(right(zPos));
      setHeight(zPos);
    }
  }
}
// overridden methods of the dictionary ADT
public Entry insert(Object k, Object v) throws InvalidKeyException  {
  Entry toReturn = super.insert(k, v); // calls our new createNode method
  rebalance(actionPos); // rebalance up from the insertion position
  return toReturn;
}
public Entry remove(Entry ent) throws InvalidEntryException {
  Entry toReturn = super.remove(ent);
  if (toReturn != null)   // we actually removed something
    rebalance(actionPos);  // rebalance up the tree
  return toReturn;
}
} // end of AVLTree class
```

Code Fragment 9.7: Auxiliary methods tallerChild and rebalance and dictionary methods insert and remove of class AVLTree.

9.3   Splay Trees

Another way we can implement the fundamental dictionary operations is to use a balanced search tree data structure known as a *splay tree*. This structure is conceptually quite different from the other balanced search trees we discuss in this chapter, for a splay tree does not use any explicit rules to enforce its balance. Instead, it applies a certain move-to-root operation, called *splaying*, after every access, in order to keep the search tree balanced in an amortized sense. The splaying operation is performed at the bottom-most node x reached during an insertion, deletion, or even a search. The surprising thing about splaying is that it allows us to guarantee an amortized running time, for insertions, deletions, and searches, that is logarithmic. The structure of a *splay tree* is simply a binary search tree T. In fact, there are no additional height, balance, or color labels that we associate with the nodes of this tree.

9.3.1   Splaying

Given an internal node x of a binary search tree T, we **splay** x by moving x to the root of T through a sequence of restructurings. The particular restructurings we perform are important, for it is not sufficient to move x to the root of T by just any sequence of restructurings. The specific operation we perform to move x up depends upon the relative positions of x, its parent y, and (if it exists) x's grandparent z. There are three cases that we consider.

zig-zig: The node x and its parent y are both left children or both right children. (See Figure 9.13.) We replace z by x, making y a child of x and z a child of y, while maintaining the inorder relationships of the nodes in T.

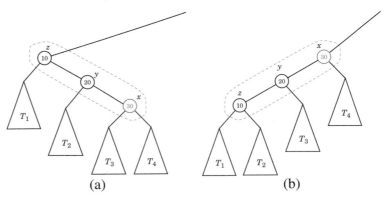

(a)   (b)

Figure 9.13: Zig-zig: (a) before; (b) after. There is another symmetric configuration where x and y are left children.

zig-zag: One of x and y is a left child and the other is a right child. (See Figure 9.14.) In this case, we replace z by x and make x have y and z as its children, while maintaining the inorder relationships of the nodes in T.

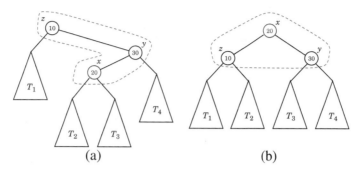

Figure 9.14: Zig-zag: (a) before; (b) after. There is another symmetric configuration where x is a right child and y is a left child.

zig: x does not have a grandparent (or we are not considering x's grandparent for some reason). (See Figure 9.15.) In this case, we rotate x over y, making x's children be the node y and one of x's former children w, so as to maintain the relative inorder relationships of the nodes in T.

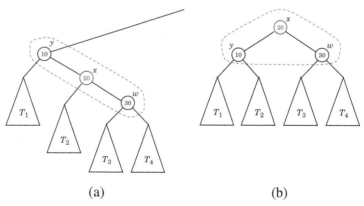

Figure 9.15: Zig: (a) before; (b) after. There is another symmetric configuration where x and w are left children.

We perform a zig-zig or a zig-zag when x has a grandparent, and we perform a zig when x has a parent but not a grandparent. A **splaying** step consists of repeating these restructurings at x until x becomes the root of T. Note that this is not the same as a sequence of simple rotations that brings x to the root. An example of the splaying of a node is shown in Figures 9.16 and 9.17.

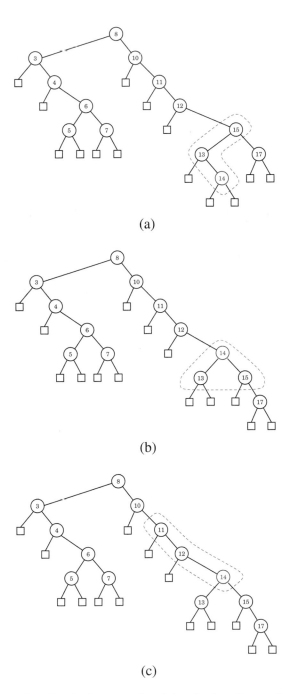

Figure 9.16: Example of splaying a node: (a) splaying the node storing 14 starts with a zig-zag; (b) after the zig-zag; (c) the next step is a zig-zig. (Continues in Figure 9.17

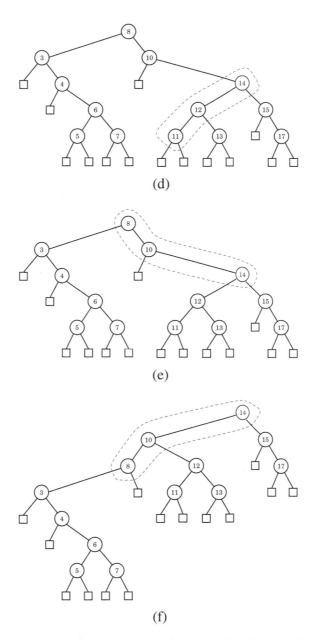

Figure 9.17: Example of splaying a node :(d) after the zig-zig; (e) the next step is again a zig-zig; (f) after the zig-zig(Continued from Figure 9.17.)

9.3.2 When to Splay

The rules that dictate when splaying is performed are as follows:

- When searching for key k, if k is found at a node x, we splay x, else we splay the parent of the external node at which the search terminates unsuccessfully. For example, the splaying in Figures 9.16 and 9.17 would be performed after searching successfully for key 14 or unsuccessfully for key 14.5.
- When inserting key k, we splay the newly created internal node where k gets inserted. For example, the splaying in Figures 9.16 and 9.17 would be performed if 14 were the newly inserted key. We show a sequence of insertions in a splay tree in Figure 9.18.

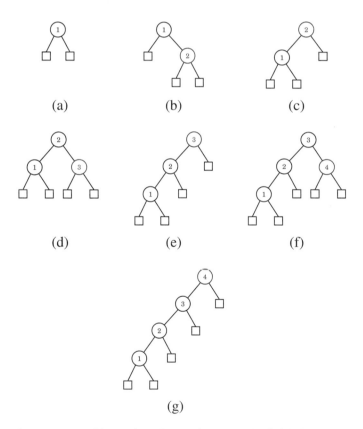

Figure 9.18: A sequence of insertions in a splay tree: (a) initial tree; (b) after inserting 2; (c) after splaying; (d) after inserting 3; (e) after splaying; (f) after inserting 4; (g) after splaying.

- When deleting a key k, we splay the parent of the node w that gets removed, that is, w is either the node storing k or one of its descendents. (Recall the removal algorithm for binary search trees.) An example of splaying following a deletion is shown in Figure 9.19.

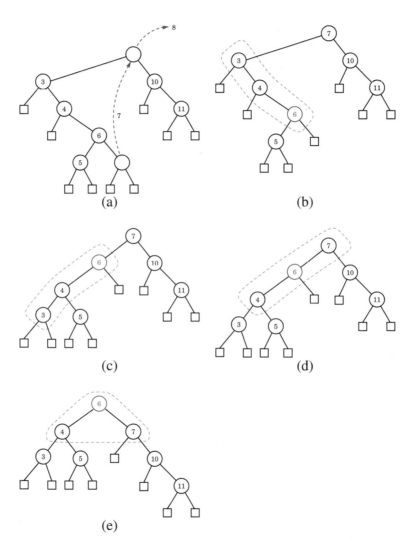

Figure 9.19: Deletion from a splay tree: (a) the deletion of 8 from node r is performed by moving to r the key of the right-most internal node v, in the left subtree of r, deleting v, and splaying the parent u of v; (b) splaying u starts with a zig-zig; (c) after the zig-zig; (d) the next step is a zig; (e) after the zig.

9.3.3   Amortized Analysis of Splaying ★

After a zig-zig or zig-zag, the depth of x decreases by two, and after a zig the depth of x decreases by one. Thus, if x has depth d, splaying x consists of a sequence of $\lfloor d/2 \rfloor$ zig-zigs and/or zig-zags, plus one final zig if d is odd. Since a single zig-zig, zig-zag, or zig affects a constant number of nodes, it can be done in $O(1)$ time. Thus, splaying a node x in a binary search tree T takes time $O(d)$, where d is the depth of x in T. In other words, the time for performing a splaying step for a node x is asymptotically the same as the time needed just to reach that node in a top-down search from the root of T.

Worst Case Time

In the worst case, the overall running time of a search, insertion, or deletion in a splay tree of height h is $O(h)$, since the node we splay might be the deepest node in the tree. Moreover, it is possible for h to be as large as n, as shown in Figure 9.18. Thus, from a worst-case point of view, a splay tree is not an attractive data structure.

In spite of its poor worst-case performance, a splay tree performs well in an amortized sense. That is, in a sequence of intermixed searches, insertions, and deletions, each operation takes on average logarithmic time. We perform the amortized analysis of splay trees using the accounting method.

Amortized Performance of Splay Trees

For our analysis, we note that the time for performing a search, insertion, or deletion is proportional to the time for the associated splaying. So let us consider only splaying time.

Let T be a splay tree with n keys, and let v be a node of T. We define the *size* $n(v)$ of v as the number of nodes in the subtree rooted at v. Note that this definition implies that the size of an internal node is one more than the sum of the sizes of its two children. We define the *rank* $r(v)$ of a node v as the logarithm in base 2 of the size of v, that is, $r(v) = \log(n(v))$. Clearly, the root of T has the maximum size $(2n + 1)$ and the maximum rank, $\log(2n + 1)$, while each external node has size 1 and rank 0.

We use cyber-dollars to pay for the work we perform in splaying a node x in T, and we assume that one cyber-dollar pays for a zig, while two cyber-dollars pay for a zig-zig or a zig-zag. Hence, the cost of splaying a node at depth d is d cyber-dollars. We keep a virtual account storing cyber-dollars at each internal node of T. Note that this account exists only for the purpose of our amortized analysis, and does not need to be included in a data structure implementing the splay tree T.

An Accounting Analysis of Splaying

When we perform a splaying, we pay a certain number of cyber-dollars (the exact value of the payment will be determined at the end of our analysis). We distinguish three cases:

- If the payment is equal to the splaying work, then we use it all to pay for the splaying.
- If the payment is greater than the splaying work, we deposit the excess in the accounts of several nodes.
- If the payment is less than the splaying work, we make withdrawals from the accounts of several nodes to cover the deficiency.

We will show, in the rest of this section, that a payment of $O(\log n)$ cyber-dollars per operation is sufficient to keep the system working, that is, to ensure that each node keeps a nonnegative account balance.

A Cyberdollar Invariant for Splaying

We use a scheme in which transfers are made between the accounts of the nodes to ensure that there will always be enough cyber-dollars to withdraw for paying for splaying work when needed.

In order to use the accounting method to perform our analysis of splaying, we maintain the following invariant:

> *Before and after a splaying, each node v of T has $r(v)$ cyber-dollars in its account.*

Note that the invariant is "financially sound," since it does not require us to make a preliminary deposit to endow a tree with zero keys.

Let $r(T)$ be the sum of the ranks of all the nodes of T. To preserve the invariant after a splaying, we must make a payment equal to the splaying work plus the total change in $r(T)$. We refer to a single zig, zig-zig, or zig-zag operation in a splaying as a splaying *substep*. Also, we denote the rank of a node v of T before and after a splaying substep with $r(v)$ and $r'(v)$, respectively. The following proposition gives an upper bound on the change of $r(T)$ caused by a single splaying substep. We will repeatedly use this lemma in our analysis of a full splaying of a node to the root.

Proposition 9.2: *Let δ be the variation of $r(T)$ caused by a single splaying sub-step (a zig, zig-zig, or zig-zag) for a node x in T. We have the following:*

- *$\delta \leq 3(r'(x) - r(x)) - 2$ if the substep is a zig-zig or zig-zag.*
- *$\delta \leq 3(r'(x) - r(x))$ if the substep is a zig.*

Justification: We use the fact (see Proposition A.1, Appendix A) that, if $a > 0$, $b > 0$, and $c > a + b$,

$$\log a + \log b \leq 2 \log c - 2. \tag{9.6}$$

Let us consider the change in $r(T)$ caused by each type of splaying substep.

zig-zig: (Recall Figure 9.13.) Since the size of each node is one more than the size of its two children, note that only the ranks of x, y, and z change in a zig-zig operation, where y is the parent of x and z is the parent of y. Also, $r'(x) = r(z)$, $r'(y) \leq r'(x)$, and $r(y) \geq r(x)$. Thus

$$
\begin{aligned}
\delta &= r'(x) + r'(y) + r'(z) - r(x) - r(y) - r(z) \\
&\leq r'(y) + r'(z) - r(x) - r(y) \\
&\leq r'(x) + r'(z) - 2r(x). \tag{9.7}
\end{aligned}
$$

Note that $n(x) + n'(z) \leq n'(x)$. Thus, by 9.6, $r(x) + r'(z) \leq 2r'(x) - 2$, that is,

$$r'(z) \leq 2r'(x) - r(x) - 2.$$

This inequality and 9.7 imply

$$
\begin{aligned}
\delta &\leq r'(x) + (2r'(x) - r(x) - 2) - 2r(x) \\
&\leq 3(r'(x) - r(x)) - 2.
\end{aligned}
$$

zig-zag: (Recall Figure 9.14.) Again, by the definition of size and rank, only the ranks of x, y, and z change, where y denotes the parent of x and z denotes the parent of y. Also, $r'(x) = r(z)$ and $r(x) \leq r(y)$. Thus

$$
\begin{aligned}
\delta &= r'(x) + r'(y) + r'(z) - r(x) - r(y) - r(z) \\
&\leq r'(y) + r'(z) - r(x) - r(y) \\
&\leq r'(y) + r'(z) - 2r(x). \tag{9.8}
\end{aligned}
$$

Note that $n'(y) + n'(z) \leq n'(x)$; hence, by 9.6, $r'(y) + r'(z) \leq 2r'(x) - 2$, Thus,

$$
\begin{aligned}
\delta &\leq 2r'(x) - 2 - 2r(x) \\
&\leq 3(r'(x) - r(x)) - 2.
\end{aligned}
$$

zig: (Recall Figure 9.15.) In this case, only the ranks of x and y change, where y denotes the parent of x. Also, $r'(y) \leq r(y)$ and $r'(x) \geq r(x)$. Thus

$$
\begin{aligned}
\delta &= r'(y) + r'(x) - r(y) - r(x) \\
&\leq r'(x) - r(x) \\
&\leq 3(r'(x) - r(x)).
\end{aligned}
$$

■

Proposition 9.3: *Let T be a splay tree with root t, and let Δ be the total variation of $r(T)$ caused by splaying a node x at depth d. We have*

$$\Delta \le 3(r(t) - r(x)) - d + 2.$$

Justification: Splaying node x consists of $p = \lceil d/2 \rceil$ splaying substeps, each of which is a zig-zig or a zig-zag, except possibly the last one, which is a zig if d is odd. Let $r_0(x) = r(x)$ be the initial rank of x, and for $i = 1, \ldots, p$, let $r_i(x)$ be the rank of x after the ith substep and δ_i be the variation of $r(T)$ caused by the ith substep. By Lemma 9.2, the total variation Δ of $r(T)$ caused by splaying node x is

$$
\begin{aligned}
\Delta &= \sum_{i=1}^{p} \delta_i \\
&\le \sum_{i=1}^{p} \left(3(r_i(x) - r_{i-1}(x)) - 2 \right) + 2 \\
&= 3(r_p(x) - r_0(x)) - 2p + 2 \\
&\le 3(r(t) - r(x)) - d + 2. \qquad \blacksquare
\end{aligned}
$$

By Proposition 9.3, if we make a payment of $3(r(t) - r(x)) + 2$ cyber-dollars towards the splaying of node x, we have enough cyber-dollars to maintain the invariant, keeping $r(v)$ cyber-dollars at each node v in T, and pay for the entire splaying work, which costs d dollars. Since the size of the root t is $2n + 1$, its rank $r(t) = \log(2n + 1)$. In addition, we have $r(x) < r(t)$. Thus, the payment to be made for splaying is $O(\log n)$ cyber-dollars. To complete our analysis, we have to compute the cost for maintaining the invariant when a node is inserted or deleted.

When inserting a new node v into a splay tree with n keys, the ranks of all the ancestors of v are increased. Namely, let $v_0, v_i, \ldots, v_d$ be the ancestors of v, where $v_0 = v$, v_i is the parent of v_{i-1}, and v_d is the root. For $i = 1, \ldots, d$, let $n'(v_i)$ and $n(v_i)$ be the size of v_i before and after the insertion, respectively, and let $r'(v_i)$ and $r(v_i)$ be the rank of v_i before and after the insertion, respectively. We have

$$n'(v_i) = n(v_i) + 1.$$

Also, since $n(v_i) + 1 \le n(v_{i+1})$, for $i = 0, 1, \ldots, d - 1$, we have the following for each i in this range:

$$r'(v_i) = \log(n'(v_i)) = \log(n(v_i) + 1) \le \log(n(v_{i+1})) = r(v_{i+1}).$$

Thus, the total variation of $r(T)$ caused by the insertion is

$$
\begin{aligned}
\sum_{i=1}^{d} \left(r'(v_i) - r(v_i) \right) &\le r'(v_d) + \sum_{i=1}^{d-1} (r(v_{i+1}) - r(v_i)) \\
&= r'(v_d) - r(v_0) \\
&\le \log(2n + 1).
\end{aligned}
$$

Therefore, a payment of $O(\log n)$ cyber-dollars is sufficient to maintain the invariant when a new node is inserted.

When deleting a node v from a splay tree with n keys, the ranks of all the ancestors of v are decreased. Thus, the total variation of $r(T)$ caused by the deletion is negative, and we do not need to make any payment to maintain the invariant when a node is deleted. Therefore, we may summarize our amortized analysis in the following proposition (which is sometimes called the "balance proposition" for splay trees):

Proposition 9.4: *Consider a sequence of m operations on a splay tree, each one a search, insertion, or deletion, starting from a splay tree with zero keys. Also, let n_i be the number of keys in the tree after operation i, and n be the total number of insertions. The total running time for performing the sequence of operations is*

$$O\left(m + \sum_{i=1}^{m} \log n_i\right),$$

which is $O(m \log n)$.

In other words, the amortized running time of performing a search, insertion, or deletion in a splay tree is $O(\log n)$, where n is the size of the splay tree at the time. Thus, a splay tree can achieve logarithmic-time, amortized performance for implementing an ordered dictionary ADT. This amortized performance matches the worst-case performance of AVL trees, $(2,4)$ trees, and red-black trees, but it does so using a simple binary tree that does not need any extra balance information stored at each of its nodes. In addition, splay trees have a number of other interesting properties that are not shared by these other balanced search trees. We explore one such additional property in the following proposition (which is sometimes called the "Static Optimality" proposition for splay trees):

Proposition 9.5: *Consider a sequence of m operations on a splay tree, each one a search, insertion, or deletion, starting from a splay tree T with zero keys. Also, let $f(i)$ denote the number of times the entry i is accessed in the splay tree, that is, its frequency, and let n denote the total number of entries. Assuming that each entry is accessed at least once, then the total running time for performing the sequence of operations is*

$$O\left(m + \sum_{i=1}^{n} f(i) \log(m/f(i))\right).$$

We omit the proof of this proposition, but it is not as hard to justify as one might imagine. The remarkable thing is that this proposition states that the amortized running time of accessing an entry i is $O(\log(m/f(i)))$.

9.4 (2,4) Trees

Some data structures we discuss in this chapter, including $(2,4)$ trees, are multi-way search trees, that is, trees with internal nodes that have two or more children. Thus, before we define $(2,4)$ trees, let us discuss multi-way search trees.

9.4.1 Multi-Way Search Trees

Recall that multi-way trees are defined so that each internal node can have many children. In this section, we discuss how multi-way trees can be used as search trees. Recall that the **entries** that we store in a search tree are pairs of the form (k,x), where k is the **key** and x is the value associated with the key. However, we do not discuss how to perform updates in multi-way search trees now, for the details for update methods depend on additional properties we might wish to maintain for multi-way trees, which we discuss in this section and Section 9.6.

Definition of a Multi-way Search Tree

Let v be a node of an ordered tree. We say that v is a *d-**node*** if v has d children. We define a ***multi-way search tree*** to be an ordered tree T that has the following properties, which are illustrated in Figure 9.20a:

- Each internal node of T has at least two children. That is, each internal node is a d-node such that $d \geq 2$.
- Each internal d-node v of T with children $v_1, \ldots, v_d$ stores an ordered set of $d-1$ key-value entries $(k_1, x_1), \ldots, (k_{d-1}, x_{d-1})$, where $k_1 \leq \cdots \leq k_{d-1}$.
- Let us conventionally define $k_0 = -\infty$ and $k_d = +\infty$. For each entry (k,x) stored at a node in the subtree of v rooted at v_i, $i = 1, \ldots, d$, we have that $k_{i-1} \leq k \leq k_i$.

That is, if we think of the set of keys stored at v as including the special fictitious keys $k_0 = -\infty$ and $k_d = +\infty$, then a key k stored in the subtree of T rooted at a child node v_i must be "in between" two keys stored at v. This simple viewpoint gives rise to the rule that a d-node stores $d-1$ regular keys, and it also forms the basis of the algorithm for searching in a multi-way search tree.

By the above definition, the external nodes of a multi-way search do not store any entries and serve only as "placeholders," as has been our convention with binary search trees (Section 9.1); hence, a binary search tree can be viewed as a special case of a multi-way search tree, where each internal node stores one entry and has two children. In addition, while the external nodes could be **null**, we make the simplifying assumption here that they are actual nodes that don't store anything.

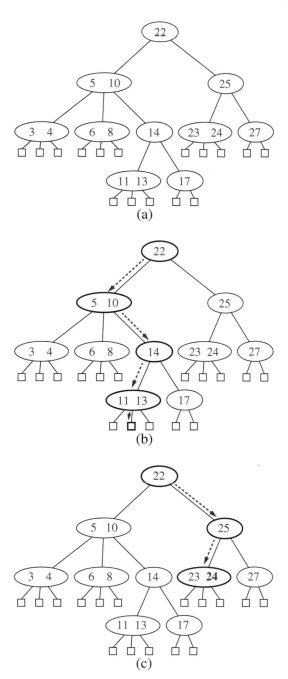

Figure 9.20: (a) A multi-way search tree T; (b) search path in T for key 12 (unsuccessful search); (c) search path in T for key 24 (successful search).

Whether internal nodes of a multi-way tree have two children or many, however, there is an interesting relationship between the number of entries and the number of external nodes.

Proposition 9.6: *An n-entry multi-way search tree has $n+1$ external nodes.*

We leave the justification of this proposition as an exercise (C-9.14).

Searching in a Multi-Way Tree

Given a multi-way search tree T, we note that searching for an entry with key k is simple. We perform such a search by tracing a path in T starting at the root. (See Figure 9.20b and c.) When we are at a d-node v during this search, we compare the key k with the keys $k_1, \ldots, k_{d-1}$ stored at v. If $k = k_i$ for some i, the search is successfully completed. Otherwise, we continue the search in the child v_i of v such that $k_{i-1} < k < k_i$. (Recall that we conventionally define $k_0 = -\infty$ and $k_d = +\infty$.) If we reach an external node, then we know that there is no entry with key k in T, and the search terminates unsuccessfully.

Data Structures for Representing Multi-way Search Trees

In Section 6.4, we discuss different ways of representing general trees. Each of these representations can also be used for multi-way search trees. In fact, in using a general tree to implement a multi-way search tree, the only additional information that we need to store at each node is the set of entries (including keys) associated with that node. That is, we need to store with v a reference to some container or collection object that stores the entries for v.

Recall that when we use a binary search tree to represent an ordered dictionary D, we simply store a reference to a single entry at each internal node. In using a multi-way search tree T to represent D, we must store a reference to the ordered set of entries associated with v at each internal node v of T. This reasoning may at first seem like a circular argument, since we need a representation of an ordered dictionary to represent an ordered dictionary. We can avoid any circular arguments, however, by using the ***bootstrapping*** technique, where we use a previous (less advanced) solution to a problem to create a new (more advanced) solution. In this case, bootstrapping consists of representing the ordered set associated with each internal node using a dictionary data structure that we have previously constructed (for example, a search table based on a sorted vector, as shown in Section 8.3.3). In particular, assuming we already have a way of implementing ordered dictionaries, we can realize a multi-way search tree by taking a tree T and storing such a dictionary at each node of T.

The dictionary we store at each node v is known as a ***secondary*** data structure, for we are using it to support the bigger, ***primary*** data structure. We denote the dictionary stored at a node v of T as $D(v)$. The entries we store in $D(v)$ will allow us to find which child node to move to next during a search operation. Specifically, for each node v of T, with children $v_1, \ldots, v_d$ and entries $(k_1, x_1), \ldots, (k_{d-1}, x_{d-1})$, we store in the dictionary $D(v)$ the entries

$$(k_1, (x_1, v_1)), (k_2, (x_2, v_2)), \ldots, (k_{d-1}, (x_{d-1}, v_{d-1})), (+\infty, (\emptyset, v_d)).$$

That is, an entry $(k_i, (x_i, v_i))$ of dictionary $D(v)$ has key k_i and value (x_i, v_i). Note that the last entry stores the special key $+\infty$.

With the above realization of a multi-way search tree T, processing a d-node v while searching for an entry of T with key k can be done by performing a search operation to find the entry $(k_i, (x_i, v_i))$ in $D(v)$ with smallest key greater than or equal to k. We distinguish two cases:

- If $k < k_i$, then we continue the search by processing child v_i. (Note that if the special key $k_d = +\infty$ is returned, then k is greater than all the keys stored at node v, and we continue the search processing child v_d).
- Otherwise ($k = k_i$), then the search terminates successfully.

Consider the space requirement for the above realization of a multi-way search tree T storing n entries. By Proposition 9.6, using any of the common realizations of ordered dictionaries (Chapter 8) for the secondary structures of the nodes of T, the overall space requirement for T is $O(n)$.

Consider next the time spent answering a search in T. The time spent at a d-node v of T during a search depends on how we realize the secondary data structure $D(v)$. If $D(v)$ is realized with a sorted vector (that is, an ordered search table), then we can process v in $O(\log d)$ time. If instead $D(v)$ is realized using an unsorted list, then processing v takes $O(d)$ time. Let d_{max} denote the maximum number of children of any node of T, and let h denote the height of T. The search time in a multi-way search tree is either $O(h d_{max})$ or $O(h \log d_{max})$, depending on the specific implementation of the secondary structures at the nodes of T (the dictionaries $D(v)$). If d_{max} is a constant, the running time for performing a search is $O(h)$, irrespective of the implementation of the secondary structures.

Thus, the primary efficiency goal for a multi-way search tree is to keep the height as small as possible, that is, we want h to be a logarithmic function of n, the total number of entries stored in the dictionary. A search tree with logarithmic height, such as this, is called a ***balanced search tree***. We discuss a balanced search tree that caps d_{max} at 4 next.

Definition of a (2,4) Tree

A multi-way search tree that keeps the secondary data structures stored at each node small and also keeps the primary multi-way tree balanced is the **(2,4) *tree***, which is sometimes called 2-4 tree or 2-3-4 tree. This data structure achieves these goals by maintaining two simple properties (see Figure 9.21):

Size Property: Every internal node has at most four children.

Depth Property: All the external nodes have the same depth.

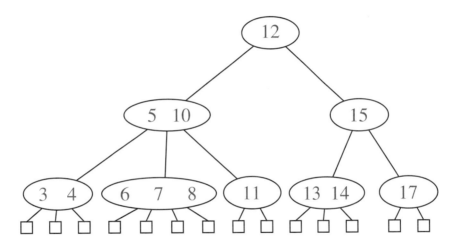

Figure 9.21: A $(2,4)$ tree.

Again, we assume that external nodes are empty and, for the sake of simplicity, we describe our search and update methods assuming that external nodes are real nodes, although this latter requirement is not strictly needed.

Enforcing the size property for $(2,4)$ trees keeps the nodes in the multi-way search tree simple. It also gives rise to the alternative name "2-3-4 tree," since it implies that each internal node in the tree has 2, 3, or 4 children. Another implication of this rule is that we can represent the dictionary $D(v)$ stored at each internal node v using an unordered list or an ordered vector, and still achieve $O(1)$-time performance for all operations (since $d_{\max} = 4$). The depth property, on the other hand, enforces an important bound on the height of a $(2,4)$ tree.

Proposition 9.7: *The height of a* $(2,4)$ *tree storing n entries is* $O(\log n)$.

Justification: Let h be the height of a $(2,4)$ tree T storing n entries. We justify the proposition by showing that the claims

$$\frac{1}{2}\log(n+1) \le h \tag{9.9}$$

and

$$h \le \log(n+1) \tag{9.10}$$

are true.

To justify these claims note first that, by the size property, we can have at most 4 nodes at depth 1, at most 4^2 nodes at depth 2, and so on. Thus, the number of external nodes in T is at most 4^h. Likewise, by the depth property and the definition of a $(2,4)$ tree, we must have at least 2 nodes at depth 1, at least 2^2 nodes at depth 2, and so on. Thus, the number of external nodes in T is at least 2^h. In addition, by Proposition 9.6, the number of external nodes in T is $n+1$. Therefore, we obtain

$$2^h \le n+1$$

and

$$n+1 \le 4^h.$$

Taking the logarithm in base 2 of each of the above terms, we get that

$$h \le \log(n+1)$$

and

$$\log(n+1) \le 2h,$$

which justifies our claims (9.9 and 9.10). ∎

Proposition 9.7 states that the size and depth properties are sufficient for keeping a multi-way tree balanced (Section 9.4.1). Moreover, this proposition implies that performing a search in a $(2,4)$ tree takes $O(\log n)$ time and that the specific realization of the secondary structures at the nodes is not a crucial design choice, since the maximum number of children d_{max} is a constant (4). We can, for example, use a simple ordered dictionary implementation, such as a vector-based search table, for each secondary structure.

9.4.2 Update Operations for (2,4) Trees

Maintaining the size and depth properties requires some effort after performing insertions and removals in a $(2,4)$ tree, however. We discuss these operations next.

Insertion

To insert a new entry (k,x), with key k, into a $(2,4)$ tree T, we first perform a search for k. Assuming that T has no entry with key k, this search terminates unsuccessfully at an external node z. Let v be the parent of z. We insert the new entry into node v and add a new child w (an external node) to v on the left of z. That is, we add entry (k,x,w) to the dictionary $D(v)$.

Our insertion method preserves the depth property, since we add a new external node at the same level as existing external nodes. Nevertheless, it may violate the size property. Indeed, if a node v was previously a 4-node, then it may become a 5-node after the insertion, which causes the tree T to no longer be a $(2,4)$ tree. This type of violation of the size property is called an ***overflow*** at node v, and it must be resolved in order to restore the properties of a $(2,4)$ tree. Let $v_1,\ldots,v_5$ be the children of v, and let $k_1,\ldots,k_4$ be the keys stored at v. To remedy the overflow at node v, we perform a ***split*** operation on v as follows (see Figure 9.22):

- Replace v with two nodes v' and v'', where
    - v' is a 3-node with children v_1,v_2,v_3 storing keys k_1 and k_2
    - v'' is a 2-node with children v_4,v_5 storing key k_4.
- If v was the root of T, create a new root node u; else, let u be the parent of v.
- Insert key k_3 into u and make v' and v'' children of u, so that if v was child i of u, then v' and v'' become children i and $i+1$ of u, respectively.

We show a sequence of insertions in a $(2,4)$ tree in Figure 9.23.

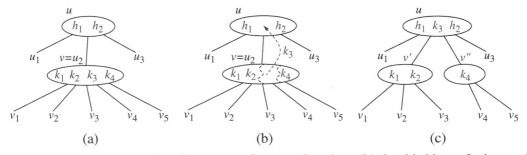

Figure 9.22: A node split: (a) overflow at a 5-node v; (b) the third key of v inserted into the parent u of v; (c) node v replaced with a 3-node v' and a 2-node v''.

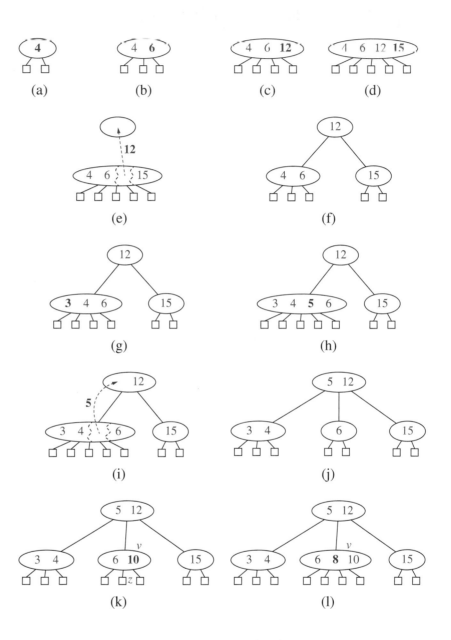

Figure 9.23: A sequence of insertions into a $(2,4)$ tree: (a) initial tree with one entry; (b) insertion of 6; (c) insertion of 12; (d) insertion of 15, which causes an overflow; (e) split, which causes the creation of a new root node; (f) after the split; (g) insertion of 3; (h) insertion of 5, which causes an overflow; (i) split; (j) after the split; (k) insertion of 10; (l) insertion of 8.

Analysis of Insertion in a (2,4) Tree

A split operation affects a constant number of nodes of the tree and $O(1)$ entries stored at such nodes. Thus, it can be implemented to run in $O(1)$ time.

As a consequence of a split operation on node v, a new overflow may occur at the parent u of v. If such an overflow occurs, it triggers in turn a split at node u. (See Figure 9.24.) A split operation either eliminates the overflow or propagates it into the parent of the current node. Hence, the number of split operations is bounded by the height of the tree, which is $O(\log n)$ by Proposition 9.7. Therefore, the total time to perform an insertion in a $(2,4)$ tree is $O(\log n)$.

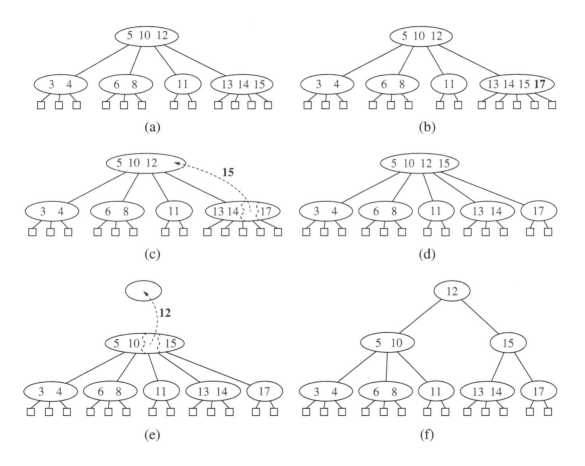

Figure 9.24: An insertion in a $(2,4)$ tree that causes a cascading split: (a) before the insertion; (b) insertion of 17, causing an overflow; (c) a split; (d) after the split a new overflow occurs; (e) another split, creating a new root node; (f) final tree.

Removal

Let us now consider the removal of an entry with key k from a $(2,4)$ tree T. We begin such an operation by performing a search in T for an entry with key k. Removing such an entry from a $(2,4)$ tree can always be reduced to the case where the entry to be removed is stored at a node v whose children are external nodes. Suppose, for instance, that the entry with key k that we wish to remove is stored in the ith entry (k_i, x_i) at a node z that has only internal-node children. In this case, we swap the entry (k_i, x_i) with an appropriate entry that is stored at a node v with external-node children as follows (see Figure 9.25d):

1. We find the right-most internal node v in the subtree rooted at the ith child of z, noting that the children of node v are all external nodes.
2. We swap the entry (k_i, x_i) at z with the last entry of v.

Once we ensure that the entry to remove is stored at a node v with only external-node children (because either it was already at v or we swapped it into v), we simply remove the entry from v (that is, from the dictionary $D(v)$) and remove the ith external node of v.

Removing an entry (and a child) from a node v as described above preserves the depth property, for we always remove an external node child from a node v with only external-node children. However, in removing such an external node we may violate the size property at v. Indeed, if v was previously a 2-node, then it becomes a 1-node with no entries after the removal (Figure 9.25d and e), which is not allowed in a $(2,4)$ tree. This type of violation of the size property is called an ***underflow*** at node v. To remedy an underflow, we check whether an immediate sibling of v is a 3-node or a 4-node. If we find such a sibling w, then we perform a ***transfer*** operation, in which we move a child of w to v, a key of w to the parent u of v and w, and a key of u to v. (See Figure 9.25b and c.) If v has only one sibling, or if both immediate siblings of v are 2-nodes, then we perform a ***fusion*** operation, in which we merge v with a sibling, creating a new node v', and move a key from the parent u of v to v'. (See Figure 9.26e and f.)

A fusion operation at node v may cause a new underflow to occur at the parent u of v, which in turn triggers a transfer or fusion at u. (See Figure 9.26.) Hence, the number of fusion operations is bounded by the height of the tree, which is $O(\log n)$ by Proposition 9.7. If an underflow propagates all the way up to the root, then the root is simply deleted. (See Figure 9.26c and d.) We show a sequence of removals from a $(2,4)$ tree in Figures 9.25 and 9.26.

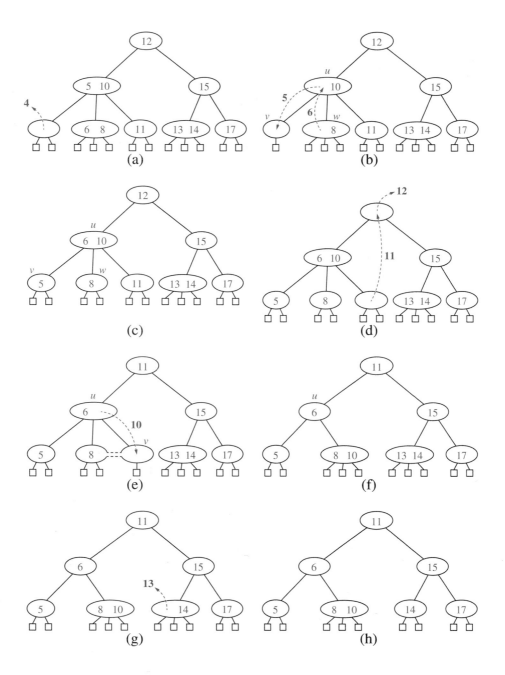

Figure 9.25: A sequence of removals from a (2,4) tree: (a) removal of 4, causing an underflow; (b) a transfer operation; (c) after the transfer operation; (d) removal of 12, causing an underflow; (e) a fusion operation; (f) after the fusion operation; (g) removal of 13; (h) after removing 13.

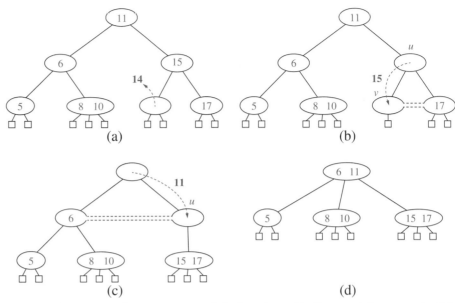

Figure 9.26: A propagating sequence of fusions in a $(2,4)$ tree: (a) removal of 14, which causes an underflow; (b) fusion, which causes another underflow; (c) second fusion operation, which causes the root to be removed; (d) final tree.

Performance of $(2,4)$ Trees

Table 9.3 summarizes the running times of the main operations of a dictionary realized with a $(2,4)$ tree. The time complexity analysis is based on the following:

- The height of a $(2,4)$ tree storing n entries is $O(\log n)$, by Proposition 9.7.
- A split, transfer, or fusion operation takes $O(1)$ time.
- A search, insertion, or removal of an entry visits $O(\log n)$ nodes.

Operation	Time
size, isEmpty	$O(1)$
find, insert, remove	$O(\log n)$
findAll	$O(\log n + s)$

Table 9.3: Performance of an n-entry dictionary realized by a $(2,4)$ tree, where s denotes the size of the iterator returned by findAll. The space usage is $O(n)$.

Thus, $(2,4)$ trees provide for fast dictionary search and update operations. $(2,4)$ trees also have an interesting relationship to the data structure we discuss next.

9.5 Red-Black Trees

Although AVL trees and $(2,4)$ trees have a number of nice properties, there are some dictionary applications for which they are not well suited. For instance, AVL trees may require many restructure operations (rotations) to be performed after a removal, and $(2,4)$ trees may require many fusing or split operations to be performed after either an insertion or removal. The data structure we discuss in this section, the red-black tree, does not have these drawbacks, however, as it requires that only $O(1)$ structural changes be made after an update in order to stay balanced.

A ***red-black tree*** is a binary search tree (see Section 9.1) with nodes colored red and black in a way that satisfies the following properties:

Root Property: The root is black.

External Property: Every external node is black.

Internal Property: The children of a red node are black.

Depth Property: All the external nodes have the same ***black depth***, defined as the number of black ancestors minus one. (Recall that a node is an ancestor of itself.)

An example of a red-black tree is shown in Figure 9.27.

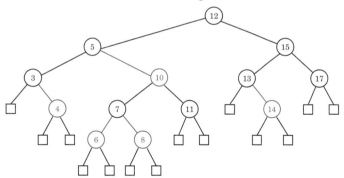

Figure 9.27: Red-black tree associated with the $(2,4)$ tree of Figure 9.21. Each external node of this red-black tree has 4 black ancestors (including itself); hence, it has black depth 3. We use the color blue instead of red. Also, we use the convention of giving an edge of the tree the same color as the child node.

As for previous types of search trees, we assume that entries are stored at the internal nodes of a red-black tree, with the external nodes being empty placeholders. Also, we assume that the external nodes are actual nodes, but we note that at the expense of slightly more complicated methods, external nodes could be **null**.

We can make the red-black tree definition more intuitive by noting an interesting correspondence between red-black trees and $(2,4)$ trees, as illustrated in Figure 9.28. Namely, given a red-black tree, we can construct a corresponding $(2,4)$ tree by merging every red node v into its parent and storing the entry from v at its parent. Conversely, we can transform any $(2,4)$ tree into a corresponding red-black tree by coloring each node black and performing the following transformation for each internal node v:

- If v is a 2-node, then keep the (black) children of v as is.

- If v is a 3-node, then create a new red node w, give v's first two (black) children to w, and make w and v's third child be the two children of v.

- If v is a 4-node, then create two new red nodes w and z, give v's first two (black) children to w, give v's last two (black) children to z, and make w and z be the two children of v.

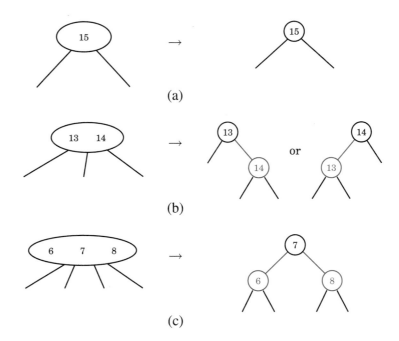

Figure 9.28: Correspondence between a $(2,4)$ tree and a red-black tree: (a) 2-node; (b) 3-node; (c) 4-node.

The correspondence between $(2,4)$ trees and red-black trees provides important intuition that we will use in our discussion of how to perform updates in red-black trees. In fact, the update algorithms for red-black trees are mysteriously complex without this intuition.

Proposition 9.8: *The height of a red-black tree storing n entries is* $O(\log n)$.

Justification: Let T be a red-black tree storing n entries, and let h be the height of T. We justify this proposition by establishing the following fact:

$$\log(n+1) \leq h \leq 2\log(n+1).$$

Let d be the common black depth of all the external nodes of T. Let T' be the $(2,4)$ tree associated with T, and let h' be the height of T'. Because of the correspondence between red-black trees and $(2,4)$ trees, we have that $h' = d$. Hence, by Proposition 9.7, $d = h' \leq \log(n+1)$. By the internal node property, $h \leq 2d$. Thus, we obtain $h \leq 2\log(n+1)$. The other inequality, $\log(n+1) \leq h$, follows from Proposition 6.10 and the fact that T has n internal nodes. ∎

We assume that a red-black tree is realized with a linked structure for binary trees (Section 6.4.2), in which we store a dictionary entry and a color indicator at each node. Thus the space requirement for storing n keys is $O(n)$. The algorithm for searching in a red-black tree T is the same as that for a standard binary search tree (Section 9.1). Thus, searching in a red-black tree takes $O(\log n)$ time.

9.5.1 Update Operations

Performing the update operations in a red-black tree is similar to that of a binary search tree, except that we must additionally restore the color properties.

Insertion

Consider now the insertion of an entry with key k into a red-black tree T, keeping in mind the correspondence between T and its associated $(2,4)$ tree T' and the insertion algorithm for T'. The algorithm initially proceeds as in a binary search tree (Section 9.1.2). Namely, we search for k in T until we reach an external node of T, and we replace this node with an internal node z, storing (k,x) and having two external-node children. If z is the root of T, we color z black, else we color z red. We also color the children of z black. This action corresponds to inserting (k,x) into a node of the $(2,4)$ tree T' with external children. In addition, this action preserves the root, external and depth properties of T, but it may violate the internal property. Indeed, if z is not the root of T and the parent v of z is red, then we have a parent and a child (namely, v and z) that are both red. Note that by the root property, v cannot be the root of T, and by the internal property (which was previously satisfied), the parent u of v must be black. Since z and its parent are red, but z's grandparent u is black, we call this violation of the internal property a ***double red*** at node z.

To remedy a double red, we consider two cases.

Case 1: ***The Sibling* w *of* v *is Black*.** (See Figure 9.29.) In this case, the double
red denotes the fact that we have created in our red-black tree T a malformed
replacement for a corresponding 4-node of the $(2,4)$ tree T', which has as its
children the four black children of u, v, and z. Our malformed replacement
has one red node (v) that is the parent of another red node (z), while we want
it to have the two red nodes as siblings instead. To fix this problem, we
perform a ***trinode restructuring*** of T. The trinode restructuring is done by
the operation restructure(z), which consists of the following steps (see again
Figure 9.29; this operation is also discussed in Section 9.2):

- Take node z, its parent v, and grandparent u, and temporarily relabel
  them as a, b, and c, in left-to-right order, so that a, b, and c will be
  visited in this order by an inorder tree traversal.
- Replace the grandparent u with the node labeled b, and make nodes a
  and c the children of b, keeping inorder relationships unchanged.

After performing the restructure(z) operation, we color b black and we color
a and c red. Thus, the restructuring eliminates the double red problem.

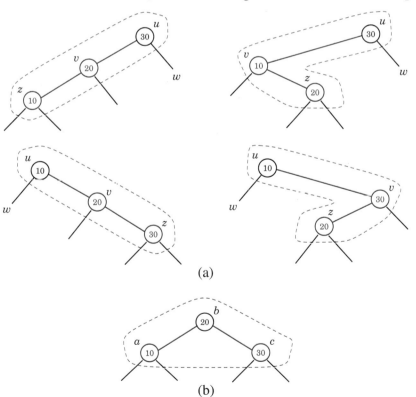

Figure 9.29: Restructuring a red-black tree to remedy a double red: (a) the four
configurations for u, v, and z before restructuring; (b) after restructuring.

Case 2: *The Sibling* w *of* v *is Red.* (See Figure 9.30.) In this case, the double red denotes an overflow in the corresponding $(2,4)$ tree T. To fix the problem, we perform the equivalent of a split operation. Namely, we do a ***recoloring***: we color v and w black and their parent u red (unless u is the root, in which case, it is colored black). It is possible that, after such a recoloring, the double red problem reappears, albeit higher up in the tree T, since u may have a red parent. If the double red problem reappears at u, then we repeat the consideration of the two cases at u. Thus, a recoloring either eliminates the double red problem at node z, or propagates it to the grandparent u of z. We continue going up T performing recolorings until we finally resolve the double red problem (with either a final recoloring or a trinode restructuring). Thus, the number of recolorings caused by an insertion is no more than half the height of tree T, that is, no more than $\log(n+1)$ by Proposition 9.8.

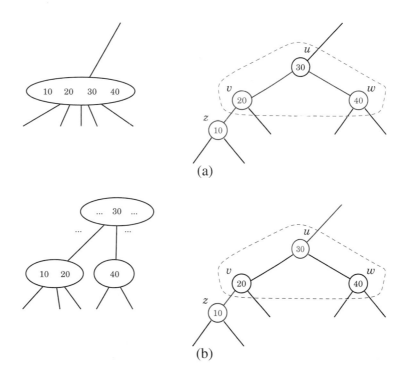

Figure 9.30: Recoloring to remedy the double red problem: (a) before recoloring and the corresponding 5-node in the associated $(2,4)$ tree before the split; (b) after the recoloring (and corresponding nodes in the associated $(2,4)$ tree after the split).

Figures 9.31 and 9.32 show a sequence of insertion operations in a red-black tree.

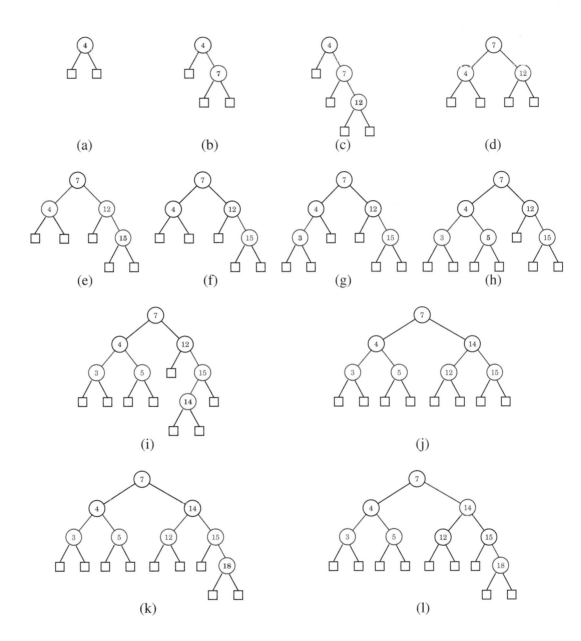

Figure 9.31: A sequence of insertions in a red-black tree: (a) initial tree; (b) insertion of 7; (c) insertion of 12, which causes a double red; (d) after restructuring; (e) insertion of 15, which causes a double red; (f) after recoloring (the root remains black); (g) insertion of 3; (h) insertion of 5; (i) insertion of 14, which causes a double red; (j) after restructuring; (k) insertion of 18, which causes a double red; (l) after recoloring. (Continues in Figure 9.32.)

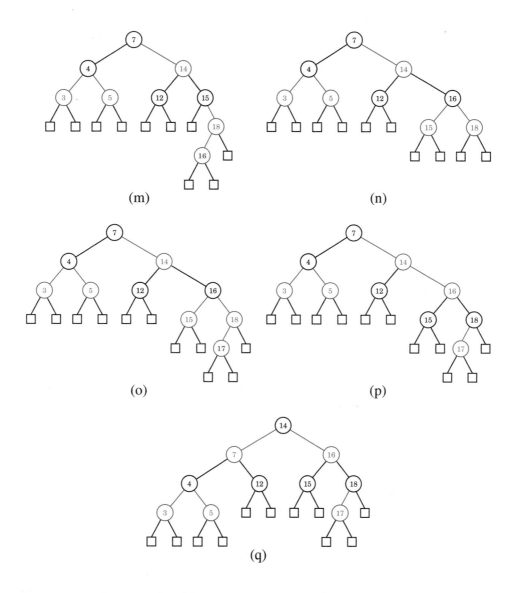

Figure 9.32: A sequence of insertions in a red-black tree : (m) insertion of 16, which causes a double red; (n) after restructuring; (o) insertion of 17, which causes a double red; (p) after recoloring there is again a double red, to be handled by a restructuring; (q) after restructuring. (Continued from Figure 9.31.)

The cases for insertion imply an interesting property for red-black trees. Namely, since the Case 1 action eliminates the double-red problem with a single trinode restructuring and the Case 2 action performs no restructuring operations, at most one restructuring is needed in a red-black tree insertion. By the above analysis and the fact that a restructuring or recoloring takes $O(1)$ time, we have the following:

Proposition 9.9: *The insertion of a key-value entry in a red-black tree storing n entries can be done in $O(\log n)$ time and requires $O(\log n)$ recolorings and one trinode restructuring (a* restructure *operation).*

Removal

Suppose now that we are asked to remove an entry with key k from a red-black tree T. Removing such an entry initially proceeds as for a binary search tree (Section 9.1.2). First, we search for a node u storing such an entry. If node u does not have an external child, we find the internal node v following u in the inorder traversal of T, move the entry at v to u, and perform the removal at v. Thus, we may consider only the removal of an entry with key k stored at a node v with an external child w. Also, as we did for insertions, we keep in mind the correspondence between red-black tree T and its associated $(2,4)$ tree T' (and the removal algorithm for T').

To remove the entry with key k from a node v of T with an external child w we proceed as follows. Let r be the sibling of w and x be the parent of v. We remove nodes v and w, and make r a child of x. If v was red (hence r is black) or r is red (hence v was black), we color r black and we are done. If, instead, r is black and v was black, then, to preserve the depth property, we give r a fictitious ***double black*** color. We now have a color violation, called the double black problem. A double black in T denotes an underflow in the corresponding $(2,4)$ tree T'. Recall that x is the parent of the double black node r. To remedy the double-black problem at r, we consider three cases.

Case 1: ***The Sibling*** **y** ***of*** **r** ***is Black and has a Red Child*** **z**. (See Figure 9.33.)
Resolving this case corresponds to a transfer operation in the $(2,4)$ tree T'. We perform a ***trinode restructuring*** by means of operation restructure(z). Recall that the operation restructure(z) takes the node z, its parent y, and grandparent x, labels them temporarily left to right as a, b, and c, and replaces x with the node labeled b, making it the parent of the other two. (See also the description of restructure in Section 9.2.) We color a and c black, give b the former color of x, and color r black. This trinode restructuring eliminates the double black problem. Hence, at most one restructuring is performed in a removal operation in this case.

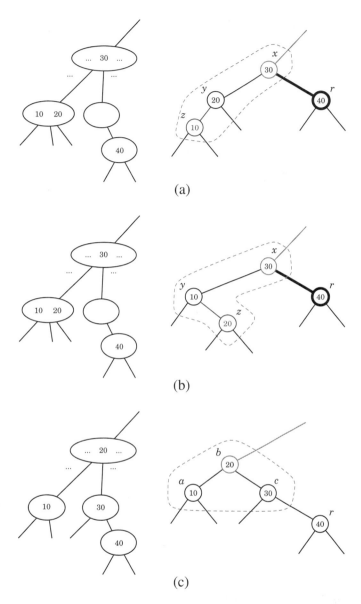

Figure 9.33: Restructuring of a red-black tree to remedy the double black problem: (a) and (b) configurations before the restructuring, where r is a right child and the associated nodes in the corresponding $(2,4)$ tree before the transfer (two other symmetric configurations where r is a left child are possible); (c) configuration after the restructuring and the associated nodes in the corresponding $(2,4)$ tree after the transfer. The grey color for node x in parts (a) and (b) and for node b in part (c) denotes the fact that this node may be colored either red or black.

Case 2: ***The Sibling*** **y** ***of*** **r** ***is Black and Both Children of*** **y** ***are Black.*** (See
Figures 9.34 and 9.35.) Resolving this case corresponds to a fusion operation
in the corresponding $(2,4)$ tree T'. We do a ***recoloring***; we color r black, we
color y red, and, if x is red, we color it black (Figure 9.34); otherwise, we
color x ***double black*** (Figure 9.35). Hence, after this recoloring, the double
black problem may reappear at the parent x of r. (See Figure 9.35.) That is,
this recoloring either eliminates the double black problem or propagates it
into the parent of the current node. We then repeat a consideration of these
three cases at the parent. Thus, since Case 1 performs a trinode restructuring
operation and stops (and, as we will soon see, Case 3 is similar), the number
of recolorings caused by a removal is no more than $\log(n+1)$.

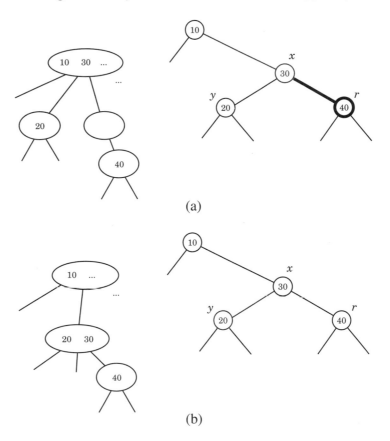

Figure 9.34: Recoloring of a red-black tree that fixes the double black problem: (a)
before the recoloring and corresponding nodes in the associated $(2,4)$ tree before
the fusion (other similar configurations are possible); (b) after the recoloring and
corresponding nodes in the associated $(2,4)$ tree after the fusion.

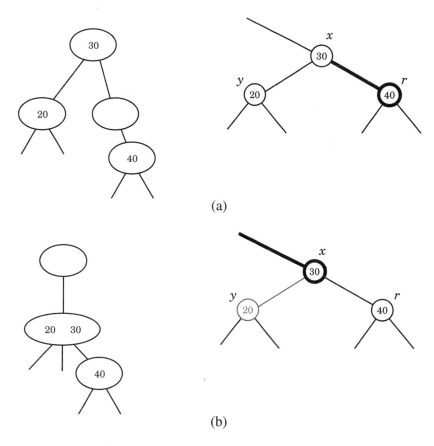

(a)

(b)

Figure 9.35: Recoloring of a red-black tree that propagates the double black problem: (a) configuration before the recoloring and corresponding nodes in the associated $(2,4)$ tree before the fusion (other similar configurations are possible); (b) configuration after the recoloring and corresponding nodes in the associated $(2,4)$ tree after the fusion.

Case 3: The Sibling y of r is Red. (See Figure 9.36.) In this case, we perform an
adjustment operation, as follows. If y is the right child of x, let z be the right
child of y; otherwise, let z be the left child of y. Execute the trinode restructuring operation restructure(z), which makes y the parent of x. Color y black
and x red. An adjustment corresponds to choosing a different representation
of a 3-node in the $(2,4)$ tree T'. After the adjustment operation, the sibling
of r is black, and either Case 1 or Case 2 applies, with a different meaning
of x and y. Note that if Case 2 applies, the double-black problem cannot
reappear. Thus, to complete Case 3 we make one more application of either
Case 1 or Case 2 above and we are done. Therefore, at most one adjustment
is performed in a removal operation.

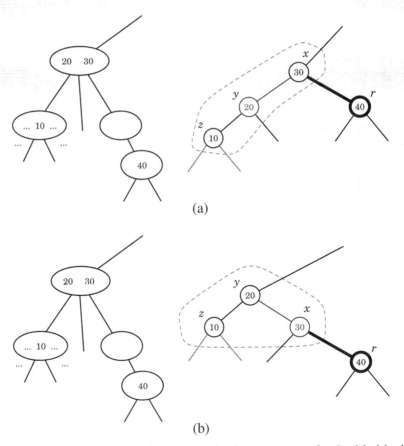

Figure 9.36: Adjustment of a red-black tree in the presence of a double black problem: (a) configuration before the adjustment and corresponding nodes in the associated $(2,4)$ tree (a symmetric configuration is possible); (b) configuration after the
adjustment with the same corresponding nodes in the associated $(2,4)$ tree.

From the above algorithm description, we see that the tree updating needed after a removal involves an upward march in the tree T, while performing at most a constant amount of work (in a restructuring, recoloring, or adjustment) per node. Thus, since any changes we make at a node in T during this upward march takes $O(1)$ time (because it affects a constant number of nodes), we have the following:

Proposition 9.10: *The algorithm for removing an entry from a red-black tree with n entries takes $O(\log n)$ time and performs $O(\log n)$ recolorings and at most one adjustment plus one additional trinode restructuring. Thus, it performs at most* two *restructure operations.*

In Figures 9.37 and 9.38, we show a sequence of removal operations on a red-black tree. We illustrate Case 1 restructurings in Figure 9.37c and d. We illustrate Case 2 recolorings at several places in Figures 9.37 and 9.38. Finally, in Figure 9.38i and j, we show an example of a Case 3 adjustment.

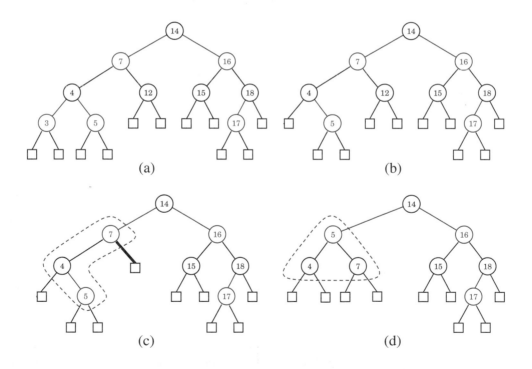

Figure 9.37: Sequence of removals from a red-black tree: (a) initial tree; (b) removal of 3; (c) removal of 12, causing a double black (handled by restructuring); (d) after restructuring.

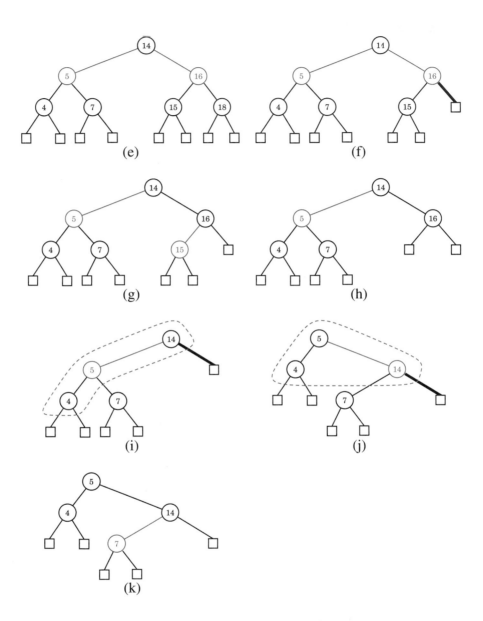

Figure 9.38: Sequence of removals in a red-black tree (continued): (e) removal of 17; (f) removal of 18, causing a double black (handled by recoloring); (g) after recoloring; (h) removal of 15; (i) removal of 16, causing a double black (handled by an adjustment); (j) after the adjustment the double black needs to be handled by a recoloring; (k) after the recoloring.

Performance of Red-Black Trees

Table 9.4 summarizes the running times of the main operations of a dictionary realized by means of a red-black tree. We illustrate the justification for these bounds in Figure 9.39.

Operation	Time
size, isEmpty	$O(1)$
find, insert, remove	$O(\log n)$
findAll	$O(\log n + s)$

Table 9.4: Performance of an n-entry dictionary realized by a red-black tree, where s denotes the size of the iterator returned by findAll. The space usage is $O(n)$.

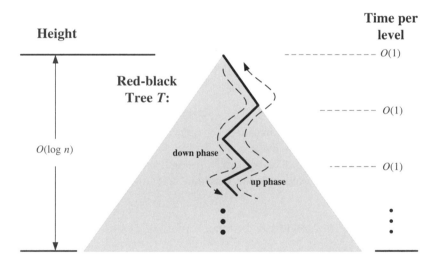

Figure 9.39: Illustrating the running time of searches and updates in a red-black tree. The time performance is $O(1)$ per level, broken into a down phase, which typically involves searching, and an up phase, which typically involves recolorings and performing local trinode restructurings (rotations).

Thus, a red-black tree achieves logarithmic worst-case running times for both searching and updating in a dictionary. The red-black tree data structure is slightly more complicated than its corresponding $(2,4)$ tree. Even so, a red-black tree has a conceptual advantage that only a constant number of trinode restructurings are ever needed to restore the balance in a red-black tree after an update.

9.5.2   Java Implementation

In Code Fragments 9.8 through 9.10, we show the major portions of a Java implementation of a dictionary realized by means of a red-black tree. The main class includes a nested class, RBNode, shown in Code Fragment 9.8, which extends the BTNode class used to represent a key-value entry of a binary search tree. It defines an additional instance variable isRed, representing the color of the node, and methods to set and return it.

```java
/** Realization of a dictionary by means of a red-black tree. */
public class RBTree extends BinarySearchTree implements Dictionary {
  public RBTree() { super(); }
  public RBTree(Comparator C) { super(C); }
  /** Nested class for the nodes of a red-black tree */
  protected static class RBNode extends BTNode {
    protected boolean isRed;  // we add a color field to a BTNode
    RBNode() {/* default constructor */}
    /** Preferred constructor */
    RBNode(Object element, BTPosition parent,
           BTPosition left, BTPosition right) {
      super(element, parent, left, right);
      isRed = false;
    }
    public boolean isRed()  {return isRed;}
    public void makeRed()  {isRed = true;}
    public void makeBlack()  {isRed = false;}
    public void setColor(boolean color)  {isRed = color;}
  }
```

Code Fragment 9.8: Instance variables, nested class, and constructor for RBTree.

Class RBTree (Code Fragments 9.8 through 9.10) extends BinarySearchTree (Code Fragments 9.2 through 9.4). We assume the parent class supports the method restructure for performing trinode restructurings (rotations); its implementation is left as an exercise (P-9.2). Class RBTree inherits methods size, isEmpty, find, and findAll from BinarySearchTree but overrides methods insert and remove. It implements these two operations by first calling the corresponding method of the parent class and then remedying any color violations that this update may have caused. Several auxiliary methods of class RBTree are not shown, but there names suggest their meanings and their implementations are straightforward.

```
/** Creates a new tree node. */
protected BTPosition createNode(Object element, BTPosition parent,
                                BTPosition left, BTPosition right) {
  return new RBNode(element,parent,left,right); // a red-black node
}
public Entry insert(Object k, Object x) throws InvalidKeyException  {
  Entry toReturn = super.insert(k, x);
  Position posZ = actionPos; // start at the insertion position
  setRed(posZ);
  if (isRoot(posZ))
    setBlack(posZ);
  else
    remedyDoubleRed(posZ); // fix a double-red color violation
  return toReturn;
}
protected void remedyDoubleRed(Position posZ)  {
  Position posV = parent(posZ);
  if (isRoot(posV))
    return;
  if (!isPosRed(posV))
    return;
  // we have a double red: posZ and posV
  if (!isPosRed(sibling(posV)))  { // Case 1: trinode restructuring
    posV = restructure(posZ);
    setBlack(posV);
    setRed(left(posV));
    setRed(right(posV));
  }
  else  { // Case 2: recoloring
    setBlack(posV);
    setBlack(sibling(posV));
    Position posU = parent(posV);
    if (isRoot(posU))
      return;
    setRed(posU);
    remedyDoubleRed(posU);
  }
}
```

Code Fragment 9.9: The dictionary ADT method insert and auxiliary methods createNode and remedyDoubleRed of class RBTree.

Methods insert (Code Fragment 9.9) and remove (Code Fragment 9.10) call the corresponding methods of the superclass first and then rebalance the tree by calling auxiliary methods to perform rotations along the path from the update position (given by the instance variable actionPos inherited from the superclass) to the root.

```
public Entry remove(Entry ent) throws InvalidEntryException {
  Entry toReturn = super.remove(ent);
  Position posR = actionPos;
  if (toReturn != null) {
    if (wasParentRed(posR) || isRoot(posR) || isPosRed(posR))
      setBlack(posR);
    else
      remedyDoubleBlack(posR);
  }
  return toReturn;
}
protected void remedyDoubleBlack(Position posR) {
  Position posX, posY, posZ;
  boolean oldColor;
  posX = parent(posR);
  posY = sibling(posR);
  if (!isPosRed(posY))  {
    posZ = redChild(posY);
    if (hasRedChild(posY))  { // Case 1: trinode restructuring
      oldColor = isPosRed(posX);
      posZ = restructure(posZ);
      setColor(posZ, oldColor);
      setBlack(posR);
      setBlack(left(posZ));
      setBlack(right(posZ));
      return;
    }
    setBlack(posR);
    setRed(posY);
    if (!isPosRed(posX))  { // Case 2: recoloring
      if (!isRoot(posX))
        remedyDoubleBlack(posX);
      return;
    }
    setBlack(posX);
    return;
  } // Case 3: adjustment
  if (posY == right(posX)) posZ = right(posY);
  else posZ = left(posY);
  restructure(posZ);
  setBlack(posY);
  setRed(posX);
  remedyDoubleBlack(posR);
}
```

Code Fragment 9.10: Method remove and auxiliary method remedyDoubleBlack of class RBTree.

9.6 External Searching in B-Trees

In this section, we study the problem of implementing an ordered dictionary for a large collection of entries that do not fit in main memory. One of the main applications of large dictionaries is in database systems.

External Memory Computations

When data cannot be held in main memory, it must be stored in ***external memory***, which is usually a disk. The time to access information on a disk is so much slower than the time used to transfer that information, so data entries on a disk are usually grouped into contiguous sections called ***blocks***. We refer to these secondary-memory blocks as ***disk blocks***. Likewise, we refer to the transfer of a block between secondary memory and main memory as a ***disk transfer***. Even though we use this terminology, the search techniques we discuss in this section also apply when the main memory is the CPU cache and the secondary memory is the main (RAM) memory, because cache lines are also collected into blocks.

There is a great time difference that exists between main memory accesses and disk accesses, equal to several orders of magnitude for many systems. Thus, the main goal of maintaining a dictionary in external memory is to minimize the number of disk transfers needed to perform a query or update. In fact, the difference in speed between disk and internal memory is so great that we should be willing to perform a considerable number of internal-memory accesses if they allow us to avoid a few disk transfers. Let us, therefore, analyze the performance of dictionary implementations by counting the number of disk transfers each would require to perform the standard dictionary search and update operations. We refer to this count as the ***I/O complexity*** of the algorithms involved.

Some Inefficient External-Memory Dictionaries

Let us consider first the simple dictionary realizations that use a list to store the entries. If the list is implemented as an unsorted doubly linked list, then insertions can be performed with $O(1)$ transfers each, but removals and searching require n transfers in the worst case, where n is the number of entries in the dictionary, since each link hop we perform could access a different block. This search time can be improved to $O(n/B)$ transfers (using a method we explore in Exercise C-9.22), where B denotes the number of nodes of the list that can fit into a block, but this is still poor performance. We could alternately implement the list using a sorted vector, that is, a search table. In this case, a search performs $O(\log_2 n)$ transfers, using the binary search algorithm, which is a nice improvement. But this solution requires n/B transfers to implement an insert or remove operation in the worst case, for we may have to access all the blocks holding the array to move elements up or down. Thus, list-based implementations of a dictionary are not efficient from an external memory standpoint.

Since these simple implementations are I/O inefficient, then perhaps we should consider the logarithmic-time strategies that use balanced binary trees (such as AVL trees or red-black trees) or other search structures with logarithmic average-case query and update times (such as skip lists). These methods store the dictionary entries at the nodes of a binary tree or a graph (for skip lists). Typically, each node accessed for a query or update in one of these structures will be in a different block. Thus, these methods typically require $O(\log_2 n)$ transfers to perform a query or update operation. This is pretty good, but we can do much better. In particular, we describe in the remainder of this section how to perform dictionary query and update operations using only $O(\log_B n)$, that is, $O(\log n/\log B)$, transfers, where B is much larger than 2.

To improve the external-memory performance of the dictionary implementations discussed above we should be willing to perform up to $O(B)$ internal-memory accesses to avoid a single disk transfer, where B denotes the size of a disk block. The hardware and software that drives the disk performs this many internal-memory accesses just to bring a block into internal memory, and, even then, this is only a small part of the cost of a disk transfer. Thus, $O(B)$ high-speed, internal-memory accesses are a small price to pay to avoid a time-consuming disk transfer.

9.6.1 (a,b) Trees

To reduce the importance of the performance difference between internal-memory accesses and external-memory accesses for searching, we can represent our dictionary using a multi-way search tree (Section 9.4.1). This approach gives rise to a generalization of the $(2,4)$ tree data structure known as the (a,b) tree.

An (a,b) tree is a multi-way search tree such that each node has between a and b children and stores between $a-1$ and $b-1$ entries. The algorithms for searching, inserting, and removing entries in an (a,b) tree are straightforward generalizations of the corresponding ones for $(2,4)$ trees. The advantage of generalizing $(2,4)$ trees to (a,b) trees is that a generalized class of trees provides a flexible search structure, where the size of the nodes and the running time of the various dictionary operations depends on the parameters a and b. By setting the parameters a and b appropriately with respect to the size of disk blocks, we can derive a data structure that achieves good external-memory performance.

Definition of an (a,b) Tree

An (a,b) **tree**, where a and b are integers, such that $2 \le a \le (b+1)/2$, is a multi-way search tree T with the following additional restrictions:

Size Property: Each internal node has at least a children, unless it is the root, and has at most b children.

Depth Property: All the external nodes have the same depth.

Proposition 9.11: *The height of an (a,b) tree storing n entries is $\Omega(\log n / \log b)$ and $O(\log n / \log a)$.*

Justification: Let T be an (a,b) tree storing n entries, and let h be the height of T. We justify the proposition by establishing the following bounds on h:

$$\frac{1}{\log b} \log(n+1) \le h \le \frac{1}{\log a} \log \frac{n+1}{2} + 1.$$

By the size and depth properties, the number n'' of external nodes of T is at least $2a^{h-1}$ and at most b^h. By Proposition 9.6, $n'' = n+1$. Thus

$$2a^{h-1} \le n+1 \le b^h.$$

Taking the logarithm in base 2 of each term, we get

$$(h-1)\log a + 1 \le \log(n+1) \le h \log b. \qquad \blacksquare$$

We recall that in a multi-way search tree T, each node v of T holds a secondary structure $D(v)$, which is itself a dictionary (Section 9.4.1). If T is an (a,b) tree, then $D(v)$ stores at most b entries. Let $f(b)$ denote the time for performing a search in a $D(v)$ dictionary. The search algorithm in an (a,b) tree is exactly like the one for multi-way search trees given in Section 9.4.1. Hence, searching in an (a,b) tree T with n entries takes $O(\frac{f(b)}{\log a} \log n)$ time. Note that if b is a constant (and thus a is also), then the search time is $O(\log n)$, independent of the specific implementation of the secondary structures.

The main application of (a,b) trees is for dictionaries stored in external memory (for example, on a disk or CD-ROM). Namely, to minimize disk accesses, we select the parameters a and b so that each tree node occupies a single disk block (so that $f(b) = 1$ if we wish to simply count block transfers). Providing the right a and b values in this context gives rise to a data structure known as the B-tree, which we will describe shortly. Before we describe this structure, however, let us discuss how insertions and removals are handled in (a,b) trees.

Update Operations

The insertion algorithm for an (a,b) tree is similar to that for a $(2,4)$ tree. An overflow occurs when an entry is inserted into a b-node v, which becomes an illegal $(b+1)$-node. (Recall that a node in a multi-way tree is a d-node if it has d children.) To remedy an overflow, we split node v by moving the median entry of v into the parent of v and replacing v with a $\lceil (b+1)/2 \rceil$-node v' and a $\lfloor (b+1)/2 \rfloor$-node v''. We can now see the reason for requiring $a \le (b+1)/2$ in the definition of an (a,b) tree. Note that as a consequence of the split, we need to build the secondary structures $D(v')$ and $D(v'')$.

Removing an entry from an (a,b) tree is similar to what was done for $(2,4)$ trees. An underflow occurs when a key is removed from an a-node v, distinct from the root, which causes v to become an illegal $(a-1)$-node. To remedy an underflow, we perform a transfer with a sibling of v that is not an a-node or we perform a fusion of v with a sibling that is an a-node. The new node w resulting from the fusion is a $(2a-1)$-node, which is another reason for requiring $a \le (b+1)/2$.

Table 9.5 shows the performance of a dictionary realized with an (a,b) tree.

Method	Time
find	$O\left(\frac{f(b)}{\log a} \log n \right)$
insert	$O\left(\frac{g(b)}{\log a} \log n \right)$
remove	$O\left(\frac{g(b)}{\log a} \log n \right)$

Table 9.5: Time bounds for fundamental methods of an n-entry dictionary realized by an (a,b) tree. The space usage is $O(n)$.

The time bounds in Table 9.5 are based on the following assumptions and facts:

- The (a,b) tree T is realized using the data structure described in Section 9.4.1, and the secondary structure of the nodes of T support search in $f(b)$ time, and split and fusion operations in $g(b)$ time, for some functions $f(b)$ and $g(b)$, which can be made to be $O(1)$ when we are only counting disk transfers.
- The height of an (a,b) tree storing n entries is $O((\log n)/(\log a))$.
- A search visits $O((\log n)/(\log a))$ nodes on a path between the root and an external node, and spends $f(b)$ time per node.
- A transfer operation takes $f(b)$ time.
- A split or fusion operation takes $g(b)$ time and builds a secondary structure of size $O(b)$ for the new node(s) created.
- An insertion or removal of an entry visits $O((\log n)/(\log a))$ nodes on a path between the root and an external node, and spends $g(b)$ time per node.

9.6.2 B-Trees

A version of the (a, b) tree data structure, which is the best known method for maintaining a dictionary in external memory, is called the "B-tree." (See Figure 9.40.) A ***B-tree of order*** d is an (a, b) tree with $a = \lceil d/2 \rceil$ and $b = d$. Since we discussed the standard dictionary query and update methods for (a, b) trees above, we restrict our discussion here to the I/O complexity of B-trees.

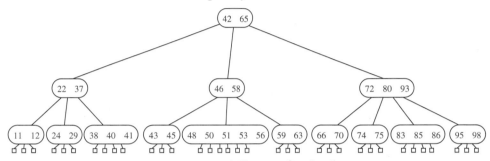

Figure 9.40: A B-tree of order 6.

An important property of B-trees is that we can choose d so that the d children references and the $d - 1$ keys stored at a node can all fit into a single disk block, implying that d is proportional to B. This choice allows us to assume that a and b are also proportional to B in the analysis of the search and update operations on (a, b) trees. Thus, $f(b)$ and $g(b)$ are both $O(1)$, for each time we access a node to perform a search or an update operation, we need only perform a single disk transfer.

As we have already observed above, each search or update requires that we examine at most $O(1)$ nodes for each level of the tree. Therefore, any dictionary search or update operation on a B-tree requires only $O(\log_{\lceil d/2 \rceil} n)$, that is, $O(\log n / \log B)$, disk transfers. For example, an insert operation proceeds down the B-tree to locate the node in which to insert the new entry. If the node would ***overflow*** (to have $d + 1$ children) because of this addition, then this node is ***split*** into two nodes that have $\lfloor (d+1)/2 \rfloor$ and $\lceil (d+1)/2 \rceil$ children, respectively. This process is then repeated at the next level up, and will continue for at most $O(\log_B n)$ levels.

Likewise, if a remove operation results in a node ***underflow*** (to have $\lceil d/2 \rceil - 1$ children), then we move references from a sibling node with at least $\lceil d/2 \rceil + 1$ children or we need to perform a ***fusion*** operation of this node with its sibling (and repeat this computation at the parent). As with the insert operation, this will continue up the B-tree for at most $O(\log_B n)$ levels. The requirement that each internal node have at least $\lceil d/2 \rceil$ children implies that each disk block used to support a B-tree is at least half full. Thus, we have the following:

Proposition 9.12: *A B-tree with n entries has I/O complexity $O(\log_B n)$ for search or update operation, and uses $O(n/B)$ blocks, where B is the size of a block.*

9.7   Exercises

For source code and help with exercises, please visit **java.datastructures.net**.

Reinforcement

R-9.1   Insert, into an empty binary search tree, entries with keys 30, 40, 24, 58, 48, 26, 11, 13 (in this order). Draw the tree after each insertion.

R-9.2   Suppose that the methods of BinarySearchTree (Code Fragments 9.2–9.4) are used to perform the updates shown in Figures 9.4, 9.5, and 9.6. What is the node referenced by actionPos after each update?

R-9.3   Dr. Amongus claims that the order in which a fixed set of entries is inserted into a binary search tree does not matter—the same tree results every time. Give a small example that proves he is wrong.

R-9.4   Dr. Amongus claims that the order in which a fixed set of entries is inserted into an AVL tree does not matter—the same AVL tree results every time. Give a small example that proves he is wrong.

R-9.5   Are the rotations in Figures 9.9 and 9.11 single or double rotations?

R-9.6   Draw the AVL tree resulting from the insertion of an entry with key 52 into the AVL tree of Figure 9.11b.

R-9.7   Draw the AVL tree resulting from the removal of the entry with key 62 from the AVL tree of Figure 9.11b.

R-9.8   Explain why performing a rotation in an n-node binary tree represented using a vector takes $\Omega(n)$ time.

R-9.9   Is the search tree of Figure 9.20a a $(2,4)$ tree? Why or why not?

R-9.10   An alternative way of performing a split at a node v in a $(2,4)$ tree is to partition v into v' and v'', with v' being a 2-node and v'' a 3-node. Which of the keys k_1, k_2, k_3, or k_4 do we store at v's parent in this case? Why?

R-9.11   Dr. Amongus claims that a $(2,4)$ tree storing a set of entries will always have the same structure, regardless of the order in which the entries are inserted. Show that he is wrong.

R-9.12   Draw four different red-black trees that correspond to the same $(2,4)$ tree.

R-9.13 Consider the sequence of keys $(5, 16, 22, 45, 2, 10, 18, 30, 50, 12, 1)$. Draw the result of inserting entries with these keys (in the given order) into
    a. An initially empty $(2,4)$ tree.
    b. An initially empty red-black tree.

R-9.14 For the following statements about red-black trees, provide a justification for each true statement and a counterexample for each false one.
    a. A subtree of a red-black tree is itself a red-black tree.
    b. The sibling of an external node is either external or it is red.
    c. There is a unique $(2,4)$ tree associated with a given red-black tree.
    d. There is a unique red-black tree associated with a given $(2,4)$ tree.

R-9.15 Draw an example red-black tree that is not an AVL tree.

R-9.16 Consider a tree T storing 100,000 entries. What is the worst-case height of T in the following cases?
    a. T is an AVL tree.
    b. T is a $(2,4)$ tree.
    c. T is a red-black tree.
    d. T is a splay tree.
    e. T is a binary search tree.

R-9.17 Perform the following sequence of operations in an initially empty splay tree and draw the tree after each set of operations.
    a. Insert keys 0, 2, 4, 6, 8, 10, 12, 14, 16, 18, in this order.
    b. Search for keys 1, 3, 5, 7, 9, 11, 13, 15, 17, 19, in this order.
    c. Delete keys 0, 2, 4, 6, 8, 10, 12, 14, 16, 18, in this order.

R-9.18 What does a splay tree look like if its entries are accessed in increasing order by their keys?

R-9.19 Give, in pseudo-code, insertion and removal algorithms for an (a,b) tree.

R-9.20 If T is a multi-way tree such that each internal node has at least five and at most eight children, for what values of a and b is T a valid (a,b) tree?

R-9.21 For what values of d is the tree T of Exercise R-9.20 an order-d B-tree?

R-9.22 Draw the result of inserting into an initially empty order-7 B-tree entries with keys $(4,40,23,50,11,34,62,78,66,22,90,59,25,72,64,77,39,12)$, in this order.

R-9.23 Show each level of recursion in performing a four-way merge-sort of the sequence given in the previous exercise.

Creativity

C-9.1 Design a variation of algorithm TreeSearch for performing the operation findAll(k) in an ordered dictionary implemented with a binary search tree T, and show that it runs in time $O(h+s)$, where h is the height of T and s is the size of the iterator returned.

C-9.2 Describe how to perform an operation removeAll(k), which removes all the entries whose keys equal k in an ordered dictionary implemented with a binary search tree T, and show that this method runs in time $O(h+s)$, where h is the height of T and s is the size of the iterator returned.

C-9.3 Draw a schematic of an AVL tree such that a single remove operation could require $\Omega(\log n)$ trinode restructurings (or rotations) from a leaf to the root in order to restore the height-balance property.

C-9.4 Show how to perform an operation, removeAll(k), which removes all entries with keys equal to K, in a dictionary implemented with an AVL tree in time $O(s \log n)$, where n is the number of entries in the dictionary and s is the size of the iterator returned.

C-9.5 If we maintain a reference to the position of the left-most internal node of an AVL tree, then operation first (Section 8.5.2) can be performed in $O(1)$ time. Describe how the implementation of the other dictionary methods needs to be modified to maintain a reference to the left-most position.

C-9.6 Show that any n-node binary tree can be converted to any other n-node binary tree using $O(n)$ rotations.

C-9.7 Let D be an ordered dictionary with n entries implemented by means of an AVL tree. Show how to implement the following operation on D in time $O(\log n + s)$, where s is the size of the iterator returned:

findAllInRange(k_1, k_2): Return an iterator of all the entries in D with key k such that $k_1 \leq k \leq k_2$.
Input: Objects (keys); *Output:* Iterator.

C-9.8 Let D be an ordered dictionary with n entries. Show how to modify the AVL tree to implement the following method for D in time $O(\log n)$:

countAllInRange(k_1, k_2): Compute and return the number of entries in D with key k such that $k_1 \leq k \leq k_2$.
Input: Objects; *Output:* Integer.

C-9.9 Show that the nodes that become unbalanced in an AVL tree after operation insertAtExternal is performed, within the execution of an insert operation, may be nonconsecutive on the path from the newly inserted node to the root.

C-9.10 Show that at most one node in an AVL tree becomes unbalanced after operation removeExternal is performed within the execution of a remove dictionary operation.

C-9.11 Show that at most one trinode restructuring operation is needed to restore balance after any insertion in an AVL tree.

C-9.12 Let T and U be $(2,4)$ trees storing n and m entries, respectively, such that all the entries in T have keys less than the keys of all the entries in U. Describe an $O(\log n + \log m)$ time method for *joining* T and U into a single tree that stores all the entries in T and U.

C-9.13 Repeat the previous problem for red-black trees T and U.

C-9.14 Justify Proposition 9.6.

C-9.15 The Boolean indicator used to mark nodes in a red-black tree as being "red" or "black" is not strictly needed when we have distinct keys. Describe a scheme for implementing a red-black tree without adding any extra space to standard binary search tree nodes. How does your scheme affect the search and update times?

C-9.16 Let T be a red-black tree storing n entries, and let k be the key of an entry in T. Show how to construct from T, in $O(\log n)$ time, two red-black trees T' and T'', such that T' contains all the keys of T less than k, and T'' contains all the keys of T greater than k. This operation destroys T.

C-9.17 Show that the nodes of any AVL tree T can be colored "red" and "black" so that T becomes a red-black tree.

C-9.18 The ***mergeable heap*** ADT consists of operations insert(k,x), removeMin(), unionWith(h), and min(), where the unionWith(h) operation performs a union of the mergeable heap h with the present one, destroying the old versions of both. Describe a concrete implementation of the mergeable heap ADT that achieves $O(\log n)$ performance for all its operations.

C-9.19 Consider a variation of splay trees, called ***half-splay trees***, where splaying a node at depth d stops as soon as the node reaches depth $\lfloor d/2 \rfloor$. Perform an amortized analysis of half-splay trees.

C-9.20 The standard splaying step requires two passes, one downward pass to find the node x to splay, followed by an upward pass to splay the node x. Describe a method for splaying and searching for x in one downward pass. Each substep now requires that you consider the next two nodes in the path down to x, with a possible zig substep performed at the end. Describe how to perform the zig-zig, zig-zag, and zig steps.

C-9.21 Describe a sequence of accesses to an n-node splay tree T, where n is odd, that results in T consisting of a single chain of internal nodes with external node children, such that the internal-node path down T alternates between left children and right children.

C-9.22 Show how to implement a dictionary in external memory using an un-ordered list so that updates execute $O(1)$ transfers and searches execute $O(n/B)$ transfers, where n is the number of entries and B is the number of list nodes that can fit into a disk block.

C-9.23 Change the rules that define red-black trees so that each red-black tree T has a corresponding $(4,8)$ tree, and vice versa.

C-9.24 Describe a modified version of the B-tree insertion algorithm so that each time we create an overflow because of a split of a node v, we redistribute entries among all of v's siblings such that each sibling holds roughly the same number of entries (possibly cascading the split up to the parent of v). What is the minimum fraction of each block that will always be filled using this scheme?

C-9.25 Suppose that instead of having the node-search function $f(d) = 1$ in an order-d B-tree T, we instead have $f(d) = \log d$. What does the asymptotic running time of performing a search in T now become?

C-9.26 Describe how to use a B-tree to implement the queue ADT so that the total number of disk transfers needed to process a sequence of n enqueue and dequeue operations is $O(n/B)$.

C-9.27 Suppose we are given a list S of n entries with integer keys such that some entries in S are colored "blue" and some entries in S are colored "red." In addition, say that a red entry e **pairs** with a blue entry f if they have the same key value. Describe an efficient external-memory algorithm for finding all the red-blue pairs in S. How many disk transfers does your algorithm perform?

C-9.28 Describe an external-memory algorithm that determines using $O(n/B)$ transfers whether a list of n integers contains an value occurring more than $n/2$ times.

C-9.29 Another possible external-memory dictionary implementation is to use a skip list, but to collect in individual blocks consecutive groups of $O(B)$ nodes on any level in the skip list. In particular, we define an **order-d B-skip list** to be such a representation of a skip list structure, where each block contains at least $\lceil d/2 \rceil$ list nodes and at most d list nodes. Let us also choose d in this case to be the maximum number of list nodes from a level of a skip list that can fit into one block. Describe insertion and removal algorithms for a B-skip list so that the expected height of the structure is $O(\log n/\log B)$.

Projects

P-9.1 Extend class BinarySearchTree (Code Fragments 9.2–9.4) to support the methods of the ordered dictionary ADT (see Section 8.5.2).

P-9.2 Implement a class RestructurableNodeBinaryTree that supports the methods of the binary tree ADT, plus a method restructure for performing a rotation operation. This class is a component of the implementation of an AVL tree given in Section 9.2.2.

P-9.3 Write a Java class that can take any red-black tree and convert it into its corresponding $(2,4)$ tree and can take any $(2,4)$ tree and convert it into its corresponding red-black tree.

P-9.4 Write a Java class that implements all the methods of the ordered dictionary ADT (see Section 8.5.2) using an AVL tree.

P-9.5 Write a Java class that implements all the methods of the ordered dictionary ADT (see Section 8.5.2) using a $(2,4)$ tree.

P-9.6 Write a Java class that implements all the methods of the ordered dictionary ADT (see Section 8.5.2) using a red-black tree.

P-9.7 Form a three-programmer team and have each member implement a different one of the previous three projects. Perform extensive experimental studies to compare the speed of these three implementations. Design three sets of experiments, each favoring a different implementation.

P-9.8   Perform an experimental study to compare the performance of a red-black tree with that of a skip list.

P-9.9   Prepare an implementation of splay trees that uses bottom-up splaying as described in this chapter and another that uses top-down splaying as described in Exercise C-9.20. Perform extensive experimental studies to see which implementation is better in practice, if any.

P-9.10 Write a Java class that implements all the methods of the ordered dictionary ADT by means of an (a,b) tree, where a and b are integer constants passed as parameters to a constructor.

P-9.11 Implement the B-tree data structure, assuming a block size of $1,024$ and integer keys. Test the number of "disk transfers" needed to process a sequence of dictionary operations.

Chapter Notes

Some of the data structures discussed in this chapter are extensively covered by Knuth in his *Sorting and Searching* book [59], and by Mehlhorn in [71]. AVL trees are due to Adel'son-Vel'skii and Landis [1], who invented this class of balanced search trees in 1962. Binary search trees, AVL trees, and hashing are described in Knuth's *Sorting and Searching* [59] book. Average-height analyses for binary search trees can be found in the books by Aho, Hopcroft, and Ullman [5] and Cormen, Leiserson, and Rivest [24]. The handbook by Gonnet and Baeza-Yates [40] contains a number of theoretical and experimental comparisons among dictionary implementations. Aho, Hopcroft, and Ullman [4] discuss $(2,3)$ trees, which are similar to $(2,4)$ trees. Red-black trees were defined by Bayer [10]. Variations and interesting properties of red-black trees are presented in a paper by Guibas and Sedgewick [45]. The reader interested in learning more about different balanced tree data structures is referred to the books by Mehlhorn [71] and Tarjan [89], and the book chapter by Mehlhorn and Tsakalidis [73]. Knuth [59] is excellent additional reading that includes early approaches to balancing trees.

B-trees were invented by Bayer and McCreight [11], and Comer [23] provides a very nice overview of this data structure. The books by Mehlhorn [71] and Samet [81] also have nice discussions about B-trees and their variants. Aggarwal and Vitter [2] study the I/O complexity of sorting and related problems, establishing upper and lower bounds, including the lower bound for sorting given in this chapter. The reader interested in further study of I/O-efficient algorithms is encouraged to examine the survey paper of Vitter [92].

Splay trees were invented by Sleator and Tarjan [84] (see also [89]).

Chapter

10

Sorting, Sets, and Selection

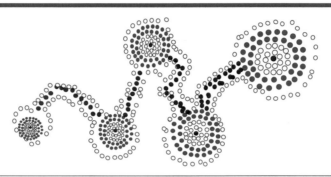

Contents

The Second Law of Thermodynamics suggests that Nature tends toward disorder. Humans, on the other hand, prefer order. Indeed, there are several advantages to keeping data in order. For example, the binary search algorithm, discussed in Section 8.3.1, works correctly only for an ordered vector. Since computers are intended to be tools for humans, we devote this chapter to the study of sorting algorithms and their applications. We recall that the sorting problem is defined as follows. Let S be a sequence of n elements that can be compared to each other according to a total order relation, that is, it is always possible to compare two elements of S to see which is larger or smaller, or if the two of them are equal. We want to rearrange S in such a way that the elements appear in increasing order (or in nondecreasing order if there are equal elements in S).

We have already presented several sorting algorithms in the previous chapters. In particular, in Section 7.1.4, we presented a simple sorting scheme, which is called PriorityQueueSort, that consists of inserting elements into a priority queue and then extracting them in nondecreasing order, by means of a series of removeMin operations. If the priority queue is implemented by means of a list, then PriorityQueueSort runs in $O(n^2)$ time and corresponds to the sorting method known as either insertion-sort or selection-sort, depending on whether the list realizing the priority queue is kept ordered or not (Section 7.2.3). If instead the priority queue is implemented by means of a heap (Section 7.3), then PriorityQueueSort runs in $O(n \log n)$ time and corresponds to the sorting method known as heap-sort (Section 7.3.5).

In this chapter, we present four other sorting algorithms, called ***merge-sort***, ***quick-sort***, ***bucket-sort***, and ***radix-sort***. We also introduce the ***set*** abstract data type and show how a simple data structure can implement the methods union and find with surprising efficiency. Throughout this chapter, we assume that a total order relation is defined over the elements to be sorted. If this relation is induced by a comparator (Section 7.1.2), we assume that a comparison test takes $O(1)$ time.

The first two algorithms we describe, merge-sort and quick-sort, are based on using recursion in an algorithmic design pattern called ***divide-and-conquer***, which is both powerful and general. We have already seen the power of recursion in describing algorithms in an elegant manner (for example, in the tree traversal techniques presented in Chapter 6). In this chapter, we show how it can be applied to solving the important sorting problem to yield algorithms running in $O(n \log n)$ time in the worst case or expected case. We also show that the $O(n \log n)$ time bound is the best possible for a comparison-based sorting algorithm. Interestingly, we show how to beat this running time, in the bucket-sort and radix-sort algorithms, by basing our algorithms on something other than comparisons, though at the cost of significantly restricting the kinds of objects we can sort.

10.1 Merge-Sort

In this section, we present a sorting technique, called *merge-sort*, which can be described in a simple and compact way using recursion.

10.1.1 Divide-and-Conquer

Merge-sort is based on an algorithmic design pattern called *divide-and-conquer*. The divide-and-conquer pattern consists of the following three steps:

1. *Divide:* If the input size is smaller than a certain threshold (say, one or two elements), solve the problem directly using a straightforward method and return the solution so obtained. Otherwise, divide the input data into two or more disjoint subsets.
2. *Recur:* Recursively solve the subproblems associated with the subsets.
3. *Conquer:* Take the solutions to the subproblems and "merge" them into a solution to the original problem.

Using Divide-and-Conquer for Sorting

Recall that in the sorting problem we are given a sequence of n objects, stored in a linked list or an array, together with some comparator defining a total order on these objects, and we are asked to produce an ordered representation of these objects. To allow for sorting of either representation, we will describe our sorting algorithm at a high level for sequences and explain the details needed to implement it for linked lists and arrays. To sort a sequence S with n elements using the three divide-and-conquer steps, the merge-sort algorithm proceeds as follows:

1. *Divide:* If S has zero or one element, return S immediately; it is already sorted. Otherwise (S has at least two elements), remove all the elements from S and put them into two sequences, S_1 and S_2, each containing about half of the elements of S; that is, S_1 contains the first $\lceil n/2 \rceil$ elements of S, and S_2 contains the remaining $\lfloor n/2 \rfloor$ elements.
2. *Recur:* Recursively sort sequences S_1 and S_2.
3. *Conquer:* Put back the elements into S by merging the sorted sequences S_1 and S_2 into a sorted sequence.

In reference to the divide step, we recall that the notation $\lceil x \rceil$ indicates the *ceiling* of x, that is, the smallest integer m, such that $x \leq m$. Similarly, the notation $\lfloor x \rfloor$ indicates the *floor* of x, that is, the largest integer k, such that $k \leq x$.

We can visualize an execution of the merge-sort algorithm by means of a binary tree T, called the *merge-sort tree*. Each node of T represents a recursive invocation (or call) of the merge-sort algorithm. We associate with each node v of T the sequence S that is processed by the invocation associated with v. The children of node v are associated with the recursive calls that process the subsequences S_1 and S_2 of S. The external nodes of T are associated with individual elements of S, corresponding to instances of the algorithm that make no recursive calls.

Figure 10.1 summarizes an execution of the merge-sort algorithm by showing the input and output sequences processed at each node of the merge-sort tree. The step-by-step evolution of the merge-sort tree is shown in Figures 10.2 through 10.5.

This algorithm visualization in terms of the merge-sort tree helps us analyze the running time of the merge-sort algorithm. In particular, since the size of the input sequence roughly halves at each recursive call of merge-sort, the height of the merge-sort tree is about $\log n$ (recall that the base of log is 2 if omitted).

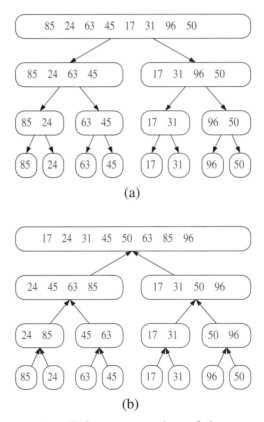

Figure 10.1: Merge-sort tree T for an execution of the merge-sort algorithm on a sequence with 8 elements: (a) input sequences processed at each node of T; (b) output sequences generated at each node of T.

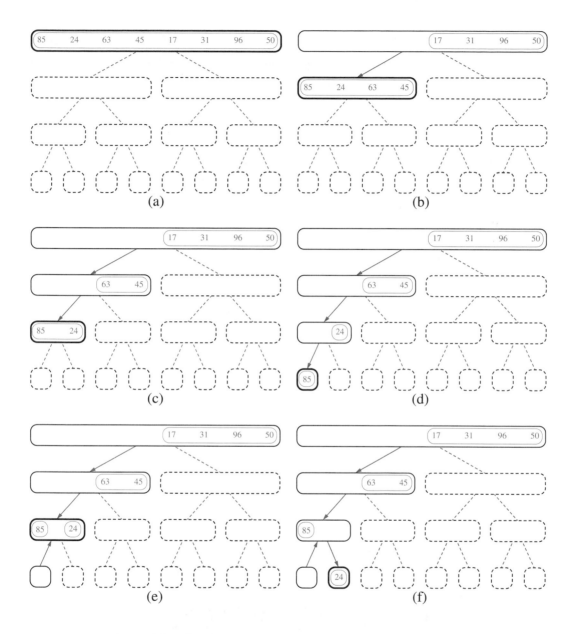

Figure 10.2: Visualization of an execution of merge-sort. Each node of the tree represents a recursive call of merge-sort. The nodes drawn with dashed lines represent calls that have not been made yet. The node drawn with thick lines represents the current call. The empty nodes drawn with thin lines represent completed calls. The remaining nodes (drawn with thin lines and not empty) represent calls that are waiting for a child invocation to return(Continues in Figure 10.3.)

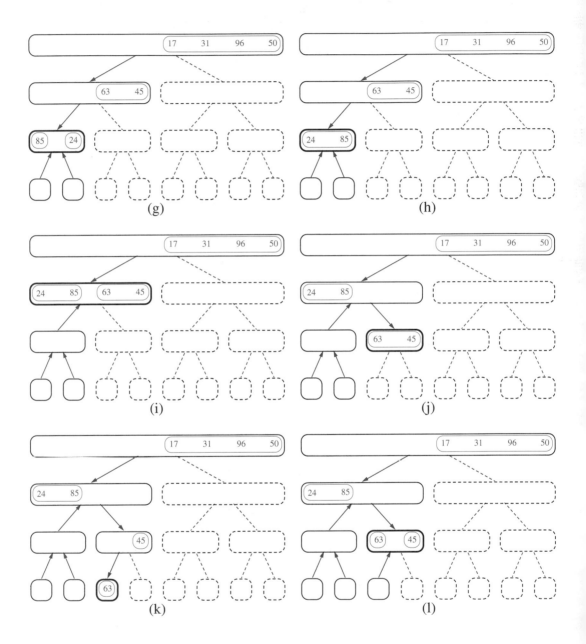

Figure 10.3: Visualization of an execution of merge-sort. Note the conquer step performed in (h). (Continues in Figure 10.4.)

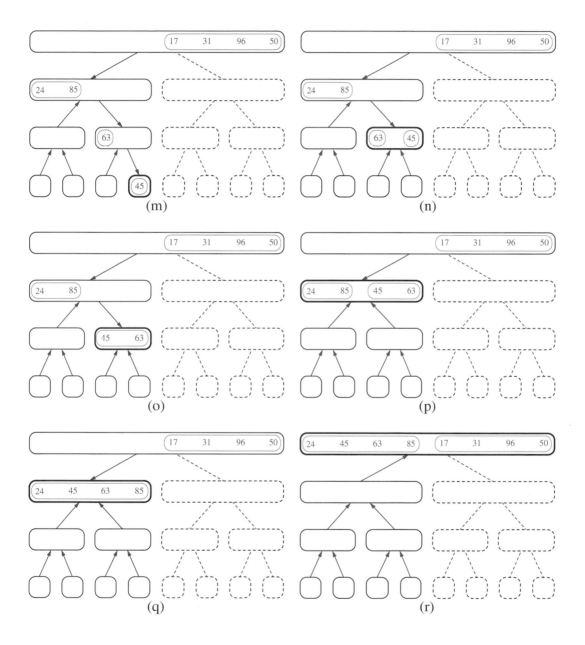

Figure 10.4: Visualization of an execution of merge-sort. Note the conquer steps performed in (o) and (q). (Continues in Fig. 10.5.)

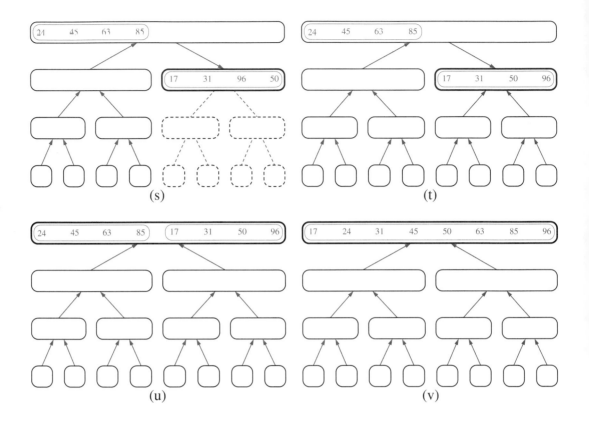

Figure 10.5: Visualization of an execution of merge-sort. Several invocations are omitted between (s) and (t). Note the conquer steps performed in (t) and (v) . (Continued from Figure 10.4.)

Proposition 10.1: *The merge-sort tree associated with an execution of merge-sort on a sequence of size n has height $\lceil \log n \rceil$.*

We leave the justification of Proposition 10.1 as a simple exercise (R-10.1). We will use this proposition to analyze the running time of the merge-sort algorithm.

Having given an overview of merge-sort and an illustration of how it works, let us consider each of the steps of this divide-and-conquer algorithm in more detail. The divide and recur steps of the merge-sort algorithm are simple; dividing a sequence of size n involves separating it at the element with rank $\lceil n/2 \rceil$, and the recursive calls simply involve passing these smaller sequences as parameters. The difficult step is the conquer step, which merges two sorted sequences into a single sorted sequence. Thus, before we present our analysis of merge-sort, we need to say more about how this is done.

10.1.2 Merging Arrays and Lists

To merge two sorted sequences, it is helpful to know if they are implemented as arrays or lists. Thus, we give detailed pseudo-code in this section describing how to merge two sorted sequences represented as arrays and as linked lists.

Merging Two Sorted Arrays

We begin with the array implementation, which we show in Code Fragment 10.1. We illustrate a step in the merge of two sorted arrays in Figure 10.6.

Algorithm merge(S_1, S_2, S):

    Input: Sorted sequences S_1 and S_2 and an empty sequence S, all of which are implemented as arrays

    Output: Sorted sequence S containing the elements from S_1 and S_2

    $i \leftarrow j \leftarrow 0$

    while $i < S_1$.size() **and** $j < S_2$.size() **do**

        if S_1.elemAtRank(i) $\leq S_2$.elemAtRank(j) **then**

            S.insertLast(S_1.elemAtRank(i)) { copy ith element of S_1 to end of S }

            $i \leftarrow i+1$

        else

            S.insertLast(S_2.elemAtRank(j)) { copy jth element of S_2 to end of S }

            $j \leftarrow j+1$

    while $i < S_1$.size() **do** {copy the remaining elements of S_1 to S}

        S.insertLast(S_1.elemAtRank(i))

        $i \leftarrow i+1$

    while $j < S_2$.size() **do** {copy the remaining elements of S_2 to S}

        S.insertLast(S_2.elemAtRank(j))

        $j \leftarrow j+1$

Code Fragment 10.1: Algorithm for merging two sorted array-based sequences.

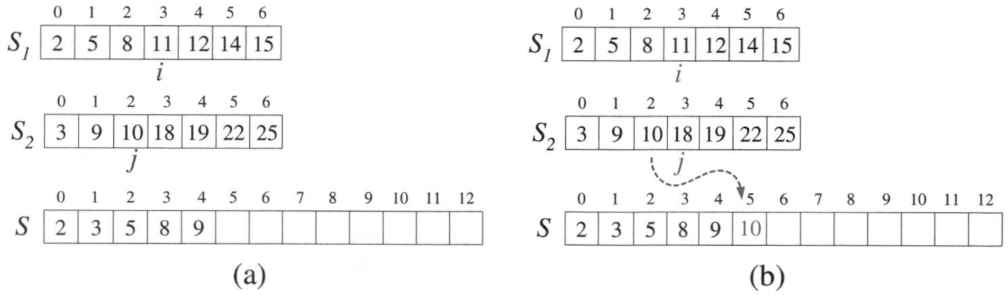

Figure 10.6: A step in the merge of two sorted arrays. We show the arrays before the copy step in (a) and after it in (b).

Merging Two Sorted Lists

In Code Fragment 10.2, we give a list-based version of algorithm merge, for merging two sorted sequences, S_1 and S_2, implemented as linked lists. The main idea is to iteratively remove a smallest element from the front of one of the two lists and add it to the end of the output sequence, S, until one of the two input lists is empty, at which point we copy the remainder of the other list to S. We show an example execution of this version of algorithm merge in Figure 10.7.

Algorithm merge(S_1, S_2, S):

    Input: Sorted sequences S_1 and S_2 and an empty sequence S, implemented as linked lists

    Output: Sorted sequence S containing the elements from S_1 and S_2

    while S_1 is not empty **and** S_2 is not empty **do**

        if S_1.first().element() $\leq S_2$.first().element() **then**

            { move the first element of S_1 at the end of S }

            S.insertLast(S_1.remove(S_1.first()))

        else

            { move the first element of S_2 at the end of S }

            S.insertLast(S_2.remove(S_2.first()))

    { move the remaining elements of S_1 to S }

    while S_1 is not empty **do**

        S.insertLast(S_1.remove(S_1.first()))

    { move the remaining elements of S_2 to S }

    while S_2 is not empty **do**

        S.insertLast(S_2.remove(S_2.first()))

Code Fragment 10.2: Algorithm merge for merging two sorted sequences implemented as linked lists.

The Running Time for Merging

We analyze the running time of the merge algorithm by making some simple observations. Let n_1 and n_2 be the number of elements of S_1 and S_2, respectively. Algorithm merge has three **while** loops. Independent of whether we are analyzing the array-based version or the list-based version, the operations performed inside each loop take $O(1)$ time each. The key observation is that during each iteration of one of the loops, one element is copied or moved from either S_1 or S_2 into S (and that element is considered no further). Since no insertions are performed into S_1 or S_2, this observation implies that the overall number of iterations of the three loops is $n_1 + n_2$. Thus, the running time of algorithm merge is $O(n_1 + n_2)$.

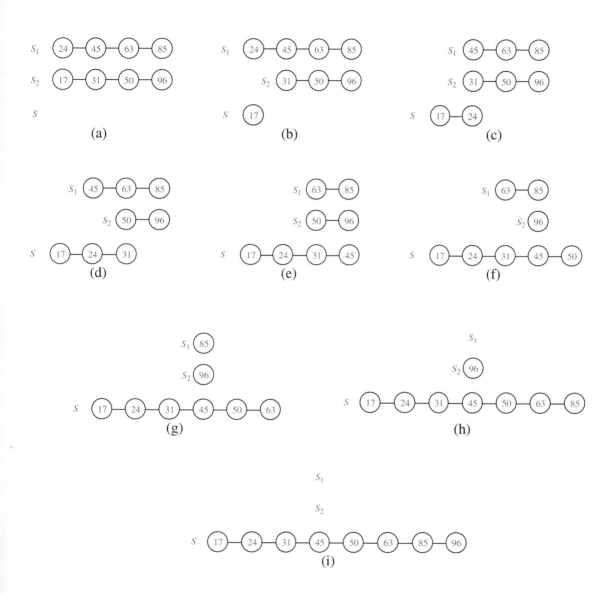

Figure 10.7: Example of execution of algorithm merge shown in Code Fragment 10.2.

10.1.3   The Running Time of Merge-Sort

Now that we have given the details of the merge-sort algorithm, in both its array-based and list-based versions, and we have analyzed the running time of the crucial merge algorithm used in the conquer step, let us analyze the running time of the entire merge-sort algorithm, assuming it is given an input sequence of n elements. For simplicity, we restrict our attention to the case where n is a power of 2. We leave it to an exercise (R-10.4) to show that the result of our analysis also holds when n is not a power of 2.

As we did in the analysis of the merge algorithm, we assume that the input sequence S and the auxiliary sequences S_1 and S_2, created by each recursive call of merge-sort, are implemented by either arrays or linked lists (the same as S), so that merging two sorted sequences can be done in linear time.

As we mentioned earlier, we analyze the merge-sort algorithm by referring to the merge-sort tree T. (Recall Figures 10.2 through 10.5.) We call the ***time spent at a node*** v of T the running time of the recursive call associated with v, excluding the time taken waiting for the recursive calls associated with the children of v to terminate. In other words, the time spent at node v includes the running times of the divide and conquer steps, but excludes the running time of the recur step. We have already observed that the details of the divide step are straightforward; this step runs in time proportional to the size of the sequence for v. In addition, as discussed above, the conquer step, which consists of merging two sorted subsequences, also takes linear time, independent of whether we are dealing with arrays or linked lists. That is, letting i denote the depth of node v, the time spent at node v is $O(n/2^i)$, since the size of the sequence handled by the recursive call associated with v is equal to $n/2^i$.

Looking at the tree T more globally, as shown in Figure 10.8, we see that, given our definition of "time spent at a node," the running time of merge-sort is equal to the sum of the times spent at the nodes of T. Observe that T has exactly 2^i nodes at depth i. This simple observation has an important consequence, for it implies that the overall time spent at all the nodes of T at depth i is $O(2^i \cdot n/2^i)$, which is $O(n)$. By Proposition 10.1, the height of T is $\lceil \log n \rceil$. Thus, since the time spent at each of the $\lceil \log n \rceil + 1$ levels of T is $O(n)$, we have the following result:

Proposition 10.2: *Algorithm merge-sort sorts a sequence S of size n in $O(n \log n)$ time, assuming two elements of S can be compared in $O(1)$ time.*

In other words, the merge-sort algorithm asymptotically matches the fast running time of the heap-sort algorithm.

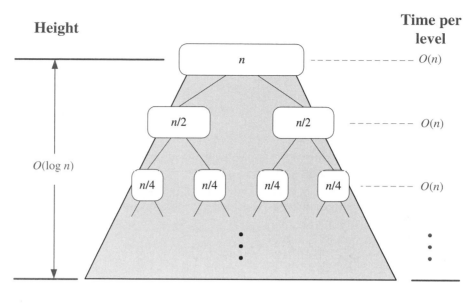

Figure 10.8: A visual time analysis of the merge-sort tree T. Each node is shown labeled with the size of its subproblem.

10.1.4 Java Implementations of Merge-Sort

In this section, we present two Java implementations of the merge-sort algorithm, one for lists and the other for arrays.

A Recursive List-Based Implementation of Merge-Sort

In Code Fragment 10.3, we show a complete Java implementation of the list-based merge-sort algorithm as a static recursive method, mergeSort. A comparator (see Section 7.1.2) is used to decide the relative order of two elements.

In this implementation, the input is a list, L, and auxiliary lists, L1 and L2, are processed by the recursive calls. Each list is modified by insertions and deletions only at the head and tail; hence, each list update takes $O(1)$ time, assuming the lists are implemented with doubly linked lists (see Table 5.4). In our code, we use class NodeList (Code Fragments 5.9–5.11) for the auxiliary lists. Thus, for a list L of size n, method mergeSort(L, c) runs in time $O(n \log n)$ provided the list L is implemented with a doubly linked list and the comparator c can compare two elements of L in $O(1)$ time.

```java
/**
 * Sort the elements of list L in nondecreasing order according
 * to comparator c, using the merge-sort algorithm.
 **/
public static void mergeSort (List L, Comparator c) {
  int n = L.size();
  if (n < 2)
    return;  // the list L is already sorted in this case
  // divide
  List L1 = new NodeList(); // first list used in recursion
  List L2 = new NodeList(); // second list used in recursion
  int i = 0;
  while (i < n/2) {
    L1.insertLast(L.remove(L.first())); // move the first n/2 elements to L1
    i++;
  }
  while (!L.isEmpty())
    L2.insertLast(L.remove(L.first())); // move the rest to L2
  // recurse
  mergeSort(L1,c);
  mergeSort(L2,c);
  //conquer
  merge(L1,L2,c,L);
}


/**
 * Merge two sorted lists, L1 and L2, into a sorted list L.
 **/
public static void merge(List L1, List L2, Comparator c, List L) {
  while (!L1.isEmpty() && !L2.isEmpty())
    if (c.compare(L1.first().element(), L2.first().element()) <= 0)
      L.insertLast(L1.remove(L1.first()));
    else
      L.insertLast(L2.remove(L2.first()));
  while(!L1.isEmpty()) // move the remaining elements of L1
    L.insertLast(L1.remove(L1.first()));
  while(!L2.isEmpty()) // move the remaining elements of L2
    L.insertLast(L2.remove(L2.first()));
}
```

Code Fragment 10.3: Methods mergeSort and merge implementing the recursive merge-sort algorithm.

A Nonrecursive Array-Based Implementation of Merge-Sort

There is a nonrecursive version of array-based merge-sort, which runs in $O(n \log n)$ time. It is a bit faster than recursive list-based merge-sort in practice, as it avoids the extra overheads of recursive calls and node creation. The main idea is to perform merge-sort bottom-up, performing the merges level-by-level going up the merge-sort tree. Given an input array of elements, we begin by merging every odd-even pair of elements into sorted runs of length two. We merge these runs into runs of length four, merge these new runs into runs of length eight, and so on, until the array is sorted. To keep the space usage reasonable, we deploy an output array that stores the merged runs (swapping input and output arrays after each iteration). We give a Java implementation in Code Fragment 10.4, where we use the built-in method System.arraycopy to copy a range of cells between two arrays.

```java
public static void mergeSort(Object[] orig, Comparator c) { // nonrecursive
    Object[] in = new Object[orig.length]; // make a new temporary array
    System.arraycopy(orig,0,in,0,in.length); // copy the input
    Object[] out = new Object[in.length]; // output array
    Object[] temp; // temp array reference used for swapping
    int n = in.length;
    for (int i=1; i < n; i*=2) { // each iteration sorts all length-2*i runs
        for (int j=0; j < n; j+=2*i) // each iteration merges two length-i pairs
            merge(in,out,c,j,i); // merge from in to out two length-i runs at j
        temp = in; in = out; out = temp; // swap arrays for next iteration
    }
    // the "in" array contains the sorted array, so re-copy it
    System.arraycopy(in,0,orig,0,in.length);
}
protected static void merge(Object[] in, Object[] out, Comparator c, int start,
        int inc) { // merge in[start..start+inc-1] and in[start+inc..start+2*inc-1]
    int x = start; // index into run #1
    int end1 = Math.min(start+inc, in.length); // boundary for run #1
    int end2 = Math.min(start+2*inc, in.length); // boundary for run #2
    int y = start+inc; // index into run #2 (could be beyond array boundary)
    int z = start; // index into the out array
    while ((x < end1) && (y < end2))
        if (c.compare(in[x],in[y]) <= 0) out[z++] = in[x++];
        else out[z++] = in[y++];
    if (x < end1) // first run didn't finish
        System.arraycopy(in, x, out, z, end1 − x);
    else if (y < end2) // second run didn't finish
        System.arraycopy(in, y, out, z, end2 − y);
}
```

Code Fragment 10.4: An implementation of the nonrecursive merge-sort algorithm.

10.1.5   Merge-Sort and Recurrence Equations ⋆

There is another way to justify that the running time of the merge-sort algorithm is $O(n \log n)$ (Proposition 10.2). Namely, we can deal more directly with the recursive nature of the merge-sort algorithm. In this section, we present such an analysis of the running time of merge-sort, and in so doing introduce the mathematical concept of a ***recurrence equation*** (also known as ***recurrence relation***).

Let the function $t(n)$ denote the worst-case running time of merge-sort on an input sequence of size n. Since merge-sort is recursive, we can characterize function $t(n)$ by means of an equation where the function $t(n)$ is recursively expressed in terms of itself. In order to simplify our characterization of $t(n)$, let us restrict our attention to the case when n is a power of 2. (We leave the problem of showing that our asymptotic characterization still holds in the general case as an exercise.) In this case, we can specify the definition of $t(n)$ as

$$t(n) = \begin{cases} b & \text{if } n \leq 1 \\ 2t(n/2) + cn & \text{otherwise.} \end{cases}$$

An expression such as the one above is called a ***recurrence equation***, since the function appears on both the left- and right-hand sides of the equal sign. Although such a characterization is correct and accurate, what we really desire is a big-Oh type of characterization of $t(n)$ that does not involve the function $t(n)$ itself. That is, we want a ***closed-form*** characterization of $t(n)$.

We can obtain a closed-form solution by applying the definition of a recurrence equation, assuming n is relatively large. For example, after one more application of the above equation, we can write a new recurrence for $t(n)$ as

$$\begin{aligned} t(n) &= 2(2t(n/2^2) + (cn/2)) + cn \\ &= 2^2 t(n/2^2) + 2(cn/2) + cn = 2^2 t(n/2^2) + 2cn. \end{aligned}$$

If we apply the equation again, we get $t(n) = 2^3 t(n/2^3) + 3cn$. At this point, we should see a pattern emerging, so that after applying this equation i times we get

$$t(n) = 2^i t(n/2^i) + icn.$$

The issue that remains, then, is to determine when to stop this process. To see when to stop, recall that we switch to the closed form $t(n) = b$ when $n \leq 1$, which will occur when $2^i = n$. In other words, this will occur when $i = \log n$. Making this substitution, then, yields

$$\begin{aligned} t(n) &= 2^{\log n} t(n/2^{\log n}) + (\log n)cn \\ &= nt(1) + cn \log n \\ &= nb + cn \log n. \end{aligned}$$

That is, we get an alternative justification of the fact that $t(n)$ is $O(n \log n)$.

10.2 Quick-Sort

The next sorting algorithm we discuss is called *quick-sort*. Like merge-sort, this algorithm is also based on the *divide-and-conquer* paradigm, but it uses this technique in a somewhat opposite manner, as all the hard work is done *before* the recursive calls.

High-Level Description of Quick-Sort

The quick-sort algorithm sorts a sequence S using a simple recursive approach. The main idea is to apply the divide-and-conquer technique, whereby we divide S into subsequences, recur to sort each subsequence, and then combine the sorted subsequences by a simple concatenation. In particular, the quick-sort algorithm consists of the following three steps (see Figure 10.9):

1. ***Divide:*** If S has at least two elements (nothing needs to be done if S has zero or one element), select a specific element x from S, which is called the ***pivot***. As is common practice, choose the pivot x to be the last element in S. Remove all the elements from S and put them into three sequences:

    - L, storing the elements in S less than x
    - E, storing the elements in S equal to x
    - G, storing the elements in S greater than x.

    Of course, if the elements of S are all distinct, then E holds just one element— the pivot itself.

2. ***Recur:*** Recursively sort sequences L and G.
3. ***Conquer:*** Put back the elements into S in order by first inserting the elements of L, then those of E, and finally those of G.

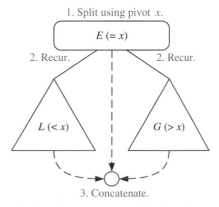

Figure 10.9: A visual schematic of the quick-sort algorithm.

Like merge-sort, the execution of quick-sort can be visualized by means of a binary recursion tree, called the *quick-sort tree*. Figure 10.10 summarizes an execution of the quick-sort algorithm by showing the input and output sequences processed at each node of the quick-sort tree. The step-by-step evolution of the quick-sort tree is shown in Figures 10.11, 10.12, and 10.13.

Unlike merge-sort, however, the height of the quick-sort tree associated with an execution of quick-sort is linear in the worst case. This happens, for example, if the sequence consists of n distinct elements and is already sorted. Indeed, in this case, the standard choice of the pivot as the largest element yields a subsequence L of size $n - 1$, while subsequence E has size 1 and subsequence G has size 0. At each invocation of quick-sort on subsequence L, the size decreases by 1. Hence, the height of the quick-sort tree is $n - 1$.

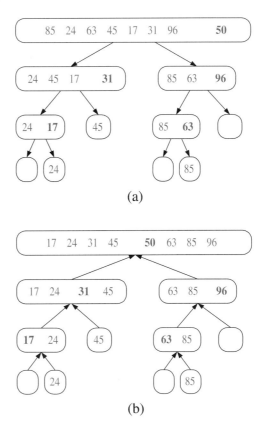

(a)

(b)

Figure 10.10: Quick-sort tree T for an execution of the quick-sort algorithm on a sequence with 8 elements: (a) input sequences processed at each node of T; (b) output sequences generated at each node of T. The pivot used at each level of the recursion is shown in bold.

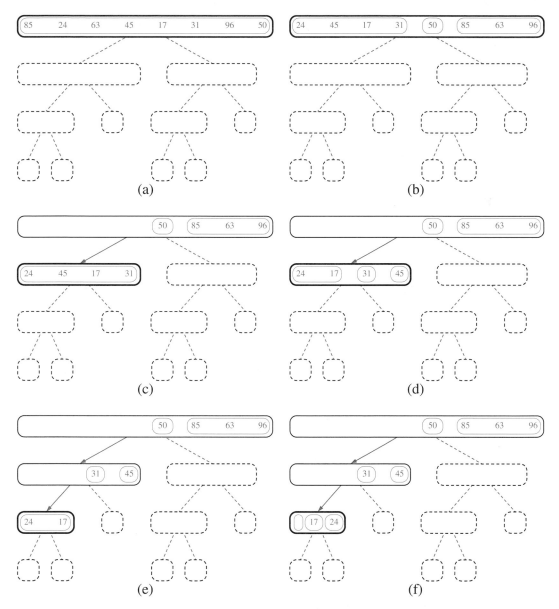

Figure 10.11: Visualization of quick-sort. Each node of the tree represents a recursive call. The nodes drawn with dashed lines represent calls that have not been made yet. The node drawn with thick lines represents the running invocation. The empty nodes drawn with thin lines represent terminated calls. The remaining nodes represent suspended calls (that is, active invocations that are waiting for a child invocation to return). Note the divide steps performed in (b), (d), and (f). (Continues in Figure 10.12.)

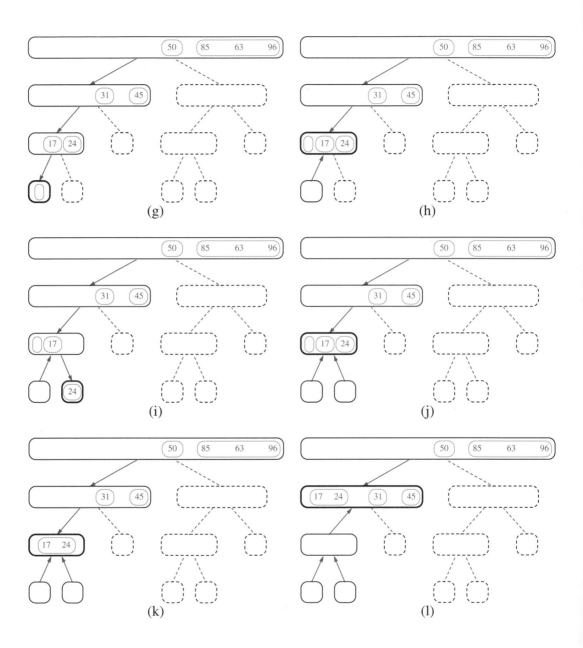

Figure 10.12: Visualization of an execution of quick-sort. Note the conquer step performed in (k). (Continues in Figure 10.13.)

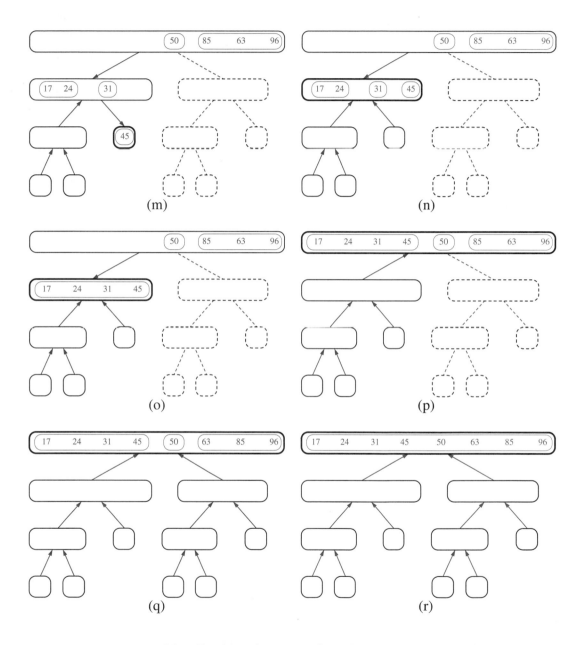

Figure 10.13: Visualization of an execution of quick-sort. Several invocations between (p) and (q) have been omitted. Note the conquer steps performed in (o) and (r). (Continued from Figure 10.12.)

Performing Quick-Sort on Arrays and Lists

In Code Fragment 10.5, we give a pseudo-code description of the quick-sort algorithm that is efficient for sequences implemented as arrays or linked lists. The algorithm follows the template for quick-sort given above, adding the detail of scanning the input sequence S backwards to divide it into the lists L, E, and G of elements that are respectively less than, equal to, and greater than the pivot. We perform this scan backwards, as removing the last element in a sequence is a constant-time operation independent of whether the sequence is implemented as an array or a linked list. We then recur on the L and G lists, and copy the sorted lists L, E, and G back to S. We perform this latter set of copies in the forward direction, since inserting elements at the end of a sequence is a constant-time operation independent of whether the sequence is implemented as an array or a linked list.

Algorithm QuickSort(S):

    Input: A sequence S implemented as an array or linked list

    Output: The sequence S in sorted order

    if S.size() ≤ 1 **then**

        return   {S is already sorted in this case}

    $p \leftarrow S$.last().element()   {the pivot}

    Let L, E, and G be empty list-based sequences

    while !S.isEmpty() **do** {scan S backwards, dividing it into L, E, and G}

        if S.last().element() $< p$ **then**

          L.insertLast(S.remove(S.last()))

        else if S.last().element() $= p$ **then**

          E.insertLast(S.remove(S.last()))

        else {the last element in S is greater than p}

          G.insertLast(S.remove(S.last())))

    QuickSort(L)   {Recur on the elements less than p}

    QuickSort(G)   {Recur on the elements greater than p}

    while !L.isEmpty() **do** {copy back to S the sorted elements less than p}

        S.insertLast(L.remove(L.first()))

    while !E.isEmpty() **do** {copy back to S the elements equal to p}

        S.insertLast(E.remove(E.first()))

    while !G.isEmpty() **do** {copy back to S the sorted elements greater than p}

        S.insertLast(G.remove(G.first()))

    return   {S is now in sorted order}

Code Fragment 10.5: Quick-sort for an input sequence S implemented with a linked list or an array.

Running Time of Quick-Sort

We can analyze the running time of quick-sort with the same technique used for merge-sort in Section 10.1.3. Namely, we can identify the time spent at each node of the quick-sort tree T and sum up the running times for all the nodes.

Examining Code Fragment 10.5, we see that the divide step and the conquer step of quick-sort can be implemented in linear time. Thus, the time spent at a node v of T is proportional to the **_input size_** $s(v)$ of v, defined as the size of the sequence handled by the invocation of quick-sort associated with node v. Since subsequence E has at least one element (the pivot), the sum of the input sizes of the children of v is at most $s(v) - 1$.

Given a quick-sort tree T, let s_i denote the sum of the input sizes of the nodes at depth i in T. Clearly, $s_0 = n$, since the root r of T is associated with the entire sequence. Also, $s_1 \leq n - 1$, since the pivot is not propagated to the children of r. Consider next s_2. If both children of r have nonzero input size, then $s_2 = n - 3$. Otherwise (one child of the root has zero size, the other has size $n - 1$), $s_2 = n - 2$. Thus, $s_2 \leq n - 2$. Continuing this line of reasoning, we obtain that $s_i \leq n - i$. As observed in Section 10.2, the height of T is $n - 1$ in the worst case. Thus, the worst-case running time of quick-sort is $O\left(\sum_{i=0}^{n-1} s_i\right)$, which is $O\left(\sum_{i=0}^{n-1}(n-i)\right)$, that is, $O\left(\sum_{i=1}^{n} i\right)$. By Proposition 3.1, $\sum_{i=1}^{n} i$ is $O(n^2)$. Thus, quick-sort runs in $O(n^2)$ worst-case time.

Given its name, we would expect quick-sort to run quickly. However, the above quadratic bound indicates that quick-sort is slow in the worst case. Paradoxically, this worst-case behavior occurs for problem instances when sorting should be easy—if the sequence is already sorted.

Going back to our analysis, note that the best case for quick-sort on a sequence of distinct elements occurs when subsequences L and G happen to have roughly the same size. That is, in the best case, we have

$$
\begin{aligned}
s_0 &= n \\
s_1 &= n - 1 \\
s_2 &= n - (1 + 2) = n - 3 \\
&\vdots \\
s_i &= n - (1 + 2 + 2^2 + \cdots + 2^{i-1}) = n - (2^i - 1).
\end{aligned}
$$

Thus, in the best case, T has height $O(\log n)$ and quick-sort runs in $O(n \log n)$ time; we leave the justification of this fact as an exercise (R-10.9).

The informal intuition behind the expected behavior of quick-sort is that at each invocation the pivot will probably divide the input sequence about equally. Thus, we expect the average running time quick-sort to be similar to the best-case running time, that is, $O(n \log n)$. We will see in the next section that introducing randomization makes quick-sort behave exactly in this way.

10.2.1   Randomized Quick-Sort

One common method for analyzing quick-sort is to assume that the pivot will always divide the sequence almost equally. We feel such an assumption would presuppose knowledge about the input distribution that is typically not available, however. For example, we would have to assume that we will rarely be given "almost" sorted sequences to sort, which are actually common in many applications. Fortunately, this assumption is not needed in order for us to match our intuition to quick-sort's behavior.

In general, we desire some way of getting close to the best-case running time for quick-sort. The way to get close to the best-case running time, of course, is for the pivot to divide the input sequence S almost equally. If this outcome were to occur, then it would result in a running time that is asymptotically the same as the best-case running time. That is, having pivots close to the "middle" of the set of elements leads to an $O(n \log n)$ running time for quick-sort.

Picking Pivots at Random

Since the goal of the partition step of the quick-sort method is to divide the sequence S almost equally, let us introduce randomization into the algorithm and pick as the pivot a ***random element*** of the input sequence. That is, instead of picking the pivot as the last element of S, we pick an element of S at random as the pivot, keeping the rest of the algorithm unchanged. This variation of quick-sort is called ***randomized quick-sort***. The following proposition shows that the expected running time of randomized quick-sort on a sequence with n elements is $O(n \log n)$. This expectation is taken over all the possible random choices the algorithm makes, and is independent of any assumptions about the distribution of the possible input sequences the algorithm is likely to be given.

Proposition 10.3: *The expected running time of randomized quick-sort on a sequence S of size n is $O(n \log n)$, assuming two elements of S can be compared in $O(1)$ time.*

Justification: We make use of a simple fact from probability theory:

> *The expected number of times that a fair coin must be flipped until it shows "heads" k times is $2k$.*

Consider a single recursive call of randomized quick-sort, and let m denote the size of the input for this call. Say that this call is "good" if the pivot chosen is such that subsequences L and G have size at least $m/4$ and at most $3m/4$ each.

Now, consider the implications of our choosing a pivot uniformly at random. Note that there are $m/2$ possible choices for the pivot for any given call of size m of the randomized quick-sort algorithm. Thus, the probability that any call is good is $1/2$ (the same as the probability a coin comes up heads).

If a node v of the quick-sort tree T, as shown in Figure 10.14, is associated with a "good" recursive call, then the input sizes of the children of v are each at most $3s(v)/4$ (which is the same as $(s(v)/(4/3))$). If we take any path in T from the root to an external node, then the length of this path is at most the number of calls that have to be made (at each node on this path) until achieving $\log_{4/3} n$ good calls. Applying the probabilistic fact reviewed above, the expected number of calls we must make until this occurs is $2\log_{4/3} n$. Thus, the expected length of any path from the root to an external node in T is $O(\log n)$. Recalling that the time spent at each level of T is $O(n)$, the expected running time of randomized quick-sort is $O(n \log n)$. ∎

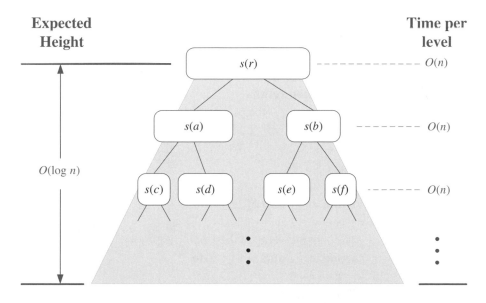

Total expected time: $O(n \log n)$

Figure 10.14: A visual time analysis of the quick-sort tree T. Each node is shown labeled with the size of its subproblem.

Actually, by using powerful facts from probability, we can show that the running time of randomized quick-sort is $O(n \log n)$ with high probability. We leave this analysis as an exercise (C-10.9) for the more mathematically inclined reader.

10.2.2 In-Place Quick-Sort

Recall from Section 7.3.5 that a sorting algorithm is **in-place** if it uses only a small amount of memory in addition to that needed for the objects being sorted themselves. The merge-sort algorithm, as we have described it above, is not in-place, and making it be in-place requires a more complicated merging method than the one we discuss in Section 10.1.2. In-place sorting is not inherently difficult, however. For, as with heap-sort, quick-sort can be adapted to be in-place.

Performing the quick-sort algorithm in-place requires a bit of ingenuity, however, for we must use the input sequence itself to store the subsequences for all the recursive calls. We show algorithm inPlaceQuickSort, which performs in-place quick-sort, in Code Fragment 10.6. Algorithm inPlaceQuickSort assumes that the input sequence, S, is given as an array of **distinct** elements. The reason for this restriction is explored in Exercise R-10.11. The extension to the general case is discussed in Exercise C-10.8.

Algorithm inPlaceQuickSort(S, a, b):
    Input: An array S of distinct elements; integers a and b
    Output: Array S with elements originally from ranks from a to b, inclusive,
        sorted in nondecreasing order from ranks a to b

    if $a \geq b$ **then return**   {at most one element in subrange}
    $p \leftarrow S[b]$ {the pivot}
    $l \leftarrow a$ {will scan rightward}
    $r \leftarrow b - 1$ {will scan leftward}
    while $l \leq r$ **do**
        {find an element larger than the pivot}
        while $l \leq r$ **and** $S[l] \leq p$ **do**
            $l \leftarrow l + 1$
        {find an element smaller than the pivot}
        while $r \geq l$ **and** $S[r] \geq p$ **do**
            $r \leftarrow r - 1$
        if $l < r$ **then**
            swap the elements at $S[l]$ and $S[r]$
    {put the pivot into its final place}
    swap the elements at $S[l]$ and $S[b]$
    {recursive calls}
    inPlaceQuickSort($S, a, l - 1$)
    inPlaceQuickSort($S, l + 1, b$)
    {we are done at this point, since the sorted subarrays are already consecutive}

Code Fragment 10.6: In-place quick-sort for an input array S.

In-place quick-sort modifies the input sequence using element swapping and does not explicitly create subsequences. Indeed, a subsequence of the input sequence is implicitly represented by a range of positions specified by a left-most rank l and a right-most rank r. The divide step is performed by scanning the array simultaneously from l forward and from r backward, swapping pairs of elements that are in reverse order, as shown in Figure 10.15. When these two indices "meet," subarrays L and G are on opposite sides of the meeting point. The algorithm completes by recurring on these two subarrays.

In-place quick-sort reduces the running time caused by the creation of new sequences and the movement of elements between them by a constant factor. We show a Java version of in-place quick-sort in Code Fragment 10.7.

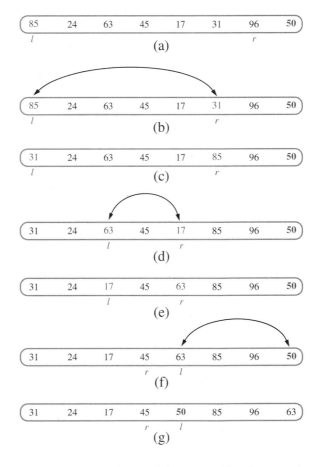

Figure 10.15: Divide step of in-place quick-sort. Index l scans the sequence from left to right, and index r scans the sequence from right to left. A swap is performed when l is at an element larger than the pivot and r is at an element smaller than the pivot. A final swap with the pivot completes the divide step.

```
public static void quickSort (Object[] S, Comparator c) {
  if (S.length < 2) return; // the array is already sorted in this case
  quickSortStep(S, c, 0, S.length−1); // recursive sort method
}
private static void quickSortStep (Object[] S, Comparator c,
                          int leftBound, int rightBound ) {
  if (leftBound >= rightBound) return; // the indices have crossed
  Object temp;  // temp object used for swapping
  Object pivot = S[rightBound];
  int leftIndex = leftBound;      // will scan rightward
  int rightIndex = rightBound−1; // will scan leftward
  while (leftIndex <= rightIndex) { // scan right until larger than the pivot
    while ( (leftIndex <= rightIndex) && (c.compare(S[leftIndex], pivot)<=0) )
      leftIndex++;
    // scan leftward to find an element smaller than the pivot
    while ( (rightIndex >= leftIndex) && (c.compare(S[rightIndex], pivot)>=0))
      rightIndex−−;
    if (leftIndex < rightIndex) { // both elements were found
      temp = S[rightIndex];
      S[rightIndex] = S[leftIndex]; // swap these elements
      S[leftIndex] = temp;
    }
  } // the loop continues until the indices cross
  temp = S[rightBound]; // swap pivot with the element at leftIndex
  S[rightBound] = S[leftIndex];
  S[leftIndex] = temp; // the pivot is now at leftIndex, so recurse
  quickSortStep(S, c, leftBound, leftIndex−1);
  quickSortStep(S, c, leftIndex+1, rightBound);
}
```

Code Fragment 10.7: A coding of in-place quick-sort, assuming distinct elements.

Unfortunately, the above implementation is not guaranteed to be in-place. Recalling Section 4.2.3, we note that we need space for a stack proportional to the depth of the recursion tree, which in this case can be as large as $n-1$. Admittedly, the expected stack depth is $O(\log n)$, which is small compared to n. Nevertheless, a simple trick lets us guarantee the stack size is $O(\log n)$. The main idea is to design a nonrecursive version of in-place quick-sort using an explicit stack to iteratively process subproblems (each of which can be represented with a pair of indices marking subarray boundaries), with each iteration involves popping the top subproblem, splitting it in two (if it is big enough), and pushing the two new subproblems. The trick is that when pushing the new subproblems, we should first push the larger subproblem and then the smaller one. In this way, the sizes of the subproblems will at least double as we go down the stack; hence, the stack can have depth at most $O(\log n)$. We leave the details of this implementation to an exercise (C-10.7).

10.3 A Lower Bound on Comparison-Based Sorting

Recapping our discussions on sorting to this point, we have described several methods with either a worst-case or expected running time of $O(n \log n)$ on an input sequence of size n. These methods include merge-sort and quick-sort, described in this chapter, as well as heap-sort, described in Section 7.3.5. A natural question to ask, then, is whether it is possible to sort any faster than in $O(n \log n)$ time.

In this section, we show that if the computational primitive used by a sorting algorithm is the comparison of two elements, then this is the best we can do—comparison-based sorting has an $\Omega(n \log n)$ worst-case lower bound on its running time. (Recall the notation $\Omega(\cdot)$ from Section 3.4.1.) To focus on the main cost of comparison-based sorting, let us only count the comparisons that a sorting algorithm performs. Since we want to derive a lower bound, this will be sufficient.

Suppose we are given a sequence $S = (x_0, x_1, \ldots, x_{n-1})$ that we wish to sort, and assume that all the elements of S are distinct (this is not really a restriction since we are deriving a lower bound). We do not care if S is implemented as an array or a linked list, for the sake of our lower bound, since we are only counting comparisons. Each time a sorting algorithm compares two elements x_i and x_j (that is, it asks, "is $x_i < x_j$?"), there are two outcomes: "yes" or "no." Based on the result of this comparison, the sorting algorithm may perform some internal calculations (which we are not counting here) and will eventually perform another comparison between two other elements of S, which again will have two outcomes. Therefore, we can represent a comparison-based sorting algorithm with a decision tree T (recall Example 6.4). That is, each internal node v in T corresponds to a comparison and the edges from node v' to its children correspond to the computations resulting from either a "yes" or "no" answer (see Figure 10.16).

It is important to note that the hypothetical sorting algorithm in question probably has no explicit knowledge of the tree T. We simply use T to represent all the possible sequences of comparisons that a sorting algorithm might make, starting from the first comparison (associated with the root) and ending with the last comparison (associated with the parent of an external node) just before the algorithm terminates its execution.

Each possible initial ordering, or **permutation**, of the elements in S will cause our hypothetical sorting algorithm to execute a series of comparisons, traversing a path in T from the root to some external node. Let us associate with each external node v in T, then, the set of permutations of S that cause our sorting algorithm to end up in v. The most important observation in our lower-bound argument is that each external node v in T can represent the sequence of comparisons for at most one permutation of S. The justification for this claim is simple: if two different permutations P_1 and P_2 of S are associated with the same external node, then there are at least two objects x_i and x_j, such that x_i is before x_j in P_1 but x_i is after x_j in P_2. At the same time, the output associated with v must be a specific reordering of S, with either x_i or x_j appearing before the other. But if P_1 and P_2 both cause the sorting algorithm to output the elements of S in this order, then that implies there is a way to trick the algorithm into outputting x_i and x_j in the wrong order. Since this cannot be allowed by a correct sorting algorithm, each external node of T must be associated with exactly one permutation of S. We use this property of the decision tree associated with a sorting algorithm to prove the following result:

Proposition 10.4: *The running time of any comparison-based algorithm for sorting an n-element sequence is* $\Omega(n \log n)$ *in the worst case.*

Justification: The running time of a comparison-based sorting algorithm must be greater than or equal to the height of the decision tree T associated with this algorithm, as described above. (See Figure 10.16.) By the above argument, each external node in T must be associated with one permutation of S. Moreover, each permutation of S must result in a different external node of T. The number of permutations of n objects is $n! = n(n-1)(n-2)\cdots 2 \cdot 1$. Thus, T must have at least $n!$ external nodes. By Proposition 6.10, the height of T is at least $\log(n!)$. This immediately justifies the proposition, because there are at least $n/2$ terms that are greater than or equal to $n/2$ in the product $n!$; hence

$$\log(n!) \geq \log\left(\frac{n}{2}\right)^{\frac{n}{2}} = \frac{n}{2} \log \frac{n}{2},$$

which is $\Omega(n \log n)$.   ■

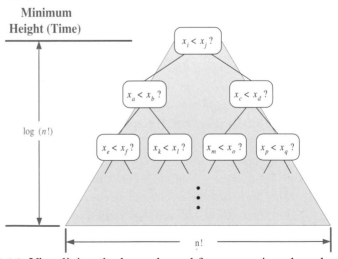

Figure 10.16: Visualizing the lower bound for comparison-based sorting.

10.4 Bucket-Sort and Radix-Sort

In the previous section, we showed that $\Omega(n \log n)$ time is necessary, in the worst case, to sort an n-element sequence with a comparison-based sorting algorithm. A natural question to ask, then, is whether there are other kinds of sorting algorithms that can be designed to run asymptotically faster than $O(n \log n)$ time. Interestingly, such algorithms exist, but they require special assumptions about the input sequence to be sorted. Even so, such scenarios often arise in practice, so discussing them is worthwhile. In this section, we consider the problem of sorting a sequence of entries, each a key-value pair.

10.4.1 Bucket-Sort

Consider a sequence S of n entries whose keys are integers in the range $[0, N-1]$, for some integer $N \geq 2$, and suppose that S should be sorted according to the keys of the entries. In this case, it is possible to sort S in $O(n+N)$ time. It might seem surprising, but this implies, for example, that if N is $O(n)$, then we can sort S in $O(n)$ time. Of course, the crucial point is that, because of the restrictive assumption about the format of the elements, we can avoid using comparisons.

The main idea is to use an algorithm called ***bucket-sort***, which is not based on comparisons, but on using keys as indices into a bucket array B that has cells indexed from 0 to $N-1$. An entry with key k is placed in the "bucket" $B[k]$, which itself is a sequence (of entries with key k). After inserting each entry of the input sequence S into its bucket, we can put the entries back into S in sorted order by enumerating the contents of the buckets $B[0], B[1], \ldots, B[N-1]$ in order. We describe the bucket-sort algorithm in Code Fragment 10.8.

Algorithm bucketSort(S):

    Input: Sequence S of entries with integer keys in the range $[0, N-1]$
    Output: Sequence S sorted in nondecreasing order of the keys

    let B be an array of N sequences, each of which is initially empty
    for each entry e in S **do**
        $k \leftarrow e.\text{key}()$
        remove e from S and insert it at the end bucket (sequence) $B[k]$
    for $i \leftarrow 0$ to $N-1$ **do**
        for each entry e in sequence $B[i]$ **do**
            remove e from $B[i]$ and insert it at the end of S

Code Fragment 10.8: Bucket-sort.

It is easy to see that bucket-sort runs in $O(n+N)$ time and uses $O(n+N)$ space. Hence, bucket-sort is efficient when the range N of values for the keys is small compared to the sequence size n, say $N = O(n)$ or $N = O(n\log n)$. Still, its performance deteriorates as N grows compared to n.

An important property of the bucket-sort algorithm is that it works correctly even if there are many different elements with the same key. Indeed, we described it in a way that anticipates such occurrences.

Stable Sorting

When sorting key-value pairs, an important issue is how equal keys are handled. Let $S = ((k_0, x_0), \ldots, (k_{n-1}, x_{n-1}))$ be a sequence of such entries. We say that a sorting algorithm is *stable* if, for any two entries (k_i, x_i) and (k_j, x_j) of S, such that $k_i = k_j$ and (k_i, x_i) precedes (k_j, x_j) in S before sorting (that is, $i < j$), entry (k_i, x_i) also precedes entry (k_j, x_j) after sorting. Stability is important for a sorting algorithm because applications may want to preserve the initial ordering of elements with the same key.

Our informal description of bucket-sort in Code Fragment 10.8 does not guarantee stability. This is not inherent in the bucket-sort method itself, however, for we can easily modify our description to make bucket-sort stable, while still preserving its $O(n+N)$ running time. Indeed, we can obtain a stable bucket-sort algorithm by always removing the *first* element from sequence S and from the sequences $B[i]$ during the execution of the algorithm.

10.4.2 Radix-Sort

One of the reasons that stable sorting is so important is that it allows the bucket-sort approach to be applied to more general contexts than to sort integers. Suppose, for example, that we want to sort entries with keys that are pairs (k, l), where k and l are integers in the range $[0, N-1]$, for some integer $N \geq 2$. In a context such as this, it is natural to define an ordering on these keys using the *lexicographical* (dictionary) convention, where $(k_1, l_1) < (k_2, l_2)$ if $k_1 < k_2$ or if $k_1 = k_2$ and $l_1 < l_2$ (Section 7.1.2). This is a pair-wise version of the lexicographic comparison function, usually applied to equal-length character strings (and it easily generalizes to tuples of d numbers for $d > 2$).

The *radix-sort* algorithm sorts a sequence S of entries with keys that are pairs, by applying a stable bucket-sort on the sequence twice; first using one component of the pair as the ordering key and then using the second component. But which order is correct? Should we first sort on the k's (the first component) and then on the l's (the second component), or should it be the other way around?

Before we answer this question, we consider the following example.

Example 10.5: *Consider the following sequence S (we show only the keys):*

$$S = ((3,3),(1,5),(2,5),(1,2),(2,3),(1,7),(3,2),(2,2)).$$

If we sort S stably on the first component, then we get the sequence

$$S_1 = ((1,5),(1,2),(1,7),(2,5),(2,3),(2,2),(3,3),(3,2)).$$

If we then stably sort this sequence S_1 using the second component, then we get the sequence

$$S_{1,2} = ((1,2),(2,2),(3,2),(2,3),(3,3),(1,5),(2,5),(1,7)),$$

which is not exactly a sorted sequence. On the other hand, if we first stably sort S using the second component, then we get the sequence

$$S_2 = ((1,2),(3,2),(2,2),(3,3),(2,3),(1,5),(2,5),(1,7)).$$

If we then stably sort sequence S_2 using the first component, then we get the sequence

$$S_{2,1} = ((1,2),(1,5),(1,7),(2,2),(2,3),(2,5),(3,2),(3,3)),$$

which is indeed sequence S lexicographically ordered.

So, from this example, we are led to believe that we should first sort using the second component and then again using the first component. This intuition is exactly right. By first stably sorting by the second component and then again by the first component, we guarantee that if two entries are equal in the second sort (by the first component), then their relative order in the starting sequence (which is sorted by the second component) is preserved. Thus, the resulting sequence is guaranteed to be sorted lexicographically every time. We leave to a simple exercise (R-10.16) the determination of how this approach can be extended to triples and other d-tuples of numbers. We can summarize this section as follows:

Proposition 10.6: *Let S be a sequence of n key-value pairs, each of which has a key $(k_1, k_2, \ldots, k_d)$, where k_i is an integer in the range $[0, N-1]$ for some integer $N \geq 2$. We can sort S lexicographically in time $O(d(n+N))$ using radix-sort.*

As important as it is, sorting is not the only interesting problem dealing with a total order relation on a set of elements. There are some applications, for example, that do not require an ordered listing of an entire set, but nevertheless call for some amount of ordering information about the set. Before we study such a problem (called "selection"), let us step back and briefly compare all of the sorting algorithms we have studied so far.

10.5   Comparison of Sorting Algorithms

At this point, it might be useful for us to take a breath and consider all the algorithms we have studied in this book to sort an n-element array, list, vector, or general sequence.

Considering Running Time and Other Factors

We have studied several methods, such as insertion-sort, and selection-sort, that have $O(n^2)$-time behavior in the average and worst case. We have also studied several methods with $O(n \log n)$-time behavior, including heap-sort, merge-sort, and quick-sort. Finally, we have studied a special class of sorting algorithms, namely, the bucket-sort and radix-sort methods, that run in linear time for certain types of keys. Certainly, the selection-sort algorithm is a poor choice in any application, since it runs in $O(n^2)$ time even in the best case. But, of the remaining sorting algorithms, which is the best?

As with many things in life, there is no clear "best" sorting algorithm from the remaining candidates. The sorting algorithm best suited for a particular application depends on several properties of that application. We can offer some guidance and observations, therefore, based on the known properties of the "good" sorting algorithms.

Insertion-Sort

If implemented well, the running time of ***insertion-sort*** is $O(n + m)$, where m is the number of ***inversions*** (that is, the number of pairs of elements out of order). Thus, insertion-sort is an excellent algorithm for sorting small sequences (say, less than 50 elements), because insertion-sort is simple to program, and small sequences necessarily have few inversions. Also, insertion-sort is quite effective for sorting sequences that are already "almost" sorted. By "almost," we mean that the number of inversions is small. But the $O(n^2)$-time performance of insertion-sort makes it a poor choice outside of these special contexts.

Merge-Sort

Merge-sort, on the other hand, runs in $O(n \log n)$ time in the worst case, which is optimal for comparison-based sorting methods. Still, experimental studies have shown that, since it is difficult to make merge-sort run in-place, the overheads needed to implement merge-sort make it less attractive than the in-place implementations of heap-sort and quick-sort for sequences that can fit entirely in a computer's main memory area. Even so, merge-sort is an excellent algorithm for situations where the input cannot all fit into main memory, but must be stored in blocks on an external memory device, such as a disk. In these contexts, the way that merge-sort processes runs of data in long merge streams makes the best use of all the data brought into main memory in a block from disk. Thus, for external memory sorting, the merge-sort algorithm tends to minimize the total number of disk reads and writes needed, which makes the merge-sort algorithm superior in such contexts.

Quick-Sort

Experimental studies have shown that if an input sequence can fit entirely in main memory, then the in-place versions of quick-sort and heap-sort run faster than merge-sort. The extra overhead needed for copying nodes or entries puts merge-sort at a disadvantage to quick-sort and heap-sort in these applications. In fact, quick-sort tends, on average, to beat heap-sort in these tests.

So, *quick-sort* is an excellent choice as a general-purpose, in-memory sorting algorithm. Indeed, it is included in the qsort sorting utility provided in C language libraries. Still, its $O(n^2)$ time worst-case performance makes quick-sort a poor choice in real-time applications where we must make guarantees on the time needed to complete a sorting operation.

Heap-Sort

In real-time scenarios where we have a fixed amount of time to perform a sorting operation and the input data can fit into main memory, the *heap-sort* algorithm is probably the best choice. It runs in $O(n \log n)$ worst-case time and can easily be made to execute in-place.

Bucket-Sort and Radix-Sort

Finally, if our application involves sorting entries with small integer keys or d-tuples of small integer keys, then *bucket-sort* or *radix-sort* is an excellent choice, for it runs in $O(d(n+N))$ time, where $[0, N-1]$ is the range of integer keys (and $d = 1$ for bucket sort). Thus, if $d(n+N)$ is significantly "below" the $n \log n$ function, then this sorting method should run faster than even quick-sort or heap-sort.

Thus, our study of all these different sorting algorithms provides us with a versatile collection of sorting methods in our algorithm engineering "toolbox."

10.6   The Set ADT and Union/Find Structures

In this section, we introduce the *set* ADT. A *set* is a container of distinct objects. That is, there are no duplicate elements in a set, and there is no explicit notion of keys or even an order. Even so, we include our discussion of sets here in a chapter on sorting, because sorting can play an important role in efficient implementations of the operations of the set ADT.

Sets and Some of Their Uses

First, we recall the mathematical definitions of the **union**, **intersection**, and **subtraction** of two sets A and B:

$$
\begin{aligned}
A \cup B &= \{x : x \in A \text{ or } x \in B\}, \\
A \cap B &= \{x : x \in A \text{ and } x \in B\}, \\
A - B &= \{x : x \in A \text{ and } x \notin B\}.
\end{aligned}
$$

Example 10.7: *Most Internet search engines store, for each word x in their dictionary database, a set, $W(x)$, of Web pages that contain x, where each Web page is identified by a unique Internet address. When presented with a query for a word x, such a search engine need only return the Web pages in the set $W(x)$, sorted according to some proprietary priority ranking of page "importance." But when presented with a two-word query for words x and y, such a search engine must first compute the intersection $W(x) \cap W(y)$, and then return the Web pages in the resulting set sorted by priority. Several search engines use the set intersection algorithm described in this section for this computation.*

Fundamental Methods of the Set ADT

The fundamental methods of the set ADT, acting on a set A, are as follows:

> union(B): Replace A with the union of A and B, that is, execute $A \leftarrow A \cup B$.
> ***Input:*** Set; ***Output:*** None.

> intersect(B): Replace A with the intersection of A and B, that is, execute $A \leftarrow A \cap B$.
> ***Input:*** Set; ***Output:*** None.

> subtract(B): Replace A with the difference of A and B, that is, execute $A \leftarrow A - B$.
> ***Input:*** Set; ***Output:*** None.

10.6.1 A Simple Set Implementation

One of the simplest ways of implementing a set is to store its elements in an ordered sequence. This implementation is included in several software libraries for generic data structures, for example. Therefore, let us consider implementing the set ADT with an ordered sequence (we consider other implementations in several exercises). Any consistent total order relation among the elements of the set can be used, provided the same order is used for all the sets.

We implement each of the three fundamental set operations using a generic version of the merge algorithm that takes, as input, two sorted sequences representing the input sets, and constructs a sequence representing the output set, be it the union, intersection, or subtraction of the input sets. Incidentally, we have defined these operations so that they modify the contents of the set A involved. Alternatively, we could have defined these methods so that they do not modify A but return a new set instead.

The generic merge algorithm iteratively examines and compares the current elements a and b of the input sequence A and B, respectively, and finds out whether $a < b$, $a = b$, or $a > b$. Then, based on the outcome of this comparison, it determines whether it should copy one of the elements a and b to the end of the output sequence C. This determination is made based on the particular operation we are performing, be it a union, intersection, or subtraction. For example, in a union operation, we proceed as follows:

- If $a < b$, we copy a to the end of C and advance to the next element of A .
- If $a = b$, we copy a to the end of C and advance to the next elements of A and B .
- If $a > b$, we copy b to the end of C and advance to the next element of B.

Performance of Generic Merging

Let us analyze the running time of generic merging. At each iteration, we compare two elements of the input sequences A and B, possibly copy one element to the output sequence, and advance the current element of A, B, or both. Assuming that comparing and copying elements takes $O(1)$ time, the total running time is $O(n_A + n_B)$, where n_A is the size of A and n_B is the size of B; that is, generic merging takes time proportional to the number of elements. Thus, we have the following:

Proposition 10.8: *The set ADT can be implemented with an ordered sequence and a generic merge scheme that supports operations* union, intersect, *and* subtract *in $O(n)$ time, where n denotes the sum of sizes of the sets involved.*

Generic Merging as a Template Method Pattern

The generic merge algorithm is based on the ***template method pattern*** (see Section 6.3.5). The template method pattern is a software engineering design pattern describing a generic computation mechanism that can be specialized by redefining certain steps. In this case we describe a method that merges two sequences into one and can be specialized by the behavior of three abstract methods.

Code Fragment 10.9 shows the class Merge providing a Java implementation of the generic merge algorithm.

```java
/** Generic merge for sorted sequences. */
public abstract class Merge {
  private Object a, b;                   // current elements in A and B
  private Iterator iterA, iterB;         // iterators for A and B
  /** Template method */
  public void merge(Sequence A, Sequence B, Comparator comp, Sequence C) {
    iterA = A.elements(); iterB = B.elements();
    boolean aExists = advanceA();  // Boolean test if there is a current a
    boolean bExists = advanceB();  // Boolean test if there is a current b
    while (aExists && bExists) {     // Main loop for merging a and b
      int x = comp.compare(a, b);
      if (x < 0) { aIsLess(a, C);  aExists = advanceA(); }
      else if (x == 0) {
        bothAreEqual(a, b, C); aExists = advanceA(); bExists = advanceB(); }
      else { bIsLess(b, C);  bExists = advanceB(); }
    }
    while (aExists) { aIsLess(a, C); aExists = advanceA(); }
    while (bExists) { bIsLess(b, C); bExists = advanceB(); }
  }
  // auxiliary methods to be specialized by subclasses
  protected void aIsLess(Object a, Sequence C) { }
  protected void bothAreEqual(Object a, Object b, Sequence C) { }
  protected void bIsLess(Object b, Sequence C) { }
  // helper methods
  private boolean advanceA() {
    if (iterA.hasNext()) { a = iterA.next(); return true; }
    return false;
  }
  private boolean advanceB() {
    if (iterB.hasNext()) { b = iterB.next(); return true; }
    return false;
  }
}
```

Code Fragment 10.9: Class Merge for generic merging.

To convert the generic Merge class into useful classes, we must extend it with classes that redefine the three auxiliary methods, aIsLess, bothAreEqual, and bIsLess. We show how union, intersection, and subtraction can be easily described in terms of these methods in Code Fragment 10.10. The auxiliary methods are redefined so that the template method merge performs as follows:

- In class UnionMerge, merge copies every element from A and B into C, but does not duplicate any element.
- In class IntersectMerge, merge copies every element that is in both A and B into C, but "throws away" elements in one set but not in the other.
- In class SubtractMerge, merge copies every element that is in A and not in B into C.

```
/** Class specializing the generic merge template to union two sets */
public class UnionMerge extends Merge {
  protected void aIsLess(Object a, Sequence C) {
    C.insertLast(a);      // add a
  }
  protected void bothAreEqual(Object a, Object b, Sequence C) {
    C.insertLast(a);      // add a (but not its duplicate b)
  }
  protected void bIsLess(Object b, Sequence C) {
    C.insertLast(b);      // add b
  }
}
/** Class specializing the generic merge template to intersect two sets */
public class IntersectMerge extends Merge {
  protected void aIsLess(Object a, Sequence C) { }
  protected void bothAreEqual(Object a, Object b, Sequence C) {
    C.insertLast(a);      // add a (but not its duplicate b)
  }
  protected void bIsLess(Object b, Sequence C) { }
}
/** Class specializing the generic merge template to subtract two sets */
public class SubtractMerge extends Merge {
  protected void aIsLess(Object a, Sequence C) {
    C.insertLast(a);      // add a
  }
  protected void bothAreEqual(Object a, Object b, Sequence C) { }
  protected void bIsLess(Object b, Sequence C) { }
}
```

Code Fragment 10.10: Classes extending the Merge class by specializing the auxiliary methods to perform set union, intersection, and subtraction, respectively.

10.6.2   Partitions with Union-Find Operations

A **partition** is a collection of disjoint sets. We define the methods of the partition ADT using position objects (Section 5.2.2), each of which stores an element x. The parition ADT then supports the following methods.

> makeSet(x): Create a singleton set containing the element x and return the position storing x in this set.
>
> union(A, B): Return the set $A \cup B$, destroying the old A and B.
>
> find(p): Return the set containing the element in position p.

A simple implementation of a partition with a total of n elements is with a collection of sequences, one for each set, where the sequence for a set A stores set positions as its elements. Each position object stores a variable, element, which references its associated element x and allows the execution of the element() method in $O(1)$ time. In addition, we also store in each position p a variable, set, which references the sequence storing p, since this sequence is representing the set containing p's element. (See Figure 10.17.) Thus, we can perform operation find(p) in $O(1)$ time, by following the set reference for p. Likewise, makeSet also takes $O(1)$ time. Operation union(A, B) requires that we join two sequences into one and update the set references of the positions in one of the two. We choose to implement this operation by removing all the positions from the sequence with smaller size, and inserting them in the sequence with larger size. Each time we take a position p from the smaller set s and insert it into the larger set t, we update the set reference for p to now point to t. Hence, the operation union(A, B) takes time $O(\min(|A|, |B|))$, which is $O(n)$, because, in the worst case, $|A| = |B| = n/2$. Nevertheless, as shown below, an amortized analysis shows this implementation to be much better than appears from this worst-case analysis.

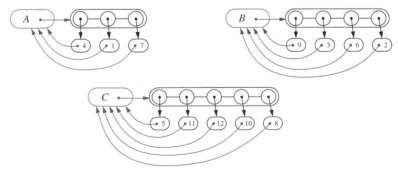

Figure 10.17: Sequence-based implementation of a partition consisting of three sets: $A = \{1, 4, 7\}$, $B = \{2, 3, 6, 9\}$, and $C = \{5, 8, 10, 11, 12\}$.

Performance of the Sequence Implementation

The above sequence implementation is simple, but it is also efficient, as the following theorem shows.

Proposition 10.9: *Performing a series of n* makeSet, union, *and* find *operations, using the above sequence-based implementation, starting from an initially empty partition takes* $O(n \log n)$ *time.*

Justification: We use the accounting method and assume that one cyber-dollar can pay for the time to perform a find operation, a makeSet operation, or the movement of a position object from one sequence to another in a union operation. In the case of a find or makeSet operation, we charge the operation itself 1 cyber-dollar. In the case of a union operation, however, we charge 1 cyber-dollar to each position that we move from one set to another. Note that we charge nothing to the union operations themselves. Clearly, the total charges to find and makeSet operations sum to be $O(n)$.

Consider, then, the number of charges made to positions on behalf of union operations. The important observation is that each time we move a position from one set to another, the size of the new set at least doubles. Thus, each position is moved from one set to another at most $\log n$ times; hence, each position can be charged at most $O(\log n)$ times. Since we assume that the partition is initially empty, there are $O(n)$ different elements referenced in the given series of operations, which implies that the total time for all the union operations is $O(n \log n)$. ∎

The amortized running time of an operation in a series of makeSet, union, and find operations, is the total time taken for the series divided by the number of operations. We conclude from the proposition above that, for a partition implemented using sequences, the amortized running time of each operation is $O(\log n)$. Thus, we can summarize the performance of our simple sequence-based partition implementation as follows.

Proposition 10.10: *Using a sequence-based implementation of a partition, in a series of n* makeSet, union, *and* find *operations starting from an initially empty partition, the amortized running time of each operation is* $O(\log n)$.

Note that in this sequence-based implementation of a partition, each find operation takes worst-case $O(1)$ time. It is the running time of the union operations that is the computational bottleneck.

In the next section, we describe a tree-based implementation of a partition that does not guarantee constant-time find operations, but has amortized time much better than $O(\log n)$ per union operation.

10.6.3   A Tree-Based Partition Implementation ⋆

An alternative data structure uses a collection of trees to store the n elements in sets, where each tree is associated with a different set. (See Figure 10.18.) In particular, we implement each tree with a linked data structure whose nodes are themselves the set position objects. We still view each position p as being a node having a variable, element, referring to its element x, and a variable, set, referring to a set containing x, as before. But now we also view each position p as also being of the "set" data type. Thus, the set reference of each position p can now point to a position, which could even be p itself. Moreover, we implement this approach so that all the positions and their respective set references together define a collection of trees.

We associate each tree with a set. For any position p, if p's set reference points back to p, then p is the ***root*** of its tree, and the name of the set containing p is "p" (that is, we will be using position names as set names in this case). Otherwise, the set reference for p points to p's parent in its tree. In either case, the set containing p is the one associated with the root of the tree containing p.

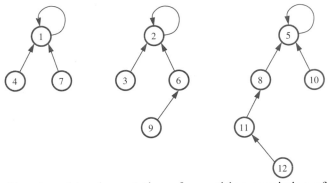

Figure 10.18: Tree-based implementation of a partition consisting of three disjoint sets: $A = \{1,4,7\}$, $B = \{2,3,6,9\}$, and $C = \{5,8,10,11,12\}$.

With this partition data structure, operation union(A,B) is called with position arguments p and q that respectively represent the sets A and B (that is, $A = p$ and $B = q$). We perform this operation by making one of the trees a subtree of the other (Figure 10.19b), which can be done in $O(1)$ time by setting the set reference of the root of one tree to point to the root of the other tree. Operation find for a position p is performed by walking up to the root of the tree containing the position p (Figure 10.19a), which takes $O(n)$ time in the worst case.

Note that this representation of a tree is a specialized data structure used to implement a partition, and is not meant to be a realization of the tree abstract data type (Section 6.1). Indeed, the representation has only "upward" links, and does not provide a way to access the children of a given node.

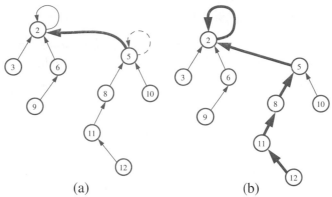

Figure 10.19: Tree-based implementation of a partition: (a) operation union(A,B); (b) operation find(p), where p denotes the position object for element 12.

At first, this implementation may seem to be no better than the sequence-based data structure, but we add the following simple heuristics to make it run faster:

Union-by-Size: Store with each position node p the size of the subtree rooted at p. In a union operation, make the tree of the smaller set become a subtree of the other tree, and update the size field of the root of the resulting tree.

Path Compression: In a find operation, for each node v that the find visits, reset the parent pointer from v to point to the root. (See Figure 10.20.)

These heuristics increase the running time of an operation by a constant factor, but as we discuss below, they significantly improve the amortized running time.

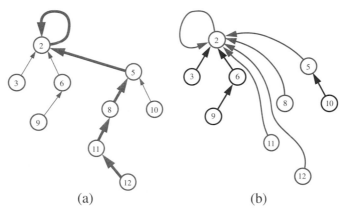

Figure 10.20: Path-compression heuristic: (a) path traversed by operation find on element 12; (b) restructured tree.

The Log-Star and Inverse Ackermann Functions

A surprising property of the tree-based partition data structure, when implemented using the union-by-size and path-compression heuristics, is that performing a series of n union and find operations takes $O(n \log^* n)$ time, where $\log^* n$ is the **log-star** function, which is the inverse of the **tower-of-twos** function. Intuitively, $\log^* n$ is the number of times that one can iteratively take the logarithm (base 2) of a number before getting a number smaller than 2. Table 10.1 shows a few sample values.

minimum n	2	$2^2 = 4$	$2^{2^2} = 16$	$2^{2^{2^2}} = 65,536$	$2^{2^{2^{2^2}}} = 2^{65,536}$
$\log^* n$	1	2	3	4	5

Table 10.1: Some values of $\log^* n$ and critical values for its inverse.

As is demonstrated in Table 10.1, for all practical purposes, $\log^* n \leq 5$. It is an amazingly slow-growing function (but one that is growing nonetheless).

In fact, the running time of a series of n partition operations implemented as above can actually be shown to be $O(n\alpha(n))$, where $\alpha(n)$ is the inverse of the **Ackermann function**, $\mathcal{A}$, which grows asymptotically even slower than $\log^* n$. Although we will not prove this fact, let us define the Ackermann function here, so as to appreciate just how quickly it grows; hence, how slowly its inverse grows. We first define an indexed Ackermann function, $\mathcal{A}_i$, as follows:

$$
\begin{aligned}
\mathcal{A}_0(n) &= 2n & \text{for } n \geq 0 \\
\mathcal{A}_i(1) &= \mathcal{A}_{i-1}(2) & \text{for } i \geq 1 \\
\mathcal{A}_i(n) &= \mathcal{A}_{i-1}(\mathcal{A}_i(n-1)) & \text{for } i \geq 1 \text{ and } n \geq 2.
\end{aligned}
$$

In other words, the Ackermann functions define a progression of functions:

- $\mathcal{A}_0(n) = 2n$ is the multiply-by-two function
- $\mathcal{A}_1(n) = 2^n$ is the power-of-two function
- $\mathcal{A}_2(n) = 2^{2^{\cdot^{\cdot^2}}}$ (with n 2's) is the tower-of-twos function
- and so on.

We then define the Ackermann function as $\mathcal{A}(n) = \mathcal{A}_n(n)$, which is an incredibly fast growing function. Likewise, the **inverse Ackermann function**,

$$\alpha(n) = \min\{m\colon \mathcal{A}(m) \geq n\},$$

is an incredibly slow growing function. It grows much slower than the $\log^* n$ function (which is the inverse of $\mathcal{A}_2(n)$), for example, and we have already noted that $\log^* n$ is a very slow-growing function.

10.7 Selection

There are a number of applications in which we are interested in identifying a single element in terms of its rank relative to an ordering of the entire set. Examples include identifying the minimum and maximum elements, but we may also be interested in, say, identifying the *median* element, that is, the element such that half of the other elements are smaller and the remaining half are larger. In general, queries that ask for an element with a given rank are called *order statistics*.

Defining the Selection Problem

In this section, we discuss the general order-statistic problem of selecting the kth smallest element from an unsorted collection of n comparable elements. This is known as the *selection* problem. Of course, we can solve this problem by sorting the collection and then indexing into the sorted sequence at rank k. Using the best comparison-based sorting algorithms, this approach would take $O(n \log n)$ time, which is obviously an overkill for the cases where $k = 1$ or $k = n$ (or even $k = 2$, $k = 3$, $k - n - 1$, or $k - n - 5$), because we can easily solve the selection problem for these values of k in $O(n)$ time. Thus, a natural question to ask is whether we can achieve an $O(n)$ running time for all values of k (including the interesting case of finding the median, where $k = \lfloor n/2 \rfloor$).

10.7.1 Prune-and-Search

This may come as a small surprise, but we can indeed solve the selection problem in $O(n)$ time for any value of k. Moreover, the technique we use to achieve this result involves an interesting algorithmic design pattern. This design pattern is known as *prune-and-search* or *decrease-and-conquer*. In applying this design pattern, we solve a given problem that is defined on a collection of n objects by pruning away a fraction of the n objects and recursively solving the smaller problem. When we have finally reduced the problem to one defined on a constant-sized collection of objects, then we solve the problem using some brute-force method. Returning back from all the recursive calls completes the construction. In some cases, we can avoid using recursion, in which case we simply iterate the prune-and-search reduction step until we can apply a brute-force method and stop. Incidentally, the binary search method described in Section 8.3.3 is an example of the prune-and-search design pattern.

10.7.2 Randomized Quick-Select

In applying the prune-and-search pattern to the selection problem, we can design a simple and practical method, called ***randomized quick-select***, for finding the kth smallest element in an unordered sequence of n elements on which a total order relation is defined. Randomized quick-select runs in $O(n)$ ***expected*** time, taken over all possible random choices made by the algorithm, and this expectation does not depend whatsoever on any randomness assumptions about the input distribution. We note though that randomized quick-select runs in $O(n^2)$ time in the ***worst case***, the justification of which is left as an exercise (R-10.21). We also provide an exercise (C-10.24) for modifying randomized quick-select to get a ***deterministic*** selection algorithm that runs in $O(n)$ ***worst-case*** time. The existence of this deterministic algorithm is mostly of theoretical interest, however, since the constant factor hidden by the big-Oh notation is relatively large in this case.

Suppose we are given an unsorted sequence S of n comparable elements together with an integer $k \in [1, n]$. At a high level, the quick-select algorithm for finding the kth smallest element in S is similar in structure to the randomized quick-sort algorithm described in Section 10.2.1. We pick an element x from S at random and use this as a "pivot" to subdivide S into three subsequences L, E, and G, storing the elements of S less than x, equal to x, and greater than x, respectively. This is the prune step. Then, based on the value of k, we then determine which of these sets to recur on. Randomized quick-select is described in Code Fragment 10.11.

Algorithm quickSelect(S, k):

    Input: Sequence S of n comparable elements, and an integer $k \in [1, n]$

    Output: The kth smallest element of S

    if $n = 1$ **then**

        return the (first) element of S.

    pick a random (pivot) element x of S and divide S into three sequences:

        • L, storing the elements in S less than x

        • E, storing the elements in S equal to x

        • G, storing the elements in S greater than x.

    if $k \leq |L|$ **then**

        quickSelect(L, k)

    else if $k \leq |L| + |E|$ **then**

        return x {each element in E is equal to x}

    else

        quickSelect($G, k - |L| - |E|$)   {note the new selection parameter}

        Code Fragment 10.11: Randomized quick-select algorithm.

10.7.3 Analyzing Randomized Quick-Select ⋆

Showing that randomized quick-select runs in $O(n)$ requires a simple probabilistic argument. The argument is based on the *linearity of expectation*, which states that if X and Y are random variables and c is a number, then

$$E(X+Y) = E(X)+E(Y) \qquad \text{and} \qquad E(cX) = cE(X),$$

where we use $E(\mathcal{Z})$ to denote the expected value of the expression $\mathcal{Z}$.

Let $t(n)$ be the running time of randomized quick-select on a sequence of size n. Since this algorithm depends on random events, its running time, $t(n)$, is a random variable. We want to bound $E(t(n))$, the expected value of $t(n)$. Say that a recursive invocation our algorithm is "good" if it partitions S so that the size of L and G is at most $3n/4$. Clearly, a recursive call is good with probability $1/2$. Let $g(n)$ denote the number of consecutive recursive calls we make, including the present one, before we get a good one. Then

$$t(n) \le bn \cdot g(n) + t(3n/4),$$

where $b \ge 1$ is a constant. Applying the linearity of expectation for $n > 1$, we get

$$E(t(n)) \le E(bn \cdot g(n) + t(3n/4)) = bn \cdot E(g(n)) + E(t(3n/4)).$$

Since a recursive call is good with probability $1/2$, and whether a recursive call is good or not is independent of its parent call being good, the expected value of $g(n)$ is the same as the expected number of times we must flip a fair coin before it comes up "heads." That is, $E(g(n)) = 2$. Thus, if we let $T(n)$ be a shorthand for $E(t(n))$, then we can write the case for $n > 1$ as

$$T(n) \le T(3n/4) + 2bn.$$

To convert this relation into a closed form, let us iteratively apply this inequality assuming n is large. So, for example, after two applications,

$$T(n) \le T((3/4)^2 n) + 2b(3/4)n + 2bn.$$

At this point, we should see that the general case is

$$T(n) \le 2bn \cdot \sum_{i=0}^{\lceil \log_{4/3} n \rceil} (3/4)^i.$$

In other words, the expected running time is at most $2bn$ times a geometric sum whose base is a positive number less than 1. Thus, by Proposition 3.3, $T(n)$ is $O(n)$.

Proposition 10.11: *The expected running time of randomized quick-select on a sequence S of size n is $O(n)$, assuming two elements of S can be compared in $O(1)$ time.*

10.8 Exercises

For source code and help with exercises, please visit **java.datastructures.net**.

Reinforcement

R-10.1 Give a complete justification of Proposition 10.1.

R-10.2 In the merge-sort tree shown in Figures 10.2 through 10.5, some edges are drawn as arrows. What is the meaning of a downward arrow? How about an upward arrow?

R-10.3 Give a complete pseudo-code description of the recursive merge-sort algorithm that takes an array as its input and output.

R-10.4 Show that the running time of the merge-sort algorithm on an n-element sequence is $O(n\log n)$, even when n is not a power of 2.

R-10.5 Suppose we are given two n-element sorted sequences A and B that should not be viewed as sets (that is, A and B may contain duplicate entries). Describe an $O(n)$-time method for computing a sequence representing the set $A \cup B$ (with no duplicates).

R-10.6 Show that $(X - A) \cup (X - B) = X - (A \cap B)$, for any three sets X, A, and B.

R-10.7 Suppose we modify the deterministic version of the quick-sort algorithm so that, instead of selecting the last element in an n-element sequence as the pivot, we choose the element at rank $\lfloor n/2 \rfloor$. What is the running time of this version of quick-sort on a sequence that is already sorted?

R-10.8 Consider again the modification of the deterministic version of the quick-sort algorithm so that, instead of selecting the last element in an n-element sequence as the pivot, we choose the element at rank $\lfloor n/2 \rfloor$. Describe the kind of sequence that would cause this version of quick-sort to run in $\Omega(n^2)$ time.

R-10.9 Show that the best-case running time of quick-sort on a sequence of size n with distinct elements is $O(n\log n)$.

R-10.10 Describe a randomized version of in-place quick-sort in pseudo-code.

R-10.11 Suppose algorithm inPlaceQuickSort (Code Fragment 10.6) is executed on a sequence with duplicate elements. Show that the algorithm still correctly sorts the input sequence, but the result of the divide step may differ from the high-level description given in Section 10.2 and may result in inefficiencies. In particular, what happens in the partition step when there are elements equal to the pivot? Is the sequence E (storing the elements equal to the pivot) actually computed? Does the algorithm recur on the subsequences L and G, or on some other subsequences? What is the running time of the algorithm if all the input elements are equal?

R-10.12 Of the $n!$ possible inputs to a given comparison-based sorting algorithm, what is the absolute maximum number of such inputs that could be sorted with just n comparisons?

R-10.13 Jonathan has a comparison-based sorting algorithm that sorts the first k elements in sequence of size n in $O(n)$ time. Give a big-Oh characterization of the biggest that k can be?

R-10.14 Is the merge-sort algorithm in Section 10.1 stable? Why or why not?

R-10.15 An algorithm that sorts key-value entries by key is said to be ***straggling*** if, any time two entries e_i and e_j have equal keys, but e_i appears before e_j in the input, then the algorithm places e_i after e_j in the output. Describe a change to the merge-sort algorithm in Section 10.1 to make it straggling.

R-10.16 Describe a radix-sort method for lexicographically sorting a sequence S of triplets (k, l, m), where k, l, and m are integers in the range $[0, N-1]$, for some $N \geq 2$. How could this scheme be extended to sequences of d-tuples $(k_1, k_2, \ldots, k_d)$, where each k_i is an integer in the range $[0, N-1]$?

R-10.17 Is the bucket-sort algorithm in-place? Why or why not?

R-10.18 Describe in pseudo-code how to perform path compression on a path of length h in $O(h)$ time in a tree-based partition union/find structure.

R-10.19 George claims he has a fast way to do path compression in a partition structure, starting at a node v. He puts v into a list L, and starts following parent pointers. Each time he encounters a new node, u, he adds u to L and updates the parent pointer of each node in L to point to u's parent. Show that George's algorithm runs in $\Omega(h^2)$ time on a path of length h.

R-10.20 Describe an in-place version of the quick-select algorithm in pseudo-code.

R-10.21 Show that the worst-case running time of quick-select on an n-element sequence is $\Omega(n^2)$.

Creativity

C-10.1 Linda claims to have an algorithm that takes an input sequence S and produces an output sequence T that is a sorting of the n elements in S.

   a. Give an algorithm, isSorted, for testing in $O(n)$ time if T is sorted.
   b. Explain why the algorithm isSorted is not sufficient to prove a particular output T to Linda's algorithm is a sorting of S.
   c. Describe what additional information Linda's algorithm could output so that her algorithm's correctness could be established on any given S and T in $O(n)$ time.

C-10.2 Given two sets A and B represented as sorted sequences, describe an efficient algorithm for computing $A \oplus B$, which is the set of elements that are in A or B, but not in both.

C-10.3 Suppose that we represent sets with balanced search trees. Describe and analyze algorithms for each of the methods in the set ADT, assuming that one of the two sets is much smaller than the other.

C-10.4 Describe and analyze an efficient method for removing all duplicates from a collection A of n elements.

C-10.5 Consider sets whose elements are integers in the range $[0, N-1]$. A popular scheme for representing a set A of this type is by means of a Boolean vector, B, where we say that x is in A if and only if $B[x] = $ **true**. Since each cell of B can be represented with a single bit, B is sometimes referred to as a *bit vector*. Describe and analyze efficient algorithms for performing the methods of the set ADT assuming this representation.

C-10.6 Consider a version of deterministic quick-sort where we pick as our pivot the median of the d last elements in the input sequence of n elements, for a fixed, constant odd number $d \geq 3$. Argue informally why this should be a good choice for pivot. What is the asymptotic worst-case running time of quick-sort in this case, in terms of n and d?

C-10.7 Describe a nonrecursive, in-place version of the quick-sort algorithm. The algorithm should still be based on the same divide-and-conquer approach, but use an explicit stack to process subproblems. Your algorithm should also guarantee the stack depth is at most $O(\log n)$.

C-10.8 Modify inPlaceQuickSort (Code Fragment 10.6) to handle the general case efficiently when the input sequence, S, may have duplicate keys.

C-10.9 Show that randomized quick-sort runs in $O(n \log n)$ time with probability $1 - \frac{1}{n^2}$, using a **Chernoff bound** stating that if we flip a coin k times, the probability that we get fewer than $k/16$ heads is less than $2^{-k/8}$.

C-10.10 Given an array A of n entries with keys equal to 0 or 1, describe an in-place method for ordering A so that all the 0's are before every 1.

C-10.11 Suppose we are given an n-element sequence S such that each element in S represents a different vote for president, where each vote is given as an integer representing a particular candidate. Design an $O(n \log n)$-time algorithm to see who wins the election S represents, assuming the candidate with the most votes wins (even if there are $O(n)$ candidates).

C-10.12 Consider the voting problem from Exercise C-10.11, but now suppose that we know the number $k < n$ of candidates running. Describe an $O(n \log k)$-time algorithm for determining who wins the election.

C-10.13 Consider the voting problem from Exercise C-10.11, but now suppose a candidate wins only if he or she gets a majority of the votes cast. Design and analyze a fast algorithm for determining the winner if there is one.

C-10.14 Show that any comparison-based sorting algorithm can be made to be stable without affecting its asymptotic running time.

C-10.15 Suppose we are given two sequences A and B of n elements, possibly containing duplicates, on which a total order relation is defined. Describe an efficient algorithm for determining if A and B contain the same set of elements. What is the running time of this method?

C-10.16 Given an array A of n integers in the range $[0, n^2 - 1]$, describe a simple method for sorting A in $O(n)$ time.

C-10.17 Let $S_1, S_2, \ldots, S_k$ be k different sequences whose elements have integer keys in the range $[0, N - 1]$, for some parameter $N \geq 2$. Describe an algorithm running in $O(n + N)$ time for sorting all the sequences (not as a union), where n denotes the total size of all the sequences.

C-10.18 Given a sequence S of n elements, on which a total order relation is defined, describe an efficient method for determining whether there are two equal elements in S. What is the running time of your method?

C-10.19 Let S be a sequence of n elements on which a total order relation is defined. An **inversion** in S is a pair of elements x and y such that x appears before y in S but $x > y$. Describe an algorithm running in $O(n \log n)$ time for determining the **number** of inversions in S.

C-10.20 Let S be a sequence of n integers. Describe a comparison-based method for sorting S in $O(n+k)$ time, where k is the number of inversions in S. (Recall the definition of inversion from Exercise C-10.19).

C-10.21 Give a sequence of n integers with $\Omega(n^2)$ inversions. (Recall the definition of inversion from Exercise C-10.19.)

C-10.22 Let A and B be two sequences of n integers each. Given an integer m, describe an $O(n\log n)$-time algorithm for determining if there is an integer a in A and an integer b in B such that $m = a+b$.

C-10.23 Given a set of n integers, describe and analyze a fast method for finding the $\lceil \log n \rceil$ integers closest to the median.

C-10.24 This problem deals with the modification of the quick-select algorithm so as to make it deterministic yet still run in $O(n)$ time on an n-element sequence. The idea is to modify the way we choose the pivot so that it is chosen deterministically, not randomly, as follows:

> Partition the set S into $\lceil n/5 \rceil$ groups of size 5 each (except possibly for one group). Sort each little set and identify the median element in this set. From this set of $\lceil n/5 \rceil$ "baby" medians, apply the selection algorithm recursively to find the median of the baby medians. Use this element as the pivot and proceed as in the quick-select algorithm.

Show that this deterministic method runs in $O(n)$ time by answering the following questions (please ignore floor and ceiling functions if that simplifies the mathematics, for the asymptotics are the same either way):

a. How many baby medians are less than or equal to the chosen pivot? How many are greater than or equal to the pivot?

b. For each baby median less than or equal to the pivot, how many other elements are less than or equal to the pivot? Is the same true for those greater than or equal to the pivot?

c. Argue why the method for finding the deterministic pivot and using it to partition S takes $O(n)$ time.

d. Based on these estimates, write a recurrence equation to bound the worst-case running time $t(n)$ for this selection algorithm (note that in the worst case there are two recursive calls—one to find the median of the baby medians and one to then recur on the larger of L and G).

e. Using this recurrence equation, show by induction that $t(n)$ is $O(n)$.

C-10.25 Bob has a set A of n nuts and a set B of n bolts, such that each nut in A has a unique matching bolt in B. Unfortunately, the nuts in A all look the same, and the bolts in B all look the same as well. The only kind of a comparison that Bob can make is to take a nut-bolt pair (a,b), such that $a \in A$ and $b \in B$, and test it to see if the threads of a are larger, smaller, or a perfect match with the threads of b. Describe and analyze an efficient algorithm for Bob to match up all of his nuts and bolts.

C-10.26 Show how to use a deterministic $O(n)$-time selection algorithm to sort a sequence of n elements in $O(n\log n)$ **worst-case** time.

C-10.27 Given an unsorted sequence S of n comparable elements, and an integer k, give an $O(n\log k)$ expected-time algorithm for finding the $O(k)$ elements that have rank $\lceil n/k \rceil, 2\lceil n/k \rceil, 3\lceil n/k \rceil$, and so on.

C-10.28 Let S be a sequence of n insert and removeMin operations, where all the keys involved are integers in the range $[0, n-1]$. Describe an algorithm running in $O(n\log^* n)$ for determining the answer to each removeMin.

C-10.29 Space aliens have given us a program, alienSplit, that can take a sequence S of n integers and partition S in $O(n)$ time into sequences $S_1, S_2, \ldots, S_k$ of size at most $\lceil n/k \rceil$ each, such that the elements in S_i are less than or equal to every element in S_{i+1}, for $i = 1, 2, \ldots, k-1$, for a fixed number, $k < n$. Show how to use alienSplit to sort S in $O(n\log n/\log k)$ time.

C-10.30 Karen has a new way to do path compression in a tree-based union/find partition data structure starting at a node v. She puts all the nodes that are on the path from v to the root in a set S. Then she then scans through S and sets the parent pointer of each node in S to its parent's parent pointer (recall that the parent pointer of the root points to itself). If this pass changed the value of any node's parent pointer, then she repeats this process, and she goes on repeating this process until she makes a scan through S that does not change any node's parent value. Show that Karen's algorithm is correct and analyze its running time for a path of length h.

Projects

P-10.1 Compare experimentally the performance of in-place quick-sort and a version of quick-sort that is not in-place.

P-10.2 Design and implement a stable version of the bucket-sort algorithm for sorting a sequence of n elements with integer keys taken from the range $[0, N-1]$, for $N \geq 2$. The algorithm should run in $O(n+N)$ time.

P-10.3 Implement merge-sort and deterministic quick-sort and perform a series of benchmarking tests to see which one is faster. Your tests should include sequences that are "random" as well as "almost" sorted.

P-10.4 Implement deterministic and randomized versions of the quick-sort algorithm and perform a series of benchmarking tests to see which one is faster. Your tests should include sequences that are very "random" looking as well as ones that are "almost" sorted.

P-10.5 Implement an in-place version of insertion-sort and an in-place version of quick-sort. Perform benchmarking tests to determine the range of values of n where quick-sort is on average better than insertion-sort.

P-10.6 Design and implement an animation for one of the sorting algorithms described in this chapter. Your animation should illustrate the key properties of this algorithm in an intuitive manner.

P-10.7 Implement the randomized quick-sort and quick-select algorithms. Design a series of benchmarking tests to test the relative speed of solving the selection problem either directly, by the quick-select method, or indirectly, by first sorting via the quick-sort method and then returning the element at the requested rank.

P-10.8 Implement an extended set ADT that includes the methods union(B), intersect(B), subtract(B), size(), isEmpty(), plus the methods equals(B), contains(e), insert(e), and remove(e) with obvious meaning.

P-10.9 Implement the tree-based union/find partition data structure with both the union-by-size and path-compression heuristics.

Chapter Notes

Knuth's classic text on *Sorting and Searching* [59] contains an extensive history of the sorting problem and algorithms for solving it, starting with the census card sorting machines of the late 19th century. Huang and Langston [50] describe how to merge two sorted lists in-place in linear time. Our set ADT is derived from the set ADT of Aho, Hopcroft, and Ullman [5]. The standard quick-sort algorithm is due to Hoare [47]. A tighter analysis of randomized quick-sort can be found in the book by Motwani and Raghavan [76]. Gonnet and Baeza-Yates [40] provide experimental comparisons and theoretical analyses of a number of different sorting algorithms. The term "prune-and-search" comes originally from the computational geometry literature (such as in the work of Clarkson [21] and Megiddo [69, 70]). The term "decrease-and-conquer" is from Levitin [64].

Chapter
11

Text Processing

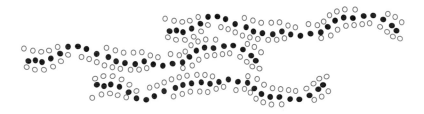

Contents

Document processing is rapidly becoming one of the dominant functions of computers. Computers are used to edit documents, to search documents, to transport documents over the Internet, and to display documents on printers and computer screens. Web "surfing" and Web searching are becoming significant and important computer applications, and many of the key computations in all of this document processing involve character strings and string pattern matching. For example, the Internet document formats HTML and XML are primarily text formats, with added tags for multimedia content. Making sense of the many terabytes of information on the Internet requires a considerable amount of text processing.

In this chapter, we study several of the fundamental text processing algorithms for quickly performing important string operations. We pay particular attention to algorithms for string searching and pattern matching, since these can often be computational bottlenecks in many document-processing applications. We also study some fundamental data structure and algorithmic issues involved in text processing, as well.

The progression of topics studied in this chapter continues to follow our abstract data type approach. The terminology and notation for the string ADT, which is used in this chapter, is defined in Section 11.1. It turns out that representing a string as an array of characters is quite simple and efficient, so we don't spend a lot of attention on string representations. Nevertheless, the string ADT includes an interesting method for string pattern matching, and we study pattern matching algorithms in Section 11.2. In Section 11.3 we study the trie data structure, which is a tree-based structure that allows for fast searching in a collection of strings. We study an important text processing problem in Section 11.4, namely, the problem of compressing a document of text so that it fits more efficiently in storage or can be transmitted more efficiently over a network. We study another text processing problem in Section 11.5, which deals with how we can measure the similarity between two documents. All of these problems are topics that arise often in Internet computations, such as Web crawlers, search engines, document distribution, and information retrieval.

In addition to having interesting applications, the topics of this chapter also highlight some important algorithmic design patterns. In particular, in the section on pattern matching, we discuss the ***brute-force method***, which is often inefficient but has wide applicability. For text compression, we study the ***greedy method***, which often allows us to approximate solutions to hard problems, and for some problems (such as in text compression) actually gives rise to optimal algorithms. Finally, in discussing text similarity, we introduce the ***dynamic programming*** design pattern, which can be applied in some special instances to solve a problem in polynomial time that appears at first to require exponential time to solve.

11.1 String Operations

At the heart of algorithms for processing text are methods for dealing with character strings. Character strings can come from a wide variety of sources, including scientific, linguistic, and Internet applications. Indeed, the following are examples of such strings:

$$P \;=\; \texttt{"CGTAAACTGCTTTAATCAAACGC"}$$
$$R \;=\; \texttt{"U.S. Men Win Soccer World Cup!"}$$
$$S \;=\; \texttt{"http://java.datastructures.net"}.$$

The first string, P, comes from DNA applications, the last string, S, is the Internet address (URL) for the Web site that accompanies this book, and the middle string, R, is a fictional news headline. In this section, we present some of the useful operations that are supported by the string ADT for processing strings such as these.

Several of the typical string processing operations involve breaking large strings into smaller strings. In order to be able to speak about the pieces that result from such operations, we use the term **substring** of an m-character string P to refer to a string of the form $P[i]P[i+1]P[i+2]\cdots P[j]$, for some $0 \le i \le j \le m-1$, that is, the string formed by the characters in P from index i to index j, inclusive. Technically, this means that a string is actually a substring of itself (taking $i = 0$ and $j = m-1$), so if we want to rule this out as a possibility, we must restrict the definition to **proper** substrings, which require that either $i > 0$ or $j < m-1$. To simplify the notation for referring to substrings, let us use $P[i..j]$ to denote the substring of P from index i to index j, inclusive. That is,

$$P[i..j] = P[i]P[i+1]\cdots P[j].$$

We use the convention that if $i > j$, then $P[i..j]$ is equal to the **null string**, which has length 0. In addition, in order to distinguish some special kinds of substrings, let us refer to any substring of the form $P[0..i]$, for $0 \le i \le m-1$, as a **prefix** of P, and any substring of the form $P[i..m-1]$, for $0 \le i \le m-1$, as a **suffix** of P. For example, if we again take P to be the string of DNA given above, then "CGTAA" is a prefix of P, "CGC" is a suffix of P, and "TTAATC" is a (proper) substring of P. Note that the null string is a prefix and a suffix of any other string.

String operations come in two flavors: those that modify the string they act on and those that simply return information about the string without actually modifying it. Java makes this distinction precise by defining the String class to represent **immutable strings**, which cannot be modified, and the StringBuffer class to represent **mutable strings**, which can be modified.

11.1.1   The Java String Class

The main operations of the Java String class are listed below:

length(): Return the length, n, of S.
Input: None; *Output:* **int**.

charAt(i): Return the character at index i in S.
Input: **int**; *Output:* **char**.

startsWith(Q): Determine if Q is a prefix of S.
Input: String; *Output:* **boolean**.

endsWith(Q): Determine if Q is a suffix of S.
Input: String; *Output:* **boolean**.

substring(i, j): Return the substring $S[i, j]$.
Input: **int** (i) and **int** (j); *Output:* String.

concat(Q): Return the concatenation of S and Q, that is, $S + Q$.
Input: String; *Output:* String.

equals(Q): Determine if Q is equal to S.
Input: String; *Output:* **boolean**.

indexOf(Q): If Q is a substring of S, return the index of the beginning of the first occurrence of Q in S, else return -1.
Input: String; *Output:* **int**.

This collection forms the typical operations for immutable strings.

Example 11.1: *Consider the following set of operations, which are performed on the string $S = $ "abcdefghijklmnop":*

Operation	*Output*
length()	16
charAt(5)	'f'
concat("qrs")	"abcdefghijklmnopqrs"
endsWith("javapop")	false
equals("abcdefghijklmnop")	true
indexOf("ghi")	6
startsWith("abcd")	true
substring(4,9)	"efghij"

With the exception of the indexOf(Q) method, which we discuss in Section 11.2, all the above methods are easily implemented simply by representing the string as an array of characters, which is the standard String implementation in Java.

11.1.2 The Java StringBuffer Class

The main methods of the Java StringBuffer class are listed below:

append(Q): Return $S + Q$, replacing S with $S + Q$.
Input: String; **Output:** StringBuffer.

insert(i, Q): Return and update S to be the string obtained by inserting Q inside S starting at index i.
Input: String; **Output:** StringBuffer.

reverse(): Reverse and return the string S.
Input: None; **Output:** StringBuffer.

setCharAt(i, ch): Set the character at index i in S to be ch.
Input: **int** (i) and **char** (ch); **Output:** None.

charAt(i): Return the character at index i in S.
Input: **int**; **Output:** **char**.

Error conditions occur when the index i is out of the bounds of the indices of the string. With the exception of the charAt method, most of the methods of the String class are not immediately available to a StringBuffer object S in Java. Fortunately, the Java StringBuffer class provides a toString() method that returns a String version of S, which can be used to access String methods.

Example 11.2: *Consider the following sequence of operations, which are performed on the mutable string that is initially* $S =$ `"abcdefghijklmnop"`:

Operation	*S*
append(`"qrs"`)	`"abcdefghijklmnopqrs"`
insert(*3,*`"xyz"`)	`"abcxyzdefghijklmnopqrs"`
reverse()	`"srqponmlkjihgfedzyxcba"`
setCharAt(*7,*`'W'`)	`"srqponmWkjihgfedzyxcba"`

Incidentally, we have not given an exhaustive listing of all methods supported by String and StringBuffer objects in Java, but the methods included above should be sufficient for most applications, such as use in instance variables. Thus, let us view the methods of the String class as defining an immutable string ADT, and let us view the methods of the StringBuffer as adding to this ADT to define a mutable string ADT.

11.2 Pattern Matching Algorithms

In the classic ***pattern matching*** problem on strings, we are given a ***text*** string T of length n and a ***pattern*** string P of length m, and want to find whether P is a substring of T. The notion of a "match" is that there is a substring of T starting at some index i that matches P, character by character, so that $T[i] = P[0]$, $T[i + 1] = P[1]$, ..., $T[i + m - 1] = P[m - 1]$. That is, $P = T[i..i + m - 1]$. Thus, the output from a pattern matching algorithm could either be some indication that the pattern P does not exist in T or an integer indicating the starting index in T of a substring matching P. This is exactly the computation performed by the indexOf method of the Java String interface. Alternatively, one may want to find all the indices where a substring of T matching P begins.

To allow for fairly general notions of a character string, we typically do not restrict the characters in T and P to explicitly come from a well-known character set, like the ASCII or Unicode character sets. Instead, we typically use the general symbol Σ to denote the character set, or ***alphabet***, from which characters in T and P can come. This alphabet Σ can, of course, be a subset of the ASCII or Unicode character sets, but it could also be something more general and is even allowed to be infinite, like positive integers. Nevertheless, since most document processing algorithms are used in applications where the underlying character set is finite, we usually assume that the size of the alphabet Σ, denoted with $|\Sigma|$, is a fixed finite constant.

In this section, we present three pattern matching algorithms (with increasing levels of difficulty).

11.2.1 Brute Force

The ***brute force*** algorithmic design pattern is a powerful technique for algorithm design when we have something we wish to search for or when we wish to optimize some function. In applying this technique in a general situation we typically enumerate all possible configurations of the inputs involved and pick the best of all these enumerated configurations.

Brute-Force Pattern Matching

In applying this technique to design the ***brute-force pattern matching*** algorithm, we derive what is probably the first algorithm that we might think of for solving the pattern matching problem—we simply test all the possible placements of P relative to T. This algorithm, shown in Code Fragment 11.1, is quite simple.

Algorithm BruteForceMatch(T,P):

    Input: Strings T (text) with n characters and P (pattern) with m characters

    Output: Starting index of the first substring of T matching P, or an indication that P is not a substring of T

    for $i \leftarrow 0$ **to** $n - m$ {for each candidate index in T} **do**

        $j \leftarrow 0$

        while $(j < m$ **and** $T[i+j] = P[j])$ **do**

            $j \leftarrow j + 1$

        if $j = m$ **then**

            return i

    return "There is no substring of T matching P."

Code Fragment 11.1: Brute-force pattern matching.

The brute-force pattern matching algorithm could not be simpler. It consists of two nested loops, with the outer loop indexing through all possible starting indices of the pattern in the text, and the inner loop indexing through each character of the pattern, comparing it to its potentially corresponding character in the text. Thus, the correctness of the brute-force pattern matching algorithm follows immediately from this exhaustive search approach.

Performance

The running time of brute-force pattern matching in the worst case is not good, however, because, for each candidate index in T, we can perform up to m character comparisons to discover that P does not match T at the current index. Referring to Code Fragment 11.1, we see that the outer **for** loop is executed at most $n - m + 1$ times, and the inner loop is executed at most m times. Thus, the running time of the brute-force method is $O((n - m + 1)m)$, which is simplified as $O(nm)$. Note that when $m = n/2$, this algorithm has quadratic runnimg time $O(n^2)$.

Example 11.3: *Suppose we are given the text string*

$$T = \texttt{"abacaabaccabacabaabb"}$$

and the pattern string

$$P = \texttt{"abacab"}.$$

In Figure 11.1 we illustrate the execution of the brute-force pattern matching algorithm on T and P.

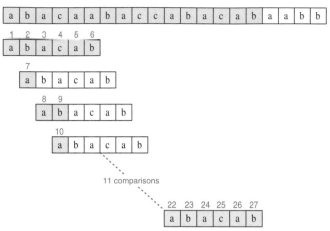

Figure 11.1: Example run of the brute-force pattern matching algorithm. The algorithm performs 27 character comparisons, indicated above with numerical labels.

11.2.2   The Boyer-Moore Algorithm

At first, we might feel that it is always necessary to examine every character in T in order to locate a pattern P as a substring. But this is not always the case, for the **Boyer-Moore** (**BM**) pattern matching algorithm, which we study in this section, can sometimes avoid comparisons between P and a sizable fraction of the characters in T. The only caveat is that, whereas the brute-force algorithm can work even with a potentially unbounded alphabet, the BM algorithm assumes the alphabet is of fixed, finite size. It works the fastest when the alphabet is moderately sized and the pattern is relatively long. Thus, the BM algorithm is ideal for searching words in documents. In this section, we describe a simplified version of the original algorithm by Boyer and Moore.

The main idea of the BM algorithm is to improve the running time of the brute-force algorithm by adding two potentially time-saving heuristics. Roughly stated, these heuristics are as follows:

Looking-Glass Heuristic: When testing a possible placement of P against T, begin the comparisons from the end of P and move backward to the front of P.

Character-Jump Heuristic: During the testing of a possible placement of P against T, a mismatch of text character $T[i] = c$ with the corresponding pattern character $P[j]$ is handled as follows. If c is not contained anywhere in P, then shift P completely past $T[i]$ (for it cannot match any character in P). Otherwise, shift P until an occurrence of character c in P gets aligned with $T[i]$.

We will formalize these heuristics shortly, but at an intuitive level, they work as an integrated team. The looking-glass heuristic sets up the other heuristic to allow us to avoid comparisons between P and whole groups of characters in T. In this case at least, we can get to the destination faster by going backwards, for if we encounter a mismatch during the consideration of P at a certain location in T, then we are likely to avoid lots of needless comparisons by significantly shifting P relative to T using the character-jump heuristic. The character-jump heuristic pays off big if it can be applied early in the testing of a potential placement of P against T.

Let us therefore get down to the business of defining how the character-jump heuristics can be integrated into a string pattern matching algorithm. To implement this heuristic, we define a function $\text{last}(c)$ that takes a character c from the alphabet and characterizes how far we may shift the pattern P if a character equal to c is found in the text that does not match the pattern. In particular, we define $\text{last}(c)$ as

- If c is in P, $\text{last}(c)$ is the index of the last (right-most) occurrence of c in P. Otherwise, we conventionally define $\text{last}(c) = -1$.

If characters can be used as indices in arrays, then the last function can be easily implemented as a look-up table. We leave the method for computing this table in $O(m + |\Sigma|)$ time, given P, as a simple exercise (R-11.6). This last function will give us all the information we need to perform the character-jump heuristic.

In Code Fragment 11.2, we show the BM pattern matching algorithm.

Algorithm $\text{BMMatch}(T, P)$:

    Input: Strings T (text) with n characters and P (pattern) with m characters
    Output: Starting index of the first substring of T matching P, or an indication
        that P is not a substring of T

    compute function last
    $i \leftarrow m - 1$
    $j \leftarrow m - 1$
    repeat
      if $P[j] = T[i]$ **then**
        if $j = 0$ **then**
          return i {a match!}
        else
          $i \leftarrow i - 1$
          $j \leftarrow j - 1$
      else
        $i \leftarrow i + m - \min(j, 1 + \text{last}(T[i]))$ { jump step }
        $j \leftarrow m - 1$
    until $i > n - 1$
    return "There is no substring of T matching P."

      Code Fragment 11.2: The Boyer-Moore pattern matching algorithm.

The jump step is illustrated in Figure 11.2. In Figure 11.3, we illustrate the execution of the Boyer-Moore pattern matching algorithm on a similar input string as in Example 11.3.

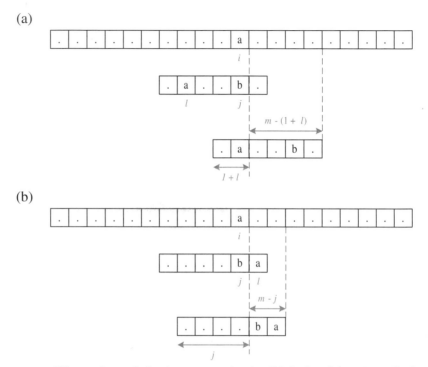

Figure 11.2: Illustration of the jump step in the BM algorithm (see Code Fragment 11.2), where we use the notation $l = \text{last}(T[i])$. We distinguish two cases: (a) $1 + l \leq j$, where we shift the pattern by $j - l$ units; (b) $j < 1 + l$, where we shift the pattern by one unit.

The correctness of the BM pattern matching algorithm follows from the fact that each time the method makes a shift, it is guaranteed not to "skip" over any possible matches. For $\text{last}(c)$ is the location of the ***last*** occurrence of c in P.

The worst-case running time of the BM algorithm is $O(nm + |\Sigma|)$. Namely, the computation of the last function takes time $O(m + |\Sigma|)$ and the actual search for the pattern takes $O(nm)$ time in the worst case, the same as the brute-force algorithm. An example of a text-pattern pair that achieves the worst case is

$$T = \overbrace{aaaaaa\cdots a}^{n}$$
$$P = b\overbrace{aa\cdots a}^{m-1}.$$

The worst-case performance, however, is unlikely to be achieved for English text.

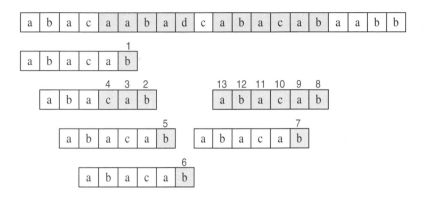

The last(c) function:

c	a	b	c	d
last(c)	4	5	3	−1

Figure 11.3: An illustration of the BM pattern matching algorithm. The algorithm performs 13 character comparisons, which are indicated with numerical labels.

Indeed, the BM algorithm is often able to skip over large portions of the text. (See Figure 11.4.) There is experimental evidence that on English text, the average number of comparisons done per text character is approximately 0.24 for a five-character pattern string. The payoff is not as great for binary strings or for very short patterns, however, in which case the KMP algorithm, discussed in Section 11.2.3, or, for very short patterns, the brute-force algorithm, may be better.

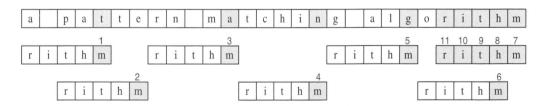

Figure 11.4: Execution of the Boyer-Moore algorithm on an English text and pattern, where a significant speedup is achieved. Note that not all text characters are examined.

A Java implementation of the BM pattern matching algorithm is shown in Code Fragment 11.3.

```java
/** Simplified version of the Boyer-Moore (BM) algorithm, which uses
 *  only the looking-glass and character-jump heuristics.
 *  @return Index of the beginning of the leftmost substring of the text
 *  matching the pattern, or -1 if there is no match.  */
public static int BMmatch (String text, String pattern) {
  int[] last = buildLastFunction(pattern);
  int n = text.length();
  int m = pattern.length();
  int i = m -1;
  if (i > n - 1)
    return -1; // no match if pattern is longer than text
  int j = m - 1;
  do {
    if (pattern.charAt(j) == text.charAt(i))
      if (j == 0)
        return i; // match
      else { // looking-glass heuristic: proceed right-to-left
        i--;
        j--;
      }
    else { // character jump heuristic
      i = i + m - Math.min(j, 1 + last[text.charAt(i)]);
      j = m - 1;
    }
  } while (i <= n - 1);
  return -1; // no match
}
public static int[] buildLastFunction (String pattern) {
  int[] last = new int[128]; // assume ASCII character set
  for (int i = 0; i < 128; i++) {
    last[i] = -1; // initialize array
  }
  for (int i = 0; i < pattern.length(); i++) {
    last[pattern.charAt(i)] = i; // implicit cast to integer ASCII code
  }
  return last;
}
```

Code Fragment 11.3: Java implementation of the BM pattern matching algorithm. The algorithm is expressed by two static methods: method BMmatch performs the matching and calls the auxiliary method buildLastFunction to compute the last function, expressed by an array indexed by the ASCII code of the character. Method BMmatch indicates the absence of a match by returning the conventional value −1.

We have actually presented a simplified version of the Boyer-Moore (BM) algorithm. The original BM algorithm achieves running time $O(n+m+|\Sigma|)$ by using an alternative shift heuristic to the partially matched text string, whenever it shifts the pattern more than the character-jump heuristic. This alternative shift heuristic is based on applying the main idea from the Knuth-Morris-Pratt pattern matching algorithm, which we discuss next.

11.2.3 The Knuth-Morris-Pratt Algorithm

In studying the worst-case performance of the brute-force and BM pattern matching algorithms on specific instances of the problem, such as that given in Example 11.3, we should notice a major inefficiency. Specifically, we may perform many comparisons while testing a potential placement of the pattern against the text, yet if we discover a pattern character that does not match in the text, then we throw away all the information gained by these comparisons and start over again from scratch with the next incremental placement of the pattern. The Knuth-Morris-Pratt (or "KMP") algorithm, discussed in this section, avoids this waste of information and, in so doing, it achieves a running time of $O(n+m)$, which is optimal in the worst case. That is, in the worst case any pattern matching algorithm will have to examine all the characters of the text and all the characters of the pattern at least once.

The Failure Function

The main idea of the KMP algorithm is to preprocess the pattern string P so as to compute a **failure function** f that indicates the proper shift of P so that, to the largest extent possible, we can reuse previously performed comparisons. Specifically, the failure function $f(j)$ is defined as the length of the longest prefix of P that is a suffix of $P[1..j]$ (note that we did **not** put $P[0..j]$ here). We also use the convention that $f(0) = 0$. Later, we will discuss how to compute the failure function efficiently. The importance of this failure function is that it "encodes" repeated substrings inside the pattern itself.

Example 11.4: *Consider the pattern string* $P =$ *"abacab" from Example 11.3. The Knuth-Morris-Pratt (KMP) failure function* $f(j)$ *for the string* P *is as shown in the following table:*

j	0	1	2	3	4	5
$P[j]$	a	b	a	c	a	b
$f(j)$	0	0	1	0	1	2

The KMP pattern matching algorithm, shown in Code Fragment 11.4, incrementally processes the text string T comparing it to the pattern string P. Each time there is a match, we increment the current indices. On the other hand, if there is a mismatch and we have previously made progress in P, then we consult the failure function to determine the new index in P where we need to continue checking P against T. Otherwise (there was a mismatch and we are at the beginning of P), we simply increment the index for T (and keep the index variable for P at its beginning). We repeat this process until we find a match of P in T or the index for T reaches n, the length of T (indicating that we did not find the pattern P in T).

Algorithm KMPMatch(T, P):

   Input: Strings T (text) with n characters and P (pattern) with m characters

   Output: Starting index of the first substring of T matching P, or an indication that P is not a substring of T

     $f \leftarrow$ KMPFailureFunction(P)   {construct the failure function f for P}

     $i \leftarrow 0$

     $j \leftarrow 0$

     while $i < n$ **do**

       if $P[j] = T[i]$ **then**

         if $j = m - 1$ **then**

           return $i - m + 1$ {a match!}

         $i \leftarrow i + 1$

         $j \leftarrow j + 1$

       else if $j > 0$ {no match, but we have advanced in P} **then**

         $j \leftarrow f(j-1)$ {j indexes just after prefix of P that must match}

       else

         $i \leftarrow i + 1$

     return "There is no substring of T matching P."

Code Fragment 11.4: The KMP pattern matching algorithm.

The main part of the KMP algorithm is the **while** loop, which performs a comparison between a character in T and a character in P each iteration. Depending upon the outcome of this comparison, the algorithm either moves on to the next characters in T and P, consults the failure function for a new candidate character in P, or starts over with the next index in T. The correctness of this algorithm follows from the definition of the failure function. Any comparisons that are skipped are actually unnecessary, for the failure function guarantees that all the ignored comparisons are redundant—they would involve comparing the same matching characters over again.

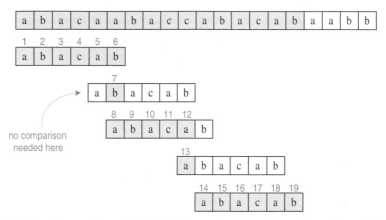

Figure 11.5: An illustration of the KMP pattern matching algorithm. The failure function f for this pattern is given in Example 11.4. The algorithm performs 19 character comparisons, which are indicated with numerical labels.

In Figure 11.5, we illustrate the execution of the KMP pattern matching algorithm on the same input strings as in Example 11.3. Note the use of the failure function to avoid redoing one of the comparisons between a character of the pattern and a character of the text. Also note that the algorithm performs fewer overall comparisons than the brute-force algorithm run on the same strings (Figure 11.1).

Performance

Excluding the computation of the failure function, the running time of the KMP algorithm is clearly proportional to the number of iterations of the **while** loop. For the sake of the analysis, let us define $k = i - j$. Intuitively, k is the total amount by which the pattern P has been shifted with respect to the text T. Note that throughout the execution of the algorithm, we have $k \leq n$. One of the following three cases occurs at each iteration of the loop.

- If $T[i] = P[j]$, then i increases by 1, and k does not change, since j also increases by 1.
- If $T[i] \neq P[j]$ and $j > 0$, then i does not change and k increases by at least 1, since in this case k changes from $i - j$ to $i - f(j-1)$, which is an addition of $j - f(j-1)$, which is positive because $f(j-1) < j$.
- If $T[i] \neq P[j]$ and $j = 0$, then i increases by 1 and k increases by 1, since j does not change.

Thus, at each iteration of the loop, either i or k increases by at least 1 (possibly both); hence, the total number of iterations of the **while** loop in the KMP pattern matching algorithm is at most $2n$. Achieving this bound, of course, assumes that we have already computed the failure function for P.

Constructing the KMP Failure Function

To construct the failure function, we use the method shown in Code Fragment 11.5, which is a "bootstrapping" process quite similar to the KMPMatch algorithm. We compare the pattern to itself as in the KMP algorithm. Each time we have two characters that match, we set $f(i) = j+1$. Note that since we have $i > j$ throughout the execution of the algorithm, $f(j-1)$ is always defined when we need to use it.

Algorithm KMPFailureFunction(P):

    Input: String P (pattern) with m characters

    Output: The failure function f for P, which maps j to the length of the longest
       prefix of P that is a suffix of $P[1..j]$

    $i \leftarrow 1$
    $j \leftarrow 0$
    $f(0) \leftarrow 0$
    while $i < m$ **do**
      if $P[j] = P[i]$ **then**
          {we have matched $j+1$ characters}
        $f(i) \leftarrow j+1$
        $i \leftarrow i+1$
        $j \leftarrow j+1$
      else if $j > 0$ **then**
          {j indexes just after a prefix of P that must match}
        $j \leftarrow f(j-1)$
      else
          {we have no match here}
        $f(i) \leftarrow 0$
        $i \leftarrow i+1$

Code Fragment 11.5: Computation of the failure function used in the KMP pattern matching algorithm. Note how the algorithm uses the previous values of the failure function to efficiently compute new values.

Algorithm KMPFailureFunction runs in $O(m)$ time. Its analysis is analogous to that of algorithm KMPMatch. Thus, we have:

Proposition 11.5: *The Knuth-Morris-Pratt algorithm performs pattern matching on a text string of length n and a pattern string of length m in $O(n+m)$ time.*

A Java implementation of the KMP pattern matching algorithm is shown in Code Fragment 11.6.

```java
public static int KMPmatch(String text, String pattern) {
  int n = text.length();
  int m = pattern.length();
  int[] fail = computeFailFunction(pattern);
  int i = 0;
  int j = 0;
  while (i < n) {
    if (pattern.charAt(j) == text.charAt(i)) {
      if (j == m − 1)
        return i − m + 1; // match
      i++;
      j++;
    }
    else if (j > 0)
      j = fail[j − 1];
    else
      i++;
  }
  return −1; // no match
}
public static int[] computeFailFunction(String pattern) {
  int[] fail = new int[pattern.length()];
  fail[0] = 0;
  int m = pattern.length();
  int j = 0;
  int i = 1;
  while (i < m) {
    if (pattern.charAt(j) == pattern.charAt(i)) { // j + 1 characters match
      fail[i] = j + 1;
      i++;
      j++;
    }
    else if (j > 0) // j follows a matching prefix
      j = fail[j − 1];
    else { // no match
      fail[i] = 0;
      i++;
    }
  }
  return fail;
}
```

Code Fragment 11.6: Java implementation of the KMP pattern matching algorithm. The algorithm is expressed by two static methods: method KMPmatch performs the matching and calls the auxiliary method computeFailFunction to compute the failure function, expressed by an array. Method KMPmatch indicates the absence of a match by returning the conventional value −1.

11.3   Tries

The pattern matching algorithms presented in the previous section speed up the search in a text by preprocessing the pattern (to compute the failure function in the KMP algorithm or the last function in the BM algorithm). In this section, we take a complementary approach, namely, we present string searching algorithms that preprocess the text. This approach is suitable for applications where a series of queries is performed on a fixed text, so that the initial cost of preprocessing the text is compensated by a speedup in each subsequent query (for example, a Web site that offers pattern matching in Shakespeare's *Hamlet* or a search engine that offers Web pages on the *Hamlet* topic).

A **trie** (pronounced "try") is a tree-based data structure for storing strings in order to support fast pattern matching. The main application for tries is in information retrieval. Indeed, the name "trie" comes from the word "re*trie*val." In an information retrieval application, such as a search for a certain DNA sequence in a genomic database, we are given a collection S of strings, all defined using the same alphabet. The primary query operations that tries support are pattern matching and **prefix matching**. The latter operation involves being given a string X, and looking for all the strings in S that contain X as a prefix.

11.3.1   Standard Tries

Let S be a set of s strings from alphabet Σ such that no string in S is a prefix of another string. A **standard trie** for S is an ordered tree T with the following properties (see Figure 11.6):

- Each node of T, except the root, is labeled with a character of Σ.
- The ordering of the children of an internal node of T is determined by a canonical ordering of the alphabet Σ.
- T has s external nodes, each associated with a string of S, such that the concatenation of the labels of the nodes on the path from the root to an external node v of T yields the string of S associated with v.

Thus, a trie T represents the strings of S with paths from the root to the external nodes of T. Note the importance of assuming that no string in S is a prefix of another string. This ensures that each string of S is uniquely associated with an external node of T. We can always satisfy this assumption by adding a special character that is not in the original alphabet Σ at the end of each string. An internal node in a standard trie T can have anywhere between 1 and d children, where d is the size of the alphabet. There is an edge going from the root r to

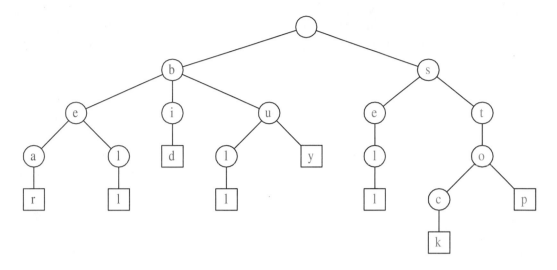

Figure 11.6: Standard trie for the strings {bear, bell, bid, bull, buy, sell, stock, stop}.

one of its children for each character that is first in some string in the collection S. In addition, a path from the root of T to an internal node v at depth i corresponds to an i-character prefix $X[0..i-1]$ of a string X of S. In fact, for each character c that can follow the prefix $X[0..i-1]$ in a string of the set S, there is a child of v labeled with character c. In this way, a trie concisely stores the common prefixes that exist among a set of strings.

If there are only two characters in the alphabet, then the trie is essentially a binary tree, with some internal nodes possibly having only one child (that is, it may be an improper binary tree). In general, if there are d characters in the alphabet, then the trie will be a multi-way tree where each internal node has between 1 and d children. In addition, there are likely to be several internal nodes in a standard trie that have fewer than d children. For example, the trie shown in Figure 11.6 has several internal nodes with only one child. We can implement a trie with a tree storing characters at its nodes.

The following proposition provides some important structural properties of a standard trie:

Proposition 11.6: *A standard trie storing a collection S of s strings of total length n from an alphabet of size d has the following properties:*

- *Every internal node of T has at most d children*
- *T has s external nodes*
- *The height of T is equal to the length of the longest string in S*
- *The number of nodes of T is $O(n)$.*

The worst case for the number of nodes of a trie occurs when no two strings share a common nonempty prefix; that is, except for the root, all internal nodes have one child.

A trie T for a set S of strings can be used to implement a dictionary whose keys are the strings of S. Namely, we perform a search in T for a string X by tracing down from the root the path indicated by the characters in X. If this path can be traced and terminates at an external node, then we know X is in the dictionary. For example, in the trie in Figure 11.6, tracing the path for "bull" ends up at an external node. If the path cannot be traced or the path can be traced but terminates at an internal node, then X is not in the dictionary. In the example in Figure 11.6, the path for "bet" cannot be traced and the path for "be" ends at an internal node. Neither such word is in the dictionary. Note that in this implementation of a dictionary, single characters are compared instead of the entire string (key). It is easy to see that the running time of the search for a string of size m is $O(dm)$, where d is the size of the alphabet. Indeed, we visit at most $m + 1$ nodes of T and we spend $O(d)$ time at each node. For some alphabets, we may be able to improve the time spent at a node to be $O(1)$ or $O(\log d)$ by using a dictionary of characters implemented in a hash table or search table. However, since d is a constant in most applications, we can stick with the simple approach that takes $O(d)$ time per node visited.

From the above discussion, it follows that we can use a trie to perform a special type of pattern matching, called ***word matching***, where we want to determine whether a given pattern matches one of the words of the text exactly. (See Figure 11.7.) Word matching differs from standard pattern matching since the pattern cannot match an arbitrary substring of the text, but only one of its words. Using a trie, word matching for a pattern of length m takes $O(dm)$ time, where d is the size of the alphabet, independent of the size of the text. If the alphabet has constant size (as is the case for text in natural languages and DNA strings), a query takes $O(m)$ time, proportional to the size of the pattern. A simple extension of this scheme supports prefix matching queries. However, arbitrary occurrences of the pattern in the text (for example, the pattern is a proper suffix of a word or spans two words) cannot be efficiently performed.

To construct a standard trie for a set S of strings, we can use an incremental algorithm that inserts the strings one at a time. Recall the assumption that no string of S is a prefix of another string. To insert a string X into the current trie T, we first try to trace the path associated with X in T. Since X is not already in T and no string in S is a prefix of another string, we will stop tracing the path at an ***internal*** node v of T before reaching the end of X. We then create a new chain of node descendents of v to store the remaining characters of X. The time to insert X is $O(dm)$, where m is the length of X and d is the size of the alphabet. Thus, constructing the entire trie for set S takes $O(dn)$ time, where n is the total length of the strings of S.

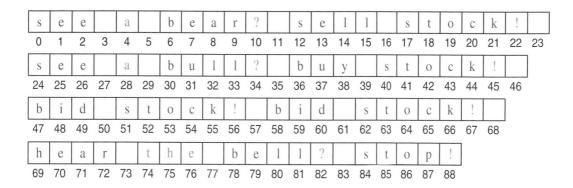

s	e	e		a		b	e	a	r	?		s	e	l	l		s	t	o	c	k	!	
0	1	2	3	4	5	6	7	8	9	10	11	12	13	14	15	16	17	18	19	20	21	22	23

s	e	e		a		b	u	l	l	?		b	u	y		s	t	o	c	k	!	
24	25	26	27	28	29	30	31	32	33	34	35	36	37	38	39	40	41	42	43	44	45	46

b	i	d		s	t	o	c	k	!		b	i	d		s	t	o	c	k	!	
47	48	49	50	51	52	53	54	55	56	57	58	59	60	61	62	63	64	65	66	67	68

h	e	a	r		t	h	e		b	e	l	l	?		s	t	o	p	!
69	70	71	72	73	74	75	76	77	78	79	80	81	82	83	84	85	86	87	88

(a)

(b)

Figure 11.7: Word matching and prefix matching with a standard trie: (a) text to be searched; (b) standard trie for the words in the text (articles and prepositions, which are also known as *stop words*, excluded), with external nodes augmented with indications of the word positions.

There is a potential space inefficiency in the standard trie that has prompted the development of the *compressed trie*, which is also known (for historical reasons) as the *Patricia trie*. Namely, there are potentially a lot of nodes in the standard trie that have only one child, and the existence of such nodes is a waste. We discuss the compressed trie next.

11.3.2 Compressed Tries

A *compressed trie* is similar to a standard trie but it ensures that each internal node in the trie has at least two children. It enforces this rule by compressing chains of single-child nodes into individual edges. (See Figure 11.8.) Let T be a standard trie. We say that an internal node v of T is *redundant* if v has one child and is not the root. For example, the trie of Figure 11.6 has eight redundant nodes. Let us also say that a chain of $k \geq 2$ edges,

$$(v_0, v_1)(v_1, v_2) \cdots (v_{k-1}, v_k),$$

is *redundant* if

- v_i is redundant for $i = 1, \ldots, k-1$
- v_0 and v_k are not redundant.

We can transform T into a compressed trie by replacing each redundant chain $(v_0, v_1) \cdots (v_{k-1}, v_k)$ of $k \geq 2$ edges into a single edge (v_0, v_k), relabeling v_k with the concatenation of the labels of nodes $v_1, \ldots, v_k$.

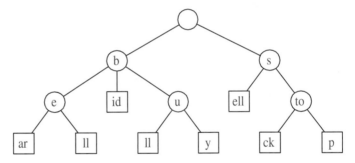

Figure 11.8: Compressed trie for the strings {bear, bell, bid, bull, buy, sell, stock, stop}. Compare this with the standard trie shown in Figure 11.6.

Thus, nodes in a compressed trie are labeled with strings, which are substrings of strings in the collection, rather than with individual characters. The advantage of a compressed trie over a standard trie is that the number of nodes of the compressed trie is proportional to the number of strings and not to their total length, as shown in the following proposition (compare with Proposition 11.6).

Proposition 11.7: *A compressed trie storing a collection S of s strings from an alphabet of size d has the following properties:*

- *Every internal node of T has at least two children and most d children*
- *T has s external nodes*
- *The number of nodes of T is $O(s)$.*

The attentive reader may wonder whether the compression of paths provides any significant advantage, since it is offset by a corresponding expansion of the node labels. Indeed, a compressed trie is truly advantageous only when it is used as an *auxiliary* index structure over a collection of strings already stored in a primary structure, and is not required to actually store all the characters of the strings in the collection.

Suppose, for example, that the collection S of strings is an array of strings $S[0]$, $S[1]$, ..., $S[s-1]$. Instead of storing the label X of a node explicitly, we represent it implicitly by a triplet of integers (i, j, k), such that $X = S[i][j..k]$; that is, X is the substring of $S[i]$ consisting of the characters from the jth to the kth included. (See the example in Figure 11.9. Also compare with the standard trie of Figure 11.7.)

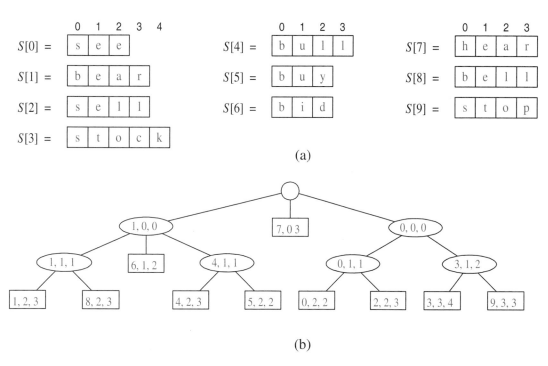

(a)

(b)

Figure 11.9: (a) Collection S of strings stored in an array. (b) Compact representation of the compressed trie for S.

This additional compression scheme allows us to reduce the total space for the trie itself from $O(n)$ for the standard trie to $O(s)$ for the compressed trie, where n is the total length of the strings in S and s is the number of strings in S. We must still store the different strings in S, of course, but we nevertheless reduce the space for the trie. In the next section, we present an application where the collection of strings can also be stored compactly.

11.3.3   Suffix Tries

One of the primary applications for tries is for the case when the strings in the collection S are all the suffixes of a string X. Such a trie is called the **suffix trie** (also known as a **suffix tree** or **position tree**) of string X. For example, Figure 11.10a shows the suffix trie for the eight suffixes of string "minimize." For a suffix trie, the compact representation presented in the previous section can be further simplified. Namely, the label of each vertex is a pair (i, j) indicating the string $X[i..j]$. (See Figure 11.10b.) To satisfy the rule that no suffix of X is a prefix of another suffix, we can add a special character, denoted with $, that is not in the original alphabet Σ at the end of X (and thus to every suffix). That is, if string X has length n, we build a trie for the set of n strings $X[i..n-1]\$$, for $i = 0, \ldots, n-1$.

Saving Space

Using a suffix trie allows us to save space over a standard trie by using several space compression techniques, including those used for the compressed trie.

The advantage of the compact representation of tries now becomes apparent for suffix tries. Since the total length of the suffixes of a string X of length n is

$$1 + 2 + \cdots + n = \frac{n(n+1)}{2},$$

storing all the suffixes of X explicitly would take $O(n^2)$ space. Even so, the suffix trie represents these strings implicitly in $O(n)$ space, as formally stated in the following proposition.

Proposition 11.8: *The compact representation of a suffix trie T for a string X of length n uses $O(n)$ space.*

Construction

We can construct the suffix trie for a string of length n with an incremental algorithm like the one given in Section 11.3.1. This construction takes $O(dn^2)$ time because the total length of the suffixes is quadratic in n. However, the (compact) suffix trie for a string of length n can be constructed in $O(n)$ time with a specialized algorithm, different from the one for general tries. This linear-time construction algorithm is fairly complex, however, and is not reported here. Still, we can take advantage of the existence of this fast construction algorithm when we want to use a suffix trie to solve other problems.

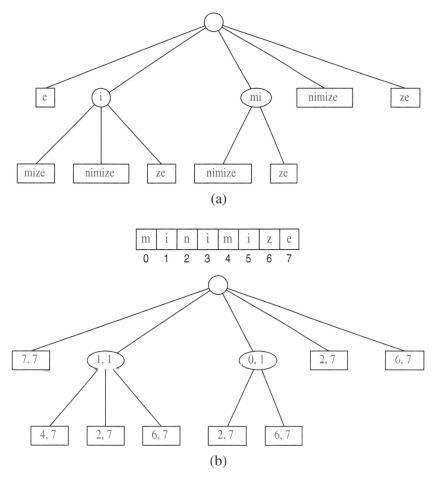

Figure 11.10: (a) Suffix trie T for the string $X = $ ''minimize''. (b) Compact representation of T, where pair (i, j) denotes $X[i..j]$.

Using a Suffix Trie

The suffix trie T for a string X can be used to efficiently perform pattern matching queries on text X. Namely, we can determine whether a pattern P is a substring of X by trying to trace a path associated with P in T. P is a substring of X if and only if such a path can be traced. The details of the pattern matching algorithm are given in Code Fragment 11.7, which assumes the following additional property on the labels of the nodes in the compact representation of the suffix trie:

> If node v has label (i, j) and Y is the string of length y associated with
> the path from the root to v (included), then $X[j - y + 1..j] = Y$.

This property ensures that we can easily compute the start index of the pattern in the text when a match occurs.

Algorithm suffixTrieMatch(T, P):

   Input: Compact suffix trie T for a text X and pattern P

   Output: Starting index of a substring of X matching P or an indication that P
     is not a substring of X

   $p \leftarrow P.\text{length}()$ { length of suffix of the pattern to be matched }
   $j \leftarrow 0$ { start of suffix of the pattern to be matched }
   $v \leftarrow T.\text{root}()$
   repeat
      $f \leftarrow$ **true** { flag indicating that no child was successfully processed }
      for each child w of v **do**
         $i \leftarrow \text{start}(v)$
         if $P[j] = T[i]$ **then**
            { process child w }
            $x \leftarrow \text{end}(w) - i + 1$
            if $p \leq x$ **then**
               { suffix is shorter than or of the same length of the node label }
               if $P[j..j + p - 1] = X[i..i + p - 1]$ **then**
                  return $i - j$ { match }
               else
                  return "P is not a substring of X"
            else
               { suffix is longer than the node label }
               if $P[j..j + x - 1] = X[i..i + x - 1]$ **then**
                  $p \leftarrow p - x$ { update suffix length }
                  $j \leftarrow j + x$ { update suffix start index }
                  $v \leftarrow w$
                  $f \leftarrow$ **false**
                  break out of the **for** loop
   until f **or** $T.\text{isExternal}(v)$
   return "P is not a substring of X"

Code Fragment 11.7: Pattern matching with a suffix trie. We denote the label of a node v with $(\text{start}(v), \text{end}(v))$, that is, the pair of indices specifying the substring of the text associated with v.

The correctness of algorithm suffixTrieMatch follows from the fact that we search down the trie T, matching characters of the pattern P one at a time until one of the following events occurs:

- We completely match the pattern P
- We get a mismatch (caught by the termination of the **for** loop without a break out)
- We are left with characters of P still to be matched after processing an external node.

Let m be the size of pattern P and d be the size of the alphabet. In order to determine the running time of algorithm suffixTrieMatch, we make the following observations:

- We process at most $m + 1$ nodes of the trie
- Each node processed has at most d children
- At each node v processed, we perform at most one character comparison for each child w of v to determine which child of v needs to be processed next (which may possibly be improved by using a fast dictionary to index the children of v)
- We perform at most m character comparisons overall in the processed nodes
- We spend $O(1)$ time for each character comparison.

Performance

We conclude that algorithm suffixTrieMatch performs pattern matching queries in $O(dm)$ time (and would possibly run even faster if we used a dictionary to index children of nodes in the suffix trie). Note that the running time does not depend on the size of the text X. Also, the running time is linear in the size of the pattern, that is, it is $O(m)$, for a constant-size alphabet. Hence, suffix tries are suited for repetitive pattern matching applications, where a series of pattern matching queries is performed on a fixed text.

We summarize the results of this section in the following proposition.

Proposition 11.9: *Let X be a text string with n characters from an alphabet of size d. We can perform pattern matching queries on X in $O(dm)$ time, where m is the length of the pattern, with the suffix trie of X, which uses $O(n)$ space and can be constructed in $O(dn)$ time.*

We explore another application of tries in the next subsection.

11.3.4   Search Engines

The World Wide Web contains a huge collection of text documents (Web pages). Information about these pages are gathered by a program called a **Web crawler**, which then stores this information in a special dictionary database. A Web **search engine** allows users to retrieve relevant information from this database, thereby identifying relevant pages on the Web containing given keywords. In this section, we present a simplified model of a search engine.

Inverted Files

The core information stored by a search engine is a dictionary, called an **inverted index** or **inverted file**, storing key-value pairs (w, L), where w is a word and L is a collection of pages containing word w. The keys (words) in this dictionary are called **index terms** and should be a set of vocabulary entries and proper nouns as large as possible. The elements in this dictionary are called **occurrence lists** and should cover as many Web pages as possible.

We can efficiently implement an inverted index with a data structure consisting of:

1. An array storing the occurrence lists of the terms (in no particular order).
2. A compressed trie for the set of index terms, where each external node stores the index of the occurrence list of the associated term.

The reason for storing the occurrence lists outside the trie is to keep the size of the trie data structure sufficiently small to fit in internal memory. Instead, because of their large total size, the occurrence lists have to be stored on disk.

With our data structure, a query for a single keyword is similar to a word matching query (See Section 11.3.1.). Namely, we find the keyword in the trie and we return the associated occurrence list.

When multiple keywords are given and the desired output are the pages containing **all** the given keywords, we retrieve the occurrence list of each keyword using the trie and return their intersection. To facilitate the intersection computation, each occurrence list should be implemented with a sequence sorted by address or with a dictionary (see, for example, the generic merge computation discussed in Section 10.6).

In addition to the basic task of returning a list of pages containing given keywords, search engines provide an important additional service by **ranking** the pages returned by relevance. Devising fast and accurate ranking algorithms for search engines is a major challenge for computer researchers and electronic commerce companies.

11.4 Text Compression

In this section, we consider an important text processing task, ***text compression***. In this problem, we are given a string X defined over some alphabet, such as the ASCII or Unicode character sets, and we want to efficiently encode X into a small binary string Y (using only the characters 0 and 1). Text compression is useful in any situation where we are communicating over a low-bandwidth channel, such as a modem line or infrared connection, and we wish to minimize the time needed to transmit our text. Likewise, text compression is also useful for storing collections of large documents more efficiently, so as to allow for a fixed-capacity storage device to contain as many documents as possible.

The method for text compression explored in this section is the ***Huffman code***. Standard encoding schemes, such as the ASCII and Unicode systems, use fixed-length binary strings to encode characters (with 7 bits in the ASCII system and 16 in the Unicode system). A Huffman code, on the other hand, uses a variable-length encoding optimized for the string X. The optimization is based on the use of character ***frequencies***, where we have, for each character c, a count $f(c)$ of the number of times c appears in the string X. The Huffman code saves space over a fixed-length encoding by using short code-word strings to encode high-frequency characters and long code-word strings to encode low-frequency characters.

To encode the string X, we convert each character in X from its fixed-length code word to its variable-length code word, and we concatenate all these code words in order to produce the encoding Y for X. In order to avoid ambiguities, we insist that no code word in our encoding is a prefix of another code word in our encoding. Such a code is called a ***prefix code***, and it simplifies the decoding of Y in order to get back X. (See Figure 11.11.) Even with this restriction, the savings produced by a variable-length prefix code can be significant, particularly if there is a wide variance in character frequencies (as is the case for natural language text in almost every spoken language).

Huffman's algorithm for producing an optimal variable-length prefix code for X is based on the construction of a binary tree T that represents the code. Each node in T, except the root, represents a bit in a code word, with each left child representing a "0" and each right child representing a "1." Each external node v is associated with a specific character, and the code word for that character is defined by the sequence of bits associated with the nodes in the path from the root of T to v. (See Figure 11.11.) Each external node v has a ***frequency*** $f(v)$, which is simply the frequency in X of the character associated with v. In addition, we give each internal node v in T a frequency, $f(v)$, that is the sum of the frequencies of all the external nodes in the subtree rooted at v.

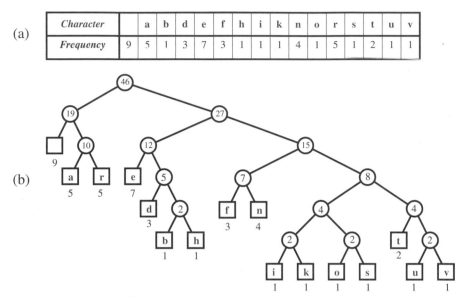

(a)

Character	a	b	d	e	f	h	i	k	n	o	r	s	t	u	v
Frequency	9	5	1	3	7	3	1	1	1	4	1	5	1	2	1	1

(b)

Figure 11.11: An illustration of an example Huffman code for the input string $X =$ "a fast runner need never be afraid of the dark": (a) frequency of each character of X; (b) Huffman tree T for string X. The code for a character c is obtained by tracing the path from the root of T to the external node where c is stored, and associating a left child with 0 and a right child with 1. For example, the code for "a" is 010, and the code for "f" is 1100.

11.4.1   The Huffman Coding Algorithm

The Huffman coding algorithm begins with each of the d distinct characters of the string X to encode being the root node of a single-node binary tree. The algorithm proceeds in a series of rounds. In each round, the algorithm takes the two binary trees with the smallest frequencies and merges them into a single binary tree. It repeats this process until only one tree is left. (See Code Fragment 11.8.)

Each iteration of the **while** loop in Huffman's algorithm can be implemented in $O(\log d)$ time using a priority queue represented with a heap. In addition, each iteration takes two nodes out of Q and adds one in, a process that will be repeated $d - 1$ times before exactly one node is left in Q. Thus, this algorithm runs in $O(n + d \log d)$ time. Although a full justification of this algorithm's correctness is beyond our scope here, we note that its intuition comes from a simple idea—any optimal code can be converted into an optimal code in which the code words for the two lowest-frequency characters, a and b, differ only in their last bit. Repeating the argument for a string with a and b replaced by a character c, gives the following:

Proposition 11.10: *Huffman's algorithm constructs an optimal prefix code for a string of length n with d distinct characters in $O(n + d \log d)$ time.*

Algorithm Huffman(X):

    Input: String X of length n with d distinct characters
    Output: Coding tree for X

    Compute the frequency $f(c)$ of each character c of X.
    Initialize a priority queue Q.
    for each character c in X **do**
        Create a single-node binary tree T storing c.
        Insert T into Q with key $f(c)$.
    while Q.size() > 1 **do**
        $f_1 \leftarrow Q$.min().key()
        $T_1 \leftarrow Q$.removeMin()
        $f_2 \leftarrow Q$.min().key()
        $T_2 \leftarrow Q$.removeMin()
        Create a new binary tree T with left subtree T_1 and right subtree T_2.
        Insert T into Q with key $f_1 + f_2$.
    return tree Q.removeMin()

Code Fragment 11.8: Huffman coding algorithm.

11.4.2 The Greedy Method

Huffman's algorithm for building an optimal encoding is an example application of an algorithmic design pattern called the **greedy method**. This design pattern is applied to optimization problems, where we are trying to construct some structure while minimizing or maximizing some property of that structure.

The general formula for the greedy method pattern is almost as simple as that for the brute-force method. In order to solve a given optimization problem using the greedy method, we proceed by a sequence of choices. The sequence starts from some well-understood starting condition, and computes the cost for that initial condition. The pattern then asks that we iteratively make additional choices by identifying the decision that achieves the best cost improvement from all of the choices that are currently possible. This approach does not always lead to an optimal solution.

But there are several problems that it does work for, and such problems are said to possess the **greedy-choice** property. This is the property that a global optimal condition can be reached by a series of locally optimal choices (that is, choices that are each the current best from among the possibilities available at the time), starting from a well-defined starting condition. The problem of computing an optimal variable-length prefix code is just one example of a problem that possesses the greedy-choice property.

11.5   Text Similarity Testing

A common text processing problem, which arises in genetics and software engineering, is to test the similarity between two text strings. In a genetics application, the two strings could correspond to two strands of DNA, which could, for example, come from two individuals, who we will consider genetically related if they have a long subsequence common to their respective DNA sequences. Likewise, in a software engineering application, the two strings could come from two versions of source code for the same program, and we may wish to determine which changes were made from one version to the next. Indeed, determining the similarity between two strings is considered such a common operation that the Unix and Linux operating systems come with a program, called `diff`, for comparing text files.

11.5.1   The Longest Common Subsequence Problem

There are several different ways we can define the similarity between two strings. Even so, we can abstract a simple, yet common, version of this problem using character strings and their subsequences. Given a string $X = x_0x_1x_2\cdots x_{n-1}$, a **subsequence** of X is any string that is of the form $x_{i_1}x_{i_2}\cdots x_{i_k}$, where $i_j < i_{j+1}$; that is, it is a sequence of characters that are not necessarily contiguous but are nevertheless taken in order from X. For example, the string $AAAG$ is a subsequence of the string $CGATAATTGAGA$. Note that the concept of **subsequence** of a string is different from the one of **substring** of a string, defined in Section 11.1.

Problem Definition

The specific text similarity problem we address here is the **longest common subsequence** (LCS) problem. In this problem, we are given two character strings, $X = x_0x_1x_2\cdots x_{n-1}$ and $Y = y_0y_1y_2\cdots y_{m-1}$, over some alphabet (such as the alphabet $\{A, C, G, T\}$ common in computational genetics) and are asked to find a longest string S that is a subsequence of both X and Y.

One way to solve the longest common subsequence problem is to enumerate all subsequences of X and take the largest one that is also a subsequence of Y. Since each character of X is either in or not in a subsequence, there are potentially 2^n different subsequences of X, each of which requires $O(m)$ time to determine whether it is a subsequence of Y. Thus, this brute-force approach yields an exponential-time algorithm that runs in $O(2^n m)$ time, which is very inefficient. In this section, we discuss how to use an algorithmic design pattern called **dynamic programming** to solve the longest common subsequence problem much faster than this.

11.5.2 Dynamic Programming

There are few algorithmic techniques that can take problems that seem to require exponential time and produce polynomial-time algorithms to solve them. Dynamic programming is one such technique. In addition, the algorithms that result from applications of the dynamic programming technique are usually quite simple—often needing little more than a few lines of code to describe some nested loops for filling in a table.

The dynamic programming technique is used primarily for *optimization* problems, where we wish to find the "best" way of doing something. Often the number of different ways of doing that "something" is exponential, so a brute-force search for the best is computationally infeasible for all but the smallest problem sizes. We can apply the dynamic programming technique in such situations, however, if the problem has a certain amount of structure that we can exploit. This structure involves the following three components:

Simple Subproblems: There has to be some way of repeatedly breaking the global optimization problem into subproblems. Moreover, there should be a simple way of defining subproblems with just a few indices, like i, j, k, and so on.

Subproblem Optimization: An optimal solution to the global problem must be a composition of optimal subproblem solutions. We should not be able to find a globally optimal solution that contains suboptimal subproblems.

Subproblem Overlap: Optimal solutions to unrelated subproblems can contain subproblems in common.

Having given the general components of a dynamic programming algorithm, we next show how to apply it to the longest common subsequence problem.

11.5.3 Applying Dynamic Programming to the LCS Problem

We can solve the longest common subsequence problem much faster than exponential time using the dynamic programming technique. As mentioned above, one of the key components of the dynamic programming technique is the definition of simple subproblems that satisfy the subproblem optimization and subproblem overlap properties.

Recall that in the LCS problem, we are given two character strings, X and Y, of length n and m, respectively, and are asked to find a longest string S that is a subsequence of both X and Y. Since X and Y are character strings, we have a natural set of indices with which to define subproblems—indices into the strings X

and Y. Let us define a subproblem, therefore, as that of computing the value $L[i,j]$, which we will use to denote the length of a longest string that is a subsequence of both $X[0..i] = x_0x_1x_2\ldots x_i$ and $Y[0..j] = y_0y_1y_2\ldots y_j$. This definition allows us to rewrite $L[i,j]$ in terms of optimal subproblem solutions. This definition depends on which of two cases we are in. (See Figure 11.12.)

- $x_i = y_j$. In this case, we have a match between the last character of $X[0..i]$ and the last character of $Y[0..j]$. We claim that this character belongs to a longest common subsequence of $X[0..i]$ and $Y[0..j]$. To justify this claim, let us suppose it is not true. There has to be some longest common subsequence $x_{i_1}x_{i_2}\ldots x_{i_k} = y_{j_1}y_{j_2}\ldots y_{j_k}$. If $x_{i_k} = x_i$ or $y_{j_k} = y_j$, then we get the same sequence by setting $i_k = i$ and $j_k = j$. Alternately, if $x_{j_k} \neq x_i$, then we can get an even longer common subsequence by adding x_i to the end. Thus, a longest common subsequence of $X[0..i]$ and $Y[0..j]$ ends with x_i. Therefore, we set

$$L[i,j] = L[i-1,j-1]+1 \quad \text{if } x_i = y_j.$$

- $x_i \neq y_j$. In this case, we cannot have a common subsequence that includes both x_i and y_j. That is, we can have a common subsequence end with x_i or one that ends with y_j (or possibly neither), but certainly not both. Therefore, we set

$$L[i,j] = \max\{L[i-1,j], L[i,j-1]\} \quad \text{if } x_i \neq y_j.$$

In order to make both of these equations make sense in the boundary cases when $i = 0$ or $j = 0$, we assign $L[i,-1] = 0$ for $i = -1,0,1,\ldots,n-1$ and $L[-1,j] = 0$ for $j = -1,0,1,\ldots,m-1$.

The above definition of $L[i,j]$ satisfies subproblem optimization, for we cannot have a longest common subsequence without also having longest common subsequences for the subproblems. Also, it uses subproblem overlap, because a subproblem solution $L[i,j]$ can be used in several other problems (namely, the problems $L[i+1,j]$, $L[i,j+1]$, and $L[i+1,j+1]$).

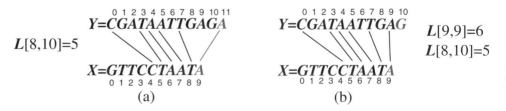

Figure 11.12: The two cases in the longest common subsequence algorithm: (a) $x_i = y_j$; (b) $x_i \neq y_j$. Note that the algorithm stores only the $L[i,j]$ values, not the matches.

The LCS Algorithm

Turning this definition of $L[i,j]$ into an algorithm is actually quite straightforward. We initialize an $(n+1) \times (m+1)$ array, L, for the boundary cases when $i = 0$ or $j = 0$. Namely, we initialize $L[i,-1] = 0$ for $i = -1,0,1,\ldots,n-1$ and $L[-1,j] = 0$ for $j = -1,0,1,\ldots,m-1$. (This is a slight abuse of notation, since in reality, we would have to index the rows and columns of L starting with 0.) Then, we iteratively build up values in L until we have $L[n-1,m-1]$, the length of a longest common subsequence of X and Y. We give a pseudo-code description of how this approach results in a dynamic programming solution to the longest common subsequence (LCS) problem in Code Fragment 11.9.

Algorithm LCS(X,Y):

    Input: Strings X and Y with n and m elements, respectively

    Output: For $i = 0,\ldots,n-1$, $j = 0,\ldots,m-1$, the length $L[i,j]$ of a longest string that is a subsequence of both the string $X[0..i] = x_0x_1x_2\cdots x_i$ and the string $Y[0..j] = y_0y_1y_2\cdots y_j$

    for $i \leftarrow -1$ to $n-1$ **do**

      $L[i,-1] \leftarrow 0$

    for $j \leftarrow 0$ to $m-1$ **do**

      $L[-1,j] \leftarrow 0$

    for $i \leftarrow 0$ to $n-1$ **do**

      for $j \leftarrow 0$ to $m-1$ **do**

        if $x_i = y_j$ **then**

          $L[i,j] \leftarrow L[i-1,j-1]+1$

        else

          $L[i,j] \leftarrow \max\{L[i-1,j], L[i,j-1]\}$

    return array L

Code Fragment 11.9: Dynamic programming algorithm for the LCS problem.

Performance

The running time of the algorithm of Code Fragment 11.9 is easy to analyze, for it is dominated by two nested **for** loops, with the outer one iterating n times and the inner one iterating m times. Since the if-statement and assignment inside the loop each requires $O(1)$ primitive operations, this algorithm runs in $O(nm)$ time. Thus, the dynamic programming technique can be applied to the longest common subsequence problem to improve significantly over the exponential-time brute-force solution to the LCS problem.

Algorithm LCS (Code Fragment 11.9) computes the length of the longest common subsequence (stored in $L[n-1, m-1]$), but not the subsequence itself. As shown in the following proposition, a simple postprocessing step can extract the longest common subsequence from the array L returned by algorithm.

Proposition 11.11: *Given a string X of n characters and a string Y of m characters, we can find the longest common subsequence of X and Y in $O(nm)$ time.*

Justification: Algorithm LCS computes $L[n-1, m-1]$, the **length** of a longest common subsequence, in $O(nm)$ time. Given the table of $L[i, j]$ values, constructing a longest common subsequence is straightforward. One method is to start from $L[n, m]$ and work back through the table, reconstructing a longest common subsequence from back to front. At any position $L[i, j]$, we can determine whether $x_i = y_j$. If this is true, then we can take x_i as the next character of the subsequence (noting that x_i is **before** the previous character we found, if any), moving next to $L[i-1, j-1]$. If $x_i \neq y_j$, then we can move to the larger of $L[i, j-1]$ and $L[i-1, j]$. (See Figure 11.13.) We stop when we reach a boundary cell (with $i = -1$ or $j = -1$). This method constructs a longest common subsequence in $O(n+m)$ additional time. ∎

L	-1	0	1	2	3	4	5	6	7	8	9	10	11
-1	0	0	0	0	0	0	0	0	0	0	0	0	0
0	0	0	1	1	1	1	1	1	1	1	1	1	1
1	0	0	1	1	2	2	2	2	2	2	2	2	2
2	0	0	1	1	2	2	2	3	3	3	3	3	3
3	0	1	1	1	2	2	2	3	3	3	3	3	3
4	0	1	1	1	2	2	2	3	3	3	3	3	3
5	0	1	1	1	2	2	2	3	4	4	4	4	4
6	0	1	1	2	2	3	3	3	4	4	5	5	5
7	0	1	1	2	2	3	4	4	4	4	5	5	6
8	0	1	1	2	3	3	4	5	5	5	5	5	6
9	0	1	1	2	3	4	4	5	5	5	6	6	6

$$0\ 1\ 2\ 3\ 4\ 5\ 6\ 7\ 8\ 9\ 10\ 11$$
$$Y = CGATAATTGAGA$$

$$X = GTTCCTAATA$$
$$0\ 1\ 2\ 3\ 4\ 5\ 6\ 7\ 8\ 9$$

Figure 11.13: Illustration of the algorithm for constructing a longest common subsequence from the array L.

11.6 Exercises

For source code and help with exercises, please visit **java.datastructures.net**.

Reinforcement

R-11.1 List the prefixes of the string $P =$"aaabbaaa" that are also suffixes of P.

R-11.2 Draw a figure illustrating the comparisons done by brute-force pattern matching for the text "aaabaadaabaaa" and pattern "aabaaa".

R-11.3 Repeat the previous problem for the BM pattern matching algorithm, not counting the comparisons made to compute the $last(c)$ function.

R-11.4 Repeat the previous problem for the KMP pattern matching algorithm, not counting the comparisons made to compute the failure function.

R-11.5 Compute a table representing the last function used in the BM pattern matching algorithm for the pattern string
> "the quick brown fox jumped over a lazy cat"
assuming the following alphabet (which starts with the space character):
> $\Sigma = \{ ,a,b,c,d,e,f,g,h,i,j,k,l,m,n,o,p,q,r,s,t,u,v,w,x,y,z\}$.

R-11.6 Assuming that the characters in alphabet Σ can be enumerated and can be used to index arrays, give an $O(m + |\Sigma|)$-time method for constructing the last function from an m-length pattern string P.

R-11.7 Compute a table representing the KMP failure function for the pattern string "cgtacgttcgtac".

R-11.8 Draw a standard trie for the following set of strings:
> $\{abab, baba, ccccc, bbaaaa, caa, bbaacc, cbcc, cbca\}$.

R-11.9 Draw a compressed trie for the set of strings given in Exercise R-11.8.

R-11.10 Draw the compact representation of the suffix trie for the string "minimize minime".

R-11.11 What is the longest prefix of the string "cgtacgttcgtacg" that is also a suffix of this string?

R-11.12 Draw the frequency array and Huffman tree for the following string: "dogs do not spot hot pots or cats".

R-11.13 Show the longest common subsequence array L for the two strings
$$X = \texttt{"skullandbones"}$$
$$Y = \texttt{"lullabybabies"}.$$
What is a longest common subsequence between these strings?

Creativity

C-11.1 Give an example of a text T of length n and a pattern P of length m that force the brute-force pattern matching algorithm to have a running time that is $\Omega(nm)$.

C-11.2 Give a justification of why the KMPFailureFunction method (Code Fragment 11.5) runs in $O(m)$ time on a pattern of length m.

C-11.3 Show how to modify the KMP string pattern matching algorithm so as to find *every* occurrence of a pattern string P that appears as a substring in T, while still running in $O(n+m)$ time. (Be sure to catch even those matches that overlap.)

C-11.4 Let T be a text of length n, and let P be a pattern of length m. Describe an $O(n+m)$-time method for finding the longest prefix of P that is a substring of T.

C-11.5 Say that a pattern P of length m is a *circular* substring of a text T of length n if there is an index $0 \leq i < m$, such that $P = T[n-m+i..n-1] + T[0..i-1]$, that is, if P is a (normal) substring of T or P is equal to the concatenation of a suffix of T and a prefix of T. Give an $O(n+m)$-time algorithm for determining whether P is a circular substring of T.

C-11.6 The KMP pattern matching algorithm can be modified to run faster on binary strings by redefining the failure function as
$$f(j) = \text{the largest } k < j \text{ such that } P[0..k-2]\widehat{p_k} \text{ is a suffix of } P[1..j],$$
where $\widehat{p_k}$ denotes the complement of the kth bit of P. Describe how to modify the KMP algorithm to be able to take advantage of this new failure function and also give a method for computing this failure function. Show that this method makes at most n comparisons between the text and the pattern (as opposed to the $2n$ comparisons needed by the standard KMP algorithm given in Section 11.2.3).

C-11.7 Modify the simplified BM algorithm presented in this chapter using ideas from the KMP algorithm so that it runs in $O(n+m)$ time.

C-11.8 Given a string X of length n and a string Y of length m, describe an $O(n + m)$-time algorithm for finding the longest prefix of X that is a suffix of Y.

C-11.9 Give an efficient algorithm for deleting a string from a standard trie and analyze its running time.

C-11.10 Give an efficient algorithm for deleting a string from a compressed trie and analyze its running time.

C-11.11 Describe an algorithm for constructing the compact representation of a suffix trie, given its noncompact representation, and analyze its running time.

C-11.12 Let T be a text string of length n. Describe an $O(n)$-time method for finding the longest prefix of T that is a substring of the reversal of T.

C-11.13 Describe an efficient algorithm to find the longest palindrome that is a suffix of a string T of length n. Recall that a *palindrome* is a string that is equal to its reversal. What is the running time of your method?

C-11.14 Given a sequence $S = (x_0, x_1, x_2, \ldots, x_{n-1})$ of numbers, describe an $O(n^2)$-time algorithm for finding a longest subsequence $T = (x_{i_0}, x_{i_1}, x_{i_2}, \ldots, x_{i_{k-1}})$ of numbers, such that $i_j < i_{j+1}$ and $x_{i_j} > x_{i_{j+1}}$. That is, T is a longest decreasing subsequence of S.

C-11.15 Define the *edit distance* between two strings X and Y of length n and m, respectively, to be the number of edits that it takes to change X into Y. An edit consists of a character insertion, a character deletion, or a character replacement. For example, the strings "algorithm" and "rhythm" have edit distance 6. Design an $O(nm)$-time algorithm for computing the edit distance between X and Y.

C-11.16 Design a greedy algorithm for making change after someone buys some candy costing x cents and the customer gives the clerk $1. Your algorithm should try to minimize the number of coins returned.

   a. Show that your greedy algorithm returns the minimum number of coins if the coins have denominations $0.25, $0.10, $0.05, and $0.01.
   b. Give a set of denominations for which your algorithm may not return the minimum number of coins. Include an example where your algorithm fails.

C-11.17 Give an efficient algorithm for determining if a pattern P is a subsequence (not substring) of a text T. What is the running time of your algorithm?

C-11.18 Let x and y be strings of length n and m respectively. Define $B(i,j)$ to be the length of the longest common substring of the suffix of length i in x and the suffix of length j in y. Design an $O(nm)$-time algorithm for computing all the values of $B(i,j)$ for $i = 1, \ldots, n$ and $j = 1, \ldots, m$.

C-11.19 Anna has just won a contest that allows her to take n pieces of candy out of a candy store for free. Anna is old enough to realize that some candy is expensive, costing dollars per piece, while other candy is cheap, costing pennies per piece. The jars of candy are numbered $0, 1, \ldots, m-1$, so that jar j has n_j pieces in it, with a price of c_j per piece. Design an $O(n+m)$-time algorithm that allows Anna to maximize the value of the pieces of candy she takes for her winnings. Show that your algorithm produces the maximum value for Anna.

C-11.20 Let three integer arrays, A, B, and C, be given, each of size n. Given an arbitrary integer x, design an $O(n^2 \log n)$-time algorithm to determine if there exist numbers $a \in A$, $b \in B$, and $c \in C$, such that $x = a+b+c$. (Hint: Use brute force first to enumerate all pairs (a,b) such that $a \in A$ and $b \in B$.)

C-11.21 Give an $O(n^2)$-time algorithm for the previous problem.

Projects

P-11.1 Perform an experimental analysis, using documents found on the Internet, of the efficiency (number of character comparisons performed) of the brute-force and KMP pattern matching algorithms for varying-length patterns.

P-11.2 Perform an experimental analysis, using documents found on the Internet, of the efficiency (number of character comparisons performed) of the brute-force and BM pattern matching algorithms for varying-length patterns.

P-11.3 Perform an experimental comparison of the relative speeds of the brute-force, KMP, and BM pattern matching algorithms. Document the time taken for coding up each of these algorithms as well as their relative running times on documents found on the Internet that are then searched using varying-length patterns.

P-11.4 Implement a compression and decompression scheme that is based on Huffman coding.

P-11.5 Create a class that implements a standard trie for a set of ASCII strings. The class should have a constructor that takes as argument a list of strings, and the class should have a method that tests whether a given string is stored in the trie.

P-11.6 Create a class that implements a compressed trie for a set of ASCII strings. The class should have a constructor that takes as argument a list of strings, and the class should have a method that tests whether a given string is stored in the trie.

P-11.7 Create a class that implements a prefix trie for an ASCII string. The class should have a constructor that takes as argument a string and a method for pattern matching on the string.

P-11.8 Implement the simplified search engine described in Section 11.3.4 for the pages of a small Web site. Use all the words in the pages of the site as index terms, excluding stop words such as articles, prepositions, and pronouns.

P-11.9 Implement a search engine for the pages of a small Web site by adding a page-ranking feature to the simplified search engine described in Section 11.3.4. Your page-ranking feature should return the most relevant pages first. Use all the words in the pages of the site as index terms, excluding stop words, such as articles, prepositions, and pronouns.

Chapter Notes

The KMP algorithm is described by Knuth, Morris, and Pratt in their journal article [60], and Boyer and Moore describe their algorithm in a journal article published the same year [15]. In their article, however, Knuth *et al.* [60] also prove that the BM algorithm runs in linear time. More recently, Cole [22] shows that the BM algorithm makes at most $3n$ character comparisons in the worst case, and this bound is tight. All of the algorithms discussed above are also discussed in the book chapter by Aho [3], albeit in a more theoretical framework, including the methods for regular-expression pattern matching. The reader interested in further study of string pattern matching algorithms is referred to the book by Stephen [85] and the book chapters by Aho [3] and Crochemore and Lecroq [26].

The trie was invented by Morrison [75] and is discussed extensively in the classic *Sorting and Searching* book by Knuth [59]. The name "Patricia" is short for "Practical Algorithm to Retrieve Information Coded in Alphanumeric" [75]. McCreight [67] shows how to construct suffix tries in linear time. An introduction to the field of information retrieval, which includes a discussion of search engines for the Web is provided in the book by Baeza-Yates and Ribeiro-Neto [8].

Chapter

12

Graphs

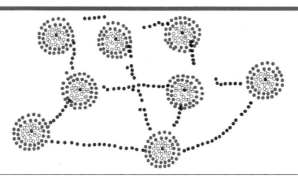

Contents

Greek mythology tells of an elaborate labyrinth that was built to house the monstrous Minotaur, which was part bull and part man. This labyrinth was so complex that neither beast nor human could escape it. No human, that is, until the Greek hero, Theseus, with the help of the king's daughter, Ariadne, decided to implement one of the algorithms discussed in this chapter. Theseus fastened a ball of thread to the door of the labyrinth and unwound it as he traversed the twisting passages in search of the monster. Theseus obviously knew about good algorithm design, for, after finding and defeating the beast, Theseus easily followed the string back out of the labyrinth to the loving arms of Ariadne.

Being able to determine which objects, such as labyrinth passages, are connected to which other objects may not always be as vitally important as it was in this story, but it is nevertheless fundamental. Connectivity information is present, for example, in city maps, where the objects are roads, and also in the routing tables for the Internet, where the objects are computers. Connectivity information is also present in the parent-child relationships defined by a binary tree, where the objects are tree nodes. Indeed, connectivity information can be defined by all kinds of relationships that exist between pairs of objects. The topic we study in this chapter—*graphs*—is therefore focused on representations and algorithms for dealing efficiently with such relationships. That is, a graph is a set of objects, called vertices, together with a collection of pairwise connections between them. By the way, this notion of a "graph" should not be confused with bar charts and function plots, as these kinds of "graphs" are unrelated to the topic of this chapter.

Graphs have applications in a host of different domains, including mapping (in geographic information systems), transportation (in road and flight networks), electrical engineering (in circuits), and computer networking (in the connections of the Internet). Because applications for graphs are so widespread and diverse, people have developed a great deal of terminology to describe different components and properties of graphs. Fortunately, since most graph applications are relatively recent developments, this terminology is fairly intuitive.

We therefore begin this chapter by reviewing much of this terminology and presenting the graph ADT, including some elementary properties of graphs. Having given the graph ADT, we then present, in Section 12.2, three main data structures for representing graphs. As with trees, traversals are important computations for graphs, and we discuss such computations in Section 12.3. We discuss directed graphs in Section 12.4, where relationships have a given direction. This topic is not addressed in subsequent sections, however, so readers or instructors with limited time may skip Section 12.4. In Sections 12.5 through 12.7 we discuss weighted graphs, where connections have a cost or distance associated with them. While weighted connections could be directed, in these sections we study the well-known shortest path and minimum spanning tree problems for undirected graphs.

12.1   The Graph Abstract Data Type

Viewed abstractly, a **graph** G is simply a set V of **vertices** and a collection E of pairs of vertices from V, called **edges**. Thus, a graph is a way of representing connections or relationships between pairs of objects from some set V. Incidentally, some books use different terminology for graphs and refer to what we call vertices as **nodes** and what we call edges as **arcs**. We use the terms "vertices" and "edges."

Edges in a graph are either **directed** or **undirected**. An edge (u, v) is said to be **directed** from u to v if the pair (u, v) is ordered, with u preceding v. An edge (u, v) is said to be **undirected** if the pair (u, v) is not ordered. Undirected edges are sometimes denoted with set notation, as $\{u, v\}$, but for simplicity we use the pair notation (u, v), noting that in the undirected case (u, v) is the same as (v, u). Graphs are typically visualized by drawing the vertices as ovals or rectangles and the edges as segments or curves connecting pairs of ovals and rectangles. The following are some examples of directed and undirected graphs.

Example 12.1: *We can visualize collaborations among the researchers of a certain discipline by constructing a graph whose vertices are associated with the researchers themselves, and whose edges connect pairs of vertices associated with researchers who have coauthored a paper or book. (See Figure 12.1.) Such edges are undirected because coauthorship is a* **symmetric** *relation; that is, if A has coauthored something with B, then B necessarily has coauthored something with A.*

Example 12.2: *We can associate with an object-oriented program a graph whose vertices represent the classes defined in the program, and whose edges indicate inheritance between classes. There is an edge from a vertex v to a vertex u if the class for v extends the class for u. Such edges are directed because the inheritance relation only goes in one direction (that is, it is* **asymmetric***).*

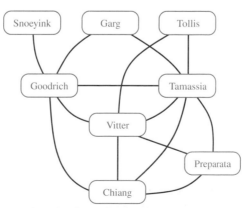

Figure 12.1: Graph of coauthorships among some authors.

If all the edges in a graph are undirected, then we say the graph is an ***undirected graph***. Likewise, a ***directed graph***, also called a ***digraph***, is a graph whose edges are all directed. A graph that has both directed and undirected edges is often called a ***mixed graph***. Note that an undirected or mixed graph can be converted into a directed graph by replacing every undirected edge (u, v) by the pair of directed edges (u, v) and (v, u). It is often useful, however, to keep undirected and mixed graphs represented as they are, for such graphs have several applications, such as that of the following example.

Example 12.3: *A city map can be modeled by a graph whose vertices are intersections or dead-ends, and whose edges are stretches of streets without intersections. This graph has both undirected edges, which correspond to stretches of two-way streets, and directed edges, which correspond to stretches of one-way streets. Thus, in this way, a graph modeling a city map is a mixed graph.*

Example 12.4: *Physical examples of graphs are present in the electrical wiring and plumbing networks of a building. Such networks can be modeled as graphs, where each connector, fixture, or outlet is viewed as a vertex, and each uninterrupted stretch of wire or pipe is viewed as an edge. Such graphs are actually components of much larger graphs, namely the local power and water distribution networks. Depending on the specific aspects of these graphs that we are interested in, we may consider their edges as undirected or directed, for, in principle, water can flow in a pipe and current can flow in a wire in either direction.*

The two vertices joined by an edge are called the ***end vertices*** (or ***endpoints***) of the edge. If an edge is directed, its first endpoint is its ***origin*** and the other is the ***destination*** of the edge. Two vertices u and v are said to be ***adjacent*** if there is an edge whose end vertices are u and v. An edge is said to be ***incident*** on a vertex if the vertex is one of the edge's endpoints. The ***outgoing edges*** of a vertex are the directed edges whose origin is that vertex. The ***incoming edges*** of a vertex are the directed edges whose destination is that vertex. The ***degree*** of a vertex v, denoted $\deg(v)$, is the number of incident edges of v. The ***in-degree*** and ***out-degree*** of a vertex v are the number of the incoming and outgoing edges of v, and are denoted $\text{indeg}(v)$ and $\text{outdeg}(v)$, respectively.

Example 12.5: *We can study air transportation by constructing a graph G, called a* **flight network***, whose vertices are associated with airports, and whose edges are associated with flights. (See Figure 12.2.) In graph G, the edges are directed because a given flight has a specific travel direction (from the origin airport to the destination airport). The endpoints of an edge e in G correspond respectively to the origin and destination for the flight corresponding to e. Two airports are adjacent* in G if there is a flight that flies between them, and an edge e is incident upon a vertex v in G if the flight for e flies to or from the airport for v. The outgoing edges of a vertex v correspond to the outbound flights from v's airport, and the incoming edges correspond to the inbound flights to v's airport. Finally, the in-degree of a vertex v of G corresponds to the number of inbound flights to v's airport, and the out-degree of a vertex v in G corresponds to the number of outbound flights.

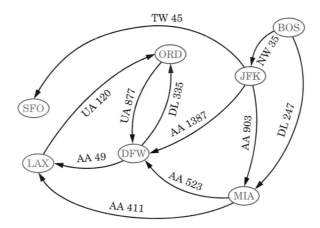

Figure 12.2: Example of a directed graph representing a flight network. The end-points of edge UA 120 are LAX and ORD; hence, LAX and ORD are adjacent. The in-degree of DFW is 3, and the out-degree of DFW is 2.

The definition of a graph refers to the group of edges as a **collection**, not a **set**, thus allowing for two undirected edges to have the same end vertices, and for two directed edges to have the same origin and the same destination. Such edges are called **parallel edges** or **multiple edges**. Parallel edges can be in a flight network (Example 12.5), in which case multiple edges between the same pair of vertices could indicate different flights operating on the same route at different times of the day. Another special type of edge is one that connects a vertex to itself. Namely, we say that an edge (undirected or directed) is a **self-loop** if its two endpoints coincide. A self-loop may occur in a graph associated with a city map (Example 12.3), where it would correspond to a "circle" (a curving street that returns to its starting point).

With few exceptions, like those mentioned above, graphs do not have parallel edges or self-loops. Such graphs are said to be **simple**. Thus, we can usually say that the edges of a simple graph are a **set** of vertex pairs (and not just a collection). Throughout this chapter, we assume that a graph is simple unless otherwise specified. This assumption simplifies the presentation of data structures and algorithms for graphs. Extending the results of this chapter to general graphs with self-loops and/or parallel edges is straightforward, though the details can be tedious.

In the propositions that follow, we explore a few important properties of graphs.

Proposition 12.6: *If G is a graph with m edges, then*

$$\sum_{v \in G} deg(v) = 2m.$$

Justification: An edge (u,v) is counted twice in the above summation; once by its endpoint u and once by its endpoint v. Thus, the total contribution of the edges to the degrees of the vertices is twice the number of edges.   ∎

Proposition 12.7: *If G is a directed graph with m edges, then*

$$\sum_{v \in G} indeg(v) \;=\; \sum_{v \in G} outdeg(v) = m.$$

Justification: In a directed graph, an edge (u,v) contributes one unit to the out-degree of its origin u and one unit to the in-degree of its destination v. Thus, the total contribution of the edges to the out-degrees of the vertices is equal to the number of edges, and similarly for the out-degrees.   ∎

We next show that a simple graph with n vertices has $O(n^2)$ edges.

Proposition 12.8: *Let G be a simple graph with n vertices and m edges. If G is undirected, then $m \leq n(n-1)/2$, and if G is directed, then $m \leq n(n-1)$.*

Justification: Suppose that G is undirected. Since no two edges can have the same endpoints and there are no self-loops, the maximum degree of a vertex in G is $n-1$ in this case. Thus, by Proposition 12.6, $2m \leq n(n-1)$. Now suppose that G is directed. Since no two edges can have the same origin and destination, and there are no self-loops, the maximum in-degree of a vertex in G is $n-1$ in this case. Thus, by Proposition 12.7, $m \leq n(n-1)$.   ∎

A *path* is a sequence of alternating vertices and edges that starts at a vertex and ends at a vertex such that each edge is incident to its predecessor and successor vertex. A *cycle* is a path with at least one edge such that its start and end vertices are the same. We say that a path is *simple* if each vertex in the path is distinct, and we say that a cycle is *simple* if each vertex in the cycle is distinct, except for the first and last one. A *directed path* is a path such that all the edges are directed and are traversed along their direction. A *directed cycle* is similarly defined. For example, in Figure 12.2, (BOS, NW 35, JFK, AA 1387, DFW) is in a directed simple path, and (LAX, UA 120, ORD, UA 877, DFW, AA 49, LAX) is a directed simple cycle. If a path P or cycle C is in simple graph, we may omit the edges in P or C, as these are well defined, in which case P is a list of adjacent vertices and C is a cycle of adjacent vertices.

Example 12.9: *Given a graph G representing a city map (see Example 12.3), we can model a couple driving to dinner at a recommended restaurant as traversing a path though G. If they know the way, and don't accidentally go through the same intersection twice, then they traverse a simple path in G. Likewise, we can model the entire trip the couple takes, from their home to the restaurant and back, as a cycle. If they go home from the restaurant in a completely different way than how they went, not even going through the same intersection twice, then their entire round trip is a simple cycle. Finally, if they travel along one-way streets for their entire trip, we can model their night out as a directed cycle.*

A **subgraph** of a graph G is a graph H whose vertices and edges are subsets of the vertices and edges of G, respectively. For example, in the flight network of Figure 12.2, vertices BOS, JFK, and MIA, and edges AA 903 and DL 247 form a subgraph. A **spanning subgraph** of G is a subgraph of G that contains all the vertices of the graph G. A graph is **connected** if, for any two vertices, there is a path between them. If a graph G is not connected, its maximal connected subgraphs are called the **connected components** of G. A **forest** is a graph without cycles. A **tree** is a connected forest, that is, a connected graph without cycles. Note that this definition of a tree is somewhat different from the one given in Chapter 6. Namely, in the context of graphs, a tree has no root. Whenever there is ambiguity, the trees of Chapter 6 should be referred to as **rooted trees**, while the trees of this chapter should be referred to as **free trees**. The connected components of a forest are (free) trees. A **spanning tree** of a graph is a spanning subgraph that is a (free) tree.

Example 12.10: *Perhaps the most talked about graph today is the Internet, which can be viewed as a graph whose vertices are computers and whose (undirected) edges are communication connections between pairs of computers on the Internet. The computers and the connections between them in a single domain, like wiley.com, form a subgraph of the Internet. If this subgraph is connected, then two users on computers in this domain can send e-mail to one another without having their information packets ever leave their domain. Suppose the edges of this subgraph form a spanning tree. This implies that, if even a single connection goes down (for example, because someone pulls a communication cable out of the back of a computer in this domain), then this subgraph will no longer be connected.*

There are a number of simple properties of trees, forests, and connected graphs.

Proposition 12.11: *Let G be an undirected graph with n vertices and m edges.*

- *If G is connected, then $m \geq n - 1$.*
- *If G is a tree, then $m = n - 1$.*
- *If G is a forest, then $m \leq n - 1$.*

We leave the justification of this proposition as an exercise (C-12.2).

12.1.1   The Graph ADT

As an abstract data type, a graph is a container of elements that are stored at the graph's *positions*—its vertices and edges. In Java, this means we can define Vertex and Edge interfaces that each extend the Position interface. Let us then introduce the following simplified graph ADT, which is suitable for vertex and edge positions in undirected graphs, that is, graphs whose edges are all undirected. Additional methods for dealing with directed edges are discussed in Section 12.4.

vertices(): Return an iterator of all the vertices of the graph.
Input: None; *Output:* Iterator of vertices.

edges(): Return an iterator of all the edges of the graph.
Input: None; *Output:* Iterator of edges.

incidentEdges(v): Return an iterator of the edges incident upon vertex v.
Input: Vertex; *Output:* Iterator of edges.

opposite(v, e): Return the endvertex of edge e distinct from vertex v; an error occurs if e is not incident on v.
Input: Vertex and edge; *Output:* Vertex.

endVertices(e): Return an array storing the end vertices of edge e.
Input: Edge; *Output:* Array of two vertices.

areAdjacent(v, w): Test whether vertices v and w are adjacent.
Input: Vertices; *Output:* Boolean.

replace(v, x): Replace the element stored at vertex v with x.
Input: Vertex and object; *Output:* Object (old element).

replace(e, x): Replace the element stored at edge e with x.
Input: Edge and object; *Output:* Object (old element).

insertVertex(x): Insert and return a new vertex storing element x.
Input: Object; *Output:* Vertex.

insertEdge(v, w, x): Insert and return a new undirected edge with end vertices v and w and storing element x.
Input: Vertices and object; *Output:* Edge.

removeVertex(v): Remove vertex v and all its incident edges and return the element stored at v.
Input: Vertex; *Output:* Object (old element).

removeEdge(e): Remove edge e and return the element stored at e.
Input: Edge; *Output:* Object (old element).

12.2 Data Structures for Graphs

There are several ways to realize the graph ADT. In this section, we discuss three popular approaches, usually referred to as the *edge list* structure, the *adjacency list* structure, and the *adjacency matrix*. In all the three representations, we use a container to store the vertices of the graph. Regarding the edges, there is a fundamental difference between the first two structures and the latter. The edge list structure and the adjacency list structure only store the edges actually present in the graph, while the adjacency matrix stores a placeholder for every pair of vertices (whether there is an edge between them or not). As we will explain in this section, this difference implies that, for a graph G with n vertices and m edges, an edge list or adjacency list representation uses $O(n+m)$ space, whereas an adjacency matrix representation uses $O(n^2)$ space.

12.2.1 The Edge List Structure

The *edge list* structure is possibly the simplest, though not the most efficient, representation of a graph G. In this representation, a vertex v of G storing an element o is explicitly represented by a vertex object. All such vertex objects are stored in a container V, such as a vector or a list. If V is a vector, for example, then we naturally think of the vertices as being numbered.

Vertex Objects

The vertex object for a vertex v storing element o has instance variables for

- A reference to o
- A reference to the position (or entry) of the vertex-object in container V.

The distinguishing feature of the edge list structure is not how it represents vertices, however, but the way in which it represents edges. In this structure, an edge e of G storing an element o is explicitly represented by an edge object. The edge objects are stored in a container E, which would typically be a list or a vector.

Edge Objects

The edge object for an edge e storing element o has instance variables for

- A reference to o
- References to the vertex objects associated with the endpoint vertices of e
- A reference to the position (or entry) of the edge-object in container E.

Visualizing the Edge List Structure

We illustrate an example of the edge list structure for a graph G in Figure 12.3.

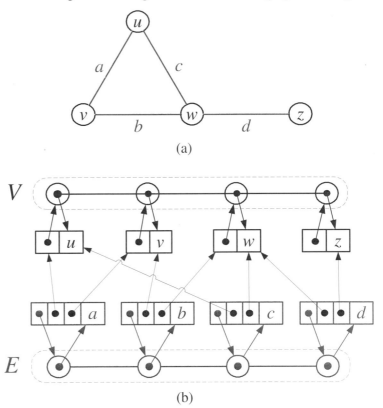

(a)

(b)

Figure 12.3: (a) A graph G; (b) schematic representation of the edge list structure for G. We visualize the elements stored in the vertex and edge objects with the element names, instead of with actual references to the element objects.

The reason this structure is called the ***edge list structure*** is that the simplest and most common implementation of the edge container E is with a list. Even so, in order to be able to conveniently search for specific objects associated with edges, we may wish to implement E with a dictionary (whose entries store the element as the key and the edge as the value) in spite of our calling this the "edge list." We may also wish to implement the container V as a dictionary for the same reason. Still, in keeping with tradition, we call this structure the edge list structure.

The main feature of the edge list structure is that it provides direct access from edges to the vertices they are incident upon. This allows us to define simple algorithms for methods endVertices(e) and opposite(v,e). Nevertheless, the "inverse" operation—that of accessing the edges that are incident upon a vertex—requires an exhaustive inspection of all the edge objects in container E. That is, in order to determine which edges are incident to a vertex v, we must examine all the edges in the edge list and check, for each one, if it happens to be incident to v. Thus, method incidentEdges(v) runs in time proportional to the number of edges in the graph, not in time proportional to the degree of vertex v. In fact, even to check if two vertices v and w are adjacent by the areAdjacent(v, w) method, requires that we search the entire edge container looking for an edge with end vertices v and w. Moreover, since removing a vertex involves removing all of its incident edges, method removeVertex also requires a complete search of the edge container E.

Performance of the Edge List Structure

Table 12.1 summarizes the performance of the edge list structure implementation of a graph under the assumption that containers V and E are realized with doubly linked lists (Section 5.3.2).

Operation	Time
vertices	$O(n)$
edges	$O(m)$
endVertices, opposite	$O(1)$
incidentEdges, areAdjacent	$O(m)$
replace	$O(1)$
insertVertex, insertEdge, removeEdge,	$O(1)$
removeVertex	$O(m)$

Table 12.1: Running times of the methods of a graph implemented with the edge list structure. The space used is $O(n+m)$, where n is the number of vertices and m is the number of edges.

Details for selected methods of the graph ADT are as follows:

- Methods vertices() and edges() are implemented by calling V.elements() and E.elements(), respectively.
- Methods incidentEdges and areAdjacent all take $O(m)$ time, since to determine which edges are incident upon a vertex v we must inspect all edges.
- Since the containers V and E are lists implemented with a doubly linked list, we can insert vertices, and insert and remove edges, in $O(1)$ time.
- The update method removeVertex(v) takes $O(m)$ time, since it requires that we inspect all the edges to find and remove those incident upon v.

Thus, the edge list representation is simple but has significant limitations.

12.2.2 The Adjacency List Structure

The *adjacency list* structure for a graph G adds extra information to the edge list structure that supports direct access to the incident edges (and thus to the adjacent vertices) of each vertex. This approach allows us to use the adjacency list structure to implement several methods of the graph ADT much faster than what is possible with the edge list structure, even though both of these two representations use an amount of space proportional to the number of vertices and edges in the graph. The adjacency list structure includes all the structural components of the edge list structure plus the following:

- A vertex object v holds a reference to a container $I(v)$, called the *incidence container* of v, whose elements store references to the edges incident on v.
- The edge object for an edge e with end vertices v and w holds references to the positions (or entries) associated with edge e in the incidence containers $I(v)$ and $I(w)$.

The Adjacency List

Traditionally, the incidence container $I(v)$ for a vertex v is realized by means of a list, which is why we call this way of representing a graph the *adjacency list* structure. Still, there may be some contexts where we wish to represent an incidence container $I(v)$ as, say, a dictionary or a priority queue, so let us stick with thinking of $I(v)$ as a generic container of edge objects.

The adjacency list structure provides direct access both from the edges to the vertices and from the vertices to their incident edges. Being able to provide access between vertices and edges in both directions allows us to speed up the performance of a number of the graph methods by using an adjacency list structure instead of an edge list structure. We illustrate the adjacency list structure of a graph in Figure 12.4. For a vertex v, the space used by the incidence container of v is proportional to the degree of v, that is, it is $O(\deg(v))$. Thus, by Proposition 12.6, the space requirement of the adjacency list structure is $O(n+m)$.

Performance of the Adjacency List Structure

All of the methods of the graph ADT that can be implemented with the edge list structure in $O(1)$ time can also be implemented in $O(1)$ time with the adjacency list structure, using essentially the same algorithms. Table 12.2 summarizes the performance of the adjacency list structure implementation of a graph, assuming that containers V and E and the incidence containers of the vertices are all implemented with doubly linked lists.

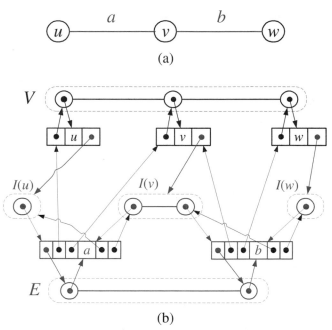

Figure 12.4: (a) A graph G; (b) schematic representation of the adjacency list structure of G. As in Figure 12.3, we visualize the elements of containers with names.

Operation	Time
vertices	$O(n)$
edges	$O(m)$
endVertices, opposite	$O(1)$
incidentEdges(v)	$O(\deg(v))$
areAdjacent(v, w)	$O(\min(\deg(v), \deg(w))$
replace	$O(1)$
insertVertex, insertEdge, removeEdge,	$O(1)$
removeVertex	$O(\deg(v))$

Table 12.2: Running times of the methods of a graph implemented with the adjacency list structure. The space used is $O(n+m)$, where n is the number of vertices and m is the number of edges.

In contrast to the edge-list way of doing things, the adjacency list structure provides improved running times for the following methods:

- Method incidentEdges(v) takes time proportional to the number of incident vertices of v, that is, $O(\deg(v))$ time.
- Method areAdjacent(u, v) can be performed by inspecting either the incidence container of u or that of v. By choosing the smaller of the two, we get $O(\min(\deg(u), \deg(v)))$ running time.
- Method removeVertex(v) takes $O(\deg(v))$ time.

12.2.3   The Adjacency Matrix Structure

Like the adjacency list structure, the ***adjacency matrix*** structure of a graph also extends the edge list structure with an additional component. In this case, we augment the edge list with a matrix (a two-dimensional array) A that allows us to determine adjacencies between pairs of vertices in constant time. As we shall see, achieving this speedup comes at a price in the space usage of the data structure.

The Components of the Adjacency Matrix Structure

In the adjacency matrix representation, we think of the vertices as being the integers in the set $\{0, 1, \ldots, n-1\}$ and the edges as being pairs of such integers. This allows us to store references to edges in the cells of a two-dimensional $n \times n$ array A. Specifically, the adjacency matrix representation extends the edge list structure as follows:

- A vertex object v stores a distinct integer key in the range $0, 1, \ldots, n-1$, called the ***index*** of v. To simplify the discussion, we may refer to the vertex with index i simply as "vertex i."
- For each pair of vertices u and w, we keep an incidence container $I(v, w)$ whose elements store references to the edges with end vertices u and w.
- The edge object for an edge e with end vertices v and w holds references to the positions (or entries) associated with edge e in the incidence containers $I(v, w)$ and $I(w, v)$.
- We keep a two-dimensional $n \times n$ array A such that the cell $A[i, j]$ holds a reference to the incidence container $I(v, w)$, where v is the vertex with index i and w is the vertex with index j.

For graphs without parallel edges, the adjacency matrix representation can be simplified by eliminating the incidence containers $I(v, w)$ and storing, in cell $A[i, j]$, a reference to the edge object for the edge e with end vertices v and w, if such an edge exists, and null otherwise. (See Figure 12.5.)

The adjacency matrix A allows us to perform method areAdjacent(v, w) in $O(1)$ time. We achieve this running time by accessing vertices v and w to determine their respective indices i and j, and then calling $I(i, j)$.isEmpty(). The optimal performance of method areAdjacent is counteracted by an increase in the space usage, however, which is now $O(n^2 + m)$, and in the running time of other methods. For example, method incidentEdges(v) now requires that we examine an entire row or column of array A and thus runs in $O(n + \deg(v))$ time. Moreover, any vertex insertions or deletions now require creating a whole new array A, of larger or smaller size, respectively, which takes time $O(n^2)$.

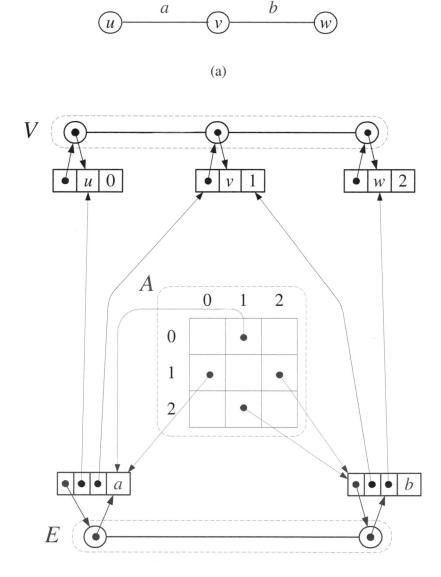

Figure 12.5: (a) A graph G without parallel edges; (b) schematic representation of the simplified adjacency matrix structure for G.

Performance of the Adjacency Matrix Structure

Table 12.3 summarizes the performance of the adjacency matrix structure implementation of a graph. From this table, we observe that the adjacency list structure is superior to the adjacency matrix in space, and is superior in time for all methods except for the areAdjacent method.

Operation	Time
vertices	$O(n)$
edges	$O(m)$
endVertices, opposite	$O(1)$
incidentEdges(v)	$O(n + \deg(v))$
areAdjacent(v, w)	$O(1)$
replace	$O(1)$
insertEdge, removeEdge,	$O(1)$
insertVertex, removeVertex	$O(n^2)$

Table 12.3: Running times of the methods of a graph implemented with the adjacency matrix structure. The space used is $O(n^2 + m)$, where n is the number of vertices and m is the number of edges.

Note that for graphs without parallel edges, the number of edges m is $O(n^2)$ and, for each vertex v, $\deg(v)$ is $O(n)$. Thus, the space requirement is $O(n^2)$ and the running time of method incidentEdges is $O(n)$.

Historically, the adjacency matrix was the first representation used for graphs. We should not find this fact surprising, however, for the adjacency matrix has a natural appeal as a mathematical structure (for example, an undirected graph has a symmetric adjacency matrix). The adjacency list structure came later, with its natural appeal in computing due to its faster methods for most algorithms (many algorithms do not use method areAdjacent) and its space efficiency.

Most of the graph algorithms we examine in this book will run efficiently when acting upon a graph stored using the adjacency list representation. In some cases, however, a trade-off occurs, where graphs with few edges are most efficiently processed with an adjacency list structure and graphs with many edges are most efficiently processed with an adjacency matrix structure.

Next, we explore a fundamental kind of algorithmic operation that we might wish to perform on a graph—traversing the edges and the vertices of that graph.

12.3 Graph Traversals

A *traversal* is a systematic procedure for exploring a graph by examining all of its vertices and edges. A traversal is efficient if it visits all the vertices and edges in time proportional to their number, that is, in linear time. In this section, we consider two efficient traversals of undirected graphs, called depth-first search and breadth-first search, respectively. In Section 12.4.1, we extend these techniques to traversals of directed graphs.

12.3.1 Depth-First Search

The first traversal algorithm we consider is ***depth-first search*** (DFS) in an undirected graph. Depth-first search is useful for performing a number of computations on graphs, including finding a path from one vertex to another, determining whether or not a graph is connected, and computing a spanning tree of a connected graph. In this section, we explain how DFS works and how it can be used.

Depth-first search in an undirected graph G is analogous to wandering in a labyrinth with a string and a can of paint without getting lost. We begin at a specific starting vertex s in G, which we initialize by fixing one end of our string to s and painting s as "visited." The vertex s is now our "current" vertex—call our current vertex u. We then traverse G by considering an (arbitrary) edge (u,v) incident to the current vertex u. If the edge (u,v) leads us to an already visited (that is, painted) vertex v, we immediately return to vertex u. If, on the other hand, (u,v) leads to an unvisited vertex v, then we unroll our string, and go to v. We then paint v as "visited," and make it the current vertex, repeating the above computation. Eventually, we will get to a "dead-end," that is, a current vertex u such that all the edges incident on u lead to vertices already visited. Thus, taking any edge incident on u will cause us to return to u. To get out of this impasse, we roll our string back up, backtracking along the edge that brought us to u, going back to a previously visited vertex v. We then make v our current vertex and repeat the above computation for any edges incident upon v that we have not looked at before. If all of v's incident edges lead to visited vertices, then we again roll up our string and backtrack to the vertex we came from to get to v, and repeat the procedure at that vertex. Thus, we continue to backtrack along the path that we have traced so far until we find a vertex that has yet unexplored edges, take one such edge, and continue the traversal. The process terminates when our backtracking leads us back to the start vertex s, and there are no more unexplored edges incident on s. This simple process traverses the edges of G in an elegant, systematic way. (See Figure 12.6.)

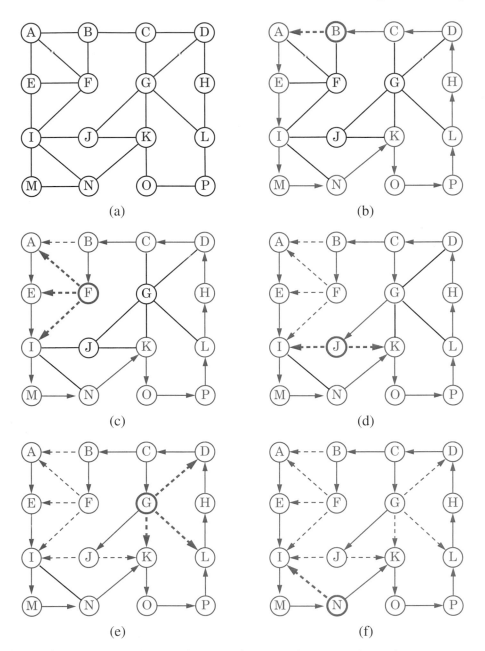

Figure 12.6: Example of depth-first search traversal on a graph starting at vertex *A*. Discovery edges are shown with solid lines and back edges are shown with dashed lines: (a) input graph; (b) path of discovery edges traced from A until back edge (B,A) is hit; (c) reaching F, which is a dead end; (d) after backtracking to C, resuming with edge (C,G), and hitting another dead end, J; (e) after backtracking to G; (f) after backtracking to N.

We can visualize a DFS traversal by orienting the edges along the direction in which they are explored during the traversal, distinguishing the edges used to discover new vertices, called *discovery edges*, or *tree edges*, from those that lead to already visited vertices, called *back edges*. (See Figure 12.6f.) In the analogy above, discovery edges are the edges where we unroll our string when we traverse them, and back edges are the edges where we immediately return without unrolling any string. As we will see, the discovery edges form a spanning tree of the connected component of the starting vertex s. We call the edges not in this tree "back edges" because, assuming that the tree is rooted at the start vertex, each such edge leads back from a vertex in this tree to one of its ancestors in the tree.

The pseudo-code for a DFS traversal starting at a vertex v follows our analogy with string and paint. We use recursion to implement the string analogy, and we assume that we have a mechanism (the paint analogy) to determine if a vertex or edge has been explored or not, and to label the edges as discovery edges or back edges. This mechanism will require additional space and may affect the running time of the algorithm. A pseudo-code description of the recursive DFS algorithm is given in Code Fragment 12.1.

Algorithm DFS(G, v):

 Input: A graph G and a vertex v of G

 Output: A labeling of the edges in the connected component of v as discovery
  edges and back edges

 label v as visited

 for all edge e in G.incidentEdges(v) **do**

  if edge e is unvisited **then**

   $w \leftarrow G$.opposite(v, e)

   if vertex w is unexplored **then**

    label e as a discovery edge

    recursively call DFS(G, w)

   else

    label e as a back edge

Code Fragment 12.1: The DFS algorithm.

There are a number of observations that we can make about the depth-first search algorithm, many of which derive from the way the DFS algorithm partitions the edges of the undirected graph G into two groups, the discovery edges and the back edges. For example, since back edges always connect a vertex v to a previously visited vertex u, each back edge implies a cycle in G, consisting of the discovery edges from u to v plus the back edge (u, v).

Proposition 12.12: *Let G be an undirected graph on which a DFS traversal starting at a vertex s has been performed. Then the traversal visits all vertices in the connected component of s, and the discovery edges form a spanning tree of the connected component of s.*

Justification: Suppose there is at least one vertex v in s's connected component not visited, and let w be the first unvisited vertex on some path from s to v (we may have $v = w$). Since w is the first unvisited vertex on this path, it has a neighbor u that was visited. But when we visited u, we must have considered the edge (u, w); hence, it cannot be correct that w is unvisited. Therefore, there are no unvisited vertices in s's connected component.

Since we only mark edges when we go to unvisited vertices, we will never form a cycle with discovery edges, that is, discovery edges form a tree. Moreover, this is a spanning tree because, as we have just seen, the depth-first search visits each vertex in the connected component of s.   ∎

In terms of its running time, depth-first search is an efficient method for traversing a graph. Note that DFS is called exactly once on each vertex, and that every edge is examined exactly twice, once from each of its end vertices. Thus, if n_s vertices and m_s edges are in the connected component of vertex s, a DFS starting at s runs in $O(n_s + m_s)$ time, provided the following conditions are satisfied:

- The graph is represented by a data structure such that creating and iterating the incidentEdges(v) iterator takes $O(\text{degree}(v))$ time, and the opposite(v, e) method takes $O(1)$ time. The adjacency list structure is one such structure, but the adjacency matrix structure is not.
- We have a way to "mark" a vertex or edge as explored, and to test if a vertex or edge has been explored in $O(1)$ time. We discuss ways of implementing DFS to achieve this goal in the next section.

Given the above assumptions, we can solve a number of interesting problems.

Proposition 12.13: *Let G be a graph with n vertices and m edges represented with an adjacency list. A DFS traversal of G can be performed in $O(n + m)$ time, and can be used to solve the following problems in $O(n + m)$ time:*

- *Testing whether G is connected*
- *Computing a spanning tree of G, if G is connected*
- *Computing the connected components of G*
- *Computing a path between two given vertices of G, if it exists*
- *Computing a cycle in G, or reporting that G has no cycles.*

The justification of Proposition 12.13 is based on algorithms that use slightly modified versions of the DFS algorithm as subroutines.

12.3.2 Implementing Depth-First Search

In this section, we discuss some of the important issues in the implementation of the depth-first search algorithm.

The Data Structures Used for Graphs and Their Positions

As we have mentioned above, the data structure we use to represent a graph has impact on the performance of the DFS algorithm. For example, an adjacency list can be used to yield a running time of $O(n+m)$ time for traversing a graph with n vertices and m edges. Using an adjacency matrix, on the other hand, would result in a running time of $O(n^2)$, since each of the n calls to the incidentEdges method would take $O(n)$ time. If the graph is **dense**, that is, it has close to $O(n^2)$ edges, then the difference between these two choices is minor, as they both would run in $O(n^2)$ time. But if the graph is **sparse**, that is, it has close to $O(n)$ edges, then the adjacency matrix approach would be much slower than the adjacency list approach.

Another important issue in the implementation of DFS deals with the way vertices and edges are represented. In particular, we need to have a way of marking vertices and edges as visited or not. There are two simple solutions, but each has drawbacks:

- We can build our vertex and edge objects to contain an explored field, which can be used by the DFS algorithm for marking. This approach is quite simple, and supports constant-time marking and unmarking, but it assumes that we are designing our graph with DFS in mind, which will not always be valid. Furthermore, this approach needlessly restricts DFS to graphs with vertices having an explored field. Thus, if we want a generic DFS algorithm that can take any graph as input, this approach has limitations.

- We can use an auxiliary hash table to store all the explored vertices and edges during the DFS algorithm. This scheme is general, in that it does not require any special fields in the positions of the graph. But this approach does not achieve worst-case constant time for marking and unmarking of vertices edges. Instead, such a hash table only supports the mark (insert) and test (find) operations in constant **expected** time (see Section 8.2).

Fortunately, there is a middle ground between requiring that each position have all the fields they will ever need for DFS and other graph algorithms, and requiring that each algorithm keep a separate mapping of vertices and edges to the labels that that algorithm needs for those positions.

The Decorator Pattern

Marking the explored vertices in a DFS traversal is an example of the ***decorator*** software engineering design pattern. This pattern is used to add ***decorations*** (also called ***attributes***) to existing objects. Each decoration is identified by a ***key*** identifying this decoration and by a ***value*** associated with the key.

The use of decorations is motivated by the need of some algorithms and data structures to add extra variables, or temporary scratch data, to objects that do not normally have such variables. Hence, a decoration is a key-value pair that can be dynamically attached to an object. In our DFS example, we would like to have "decorable" vertices and edges with an ***explored*** decoration and a Boolean value.

We can realize the decorator pattern for any position by allowing it to be decorated. This allows us to add labels to vertices and edges, for example, without requiring that we know in advance the kinds of labels that we will need. We can simply require that our vertices and edges implement a ***decorable position*** ADT, which inherits from both the position ADT and the map ADT (Section 8.1). Namely, the methods of the decorable position ADT are the union of the methods of the position ADT and of the map ADT, that is, in addition to the standard size and isEmpty methods, a decorable position would support the following:

element(): Return the element stored at this position.

put(k, x): Map the decoration value x to the key k, returning the old value for k, or **null** if this is a new value for k.

get(k): Get the decoration value x assigned to k, or **null** if there is no mapping for k.

remove(k): Remove the decoration mapping for k, returning the old value, or **null** if there is none.

entries(): Return all the key-decoration pairs for this position.

The map methods of a decorable position p provide a simple mechanism for accessing and setting the decorations of p. For example, we use p.get(k) to obtain the value of the decoration with key k and we use p.put(k, x) to set the value of the decoration with key k to x. Moreover, the key k can be any object, including a special explored object our DFS algorithm might create.

The decorable position ADT can be implemented as an object that stores an element plus a map. In principle, the running times of the methods of a decorable position depend on the implementation of the underlying map. However, most algorithms (including DFS) use a small constant number of decorations. Thus, irrespective of the implementation of the map, the decorable position methods will run in $O(1)$ worst-case time.

Using decorable positions, the complete DFS traversal algorithm can be described in more detail, as shown in Code Fragment 12.2.

Algorithm DFS(G, v, k):

   Input: A graph G with decorable vertices and edges, a vertex v of G, and a decoration key k

   Output: A decoration of the vertices of in the connected component of v with key k and value VISITED and of the edges in the connected component of v with key k and values DISCOVERY and BACK, according to a depth-first search traversal of G

  v.put(k, VISITED)

  for all edge e in G.incidentEdges(v) **do**

    if e.get(k) = null **then**

      $w \leftarrow G$.opposite(v, e)

      if w.get(k) = null **then**

        e.put(k, DISCOVERY)

        DFS(G, w, k)

      else

        e.put(k, BACK)

Code Fragment 12.2: DFS on a graph with decorable edges and vertices.

A Generic DFS Implementation in Java

In Code Fragments 12.3 and 12.4, we show a Java implementation of a generic depth-first search traversal using an abstract class, DFS. Its behavior can be specialized for a particular application by defining method execute, which activates the computation, and redefining the following methods, which are called at various times by the recursive template method dfsTraversal.

- initResult(): called at the beginning of the execution of dfsTraversal.
- startVisit(Vertex v): called at the beginning of dfsTraversal at v.
- traverseDiscovery(Edge e, Vertex v): called when a discovery edge e out of v is traversed.
- traverseBack(Edge e, Vertex v): called when a back edge e out of v is traversed.
- isDone(): called to determine whether to end the traversal early.
- finishVisit(Vertex v): called when we are finished exploring from v.
- result(): called to return the output of dfsTraversal.

```
/** Generic depth first search traversal of a graph using the template method
  * pattern. A subclass should override various methods to add functionality. */
public abstract class DFS {
  protected Graph G;                    // The graph being traversed
  protected Object visitResult;         // The result of the traversal
  protected static Object STATUS = new Object();    // The status attribute
  protected static Object VISITED = new Object();    // Visited value
  protected static Object UNVISITED = new Object(); // Unvisited value
  /** Execute a depth first search traversal on graph g, starting
    * from a vertex v, optionally passing in an information object (info)
    */
  public abstract Object execute(Graph g, Vertex start, Object info);
  /** Initialize the graph g for a traversal. */
  protected void init(Graph g) {
    G = g;
    for(Iterator vertices = g.vertices(); vertices.hasNext(); )
      unVisit((DecorablePosition)vertices.next());
    for(Iterator edges = g.edges(); edges.hasNext(); )
      unVisit((DecorablePosition)edges.next());
  }
  /** Mark a position as visited.       */
  protected void visit(DecorablePosition p) { p.put(STATUS, VISITED); }
  /** Mark a position as unvisited.      */
  protected void unVisit(DecorablePosition p) { p.put(STATUS, UNVISITED); }
  /** Test if a position has been visited. */
  protected boolean isVisited(DecorablePosition p) {
    return (p.get(STATUS) == VISITED);
  }
  // Auxiliary methods (all initially null) for specializing a generic DFS
  /** Initializes result (called first, once per vertex visited). */
  protected void initResult() {}
  /** Called when we encounter a vertex (v). */
  protected void startVisit(Vertex v) {}
  /** Called after we finish the visit for a vertex (v). */
  protected void finishVisit(Vertex v) {}
  /** Called when we traverse a discovery edge (e) from a vertex (from). */
  protected void traverseDiscovery(Edge e, Vertex from) {}
  /** Called when we traverse a back edge (e) from a vertex (from). */
  protected void traverseBack(Edge e, Vertex from) {}
  /** Determines whether the traversal is done early. */
  protected boolean isDone() { return false; /* default value */ }
  /** Returns a result of a visit (if needed). */
  protected Object result() { return null; /* default value */ }
```

Code Fragment 12.3: Instance variables and support methods of class DFS, which performs a generic DFS traversal. The methods visit, unVisit, and isVisited are implemented using decorable positions. (Continues in Code Fragment 12.4.)

```
/** Recursive template method for a generic DFS traversal.
 * @param v Start vertex of the traversal
 * @return result of the traversal
 */
protected Object dfsTraversal(Vertex v) {
  initResult();
  if (!isDone())
    startVisit(v);
  if (!isDone()) {
    visit(v);
    for (Iterator inEdges = G.incidentEdges(v); inEdges.hasNext(); ) {
      Edge nextEdge = (Edge) inEdges.next();
      if (!isVisited(nextEdge)) {
        // found an unexplored edge, explore it
        visit(nextEdge);
        Vertex w = G.opposite(v, nextEdge);
        if (!isVisited(w)) {
          // w is unexplored, this is a discovery edge
          traverseDiscovery(nextEdge, v);
          if (isDone())
            break;
          visitResult = dfsTraversal(w);
          if (isDone())
            break;
        }
        else {
          // w is explored, this is a back edge
          traverseBack(nextEdge, v);
          if (isDone())
            break;
        }
      }
    }
  }
  if(!isDone())
    finishVisit(v);
  return result();
}
} // end of DFS abstract class
```

Code Fragment 12.4: The main template method dfsTraversal of class DFS, which performs a generic DFS traversal of a graph.

Using the Template Method Pattern for DFS

Our generic depth-first search traversal is based on the template method pattern (see Section 6.3.5), which describes a generic computation mechanism that can be specialized by redefining certain steps.

The mechanism used to identify the vertices and edges that have already been visited (explored) during the traversal is encapsulated in the calls to methods isVisited, visit, and unVisit. Our implementation (see Code Fragment 12.3) assumes that the vertices and edges are decorable positions. Alternatively, we can set up a dictionary of positions and store the visited vertices and edges in it.

For us to do anything interesting with the dfsTraversal, we must extend the DFS class and redefine some of the auxiliary methods of Code Fragment 12.3 to do something nontrivial. This approach conforms to the template method pattern, for these methods specialize the behavior of the template method dfsTraversal.

Extending Generic DFS for Interesting Algorithms

In Code Fragments 12.5 through 12.7, we illustrate, in classes that extend DFS, some interesting uses of the dfsTraversal method. Class ConnectivityDFS (Code Fragment 12.5), for instance, tests whether the graph is connected. It counts the vertices reachable by a DFS traversal starting at a vertex and compares this number with the total number of vertices of the graph.

```java
/** This class specializes DFS to determine whether the graph is connected. */
public class ConnectivityDFS extends DFS {
  protected int reached;
  public Object execute(Graph g, Vertex start, Object info) {
    init(g);
    int n = 0;
    Iterator V = G.vertices();
    while (V.hasNext()) {
      V.next();
      n++;
    }
    reached = 0;
    dfsTraversal(start);
    return new Boolean(reached == n);
  }
  protected void startVisit(Vertex v) { reached++; }

}
```

Code Fragment 12.5: Specialization of class DFS to test if the graph is connected.

Class FindPathDFS (Code Fragment 12.6) finds a path between a pair of given start and target vertices. It performs a depth-first search traversal beginning at the start vertex. We maintain the path of discovery edges from the start vertex to the current vertex. When we encounter an unexplored vertex, we add it to the end of the path, and when we finish processing a vertex, we remove it from the path. The traversal is terminated when the target vertex is encountered, and the path is returned as an iterator of vertices. Note that the path found by this class consists of discovery edges.

```
/** This class specializes DFS to find a path between the start vertex
 * and a given target vertex.  */
public class FindPathDFS extends DFS {
  protected List path;
  protected boolean done;
  protected Vertex target;
  /** @param info target vertex of the path
   * @return {@link Iterator} of the vertices and edges in a path
   * from the start vertex to the target vertex, or an empty iterator
   * if no such path exists in the graph */
  public Object execute(Graph g, Vertex start, Object info) {
    init(g);
    path = new NodeList();
    done = false;
    target = (Vertex) info; // target vertex is stored in info parameter
    dfsTraversal(start);
    return path.elements();
  }
  protected void startVisit(Vertex v) {
    path.insertLast(v); // add vertex v to path
    if (v == target)
      done = true;
  }
  protected void finishVisit(Vertex v) {
    path.remove(path.last());     // remove v from path
    if(!path.isEmpty())           // if v is not the start vertex
      path.remove(path.last());   // remove discovery edge into v from path
  }
  protected void traverseDiscovery(Edge e, Vertex from) {
    path.insertLast(e); // add edge e to the path
  }
  protected boolean isDone() { return done; }
}
```

Code Fragment 12.6: Specialization of class DFS to find a path between start and target vertices.

Class FindCycleDFS (Code Fragment 12.7) finds a cycle in the connected component of a given vertex v, by performing a depth-first search traversal from v that terminates when a back edge is found. It returns a (possibly empty) iterator of the edges in the cycle formed by the found back edge.

```
public class FindCycleDFS extends DFS { // find a cycle from a start vertex
  protected List cycle; // sequence of edges of the cycle
  protected boolean done;
  protected Vertex cycleStart;
  public Object execute(Graph g, Vertex start, Object info) {
    init(g);
    cycle = new NodeList();
    done = false;
    dfsTraversal(start);
    // remove the vertices and edges from start to cycleStart
    if (!cycle.isEmpty() && start != cycleStart) {
      Iterator pos = cycle.positions();
      while (pos.hasNext()) {
        Position p = (Position) pos.next();
        cycle.remove(p);                      // remove vertex from cycle
        p = (Position) pos.next();
        Edge e = (Edge) p.element();          // remove edge from cycle
        cycle.remove(p);
        Vertex[] endv = g.endVertices(e);
        if ((endv[0] == cycleStart) || (endv[1] == cycleStart )) break;
      }
    }
    return cycle.elements(); // iterator of the vertices and edges of the cycle
  }
  protected void startVisit(Vertex v) { cycle.insertLast(v); /* add v to cycle */ }
  protected void finishVisit(Vertex v) {
    cycle.remove(cycle.last());    // remove v from cycle
    if (!cycle.isEmpty()) cycle.remove(cycle.last()); // remove edge into v from cycle
  }
  protected void traverseDiscovery(Edge e, Vertex from) { cycle.insertLast(e); }
  protected void traverseBack(Edge e, Vertex from) {
    cycle.insertLast(e);                      // back edge e creates a cycle
    cycleStart = G.opposite(from, e);
    cycle.insertLast(cycleStart);             // first vertex completes the cycle
    done = true;
  }
  protected boolean isDone() {  return done; }
}
```

Code Fragment 12.7: Specialization of class DFS to find a cycle in the connected component of the start vertex.

12.3.3 Breadth-First Search

In this section, we consider the ***breadth-first search*** (BFS) traversal algorithm. Like DFS, BFS traverses a connected component of a graph, and in so doing defines a useful spanning tree. BFS is less "adventurous" than DFS, however. Instead of wandering the graph, BFS proceeds in rounds and subdivides the vertices into *levels*. BFS can also be thought of as a traversal using a string and paint, with BFS unrolling the string in a more conservative manner.

BFS starts at vertex s, which is at level 0 and defines the "anchor" for our string. In the first round, we let out the string the length of one edge and we visit all the vertices we can reach without unrolling the string any farther. In this case, we visit, and paint as "visited," the vertices adjacent to the start vertex s—these vertices are placed into level 1. In the second round, we unroll the string the length of two edges and we visit all the new vertices we can reach without unrolling our string any farther. These new vertices, which are adjacent to level 1 vertices and not previously assigned to a level, are placed into level 2, and so on. The BFS traversal terminates when every vertex has been visited.

Pseudo-code for a BFS starting at a vertex s is shown in Code Fragment 12.8. We use auxiliary space to label edges, mark visited vertices, and store containers associated with levels. That is, the containers L_0, L_1, L_2, and so on, store the vertices that are in level 0, level 1, level 2, and so on. These containers could, for example, be implemented as queues. They also allow BFS to be nonrecursive.

Algorithm BFS(s):
    initialize container L_0 to contain vertex s
    $i \leftarrow 0$
    while L_i is not empty **do**
      create container L_{i+1} to initially be empty
      for all vertex v in L_i **do**
        for all edge e in G.incidentEdges(v) **do**
          if edge e is unexplored **then**
            $w \leftarrow G$.opposite(v, e)
            if vertex w is unexplored **then**
              label e as a discovery edge
              insert w into L_{i+1}
          else
            label e as a cross edge
      $i \leftarrow i+1$

Code Fragment 12.8: The BFS algorithm.

We illustrate a BFS traversal in Figure 12.7.

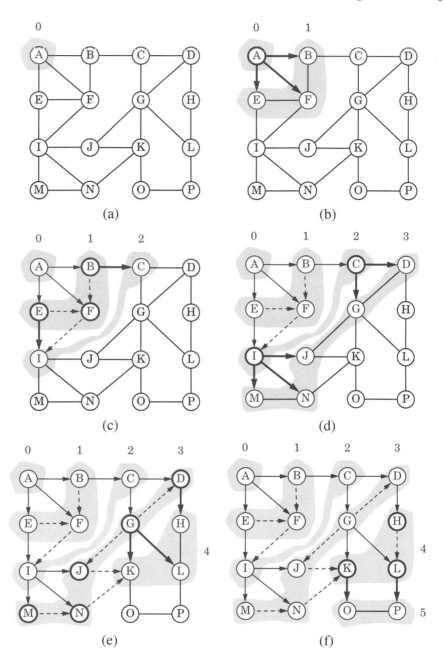

Figure 12.7: Example of breadth-first search traversal, where the edges incident on a vertex are explored by the alphabetical order of the adjacent vertices. The discovery edges are shown with solid lines and the cross edges are shown with dashed lines: (a) graph before the traversal; (b) discovery of level 1; (c) discovery of level 2; (d) discovery of level 3; (e) discovery of level 4; (f) discovery of level 5.

One of the nice properties of the BFS approach is that, in performing the BFS traversal, we can label each vertex by the length of a shortest path (in terms of the number of edges) from the start vertex s. In particular, if vertex v is placed into level i by a BFS starting at vertex s, then the length of a shortest path from s to v is i.

As with DFS, we can visualize the BFS traversal by orienting the edges along the direction in which they are explored during the traversal, and by distinguishing the edges used to discover new vertices, called ***discovery edges***, from those that lead to already visited vertices, called ***cross edges***. (See Figure 12.7f.) As with the DFS, the discovery edges form a spanning tree, which in this case we call the BFS tree. We do not call the nontree edges "back edges" in this case, however, for none of them connects a vertex to one of its ancestors. Every nontree edge connects a vertex v to another vertex that is neither v's ancestor nor its descendent.

The BFS traversal algorithm has a number of interesting properties, some of which we explore in the proposition that follows.

Proposition 12.14: *Let G be an undirected graph on which a BFS traversal starting at vertex s has been performed. Then*

- *The traversal visits all vertices in the connected component of s.*
- *The discovery-edges form a spanning tree T, which we call the BFS tree, of the connected component of s.*
- *For each vertex v at level i, the path of the BFS tree T between s and v has i edges, and any other path of G between s and v has at least i edges.*
- *If (u,v) is an edge that is not in the BFS tree, then the level numbers of u and v differ by at most 1.*

We leave the justification of this proposition as an exercise (C-12.14). The analysis of the running time of BFS is similar to the one of DFS, which implies the following.

Proposition 12.15: *Let G be a graph with n vertices and m edges represented with the adjacency list structure. A BFS traversal of G takes $O(n+m)$ time. Also, there exist $O(n+m)$-time algorithms based on BFS for the following problems:*

- *Testing whether G is connected*
- *Computing a spanning tree of G, if G is connected*
- *Computing the connected components of G*
- *Given a start vertex s of G, computing, for every vertex v of G, a path with the minimum number of edges between s and v, or reporting that no such path exists.*
- *Computing a cycle in G, or reporting that G has no cycles.*

12.4 Directed Graphs

In this section, we consider issues that are specific to directed graphs. Recall that a directed graph (***digraph***), is a graph whose edges are all directed.

Methods Dealing with Directed Edges

When we allow for some or all the edges in a graph to be directed, we should add the following two methods to the graph ADT in order to deal with edge directions.

isDirected(e): Test whether edge e is directed.
Input: Edge; ***Output:*** Boolean.

insertDirectedEdge(v, w, o): Insert and return a new directed edge with origin v and destination w and storing element o.
Input: Vertices and object; ***Output:*** Edge.

Also, if an edge e is directed, the method endVertices(e) should return an array A such that $A[0]$ is the origin of e and $A[1]$ is the destination of e. The running time for the method isDirected(e) should be $O(1)$, and the running time of the method insertDirectedEdge(v, w, o) should match that of undirected edge insertion.

Reachability

One of the most fundamental issues with directed graphs is the notion of ***reachability***, which deals with determining where we can get to in a directed graph. A traversal in a directed graph always goes along directed paths, that is, paths where all the edges are traversed according to their respective directions. Given vertices u and v of a digraph $\vec{G}$, we say that u ***reaches*** v (and v is ***reachable*** from u) if $\vec{G}$ has a directed path from u to v. We also say that a vertex v reaches an edge (w, z) if v reaches the origin vertex w of the edge.

A digraph $\vec{G}$ is ***strongly connected*** if for any two vertices u and v of $\vec{G}$, u reaches v and v reaches u. A ***directed cycle*** of $\vec{G}$ is a cycle where all the edges are traversed according to their respective directions. (Note that $\vec{G}$ may have a cycle consisting of two edges with opposite direction between the same pair of vertices.) A digraph $\vec{G}$ is ***acyclic*** if it has no directed cycles. (See Figure 12.8 for some examples.)

The ***transitive closure*** of a digraph $\vec{G}$ is the digraph $\vec{G}^*$ such that the vertices of $\vec{G}^*$ are the same as the vertices of $\vec{G}$, and $\vec{G}^*$ has an edge (u, v), whenever $\vec{G}$ has a directed path from u to v. That is, we define $\vec{G}^*$ by starting with the digraph $\vec{G}$ and adding in an extra edge (u, v) for each u and v such that v is reachable from u (and there isn't already an edge (u, v) in $\vec{G}$).

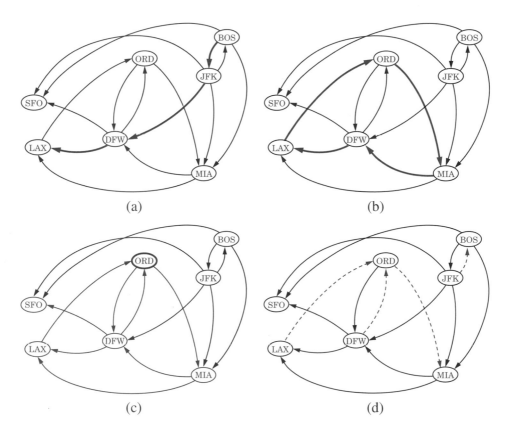

Figure 12.8: Examples of reachability in a digraph: (a) a directed path from BOS to LAX is drawn in blue; (b) a directed cycle (ORD, MIA, DFW, LAX, ORD) is shown in blue; its vertices induce a strongly connected subgraph; (c) the subgraph of the vertices and edges reachable from ORD is shown in blue; (d) removing the dashed blue edges gives an acyclic digraph.

Interesting problems that deal with reachability in a digraph $\vec{G}$ include the following:

- Given vertices u and v, determine whether u reaches v.
- Find all the vertices of $\vec{G}$ that are reachable from a given vertex s.
- Determine whether $\vec{G}$ is strongly connected.
- Determine whether $\vec{G}$ is acyclic.
- Compute the transitive closure $\vec{G}^*$ of $\vec{G}$.

In the remainder of this section, we explore some efficient algorithms for solving these problems.

12.4.1 Traversing a Digraph

As with undirected graphs, we can explore a digraph in a systematic way with methods akin to the depth-first search (DFS) and breadth-first search (BFS) algorithms defined previously for undirected graphs (Sections 12.3.1 and 12.3.3). Such explorations can be used, for example, to answer reachability questions. The directed depth-first search and breadth-first search methods we develop in this section for performing such explorations are very similar to their undirected counterparts. In fact, the only real difference is that the directed depth-first search and breadth-first search methods only traverse edges according to their respective directions.

The directed version of DFS starting at a vertex v can be described by the recursive algorithm in Code Fragment 12.9. (See Figure 12.9.)

Algorithm DirectedDFS(v):

     Mark vertex v as visited.

     for each outgoing edge (v, w) of v **do**

         if vertex w has not been visited **then**

             Recursively call DirectedDFS(w).

Code Fragment 12.9: The DirectedDFS algorithm.

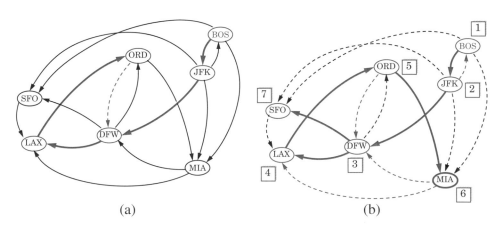

(a)   (b)

Figure 12.9: An example of a DFS in a digraph: (a) intermediate step, where, for the first time, an already visited vertex (DFW) is reached; (b) the completed DFS. The tree edges are shown with solid blue lines, the back edges are shown with dashed blue lines, and the forward and cross edges are shown with dashed black lines. The order in which the vertices are visited is indicated by a label next to each vertex. The edge (ORD,DFW) is a back edge, but (DFW,ORD) is a forward edge. Edge (BOS,SFO) is a forward edge, and (SFO,LAX) is a cross edge.

A DFS on a digraph $\vec{G}$ partitions the edges of $\vec{G}$ reachable from the starting vertex into ***tree edges*** or ***discovery edges***, which lead us to discover a new vertex, and ***nontree edges***, which take us to a previously visited vertex. The tree edges form a tree rooted at the starting vertex, called the ***depth-first search*** tree, and there are three kinds of nontree edges:

- ***back edges***, which connect a vertex to an ancestor in the DFS tree
- ***forward edges***, which connect a vertex to a descendent in the DFS tree
- ***cross edges***, which connect a vertex to a vertex that is neither its ancestor nor its descendent.

Refer back to Figure 12.9b to see an example of each type of nontree edge.

Proposition 12.16: *Let $\vec{G}$ be a digraph. Depth-first search on $\vec{G}$ starting at a vertex s visits all the vertices of $\vec{G}$ that are reachable from s. Also, the DFS tree contains directed paths from s to every vertex reachable from s.*

Justification: Let V_s be the subset of vertices of $\vec{G}$ visited by DFS starting at vertex s. We want to show that V_s contains s and every vertex reachable from s belongs to V_s. Suppose now, for the sake of a contradiction, that there is a vertex w reachable from s that is not in V_s. Consider a directed path from s to w, and let (u, v) be the first edge on such a path taking us out of V_s, that is, u is in V_s but v is not in V_s. When DFS reaches u, it explores all the outgoing edges of u, and thus must reach also vertex v via edge (u, v). Hence, v should be in V_s, and we have obtained a contradiction. Therefore, V_s must contain every vertex reachable from s. ∎

Analyzing the running time of the directed DFS method is analogous to that for its undirected counterpart. In particular, a recursive call is made for each vertex exactly once, and each edge is traversed exactly once (from its origin). Hence, if n_s vertices and m_s edges are reachable from vertex s, a directed DFS starting at s runs in $O(n_s + m_s)$ time, provided the digraph is represented with a data structure that supports constant-time vertex and edge methods. The adjacency list structure satisfies this requirement, for example.

By Proposition 12.16, we can use DFS to find all the vertices reachable from a given vertex, and hence to find the transitive closure of $\vec{G}$. That is, we can perform a DFS, starting from each vertex v of $\vec{G}$, to see which vertices w are reachable from v, adding an edge (v, w) to the transitive closure for each such w. Likewise, by repeatedly traversing digraph $\vec{G}$ with a DFS, starting in turn at each vertex, we can easily test whether $\vec{G}$ is strongly connected. Namely, $\vec{G}$ is strongly connected if each DFS visits all the vertices of $\vec{G}$.

Thus, we may immediately derive the proposition that follows.

Proposition 12.17: *Let $\vec{G}$ be a digraph with n vertices and m edges. The following problems can be solved by an algorithm that traverses $\vec{G}$ n times using DFS, runs in $O(n(n+m))$ time, and uses $O(n)$ auxiliary space:*

- *Computing, for each vertex v of $\vec{G}$, the subgraph reachable from v*
- *Testing whether $\vec{G}$ is strongly connected*
- *Computing the transitive closure $\vec{G}^*$ of $\vec{G}$.*

Testing for Strong Connectivity

Actually, we can determine if a directed graph $\vec{G}$ is strongly connected much faster than this, just using two depth-first searches. We begin by performing a DFS of our directed graph $\vec{G}$ starting at an arbitrary vertex s. If there is any vertex of $\vec{G}$ that is not visited by this DFS, and is not reachable from s, then the graph is not strongly connected. So, if this first DFS visits each vertex of $\vec{G}$, then we reverse all the edges of $\vec{G}$ (using the reverseDirection method) and perform another DFS starting at s in this "reverse" graph. If every vertex of $\vec{G}$ is visited by this second DFS, then the graph is strongly connected, for each of the vertices visited in this DFS can reach s. Since this algorithm makes just two DFS traversals of $\vec{G}$, it runs in $O(n+m)$ time.

Directed Breadth-First Search

As with DFS, we can extend breadth-first search (BFS) to work for directed graphs. The algorithm still visits vertices level by level and partitions the set of edges into *tree edges* (or *discovery edges*), which together form a directed *breadth-first search* tree rooted at the start vertex, and *nontree edges*. Unlike the directed DFS method, however, the directed BFS method only leaves two kinds of nontree edges: *back edges*, which connect a vertex to one of its ancestors, and *cross edges*, which connect a vertex to another vertex that is neither its ancestor nor its descendent. There are no forward edges, which is a fact we explore in an exercise (C-12.10).

12.4.2 Transitive Closure

In this section, we explore an alternative technique for computing the transitive closure of a digraph. Let $\vec{G}$ be a digraph with n vertices and m edges. We compute the transitive closure of $\vec{G}$ in a series of rounds. We initialize $\vec{G}_0 = \vec{G}$. We also arbitrarily number the vertices of $\vec{G}$ as $v_1, v_2, \ldots, v_n$. We then begin the computation of the rounds, beginning with round 1. In a generic round k, we construct digraph $\vec{G}_k$ starting with $\vec{G}_k = \vec{G}_{k-1}$ and adding to $\vec{G}_k$ the directed edge (v_i, v_j) if digraph $\vec{G}_{k-1}$ contains both the edges (v_i, v_k) and (v_k, v_j). In this way, we will enforce a simple rule embodied in the proposition that follows.

Proposition 12.18: *For $i = 1, \ldots, n$, digraph $\vec{G}_k$ has an edge (v_i, v_j) if and only if digraph $\vec{G}$ has a directed path from v_i to v_j, whose intermediate vertices (if any) are in the set $\{v_1, \ldots, v_k\}$. In particular, $\vec{G}_n$ is equal to $\vec{G}^*$, the transitive closure of $\vec{G}$.*

Proposition 12.18 suggests a simple algorithm for computing the transitive closure of $\vec{G}$ that is based on the series of rounds we described above. This algorithm is known as the ***Floyd-Warshall algorithm***, and its pseudo-code is given in Code Fragment 12.10. From this pseudo-code, we can easily analyze the running time of the Floyd-Warshall algorithm assuming that the data structure representing G supports methods areAdjacent and insertDirectedEdge in $O(1)$ time. The main loop is executed n times and the inner loop considers each of $O(n^2)$ pairs of vertices, performing a constant-time computation for each one. Thus, the total running time of the Floyd-Warshall algorithm is $O(n^3)$.

Algorithm FloydWarshall($\vec{G}$):

    Input: A digraph $\vec{G}$ with n vertices
    Output: The transitive closure $\vec{G}^*$ of $\vec{G}$

    let $v_1, v_2, \ldots, v_n$ be an arbitrary numbering of the vertices of $\vec{G}$
    $\vec{G}_0 \leftarrow \vec{G}$
    for $k \leftarrow 1$ to n **do**
        $\vec{G}_k \leftarrow \vec{G}_{k-1}$
        for all i, j in $\{1, \ldots, n\}$ with $i \neq j$ and $i, j \neq k$ **do**
            if both edges (v_i, v_k) and (v_k, v_j) are in $\vec{G}_{k-1}$ **then**
                add edge (v_i, v_j) to $\vec{G}_k$ (if it is not already present)
    return $\vec{G}_n$

Code Fragment 12.10: Pseudo-code for the Floyd-Warshall algorithm. This algorithm computes the transitive closure $\vec{G}^*$ of G by incrementally computing a series of digraphs $\vec{G}_0, \vec{G}_1, \ldots, \vec{G}_n$, where for $k = 1, \ldots, n$.

This description is actually an example of an algorithmic design pattern known as dynamic programming, which is discussed in more detail in Section 11.5.2. From the above description and analysis we may immediately derive the following proposition.

Proposition 12.19: *Let $\vec{G}$ be a digraph with n vertices, and let $\vec{G}$ be represented by a data structure that supports lookup and update of adjacency information in $O(1)$ time. Then the Floyd-Warshall algorithm computes the transitive closure $\vec{G}^*$ of $\vec{G}$ in $O(n^3)$ time.*

We illustrate an example run of the Floyd-Warshall algorithm in Figure 12.10.

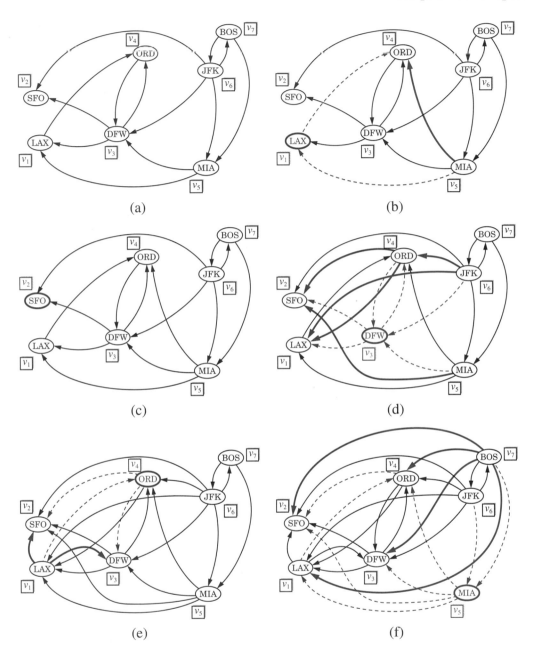

Figure 12.10: Sequence of digraphs computed by the Floyd-Warshall algorithm: (a) initial digraph $\vec{G} = \vec{G}_0$ and numbering of the vertices; (b) digraph $\vec{G}_1$; (c) $\vec{G}_2$; (d) $\vec{G}_3$; (e) $\vec{G}_4$; (f) $\vec{G}_5$. Note that $\vec{G}_5 = \vec{G}_6 = \vec{G}_7$. If digraph $\vec{G}_{k-1}$ has the edges (v_i, v_k) and (v_k, v_j), but not the edge (v_i, v_j), in the drawing of digraph $\vec{G}_k$, we show edges (v_i, v_k) and (v_k, v_j) with dashed blue lines, and edge (v_i, v_j) with a thick blue line.

Performance of the Floyd-Warshall Algorithm

The running time of the Floyd-Warshall algorithm might appear to be slower than performing a DFS of a directed graph from each of its vertices, but this depends upon the representation of the graph. If a graph is represented using an adjacency matrix, then running the DFS method once on a directed graph $\vec{G}$ takes $O(n^2)$ time (we explore the reason for this in Exercise R-12.9). Thus, running DFS n times takes $O(n^3)$ time, which is no better than a single execution of the Floyd-Warshall algorithm, but the Floyd-Warshall algorithm would be much simpler to implement. Nevertheless, if the graph is represented using an adjacency list structure, then running the DFS algorithm n times would take $O(n(n+m))$ time to compute the transitive closure. Even so, if the graph is **dense**, that is, if it has $\Omega(n^2)$ edges, then this approach still runs in $O(n^3)$ time and is more complicated than a single instance of the Floyd-Warshall algorithm. The only case where repeatedly calling the DFS method is better is when the graph is not dense and is represented using an adjacency list structure.

12.4.3 Directed Acyclic Graphs

Directed graphs without directed cycles are encountered in many applications. Such a digraph is often referred to as a **directed acyclic graph**, or **DAG**, for short. Applications of such graphs include the following:

- Inheritance between classes of a Java program
- Prerequisites between courses of a degree program
- Scheduling constraints between the tasks of a project.

Example 12.20: *In order to manage a large project, it is convenient to break it up into a collection of smaller tasks. The tasks, however, are rarely independent, because scheduling constraints exist between them. (For example, in a house building project, the task of ordering nails obviously precedes the task of nailing shingles to the roof deck.) Clearly, scheduling constraints cannot have circularities, because they would make the project impossible. (For example, in order to get a job you need to have work experience, but in order to get work experience you need to have a job.) The scheduling constraints impose restrictions on the order in which the tasks can be executed. Namely, if a constraint says that task a must be completed before task b is started, then a must precede b in the order of execution of the tasks. Thus, if we model a feasible set of tasks as vertices of a directed graph, and we place a directed edge from v to w whenever the task for v must be executed before the task for w, then we define a directed acyclic graph.*

The above example motivates the following definition. Let $\vec{G}$ be a digraph with n vertices. A *topological ordering* of $\vec{G}$ is an ordering $v_1,\ldots,v_n$ of the vertices of $\vec{G}$ such that for every edge (v_i, v_j) of $\vec{G}$, $i < j$. That is, a topological ordering is an ordering such that any directed path in $\vec{G}$ traverses vertices in increasing order. (See Figure 12.11.) Note that a digraph may have more than one topological ordering.

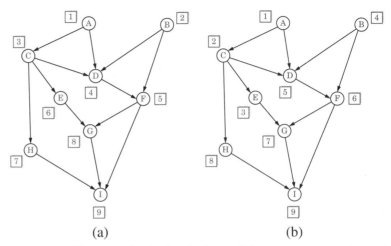

(a)   (b)

Figure 12.11: Two topological orderings of the same acyclic digraph.

Proposition 12.21: *$\vec{G}$ has a topological ordering if and only if it is acyclic.*

Justification: The necessity (the "only if" part of the statement) is easy to demonstrate. Suppose $\vec{G}$ is topologically ordered. Assume, for the sake of a contradiction, that $\vec{G}$ has a cycle consisting of edges $(v_{i_0}, v_{i_1}), (v_{i_1}, v_{i_2}), \ldots, (v_{i_{k-1}}, v_{i_0})$. Because of the topological ordering, we must have $i_0 < i_1 < \cdots < i_{k-1} < i_0$, which is clearly impossible. Thus, $\vec{G}$ must be acyclic.

We now argue the sufficiency of the condition (the "if" part of the statement). Suppose $\vec{G}$ is acyclic. We will give an algorithmic description of how to build a topological ordering for $\vec{G}$. Since $\vec{G}$ is acyclic, $\vec{G}$ must have a vertex with no incoming edges (that is, with in-degree 0). Let v_1 be such a vertex. Indeed, if v_1 did not exist, then in tracing a directed path from an arbitrary start vertex we would eventually encounter a previously visited vertex, thus contradicting the acyclicity of $\vec{G}$. If we remove v_1 from $\vec{G}$, together with its outgoing edges, the resulting digraph is still acyclic. Hence, the resulting digraph also has a vertex with no incoming edges, and we let v_2 be such a vertex. By repeating this process until the digraph becomes empty, we obtain an ordering $v_1,\ldots,v_n$ of the vertices of $\vec{G}$. Because of the above construction, if (v_i, v_j) is an edge of $\vec{G}$, then v_i must be deleted before v_j can be deleted, and thus $i < j$. Thus, $v_1,\ldots,v_n$ is a topological ordering.

■

Proposition 12.21's justification suggests an algorithm (Code Fragment 12.11), called *topological sorting*, for computing a topological ordering of a digraph.

Algorithm TopologicalSort($\vec{G}$):

    Input: A digraph $\vec{G}$ with n vertices.

    Output: A topological ordering $v_1, \ldots, v_n$ of $\vec{G}$.

    $S \leftarrow$ an initially empty stack.

    for all u in $\vec{G}$.vertices() **do**

        Let incounter(u) be the in-degree of u.

        if incounter(u) $= 0$ **then**

            S.push(u)

    $i \leftarrow 1$

    while !S.isEmpty() **do**

        $u \leftarrow S$.pop()

        Let u be vertex number i in the topological ordering.

        $i \leftarrow i+1$

        for all outgoing edge (u, w) of u **do**

            incounter(w) $\leftarrow$ incounter(w) $- 1$

            if incounter(w) $= 0$ **then**

                S.push(w)

Code Fragment 12.11: Pseudo-code for the topological sorting algorithm. (We show an example application of this algorithm in Figure 12.12.)

Proposition 12.22: *Let $\vec{G}$ be a digraph with n vertices and m edges. The topological sorting algorithm runs in $O(n+m)$ time using $O(n)$ auxiliary space, and either computes a topological ordering of $\vec{G}$ or fails to number some vertices, which indicates that $\vec{G}$ has a directed cycle.*

Justification: The initial computation of in-degrees and setup of the incounter variables can be done with a simple traversal of the graph, which takes $O(n+m)$ time. We use the decorator pattern to associate counter attributes with the vertices. Say that a vertex u is *visited* by the topological sorting algorithm when u is removed from the stack S. A vertex u can be visited only when incounter(u) $= 0$, which implies that all its predecessors (vertices with outgoing edges into u) were previously visited. As a consequence, any vertex that is on a directed cycle will never be visited, and any other vertex will be visited exactly once. The algorithm traverses all the outgoing edges of each visited vertex once, so its running time is proportional to the number of outgoing edges of the visited vertices. Therefore, the algorithm runs in $O(n+m)$ time. Regarding the space usage, observe that the stack S and the incounter variables attached to the vertices use $O(n)$ space. ∎

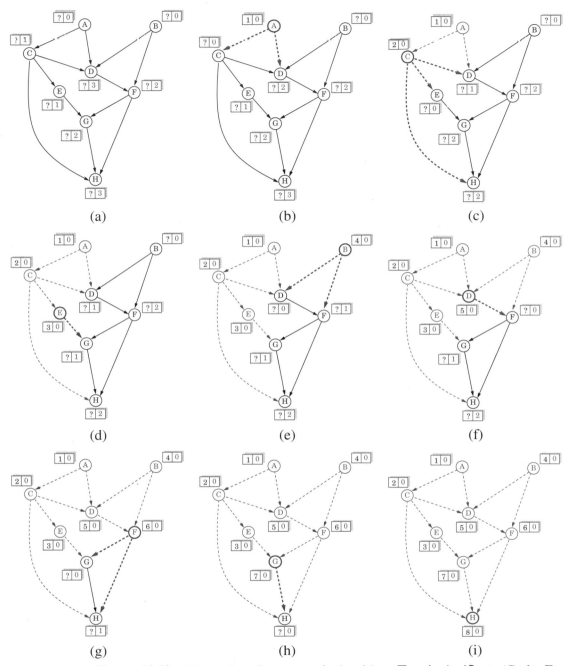

Figure 12.12: Example of a run of algorithm TopologicalSort (Code Fragment 12.11): (a) initial configuration; (b–i) after each while-loop iteration. The vertex labels show the vertex number and the current incounter value. The edges traversed are shown with dashed blue arrows. Thick lines denote the vertex and edges examined in the current iteration.

As a side effect, the topological sorting algorithm of Code Fragment 12.11 also tests whether the input digraph $\vec{G}$ is acyclic. Indeed, if the algorithm terminates without ordering all the vertices, then the subgraph of the vertices that have not been ordered must contain a directed cycle. (See Figure 12.13.)

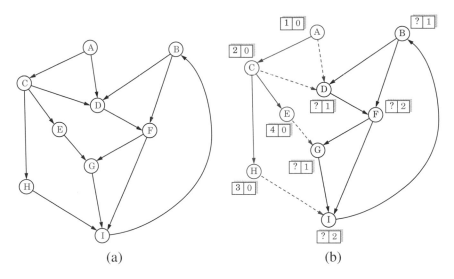

(a)   (b)

Figure 12.13: Detecting a directed cycle: (a) input digraph; (b) after algorithm TopologicalSort (Code Fragment 12.11) terminates, the subgraph of the vertices with undefined number contains a directed cycle.

Next we present an application of directed graph traversal in Java.

12.4.4 Application: Garbage Collection in Java ★

In some languages, like C and C++, the memory space for objects must be explicitly allocated and deallocated by the programmer. This memory-allocation duty is often overlooked by beginning programmers, and, when done incorrectly, it can even be the source of frustrating programming errors for experienced programmers. Thus, the designers of other languages, like Java, place the burden of memory management on the run-time environment. A Java programmer does not have to explicitly deallocate the memory for some object when its life is over. Instead, the *garbage collector* mechanism deallocates the memory for such objects.

Recall that in Java the memory for most objects is allocated from the memory heap (see Section 4.3.4). In addition, the running threads in a Java program (see Section 4.3.5) store the current space for their instance variables on their respective Java stacks (see Section 4.2.3). Since the instance variables in the Java stacks can refer to objects in the memory heap, all the variables and objects in the Java stacks of running threads are called *root objects*. All those objects that can be reached by following object references that start from a root object are called *live objects*. The live objects are the active objects currently being used by the running program; these objects should *not* be deallocated. For example, a running Java program may store in a variable a reference to a sequence S that is implemented using a doubly linked list. The reference variable to S is a root object, while the object for S is a live object, as are all the node objects that are referenced from this object and all the elements that are referenced from these node objects.

From time to time, the Java virtual machine (JVM) may notice that the available free space in the memory heap is becoming scarce. At such times, the JVM will probably elect to reclaim the space that is being used for objects that are no longer live. This reclamation process is known as *garbage collection*. There are several different algorithms for garbage collection, but one of the most used is the *mark-sweep algorithm*. Therefore, let us consider the steps that we would need to implement to design a Java virtual machine that uses mark-sweep garbage collection algorithm.

The Mark-Sweep Algorithm

In the mark-sweep garbage collection algorithm, we associate with each object a "mark" bit that identifies if that object is live or not. When we determine at some point that garbage collection is needed, we suspend all other running threads and clear all of the mark bits of objects currently allocated in the memory heap. We then trace through the Java stacks of the currently running threads and we mark as "live" all of the (root) objects in these stacks. We must then determine all of the other live objects—the ones that are reachable from the root objects. To do this efficiently, we should use the directed-graph version of the depth-first search traversal. In this case, each object in the memory heap is viewed as a vertex in a directed graph, and the reference from one object to another is viewed as an edge. By performing a directed DFS from each root object, we can correctly identify and mark each live object. This process is known as the "mark" phase. Once this process has completed, we then scan through the memory heap and reclaim any space that is being used for an object that has not been marked. This scanning process is known as the "sweep" phase, and when it completes, we resume running the suspended threads. Thus, the mark-sweep garbage collection algorithm will reclaim unused space in time proportional to the number of live objects and their references plus the size of the memory heap.

Performing DFS In-place

The mark-sweep algorithm is an effective way of reclaiming unused space in the memory heap, but there is an important issue we must face during the mark phase. Since we are probably reclaiming memory space at a time when free memory is scarce, we must take special care not to use much extra space during the garbage collection itself. The trouble is that the DFS algorithm, as we have described it, can use as much extra space as there are vertices in the graph. In the case of garbage collection, the vertices in our graph are the objects in the memory heap. We probably don't have this much memory to use, so our only alternative is to find a way to perform DFS in-place rather than recursively, that is, we must perform DFS using only a constant amount of additional storage. Fortunately, it is possible to perform DFS in-place.

The main idea for performing DFS in-place is to simulate the recursion stack using the edges of the graph (which in the case of garbage collection correspond to object references). Whenever we traverse an edge from a visited vertex v to a new vertex w, we change the edge (v, w) stored in v's adjacency list to point back to v's parent in the DFS tree. When we return back to v (simulating the return from the "recursive" call at w), we can now switch the edge we modified to point back to w as it did before. Of course, we need to have some way of identifying which edge we need to change back. One possibility is to number the references going out of v as 1, 2, and so on, and store, in addition to the mark bit (which we are using for the "visited" tag in our DFS), a count identifier that tells us which edges we have modified.

Using a count identifier of course requires an extra word of storage per object. This extra word can be avoided in some implementations, however. For example, many implementations of the Java virtual machine represent an object as a composition of a reference with a type identifier (which indicates if this object is an Integer or Vector or some other type) and as a reference to the other objects or data fields for this object. Since the type reference is always supposed to be the first element of the composition in such implementations, we can use this reference to "mark" the edge we changed when leaving an object v and going to some object w in our DFS. We simply swap the reference at v that refers to the type of v with the reference at v that refers to w. When we return to v, we can quickly identify the edge (v, w) we changed, because it will be the first reference in the composition for v, and the position of the reference to v's type will tell us the place were this edge belongs in v's adjacency list. Thus, whether we use this edge-swapping trick or a count identifier, we can implement DFS in-place without affecting its asymptotic running time.

12.5   Weighted Graphs

As we saw in Section 12.3.3, the breadth-first search strategy can be used to find a shortest path from some starting vertex to every other vertex in a connected graph. This approach makes sense in cases where each edge is as good as any other, but there are many situations where this approach is not appropriate. For example, we might be using a graph to represent a computer network (such as the Internet), and we might be interested in finding the fastest way to route a data packet between two computers. In this case, it is probably not appropriate for all the edges to be equal to each other, for some connections in a computer network are typically much faster than others (for example, some edges might represent slow phone-line connections while others might represent high-speed, fiber-optic connections). Likewise, we might want to use a graph to represent the roads between cities, and we might be interested in finding the fastest way to travel cross-country. In this case, it is again probably not appropriate for all the edges to be equal to each other, for some inter-city distances will likely be much larger than others. Thus, it is natural to consider graphs whose edges are not weighted equally.

A *weighted graph* is a graph that has a numeric (for example, integer) label $w(e)$ associated with each edge e, called the *weight* of edge e. We show an example of a weighted graph in Figure 12.14.

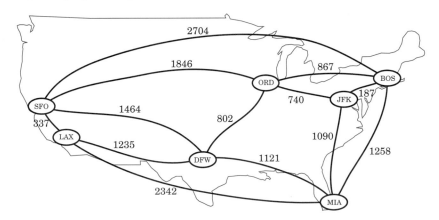

Figure 12.14: A weighted graph whose vertices represent major U.S. airports and whose edge weights represent distances in miles. This graph has a path from JFK to LAX of total weight 2,777 (going through ORD and DFW). This is the minimum weight path in the graph from JFK to LAX.

In the remaining sections of this chapter, we study weighted graphs.

12.6 Shortest Paths

Let G be a weighted graph. The **length** (or weight) of a path is the sum of the weights of the edges of P. That is, if $P = ((v_0, v_1), (v_1, v_2), \ldots, (v_{k-1}, v_k))$, then the length of P, denoted $w(P)$, is defined as

$$w(P) = \sum_{i=0}^{k-1} w((v_i, v_{i+1})).$$

The **distance** from a vertex v to a vertex u in G, denoted $d(v, u)$, is the length of a minimum length path (also called **shortest path**) from v to u, if such a path exists.

People often use the convention that $d(v, u) = +\infty$ if there is no path at all from v to u in G. Even if there is a path from v to u in G, the distance from v to u may not be defined, however, if there is a cycle in G whose total weight is negative. For example, suppose vertices in G represent cities, and the weights of edges in G represent how much money it costs to go from one city to another. If someone were willing to actually pay us to go from say JFK to ORD, then the "cost" of the edge (JFK,ORD) would be negative. If someone else were willing to pay us to go from ORD to JFK, then there would be a negative-weight cycle in G and distances would no longer be defined. That is, anyone could now build a path (with cycles) in G from any city A to another city B that first goes to JFK and then cycles as many times as he or she likes from JFK to ORD and back, before going on to B. The existence of such paths would allow us to build arbitrarily low negative-cost paths (and in this case make a fortune in the process). But distances cannot be arbitrarily low negative numbers. Thus, any time we use edge weights to represent distances, we must be careful not to introduce any negative-weight cycles.

Suppose we are given a weighted graph G, and we are asked to find a shortest path from some vertex v to each other vertex in G, viewing the weights on the edges as distances. In this section, we explore efficient ways of finding all such shortest paths, if they exist. The first algorithm we discuss is for the simple, yet common, case when all the edge weights in G are nonnegative (that is, $w(e) \geq 0$ for each edge e of G); hence, we know in advance that there are no negative-weight cycles in G. Recall that the special case of computing a shortest path when all weights are equal to one was solved with the BFS traversal algorithm presented in Section 12.3.3.

There is an interesting approach for solving this **single-source** problem based on the **greedy method** design pattern (Section 11.4.2). Recall that in this pattern we solve the problem at hand by repeatedly selecting the best choice from among those available in each iteration. This paradigm can often be used in situations where we are trying to optimize some cost function over a collection of objects. We can add objects to our collection, one at a time, always picking the next one that optimizes the function from among those yet to be chosen.

12.6.1   Dijkstra's Algorithm

The main idea in applying the greedy method pattern to the single-source shortest-path problem is to perform a "weighted" breadth-first search starting at v. In particular, we can use the greedy method to develop an algorithm that iteratively grows a "cloud" of vertices out of v, with the vertices entering the cloud in order of their distances from v. Thus, in each iteration, the next vertex chosen is the vertex outside the cloud that is closest to v. The algorithm terminates when no more vertices are outside the cloud, at which point we have a shortest path from v to every other vertex of G. This approach is a simple, but nevertheless powerful, example of the greedy method design pattern.

A Greedy Method for Finding Shortest Paths

Applying the greedy method to the single-source, shortest-path problem, results in an algorithm known as ***Dijkstra's algorithm***. When applied to other graph problems, however, the greedy method may not necessarily find the best solution (such as in the so-called ***traveling salesman problem***, in which we wish to find the shortest path that visits all the vertices in a graph exactly once). Nevertheless, there are a number of situations in which the greedy method allows us to compute the best solution. In this chapter, we discuss two such situations: computing shortest paths and constructing a minimum spanning tree.

In order to simplify the description of Dijkstra's algorithm, we assume, in the following, that the input graph G is undirected (that is, all its edges are undirected) and simple (that is, it has no self-loops and no parallel edges). Hence, we denote the edges of G as unordered vertex pairs (u, z).

In Dijkstra's algorithm for finding shortest paths, the cost function we are trying to optimize in our application of the greedy method is also the function that we are trying to compute—the shortest path distance. This may at first seem like circular reasoning until we realize that we can actually implement this approach by using a "bootstrapping" trick, consisting of using an approximation to the distance function we are trying to compute, which in the end will be equal to the true distance.

Edge Relaxation

Let us define a label $D[u]$ for each vertex u in V, which we use to approximate the distance in G from v to u. The meaning of these labels is that $D[u]$ will always store the length of the best path we have found ***so far*** from v to u. Initially, $D[v] = 0$ and $D[u] = +\infty$ for each $u \neq v$, and we define the set C, which is our "***cloud***" of vertices, to initially be the empty set $\emptyset$. At each iteration of the algorithm, we select a vertex u not in C with smallest $D[u]$ label, and we pull u into C. In the very first iteration we will, of course, pull v into C. Once a new vertex u is pulled into C, we then update the label $D[z]$ of each vertex z that is adjacent to u and is outside of C, to reflect the fact that there may be a new and better way to get to z via u. This update operation is known as a ***relaxation*** procedure, for it takes an old estimate and checks if it can be improved to get closer to its true value. (A metaphor for why we call this a relaxation comes from a spring that is stretched out and then "relaxed" back to its true resting shape.) In the case of Dijkstra's algorithm, the relaxation is performed for an edge (u,z) such that we have computed a new value of $D[u]$ and wish to see if there is a better value for $D[z]$ using the edge (u,z). The specific edge relaxation operation is as follows:

Edge Relaxation:

$$\textbf{if } D[u] + w((u,z)) < D[z] \textbf{ then}$$
$$D[z] \leftarrow D[u] + w((u,z))$$

We give the pseudo-code for Dijkstra's algorithm in Code Fragment 12.12. Note that we use a priority queue Q to store the vertices outside of the cloud C.

Algorithm ShortestPath(G, v):

   Input: A simple undirected weighted graph G with nonnegative edge weights, and a distinguished vertex v of G.

   Output: A label $D[u]$, for each vertex u of G, such that $D[u]$ is the length of a shortest path from v to u in G

   Initialize $D[v] \leftarrow 0$ and $D[u] \leftarrow +\infty$ for each vertex $u \neq v$.
   Let a priority queue Q contain all the vertices of G using the D labels as keys.
   while Q is not empty **do**
      {pull a new vertex u into the cloud}
      $u \leftarrow Q$.removeMin()
      for each vertex z adjacent to u such that z is in Q **do**
         {perform the ***relaxation*** procedure on edge (u,z)}
         if $D[u] + w((u,z)) < D[z]$ **then**
            $D[z] \leftarrow D[u] + w((u,z))$
            Change to $D[z]$ the key of vertex z in Q.
   return the label $D[u]$ of each vertex u

Code Fragment 12.12: Dijkstra's algorithm for the single-source shortest path problem.

We illustrate several iterations of Dijkstra's algorithm in Figures 12.15 and 12.16.

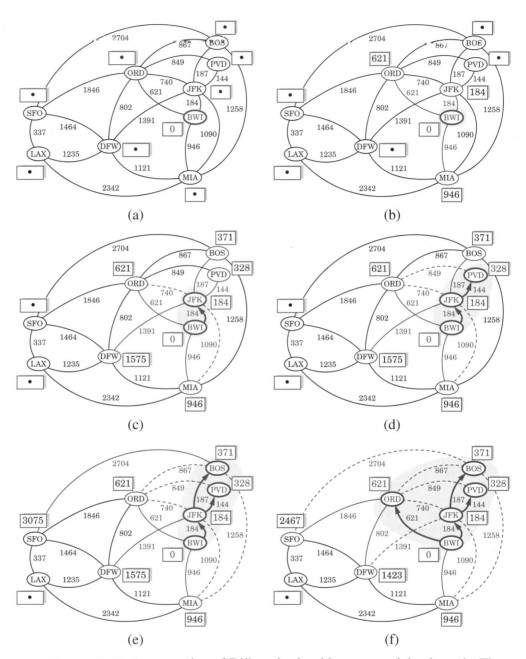

Figure 12.15: An execution of Dijkstra's algorithm on a weighted graph. The start vertex is BWI. A box next to each vertex v stores the label $D[v]$. The symbol ● is used instead of $+\infty$. The edges of the shortest-path tree are drawn as thick blue arrows, and for each vertex u outside the "cloud" we show the current best edge for pulling in u with a solid blue line.

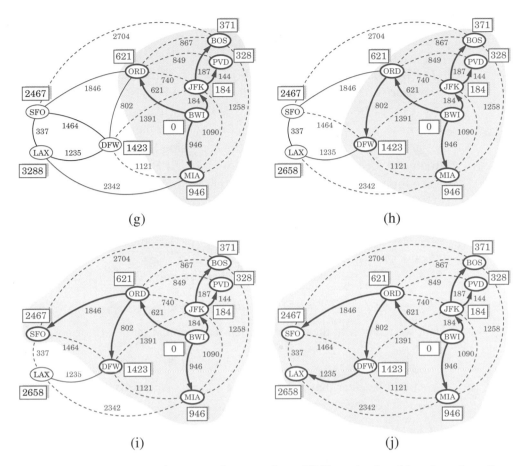

Figure 12.16: An example execution of Dijkstra's algorithm (continued).

Why It Works

The interesting, and possibly even a little surprising, aspect of the Dijkstra algorithm is that, at the moment a vertex u is pulled into C, its label $D[u]$ stores the correct length of a shortest path from v to u. Thus, when the algorithm terminates, it will have computed the shortest-path distance from v to every vertex of G. That is, it will have solved the single-source shortest path problem.

It is probably not immediately clear why Dijkstra's algorithm correctly finds the shortest path from the start vertex v to each other vertex u in the graph. Why is it that the distance from v to u is equal to the value of the label $D[u]$ at the time vertex u is pulled into the cloud C (which is also the time u is removed from the priority queue Q)? The answer to this question depends on there being no negative-weight edges in the graph, for it allows the greedy method to work correctly, as we show in the proposition that follows.

Proposition 12.23: *In Dijkstra's algorithm, whenever a vertex u is pulled into the cloud, the label D[u] is equal to d(v,u), the length of a shortest path from v to u.*

Justification: Suppose that $D[t] > d(v,t)$ for some vertex t in V, and let u be the ***first*** vertex the algorithm pulled into the cloud C (that is, removed from Q) such that $D[u] > d(v,u)$. There is a shortest path P from v to u (for otherwise $d(v,u) = +\infty = D[u]$). Let us therefore consider the moment when u is pulled into C, and let z be the first vertex of P (when going from v to u) that is not in C at this moment. Let y be the predecessor of z in path P (note that we could have $y = v$). (See Figure 12.17.) We know, by our choice of z, that y is already in C at this point. Moreover, $D[y] = d(v,y)$, since u is the ***first*** incorrect vertex. When y was pulled into C, we tested (and possibly updated) $D[z]$ so that we had at that point

$$D[z] \le D[y] + w((y,z)) = d(v,y) + w((y,z)).$$

But since z is the next vertex on the shortest path from v to u, this implies that

$$D[z] = d(v,z).$$

But we are now at the moment when we are picking u, not z, to join C; hence,

$$D[u] \le D[z].$$

It should be clear that a subpath of a shortest path is itself a shortest path. Hence, since z is on the shortest path from v to u,

$$d(v,z) + d(z,u) = d(v,u).$$

Moreover, $d(z,u) \ge 0$ because there are no negative-weight edges. Therefore,

$$D[u] \le D[z] = d(v,z) \le d(v,z) + d(z,u) = d(v,u).$$

But this contradicts the definition of u; hence, there can be no such vertex u.   ■

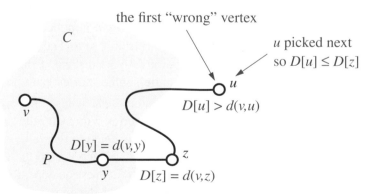

Figure 12.17: A schematic illustration for the justification of Proposition 12.23.

The Running Time of Dijkstra's Algorithm

In this section, we analyze the time complexity of Dijkstra's algorithm. We denote with n and m, the number of vertices and edges of the input graph G, respectively. We assume that the edge weights can be added and compared in constant time. Because of the high level of the description we gave for Dijkstra's algorithm in Code Fragment 12.12, analyzing its running time requires that we give more details on its implementation. Specifically, we should indicate the data structures used and how they are implemented.

Let us first assume that we are representing the graph G using an adjacency list structure. This data structure allows us to step through the vertices adjacent to u during the relaxation step in time proportional to their number. It still does not settle all the details for the algorithm, however, for we must say more about how to implement the other principle data structure in the algorithm—the priority queue Q.

An efficient implementation of the priority queue Q uses a heap (Section 7.3). This allows us to extract the vertex u with smallest D label (call to the removeMin method) in $O(\log n)$ time. As noted in the pseudo-code, each time we update a $D[z]$ label we need to update the key of z in the priority queue. Thus, we actually need a heap implementation of an adaptable priority queue (Section 7.4). If Q is an adaptable priority queue implemented as a heap, then this key update can, for example, be done using the replaceKey(e,k), where e is the entry storing the key for the vertex z. If e is location-aware, then we can easily implement such key updates in $O(\log n)$ time, since a location-aware entry for vertex z would allow Q to have immediate access to the entry e storing z in the heap (see Section 7.4.2). Assuming this implementation of Q, Dijkstra's algorithm runs in $O((n+m)\log n)$ time.

Referring back to Code Fragment 12.12, the details of the running-time analysis are as follows:

- Inserting all the vertices in Q with their initial key value can be done in $O(n\log n)$ time by repeated insertions, or in $O(n)$ time using bottom-up heap construction (see Section 7.3.6).
- At each iteration of the **while** loop, we spend $O(\log n)$ time to remove vertex u from Q, and $O(\text{degree}(v)\log n)$ time to perform the relaxation procedure on the edges incident on u.
- The overall running time of the **while** loop is

$$\sum_{v \in G}(1 + \text{degree}(v))\log n,$$

which is $O((n+m)\log n)$ by Proposition 12.6.

Note that if we wish to express the running time as a function of n only, then it is $O(n^2 \log n)$ in the worst case.

An Alternative Implementation for Dijkstra's Algorithm

Let us now consider an alternative implementation for the adaptable priority queue Q using an unsorted sequence. This, of course, requires that we spend $O(n)$ time to extract the minimum element, but it allows for very fast key updates, provided Q supports location-aware entries (Section 7.4.2). Specifically, we can implement each key update done in a relaxation step in $O(1)$ time—we simply change the key value once we locate the entry in Q to update. Hence, this implementation results in a running time that is $O(n^2 + m)$, which can be simplified to $O(n^2)$ since G is simple.

Comparing the Two Implementations

We have two choices for implementing the adaptable priority queue with location-aware entries in Dijkstra's algorithm: a heap implementation, which yields a running time of $O((n+m)\log n)$, and an unsorted sequence implementation, which yields a running time of $O(n^2)$. Since both implementations would be fairly simple to code up, they are about equal in terms of the programming sophistication needed. These two implementations are also about equal in terms of the constant factors in their worst-case running times. Looking only at these worst-case times, we prefer the heap implementation when the number of edges in the graph is small (that is, when $m < n^2/\log n$), and we prefer the sequence implementation when the number of edges is large (that is, when $m > n^2/\log n$).

Proposition 12.24: *Given a simple undirected weighted graph G with n vertices and m edges, such that the weight of each edge is nonnegative, and a vertex v of G, Dijkstra's algorithm computes the distance from v to all other vertices of G in $O((n+m)\log n)$ worst-case time, or, alternatively, in $O(n^2)$ worst-case time.*

In Exercise R-12.16, we explore how to modify Dijkstra's algorithm to output a tree T rooted at v, such that the path in T from v to a vertex u is a shortest path in G from v to u.

Programming Dijkstra's Algorithm in Java

Having given a pseudo-code description of Dijkstra's algorithm, let us now present Java code for performing Dijkstra's algorithm, assuming we are given an undirected graph with positive integer weights. We express the algorithm by means of class Dijkstra (Code Fragments 12.13–12.15), which uses a weight decoration for each edge e to extract e's weight. Class Dijkstra assumes that each edge has a *weight* decoration.

```
/* Dijkstra's algorithm for the single-source shortest path problem
 * in an undirected graph whose edges have integer weights.
 */
public class Dijkstra {
  /** Infinity value. */
  public static final int INFINITE = Integer.MAX_VALUE;
  /** Input graph. */
  protected Graph graph;
  /** Decoration key for edge weights */
  protected Object WEIGHT;
  /** Auxiliary priority queue. */
  protected AdaptablePriorityQueue Q;
  /** Executes Dijkstra's algorithm.
   * @param g Input graph
   * @param s Source vertex
   * @param w Weight decoration object
   */
  public void execute(Graph g, Vertex s, Object w) {
    graph = g;
    WEIGHT = w;
    Q = new HeapAdaptablePriorityQueue(new DefaultComparator());
    dijkstraVisit(s);
  }
  /** Get the distance of a vertex from the source vertex.
   * @param u Start vertex for the shortest path tree
   */
  public int getDist(Vertex u) {
    return ((Integer) u.get(DIST)).intValue();
  }
```

Code Fragment 12.13: Class Dijkstra implementing Dijkstra's algorithm. (Continues in Code Fragment 12.14.)

The main computation of Dijkstra's algorithm is performed by method dijkstraVisit. An adaptable priority queue Q supporting location-aware entries (Section 7.4.2) is used. We insert a vertex u into Q with method insert, which returns the location-aware entry of u in Q. We "attach" to u its entry in Q by means of method setEntry, and we retrieve the entry of u by means of method getEntry. Note that associating entries to the vertices is an instance of the decorator design pattern (Section 12.3.2). Instead of using an additional data structure for the labels $D[u]$, we exploit the fact that $D[u]$ is the key of vertex u in Q, and thus $D[u]$ can be retrieved given the entry for u in Q. Changing the label of a vertex z to d in the relaxation procedure corresponds to calling method replaceKey(e,d), where e is the location-aware entry for z in Q.

```java
/** The actual execution of Dijkstra's algorithm.
 * @param v source vertex.
 */
protected void dijkstraVisit (Vertex v) {
  // store all the vertices in priority queue Q
  for (Iterator vertices = graph.vertices(); vertices.hasNext();) {
    Vertex u = (Vertex) vertices.next();
    int u_dist;
    if (u==v)
      u_dist = 0;
    else
      u_dist = INFINITE;

    Entry u_entry = Q.insert(new Integer(u_dist), u);
    setEntry(u, u_entry);
  }
  // grow the cloud, one vertex at a time
  while (!Q.isEmpty()) {
    // remove from Q and insert into cloud a vertex with minimum distance
    Entry u_entry = Q.min();
    Vertex u = getVertex(u_entry);
    int u_dist = getDist(u_entry);
    Q.remove(u_entry); // remove u from the priority queue
    setDist(u, u_dist); // the distance of u is final
    removeEntry(u); // remove the entry decoration of u
    if (u_dist == INFINITE)
      continue; // unreachable vertices are not processed
    // examine all the neighbors of u and update their distances
    for (Iterator edges = graph.incidentEdges(u); edges.hasNext();) {
      Edge e = (Edge) edges.next();
      Vertex z = graph.opposite(u,e);
      Entry z_entry = getEntry(z);
      if (z_entry != null) { // check that z is in Q, i.e., not in the cloud
        int e_weight = weight(e);
        int z_dist = getDist(z_entry);
        if ( u_dist + e_weight < z_dist ) // relaxation of edge e = (u,z)
          Q.replaceKey(z_entry, new Integer(u_dist + e_weight));
      }
    }
  }
}
```

Code Fragment 12.14: Method dijkstraVisit of class Dijkstra. (Continues in Code Fragment 12.15.)

```java
/** Get the weight of an edge
 */
protected int weight(Edge e) {
    return ((Integer) e.get(WEIGHT)).intValue();
}
/** Attribute for vertex distances
 */
protected Object DIST = new Object();
/** Set the distance of a vertex.
 */
protected void setDist(Vertex v, int d) {
    v.put(DIST, new Integer(d));
}
/** Decoration key for entries in the priority queue
 */
protected Object ENTRY = new Object();
/** Get the entry decoration of a vertex.
 */
protected Entry getEntry(Vertex v) {
    return (Entry) v.get(ENTRY);
}
/** Set the entry decoration of a vertex
 */
protected void setEntry(Vertex v, Entry e) {
    v.put(ENTRY, e);
}
/** Remove the entry decoration of a vertex
 */
protected void removeEntry(Vertex v) {
    v.remove(ENTRY);
}
/** Get the vertex associated with an entry
 */
protected Vertex getVertex(Entry e) {
    return (Vertex) e.value();
}
/** Get the distance of a vertex given its entry
 */
protected int getDist(Entry e) {
    return ((Integer) e.key()).intValue();
}
} // end of Dijkstra class
```

Code Fragment 12.15: Auxiliary methods of class Dijkstra. They assume that the vertices of the graph are decorable. (Continued from Code Fragment 12.14.)

12.7 Minimum Spanning Trees

Suppose we wish to connect all the computers in a new office building using the least amount of cable. We can model this problem using a weighted graph G whose vertices represent the computers, and whose edges represent all the possible pairs (u, v) of computers, where the weight $w((v, u))$ of edge (v, u) is equal to the amount of cable needed to connect computer v to computer u. Rather than computing a shortest path tree from some particular vertex v, we are interested instead in finding a (free) tree T that contains all the vertices of G and has the minimum total weight over all such trees. Methods for finding such a tree are the focus of this section.

Problem Definition

Given a weighted undirected graph G, we are interested in finding a tree T that contains all the vertices in G and minimizes the sum

$$w(T) = \sum_{(v,u) \in T} w((v, u)).$$

A tree, such as this, that contains every vertex of a connected graph G is said to be a ***spanning tree***, and the problem of computing a spanning tree T with smallest total weight is known as the ***minimum spanning tree*** (or ***MST***) problem.

The development of efficient algorithms for the minimum spanning tree problem predates the modern notion of computer science itself. In this section, we discuss two classic algorithms for solving the MST problem. These algorithms are both applications of the ***greedy method***, which, as was discussed briefly in the previous section, is based on choosing objects to join a growing collection by iteratively picking an object that minimizes some cost function. The first algorithm we discuss is Kruskal's algorithm, which "grows" the MST in clusters by considering edges in order of their weights. The second algorithm we discuss is the Prim-Jarník algorithm, which grows the MST from a single root vertex, much in the same way as Dijkstra's shortest-path algorithm.

As in Section 12.6.1, in order to simplify the description of the algorithms, we assume, in the following, that the input graph G is undirected (that is, all its edges are undirected) and simple (that is, it has no self-loops and no parallel edges). Hence, we denote the edges of G as unordered vertex pairs (u, z).

Before we discuss the details of these algorithms, however, let us give a crucial fact about minimum spanning trees that forms the basis of the algorithms.

A Crucial Fact about Minimum Spanning Trees

The two MST algorithms we discuss are based on the greedy method, which in this case depends crucially on the following fact. (See Figure 12.18.)

e Belongs to a Minimum Spanning Tree

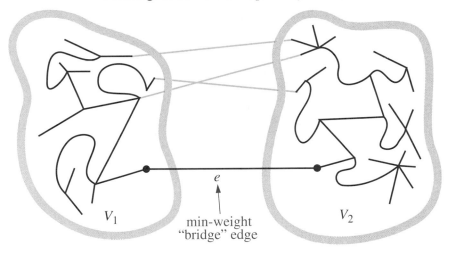

Figure 12.18: An illustration of the crucial fact about minimum spanning trees.

Proposition 12.25: *Let G be a weighted connected graph, and let V_1 and V_2 be a partition of the vertices of G into two disjoint nonempty sets. Furthermore, let e be an edge in G with minimum weight from among those with one endpoint in V_1 and the other in V_2. There is a minimum spanning tree T that has e as one of its edges.*

Justification: Let T be a minimum spanning tree of G. If T does not contain edge e, the addition of e to T must create a cycle. Therefore, there is some edge f of this cycle that has one endpoint in V_1 and the other in V_2. Moreover, by the choice of e, $w(e) \leq w(f)$. If we remove f from $T \cup \{e\}$, we obtain a spanning tree whose total weight is no more than before. Since T was a minimum spanning tree, this new tree must also be a minimum spanning tree. ∎

In fact, if the weights in G are distinct, then the minimum spanning tree is unique; we leave the justification of this less crucial fact as an exercise (C-12.18). In addition, note that Proposition 12.25 remains valid even if the graph G contains negative-weight edges or negative-weight cycles, unlike the algorithms we presented for shortest paths.

12.7.1 Kruskal's Algorithm

The reason Proposition 12.25 is so important is that it can be used as the basis for building a minimum spanning tree. In Kruskal's algorithm, it is used to build the minimum spanning tree in clusters. Initially, each vertex is in its own cluster all by itself. The algorithm then considers each edge in turn, ordered by increasing weight. If an edge e connects two different clusters, then e is added to the set of edges of the minimum spanning tree, and the two clusters connected by e are merged into a single cluster. If, on the other hand, e connects two vertices that are already in the same cluster, then e is discarded. Once the algorithm has added enough edges to form a spanning tree, it terminates and outputs this tree as the minimum spanning tree.

We give pseudo-code for Kruskal's MST algorithm in Code Fragment 12.16 and we show the working of this algorithm in Figures 12.19, 12.20, and 12.21.

Algorithm Kruskal(G):

    Input: A simple connected weighted graph G with n vertices and m edges

    Output: A minimum spanning tree T for G

  for each vertex v in G **do**

    Define an elementary cluster $C(v) \leftarrow \{v\}$.

  Initialize a priority queue Q to contain all edges in G, using the weights as keys.

  $T \leftarrow \emptyset$ $\{T$ will ultimately contain the edges of the MST$\}$

  while T has fewer than $n - 1$ edges **do**

    $(u, v) \leftarrow Q.\mathsf{removeMin}()$

    Let $C(v)$ be the cluster containing v, and let $C(u)$ be the cluster containing u.

    if $C(v) \neq C(u)$ **then**

      Add edge (v, u) to T.

      Merge $C(v)$ and $C(u)$ into one cluster, that is, union $C(v)$ and $C(u)$.

  return tree T

    Code Fragment 12.16: Kruskal's algorithm for the MST problem.

As mentioned before, the correctness of Kruskal's algorithm follows from the crucial fact about minimum spanning trees, Proposition 12.25. Each time Kruskal's algorithm adds an edge (v, u) to the minimum spanning tree T, we can define a partitioning of the set of vertices V (as in the proposition) by letting V_1 be the cluster containing v and letting V_2 contain the rest of the vertices in V. This clearly defines a disjoint partitioning of the vertices of V and, more importantly, since we are extracting edges from Q in order by their weights, e must be a minimum-weight edge with one vertex in V_1 and the other in V_2. Thus, Kruskal's algorithm always adds a valid minimum spanning tree edge.

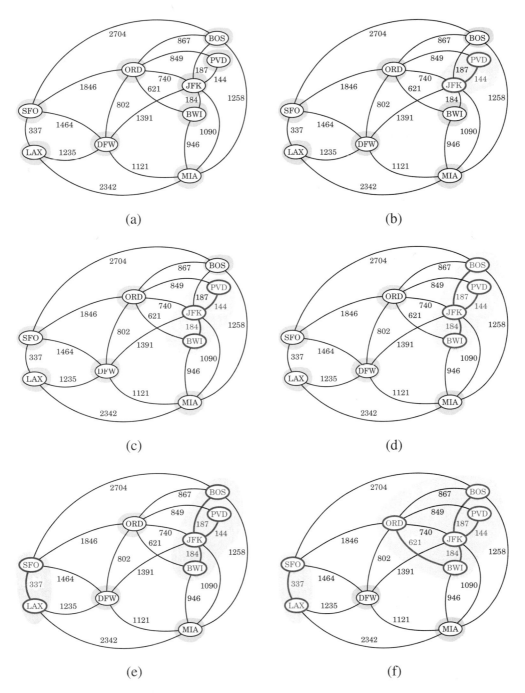

Figure 12.19: Example of an execution of Kruskal's MST algorithm on a graph with integer weights. We show the clusters as shaded regions and we highlight the edge being considered in each iteration. (Continues in Figure 12.20.)

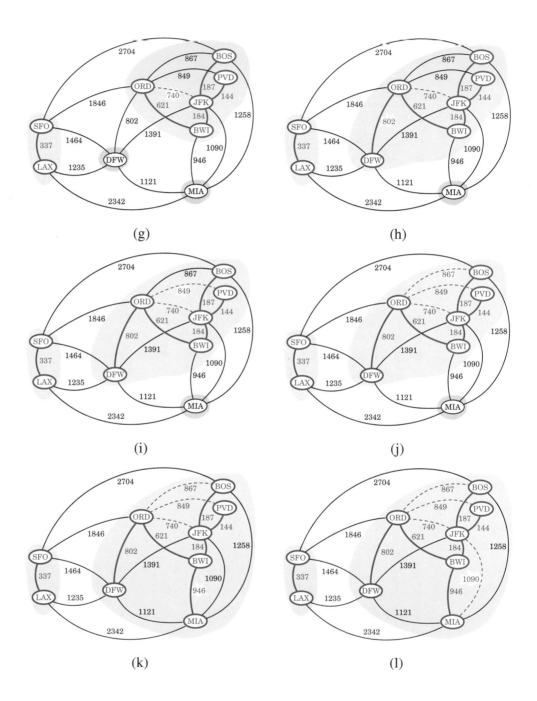

Figure 12.20: An example of an execution of Kruskal's MST algorithm. Rejected edges are shown dashed. (Continues in Figure 12.21.)

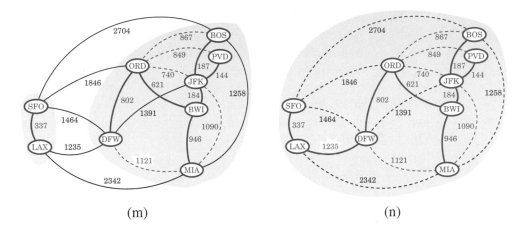

(m)   (n)

Figure 12.21: Example of an execution of Kruskal's MST algorithm (continued). The edge considered in (n) merges the last two clusters, which concludes this execution of Kruskal's algorithm. (Continued from Figure 12.20.)

The Running Time of Kruskal's Algorithm

In this section, we analyze the time complexity of Kruskal's algorithm. We denote the number of vertices and edges of the input graph G with n and m, respectively. We assume that the edge weights can be compared in constant time. Because of the high level of the description we gave for Kruskal's algorithm in Code Fragment 12.16, analyzing its running time requires that we give more details on its implementation. Specifically, we should indicate the data structures used and how they are implemented.

We can implement the priority queue Q using a heap. Thus, we can initialize Q in $O(m \log m)$ time by repeated insertions, or in $O(m)$ time using bottom-up heap construction (see Section 7.3.6). In addition, at each iteration of the **while** loop, we can remove a minimum-weight edge in $O(\log m)$ time, which actually is $O(\log n)$, since G is simple. Thus, the total time spent performing priority queue operations is no more than $O(m \log n)$.

We can represent each cluster C using one of the union-find partition data structures discussed in Section 10.6.2. Recall that the sequence-based union-find structure allows us to perform a series of N union and find operations in $O(N \log N)$ time, and the tree-based version can implement such a series of operations in $O(N \log^* N)$ time. Thus, since we perform $n - 1$ calls to methodunion and at most m calls to find, the total time spent on merging clusters and determining the clusters that vertices belong to is no more than $O(m \log n)$ using the sequence-based approach or $O(m \log^* n)$ using the tree-based approach.

Therefore, using arguments similar to those used in the analysis of Dijkstra's algorithm, we conclude that the running time of Kruskal's algorithm is $O((n + m)\log n)$, which can be simplified as $O(m\log n)$, since G is simple and connected. We summarize as follows.

Proposition 12.26: *Given a simple connected weighted graph G with n vertices and m edges, Kruskal's algorithm constructs a minimum spanning tree for G in $O(m\log n)$ time.*

12.7.2 The Prim-Jarník Algorithm

In the Prim-Jarník algorithm, we grow a minimum spanning tree from a single cluster starting from some "root" vertex v. The main idea is similar to that of Dijkstra's algorithm. We begin with some vertex v, defining the initial "cloud" of vertices C. Then, in each iteration, we choose a minimum-weight edge $e = (v, u)$, connecting a vertex v in the cloud C to a vertex u outside of C. The vertex u is then brought into the cloud C and the process is repeated until a spanning tree is formed. Again, the crucial fact about minimum spanning trees comes to play, for by always choosing the smallest-weight edge joining a vertex inside C to one outside C, we are assured of always adding a valid edge to the MST.

To efficiently implement this approach, we can take another cue from Dijkstra's algorithm. We maintain a label $D[u]$ for each vertex u outside the cloud C, so that $D[u]$ stores the weight of the best current edge for joining u to the cloud C. These labels allow us to reduce the number of edges that we must consider in deciding which vertex is next to join the cloud. We give the pseudo-code in Code Fragment 12.17.

Let n and m denote the number of vertices and edges of the input graph G, respectively. The implementation issues for the Prim-Jarník algorithm are similar to those for Dijkstra's algorithm. If we implement the adaptable priority queue Q as a heap that supports location-aware entries (Section 7.4.2), then we can extract the vertex u in each iteration in $O(\log n)$ time. In addition, we can update each $D[z]$ value in $O(\log n)$ time, as well, which is a computation considered at most once for each edge (u, z). The other steps in each iteration can be implemented in constant time. Thus, the total running time is $O((n + m)\log n)$, which is $O(m\log n)$. Hence, we can summarize as follows:

Proposition 12.27: *Given a simple connected weighted graph G with n vertices and m edges, the Prim-Jarník algorithm constructs a minimum spanning tree for G in $O(m\log n)$ time.*

Algorithm PrimJarnik(G):

    Input: A weighted connected graph G with n vertices and m edges

    Output: A minimum spanning tree T for G

  Pick any vertex v of G

  $D[v] \leftarrow 0$

  for each vertex $u \neq v$ **do**

    $D[u] \leftarrow +\infty$

  Initialize $T \leftarrow \emptyset$.

  Initialize a priority queue Q with an entry $((u, \text{null}), D[u])$ for each vertex u, where (u, null) is the element and $D[u])$ is the key.

  while Q is not empty **do**

    $(u, e) \leftarrow Q.\text{removeMin}()$

    Add vertex u and edge e to T.

    for each vertex z adjacent to u such that z is in Q **do**

      {perform the relaxation procedure on edge (u, z)}

      if $w((u, z)) < D[z]$ **then**

        $D[z] \leftarrow w((u, z))$

        Change to $(z, (u, z))$ the element of vertex z in Q.

        Change to $D[z]$ the key of vertex z in Q.

  return the tree T

    Code Fragment 12.17: The Prim-Jarník algorithm for the MST problem.

We illustrate the Prim-Jarník algorithm in Figures 12.22 through 12.24.

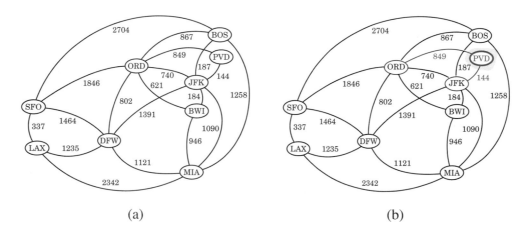

              (a)   (b)

Figure 12.22: An illustration of the Prim-Jarník algorithm. (Continues in Figure 12.23.)

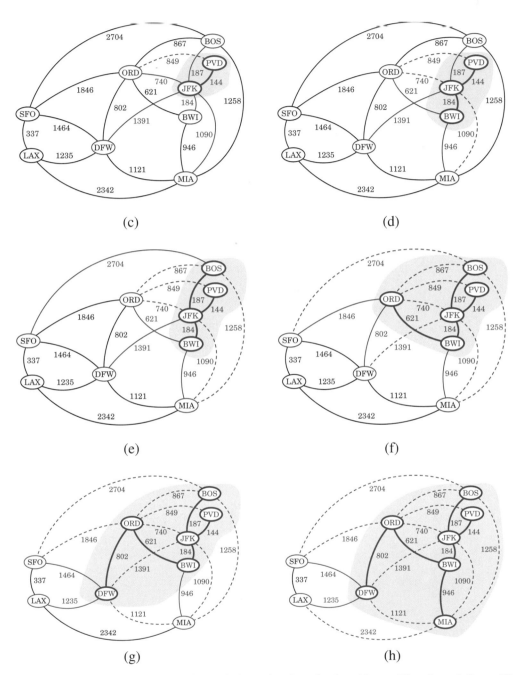

Figure 12.23: An illustration of the Prim-Jarník algorithm. (Continued from Figure 12.22; continues in Figure 12.24.)

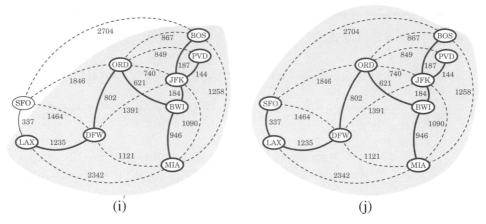

Figure 12.24: An illustration of the Prim-Jarník algorithm. (Continued from Figure 12.23.)

A Comparison of the Above MST Algorithms

Although each of the above algorithms for computing minimum spanning trees has the same worst-case running time, each one achieves this running time using different data structures and different approaches to building the minimum spanning tree.

Concerning auxiliary data structures, Kruskal's algorithm uses a priority queue, to store edges, and a collection of sets, implemented with lists, to store clusters. The Prim-Jarník algorithm uses only a priority queue, to store vertex-edge pairs. Thus, from an ease of programming viewpoint, the Prim-Jarník algorithm is preferable. Indeed, the Prim-Jarník algorithm is so similar to Dijkstra's algorithm that an implementation of Dijkstra's algorithm could be converted into an implementation for the Prim-Jarník algorithm without much effort.

In terms of the constant factors, the two algorithms are fairly similar in that they both have relatively small constant factors in their asymptotic running times.

12.8 Exercises

For source code and help with exercises, please visit **java.datastructures.net**.

Reinforcement

R-12.1 Draw a simple undirected graph G that has 12 vertices, 18 edges, and 3 connected components. Why would it be impossible to draw G with 3 connected components if G had 66 edges?

R-12.2 Let G be a simple connected graph with n vertices and m edges. Explain why $O(\log m)$ is $O(\log n)$.

R-12.3 Draw a simple connected directed graph with 8 vertices and 16 edges such that the in-degree and out-degree of each vertex is 2. Show that there is a single (nonsimple) cycle that includes all the edges of your graph, that is, you can trace all the edges in their respective directions without ever lifting your pencil. (Such a cycle is called an ***Euler tour***.)

R-12.4 Repeat the previous problem and then remove one edge from the graph. Show that now there is a single (nonsimple) path that includes all the edges of your graph. (Such a path is called an ***Euler path***.)

R-12.5 Bob loves foreign languages and wants to plan his course schedule for the following years. He is interested in the following nine language courses: LA15, LA16, LA22, LA31, LA32, LA126, LA127, LA141, and LA169. The course prerequisites are:

- LA15: (none)
- LA16: LA15
- LA22: (none)
- LA31: LA15
- LA32: LA16, LA31
- LA126: LA22, LA32
- LA127: LA16
- LA141: LA22, LA16
- LA169: LA32.

Find the sequence of courses that allows Bob to satisfy all the prerequisites.

R-12.6 Suppose we represent a graph G having n vertices and m edges with the edge list structure. Why, in this case, does the insertVertex method run in $O(1)$ time while the removeVertex method runs in $O(m)$ time?

R-12.7 Let G be a graph whose vertices are the integers 1 through 8, and let the adjacent vertices of each vertex be given by the table below:

vertex	adjacent vertices
1	(2, 3, 4)
2	(1, 3, 4)
3	(1, 2, 4)
4	(1, 2, 3, 6)
5	(6, 7, 8)
6	(4, 5, 7)
7	(5, 6, 8)
8	(5, 7)

Assume that, in a traversal of G, the adjacent vertices of a given vertex are returned in the same order as they are listed in the above table.

a. Draw G.
b. Give the sequence of vertices of G visited using a DFS traversal starting at vertex 1.
c. Give the sequence of vertices visited using a BFS traversal starting at vertex 1.

R-12.8 Would you use the adjacency list structure or the adjacency matrix structure in each of the following cases? Justify your choice.

a. The graph has 10,000 vertices and 20,000 edges, and it is important to use as little space as possible.
b. The graph has 10,000 vertices and 20,000,000 edges, and it is important to use as little space as possible.
c. You need to answer the query areAdjacent as fast as possible, no matter how much space you use.

R-12.9 Explain why the DFS traversal runs in $O(n^2)$ time on an n-vertex simple graph that is represented with the adjacency matrix structure.

R-12.10 Draw the transitive closure of the directed graph shown in Figure 12.2.

R-12.11 Compute a topological ordering for the directed graph drawn with solid edges in Figure 12.8d.

R-12.12 Can we use a queue instead of a stack as an auxiliary data structure in the topological sorting algorithm shown in Code Fragment 12.11? Why or why not?

R-12.13 Draw a simple, connected, weighted graph with 8 vertices and 16 edges, each with unique edge weights. Identify one vertex as a "start" vertex and illustrate a running of Dijkstra's algorithm on this graph.

R-12.14 Show how to modify the pseudo-code for Dijkstra's algorithm for the case when the graph may contain parallel edges and self-loops.

R-12.15 Show how to modify the pseudo-code for Dijkstra's algorithm for the case when the graph is directed and we we want to compute shortest directed paths from the source vertex to all the other vertices.

R-12.16 Show how to modify the pseudo-code for Dijkstra's algorithm to not only output the distance from v to each vertex in G, but also to output a tree T rooted at v such that the path in T from v to a vertex u is actually a shortest path in G from v to u.

R-12.17 There are eight small islands in a lake, and the state wants to build seven bridges to connect them so that each island can be reached from any other one via one or more bridges. The cost of constructing a bridge is proportional to its length. The distances between pairs of islands are given in the following table.

	1	2	3	4	5	6	7	8
1	-	240	210	340	280	200	345	120
2	-	-	265	175	215	180	185	155
3	-	-	-	260	115	350	435	195
4	-	-	-	-	160	330	295	230
5	-	-	-	-	-	360	400	170
6	-	-	-	-	-	-	175	205
7	-	-	-	-	-	-	-	305
8	-	-	-	-	-	-	-	-

Find which bridges to build to minimize the total construction cost.

R-12.18 Draw a simple, connected, undirected, weighted graph with 8 vertices and 16 edges, each with unique edge weights. Illustrate the execution of Kruskal's algorithm on this graph. (Note that there is only one minimum spanning tree for this graph.)

R-12.19 Repeat the previous problem for the Prim-Jarník algorithm.

R-12.20 Consider the unsorted sequence implementation of the priority queue Q used in Dijkstra's algorithm. Why is, in this case, is the best-case running time of Dijkstra's algorithm $O(n^2)$ on an n-vertex graph?

R-12.21 Describe the meaning of the graphical conventions used in Figure 12.6 illustrating a DFS traversal. What do the colors blue and black refer to? What do the arrows signify? How about thick lines and dashed lines?

R-12.22 Repeat Exercise R-12.21 for Figure 12.7 illustrating a BFS traversal.

R-12.23 Repeat Exercise R-12.21 for Figure 12.9 illustrating a directed DFS traversal.

R-12.24 Repeat Exercise R-12.21 for Figure 12.10 illustrating the Floyd-Warshall algorithm.

R-12.25 Repeat Exercise R-12.21 for Figure 12.12 illustrating the topological sorting algorithm.

R-12.26 Repeat Exercise R-12.21 for Figures 12.15 and 12.16 illustrating Dijkstra's algorithm.

R-12.27 Repeat Exercise R-12.21 for Figures 12.19 and 12.21 illustrating Kruskal's algorithm.

R-12.28 Repeat Exercise R-12.21 for Figures 12.22 and 12.23 illustrating the Prim-Jarník algorithm.

R-12.29 How many edges are in the transitive closure of a graph that consists of a simple directed path of n vertices?

R-12.30 Given a complete binary tree T with n nodes, consider a directed graph $\vec{G}$ having the nodes of T as its vertices. For each parent-child pair in T, create a directed edge in $\vec{G}$ from the parent to the child. Show that the transitive closure of $\vec{G}$ has $O(n \log n)$ edges.

R-12.31 A simple undirected graph is a ***complete*** if it contains an edge between every pair of distinct vertices. What does a depth-first search tree of a complete graph look like?

R-12.32 Recalling the definition of a complete graph from Exercise R-12.31, what does a breadth-first search tree of a complete graph look like?

Creativity

C-12.1 Say that an n-vertex directed acyclic graph $\vec{G}$ is **compact** if there is some way of numbering the vertices of $\vec{G}$ with the integers from 0 to $n-1$ such that $\vec{G}$ contains the edge (i, j) if and only if $i < j$, for all i, j in $[0, n-1]$. Give an $O(n^2)$ time algorithm for detecting if $\vec{G}$ is compact.

C-12.2 Justify Proposition 12.11.

C-12.3 Describe the details of an $O(n+m)$ time algorithm for computing **all** the connected components of an undirected graph G with n vertices and m edges.

C-12.4 Let T be the spanning tree rooted at the start vertex produced by the depth-first search of a connected, undirected graph G. Argue why every edge of G not in T goes from a vertex in T to one of its ancestors, that is, it is a **back edge**.

C-12.5 Suppose we wish to represent an n-vertex graph G using the edge list structure, assuming that we identify the vertices with the integers in the set $\{0, 1, \ldots, n-1\}$. Describe how to implement the container E to support $O(\log n)$-time performance for the areAdjacent method. How are you implementing the method in this case?

C-12.6 Tamarindo University and many other schools worldwide are doing a joint project on multimedia. A computer network is built to connect these schools using communication links that form a free tree. The schools decide to install a file server at one of the schools to share data among all the schools. Since the transmission time on a link is dominated by the link setup and synchronization, the cost of a data transfer is proportional to the number of links used. Hence, it is desirable to choose a "central" location for the file server. Given a free tree T and a node v of T, the *eccentricity* of v is the length of a longest path from v to any other node of T. A node of T with minimum eccentricity is called a *center* of T.

    a. Design an efficient algorithm that, given an n-node free tree T, computes a center of T.

    b. Is the center unique? If not, how many distinct centers can a free tree have?

C-12.7 Show that, if T is a BFS tree produced for a connected graph G, then, for each vertex v at level i, the path of T between s and v has i edges, and any other path of G between s and v has at least i edges.

C-12.8 The time delay of a long-distance call can be determined by multiplying a small fixed constant by the number of communication links on the telephone network between the caller and callee. Suppose the telephone network of a company named RT&T is a free tree. The engineers of RT&T want to compute the maximum possible time delay that may be experienced in a long-distance call. Given a free tree T, the *diameter* of T is the length of a longest path between two nodes of T. Give an efficient algorithm for computing the diameter of T.

C-12.9 A company named RT&T has a network of n switching stations connected by m high-speed communication links. Each customer's phone is directly connected to one station in his or her area. The engineers of RT&T have developed a prototype video-phone system that allows two customers to see each other during a phone call. In order to have acceptable image quality, however, the number of links used to transmit video signals between the two parties cannot exceed 4. Suppose that RT&T's network is represented by a graph. Design an efficient algorithm that computes, for each station, the set of stations it can reach using no more than 4 links.

C-12.10 Explain why there are no forward nontree edges with respect to a BFS tree constructed for a directed graph.

C-12.11 An independent set of an undirected graph $G = (V,E)$ is a subset I of V such that no two vertices in I are adjacent. That is, if $u, v \in I$, then $(u, v) \notin E$. A *maximal independent set* M is an independent set such that, if we were to add any additional vertex to M, then it would not be independent any more. Every graph has a maximal independent set. (Can you see this? This question is not part of the exercise, but it is worth thinking about.) Give an efficient algorithm that computes a maximal independent set for a graph G. What is this method's running time?

C-12.12 An *Euler tour* of a directed graph $\vec{G}$ with n vertices and m edges is a cycle that traverses each edge of $\vec{G}$ exactly once according to its direction. Such a tour always exists if $\vec{G}$ is connected and the in-degree equals the out-degree of each vertex in $\vec{G}$. Describe an $O(n+m)$-time algorithm for finding an Euler tour of such a digraph $\vec{G}$.

C-12.13 Let G be an undirected graph G with n vertices and m edges. Describe an $O(n+m)$-time algorithm for traversing each edge of G exactly once in each direction.

C-12.14 Justify Proposition 12.14.

C-12.15 Give an example of an n-vertex simple graph G that causes Dijkstra's algorithm to run in $\Omega(n^2 \log n)$ time when its implemented with a heap.

C-12.16 Give an example of a weighted directed graph $\vec{G}$ with negative-weight edges, but no negative-weight cycle, such that Dijkstra's algorithm incorrectly computes the shortest-path distances from some start vertex v.

C-12.17 Consider the following greedy strategy for finding a shortest path from vertex *start* to vertex *goal* in a given connected graph.

   1: Initialize *path* to *start*.
   2: Initialize *VisitedVertices* to $\{start\}$.
   3: If *start=goal*, return *path* and exit. Otherwise, continue.
   4: Find the edge *(start,v)* of minimum weight such that v is adjacent to *start* and v is not in *VisitedVertices*.
   5: Add v to *path*.
   6: Add v to *VisitedVertices*.
   7: Set *start* equal to v and go to step 3.

   Does this greedy strategy always find a shortest path from *start* to *goal*? Either explain intuitively why it works, or give a counter example.

C-12.18 Show that if all the weights in a connected weighted graph G are distinct, then there is exactly one minimum spanning tree for G.

C-12.19 Design an efficient algorithm for finding a **longest** directed path from a vertex s to a vertex t of an acyclic weighted digraph $\vec{G}$. Specify the graph representation used and any auxiliary data structures used. Also, analyze the time complexity of your algorithm.

C-12.20 Consider a diagram of a telephone network, which is a graph G whose vertices represent switching centers, and whose edges represent communication lines joining pairs of centers. Edges are marked by their bandwidth, and the bandwidth of a path is the bandwidth of its lowest bandwidth edge. Give an algorithm that, given a diagram and two switching centers a and b, outputs the maximum bandwidth of a path between a and b.

C-12.21 Computer networks should avoid single points of failure, that is, network nodes that can disconnect the network if they fail. We say a connected graph G is **biconnected** if it contains no vertex whose removal would divide G into two or more connected components. Give an $O(n+m)$-time algorithm for adding at most n edges to a connected graph G, with $n \geq 3$ vertices and $m \geq n-1$ edges, to guarantee that G is biconnected.

C-12.22 NASA wants to link n stations spread over the country using communication channels. Each pair of stations has a different bandwidth available, which is known a priori. NASA wants to select $n - 1$ channels (the minimum possible) in such a way that all the stations are linked by the channels and the total bandwidth (defined as the sum of the individual bandwidths of the channels) is maximum. Give an efficient algorithm for this problem and determine its worst-case time complexity. Consider the weighted graph $G = (V, E)$, where V is the set of stations and E is the set of channels between the stations. Define the weight $w(e)$ of an edge $e \in E$ as the bandwidth of the corresponding channel.

C-12.23 Suppose you are given a *timetable*, which consists of:

- A set $\mathcal{A}$ of n airports, and for each airport $a \in \mathcal{A}$, a minimum connecting time $c(a)$
- A set $\mathcal{F}$ of m flights, and the following, for each flight $f \in \mathcal{A}$:
  - Origin airport $a_1(f) \in \mathcal{A}$
  - Destination airport $a_2(f) \in \mathcal{A}$
  - Departure time $t_1(f)$
  - Arrival time $t_2(f)$.

Describe an efficient algorithm for the flight scheduling problem. In this problem, we are given airports a and b, and a time t, and we wish to compute a sequence of flights that allows one to arrive at the earliest possible time in b when departing from a at or after time t. Minimum connecting times at intermediate airports should be observed. What is the running time of your algorithm as a function of n and m?

C-12.24 Let $\vec{G}$ be a weighted digraph with n vertices. Design a variation of Floyd-Warshall's algorithm for computing the lengths of the shortest paths from each vertex to every other vertex in $O(n^3)$ time.

C-12.25 Inside the Castle of Asymptopia there is a maze, and along each corridor of the maze there is a bag of gold coins. The amount of gold in each bag varies. A noble knight, named Sir Paul, will be given the opportunity to walk through the maze, picking up bags of gold. He may enter the maze only through a door marked "ENTER" and exit through another door marked "EXIT." While in the maze he may not retrace his steps. Each corridor of the maze has an arrow painted on the wall. Sir Paul may only go down the corridor in the direction of the arrow. There is no way to traverse a "loop" in the maze. Given a map of the maze, including the amount of gold in and the direction of each corridor, describe an algorithm to help Sir Paul pick up the most gold.

C-12.26 Suppose we are given a directed graph $\vec{G}$ with n vertices, and let M be the $n \times n$ adjacency matrix corresponding to $\vec{G}$.

a. Let the product of M with itself (M^2) be defined, for $1 \le i, j \le n$, as follows:

$$M^2(i,j) = M(i,1) \odot M(1,j) \oplus \cdots \oplus M(i,n) \odot M(n,j),$$

where "$\oplus$" is the Boolean **or** operator and "$\odot$" is Boolean **and**. Given this definition, what does $M^2(i,j) = 1$ imply about the vertices i and j? What if $M^2(i,j) = 0$?

b. Suppose M^4 is the product of M^2 with itself. What do the entries of M^4 signify? How about the entries of $M^5 = (M^4)(M)$? In general, what information is contained in the matrix M^p?

c. Now suppose that $\vec{G}$ is weighted and assume the following:
   1: for $1 \le i \le n$, $M(i,i) = 0$.
   2: for $1 \le i, j \le n$, $M(i,j) = weight(i,j)$ if $(i,j) \in E$.
   3: for $1 \le i, j \le n$, $M(i,j) = \infty$ if $(i,j) \notin E$.
   Also, let M^2 be defined, for $1 \le i, j \le n$, as follows:

$$M^2(i,j) = \min\{M(i,1) + M(1,j), \ldots, M(i,n) + M(n,j)\}.$$

If $M^2(i,j) = k$, what may we conclude about the relationship between vertices i and j?

C-12.27 A graph G is **bipartite** if its vertices can be partitioned into two sets X and Y such that every edge in G has one end vertex in X and the other in Y. Design and analyze an efficient algorithm for determining if an undirected graph G is bipartite (without knowing the sets X and Y in advance).

C-12.28 There is an old MST algorithm, called **Barůvka's algorithm**, which works as follows on a weighted graph G with n vertices and m edges:

Let T be a subgraph of G initially containing just the vertices in V.
while T has fewer than $n - 1$ edges **do**
  for each connected component C_i of T **do**
    Find a lowest-weight edge (v,u) in E with $v \in C_i$ and $u \notin C_i$.
    Add (v,u) to T (unless it is already in T).
return T

Argue why this algorithm is correct and why it runs in $O(m \log n)$ time.

C-12.29 Let G be a graph with n vertices and m edges such that all the edge weights in G are integers in the range $[1,n]$. Give an algorithm for finding a minimum spanning tree for G in $O(m \log^* n)$ time.

Projects

P-12.1 Write a class implementing a simplified graph ADT that has only methods relevant to undirected graphs and does not include update methods, using the adjacency matrix structure. Your class should include a constructor method that takes two containers (for example, sequences)—a container V of vertex elements and a container E of pairs of vertex elements—and produces the graph G that these two containers represent.

P-12.2 Implement the simplified graph ADT described in Project P-12.1, using the adjacency list structure.

P-12.3 Implement the simplified graph ADT described in Project P-12.1, using the edge list structure.

P-12.4 Extend the class of Project P-12.2 to support update methods.

P-12.5 Extend the class of Project P-12.2 to support all the methods of the graph ADT (including methods for directed edges).

P-12.6 Implement a generic BFS traversal using the template method pattern.

P-12.7 Implement the topological sorting algorithm.

P-12.8 Implement the Floyd-Warshall transitive closure algorithm.

P-12.9 Design an experimental comparison of repeated DFS traversals versus the Floyd-Warshall algorithm for computing the transitive closure of a digraph.

P-12.10 Implement Kruskal's algorithm assuming that the edge weights are integers.

P-12.11 Implement the Prim-Jarník algorithm assuming that the edge weights are integers.

P-12.12 Perform an experimental comparison of two of the minimum spanning tree algorithms discussed in this chapter (Kruskal and Prim-Jarník). Develop an extensive set of experiments to test the running times of these algorithms using randomly generated graphs.

Chapter Notes

The depth-first search method is a part of the "folklore" of computer science, but Hopcroft and Tarjan [48, 88] are the ones who showed how useful this algorithm is for solving several different graph problems. Knuth [58] discusses the topological sorting problem. The simple linear-time algorithm that we describe for determining if a directed graph is strongly connected is due to Kosaraju. The Floyd-Warshall algorithm appears in a paper by Floyd [34] and is based upon a theorem of Warshall [95]. The mark-sweep garbage collection method we describe is one of many different algorithms for performing garbage collection. We encourage the reader interested in further study of garbage collection to examine the book by Jones [53]. To learn about different algorithms for drawing graphs, please see the book chapter by Tamassia [86], the annotated bibliography of Di Battista *et al.* [28], or the book by Di Battista *et al.* [29]. The first known minimum spanning tree algorithm is due to Barůvka [9], and was published in 1926. The Prim-Jarník algorithm was first published in Czech by Jarník [52] in 1930 and in English in 1957 by Prim [79]. Kruskal published his minimum spanning tree algorithm in 1956 [61]. The reader interested in further study of the history of the minimum spanning tree problem is referred to the paper by Graham and Hell [43]. The current asymptotically fastest minimum spanning tree algorithm is a randomized method of Karger, Klein, and Tarjan [54] that runs in $O(m)$ expected time.

Dijkstra [30] published his single-source, shortest path algorithm in 1959. The reader interested in further study of graph algorithms is referred to the books by Ahuja, Magnanti, and Orlin [6], Cormen, Leiserson, and Rivest [24], Even [32], Gibbons [38], Mehlhorn [72], and Tarjan [89], and the book chapter by van Leeuwen [91]. Incidentally, the running time for the Prim-Jarník algorithm, and also that of Dijkstra's algorithm, can actually be improved to be $O(n \log n + m)$ by implementing the queue Q with either of two more sophisticated data structures, the "Fibonacci Heap" [36] or the "Relaxed Heap" [31]. The reader interested in these implementations is referred to the papers that describe the implementation of these structures, and how they can be applied to the shortest-path and minimum spanning tree problems.

Appendix

A   Useful Mathematical Facts

In this appendix we give several useful mathematical facts. We begin with some combinatorial definitions and facts.

Logarithms and Exponents

The logarithm function is defined as

$$\log_b a = c \qquad \text{if} \qquad a = b^c.$$

The following identities hold for logarithms and exponents:

1. $\log_b ac = \log_b a + \log_b c$
2. $\log_b a/c = \log_b a - \log_b c$
3. $\log_b a^c = c \log_b a$
4. $\log_b a = (\log_c a)/\log_c b$
5. $b^{\log_c a} = a^{\log_c b}$
6. $(b^a)^c = b^{ac}$
7. $b^a b^c = b^{a+c}$
8. $b^a/b^c = b^{a-c}$

In addition, we have the following:

Proposition A.1: *If $a > 0$, $b > 0$, and $c > a + b$, then*

$$\log a + \log b \le 2 \log c - 2.$$

Justification: It is enough to show that $ab < c^2/4$. We can write

$$
\begin{aligned}
ab &= \frac{a^2 + 2ab + b^2 - a^2 + 2ab - b^2}{4} \\
&= \frac{(a+b)^2 - (a-b)^2}{4} \le \frac{(a+b)^2}{4} < \frac{c^2}{4}.
\end{aligned}
$$
■

The **natural logarithm** function $\ln x = \log_e x$, where $e = 2.71828\ldots$, is the value of the following progression:

$$e = 1 + \frac{1}{1!} + \frac{1}{2!} + \frac{1}{3!} + \cdots.$$

In addition,

$$e^x = 1 + \frac{x}{1!} + \frac{x^2}{2!} + \frac{x^3}{3!} + \cdots$$

$$\ln(1+x) = x - \frac{x^2}{2!} + \frac{x^3}{3!} - \frac{x^4}{4!} + \cdots.$$

There are a number of useful inequalities relating to these functions (which derive from these definitions).

Proposition A.2: *If $x > -1$,*

$$\frac{x}{1+x} \leq \ln(1+x) \leq x.$$

Proposition A.3: *For $0 \leq x < 1$,*

$$1 + x \leq e^x \leq \frac{1}{1-x}.$$

Proposition A.4: *For any two positive real numbers x and n,*

$$\left(1 + \frac{x}{n}\right)^n \leq e^x \leq \left(1 + \frac{x}{n}\right)^{n+x/2}.$$

Integer Functions and Relations

The "floor" and "ceiling" functions are defined respectively as follows:

1. $\lfloor x \rfloor$ = the largest integer less than or equal to x.
2. $\lceil x \rceil$ = the smallest integer greater than or equal to x.

The **modulo** operator is defined for integers $a \geq 0$ and $b > 0$ as

$$a \bmod b = a - \left\lfloor \frac{a}{b} \right\rfloor b.$$

The **factorial** function is defined as

$$n! = 1 \cdot 2 \cdot 3 \cdot \cdots \cdot (n-1)n.$$

The binomial coefficient is

$$\binom{n}{k} = \frac{n!}{k!(n-k)!},$$

which is equal to the number of different **combinations** one can define by choosing k different items from a collection of n items (where the order does not matter). The name "binomial coefficient" derives from the **binomial expansion**:

$$(a+b)^n = \sum_{k=0}^{n} \binom{n}{k} a^k b^{n-k}.$$

We also have the following relationships.

Proposition A.5: *If* $0 \leq k \leq n$, *then*

$$\left(\frac{n}{k}\right)^k \leq \binom{n}{k} \leq \frac{n^k}{k!}.$$

Proposition A.6 (Stirling's Approximation):

$$n! = \sqrt{2\pi n} \left(\frac{n}{e}\right)^n \left(1 + \frac{1}{12n} + \varepsilon(n)\right),$$

where $\varepsilon(n)$ *is* $O(1/n^2)$.

The **Fibonacci progression** is a numeric progression such that $F_0 = 0$, $F_1 = 1$, and $F_n = F_{n-1} + F_{n-2}$ for $n \geq 2$.

Proposition A.7: *If* F_n *is defined by the Fibonacci progression, then* F_n *is* $\Theta(g^n)$, *where* $g = (1 + \sqrt{5})/2$ *is the so-called* **golden ratio**.

Summations

There are a number of useful facts about summations.

Proposition A.8: *Factoring summations:*

$$\sum_{i=1}^{n} a f(i) = a \sum_{i=1}^{n} f(i),$$

provided a *does not depend upon* i.

Proposition A.9: *Reversing the order:*

$$\sum_{i=1}^{n} \sum_{j=1}^{m} f(i,j) = \sum_{j=1}^{m} \sum_{i=1}^{n} f(i,j).$$

One special form of summation is a **telescoping sum**:

$$\sum_{i=1}^{n}(f(i) - f(i-1)) = f(n) - f(0),$$

which arises often in the amortized analysis of a data structure or algorithm.

The following are some other facts about summations that arise often in the analysis of data structures and algorithms.

Proposition A.10: $\sum_{i=1}^{n} i = n(n+1)/2$.

Proposition A.11: $\sum_{i=1}^{n} i^2 = n(n+1)(2n+1)/6$.

Proposition A.12: *If $k \geq 1$ is an integer constant, then*

$$\sum_{i=1}^{n} i^k \text{ is } \Theta(n^{k+1}).$$

Another common summation is the **geometric sum**, $\sum_{i=0}^{n} a^i$, for any fixed real number $0 < a \neq 1$.

Proposition A.13:

$$\sum_{i=0}^{n} a^i = \frac{a^{n+1} - 1}{a - 1},$$

for any real number $0 < a \neq 1$.

Proposition A.14:

$$\sum_{i=0}^{\infty} a^i = \frac{1}{1 - a}$$

for any real number $0 < a < 1$.

There is also a combination of the two common forms, called the **linear exponential** summation, which has the following expansion:

Proposition A.15: *For $0 < a \neq 1$, and $n \geq 2$,*

$$\sum_{i=1}^{n} i a^i = \frac{a - (n+1)a^{(n+1)} + na^{(n+2)}}{(1-a)^2}.$$

The nth **Harmonic number** H_n is defined as

$$H_n = \sum_{i=1}^{n} \frac{1}{i}.$$

Proposition A.16: *If H_n is the nth harmonic number, then H_n is $\ln n + \Theta(1)$.*

Basic Probability

We review some basic facts from probability theory. The most basic is that any statement about a probability is defined upon a **sample space** S, which is defined as the set of all possible outcomes from some experiment. We leave the terms "outcomes" and "experiment" undefined in any formal sense.

Example A.17: *Consider an experiment that consists of the outcome from flipping a coin five times. This sample space has 2^5 different outcomes, one for each different ordering of possible flips that can occur.*

Sample spaces can also be infinite, as the following example illustrates.

Example A.18: *Consider an experiment that consists of flipping a coin until it comes up heads. This sample space is infinite, with each outcome being a sequence of i tails followed by a single flip that comes up heads, for $i \in \{1, 2, 3, \ldots\}$.*

A **probability space** is a sample space S together with a probability function Pr that maps subsets of S to real numbers in the interval $[0, 1]$. It captures mathematically the notion of the probability of certain "events" occurring. Formally, each subset A of S is called an **event**, and the probability function Pr is assumed to possess the following basic properties with respect to events defined from S:

1. $\Pr(\emptyset) = 0$.
2. $\Pr(S) = 1$.
3. $0 \le \Pr(A) \le 1$, for any $A \subseteq S$.
4. If $A, B \subseteq S$ and $A \cap B = \emptyset$, then $\Pr(A \cup B) = \Pr(A) + \Pr(B)$.

Two events A and B are **independent** if

$$\Pr(A \cap B) = \Pr(A) \cdot \Pr(B).$$

A collection of events $\{A_1, A_2, \ldots, A_n\}$ is **mutually independent** if

$$\Pr(A_{i_1} \cap A_{i_2} \cap \cdots \cap A_{i_k}) = \Pr(A_{i_1}) \Pr(A_{i_2}) \cdots \Pr(A_{i_k}).$$

for any subset $\{A_{i_1}, A_{i_2}, \ldots, A_{i_k}\}$.

The **conditional probability** that an event A occurs, given an event B, is denoted as $\Pr(A|B)$, and is defined as the ratio

$$\frac{\Pr(A \cap B)}{\Pr(B)},$$

assuming that $\Pr(B) > 0$.

An elegant way for dealing with events is in terms of ***random variables***. Intuitively, random variables are variables whose values depend upon the outcome of some experiment. Formally, a ***random variable*** is a function X that maps outcomes from some sample space S to real numbers. An ***indicator random variable*** is a random variable that maps outcomes to the set $\{0,1\}$. Often in data structure and algorithm analysis we use a random variable X to characterize the running time of a randomized algorithm. In this case, the sample space S is defined by all possible outcomes of the random sources used in the algorithm.

We are most interested in the typical, average, or "expected" value of such a random variable. The ***expected value*** of a random variable X is defined as

$$\mathbf{E}(X) = \sum_x x \Pr(X = x),$$

where the summation is defined over the range of X (which in this case is assumed to be discrete).

Proposition A.19 (The Linearity of Expectation): *Let X and Y be two arbitrary random variables. Then*

$$\mathbf{E}(X + Y) = \mathbf{E}(X) + \mathbf{E}(Y).$$

Example A.20: *Let X be a random variable that assigns the outcome of the roll of two fair dice to the sum of the number of dots showing. Then $\mathbf{E}(X) = 7$.*

Justification: *To justify this claim, let X_1 and X_2 be random variables corresponding to the number of dots on each die. Thus, $X_1 = X_2$ (i.e., they are two instances of the same function) and $\mathbf{E}(X) = \mathbf{E}(X_1 + X_2) = \mathbf{E}(X_1) + \mathbf{E}(X_2)$. Each outcome of the roll of a fair die occurs with probability $1/6$. Thus*

$$\mathbf{E}(X_i) = \frac{1}{6} + \frac{2}{6} + \frac{3}{6} + \frac{4}{6} + \frac{5}{6} + \frac{6}{6} = \frac{7}{2},$$

for $i = 1, 2$. Therefore, $E(X) = 7$.   ∎

Two random variables X and Y are ***independent*** if

$$\Pr(X = x | Y = y) = \Pr(X = x),$$

for all real numbers x and y.

Proposition A.21: *If two random variables X and Y are independent, then*

$$\mathbf{E}(XY) = \mathbf{E}(X)\mathbf{E}(Y).$$

Example A.22: *Let X be a random variable that assigns the outcome of a roll of two fair dice to the product of the number of dots showing. Then $E(X) = 49/4$.*

Justification: *Let X_1 and X_2 be random variables denoting the number of dots on each die. The variables X_1 and X_2 are clearly independent; hence*

$$E(X) = E(X_1 X_2) = E(X_1)E(X_2) = (7/2)^2 = 49/4.$$

■

Useful Mathematical Techniques

To compare the growth rates of different functions, it is sometimes helpful to apply the following rule.

Proposition A.23 (L'Hôpital's Rule): *If we have $\lim_{n \to \infty} f(n) = +\infty$ and we have $\lim_{n \to \infty} g(n) = +\infty$, then $\lim_{n \to \infty} f(n)/g(n) = \lim_{n \to \infty} f'(n)/g'(n)$, where $f'(n)$ and $g'(n)$ respectively denote the derivatives of $f(n)$ and $g(n)$.*

In deriving an upper or lower bound for a summation, it is often useful to **split a summation** as follows:

$$\sum_{i=1}^{n} f(i) = \sum_{i=1}^{j} f(i) + \sum_{i=j+1}^{n} f(i).$$

Another useful technique is to **bound a sum by an integral**. If f is a nondecreasing function, then, assuming the following terms are defined,

$$\int_{a-1}^{b} f(x)\,dx \le \sum_{i=a}^{b} f(i) \le \int_{a}^{b+1} f(x)\,dx.$$

There is a general form of recurrence relation that arises in the analysis of divide-and-conquer algorithms:

$$T(n) = aT(n/b) + f(n),$$

for constants $a \ge 1$ and $b > 1$.

Proposition A.24: *Let $T(n)$ be defined as above. Then*

1. *If $f(n)$ is $O(n^{\log_b a - \varepsilon})$, for some constant $\varepsilon > 0$, then $T(n)$ is $\Theta(n^{\log_b a})$.*
2. *If $f(n)$ is $\Theta(n^{\log_b a} \log^k n)$, for a fixed nonnegative integer $k \ge 0$, then $T(n)$ is $\Theta(n^{\log_b a} \log^{k+1} n)$.*
3. *If $f(n)$ is $\Omega(n^{\log_b a + \varepsilon})$, for some constant $\varepsilon > 0$, and if $af(n/b) \le cf(n)$, then $T(n)$ is $\Theta(f(n))$.*

This proposition is known as the **master method** for characterizing divide-and-conquer recurrence relations asymptotically.

Bibliography

[1] G. M. Adel'son-Vel'skii and Y. M. Landis, "An algorithm for the organization of information," *Doklady Akademii Nauk SSSR*, vol. 146, pp. 263–266, 1962. English translation in *Soviet Math. Dokl.*, **3**, 1259–1262.

[2] A. Aggarwal and J. S. Vitter, "The input/output complexity of sorting and related problems," *Commun. ACM*, vol. 31, pp. 1116–1127, 1988.

[3] A. V. Aho, "Algorithms for finding patterns in strings," in *Handbook of Theoretical Computer Science* (J. van Leeuwen, ed.), vol. A. Algorithms and Complexity, pp. 255–300, Amsterdam: Elsevier, 1990.

[4] A. V. Aho, J. E. Hopcroft, and J. D. Ullman, *The Design and Analysis of Computer Algorithms*. Reading, MA: Addison-Wesley, 1974.

[5] A. V. Aho, J. E. Hopcroft, and J. D. Ullman, *Data Structures and Algorithms*. Reading, MA: Addison-Wesley, 1983.

[6] R. K. Ahuja, T. L. Magnanti, and J. B. Orlin, *Network Flows: Theory, Algorithms, and Applications*. Englewood Cliffs, NJ: Prentice Hall, 1993.

[7] K. Arnold and J. Gosling, *The Java Programming Language*. The Java Series, Reading, Mass.: Addison-Wesley, 1996.

[8] R. Baeza-Yates and B. Ribeiro-Neto, *Modern Information Retrieval*. Reading, Mass.: Addison-Wesley, 1999.

[9] O. Baruvka, "O jistem problemu minimalnim," *Praca Moravske Prirodovedecke Spolecnosti*, vol. 3, pp. 37–58, 1926. (in Czech).

[10] R. Bayer, "Symmetric binary B-trees: Data structure and maintenance," *Acta Informatica*, vol. 1, no. 4, pp. 290–306, 1972.

[11] R. Bayer and McCreight, "Organization of large ordered indexes," *Acta Inform.*, vol. 1, pp. 173–189, 1972.

[12] J. L. Bentley, "Programming pearls: Writing correct programs," *Communications of the ACM*, vol. 26, pp. 1040–1045, 1983.

[13] J. L. Bentley, "Programming pearls: Thanks, heaps," *Communications of the ACM*, vol. 28, pp. 245–250, 1985.

[14] G. Booch, *Object-Oriented Analysis and Design with Applications*. Redwood City, CA: Benjamin/Cummings, 1994.

[15] R. S. Boyer and J. S. Moore, "A fast string searching algorithm," *Communications of the ACM*, vol. 20, no. 10, pp. 762–772, 1977.

[16] G. Brassard, "Crusade for a better notation," *SIGACT News*, vol. 17, no. 1, pp. 60–64, 1985.

[17] T. Budd, *An Introduction to Object-Oriented Programming*. Reading, Mass.: Addison-Wesley, 1991.

[18] M. Campione and H. Walrath, *The Java Tutorial: Programming for the Internet*. Reading, Mass.: Addison Wesley, 1996.

[19] L. Cardelli and P. Wegner, "On understanding types, data abstraction and polymorphism," *ACM Computing Surveys*, vol. 17, no. 4, pp. 471–522, 1985.

[20] S. Carlsson, "Average case results on heapsort," *BIT*, vol. 27, pp. 2–17, 1987.

[21] K. L. Clarkson, "Linear programming in $O(n3^{d^2})$ time," *Inform. Process. Lett.*, vol. 22, pp. 21–24, 1986.

[22] R. Cole, "Tight bounds on the complexity of the Boyer-Moore pattern matching algorithm," *SIAM Journal on Computing*, vol. 23, no. 5, pp. 1075–1091, 1994.

[23] D. Comer, "The ubiquitous B-tree," *ACM Comput. Surv.*, vol. 11, pp. 121–137, 1979.

[24] T. H. Cormen, C. E. Leiserson, and R. L. Rivest, *Introduction to Algorithms*. Cambridge, MA: MIT Press, 1990.

[25] G. Cornell and C. S. Horstmann, *Core Java*. Mountain View, CA: SunSoft Press, 1996.

[26] M. Crochemore and T. Lecroq, "Pattern matching and text compression algorithms," in *The Computer Science and Engineering Handbook* (A. B. Tucker, Jr., ed.), ch. 8, pp. 162–202, CRC Press, 1997.

[27] S. A. Demurjian, Sr., "Software design," in *The Computer Science and Engineering Handbook* (A. B. Tucker, Jr., ed.), ch. 108, pp. 2323–2351, CRC Press, 1997.

[28] G. Di Battista, P. Eades, R. Tamassia, and I. G. Tollis, "Algorithms for drawing graphs: an annotated bibliography," *Comput. Geom. Theory Appl.*, vol. 4, pp. 235–282, 1994.

[29] G. Di Battista, P. Eades, R. Tamassia, and I. G. Tollis, *Graph Drawing*. Upper Saddle River, NJ: Prentice Hall, 1999.

[30] E. W. Dijkstra, "A note on two problems in connexion with graphs," *Numerische Mathematik*, vol. 1, pp. 269–271, 1959.

[31] J. R. Driscoll, H. N. Gabow, R. Shrairaman, and R. E. Tarjan, "Relaxed heaps: An alternative to Fibonacci heaps with applications to parallel computation.," *Commun. ACM*, vol. 31, pp. 1343–1354, 1988.

[32] S. Even, *Graph Algorithms*. Potomac, Maryland: Computer Science Press, 1979.

[33] D. Flanagan, *Java in a Nutshell*. O'Reilly, 4th ed., 2002.

[34] R. W. Floyd, "Algorithm 97: Shortest path," *Communications of the ACM*, vol. 5, no. 6, p. 345, 1962.

[35] R. W. Floyd, "Algorithm 245: Treesort 3," *Communications of the ACM*, vol. 7, no. 12, p. 701, 1964.

[36] M. L. Fredman and R. E. Tarjan, "Fibonacci heaps and their uses in improved network optimization algorithms," *J. ACM*, vol. 34, pp. 596–615, 1987.

[37] E. Gamma, R. Helm, R. Johnson, and J. Vlissides, *Design Patterns: Elements of Reusable Object-Oriented Software*. Reading, Mass.: Addison-Wesley, 1995.

[38] A. M. Gibbons, *Algorithmic Graph Theory*. Cambridge, UK: Cambridge University Press, 1985.

[39] A. Goldberg and D. Robson, *Smalltalk-80: The Language*. Reading, Mass.: Addison-Wesley, 1989.

[40] G. H. Gonnet and R. Baeza-Yates, *Handbook of Algorithms and Data Structures in Pascal and C*. Reading, Mass.: Addison-Wesley, 1991.

[41] G. H. Gonnet and J. I. Munro, "Heaps on heaps," *SIAM Journal on Computing*, vol. 15, no. 4, pp. 964–971, 1986.

[42] M. T. Goodrich, M. Handy, B. Hudson, and R. Tamassia, "Accessing the internal organization of data structures in the JDSL library," in *Proc. Workshop on Algorithm Engineering and Experimentation* (M. T. Goodrich and C. C. McGeoch, eds.), vol. 1619 of *Lecture Notes Comput. Sci.*, pp. 124–139, Springer-Verlag, 1999.

[43] R. L. Graham and P. Hell, "On the history of the minimum spanning tree problem," *Annals of the History of Computing*, vol. 7, no. 1, pp. 43–57, 1985.

[44] R. L. Graham, D. E. Knuth, and O. Patashnik, *Concrete Mathematics*. Reading, Mass.: Addison-Wesley, 1989.

[45] L. J. Guibas and R. Sedgewick, "A dichromatic framework for balanced trees," in *Proc. 19th Annu. IEEE Sympos. Found. Comput. Sci.*, Lecture Notes Comput. Sci., pp. 8–21, Springer-Verlag, 1978.

[46] Y. Gurevich, "What does $O(n)$ mean?," *SIGACT News*, vol. 17, no. 4, pp. 61–63, 1986.

[47] C. A. R. Hoare, "Quicksort," *The Computer Journal*, vol. 5, pp. 10–15, 1962.

[48] J. E. Hopcroft and R. E. Tarjan, "Efficient algorithms for graph manipulation," *Communications of the ACM*, vol. 16, no. 6, pp. 372–378, 1973.

[49] C. S. Horstmann, *Computing Concepts in Java*. New York: John Wiley, and Sons, 1998.

[50] B. Huang and M. Langston, "Practical in-place merging," *Communications of the ACM*, vol. 31, no. 3, pp. 348–352, 1988.

[51] J. JáJá, *An Introduction to Parallel Algorithms*. Reading, Mass.: Addison-Wesley, 1992.

[52] V. Jarnik, "O jistem problemu minimalnim," *Praca Moravske Prirodovedecke Spolecnosti*, vol. 6, pp. 57–63, 1930. (in Czech).

[53] R. E. Jones, *Garbage Collection: Algorithms for Automatic Dynamic Memory Management*. John Wiley and Sons, 1996.

[54] D. R. Karger, P. Klein, and R. E. Tarjan, "A randomized linear-time algorithm to find minimum spanning trees," *Journal of the ACM*, vol. 42, pp. 321–328, 1995.

[55] R. M. Karp and V. Ramachandran, "Parallel algorithms for shared memory machines," in *Handbook of Theoretical Computer Science* (J. van Leeuwen, ed.), pp. 869–941, Amsterdam: Elsevier/The MIT Press, 1990.

[56] P. Kirschenhofer and H. Prodinger, "The path length of random skip lists," *Acta Informatica*, vol. 31, pp. 775–792, 1994.

[57] D. E. Knuth, "Big omicron and big omega and big theta," in *SIGACT News*, vol. 8, pp. 18–24, 1976.

[58] D. E. Knuth, *Fundamental Algorithms*, vol. 1 of *The Art of Computer Programming*. Reading, MA: Addison-Wesley, 3rd ed., 1997.

[59] D. E. Knuth, *Sorting and Searching*, vol. 3 of *The Art of Computer Programming*. Reading, MA: Addison-Wesley, 2nd ed., 1998.

[60] D. E. Knuth, J. H. Morris, Jr., and V. R. Pratt, "Fast pattern matching in strings," *SIAM Journal on Computing*, vol. 6, no. 1, pp. 323–350, 1977.

[61] J. B. Kruskal, Jr., "On the shortest spanning subtree of a graph and the traveling salesman problem," *Proc. Amer. Math. Soc.*, vol. 7, pp. 48–50, 1956.

[62] N. G. Leveson and C. S. Turner, "An investigation of the Therac-25 accidents," *IEEE Computer*, vol. 26, no. 7, pp. 18–41, 1993.

[63] R. Levisse, "Some lessons drawn from the history of the binary search algorithm," *The Computer Journal*, vol. 26, pp. 154–163, 1983.

[64] A. Levitin, "Do we teach the right algorithm design techniques?," in *30th ACM SIGCSE Symp. on Computer Science Education*, pp. 179–183, 1999.

[65] T. Lindholm and F. Yellin, *The Java Virtual Machine Specification*. Reading, Mass.: Addison-Wesley, 1997.

[66] B. Liskov and J. Guttag, *Abstraction and Specification in Program Development*. Cambridge, Mass./New York: The MIT Press/McGraw-Hill, 1986.

[67] E. M. McCreight, "A space-economical suffix tree construction algorithm," *Journal of Algorithms*, vol. 23, no. 2, pp. 262–272, 1976.

[68] C. J. H. McDiarmid and B. A. Reed, "Building heaps fast," *Journal of Algorithms*, vol. 10, no. 3, pp. 352–365, 1989.

[69] N. Megiddo, "Linear-time algorithms for linear programming in R^3 and related problems," *SIAM J. Comput.*, vol. 12, pp. 759–776, 1983.

[70] N. Megiddo, "Linear programming in linear time when the dimension is fixed," *J. ACM*, vol. 31, pp. 114–127, 1984.

[71] K. Mehlhorn, *Data Structures and Algorithms 1: Sorting and Searching*, vol. 1 of *EATCS Monographs on Theoretical Computer Science*. Heidelberg, Germany: Springer-Verlag, 1984.

[72] K. Mehlhorn, *Data Structures and Algorithms 2: Graph Algorithms and NP-Completeness*, vol. 2 of *EATCS Monographs on Theoretical Computer Science*. Heidelberg, Germany: Springer-Verlag, 1984.

[73] K. Mehlhorn and A. Tsakalidis, "Data structures," in *Handbook of Theoretical Computer Science* (J. van Leeuwen, ed.), vol. A. Algorithms and Complexity, pp. 301–341, Amsterdam: Elsevier, 1990.

[74] M. H. Morgan, *Vitruvius: The Ten Books on Architecture*. New York: Dover Publications, Inc., 1960.

[75] D. R. Morrison, "PATRICIA—practical algorithm to retrieve information coded in alphanumeric," *Journal of the ACM*, vol. 15, no. 4, pp. 514–534, 1968.

[76] R. Motwani and P. Raghavan, *Randomized Algorithms*. New York, NY: Cambridge University Press, 1995.

[77] T. Papadakis, J. I. Munro, and P. V. Poblete, "Average search and update costs in skip lists," *BIT*, vol. 32, pp. 316–332, 1992.

[78] P. V. Poblete, J. I. Munro, and T. Papadakis, "The binomial transform and its application to the analysis of skip lists," in *Proceedings of the European Symposium on Algorithms (ESA)*, pp. 554–569, 1995.

[79] R. C. Prim, "Shortest connection networks and some generalizations," *Bell Syst. Tech. J.*, vol. 36, pp. 1389–1401, 1957.

[80] W. Pugh, "Skip lists: a probabilistic alternative to balanced trees," *Commun. ACM*, vol. 33, no. 6, pp. 668–676, 1990.

[81] H. Samet, *The Design and Analysis of Spatial Data Structures*. Reading, MA: Addison-Wesley, 1990.

[82] R. Schaffer and R. Sedgewick, "The analysis of heapsort," *Journal of Algorithms*, vol. 15, no. 1, pp. 76–100, 1993.

[83] R. Sedgewick and P. Flajolet, *An Introduction to the Analysis of Algorithms.* Reading, Mass.: Addison-Wesley, 1996.

[84] D. D. Sleator and R. E. Tarjan, "Self-adjusting binary search trees," *J. ACM*, vol. 32, no. 3, pp. 652–686, 1985.

[85] G. A. Stephen, *String Searching Algorithms.* World Scientific Press, 1994.

[86] R. Tamassia, "Graph drawing," in *Handbook of Discrete and Computational Geometry* (J. E. Goodman and J. O'Rourke, eds.), ch. 44, pp. 815–832, Boca Raton, FL: CRC Press LLC, 1997.

[87] R. Tarjan and U. Vishkin, "An efficient parallel biconnectivity algorithm," *SIAM J. Comput.*, vol. 14, pp. 862–874, 1985.

[88] R. E. Tarjan, "Depth first search and linear graph algorithms," *SIAM Journal on Computing*, vol. 1, no. 2, pp. 146–160, 1972.

[89] R. E. Tarjan, *Data Structures and Network Algorithms*, vol. 44 of *CBMS-NSF Regional Conference Series in Applied Mathematics.* Philadelphia, PA: Society for Industrial and Applied Mathematics, 1983.

[90] A. B. Tucker, Jr., *The Computer Science and Engineering Handbook.* CRC Press, 1997.

[91] J. van Leeuwen, "Graph algorithms," in *Handbook of Theoretical Computer Science* (J. van Leeuwen, ed.), vol. A. Algorithms and Complexity, pp. 525–632, Amsterdam: Elsevier, 1990.

[92] J. S. Vitter, "Efficient memory access in large-scale computation," in *Proc. 8th Sympos. Theoret. Aspects Comput. Sci.*, Lecture Notes Comput. Sci., Springer-Verlag, 1991.

[93] J. S. Vitter and W. C. Chen, *Design and Analysis of Coalesced Hashing.* New York: Oxford University Press, 1987.

[94] J. S. Vitter and P. Flajolet, "Average-case analysis of algorithms and data structures," in *Algorithms and Complexity* (J. van Leeuwen, ed.), vol. A of *Handbook of Theoretical Computer Science*, pp. 431–524, Amsterdam: Elsevier, 1990.

[95] S. Warshall, "A theorem on boolean matrices," *Journal of the ACM*, vol. 9, no. 1, pp. 11–12, 1962.

[96] J. W. J. Williams, "Algorithm 232: Heapsort," *Communications of the ACM*, vol. 7, no. 6, pp. 347–348, 1964.

[97] M. R. Williams, *A History of Computing Technology.* Prentice-Hall, Inc., 1985.

[98] D. Wood, *Data Structures, Algorithms, and Performance.* Reading, Mass.: Addison-Wesley, 1993.